A COMPLETE GUIDE TO HERALDRY

A. C. FOX-DAVIES

A Complete Guide to
HERALDRY

Revised and annotated by
J. P. BROOKE-LITTLE
Norroy and Ulster King of Arms

BONANZA BOOKS

Copyright © Thomas Nelson and Sons Ltd 1969

Reprinted with revisions by Dr Charles A. Franklyn 1949,
1950, 1951, 1954, 1956, 1961

Published 1985 by Bonanza Books, distributed by Crown
Publishers, Inc.

Library of Congress Cataloging in Publication Data

Fox-Davies, Arthur Charles, 1871–1928
    A complete guide to heraldry
    Reprint. Originally published: London: Nelson, 1969
    1. Heraldry—Great Britain. I. Brook-Little, J. P.
(John Philip) II. Title
CR492. F723 1985   929.6′ 0941   84-29280

Printed in England

Contents

Preface

When I was about twelve years old, the *Complete Guide* became my first cicerone through the fields of armory. Fox-Davies' style can be didactic, long-winded and often curiously ungrammatical, but I never, even as a child, found it dull. Every time I opened the book I was fascinated and instructed. It really was a complete guide, and no other book on heraldry of the many that I have ever read has covered the same wide field with comparable fidelity. Fox-Davies saw heraldry as an actual living science, and his aim in the *Complete Guide* was to correct ancient myths and detail current practice. He has been dubbed a pedant, a dogmatist and unscholarly by the medievalists, but such attacks are superficial. Essentially, his object was, as I have stated, to expound and comment on heraldic practice, but he had a much more open and informed mind on the history of armory than he was credited with by his critics. The last paragraph of Chapter 8 and the first two pages of Chapter 9 contain much liberal thinking, and he frequently makes casual observations, such as on the origin of the arms of the See of Canterbury or on the cross botonny which were later justified by the researches of heraldic scholars.

When the Publishers approached me and asked if I would revise the *Complete Guide*, I refused; for to me it is, as it has always been, a classic in its field, and to revise it would be to rewrite it—an overwhelming labour, ending in the birth of what could only be a bastard work. However, I did agree, and enthusiastically, to annotate it, so that it might continue to be a comprehensive guide to modern heraldic practice. I read the book from cover to cover on the *Queen Elizabeth*. I made 564 notes to check, augment or correct statements made by Fox-Davies. Thereafter I set to work on this formidable assignment. In many cases I found his statements correct, in others the information he gave was out of date, and in only a very few instances was he actually inaccurate. As Fox-Davies does not usually quote his sources, I could not check every statement in the book; in many cases where he cites examples of the bearing of arms, his 'authority' is no better than Papworth's *Ordinary of British Armorials*, and it would be a life's work to check the entries in Papworth. All I have really tried to do is, by detailing twentieth-century official heraldic practice, to make the book as valuable to the student of heraldry today as it was when it was first published. Indeed, it should be more valuable, because the reader will be able to see exactly how heraldry and heraldic thought has evolved during the past half century.

I stipulated that Fox-Davies' original text should stand unaltered. Except where an obvious anachronism has been corrected either in this or in the 1949 edition, which contained revisions by Dr. Charles Franklyn, no attempt has been made in the text to alter Fox-Davies' opinions or to tamper with his style.

In Chapter 23 ("Marks of Bastardy"), Fox-Davies has an almost aggressive sympathy for the illegitimate child, and this made me wonder whether he himself had a wavy line in his pedigree. I made some investigations, and was rewarded by making the acquaintance of a nephew of his, the Rev. M. E. Fox-Davies, who was kind enough to meet me and to lend me a most interesting and detailed privately-printed pedigree of the family.

From this it appears that the first known progenitor of the family was one Thomas, son of David Davies, of Carmarthen, who was baptized at St. Peter's Church there in 1770. He married Jane Edmond of Carmarthen and had eight sons and six daughters. Charles, the youngest son, lived most of his life in Cardigan, where he married Mary Herring, the daughter of the Baptist Minister there. They had several children, the eldest, Thomas Edmond, being the author's father. The second son, John Herring Davies, was an early trickle down the brain drain, being Professor of Chemistry in the Medical and Surgical College of New Jersey. He married, and some of his descendants are doubtless still living in America.

Thomas Edmond Davies was baptized at the Hope (Congregational) Chapel, Cardigan, in 1839. In 1868 he married Maria Jane, daughter and co-heir of John Fox of Coalbrookdale, Shropshire.

In 1886 arms were granted to Thomas Edmond Davies with limitation to him and his descendants and to the other descendants of his late father, Charles Davies. Then, in 1894, he received a Royal Licence authorizing him and his issue by his wife Maria Jane to assume the surname of Fox in addition to and before that of Davies. Lastly, in 1905, arms were granted for Fox. In all these armorial transactions the hand of Thomas Edmond's second son, Arthur Charles, is readily discernable.

The author, born in 1871, was educated at Ackworth, a Quaker school in Yorkshire. He never attended University, but was called to the Utter Bar on "Grand Night" 1906 by the famous advocate Sir Edward Clark, then Treasurer of Lincoln's Inn. He had a reasonably lucrative practice at the Bar, but his claim to fame must be based on his heraldic writings. The most noted of these are: his editions of *Fairbairn's Book of Crests* (1893 and 1895), *The Book of Public Arms* (1894), *Armorial Families* (1895 and several later editions), *The Art of Heraldry* (1904), *The Right to Bear Arms* (1899, revised 1900), his edition of *Boutell's Heraldry* (1906), *Heraldic Badges* (1906), and this present work, which is based on his magnificent *The Art of Heraldry*. He also edited various periodicals, wrote a number of novels, edited and partly wrote *The History of the Noble House of Stourton* (1899), and took part in several peerage cases.

He married Mary Ellen Blanche Cookes in 1901, and had two children. His wife wrote a number of stories and serials under the pseudonym of 'Mary Proctor', and as 'C. Helard' had a certain reputation as a designer of book plates. Figures 282 and 283 in this book are the work of Mrs Fox-Davies.

Arthur Charles died in 1928, and it is a matter of some considerable satisfaction to me that the mantle of the author of my heraldic *vade mecum* should have touched my shoulders. Fifty-nine years after the *Complete Guide* was first published, I am concluding the Preface of this book which will, I hope, prove as valuable to those who study it as it has been to me.

J.B.-L.

Heyford House, May 1969

Introduction

Too frequently it is the custom to regard the study of the science of Armory as
that of a subject which has passed beyond the limits of practical politics. Heraldry
has been termed 'the shorthand of History', but nevertheless the study of that
shorthand has been approached too often as if it were but the study of a dead
language. The result has been that too much faith has been placed in the works of
older writers, whose dicta have been accepted as both unquestionably correct at
the date they wrote, and, as a consequence, equally binding at the present day.

Since the *Boke of St Albans* was written, into the heraldic portion of which the
author managed to compress an unconscionable amount of rubbish, books and
treatises on the subject of Armory have issued from the press in a constant succession. A few of them stand a head and shoulders above the remainder. The said
remainder have already sunk into oblivion. Such a book as Guillim must of
necessity rank in the forefront of any armorial bibliography; but any one seeking
to judge the Armory of the present day by the standards and ethics adopted by
that writer, would find himself making mistake after mistake, and led hopelessly
astray. There can be very little doubt that the *Display of Heraldry* is an accurate
representation of the laws of Armory which governed the use of Arms at the date
the book was written; and it correctly puts forward the opinions which were then
accepted concerning the past history of the science.

There are two points, however, which must be borne in mind.

The first is that the critical desire for accuracy which fortunately seems to
have been the keynote of research during the nineteenth century, has produced
students of Armory whose investigations into facts have swept away the fables,
the myths, and the falsehood which had collected around the ancient science, and
which in their preposterous assertions had earned for Armory a ridicule, a contempt, and a disbelief which the science itself, and moreover the active practice
of the science, had never at any time warranted or deserved. The desire to gratify
the vanity of illustrious patrons rendered the mythical traditions attached to
Armory more difficult to explode than in the cases of those other sciences in which
no one has a personal interest in upholding the wrong; but a study of the scientific
works of bygone days, and the comparison, for example, of a sixteenth or seventeenth century medical book with a similar work of the present day, will show
that all scientific knowledge during past centuries was a curious conglomeration
of unquestionable fact, interwoven with and partly obscured by a vast amount of
false information, which now can either be dismissed as utter rubbish or contro-
verted and disproved on the score of being plausible untruth. Consequently,
Armory, no less than medicine, theology, or jurisprudence, should not be lightly
esteemed because our predecessors knew less about the subject than is known at the
present day, or because they believed implicitly dogma and tradition which we

ourselves know to be and accept as exploded. Research and investigation constantly goes on, and every day adds to our knowledge.

The second point, which perhaps is the most important, is the patent fact that Heraldry and Armory are not a dead science, but are an actual living reality. Armory may be a quaint survival of a time with different manners and customs, and different ideas from our own, but the word 'Finis' has not yet been written to the science, which is still slowly developing and altering and changing as it is suited to the altered manners and customs of the present day. I doubt not that this view will be a startling one to many who look upon Armory as indissolubly associated with parchments and writings already musty with age. But so long as the Sovereign has the power to create a new order of Knighthood, and attach thereto Heraldic insignia, so long as the Crown has the power to create a new coronet, or to order a new ceremonial, so long as new coats of arms are being called into being—for so long is it idle to treat Armory and Heraldry as a science incapable of further development, or as a science which in recent periods has not altered in its laws.

The many mistaken ideas upon Armory, however, are not all due to the two considerations which have been put forward. Many are due to the fact that the hand-books of Armory professing to detail the laws of the science have not always been written by those having complete knowledge of their subject. Some statement appears in a text-book of Armory, it is copied into book after book, and accepted by those who study Armory as being correct; whilst all the time it is absolutely wrong, and has never been accepted or acted upon by the Officers of Arms. One instance will illustrate my meaning. There is scarcely a text-book of Armory which does not lay down the rule, that when a crest issues from a coronet it must not be placed upon a wreath. Now there is no rule whatever upon the subject; and instances are frequent, both in ancient and in modern grants, in which coronets have been granted to be borne upon wreaths; and the wreath should be inserted or omitted *according to the original grant of the crest*. Consequently, the so-called rule must be expunged.

Another fruitful source of error is the effort which has frequently been made to assimilate the laws of Armory prevailing in the three different kingdoms into one single series of rules and regulations. Some writers have even gone so far as to attempt to assimilate with our own the rules and regulations which hold upon the Continent. As a matter of fact, many of the laws of Arms in England and Scotland are radically different; and care needs to be taken to point out these differences.

The truest way to ascertain the laws of Armory is by deduction from known facts. Nevertheless, such a practice may lead one astray, for the number of exceptions to any given rule in Armory is always great, and it is sometimes difficult to tell what is the rule, and which are the exceptions. Moreover, the Sovereign, as the fountain of honour, can over-ride any rule or law of Arms; and many exceptional cases which have been governed by specific grants have been accepted in times past as demonstrating the laws of Armory, when they have been no more than instances of exceptional favour on the part of the Crown.

In England no one is compelled to bear Arms; but should he desire to do so, the Inland Revenue, until the end of 1944, required a payment of one or two guineas annually, according to the method of usage. From this source the yearly revenue exceeded £70,000. This affords pretty clear evidence that Armory is still decidedly popular, and that its use and display are extensive; but at the same time it would be foolish to suppose that the estimation in which Armory is held, is equal to, or approaches, the romantic value which in former days was attached to the inheritance of Arms. The result of this has been—and it is not to be wondered at—that ancient examples are accepted and extolled beyond what should be the case. It should be borne in mind that the very ancient examples of Armory which have come down to us, may be examples of the handicraft of ignorant individuals; and it is not safe to accept unquestioningly laws of Arms which are deduced from Heraldic *handicraft* of other days. Most of them are correct, because as a rule such handicraft was done under supervision; but there is always the risk that it has not been; and *this risk should be borne in mind* when estimating the value of any particular example of Armory as proof or contradiction of any particular Armorial law. There were 'heraldic stationers' before the present day.

A somewhat similar consideration must govern the estimate of the Heraldic art of a former day. To every action we are told there is a reaction; and the reaction of the present day, admirable and commendable as it undoubtedly is, which has taken the art of Armory back to the style in vogue in past centuries, needs to be kept within intelligent bounds. That the freedom of design and draughtsmanship of the old artists should be copied is desirable; but at the same time there is not the slightest necessity to copy, and to deliberately copy, the crudeness of execution which undoubtedly exists in much of the older work. The revulsion from what has been aptly styled 'the die-sinker school of heraldry' has caused some artists to produce Heraldic drawings which (though doubtless modelled upon ancient examples) are grotesque to the last degree, and can be described in no other way.

In conclusion, I have to repeat my grateful acknowledgments to the many individuals who assisted me in the preparation of my *Art of Heraldry*, upon which this present volume is founded, and whose work I have again made use of.

A. C. FOX-DAVIES

23 OLD BUILDINGS,
LINCOLN'S INN, W.C.

1 · The Origin of Armory

Armory is that science of which the rules and the laws govern the use, display, meaning, and knowledge of the pictured signs and emblems appertaining to shield, helmet, or banner. Heraldry has a wider meaning, for it comprises everything within the duties of a herald; and whilst Armory undoubtedly is Heraldry, the regulation of ceremonials and matters of pedigree, which are really also within the scope of Heraldry, most decidedly are not Armory.

'Armory' relates only to the emblems and devices. 'Armoury' relates to the weapons themselves as weapons of warfare, or to the place used for the storing of the weapons. But these distinctions of spelling are modern.

The word 'Arms', like many other words in the English language, has several meanings, and at the present day is used in several senses. It may mean the weapons themselves; it may mean the limbs upon the human body. Even from the heraldic point of view it may mean the entire achievement, but usually it is employed in reference to the device upon the shield only.

Of the exact origin of arms and armory nothing whatever is definitely known, and it becomes difficult to point to any particular period as the period covering the origin of armory, for the very simple reason that it is much more difficult to decide what is or is not to be admitted as armorial.

Until comparatively recently heraldic books referred armory indifferently to the tribes of Israel, to the Greeks, to the Romans, to the Assyrians and the Saxons; and we are equally familiar with the 'Lion of Judah' and the 'Eagle of the Cæsars'. In other directions we find the same sort of thing, for it has ever been the practice of semi-civilised nations to bestow or to assume the virtues and the names of animals and of deities as symbols of honour. We scarcely need refer to the totems of the North American Indians for proof of such a practice. They have reduced the subject almost to an exact science; and there cannot be the shadow of a doubt that it is to this semi-savage practice that armory is to be traced if its origin is to be followed out to its logical and most remote beginning. Equally is it certain that many recognised heraldic figures, and more particularly those mythical creatures of which the armorial menagerie alone has now cognisance, are due to the art of civilisations older than our own, and the legends of those civilisations which have called these mythical creatures into being.

The widest definition of armory would have it that any pictorial badge which is used by an individual or a family with the meaning that it is a badge indicative of that person or family, and adopted and repeatedly used in that sense, is heraldic. If such be your definition, you may ransack the Scriptures for the arms of the tribes of Israel, the writings of the Greek and Roman poets for the decorations of the armour and the persons of their heroes, mythical and actual, and you may annex numberless 'heraldic' instances from the art of Nineveh, of Babylon, and of Egypt. Your heraldry is of the beginning and from the beginning. It *is* fact, but is it heraldry? The statement in the *Boke of St Albans* that Christ was a gentleman of coat armour is a fable, and due distinction must be had between the fact and the fiction in this as in all other similar cases.

Mr G. W. Eve, in his *Decorative Heraldry*, alludes to and illustrates many striking examples of figures of an embryonic type of heraldry, of which the best are one from a Chaldean bas-relief 4000 B.C., the earliest known device that can in any way be called heraldic, and another, a device from a Byzantine silk of the tenth century. Mr Eve certainly seems inclined to follow the older heraldic writers in giving as wide an interpretation as possible to the word heraldic, but it is significant that none of these early instances which he gives appear to have any relation to a shield, so that, even if it be conceded that the figures are heraldic, they certainly cannot be said to be armorial. But doubtless the inclusion of such instances is due to an attempt, conscious or unconscious, on the part of the writers who have taken their stand on the side of great antiquity to so frame the definition of armory that it shall include everything heraldic, and due perhaps somewhat to the half unconscious reasoning that these mythical animals, and more especially the peculiarly heraldic positions they are depicted in, which nowadays we only know as part of armory, and which exist nowhere else within our knowledge save within the charmed circle of heraldry, must be evidence of the great antiquity of that science or art, call it which you will. But it is a false deduction, due to a confusion of premise and conclusion. We find certain figures at the present day purely heraldic—we find those figures fifty centuries ago. It certainly seems a correct conclusion that, therefore, heraldry must be of that age. But is not the real conclusion, that, our heraldic figures being so old, it is evident that the figures originated long before heraldry was ever thought of, and that instead of these mythical figures having been originated by the necessities of heraldry, and being part, or even the rudimentary origin of heraldry, they had existed *for other reasons and purposes*—and that when the science of heraldry sprang into being, it found the *whole range* of its forms and charges already existing, and that *none* of these figures owe their being to heraldry? The gryphon is supposed to have *originated*, as is the double-headed eagle, from the dimidiation of two coats of arms resulting from impalement by reasons of marriage. Both these figures were known ages earlier. Thus departs yet another of the little fictions which past writers on armory have fostered and perpetuated. Whether the ancient Egyptians and Assyrians knew they were depicting mythical animals, and did it, intending them to be symbolical of attributes of their deities, something beyond what they were familiar with in their ordinary life, we do not know; nor indeed have we any certain knowledge that there have never been animals of which their figures are but imperfect and crude representations.

But it does not necessarily follow that because an Egyptian artist drew a certain figure, which figure is now appropriated to the peculiar use of armory, that he knew anything whatever of the laws of armory. Further, where is this argument to end? There is nothing peculiarly heraldic about the lion passant, statant, dormant, couchant, or salient, and though heraldic artists may for the sake of artistic appearance distort the brute away from his natural figure, the rampant is alone the position which exists not in nature; and if the argument is to be applied to the

2

bitter end, heraldry must be taken back to the very earliest instance which exists of any representation of a lion. The proposition is absurd. The ancient artists drew their lions how they liked, regardless of armory and its laws, which did not then exist; and, from decorative reasons, they evolved a certain number of methods of depicting the positions of *e.g.* the lion and the eagle to suit their decorative purposes. When heraldry came into existence it came in as an adjunct of decoration, and it necessarily followed that the whole of the positions in which the craftsmen found the eagle or the lion depicted were appropriated with the animals for heraldry. That this appropriation for the exclusive purposes of armory has been silently acquiesced in by the decorative artists of later days is simply proof of the intense power and authority which accrued later to armory, and which was in fact attached to anything relating to privilege and prerogative. To put it baldly, the dominating authority of heraldry and its dogmatic protection by the Powers that were, appropriated certain figures to its use, and then defied anyone to use them for more humble decorative purposes not allied with armory. And it is the trail of this autocratic appropriation, and from the decorative point of view this arrogant appropriation, which can be traced in the present idea that a griffin or a spread eagle, for example, must be heraldic. Consequently the argument as to the antiquity of heraldry which is founded upon the discovery of the heraldic creature in the remote ages goes by the board. One practical instance may perhaps more fully demonstrate my meaning. There is one figure, probably the most beautiful of all of those which we owe to Egypt, which is now rapidly being absorbed into heraldry. I refer to the Sphinx. This, whilst strangely in keeping with the remaining mythical heraldic figures, for some reason or other escaped the exclusive appropriation of armorial use until within modern times. One of the earliest instances of its use in recognised armory occurs in the grant to Sir John Moore, K.B., the hero of Corunna, and another will be found in the augmentation granted to Admiral Sir Alexander Cochrane, K.B. Since then it has been used on some number of occasions. It certainly remained, however, for a former Garter King of Arms to evolve from the depths of his imagination a position which no Egyptian sphinx ever occupied, when he granted two of them as supporters to Sir Edward Malet, G.C.B. The Sphinx has also been adopted as the badge of one of his Majesty's regiments, and I have very little doubt that the Sphinx will figure in some of the grants to commemorate fortunes made in Egypt, or lifetimes spent in the Egyptian services. If this be so, the dominating influence of armory will doubtless in the course of another century have given to the Sphinx, as it has to many other objects, a distinctly heraldic nature and character in the mind of the 'man in the street' to which we nowadays so often refer the arbitrament between conflicting opinions. Perhaps in the even yet more remote future, when the world in general accepts as a fact that armory did not exist at the time of the Norman Conquest, we shall have some interesting and enterprising individual writing a book to demonstrate that because the Sphinx existed in Egypt long before the days of Cleopatra, heraldry must of necessity be equally antique.

I have no wish, however, to dismiss thus lightly the subject of the antiquity of heraldry, because there is one side of the question which I have not yet touched upon, and that is, the symbolism of these ancient and so called heraldic examples.

3

There is no doubt whatever that symbolism forms an integral part of armory; in fact there is no doubt that armory *itself* as a whole is nothing more or less than a kind of symbolism. I have no sympathy whatever with many of the ideas concerning this symbolism, which will be found in nearly all heraldic books before the day of J. R. Planché, Somerset Herald, who fired the train which exploded then and for ever the absurd ideas of former writers. That an argent field meant purity, that a field of gules meant royal or even martial ancestors, that a saltire meant the capture of a city, or a lion rampant noble and enviable qualities, I utterly deny. But that nearly every coat of arms for any one of the name of Fletcher bears upon it in some form or another an arrow or an arrow-head, because the origin of the names come from the occupation of the fletcher, who was an arrow-maker, is true enough. Symbolism of that kind will be found constantly in armory, as in the case of the foxes and foxes' heads in the various coats of Fox, the lions in the coats of arms of Lyons, the horse in the arms of Trotter, and the acorns in the arms of Oakes; in fact by far the larger proportion of the older coats of arms, where they can be traced to their real origin, exhibit some such derivation. There is another kind of symbolism which formerly, and still, favours the introduction of swords and spears and bombshells into grants of arms to military men, that gives bezants to bankers and those connected with money, and that assigns woolpacks and cotton-plants to the shields of textile merchants; but that is a sane and reasonable symbolism, which the reputed symbolism of the earlier heraldry books was not.

It has yet to be demonstrated, however, though the belief is very generally credited, that all these very ancient Egyptian and Assyrian figures of a heraldic character had anything of symbolism about them. But even granting the whole symbolism which is claimed for them, we get but little further. There is no doubt that the eagle from untold ages has had an imperial symbolism which it still possesses. But that symbolism is not necessarily heraldic, and it is much more probable that heraldry appropriated both the eagle and its symbolism ready made, and together: consequently, if, as we have shown, the *existence* of the eagle is not proof of the coeval existence of heraldry, no more is the existence of the *symbolical* imperial eagle. For if we are to regard all symbolism as heraldic, where are we either to begin or to end? Church vestments and ecclesiastical emblems are symbolism run riot; in fact they are little else: but by no stretch of imagination can these be considered heraldic with the exception of the few (for example the crosier, the mitre, and the pallium) which heraldry has appropriated ready made. Therefore, though heraldry appropriated ready made from other decorative art, and from nature and handicraft, the whole of its charges, and though it is evident heraldry also appropriated ready made a great deal of its symbolism, neither the earlier existence of the forms which it appropriated, nor the earlier existence of their symbolism, can be said to weigh at all as determining factors in the consideration of the age of heraldry. Sloane Evans in his *Grammar of Heraldry* (p. ix) gives the following instances as evidence of the greater antiquity and they are worthy at any rate of attention if the matter is to be impartially considered.

The antiquity of ensigns and symbols may be proved by reference to Holy Writ.

1. 'Take ye the sum of all the congregation of the children of Israel, after their

families, by the house of their fathers, with the number of their names. . . . And they assembled all the congregation together on the first day of the second month; and they declared their pedigrees after their families, by the house of their fathers, according to the number of the names, from twenty years old and upward. . . . And the children of Israel shall pitch their tents, every man by his own camp, and every man by his own standard, throughout their hosts' (Numbers i. 2, 18, 52).

2. 'Every man of the children of Israel shall pitch by his own standard, with the ensign of their father's house' (Numbers ii. 2).

3. 'And the children of Israel did according to all that the Lord commanded Moses: so they pitched by their standards, and so they set forward, every one after their families, according to the house of their fathers' (Numbers ii. 34).

The Latin and Greek poets and historians afford numerous instances of the use of symbolic ornaments and devices. It will be sufficient in this work to quote from Æschylus and Virgil, as poets: Herodotus and Tacitus, as historians.

Æschylus. *Septem contra Thebas*

The poet here introduces a dialogue between Eteocles, King of Thebes, the women who composed the chorus, and a herald (κῆρυξ), which latter is pointing out the seven captains or chiefs of the army of Adrastus against Thebes; distinguishing one from another by the emblematical devices upon their shields.

1. TYDEUS.

Τοιαῦν ἀϋτῶν—νυκτὸς ὀφθαλμὸς πρέπει. Lines 380–6.

. . . Frowning he speaks, and shakes
The dark crest streaming o'er his shaded helm
In triple wave; whilst dreadful ring around
The brazen bosses of his shield, impress'd
With his proud argument: 'A sable sky
Burning with stars; and in the midst full orb'd
A silver moon;' the eye of night o'er all,
Awful in beauty, forms her peerless light.

2. CAPANEUS.

Ἔχει δὲ σῆμα,—ΠΡΗΣΩ ΠΟΛΙΝ. Lines 428–30.

On his proud shield portray'd: 'A naked man
Waves in his hand a blazing torch;' beneath
In golden letters—'I will fire the city.'

3. ETEOCLUS.

Ἐσχημάτισται,—πυργωμάτων. Lines 461–5.

. . . No mean device
Is sculptured on his shield: 'A man in arms,
His ladder fix'd against the enemies' walls,
Mounts, resolute, to rend their rampires down;'
And cries aloud (the letters plainly mark'd),
'Not Mars himself shall beat me from the Tow'rs.'

4. HIPPOMEDON.

Ὁ σηματουργὸς—φόβον βλέπων. Lines 487–94.

. . . On its orb, no vulgar artist
Expressed this image: 'A Typhæus huge,

5

Disgorging from his foul enfounder'd jaws,
In fierce effusion wreaths of dusky smoke.
Signal of kindling flames; its bending verge
With folds of twisted serpents border'd round.'
With shouts the giant chief provokes the war,
And in the ravings of outrageous valour
Glares terror from his eyes . . . .

5. PARTHENOPÆUS.

Ὸν μήν ἀκόμπαστος—ἴαπτεσθαι Βέλη. Lines 534-40.

. . . Upon his clashing shield,
Whose orb sustains the storm of war, he bears
The foul disgrace of Thebes: 'A rav'nous Sphynx
Fixed to the plates: the burnish'd monster round
Pours a portentous gleam: beneath her lies
A Theban mangled by her cruel fangs:'
'Gainst this let each brave arm direct the spear

6. AMPHIARAUS.

Τοιαῦθ ὁ μάντις—βλαστανει βουλευματα. Lines 587-91.

So spoke the prophet; and with awful port
Advanc'd his massy shield, the shining orb
Bearing no impress, for his gen'rous soul
Wishes to be, not to appear, the best;
And from the culture of his modest worth
Bears the rich fruit of great and glorious deeds.

7. POLYNICES.

Εχει δὲ—τᾰ ξευρηματα. Lines 639-46.

. . . His well-orb'd shield he holds,
New wrought, and with a double impress charg'd:
A warrior, blazing all in golden arms,
A female form of modest aspect leads,
Expressing justice, as th' inscription speaks,
'Yet once more to his country, and once more
To his Paternal Throne I will restore him'—
Such their devices . . . .

Virgil. *The Æneid*

1. Atque hic exultans—insigne decorum. *Lib. ii. lines 386-92.*

Choræbus, with youthful hopes beguil'd,
Swol'n with success, and of a daring mind,
This new invention fatally design'd.
'My friends,' said he, 'since fortune shows the way,
'Tis fit we should the auspicious guide obey.
For what has she these Grecian arms bestowed,
But their destruction, and the Trojans' good?
Then change we shields, and their devices bear:
Let fraud supply the want of force in war.
They find us arms.' This said, himself he dress'd
In dead Androgeos' spoils, his upper best,
His painted buckler, and his plumy crest.

2. Post hos insignem—serpentibus hydram. *Lib. vii. lines 655–8.*

> Next Aventinus drives his chariot round
> The Latian plains, with palms and laurels crown'd.
> Proud of his steeds, he smokes along the field;
> His father's hydra fills his ample shield;
> A hundred serpents his about the brims;
> The son of Hercules he justly seems,
> By his broad shoulders and gigantic limbs.

3. Sequitur pulcherrimus Astur—insigne paternæ. *Lib. x. lines 180–8.*

> Fair Astur follows in the wat'ry field,
> Proud of his manag'd horse, and painted shield.
> Thou muse, the name of Cinyras renew,
> And brave Cupavo follow'd but by few;
> Whose helm confess'd the lineage of the man,
> And bore, with wings display'd, a silver swan.
> Love was the fault of his fam'd ancestry.
> Whose forms and fortunes in his Ensigns fly.

Herodotus

1. CLIO, § 171.

Καί σφι τριξὰ ἐξευρήματα ἔγένετο—τὰ σημήϊα ποιέεσθαι.

And to them is allowed the invention of three things, which have come into use among the Greeks: For the Carians seem to be the first who put crests upon their helmets and sculptured devices upon their shields.

2. CALLIOPE, § 74.

Ὁ δὲτερος τῶν λόγων—ἐπίοημον ἄγκυραν.

Those who deny this statement assert that he (Sophanes) bare on his shield, as a device, an anchor.

Tacitus. *The Annals.* Lib. I

1. Tum redire paulatim—in sedes referunt. *Cap. 28.*

They relinquished the guard of the gates; and the Eagles and other Ensigns, which in the beginning of the Tumult they had thrown together, were now restored each to its distinct station.

Potter in his *Antiquities of Greece* (Dunbar's edition, Edinburgh, 1824, vol. ii, page 79), thus speaks of the ensigns or flags (σημεῖα) used by the Grecians in their military affairs: 'Of these there were different sorts, several of which were adorned with images of animals, or other things bearing peculiar relations to the cities they belong to. The Athenians, for instance, bore an *owl* in their ensigns (Plutarchus Lysandro), as being sacred to Minerva, the protectress of their city; the Thebans a *Sphynx* (*idem*, Pelopidas, Cornelius Nepos, Epaminondas), in memory of the famous monster overcome by Œdipus. The Persians paid divine honours to the sun, and therefore represented him in their ensigns' (Curtius, lib. 3). Again (on page 150), speaking of the ornaments and devices on their ships, he says: 'Some other things there are in the prow and stern that deserve our notice, as those ornaments wherewith the extremities of the ship were beautified, commonly called ἀβϱονεα (or νεῶν ϰοϱωνίδες), in Latin, *Corymbi*. The form of them sometimes represented helmets, sometimes living creatures, but most frequently was winded into a round compass, whence they are so commonly named *Corymbi* and *Coronæ*. To the ἀϰϱοστόλια in the prow, answered the ἄφγαστα in the stern, which were often of an orbicular figure, or fashioned like wings, to which a little shield called ἀσπιδειον, or ἀσπιδίσϰη, was frequently affixed; sometimes a piece of wood was erected, whereon ribbons of divers colours were hung, and served instead of a flag to distinguish the ship. Χηνίσϰος was so called from Χὴν, *a Goose*, whose figure it resembled, because geese were looked on as fortunate omens to mariners, for that they swim on the top of the waters and sink not. Παϱάσημον was the flag whereby ships were distinguished from one another; it was placed in the prow, just below the στόλος, being sometimes carved, and frequently painted, whence it is in Latin termed *pictura*, representing the form of a *mountain*, a *tree*, a *flower*, or any other thing, wherein it was distinguished from what was called *tutela*, or the safeguard of the ship, which always represented *some one of the gods*, to whose care and protection the ship was recommended; for which reason it was held sacred. Now and then we find the *tutela* taken for the Παϱάσημον and perhaps sometimes the images of gods might be represented on the flags; by some it is placed also in the prow, but by most authors of credit assigned to the stern. Thus Ovid in his Epistle to Paris:

> Accipit et pictos puppis adunca Deos.
> The stern with painted deities richly shines.

'The Ship wherein Europa was conveyed from Phœnicia into Crete had a *bull* for its flag, and *Jupiter* for its tutelary deity. The Bœotian ships had for their tutelar god *Cadmus*, represented with a *dragon* in his hand, because he was the founder of Thebes, the principal city of Bœotia. The name of the ship was usually taken from the flag, as appears in the following passage of Ovid, where he tells us his ship received its name from the helmet painted upon it:

> Est mihi, sitque, precor, flavæ tutela Minervæ,
> Navis et à pictâ casside nomen habit.

> Minerva is the goddess I adore,
> And may she grant the blessings I implore;
> The ship its name a painted helmet gives.

'Hence comes the frequent mention of ships called *Pegasi*, *Scyllæ*, *Bulls*, *Rams*, *Tigers*, &c., which the poets took liberty to represent as living creatures that transported their riders from one country to another; nor was there (according to some) any other ground for those known fictions of Pegasus, the winged Bellerophon, or the Ram which is reported to have carried Phryxus to Colchos.'

To quote another very learned author: 'The system of hieroglyphics, or symbols, was adopted into every mysterious institution, for the purpose of concealing the most sublime secrets of religion from the prying curiosity of the vulgar; to whom nothing was exposed but the beauties of the morality.' (See Ramsay's *Travels of Cyrus*, lib. 3.) 'The old Asiatic style, so highly figurative, seems, by what we find of its remains in the prophetic language of the sacred writers, to have been evidently fashioned to the mode of the ancient hieroglyphics; for as in hieroglyphic writing the sun, moon, and stars were used to represent states and empires, kings, queens, and nobility—their eclipse and extinction, temporary disasters, or entire overthrow—fire and flood, desolation by war and famine; plants or animals, the qualities of particular persons, &c.; so, in like manner, the Holy Prophets call kings and empires by the names of the heavenly luminaries; their misfortunes and overthrow are represented by eclipses and extinction; stars falling from the firmament are employed to denote the destruction of the nobility; thunder and tempestuous winds, hostile invasions; lions, bears, leopards, goats, or high trees, leaders of armies, conquerors, and founders of empires; royal dignity is described by purple, or a crown; iniquity by spotted garments; a warrior by a sword or bow; a powerful man, by a gigantic stature; a judge by balance, weights, and measures— in a word, the prophetic style seems to be a speaking hieroglyphic.'

It seems to me, however, that the whole of these are no more than symbolism, though they are undoubtedly symbolism of a high and methodical order, little removed from our own armory. Personally I do not consider them to be armory, but if the word is to be stretched to the utmost latitude to permit of their inclusion, one certain conclusion follows. That if the heraldry of that day had an orderly existence, it most certainly came absolutely to an end and disappeared. Armory as we know it, the armory of today, which as a system is traced back to the period of the Crusades, is no mere continuation by adoption. It is a distinct development and a re-development *ab initio*. Undoubtedly there is a period in the early development of European civilisation which is destitute alike of armory, or of anything of that nature. The civilisation of Europe is not the civilisation of Egypt, of Greece, or of Rome, nor a continuation thereof, but a new development, and though each of these in its turn attained a high degree of civilisation and may have separately developed a heraldic symbolism much akin to armory, as a natural consequence of its own development, as the armory we know is a development of its own consequent upon the rise of our own civilisation, nevertheless it is unjustifiable to attempt to establish continuity between the ordered symbolism of earlier but distinct civilisations, and our own present system of armory. The one and only civilisation which has preserved its continuity is that of the Jewish race. In spite of persecution the Jews have preserved unchanged the minutest details of ritual law and ceremony, the causes of their suffering. Had heraldry, which is and has always been a matter of pride, formed a part of their distinctive life we should find it still existing. Yet the fact remains that no trace of Jewish heraldry can be found until modern times. Consequently I accept unquestioningly the conclusions of the late J. R. Planché, Somerset Herald, who unhesitatingly asserted that armory did not exist at the time of the Conquest, basing his conclusions principally upon the entire absence of armory from the seals of that period, and the Bayeux tapestry.

The family tokens (*mon*) of the Japanese, however, fulfil very nearly all of the essentials of armory, although considered heraldically they may appear somewhat peculiar to European eyes. Though perhaps never forming the entire decoration of a shield, they do appear upon weapons and armour, and are used most lavishly in the decoration of clothing, rooms, furniture, and in fact almost every conceivable object, being employed for *decorative* purposes in precisely the same manners and methods that armorial devices are decoratively made use of in this

1 *Kiku-non-hana-mon. State* Mon *of Japan.*

9

2 *Kiri-mon.* Mon
of the Mikado.

3 *Awoï-mon.* Mon of the
House of Minamoto
Tokugawa.

4 Mon *of the House of*
Minamoto Ashikaya.

5 *Tomoye.*
Mon *of the*
House of Arina.

6 *Double eagle on a coin*
(*drachma*) *under the Orthogide*
of Kaifa Naçr Edin Mahmud,
1217.

country. A Japanese of the upper classes always has his *mon* in three places upon his *kimono,* usually at the back just below the collar and on either sleeve. The Japanese servants also wear their service badge in much the same manner that in olden days the badge was worn by the servants of a nobleman. The design of the service badge occupies the whole available surface of the back, and is reproduced in a miniature form on each lappel of the *kimono.* Unfortunately, like armorial bearings in Europe, but to a far greater extent, the Japanese *mon* has been greatly pirated and abused.

1, 'Kiku-non-hana-mon,' formed from the conventionalised bloom (*hana*) of the chrysanthemum, is the *mon* of the State. It is formed of sixteen petals arranged in a circle, and connected on the outer edge by small curves.

2, 'Kiri-mon,' is the personal *mon* of the Mikado, formed of the leaves and flower of the *Paulowna imperialis,* conventionally treated.

3, 'Awoï-mon,' is the *mon* of the House of Minamoto Tokugawa, and is composed of three sea leaves (*Asarum*). The Tokugawa reigned over the country as *Shogune* from 1603 until the last revolution in 1867, before which time the Emperor (the Mikado) was only nominally the ruler.

4 shows the *mon* of the House of Minamoto Ashikaya, which from 1336 until 1573 enjoyed the Shogunat.

5 shows the second *mon* of the House of Arina, Toymote, which is used, however, throughout Japan as a sign of luck.

The Saracens and the Moors, to whom we owe the origin of so many of our recognised heraldic charges and the derivation of some of our terms (*e.g.* 'gules', from the Persian *gul,* and 'azure' from the Persian *lazur*) had evidently on their part something more than the rudiments of armory, as 6 to 11 will indicate.

One of the best definitions of a coat of arms that I know, though this is not perfect, requires the twofold qualification that the design must be hereditary and must be connected with armour. And there can be no doubt that the theory of armory as we now know it is governed by those two ideas. The shields and the crests, if any decoration of a helmet is to be called a crest, of the Greeks and the Romans undoubtedly come within the one requirement. Also were they indicative of and perhaps intended to be symbolical of the owner. They lacked, however, heredity, and we have no proof that the badges we read of, or the decorations of shield and helmet, were continuous even during a single lifetime. Certainly as we now understand the term there must be both continuity of use, if the arms be impersonal, or heredity if the arms be personal. Likewise must there be their use as decorations of the implements of warfare.

If we exact these qualifications as essential, armory as a fact and as a science is a product of later days, and is the evolution from the idea of tribal badges and tribal means and methods of honour applied to the decoration of implements of warfare. It is the conjunction and association of these two distinct ideas to which is added the no less important idea of heredity. The civilisation of England before the Conquest has left us no trace of any sort or kind that the Saxons, the Danes, or the Celts either knew or practised armory. So that if armory as we know it is to be traced to the period of the Norman Conquest, we must look for it as an adjunct of the altered civilisation and the altered law which Duke William brought into this country. Such evidence as exists is to the contrary, and there is nothing that can be truly termed armorial in that marvellous piece of cotemporaneous workmanship known as the Bayeux tapestry.

Concerning the Bayeux tapestry and the evidence it affords, Woodward and Burnett's *Treatise on Heraldry*, apparently following Planché's conclusions, remarks: 'The evidence afforded by the famous tapestry preserved in the public library of Bayeux, a series of views in sewed work representing the invasion and conquest of England by WILLIAM the Norman, has been appealed to on both sides of this controversy, and has certainly an important bearing on the question of the antiquity of coat-armour. This panorama of seventy-two scenes is on probable grounds believed to have been the work of the Conqueror's Queen MALTIDA and her maidens; though the French historian THIERRY and others ascribe it to the Empress MAUD, daughter of HENRY III. The latest authorities suggest the likelihood of its having been wrought as a decoration of the Cathedral of Bayeux, when rebuilt by WILLIAM's uterine brother ODO, Bishop of that See, in 1077. The exact correspondence which has been discovered between the length of the tapestry and the inner circumference of the nave of the cathedral greatly favours this supposition. This remarkable work of art, as carefully drawn in colour in 1818 by Mr C. STOTHARD, is reproduced in the sixth volume of the *Vetusta Monumenta*; and more recently an excellent copy of it from autotype plates has been published by the Arundel Society.[1] Each of its scenes is accompanied by a Latin description, the whole uniting into a graphic history of the event commemorated. We see HAROLD taking leave of EDWARD THE CONFESSOR; riding to Bosham with his hawk and hounds; embarking for France; landing there and being captured by the Count of Ponthieu; redeemed by WILLIAM of Normandy, and in the midst of his Court aiding him against CONAN, Count of BRETAGNE; swearing on the sacred relics to recognise WILLIAM's claim of succession to the English throne, and then re-embarking for England. On his return, we have him recounting the incidents of his journey to EDWARD THE CONFESSOR, to whose funeral obsequies we are next introduced. Then we have HAROLD receiving the crown from the English people, and ascending the throne; and WILLIAM, apprised of what had taken place, consulting with his half-brother ODO about invading England. The war preparations of the Normans, their embarkation, their landing, their march to Hastings, and formation of a camp there, form the subjects of successive scenes; and finally we have the battle of Hastings, with the death of Harold and the flight of the English. In this remarkable piece of work we have figures of more than six hundred persons, and seven hundred animals, besides thirty-seven buildings, and forty-one ships or boats. There are of course also numerous shields of warriors, of which some are round, others kite-shaped, and on some of the latter are rude figures, of dragons or other imaginary animals, as well as crosses of different forms, and spots. On one hand it requires little imagination to find the cross *patée* and the cross *botonnée* of heraldry prefigured on two of these shields. But there are several fatal objections to regarding these figures as incipient *armory*, namely that while the most prominent persons of the time are depicted, most of them repeatedly, none of these is ever represented twice as bearing the same device, nor

1. One of the most beautiful as well as the most definitive works on the tapestry was published by Phaidon in 1957. It is entitled *The Bayeux Tapestry*, and contains contributions by leading experts in history, palaeography, textiles, costumes and armour.

7 *Device of the Mameluke Emir Toka Timur, Governor of Rahaba, 1350.*

8 *Lily on the Bab-al-Hadid gate at Damascus.*

9 *Device of the Emir Arkatây (a band between two keys).*

10 *Device of the Mameluke Emir Schaikhu.*

11 *Device of Abu Abdallah, Mohammed ibn Naçr, King of Granada, said to be the builder of the Alhambra (1231–1272).*

is there one instance of any resemblance in the rude designs described to the bearings actually used by the descendants of the persons in question. If a personage so important and so often depicted as the Conqueror had borne arms, they could not fail to have had a place in a nearly contemporary work, and more especially if it proceeded from the needle of his wife.'

Lower, in his *Curiosities of Heraldry*, clinches the argument when he writes: 'Nothing but disappointment awaits the curious armorist who seeks in this venerable memorial the pale, the bend, and other early elements of arms. As these would have been much more easily imitated with the needle than the grotesque figures before alluded to, we may safely conclude that personal arms had not yet been introduced.' The *Treatise on Heraldry* proceeds: 'The Second Crusade took place in 1147; and in MONTFAUCON's plates of the no longer extant windows of the Abbey of St Denis, representing that historical episode, there is not a trace of an armorial ensign on any of the shields. That window was probably executed at a date when the memory of that event was fresh; but in MONTEFAUCON's time, the beginning of the eighteenth century, the *Science héroïque* was matter of such moment in France that it is not to be believed that the armorial figures on the shields, had there been any, would have been left out.

Surely, if anywhere, we might have expected to have found evidence of armory, if it had then existed, in the Bayeux Tapestry. Neither do the seals nor the coins of the period produce a shield of arms. Nor amongst the host of records and documents which have been preserved to us do we find any reference to armorial bearings. The intense value and estimation attached to arms in the fourteenth and fifteenth centuries, which has steadily though slowly declined since that period, would lead one to suppose that had arms existed as we know them at an earlier period, we should have found some definite record of them in the older chronicles. There are no such references, and no coat of arms in use at a later date can be relegated to the Conquest or any anterior period. Of arms, as we know them, there are *isolated examples* in the early part of the twelfth century, *perhaps* also at the end of the eleventh. At the period of the Third Crusade (1189) they were in actual existence as hereditary decorations of weapons of warfare.

Luckily, for the purposes of deductive reasoning, human nature remains much the same throughout the ages, and, dislike it as we may, vanity now and vanity in olden days was a great lever in the determination of human actions. A noticeable result of civilisation is the effort to suppress any sign of natural emotion; and if the human race at the present day is not unmoved by a desire to render its appearance attractive, we may rest very certainly assured that in the twelfth and thirteenth centuries this motive was even more pronounced, and still yet more pronounced at a more remote distance of time. Given an opportunity of ornament, there you will find ornament and decoration. The ancient Britons, like the Maoris of today, found their opportunities restricted to their skins. The Maoris tattoo themselves in intricate patterns, the ancient Britons used woad, though history is silent as to whether they were content with flat colour or gave their preference to patterns. It is unnecessary to trace the art of decoration through embroidery upon clothes, but there is no doubt that as soon as shields came into use they were painted and decorated, though I hestitate to follow practically the whole of heraldic writers in the statement that it was *the necessity for distinction in battle* which accounted for the decoration of shields. Shields were painted and decorated, and helmets were adorned with all sorts of ornament, long *before* the closed helmet made it impossible to recognise a man by his facial peculiarities and distinctions. We have then this underlying principle of vanity, with its concomitant result of personal decoration and adornment. We have the relics of savagery which caused a man to be nicknamed from some animal. The conjunction of the two produces the effort to apply the opportunity for decoration and the vanity of the animal nickname to each other.

We are fast approaching armory. In those days every man fought, and his weapons were the most cherished of his personal possessions. The sword his father fought with, the shield his father carried, the banner his father followed would naturally be amongst the articles a son would be most eager to possess. Herein are the rudiments of the idea of heredity in armory; and the science of armory as we know it begins to slowly evolve itself from that point, for the son would naturally take a pride in upholding the fame which had clustered round the pictured signs and emblems under which his father had warred.

Another element then appeared which exercised a vast influence upon armory. Europe rang from end to end with the call to the Crusades. We may or we may not understand the fanaticism which gripped the whole of the Christian world and sent it forth to fight the Saracens. That has little to do with it. The result was the collection together in a comparatively restricted space of all that was best and noblest amongst the human race at that time. And the spirit of emulation caused nation to vie with nation, and individual with individual in the performance of illustrious feats of honour. War was elevated to the dignity of a sacred duty, and the implements of warfare rose in estimation. It is easy to understand the glory therefore that attached to arms, and the slow evolution which I have been endeavouring to indicate became a concrete fact, and it is due to the Crusades that the origin of armory as we now know it was practically coeval throughout Europe, and also that a large proportion of the charges and terms and rules of heraldry are identical in all European countries.

The next dominating influence was the introduction, in the early part of the thirteenth century, of the closed helmet. This hid the face of the wearer from his followers and necessitated some means by which the latter could identify the man under whom they served. What more natural than that they should identify him by the decoration of his shield and the ornaments of his helmet, and by the coat or surcoat which he wore over his coat of mail?

This surcoat had afforded another opportunity of decoration, and it had been decorated with the same signs that the wearer had painted on his shield, hence the term 'coat of arms'. This textile coat was in itself a product of the Crusades. The Crusaders went in their metal armour from the cooler atmospheres of Europe to the intolerable heat of the East. The surcoat and the lambrequin alike protected the metal armour and the metal helmet from the rays of the sun and the resulting discomfort to the wearer, and were also found very effective as a preventative of the rust resulting from rain and damp upon the metal. By the time that the closed helmet had developed the necessity of distinction and the identification of man with the pictured signs he wore or carried, the evolution of armory into the science we know was practically complete.

13

2 · The status and the meaning of a coat of arms in Great Britain

It would be foolish and misleading to assert that the possession of a coat of arms at the present date has anything approaching the dignity which attached to it in the days of long ago; but one must trace this through the centuries which have passed in order to form a true estimate of it, and also properly to appreciate a coat of arms at the present time. It is necessary to go back to the Norman Conquest and the broad dividing lines of social life in order to obtain a correct knowledge. The Saxons had no armory, though they had a very perfect civilisation. This civilisation William the Conqueror upset, introducing in its place the system of feudal tenure with which he had been familiar on the Continent. Briefly, this feudal system may be described as the partition of the land amongst the barons, earls, and others, in return for which, according to the land they held, they accepted a liability of military service for themselves and so many followers. These barons and earls in their turn sublet the land on terms advantageous to themselves, but nevertheless requiring from those to whom they sublet the same military service which the King had exacted from themselves proportionate with the extent of the sublet lands. Other subdivisions took place, but always with the same liability of military service, until we come to those actually holding and using the lands, enjoying them subject to the liability of military service attached to those particular lands. Every man who held land under these conditions—and it was impossible to hold land without them— was of the upper class. He was *nobilis* or *known*, and of a rank distinct, apart, and absolutely separate from the remainder of the population, who were at one time actually serfs, and for long enough afterwards, of no higher social position than they had enjoyed in their period of servitude. This wide distinction between the upper and lower classes, which existed from one end of Europe to the other, was the very root and foundation of armory. It cannot be too greatly insisted upon. There were two qualitative terms, 'gentle' and 'simple', which were applied to the upper and lower classes respectively. Though now becoming archaic and obsolete, the terms 'gentle' and 'simple' are still occasionally to be met with used in that original sense; and the two adjectives 'gentle' and 'simple', in the everyday meanings of the words, are derived from, and are a *later* growth from, the original usage with the meaning of the upper and lower classes; because the quality of being gentle was supposed to exist in that class of life referred to as gentle, whilst the quality of simplicity was supposed to be an attribute of the lower class. The word gentle is derived from the Latin word *gens* (*gentilis*), meaning a man, because those were *men* who were not serfs. Serfs and slaves were nothing accounted of. The word 'gentleman' is a *derivative* of the word gentle, and a gentleman was a member of the gentle or upper class, and gentle qualities were so termed because they were the qualities supposed to belong to the gentle class. A man was not a gentleman, even in those days, because he happened to possess personal qualities usually associated with the gentle class; a man was a gentleman if he belonged to the gentle or upper class and not otherwise, so that 'gentleman' was an identical term for one to whom the word *nobilis* was applied, both being names for members of the upper class. To all intents and purposes at that date there was no middle class at all. The kingdom was the land; and the trading community who dwelt in the towns were of little account save as milch kine for the purposes of taxation. The social position conceded to them by the upper class was little, if any, more than was conceded to the lower classes, whose life and liberties were held very cheaply. Briefly to sum up, therefore, there were but the two classes in existence, of which the upper class were those who held the land, who had military obligations, and who were noble, or in other words gentle. Therefore all who held land were gentlemen; because they held land they had to lead their servants and followers into battle, and they themselves were personally responsible for the appearance of so many followers, when the King summoned them to war. Now we have seen in the previous chapter that arms became necessary to the leader that his followers might distinguish him in battle. Consequently all who held land having, because of that land, to be responsible for followers in battle, found it necessary to use arms. The corollary is therefore evident, that all who held lands of the King were gentlemen or noble, and used arms; and as a consequence all who possessed arms were gentlemen, for they would not need or use arms, nor was their armour of a character upon which they could display arms, unless they were leaders. The leaders, we have seen, were the land-owning or upper class; therefore every one who had arms was a gentleman, and every gentleman had arms. But the status of gentlemen existed before there were coats of arms, and the later inseparable connection between the two was an evolution.

The preposterous prostitution of the word gentleman in these latter days is due to the almost universal attribute of human nature which declines to admit itself as of other than gentle rank; and in the eager desire to write itself gentleman, it has deliberately accepted and ordained a meaning to the word which it did not formerly possess, and has attributed to it and allowed it only such a definition as would enable almost anybody to be included within its ranks.

The word gentleman nowadays has become meaningless as a word in an ordinary vocabulary; and to use the word with its original and true meaning, it is necessary now to consider it as purely a technical term. We are so accustomed to employ the word nowadays in its unrestricted usage that we are apt to overlook the fact that such a usage is comparatively modern. The following extract from *The Right to Bear Arms* will prove that its real meaning was understood and was decided by law so late as the seventeenth century to be 'a man entitled to bear arms':

15

The following case in the Earl Marshal's Court, which hung upon the definition of the word, conclusively proves my contention:

'*21st November* 1637. W. Baker, gent., humbly sheweth that having some occasion of conference with Adam Spencer of Broughton under the Bleane, co. Cant., on or about 28th July last, the said Adam did in most base and opprobrious tearmes abuse your petitioner, calling him a base, lying fellow, &c. &c. The defendant pleaded that Baker is noe Gentleman, and soe not capable of redresse in this court. Le Neve, Clarenceux, is directed to examine the point raised, and having done so, declared as touching the gentry of William Baker, that Robert Cooke, Clarenceux King of Arms, did make a declaration 10th May 1573, under his hand and seale of office, that George Baker of London, sonne of J. Baker of the same place, sonne of Simon Baker of Feversham, co. Cant., was a bearer of tokens of honour, and did allow and confirm to the said George Baker and to his posterity, and to the posterity of Christopher Baker, these Arms, &c. &c. And further, Le Neve has received proof that the petitioner, William Baker, is the son of William Baker of Kingsdowne, co. Cant., who was the brother of George Baker, and son of Christopher aforesaid.' The judgment is not stated. (The original Confirmation of Arms by Cooke, 10th May 1573, may now be seen in the British Museum. *Genealogist* for 1889, p. 242.)[2]

It has been shown that originally practically all who held land bore arms. It has also been shown that armory was an evolution, and as a consequence it did not start, in this country at any rate, as a ready-made science with all its rules and laws completely known or promulgated. There is not the slightest doubt that, in the earliest infancy of the science, arms were assumed and chosen without the control of the Crown; and one would not be far wrong in assuming that, so long as the rights accruing from prior appropriation of other people were respected, a landowner finding the necessity of arms in battle, was originally at liberty to assume what arms he liked.

That period, however, was of but brief duration, for we find as early as 1390,

2. Here Fox-Davies is quoting himself, for *The Right to Bear Arms* by 'X' (revised edition, 1900) was, in fact, his own book. Whilst it is true that many cases brought before the Court of Chivalry turned on the question of a man's gentility and whilst the simplest way of proving gentility was to establish a right to arms, the insignia of gentility, the meaning of the word gentleman was not 'a man entitled to bear arms'. A man who bore arms was 'a gentleman of coat armour' but a man could also be accounted gentle even although he had no arms. The difficulty was that it was less easy to prove gentility when there were no arms.

The preamble to grants of arms in the fifteenth, sixteenth and seventeenth centuries invariably recites that the petitioner is a gentleman and that, because he is a gentleman, the granting king of arms cannot do less than assign to him the insignia proper to his rank and condition. The following excerpt from the translation of the text of a grant of arms to Richard Andrews of Synton, Worcestershire, made on 25 May 1529 by Sir Thomas Wriothesley, Garter, is a typical example:

'I . . . am well advertised and informed that Richard Andrews, of Synton, in the county of Worcester, *gentleman* (my italics), has carried himself virtuously and honourably behaved, so that he is well deserving and worthy that in future and for ever, he and his posterity be in all places honourably admitted, renowned and reckoned among the number and of the company of other ancient gentle and noble men.'

It is true that a few grants of arms read like patents of gentility, but the vast majority read as they are intended to be understood, namely as recognitions of existing gentility. It is important to bear this in mind when reading Fox-Davies' next paragraphs.

Reports of Heraldic Cases in the Court of Chivalry 1623–1732, prepared from records of the Court by G. D. Squibb, Q.C., F.S.A. (now Norfolk Herald Extraordinary) was published by the Harleian Society in 1956 (Volume 107, marked 1955) and contains much of genealogical as well as of heraldic interest.

from the celebrated Scrope and Grosvenor case, (1) that a man could have obtained at that time a definite right to his arms, (2) that this right could be enforced against another, and we find, what is more important, (3) that the Crown and the Sovereign had supreme control and jurisdiction over arms, and (4) that the Sovereign could and did grant arms. From that date down to the present time the Crown, both by its own direct action and by the action of the Kings of Arms to whom its delegates powers for the purpose, in Letters Patent under the Great Seal, specifically issued to each separate King of Arms upon his appointment, has continued to grant armorial bearings. Some numbers of early grants of arms direct from the Crown have been printed in the *Genealogical Magazine*, and some of the earliest distinctly recite that the recipients are made noble and created gentlemen, and that the arms are given them *as the sign of their nobility*. The class of persons to whom grants of arms were made in the earliest days of such instruments is much the same as the class which obtain grants of arms at the present day, and the successful trader or merchant is now at liberty, as he was in the reign of Henry VIII and earlier, to raise himself to the rank of a gentleman by obtaining a grant of arms. A family must make its start at some time or other; let this start be made honestly, and not by the appropriation of the arms of some other man.

The illegal assumption of arms began at an early date; and in spite of the efforts of the Crown, which have been more or less continuous and repeated, it has been found that the use of 'other people's' arms has continued. In the reign of Henry V a very stringent proclamation was issued on the subject; and in the reigns of Queen Elizabeth I and her successors, the Kings of Arms were commanded to make perambulations throughout the country for the purpose of pulling down and defacing improper arms, of recording arms properly borne by authority, and of compelling those who used arms without authority to obtain authority for them or discontinue their use. These perambulations were termed Visitations. The subject of Visitations, and in fact the whole subject of the right to bear arms, is dealt with at length in the book to which reference has been already made namely, 'The Right to Bear Arms'.[3]

The glory of a descent from a long line of armigerous ancestors, the glory and the pride of race inseparably interwoven with the inheritance of a name which has been famous in history, the fact that some arms have been designed to commemorate heroic achievements, the fact that the display of a particular coat of arms has been the method, which society has countenanced, of advertising to the world that one is of the upper class or a descendant of some ancestor who performed some glorious deed to which the arms have reference, the fact that arms

---

3. This passing reference to the Visitations should not suggest to the student of heraldry that they are of little importance. The visitation records are of paramount importance to the genealogist, armorist and social historian. The first regular visitations took place in 1530, although there had been earlier sporadic visitations by kings of arms (see *Heralds and Heraldry in the Middle Ages* by A. R. (now Sir Anthony) Wagner (2nd edition 1956) page 106 et seq.). Although the first and last visitations did not cover all the counties of England, during the period 1530 to 1687 each county was visited about five times. Many of these visitations have been published by The Harleian Society and others, and so can be consulted by the student. Most of the original visitations are in the library of the College of Arms, but the printed versions, though not always accurate, provide an invaluable corpus of material. For further information, see G. D. Squibb's booklet, *Visitation Pedigrees and the Genealogist* (1964).

themselves are the very sign of a particular descent or of a particular rank, have all tended to cause a false and fictitious value to be placed upon all these pictured emblems which as a whole they have never possessed, and which I believe they were never intended to possess. It is *because* they were the prerogative and the sign of aristocracy that they have been coveted so greatly, and consequently so often assumed improperly. Now aristocracy and social position are largely a matter of personal assertion. A man assumes and asserts for himself a certain position, which position is gradually and imperceptibly but continuously increased and elevated as its assertion is reiterated. There is no particular moment in a man's life at the present time, the era of the great middle class, at which he visibly steps from a plebeian to a patrician standing. And when he has fought and talked the world into conceding him a recognised position in the upper classes, he naturally tries to obliterate the fact that he or 'his people' were ever of any other social position, and he hesitates to perpetually date his elevation to the rank of gentility by obtaining a grant of arms and thereby admitting that before that date he and his people were plebeian. Consequently he waits until some circumstance compels an application for a grant, and the consequence is that he thereby post-dates his actual technical gentility to a period long subsequent to the recognition by Society of his position in the upper classes.

Arms are the sign of the technical rank of gentility. The possession of arms is a matter of hereditary privilege, which privilege the Crown is willing should be obtained upon certain terms by any who care to possess it, who live according to the style and custom which is usual amongst gentle people. And so long as the possession of arms is a matter of privilege, even though this privilege is no greater than is consequent upon payment of certain fees to the Crown and its officers; for so long will that privilege possess a certain prestige and value, though this may not be very great. Arms have never possessed any greater value than attaches to a matter of privilege; and (with singularly few exceptions) in every case, be it of a peer or baronet, of knight or of simple gentleman, this privilege has been obtained or has been regularised by the payment at some time or other of fees to the Crown and its officers. And the *only* difference between arms granted and paid for yesterday and arms granted and paid for five hundred years ago is the simple moral difference which attaches to the dates at which the payments were made.

Gentility is merely hereditary rank, emanating, with all other rank, from the Crown, the sole fountain of honour. It is idle to make the word carry a host of meanings it was never intended to. Arms being the sign of the technical rank of gentility, the use of arms is the advertisement of one's claim to that gentility. Arms mean nothing more. By coronet, supporters, and helmet can be indicated one's place in the scale of precedence; by adding arms for your wife you assert that she also is of gentle rank; your quarterings show the other gentle families you represent; difference marks will show your position in your own family (not a very important matter); augmentations indicate the deeds of your ancestors which the Sovereign thought worthy of being held in especial remembrance. *By the use of a certain coat of arms, you assert your descent from the person to whom those arms were granted, confirmed, or allowed.* That is the beginning and end of armory. Why seek to make it mean more?

However heraldry is looked upon, it must be admitted that from its earliest infancy armory possessed two essential qualities. It was the definite sign of hereditary nobility and rank, and it was practically an integral part of warfare; but also from its earliest infancy it formed a means of decoration. It would be a rash statement to assert that armory has lost its actual military character even now, but it certainly possessed it undiminished so long as tournaments took place, for the armory of the tournament was of a mugh higher standard than the armory of the battlefield. Armory as an actual part of warfare existed as a means of decoration for the implements of warfare, and as such it certainly continues in some slight degree to the present day.

Armory in that bygone age, although it existed as the symbol of the lowest hereditary rank, was worn and used in warfare, for purposes of pageantry, for the indication of ownership, for decorative purposes, for the needs of authenticity in seals, and for the purposes of memorials in records, pedigrees, and monuments. All those uses and purposes of armory can be traced back to a period coeval with that to which our certain knowledge of the existence of armory runs. Of all those usages and purposes, one only, that of the use of armorial bearings in actual battle, can be said to have come to an end, and even that not entirely so; the rest are still with us in actual and extensive existence. I am not versed in the minutiæ of army matters or army history, but I think I am correct in saying that there was no such thing as a regular standing army or a national army until the reign of Henry VIII. Prior to that time the methods of the feudal system supplied the wants of the country. The actual troops were in the employment, not of the Crown, but of the individual leaders. The Sovereign called upon, and had the right to call upon, those leaders to provide troops; but as those troops were not in the direct employment of the Crown, they wore the liveries and heraldic devices of their leaders. The leaders wore their own devices, originally for decorative reasons, and later that they might be distinguished by their particular followers: hence the actual use in battle in former days of private armorial bearings. And even yet the practice is not wholly extinguished, for the tartans of the Gordon and Cameron Highlanders are a relic of the usages of these former days. With the formation of a standing army, and the direct service of the troops to the Crown, the liveries and badges of those who had formerly been responsible for the troops gave way to the liveries and badges of the Crown. The uniform of the Beefeaters is a good example of the method in which in the old days a servant wore the badge and livery of his lord. The Beefeaters wear the scarlet livery of the Sovereign, and wear the badge of the Sovereign still. Many people will tell you, by the way, that the uniform of a Beefeater is identical now with what it was in the days of Henry VIII. It isn't. In accordance with the strictest laws of armory, the badge, embroidered on the front and back of the tunic, has changed, and is now the triple badge—the rose, the thistle, and the shamrock—of the triple kingdom of Great Britain and Ireland. Every soldier who wears a scarlet coat, the livery of his Sovereign, every regiment that carries its colours, every saddle-cloth with a Royal emblem thereupon, is evidence that the use of armory in battle still exists in a small degree to the present day; but circumstances have altered. The troops no longer attack to the cry of 'A Warwick! a Warwick!' they serve His Majesty the King and wear his livery and devices. They no longer carry the banner of their officer, whose servants and tenants they would formerly have been; the regiment cherishes

19

instead the banner of the armorial bearings of His Majesty. Within the last few years, probably within the lifetime of all my readers, there has been striking evidence of the manner in which circumstances alter everything. The Zulu War put an end to the practice of taking the colours of a regiment into battle; the South African War saw khaki substituted universally for the scarlet livery of His Majesty; and to have found upon a South African battlefield the last remnant of the armorial practices of the days of chivalry, one would have needed, I am afraid, to examine the buttons of the troopers. Still the scarlet coat exists in the army on parade: the Life Guards wear the Royal Cross of St George and the Star of the Garter, the Scot Greys have the Royal Saltire of St Andrew, and the Gordon Highlanders have the Gordon crest of the Duke of Richmond and Gordon; and there are many other similar instances.

It is foolish to contend that armory has ceased to exist, save as an interesting survival of the past. It is a living reality, more *widely* in use at the present day than ever before. Certainly the military side of armory has sunk in importance till it is now utterly overshadowed by the decorative, but the fact that armory still exists as the sign and adjunct of hereditary rank utterly forbids one to assert that armory is dead, and though this side of armory is also now partly overshadowed by its decorative use, armory must be admitted to be still alive whilst its laws can still be altered. When, if ever, rank is finally swept away, and when the Crown ceases to grant arms, and people cease to use them, then armory will be dead, and can be treated as the study of a dead science.

PLATE I

The Royal Arms

3 · The heralds and officers of arms

The Crown is the Fountain of Honour, having supreme control of coat-armour. This control in all civilised countries is one of the appanages of sovereignty, but from an early period much of the actual control has been delegated to the Heralds and Kings of Arms. The word Herald is derived from the Anglo-Saxon—*here*, an army, and *wald*, strength or sway—though it has probably come to us from the German word *Herold*.

In the last years of the twelfth century there appeared at festal gatherings persons mostly habited in richly coloured clothing, who delivered invitations to the guests, and, side by side with the stewards, superintended the festivities. Many of them were minstrels, who, after tournaments or battle, extolled the deeds of the victors. These individuals were known in Germany as *Garzune*.

Originally every powerful leader has his own herald, and the dual character of minstrel and messenger led the herald to recount the deeds of his master, and, as a natural consequence, of his master's ancestors. In token of their office they wore the coats of arms of the leaders they served; and the original status of a herald was that of a non-combatant messenger. When tournaments came into vogue it was natural that someone should examine the arms of those taking part, and from this the duties of the herald came to include a knowledge of coat-armour. As the Sovereign assumed or arrogated the control of arms, the right to grant arms, and the right of judgment in disputes concerning arms, it was but the natural result that the personal heralds of the Sovereign should be required to have a knowledge of the arms of his principal subjects, and should obtain something in the nature of a cognisance or control and jurisdiction over those arms; for doubtless the actions of the Sovereign would often depend upon the knowledge of his heralds.

The process of development in this country will be more easily understood when it is remembered that the Marshal or Earl Marshal was in former times, with the Lord High Constable, the first in *military* rank under the King, who usually led his army in person, and to the Marshal was deputed the ordering and arrangement of the various bodies of troops, regiments, bands of retainers, &c., which ordering was at first facilitated and at length entirely determined by the use of various pictorial ensigns, such as standards, banners, crests, cognisances, and badges. The due arrangement and knowledge of these various ensigns became first the necessary study and then the ordinary duty of these officers of the Marshal, and their possession of such knowledge, which soon in due course had to be written down and tabulated, secured to them an important part in medieval life. The result was that at an early period we find them employed in semi-diplomatic missions, such as carrying on negotiations between contending armies on the field, bearing declarations of war, challenges from one sovereign to another, besides arranging the ceremonial not only of battles and tournaments, but also of coronations, Royal baptisms, marriages, and funerals.

From the fact that neither King of Arms nor Herald is mentioned as officiating in the celebrated Scrope and Grosvenor case, of which very full particulars have come down to us, it is evident that the control of arms had not passed either in fact or in theory from the Crown to the officers of arms at that date. Konrad Grünenberg, in his *Wappencodex* ('Roll of Arms'), the date of which is 1483, gives a representation of a *helmschau* (literally helmet-show), here reproduced (12), which includes the figure of a herald. Long before that date, however, the position of a herald in England was well defined, for we find that on 5 January 1420, the King appointed William Bruges to be Garter King of Arms.[4] It is usually considered in England that it would be found that in Germany armory reached its highest point of evolution. Certainly German heraldic art is in advance of our own, and it is curious to read in the latest and one of the best of German heraldic books that 'from the very earliest times heraldry was carried to a higher degree of perfection and thoroughness in England than elsewhere, and that it has maintained itself at the same level until the present day. In other countries, for the most part, heralds no longer have any existence but in name.'

Long before there was any College of Arms, the Marshal, afterwards the Earl Marshal, had been appointed. The Earl Marshal is now head of the College of Arms,[5] and to him has been delegated the whole of the control both of armory and of the College, with the exception of that part which the Crown has retained in its own hands. After the Earl Marshal come the Kings of Arms, the Heralds of Arms, and the Pursuivants of Arms.

The title of King of Arms, or, as it was more anciently written, King of Heralds, was no doubt originally given to the chief or principal officer, who presided over the heralds of a kingdom, or some principal province, which heraldic writers formerly termed *marches*; or else the title was conferred upon the officer of arms attendant upon some particular order of knighthood. Garter King of Arms, who is immediately attached to that illustrious order, is likewise Principal King of Arms, and these, although separate and distinct offices, are and have been always united in one person. Upon the revival and new modelling of the Order of the Bath, in the reign of George the First, a King of Arms was created and attached to it, by the title of Bath King of Arms; and King George III, upon the institution of the Hanoverian Guelphic Order of Knighthood, annexed to that order a King of Arms, by the appellation of Hanover. At the time of the creation of his office, Bath King of Arms was given Wales as his province, the intention

4. The date of Bruges' appointment is now known to have been *c.* 30 June 1415. See note 6.
5. The term 'head' can be misleading when considering the position of the Earl Marshal vis-à-vis the corporation of the Kings, Heralds and Pursuivants of Arms, commonly called the College of Arms or Heralds' College. The Earl Marshal is not a member of the Corporation. He has no share in the freehold of the College of Arms which was granted to certain of the royal heralds and their successors in office by King Philip and Queen Mary in 1555, but he has a general supervision of officers of arms and their conduct and also of coats of arms. His position in regard to the corporation has been likened to that of a Visitor to a College, and perhaps this is the most apt description of a complex relationship.

12 Helmschan *or Helmet-Show. (From Konrad Grünenberg's* Wappencodex zu München.) *End of fifteenth century.*

being that he should rank with the others, granting arms in his own province, but he was not, nor was Hanover, nor is the King of Arms of the Order of St Michael and St George, a member (as such) of the corporation of the College of Arms. The members of that corporation considered that the gift of the province of Wales, the jurisdiction over which they had previously possessed, to Bath King was an infringement of their chartered privileges. The dispute was referred to the

23

law officers of the Crown, whose opinion was in favour of the corporate body.

Berry in his *Encyclopædia Heraldica* further remarks: 'The Kings of Arms of the provincial territories have the titles of *Clarenceux* and *Norroy*, the jurisdiction of the former extending over the south, east, and west parts of England, from the river Trent southwards; and that of the latter, the remaining part of the kingdom northward of that river. Kings of Arms have been likewise assigned other provinces over different kingdoms and dominions, and besides Ulster King of Arms for Ireland, and Lyon King of Arms for Scotland, others were nominated for particular provinces abroad, when united to the Crown of England, such as *Aquitaine*, *Anjou*, and *Guyenne*, who were perhaps at their first creation intended only for the services of the places whose titles they bore, when the same should be entirely subdued to allegiance to the Crown of England, and who, till that time, might have had other provinces allotted to them, either provisionally or temporarily, within the realm of England.

There were also other Kings of Arms, denominated from the dukedoms or earldoms which our princes enjoyed before they came to the throne, as *Lancaster*, *Gloucester*, *Richmond*, and *Leicester*, the three first having marches, or provinces, and the latter a similar jurisdiction. Windsor, likewise, was a local title, but it is doubtful whether that officer was ever a King of Arms. *Marche* also assumed that appellation, from his provincial jurisdiction over a territory so called.

But although anciently there were at different periods several Kings of Arms in England, only two provincial Kings of Arms have, for some ages, been continued in office, viz. Clarenceux and Norroy, whose provinces or marches are, as before observed, separated by the river Trent, the ancient limits of the escheaters, when there were only two in the kingdom, and the jurisdiction of the wardens of the forests.[6]

Norroy is considered the most ancient title, being the only one in England taken from the local situation of his province, unless *Marche* should be derived

6. The notes on various heraldic titles which follow are, in the main, accurate, although Fox-Davies did not have the benefit of the scholarly investigations of the late Hugh Stanford London, Norfolk Herald Extraordinary. The fruit of his labours was published in 1963 under the title *The College of Arms, London*, being the sixteenth and final monograph published by the London Survey Committee. To this work, edited by Walter H. Godfrey, C.B.E., F.S.A., F.R.I.B.A., and by Sir Anthony Wagner, K.C.V.O., D.Litt., F.S.A., Garter King of Arms, London contributed a complete list of all known officers of arms together with details of their personal arms where these are known.

Students of heraldry who are interested in the titles, biographies and arms of heralds are advised to consult this work. To Fox-Davies' comments I would only add the following few notes.

Falcon: the last officer to hold this title was H. F. Stephenson, who was created Falcon Herald Extraordinary in 1813; but the last officer in ordinary appears to have been John Yonge, *temp.* Henry VII.

Lancaster: the holder of this title was originally a private herald in the service of the Duke of Lancaster. One such is mentioned *c.* 1354.

Ireland: the date 1482 is clearly erroneous. The regnal year 6 Richard II is 1382/3, and this is presumably what is intended. In fact the first mention of Ireland is *c.* 1370.

Garter: here Fox-Davies asserts, quoting Anstis, that the office of Garter must have been instituted between 22 May and 3 September 1417; elsewhere he states that the first Garter, William Bruges, was appointed 5 January 1420. London dates his creation as *c.* 30 June 1415, and before 4 July of that year.

from the same cause. The title of *Norroy* was anciently written *Norreys* and *Norreis*, King of Arms of the people residing in the north; *Garter* being styled *Roy des Anglois*, of the people, and not *d'Angleterre*, of the kingdom, the inhabitants of the north being called *Norreys*,★ as we are informed by ancient historians.

It appears that there was a King of Arms for the parts or people on the north of Trent as early as the reign of Edward I, from which, as Sir Henry Spelman observes, it may be inferred that the southern, eastern, and western parts had principal heralds, or Kings of Arms, although their titles at that early age cannot now be ascertained.

Norroy had not the title of King till after the reign of Edward II. It was appropriated to a King of Heralds, expressly called *Rex Norroy*, *Roy d'Armes del North*, *Rex Armorum del North*, *Rex de North*, and *Rex Norroy du North*; and the term *Roy Norreys* likewise occurs in the Pell Rolls of the 22nd Edward III; but from that time till the 9th of Richard II no farther mention is made of any such officer, from which it is probable a different person enjoyed the office by some other title during that interval, particularly as the office was actually executed by other Kings of Arms, immediately after that period. *John Otharlake, Marche King of Arms*, executed it in the 9th of Richard II, *Richard del Brugg, Lancaster King of Arms*, 1st Henry IV, and *Ashwell, Boys*, and *Tindal*, successively *Lancaster Kings of Arms*, until the end of that monarch's reign.

Edward IV replaced this province under a King of Arms, and revived the dormant title of *Norroy*. But in the Statute of Resumptions, made 1st Henry VII, a clause was inserted that the same should not extend to *John Moore*, otherwise *Norroy*, chief Herald King of Arms of the north parts of this realm of England, so appointed by King Edward IV by his Letters Patent, bearing date 9 July, in the eighteenth year of his reign. It has since continued without interruption.

Falcon King of Arms seems the next who had the title of King conferred upon him, and was so named from one of the Royal badges of King Edward III, and it was afterwards given to a herald and pursuivant, under princes who bore the falcon as a badge or cognisance, and it is difficult to ascertain whether this officer was considered a king, herald, or pursuivant. *Froissart* in 1395 calls *Faucon* only a herald, and in 1364 mentions this officer as a King of Arms belonging to the King of England; but it is certain that in the 18th Richard II there was a King of Arms by that appellation, and so continued until the reign of Richard III, if not later; but at what particular period of time the officer was discontinued cannot be correctly ascertained.

Windsor has been considered by some writers to have been the title of a King of Arms, from an abbreviation in some old records, which might be otherwise translated. There is, however, amongst the Protections in the Chancery records, one granted in the 49th Edward III to *Stephen de Windesore, Heraldo Armorum rege dicto*, which seems to favour the conjecture, and other records might be quoted

---

★ 'Norreys and Surreis, that service aught the kyng,
With horse and harneis at Carlele, made samning.'

See Langtoft's Chronicle treating of the Wars of Edward I against the Scots.

'Bot Sir John de Waleis taken was, in a pleyne,
Throgh Spring of Norreis men that were certeyn.'

Ibid., *Australes se Norensibus opposuerunt*. M. Oaris, under the year 1237.

for and against this supposition, which might have arisen through mistake in the entries, as they contradict one another.

Marche seems the next in point of antiquity of creation; but although Sir Henry Spelman says that King Edward IV descended from the *Earls of Marche*, promoted *Marche Herald* to be a King of Arms, giving him, perhaps, the marches for his province, it is pretty clearly ascertained that it was of a more early date, from the express mention of *March Rex Heraldorum* and *March Rex Heraldus* in records of the time of Richard II, though it may be possible that it was then only a nominal title, and did not become a real one till the reign of Edward IV, as mentioned by Spelman.

Lancaster King of Arms was, as the same author informs us, so created by Henry IV in relation to his own descent from the Lancastrian family, and the county of Lancaster assigned to him as his province; but *Edmondson* contends 'that that monarch superadded the title of Lancaster to that of Norroy, or King of the North, having, as it may be reasonably conjectured, given this province north of Trent, within which district Lancaster was situated, to him who had been formerly his officer of arms, by the title of that dukedom, and who might, according to custom, in some instances of former ages, retain his former title and surname of heraldship, styling himself *Lancaster Roy d'Armes del North.*'

Leicester King of Arms was a title similar to that of *Lancaster*, and likewise a creation to the same Sovereign, Henry IV, who was also Earl of Leicester before he assumed the crown, and was given to a person who was before that time a herald. It appears that *Henry Grene* was *Leicester Herald*, 9th King Richard II, and in the 13th of the same reign is called *a Herald of the Duke of Guyen and Lancaster*, but prior to the coronation of Henry IV he was certainly a King of Heralds, and so styled in a privy seal dated antecedent to that ceremony. A similar instrument of the tenth year of that monarch's reign also mentions *Henry Grene*, otherwise *Leicester King of Arms*.

As it is evident that, during the reign of Henry IV, *Lancaster King of Arms* has under that title the province of the north, *Mr Edmondson*, with good reason, supposes that the southern province, or part of that which is now under Clarenceux, might at that time be under this *Leicester*, especially as the title of *Clarenceux* was not in being till after the 3rd of Henry V, when, or soon after, the title of *Leicester* might have become extinct by the death of that officer; for although *Leicester King of Arms* went over into France with Henry V in the third year of his reign, yet he is not mentioned in the constitutions made by the heralds at Roan in the year 1419–20.

Clarenceux, the next King of Arms in point of creation, is a title generally supposed to have been taken from *Clare*, in Suffolk, the castle at that place being the principal residence of the ancient Earls of Hereford, who were, from thence, though very improperly, called *Earls of Clare*, in the same manner as the Earls of Pembroke were often named *Earls of Strigoil and Chepstow*; the Earl of Hampshire, *Earl of Winchester*, the Earl of Derby, *Earl of Tuttebury*; the Earl of Sussex, *Earl of Chichester* &c. King Edward III created his third son Lionel *Duke of Clarence*, instead of the monosyllable *Clare* (from his marriage with the grand-daughter of the late Earl), but Lionel dying without issue male, Henry IV created his younger son Thomas *Duke of Clarence*, who being slain without issue 9th of Henry V, the honour remained in the Crown, until King Edward IV conferred it upon his own brother. Mr Sandford tells us that *Clarence* is the country about the town, castle, and honour of *Clare*, from which duchy the name of *Clarenceux King of Arms* is derived. Spelman, however, contends that it is a mistake in attributing the institution of *Clarenceux* to King Edward IV after the honour of *Clarence* devolved as an excheat to the Crown upon the untimely death of his brother George, as he found William Horsely called by this title in the reign of Henry V and also Roger Lygh, under King Henry VI; and it is conjectured that the office of *Clarenceux King of Arms* is not more ancient than the reign of Edward III.

Gloucester Herald, frequently mentioned by historians was originally the herald of the great Humphry, Duke of Gloucester, of whom mention is made upon record in the 10th of Henry VI; and Richard, brother to Edward IV, who was created Duke of Gloucester, is said to have had a herald by that title during the reign of his brother, and who was attendant as such at the funeral of that monarch. In a manuscript in the Ashmolean collection, it is stated that Richard Champnay attended as Gloucester King of Arms at the coronation of Richard III upon the 7 July following his usurpation of the crown; but it appears by more authentic record that this Richard Champnay was, by the style and title of Herald of Arms, on 18 September, in the first year of his usurpation, by patent created a King of Arms and Principal Herald of the parts of Wales, by the style and title of Gloucester, giving him licence and authority to execute all and singular that by law or custom in former times belonged to the office of King of Arms. It is supposed that the office ceased upon his death, which in all probability took place before that of the usurper.

Richmond King of Arms. A herald called *Richmond* is frequently mentioned, as well belonging to the Crown as of the nobility. But the records of the reign of King Henry VII, who had before his elevation to the throne been Earl of Richmond, contain many entries of *Richmond King of Arms*; but although somewhat vague in the description, sufficiently bear out the conjecture that Henry VII, previous to his coronation, created a new King of Arms by the title of *Richmond*, although no regular patent of creation has ever been found.

Sir Henry Spelman informs us that, in addition to the two Kings of Arms for the two Heraldic provinces bounded north and south by the river Trent, there were also two provincial kings for the dominions of our Sovereign in France, styled *Guyenne* and *Agincourt* (omitting *Aquitaine* and *Anjou*, which were certainly in being at the same time), and another for *Ireland* by that name, altered by King Edward VI into *Ulster*.

Ireland King of Arms first occurs upon record *c.* 1370, mentioned by *Froissart*, where he is called *Chandos le Roy d'Ireland*. A regular succession of officers, by the title of Ireland King of Arms, continued from that time till the reign of King Edward IV, but from the death of that monarch till the creation of Ulster by Edward VI it is uncertain whether the title existed, or what became of the office.

Edward VI altered the title of Ireland King of Arms into that of Ulster, or rather considered it as a new institution, from the words of his journal: '2 Feb. There was a King of Arms made for Ireland, whose name was *Ulster*, and his province was all Ireland; and he was the fourth King of Arms, and the first Herald of Ireland.' The patent passed under the Great Seal of England. (See note 17 on page 39.)

Guyenne, a part of Aquitaine, in France, a province belonging to the British Crown, gave title not only to a King of Arms, but to a herald likewise, and Sir Henry Spelman dates its creation in the time of Edward I, although it is somewhat doubtful, and thought to be in the reign of Edward III. Guyenne Herald appears upon record during the reign of Henry VI, and though Kings of Arms were frequently styled heralds in old records, it is more than probable both offices were in existence at the same time. From the time of Edward IV no such officers belonging to the Crown of England seem to have been continued, and it is doubtful whether they ever held in constant succession from their first creation.

Aquitaine, which included what were afterwards called Guyenne, Xantoigne, Gascoigne, and some islands, gave title to a King of Heralds as early as the reign of Edward III, and it is conjectured to have been an officer belonging to the Black Prince, who had the principality of Aquitaine given to him by his father; but although this officer is mentioned in the reign of Richard II and 3rd of Henry V, no record occurs after the latter period.

Agincourt was also a title conferred upon a herald, in memory of that signal victory; and lands were granted to him for life, 6th Henry V, as mentioned by Sir Henry Spelman; but whether the office was continued, or any particular province assigned to this officer, cannot be ascertained.

Anjou King of Arms was likewise an officer of King Henry VI, and attendant upon John, Duke of Bedford, when Regent of France, who assumed the title of Duke of Anjou. But upon the death of the Duke of Bedford, this officer was promoted to Lancaster King of Arms; and in all probability the title of Anjou as a King of Heralds, was discontinued.

Volant also occurs upon record in the 28th Edward III, and *Vaillant, le Roy Vaillant Heraud*, and *le Roy Vailland*, are likewise mentioned in 1395.

Henry V instituted the office of Garter King of Arms; but at what particular period is rather uncertain, although Mr Anstis has clearly proved that it must have taken place after 22 May, and before 3 September, in the year 1417.

Stephen Martin Leake, Esq., who filled the office, sums up its duties in the following words: 'Garter was instituted by King Henry V, A.D. 1417, for the service of the Most Noble Order of the Garter, which was made sovereign within the office of arms over all other officers, subject to the Crown of England, by the name of Garter King of Arms of England. In this patent he is styled Principal King of English Arms, and Principal Officer of Arms of the Most Noble Order of the Garter, and has power to execute the said office by himself or deputy, being an herald. By the constitution of his office, he must be a native of England, and a gentleman bearing arms. To him belongs the correction of arms, and all ensigns of honour, usurped or borne unjustly, and also to grant arms to deserving persons, and supporters to the nobility and Knights of the Bath; to go next before the sword in solemn proceeding, none interposing, except the constable and marshal; to administer the oath to all the officers of arms; to have a habit like the registrar of the order; baron's service in the court; lodgings in Windsor Castle; to bear his white rod with a banner of the ensigns of the order thereon before the Sovereign; also when any lord shall enter the Parliament chamber, to assign him his place, accordingly to his dignity and degree; to carry the ensign of the order to foreign princes, and to do, or procure to be done, what the Sovereign shall enjoin, relating to the order; with other duties incident to his office of principal King of Arms, for the execution whereof he hath a salary of one hundred pounds a year, payable at the Exchequer, and an hundred pounds more out of the revenue of the order, besides fees.'

Bath King of Arms was created 11th George I, in conformity with the statues established by His Majesty for the government of the Order of the Bath, and in obedience to those statutes was nominated and created by the Great Master of the Order denominated *Bath*, and in Latin, *Rex armorum Honoratissimi Ordinis Militaris de Balneo*. These statutes direct that this officer shall, in all the ceremonies of the order, he habited in a white mantle lined with red, having on the right shoulder the badge of the order, and under it a surcoat of white silk, lined and edged with red; that he shall wear on his breast, hanging to a golden chain about his neck, an escocheon of gold, enamelled with the arms of the order, impaling the arms of the Sovereign, crowned with the Imperial crown. That at all coronations he shall precede the companions of the order, and shall carry and wear his crown as other Kings of Arms are obliged to do. That the chain, escocheon, rod, and crown, shall be of the like materials, value, and weight, with those borne and used by Garter Principal King of Arms, and of the like fashion, the before specified variations only excepted: and that besides the duties required of him in the several other articles of the statutes, he shall diligently perform whatever the Sovereign of Great Master shall further command. On 14 January 1725, His Majesty was further pleased by his Royal sign-manual, to erect, make, constitute, and ordain the then Bath King of Arms, *Gloucester* King of Arms, and principal Herald of the parts of Wales, and to direct letters patent to be made out and pass the Great Seal, empowering him to grant arms and crests to persons residing within the dominions of Wales, either jointly with Garter, or singly by himself, with the consent and at the pleasure of the Earl Marshal, or his deputy for the time being, and for the future that the office of Gloucester should be inseparably annexed, united, and perpetually consolidated with the office of *Bath King of Arms, of the Most Honourable Military Order of the Bath, and Gloucester King of Arms, and principal Herald of the parts of Wales*. And also that he, for the dignity of the order, should in all assemblies and at all times have and take place and precedency above and before all other provincial Kings of Arms whatsoever.'

This armorial jurisdiction, however, was subsequently annulled, as has been previously explained.

Concerning the heralds Berry remarks: 'In former ages, when honour and chivalry were at their height, these officers were held in great estimation, as appears by the ceremonies which attended their creations, which was by the Sovereign himself or by special commission from him, and, according to Gerard Leigh, was after the following manner: The King asked the person to be so created whether he were a gentleman of blood or of second coat-armour; if he was not, the King gave him lands and fees, and assigned him and his heirs proper arms. Then, as the messenger was brought in by the herald of the province, so the pursuivant was brought in by the eldest herald, who, at the prince's command, performed all the ceremonies, as turning the coat of arms, setting the manacles thereof on the arms of the pursuivant and putting about his neck the collar of SS, and when he was named, the prince himself took the cup from the herald, which was gilt, and poured the water and wine upon the head of the pursuivant, creating him by the name of *our herald*, and the King, when the oath was administered, gave the same cup to the new herald.

Upton sums up the business of a herald thus: That it was their office to create under officers, to number the people, to commence treaties of matrimony and of peace between princes, to visit kingdoms and regions, and to be present at martial exploits, &c., and they were to wear a coat of their master's arms, wearing the same in conflicts and tournaments, in riding through foreign countries, and at all great entertainments, coronations of kings and queens, and the solemnities of princes, dukes, and other great lords.

In the time of King Richard II there belonged to the King of Arms and heralds the following fees, viz.: at the coronation of the King, a bounty of £100; when the King first displayed his banners, 100 marks; when the King's son was made a knight, 40 marks; when the prince and a duke first display their banners, £20; if it be a marquis, 20 marks; if an earl, £10; if a baron, 5 marks of silver crowns, or 15 nobles; and if a knight bachelor, newly made a banneret, 3 marks, or 10 nobles; when the King is married, the said King of Arms and heralds to have £50; when the Queen has a child christened, a largess at the Queen's pleasure, or of the lords of the council, which was sometimes £100, and at others 100 marks, more or less; and when she is churched, such another largess; when princesses, duchesses, marchionesses, countesses, and baronesses have a child christened, and when they are churched, a largess suitable to their quality and pleasure; as often as the King wears his crown, or holds Royal state, especially at the four great festivals of Christmas, Easter, Whitsuntide, and All Saints, to every one of the three Kings of Arms present when the King goes to the chapel to mass, a largess at the King's pleasure; when a maiden princess, or daughter of a duke, marquis, earl, or baron is married, there belongs to the said Kings of Arms, if present, the upper garment she is married in; if there be a combat within lists, there belong to the Kings of Arms, if present, and if not to the other heralds present, their pavilions; and if one of the combatants is vanquished, the Kings of Arms and heralds who are present shall have all the accountrements of the person so vanquished, and all other armour that falls to the ground; when subjects rebel, and fortify any camp or place, and afterwards quit the same, and fly, without a battle, there appertain to the said Kings of Arms and heralds who are present all the carts, carriages, and tools left behind; and, at New Year's Tide, all the noblemen and knights of the court used to give the heralds New Year's gifts. Beside the King's heralds, in former times, divers noblemen had heralds and pursuivants, who went with their lords, with the King's heralds, when attending the King.

The fees of the King's heralds and pursuivants of arms have since varied, and, besides fees upon creations of peers, baronets, and knights, they have still donations for attendance at court upon the festivals of Christmas, Easter, Whitsuntide, All Saints, and St George's Day; fees upon installation of Knights of the Garter and Bath, Royal marriages, funerals, public solemnities, &c., with small salaries paid from the Exchequer; but their ancient fees from the nobility, upon certain occasions, have been long discontinued, and their principal emolument arises from grants of arms, the tracing of genealogies, and recording the same in the Registers of the College of Arms.'[7]

The present *heralds* are six in number, viz.:

Windsor Herald, which title was instituted 38th of Edward III, when that monarch was in France.

Chester Herald, instituted in the same reign.

Richmond Herald, instituted by King Edward IV.

Somerset Herald, instituted by King Henry VIII about the time when that monarch created his son Henry Fitzroy Duke of Somerset.

York Herald, instituted by King Edward III in honour of his son, whom he created Duke of York.

Lancaster Herald, also instituted by Edward III when he created his son Duke of Lancaster.

The heralds were first incorporated as a college by Richard III. They were styled the Corporation of Kings, Heralds, and Pursuivants of Arms.[8]

Concerning Pursuivants of Arms, Berry remarks that these officers, who are the lowest in degree amongst officers of arms, 'were, as the name implies, followers, marshals, or messengers attendant upon the heralds. Pursuivants were formerly created by the nobility (who had, likewise, heralds of arms) with great ceremony in the following manner. One of the heralds, wearing his master's coat, leading the person to be created pursuivant by the left hand, and holding a cup full of wine and water in his right, came into the presence of the lord and master of him who was to be created, and of whom the herald asked by what name he would have his pursuivant called, which the lord having mentioned, the herald then poured part of the wine and water upon his head, calling him by the name so

---

7. The present salaries of the Officers of Arms are as follows: Garter King of Arms, £49 1s. 4d.; the Provincial Kings, £20 5s. 0d.; Heralds, £17 16s. 0d. and Pursuivants, £13 19s. 0d. These salaries are paid at the office of the Chamberlain of the Household, and not by the Exchequer. In fact the heralds' salaries were cut when William IV came to the throne. Previously Garter had received £100, the Provincial Kings £40, Heralds 40 marks (i.e. £26 13s. 4d.) and Pursuivants £20. Largesse is still paid on the festivals mentioned (which should include the Epiphany and All Saints' Day) to those officers who appear personally at St James's Palace between 12 mid-day and 1 p.m., and sign their names in the book provided.

8. The charter of King Richard III was dated 2 March 1483/4. It both incorporated the heralds and granted them a residence known as Coldharbour. Their sojourn here was brief for, when Henry VII defeated Richard III at Bosworth in 1485 and ascended the throne, he took Coldharbour from the heralds and granted it to his mother. The heralds were reincorporated by King Philip and Queen Mary by a Charter dated 18 July 1555 and given Derby Place on the site of which the present College of Arms now stands. The old house, once a residence of the Stanleys, Earls of Derby, was destroyed in the fire of 1666. The heralds also received a Charter from King Edward VI, dated 4 June 1549. This Charter set forth and confirmed their liberties and privileges, many of which, such as freedom from jury service, they still enjoy. This Charter and that of Philip and Mary are preserved at the College of Arms; Richard's Charter is among the Cottonian manuscripts at the British Museum.

It is far more likely that the name Bluemantle (normally one word, not two) is derived from the mantle worn by knights of the Garter. The first Bluemantle appears during the reign of Henry V, not Edward III, and the creation of the office may well have been connected with that of Garter in 1415, although there is no documentary evidence to support this contention. As the first mention of the office of Rouge Croix is in 1418–19, it is just possible that Bluemantle may antedate Rouge Croix in antiquity.

assigned to him. The herald then took the coat of his lord, and put it over his head athwart, so that part of the coat made for the arms before and behind, and the longer part of it on both sides of the arms of the person created, and in which way the pursuivant was always to wear it. This done, an oath of fidelity was administered to the new-made pursuivant, and the ceremony concluded.'

This curious method of the wearing of the tabard by a pursuivant has long since been discontinued, if indeed it was ever generally adopted, a point on which I have by no means been able to satisfy myself.

The appointment of heralds and pursuivants of arms by the nobility has long been discontinued, and there are now only four pursuivants belonging to the College of Arms, viz.:

Rouge-Croix, the first in point of antiquity of creation, is so styled from the red cross of St George, the Patron Saint of England.

Blue-Mantle, so called by King Edward III, in honour of the French coat which he assumed, being blue.

Rouge-Dragon, so styled from the red dragon, one of the supporters of the Royal arms of King Henry VII (who created this pursuivant), and also the badge of Wales, and

Portcullis, also instituted by Henry VII, and so named from that badge, or cognisance, used by him.

The duties of a pursuivant are similar to those of a herald; he assists in all public processions, or ceremonies, such as Royal marriages, funerals, installations, &c., and has certain fees for attendance upon such occasions. Pursuivants likewise receive fees upon creations of peers, baronets, and knights, and also donations for attending court upon the principal festivals of Christmas, Easter, Whit-Sunday, All Saints, and St George's Day, and a small salary payable out of the Exchequer. They wear a tabard of damask silk, embroidered with the Royal arms, like the heralds, but no collar of SS.[9]

Of the Heraldic Executive in Scotland Sir James Balfour Paul, in his book *Heraldry in relation to Scottish History and Art*, writes: 'At one period the Lyon was solemnly crowned at his inauguration, and vested with his tabard and baton of office.' The ceremony was a very elaborate one, and is fully described by Sir James Balfour in a MS., now in the Advocates' Library. There is also an account of the coronation of Sir Alexander Durham, when Laurie, the minister of the Tron Kirk, preached from the text, 'What shall be done to the man whom the king delighteth to honour?' The crown was of gold, and exactly similar to the Imperial crown of Scotland, save that it had no jewels. Now the Lyon's crown is the same as that of the English Kings of Arms. The crown is only worn at Royal coronations. At that of Charles I at Edinburgh in 1633, the Lyon carried the vessel containing the sacred oil. In addition to his strictly armorial appointment, the Lyon is also a King of Arms of the Most Ancient and Most Noble Order of the Thistle.

Heralds and pursuivants formed an important part from very early times not

9. See note 7 for a correct list of festivals on which largesse is disbursed. The pursuivants, like the other officers, no longer receive fees on the creation of dignities. Their right to such fees is specifically excepted from their privileges in their Letters Patent of creation.

only of the Royal Household, but also of those of the higher nobility, many of whom had private heralds. Of these officers there is a very full list given by Dr Dickson in the preface to the Lord Treasurer's Accounts. Of heralds who were or ultimately became part of the King's Household we meet with Rothesay, Marchmont, Snowdon, Albany, Ross, and Islay; Ireland, Orkney, and Carrick are also mentioned as heralds, but it is doubtful whether the first and last were ever more than pursuivants. Of the latter class of officers the following were in the Royal establishment: Carrick, Bute, Dingwall, Kintyre, Ormonde, Unicorn; but we also find Aliszai or Alishay, Dragance, Diligens, Montrose, Falkland, Ireland, Daranway, Garioch, Ettrick, Hales, Lindsay, Endure, Douglas, and Angus. Of the latter Garioch was created by James IV for his brother John, Earl of Mar; Hailes in 1488, when Lord Hailes was made Earl of Bothwell; while Lindsay and Endure were both evidently attached to the Lindsay family, as were Douglas and Angus to the noblemen whose titles they bore. In 1403 Henry IV of England granted a pursuivant under the title of Shrewsbury to George, Earl of March, for services rendered at the battle of that name, but we do not find that the office was continued.

In Scotland heralds appear at an early date, though none are mentioned as attending the coronation of Alexander III in 1249; nor is there any account of any such officers accompanying that sovereign when he did homage to Edward I at Westminster in 1278. In the next century, however, armorial bearings were quite well known in Scotland, and there is an entry in the Exchequer Rolls on 10 October 1337 of a payment of £32 6s. Scots for the making of seventeen armorial banners, and in 1364 there is another to the heralds for services at the tournaments; while William Petillock, herald, has a grant from David II of three husbandlands in Bonjedward, and Allan Fawsyde gets a gift of the forfeited estate of one Coupland, a herald (*temp.* Edward Baliol).* The first mention of a herald, under his official designation, which I have met with in our records occurs in 1365, when there is a confirmation under the Great Seal by David II of a charter by Dugal M'Dowille to John Trupour or Trumpour 'nunc dicto Carric heraldo'. Sir James Balfour Paul tells us that the Lyon and his heralds attended the coronation of Robert II at Holyrood on 23 May 1371, but whether or not this is true — and I have not been able to verify it — it is certain that a Lyon Herald existed very shortly after that date, as the Exchequer Rolls mention the payment of a certain sum to such an officer in 1377; in 1379 Froissart says that a herald was sent by Robert II to London to explain that the truce had been infringed without his will and against his knowledge, and on 8 April 1381 a warrant was issued in London for a licence to 'Lion Heraud' of the King of Scots, authorising him to take away a complete suit of armour which he had bought in that city. It is not, however, till 1388 that we find Lyon accorded the Royal style. In that year a payment is made 'Leoni regi heraldorum', but at the audit following the battle of Otterburn he is called *defunctus*, which suggests that he had been slain on that well-fought field. The Lyon appears in several embassies about this period both to England and France, and one Henry Greve, described in the English Issue Rolls as 'King of Scottish Heralds', was at the Tower of London in 1399, either at or immediately after the coronation of Henry IV. From 1391 onwards there is frequent mention of one

---

* Robertson, *Index*, pp. 59, no. 5; 37, roll i, no. 9.

13 *Officers of Arms as represented in the famous Tournament Roll of Henry VIII, now preserved in the College of Arms.*

14. *The velvet tabard of Sir William Dugdale, Garter King of Arms from 26 April 1677 to 10 February 1686.*

Douglas, 'Herald of the King', and in 1421 he is styled 'Lyon Herald'.[10]

Of the German officers of arms they, like the English, are divided into three classes, known as *Wappenkönige*, *Herolde*, and *Persevanten*. These, like our own officers, had peculiar titles; for example *Suchenwirt* (an Austrian ducal herald),

10. Although Lyon is created by the Crown, the Scottish heralds and pursuivants, both in ordinary and extraordinary, are appointed by Lyon. The extraordinary officers are usually appointed for a specific purpose and for a specific period; pursuivants hold their offices 'during pleasure' and heralds are appointed for life. When Sir James Balfour Paul was Lyon, all officers were appointed during pleasure, but this was later considered to be wrong in the case of heralds, whose office is of a permanent character, as are priestly orders, to which the office of herald has been likened.

34

Lub-den Frumen (a Lichtenstein pursuivant), *Jerusalem* (a herald of the Limmer Palatinate), *Romreich* (an Imperial herald). About the middle of the sixteenth century, the official names of the heralds fell into disuse; they began to make use of their ancestral names with the title of *Edel* and *Ehrenvest* (noble and honourable), but this did not last long, and the heralds found themselves thrown back into the old ways, into which the knightly accoutrements had already wandered.

The official dress of an officer of arms as such in Great Britain is merely his tabard (13, 14, 15). This garment in style and shape has remained unchanged in this country from the earliest known period of which representations of officers of arms exist; but whilst the tabard itself has remained unaltered in its style, the arms thereupon have constantly changed, these always being the arms of the Sovereign for the time being. The costume worn with the tabard has naturally been subject to many changes, but it is doubtful if any attempt to regulate such costume was ever officially made prior to the reign of Queen Victoria. The tabard of a pursuivant is of damask silk; that of a herald, of satin; and that of a king of arms, of velvet.

15 is a representation of the first Garter King of Arms, William Bruges, appointed 5 January 1420.[11] He is represented as carrying a white staff, a practice which has been recently revived, white wands being carried by all the heralds at the public funeral of the Right Hon. W. E. Gladstone.[12] In Germany the wands of the heralds were later painted with the colours of the escutcheons of the Sovereign to whom they were attached. There was formerly no official hat for an officer of arms in England, and confirmation of this is to be found in the fact that Dallaway mentions a special licence to Wriothesley Garter giving him permission to wear a cap on account of his great age. Obviously, however, a tabard requires other clothing to be worn with it. The heralds in Scotland, not so long ago, when making public proclamations were content to appear in the ordinary elastic-side boots and cloth trousers of everyday life. This gave way for a brief period, in which Court dress was worn below the tabard, but now, as in England, the recognised uniform of a member of the Royal Household is worn. In England, owing to the less frequent ceremonial appearances of the heralds, and the more scrupulous control which has been exercised, no such anachronisms as were perpetuated in Scotland have been tolerated, and it has been customary for the officers of arms to wear their uniform as members of the Sovereign's Household (in which uniform they attend the levees) beneath the tabard when making proclamations at the opening of Parliament or on similar occasions. At a coronation and at some other full State ceremonies they wear knee-breeches. At the late ceremony of the coronation of King Edward VII, a head-dress was designed for the officers of arms.

15 William Bruges, the first Garter King of Arms, appointed 5 January 1420.[11] (From an illuminated MS. in the Bodleian Library at Oxford.)

11. See note 6 *sub* Garter for the date of the creation of the office of Garter.

12. A Warrant from the Earl Marshal dated 2 December 1906 ordained that all Officers of Arms should carry staves indicative of their rank on state occasions. In pursuance of this order, black staves, ensigned with the badges of the various officers, were prepared. These were used until 1953, when new staves were introduced for the coronation of Queen Elizabeth II. These are white staves with gilt handles ensigned with a blue dove within a coronet: the crest of the Corporation of the College of Arms. Officers extraordinary do not have the coronet on their staves, and Clarenceux King of Arms, the only King of Arms who does not have a special sceptre, has a band of gold encircling the middle of his stave.

35

16 *A Herald* (temp. *Hen. VIII*).   17 *A State Trumpeter* (temp. *Hen. VIII*).

These caps are of black velvet embroidered at the side with a rose, a thistle, or a harp, respectively for the English, Scottish, and Irish officers of arms.[13]

A great deal of confusion has arisen between the costume and the functions of a Herald and a Trumpeter, though the confusion has been confined to the minds of the uninitiated and the theatrical stage. The whole subject was very amusingly dealt with in the *Genealogical Magazine* in an article by Mr G. Ambrose Lee, Bluemantle, and the illustrations which he gives of the relative dresses of the Heralds and the Trumpeters at different periods (see 16–19) are interesting. Briefly, the matter can be summed up in the statement that there never was a Trumpeter who made a proclamation, or wore a tabard, and there never was a Herald who blew a trumpet. The Trumpeters nearly always accompanied the Heralds to proclaim their presence and call attention to their proclamation.

In France the Heralds were formed into an incorporation by Charles VI in 1406, their head being Mountjoye, King of Arms, with ten heralds and pursuivants under him. It will be noticed that this incorporation is earlier than that of the College of Arms in England. The Revolution played havoc with the French Records, and no College of Arms now exists in France. But it is doubtful whether at any time it reached the dignity or authority which its English counterpart has enjoyed in former times.

20 represents a French Herald of the early part of the fifteenth century. It is taken from a representation of the Rally of the Parisians against King Charles VI in 1413, to be found in a MS. edition of Froissart, formerly in the Royal Library at Paris.

All the Heralds and Kings of Arms (but not the Pursuivants) wear the curious

13. In the Warrant which lays down the design of this hat, the Irish version bore a crowned shamrock, not a harp. The hat is still worn by Officers of Arms on the occasion of the annual service of the Order of the Garter; on other occasions they wear a black beaver cocked hat, those of Kings of Arms being crested with white ostrich feathers, and those of other officers with black.

The design of these hats, together with definitive regulations for the uniforms of the English Officer of Arms, were laid down in an Earl Marshal's Warrant dated 5 August 1929. Levee dress, consisting of scarlet coat with tails trimmed with gold, overalls and wellingtons, is now rarely worn. On state occasions full dress is worn. This consists of scarlet coat trimmed with gold (the amount of gold varies according to rank) and black knee breeches and stockings. On certain great occasions, such as a coronation, white breeches and stockings are worn.

18 *A State Trumpeter and a Herald at the coronation of James I.* 19 *Peace proclaimed at the Royal Exchange after the Crimean War.*

collar of SS about which there has been so much discussion. The form has remained unchanged, save that the badge is the badge for the time being of the Sovereign. The Heralds have their collars of SS of silver, whilst those of a King of Arms are of silver gilt, and the latter have the further distinction that a portcullis is introduced on each shoulder. The Heralds and Kings of Arms usually place these collars round their shields in representations of their arms. Collars of SS are also worn by Serjeants-at-Arms, and by the Lord Chief Justice.

The English Heralds have no equivalent badge to that which the Scottish Heralds wear suspended from their necks by a ribbon. In Ireland both Heralds and Pursuivants wear a badge.[14]

In addition each King of Arms has his crown; the only occasion, however, upon which this is worn being at the ceremony of a coronation. The crown is of silver gilt, formed of a circle upon which is inscribed part of the first verse of the 51st Psalm, viz. 'Miserere mei Deus secundum magnam misericordiam tuam': the rim is surmounted of sixteen leaves, in shape resembling the oak-leaf, every alternate one being somewhat higher than the remainder. Nine of these leaves are shown in a representation of it. The cap is of crimson satin, closed at the top by a gold tassel, and turned up with ermine.

Garter King of Arms has a baton or 'sceptre' of silver gilt, about two feet in length, the top being of gold, of four sides of equal height, but of unequal breadth. On the two larger sides are the arms of St George impaling the Sovereign's, and on the two lesser sides the arms of St George surrounded by the Garter and motto, the whole ensigned with an Imperial crown. This 'sceptre' has sometimes been placed in bend behind the arms of Garter King. Lyon King of Arms has a baton of blue enamel with gold extremities, the baton being powdered with roses, thistles, and fleurs-de-lis. Sir James Balfour Paul, in his *Heraldry in Relation to Scottish History and Art*, remarks that this is one of the few pieces of British official regalia which is still adorned with the ancient ensigns of France. But knowing how strictly all official regalia in England is required to have the armorial

20 *A French Herald of the early part of the fifteenth century.*

14. This matter has now been put right. King George VI sanctioned the use of a neck badge by the English heralds and pursuivants, and the design was laid down in an Earl Marshal's Warrant dated 6 March 1950. By this Warrant, heralds and pursuivants are permitted to wear a jewel of silver gilt enamelled with the royal arms. This is worn round the neck when in uniform or when decorations are commonly worn, suspended from a ribbon of red taffeta silk two inches wide. When decorations are worn, it may be worn in miniature.

devices thereupon changed, as the Royal arms and badges change, there can be very little doubt that the appearance of the fleur-de-lis in this case is due to an oversight. The baton happens to be that of a former Lyon King of Arms, which really should long since have been discarded and a new one substituted. Two batons are usually placed in saltire behind the arms of Lyon King of Arms.[15]

Ulster King of Arms has a staff of office which, however, really belongs to his office as Knight Attendant on the Most Illustrious Order of St Patrick.

The Scottish Heralds each have a rod of ebony tipped with ivory, which has been sometimes stated to be a rod of office. This, however, is not the case and the the explanation of their possession of it is very simple. They are constantly called upon by virtue of their office to make from the Market Cross in Edinburgh the Royal Proclamations. Now these Proclamations are read from printed copies which in size of type and paper are always of the nature of a poster. The Herald would naturally find some difficulty in holding up a large piece of paper of this size on a windy day, in such a manner that it was easy to read from; consequently he winds it round his ebony staff, slowly unwinding it all the time as he reads.

Garter King of Arms, Lyon King of Arms, and Ulster King of Arms all possess badges of their offices which they wear about their necks.

The badge of Garter is of gold, having on both sides the arms of St George, impaled with those of the Sovereign, within the Garter and motto, enamelled in their proper colours, and ensigned with the Royal crown.

The badge of Lyon King of Arms is oval, and is worn suspended by a broad green ribbon. The badge proper consists on the obverse of the effigy of St Andrew bearing his cross before him, with a thistle beneath, all enamelled in the proper colours on an azure ground. The reverse contains the arms of Scotland, having in the lower parts of the badge a thistle, as on the other side; the whole surmounted with the Imperial crown.

The badge of 'Ulster' is of gold, containing on one side the cross of St Patrick, or, as it is described in the statutes, 'The cross gules of the Order upon a field argent, impaled with the arms of the Realm of Ireland,' and both encircled with the motto, 'Quis Separabit', and the date of the institution of the Order, MDCCLXXXIII. The reserve exhibits the arms of the office of Ulster, viz.: 'Or, a cross gules, on a chief of the last a lion of England between a harp and portcullis, all of the first,' placed on a ground of green enamel, surrounded by a gold border with shamrocks, surmounted by an Imperial crown, and suspended by a sky-blue riband from the neck.

The arms of the Corporation of the College of Arms are: Argent, a cross gules between four doves, the dexter wing of each expanded and inverted azure. Crest: on a dual coronet or, a dove rising azure. Supporters: two lions rampant guardant argent, ducally gorged or.

The official arms of the English Kings of Arms are:

Garter King of Arms. Argent, a cross gules, on a chief azure, a ducal coronet

---

15. The same baton is still in use. In addition to the emblems mentioned, it also is strewn with the Irish harp. There seems little doubt that it was in use before the French Arms were discarded from the royal arms in 1801. The baton has the royal arms of Scotland on one end, and the effigy of St Andrew with the motto of the Order of the Thistle on the other.

encircled with a garter, between a lion passant guardant on the dexter and a fleur-de-lis on the sinister all or.

Clarenceux King of Arms. Argent, a cross gules, on a chief of the second a lion passant guardant or, crowned of the last.

Norroy King of Arms. Argent, a cross gules, on a chief of the second a lion passant guardant crowned of the first, between a fleur-de-lis on the dexter and a key on the sinister of the last.

Badges have never been officially assigned to the various Heralds by any specific instruments of grant or record; but from a remote period certain of the Royal badges relating to their titles have been used by various Heralds, viz.:

Lancaster. The red rose of Lancaster ensigned by the Royal crown.

York. The white rose of York *en soleil* ensigned by the Royal crown.

Richmond. The red rose of Lancaster impaled with the white rose *en soleil* of York, the whole ensigned with the Royal crown.

Windsor. Rays of the sun issuing from clouds.

The four Pursuivants make use of the badges from which they derive their titles.[16]

The official arms of Lyon King of Arms and of Lyon Office are the same, namely: Argent, a lion sejant full-faced gules, holding in the dexter paw a thistle slipped vert and in the sinister a shield of the second; on a chief azure, a St Andrew's cross of the field.

There are no official arms for Ulster's Office, that office, unlike the College of Arms, not being a corporate body, but the official arms of Ulster King of Arms are: Or, a cross gules, on a chief of the last a lion passant guardant between a harp and a portcullis all of the field.[17]

16. In order to place the badges of the heralds and pursuivants on an official footing, in 1959 Queen Elizabeth II approved the form which their badges should take. In addition to the four given above the following badges were approved:

Chester: A gold garb ensigned by the Royal Crown. Previously the garb of Chester had not been crowned.

Somerset: A gold portcullis ensigned by the Royal Crown.

The sunburst badge of Windsor Herald is now ensigned with the Royal Crown.

The pursuivants' badges are:

Rouge Croix: A red cross.

Bluemantle: A blue mantle lined with ermine and having gold tassels.

Rouge Dragon: A red dragon passant on a green mount.

Portcullis: A gold portcullis.

Badges were also approved for three of the extraordinary offices,

Arundel Herald Extraordinary. A silver horse at speed holding in its mouth a sprig of oak, the leaves green, the acorns gold.

Norfolk Herald Extraordinary: Two silver ostrich feathers crossed in saltire each with a gold chain laid along the quill.

Fitzalan Pursuivant Extraordinary: A green sprig of oak, the acorns gold.

17. By the Irish Free State Treaty of 1922, H.M. Ulster Office, Dublin Castle, was reserved as a Crown Office and the then Ulster King of Arms, Sir Nevile Rodwell Wilkinson, K.C.V.O., remained in office until his death on 22 December 1940. As Southern Ireland had become a sovereign independent republic in 1937 the office of Ulster was not continued, but was united to that of Norroy. The first holder of the combined office was Major (later Sir) Algar Henry Stafford Howard, who was appointed on 1 April 1943.

Norroy and Ulster has jurisdiction in Northern Ireland where he grants arms conjointly with

Garter. The Irish grant fees are still lower than those which pertain in England, and Irish grants of arms are entered in special books of record at the College of Arms.

When heraldic jurisdiction in Ireland was divided, the Government of Ireland appointed a Chief Herald, a civil servant attached to the Ministry of Education, who grants arms in the Republic and arranges for genealogical work to be undertaken. He still resides in Dublin Castle, and the office is now known as the Genealogical Office. Copies of the Irish records have been deposited in the College of Arms.

At the time of writing no arms have been assigned to the new combined office, the penultimate holder of which, Mr Aubrey John Toppin, C.V.O. (later Maltravers Herald Extraordinary), used the arms of office of Norroy impaling those of Ulster on his official seal.

21 *Brass in the Scarisbrick Chapel of Ormskirk Church, co. Lancs., to a member of the Scarisbrick family of that name. Arms: Gules, three mullets in bend between two bendlets engrailed argent. (From a rubbing by Walter J. Kaye.)*

4 · Heraldic brasses

By WALTER J. KAYE, JUNR., B.A., F.S.A., F.S.A. SCOT.

Member of the Monumental Brass Society, London;
Honorary Member of the Spalding Gentleman's Society;
Author of A Brief History of Gosberton, in the County of Lincoln

Monumental brasses do not merely afford a guide to the capricious changes of fashion in armour, in ecclesiastical vestments (which have altered but little), and in legal, civilian, and feminine costume, but they provide us also with a vast number of admirable specimens of heraldic art. The vandal and the fanatic have robbed us of many of these beautiful memorials, but of those which survive to our own day the earliest on the continent of Europe marks the last resting-place of Abbot Ysowilpe, 1231, at Verden, in Hanover. In England there was once a brass, which unfortunately disappeared long ago, to an Earl of Bedford, in St Paul's Church, Bedford, of the year 1208, leaving 1277 as the date of the earliest one.

Latten (Fr. *laiton*), the material of which brasses were made, was at an early date manufactured in large quantities at Cologne, whence plates of this metal came to be known as cullen (Köln) plates; these were largely exported to other countries, and the Flemish workmen soon attained the greatest proficiency in their engraving. Flemish brasses are usually large and rectangular, having the space between the figure and the marginal inscription filled either by diaper work or by small figures in niches. Brasses vary considerably in size: the matrix of Bishop Beaumont's brass in Durham Cathedral measures about 16 feet by 8 feet, and the memorial to Griel van Ruwescuere, in the chapel of the Lady Superior of the Béguinage at Bruges, is only about 1 foot square. Brazen effigies are more numerous in England in the eastern and southern counties, than in parts more remote from the continent of Europe.

40

Armorial bearings are displayed in a great variety of ways on monumental brasses, some of which are exhibited in the rubbings selected for illustration. In most cases separate shields are placed above and below the gures. They occur also in the spandrils of canopies and in the shafts and finials of the same, as well as in the centre and at the angles of border-fillets. They naturally predominate in the memorials of warriors, where we find them emblazoned not only on shield and pennon but on the scabbard and ailettes, and on the jupon, tabard, and cuirass also, while crests frequently occur on the tilting-helm. In one case (the brass of Sir Peter Legh, 1527, at Winwick, co. Lancaster) they figure upon the priestly chasuble. Walter Pescod, the merchant of Boston, Lincolnshire, 1398, wears a gown adorned with peascods—a play upon his name; and many a merchant's brass bears his coat of arms and merchant's mark beside, pointing a moral to not a few at the present day. The fifteenth and sixteenth centuries witnessed the greatest profusion in heraldic decoration in brasses, when the tabard and the heraldic mantle were evolved. A good example of the former remains in the parish church of Ormskirk, Lancashire, in the brass commemorating a member of the Scarisbrick family, c. 1500 (21). Ladies were accustomed at this time to wear their husband's arms upon the mantle or outer garment and their own upon the kirtle, but the fashion which obtained at a subsequent period was to emblazon the husband's arms on the dexter and their own on the sinister side of the mantle (22).

The majority of such monuments, as we behold them now, are destitute of any indications of metals or tinctures, largely owing to the action of the varying degrees of temperature in causing contraction and expansion. Here and there, however, we may still detect traces of their pristine glory. But these matters received due attention from the engraver. To represent *or*, he left the surface of the brass untouched, except for gilding or perhaps polishing; this universal method has solved many heraldic problems. Lead or some other white metal was inlaid to indicate *argent*, and the various tinctures were supplied by the excision of a portion of the plate, thereby forming a depression, which was filled up by pouring in some resinous substance of the requisite colour. The various kinds of fur used in armory may be readily distinguished, with the sole exception of *vair* (*argent* and *azure*), which presents the appearance of a row of small upright shields alternating with a similar row reversed.

22 *Brass of Margaret (daughter of Henry Percy, Earl of Northumberland), second wife of Henry, 1st Earl of Cumberland, in Skipton Parish Church. Arms: On the dexter side those of the Earl of Cumberland, on the sinister side those of Percy.*

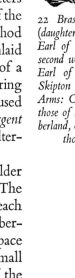

The earliest brass extant in England is that to Sir John D'Aubernoun, the elder (23), at Stoke D'Abernon, in Surrey, which carries us back to the year 1277. The simple marginal inscription in Norman-French, surrounding the figure, and each Lombardic capital of which is set in its own matrix, reads: 'Sire: John: Daubernoun: Chivaler: Gist: Icy: Deu: De: Sa: Alme: Eyt: Mercy:'* In the space between the inscription and the upper portion of the figure were two small shields, of which the dexter one alone remains, charged with the arms of the knight: 'Azure, a chevron, or'. Sir John D'Aubernoun is represented in a complete panoply of chain mail—his head being protected by a *coif de mailles*, which is joined to the *hauberk* or mail shirt, which extends to the hands, having apparently no divisions for the fingers, and being tightened by straps at the wrists. The legs, which are not crossed, are covered by long *chausses*, or stockings of mail, protected at the knees by *poleyns* or *genouillères* of *cuir bouilli* richly ornamented by

* Here lieth Sir John D'Aubernoun, knight. On his soul may God have mercy.

41

23 *Brass of Sir John D'Aubernoun at Stoke D'Abernon. Arms: Azure, a chevron or. (From a rubbing by Walter J. Kaye.)*

24 *Brass of Sir Roger de Trumpington at Trumpington. Arms: Azure, crusilly and two trumpets palewise or. (From a rubbing by Walter J. Kaye.)*

25 *Brass of Sir Robert de Septvans in Chartham Church.*

elaborate designs. A surcoat, probably of linen, depends from the shoulders to a little below the knees, and is cut away to a point above the knee. This garment is tightly confined (as the creases in the surcoat show) at the waist by a girdle, and over it is passed a *guige* whereto the long sword is attached. 'Pryck' spurs are fixed to the instep, and the feet rest upon a lion, whose mouth grasps the lower portion of a lance. The lance bears a pennon charged with a chevron, as also is the small heater-shaped shield borne on the knight's left arm. The whole composition measures about eight feet by three.

Heraldry figures more prominently in our second illustration, the brass to Sir Roger de Trumpington, 1289 (24). This fine effigy lies under the canopy of an altar-tomb, so called, in the Church of St Michael and All Angels, Trumpington, Cambridgeshire. It portrays the knight in armour closely resembling that already described, with these exceptions: the head rests upon a huge *heaume*, or tilting-helm, attached by a chain to the girdle, and the neck is here protected from side-thrusts by *ailettes* or oblong plates fastened behind the shoulders, and bearing the arms of Sir Roger. A dog here replaces the lion at the feet, the lance and pennon are absent, and the shield is rounded to the body. On this brass the arms not only occur upon the shield, but also upon the ailettes, and are four times repeated on the scabbard. They afford a good example of 'canting' arms: 'Azure, crusilly and two trumpets palewise or, with a label of five points in chief, for difference.' It is interesting also to notice that the engraver had not completed his task, for the short horizontal lines across the dexter side of the shield indicate his intention of cutting away the surface of the field.

Sir Robert de Setvans (formerly Septvans), whose beautiful brass may be seen at Chartham, Kent, is habited in a surcoat whereon, together with the shield and ailettes, are seven winnowing fans—another instance of canting arms (25). This one belongs to a somewhat later date, 1307.

Our next example is a mural effigy to Sir William de Aldeburgh, *c.* 1360, from the north aisle of Aldborough Church, near Boroughbridge, Yorkshire (26). He is attired like the 'veray parfite gentil knight' of Chaucer, in a *bascinet* or steel cap, to which is laced the *camail* or tippet of chain mail, and a hauberk almost concealed by a *jupon*, whereon are emblazoned his arms: 'Azure, a fess indented argent, between three crosslets botony, or.' The first crosslet is charged with an annulet, probably as a mark of cadency. The engraver has omitted the indenture upon the fess, which, however, appears upon the shield. The knight's arms are protected by *epaulières*, *brassarts*, *coutes*, and *vambraces*; his hands, holding a heart, by gauntlets of steel. An elaborate baldric passes round his waist, from which are suspended, on the left, a cross-hilted sword, in a slightly ornamented scabbard; on the right, a *misericorde*, or dagger of mercy. The thighs are covered by *cuisses*—steel plates, here deftly concealed probably by satin or velvet secured by metal studs—the knees by *genouillères*, the lower leg by *jambes*, which reveal chausses of mail at the interstices. Sollerets, or long, pointed shoes, whereto are attached rowel spurs, complete his outfit. The figure stands upon a bracket bearing the name 'Will's de Aldeburgh'.

The parish church of Eastington, Gloucestershire, contains a brass to Elizabeth Knevet, which is illustrated and decribed by Mr Cecil T. Davis at page 117 of his excellent work on the *Monumental Brasses of Gloucestershire*.* The block (27), which presents a good example of the heraldic mantle, has been very kindly placed at my disposal by Mr Davis. To confine our description to the heraldic portion of the brass, we find the following arms upon the mantle:

* *Monumental Brasses of Gloucestershire*, by C. T. Davis. London: Phillimore & Co., 1899.

26 Brass of Sir William de Aldeburgh at Aldborough, Yorks. Arms: Azure, a fesse argent between three cross crosslets or. (From a rubbing by Walter J. Kaye.)

'Quarterly, 1. argent, a bend sable, within a bordure engrailed azure (Knevet); 2. argent, a bend azure, and chief, gules (Cromwell); 3. chequy or and gules, a chief ermine (Tatshall); 4. chequy or and gules, a bend ermine (De Cailly or Clifton); 9. pale of six within a bordure bezanté . . . 6. bendy of six, a canton . . .'★

A coat of arms occurs also at each corner of the slab: 'Nos. 1 and 4 are on ordinary shields, and 2 and 3 on lozenges. Nos. 1 and 3 are charged with the same bearings as are on her mantle. No. 2, on a lozenge, quarterly, 1. Knevet; 2. Cromwell; 3. Tatshall; 4. Cailli; 5. De Woodstock; 6. paly of six within a bordure; 7. bendy of six, a canton; 8. or, a chevron gules (Stafford); 9. azure, a bend cottised between six lioncels rampant, or (de Bohun). No. 4 similar to No. 1, with the omission of 2 and 3.'[18]

In later times thinner plates of metal were employed, a fact which largely contributed to preclude much of the boldness in execution hitherto displayed. A prodigality in shading, either by means of parallel lines or by cross-hatching, also tended to mar the beauty of later work of this kind. Nevertheless there are some good brasses of the Stuart period. These sometimes consist of a single quadrangular plate, with the upper portion occupied by armorial bearings and emblematical figures, the centre by an inscription, and the lower portion by a representation of the deceased, as at Forcett, in the North Riding of Yorkshire. Frequently, however, as at Rotherham and Rawmarsh, in the West Riding of the same county, the inscription is surmounted by a view of the whole family, the father kneeling on a cushion at a fald-stool, with his sons in a similar attitude behind him, and the mother likewise engaged with her daughters on the opposite side, while the armorial insignia find a place on separate shields above.

27 Brass of Elizabeth Knevet.

★ The arms are quoted by Mr Davis from Bigland's *Gloucestershire*, vol. 1, p. 539.

18. Ralph Bigland, although an officer of arms (he was Garter from 1822 to 1831) and an industrious herald, had not investigated this brass properly. The subject of the brass is Elizabeth, daughter of Sir William Knevet (or Knyvet) of Buckenham, Norfolk, by his second wife Joan, sister of Edward Duke of Buckingham.

The quarterings should be blazoned: 1. argent, a bend within a bordure engrailed sable (Knevet); 2. argent, a chief gules, over all a bend azure (Cromwell); 3. Chequy or and gules, a chief ermine (Tattershall); 4. Chequy or and gules, a bend ermine (Clifton); 5. Paly of six (in the illustration it looks like three palets) argent and gules, a bordure azure bezanty (Basset of Weldon); 6. Or four bends azure, a canton argent (Rowton or this quartering might possibly be intended for Fitz Oates); bendy of six or and azure, a canton Ermine, which was another Knevet quartering.

5 · The component parts of an achievement

We now come to the science of armory and the rules governing the display of these marks of honour. The term 'coat of arms', as we have seen, is derived from the textile garment or 'surcoat' which was worn over the armour, and which bore in embroidery a duplication of the design upon the shield. There can be very little doubt that arms themselves are older than the fact of the surcoat or the term 'coat of arms'. The entire heraldic or armorial decoration which any one is entitled to bear may consist of many things. It must as a minimum consist of a shield of arms, for whilst there are many coats of arms in existence, and many still rightly in use at the present day, to which no crest belongs, a crest in this country cannot lawfully exist without its complementary coat of arms. For the last two centuries certainly, and probably nearly three centuries, no original grant of personal arms has ever been issued without it containing the grant of a crest except in the case of a grant to a woman, who of course cannot bear or transmit a crest; or else in the case of arms borne in right of women or descent from women, through whom naturally no right to a crest could have been transmitted. The grants which I refer to as exceptions are those of quarterings and impalements to be borne with other arms, or else exemplifications following upon the assumption of name and arms which in fact and theory are regrants of previously existing arms, in which cases the regrant is of the original coat with or without a crest, as the case may be, and as the arms theretofor existed. Grants of *impersonal* arms also need not include a crest.

As it has been impossible for the last two centuries to obtain a grant of arms without its necessarily accompanying grant of crest, a decided distinction attaches to the lawful possession of arms which have no crest belonging to them, for of necessity the arms must be at least two hundred years old. Bearing this in mind, one cannot but wonder at the actions of some ancient families like those of Astley and Pole, who, lawfully possessing arms concerning which there is and can be no doubt or question, yet nevertheless invent and use crests which have no authority.

One instance and one only do I know where a crest has had a legitimate existence without any coat of arms. This case is that of the family of Buckworth, who at the time of the Visitations exhibited arms and crest. The arms infringed upon those of another family, and no sufficient proof could be produced to compel their admission as borne of right. The arms were respited for further proof, while the crest was allowed, presumably tentatively, and whilst awaiting the further proof

45

for the arms; no proof, however, was made.[19] The arms and crest remained in this position until the year 1806, when Sir Buckworth Buckworth-Herne, whose father had assumed the additional name of Herne, obtained a Royal Licence to bear the name of Soame in addition to and after those of Buckworth-Herne, with the arms of Soame quarterly with the arms of Buckworth. It then became necessary to prove the right to these arms of Buckworth, and they were accordingly regranted with the trifling addition of an ermine spot upon the chevron: consequently this solitary instance has now been rectified, and I cannot learn of any other instance where these exceptional circumstances have similarly occurred; and there never has been a grant of a crest alone unless arms have been in existence previously.

Whilst arms may exist alone, and the decoration of a shield form the only armorial ensign of a person, such need not be the case; and it will usually be found that the armorial bearings of an ordinary commoner consist of shield, crest, and motto. To these must naturally be added the helmet and mantling, which become an essential to other than an abbreviated achievement when a crest has to be displayed. It should be remembered, however, that the helmet is not specifically granted, and apparently is a matter of inherent right, so that a person would not be in the wrong in placing a helmet and mantling above a shield even when no crest exists to surmount the helmet. The motto is usually to be found but is not a necessity, and there are many more coats of arms which have never been used with a motto than shields which exist without a crest. Sometimes a *cri-de-guerre* will be found instead of or in addition to a motto. The escutcheon may have supporters, or it may be displayed upon an eagle or a lymphad, &c., for which particular additions no other generic term has yet been coined save the very inclusive one of 'exterior ornaments'. A coronet of rank may form a part of the achievement, and the shield may be encircled by the 'ribbons' or the 'circles' or by the Garter, of the various Orders of Knighthood, and by their collars. Below it may depend the badge of a Baronet of Nova Scotia, or of an Order of Knighthood, and added to it may possibly be what is termed a compartment, though this is a feature almost entirely peculiar to Scottish armory. There is also the crowning distinction of a badge; and of all armorial insignia this is the most cherished, for the existing badges are but few in number. The escutcheon may be placed in front of the crosiers of a bishop, the batons of the Earl Marshal, or similar ornaments. It may be displayed upon a mantle of estate, or it may be borne beneath a pavilion. With two more additions the list is complete, and these are the banner and the standard. For these several features of armory reference must be made to the various chapters in which they are treated.

Suffice it here to remark that whilst the term 'coat of arms' has through the slipshod habits of English philology come to be used to signify a representation of any heraldic bearing, the correct term for the whole emblazonment is an 'achievement', a term most frequently employed to signify the whole, but which can correctly be used to signify anything which a man is entitled to represent of an

---

19. This is a very curious case. In the 1619 visitation of Cambridgeshire the following arms were entered for Buckworth: quarterly, 1 and 4 blank; 2 Everard and 3 Ridick. The crest is untinctured, and consists of a man's head in a helm, the visor raised. The same arms are entered in the 1684 visitation of the same county but in neither visitation were the arms respited for proof as Fox-Davies states, indeed the visiting heralds made no comments whatever on this singular coat.

armorial character. Had not the recent revival of interest in armory taken place, we should have found a firmly rooted and even yet more slipshod declension, for a few years ago the habit of the uneducated in styling anything stamped upon a sheet of note-paper 'a crest', was fast becoming stereotyped into current acceptance.

6 · The shield

The shield is the most important part of the achievement, for on it are depicted the signs and emblems of the house to which it appertains; the difference marks expressive of the cadency of the members within that house; the augmentations of honour which the Sovereign has conferred; the quarterings inherited from families which are represented, and the impalements of marriage; and it is with the shield principally that the laws of armory are concerned, for everything else is dependent upon the shield, and falls into comparative insignificance alongside of it.

Let us first consider the shield itself, without reference to the charges it carries. A shield may be depicted in any fashion and after any shape that the imagination can suggest, which shape and fashion have been accepted at any time as the shape and fashion of a shield. There is no law upon the subject. The various shapes adopted in emblazonments in past ages, and used at the present time in imitation of past usage—for luckily the present period has evolved no special shield of its own—are purely the result of artistic design, and have been determined at the periods they have been used in heraldic art by no other consideration than the particular theory of design that has happened to dominate the decoration, and the means and ends of such decoration of that period. The lozenge certainly is reserved for and indicative of the achievements of the female sex, but, save for this one exception, the matter may be carried further, and arms be depicted upon a banner, a parallelogram, a square, a circle, or an oval; and even then one would be correct, for the purposes of armory, in describing such figures as shields on all occasions on which they are made the vehicles for the emblazonment of a design which properly and originally should be borne upon a shield. Let no one think that a design ceases to be a coat of arms if it is not displayed upon a shield. Many people have thought to evade the authority of the Crown as the arbiter of coat-armour, and the penalties of taxation imposed by the Revenue, by using designs without depicting them upon a shield. This little deception has always been borne in mind, for we find in the Royal Warrants of Queen Elizabeth commanding the Visitations

28 *Taken from the tomb of Geoffrey Plantagenet, Count of Anjou.*

that the King of Arms to whom the warrant was addressed was to 'correcte, cumptrolle and refourme all mann' of armes, crests, cognizaunces and devices unlawfull or unlawfully usurped, borne or taken by any p'son or p'sons within the same p'vince cont²ry to the due order of the laws or armes, and the same to rev'se, put downe or otherwise deface at his discrecon as well in coote armors, helmes, standerd, pennons and hatchments of tents and pavilions, as also in plate jewells, pap', parchement, wyndowes, gravestones and monuments, or elsewhere wheresoev' they be sett or placed, whether they be in shelde, schoocheon, lozenge, square, rundell or otherwise howsoev' cont²rie to the autentiq' and auncient lawes, customes, rules, privileges and orders of armes.'

The Act 32 & 33 Victoria, section 19, defines (for the purpose of the taxation it enforced) armorial bearings to mean and include 'any armorial bearing, crest, or ensign, by whatever name the same shall be called, and whether such armorial bearing, crest, or ensign shall be registered in the College of Arms or not.'[20]

The shape of the shield throughout the rest of Europe has also varied between wide extremes, and at no time has any one particular shape been assigned to or peculiar to any country, rank, or condition, save possibly with one exception, namely, that the use of the cartouche or oval seems to have been very nearly universal with ecclesiastics in France, Spain, and Italy, though never reserved exclusively for their use. Probably this was an attempt on the part of the Church to get away from the military character of the shield. It is in keeping with the rule by which, even at the present day, a bishop or a cardinal bears neither helmet nor crest, using in place thereof his ecclesiastical mitre or tasselled hat, and by which the clergy, both abroad and in this country, seldom made use of a crest in depicting their arms. A clergyman in this country, however, has never been denied the right of using a crest (if he possesses one and chooses to display it) until he reaches episcopal rank. A grant of arms to a clergyman at the present day depicts his achievement with helmet, mantling, and crest in identical form with those adopted for any one else. But the laws of armory, official and amateur, have always denied the right to make use of a crest to bishop, archbishop, and cardinal.

At the present day, if a grant of arms is made to a bishop of the Established Church, the emblazonment at the head of his patent consists of shield and mitre only. The laws of the Church of England, however, require no vow of celibacy from its ecclesiastics, and consequently the descendants of a bishop would be placed in the position of having no crest to display if the bishop and his requirements were alone considered. So that in the case of a grant to a bishop the crest is granted for his descendants in a separate clause, being depicted by itself in the body of the patent apart from the emblazonment 'in the margin hereof', which in an ordinary patent is an emblazonment of the whole achievement. A similar method is usually adopted in cases in which the actual patentee is a woman, and where, by the limitations attached to the patent being extended beyond herself,

20. Section 19 of this Act, which should properly be referred to as 32 and 33 Victoria, chapter 14, made it an offence 'to wear or use' armorial bearings (as defined above) without obtaining an annual licence to do so. This licence cost £1 1s. 0d. or £2 2s. 0d. if the arms were also 'painted, marked or affixed on or to any carriage'. As the definition of the expression 'Armorial Bearings' suggests, the issue of a licence in no way authenticated the arms used. The Act was repealed with effect from 1 January 1945.

males are brought in who will bear the arms granted to the patentee as their pronominal arms. In these cases the arms of the patentee are depicted upon a lozenge at the head of the patent, the crest being depicted separately elsewhere.

Whilst shields were actually used in warfare the utilitarian article largely governed the shape of the artistic representation, but after the fifteenth century the latter gradually left the beaten track of utility and passed wholly into the cognisance of art and design. The earliest shape of all is the long, narrow shape, which is now but seldom seen. This was curved to protect the body, which it nearly covered, and an interesting example of this is to be found in the monumental slab of champlevé enamel, part of the tomb of Geoffrey Plantagenet, Count of Anjou (28), the ancestor of our own Royal dynasty of Plantagenet, who died in the year 1150. This tomb was formerly in the cathedral of Le Mans, and is now in the museum there. I shall have occasion again to refer to it. The shield is blue; the lions are gold.

Other forms of the same period are found with curved tops, in the shape of an inverted pear, but the form known as the heater-shaped shield is to all intents and purposes the earliest shape which was used for armorial purposes.

The church of St Elizabeth at Marburg, in Hesse, affords examples of shields which are exceedingly interesting, inasmuch as they are original and contemporary even if only pageant shields. Those which now remain are the shields of the Landgrave Konrad of Thuringia (d. 1241) and of Henry of Thuringia (d. 1298).

29 *Shield of the Landgrave Konrad of Thuringia* (d. *1241*).

The shield of the former (see 29) is 90 centimetres high and 74 wide. Konrad was Landgrave of Thuringia and Grand Master of the Teutonic Order of Knighthood. His arms show the lion of Thuringia barry of gules and argent on a field of azure, and between the hind feet a small shield, with the arms of the Teutonic Order of Knights. The only remains of the lion's mane are traces of the nails. The body of the lion is made of pressed leather, and the yellow claws have been supplied with a paint-brush. A precious stone probably represented the eye.

The making and decorating of the shields lay mostly in the hands of the herald painters, known in Germany as *Schilter*, who, in addition to attending to the shield and crest, also had charge of all the riding paraphernalia, because most of

49

the articles comprised therein were heraldically decorated. Many of these shield-workers' fraternities won widespread fame for themselves, and enjoyed great consideration at that time.

Thus the *History of a Celebrated Painters' Guild on the Lower Rhine* tells us of costly shields which the shield-workers of Paris had supplied around 1260. Vienna, too, was the home of a not unimportant shield-workers' guild, and the town archives of Vienna contain writings of the fifteenth century treating of this subject. For instance, we learn that in an order of St Luke's parish, 28 June 1446, with regard to the masterpiece of a member of the guild:

'Item, a shield-worker shall make four new pieces of work with his own hand, a jousting saddle, a leather apron, a horse's head-piece, and a jousting shield, that shall he do in eight weeks, and must be able to paint it with his own hand, as Knight and man-at-arms shall direct.'

The shield was of wood, covered with linen or leather, the charges in relief and painted. Leather plastic was very much esteemed in the early Middle Ages. The leather was soaked in oil, and pressed or beaten into shape. Besides piecing and leather plastic, pressed linen (linen dipped in chalk and lime) was also used, and a kind of tempera painting on a chalk background. After the shield was decorated with the charges, it was frequently strengthened with metal clasps, or studs, particularly those parts which were more especially exposed to blows and pressure. These clasps and nails originally had no other object than to make the shield stronger and more durable, but later on their nature was misunderstood; they were treated and used as genuine heraldic charges, and stereotyped into hereditary designs. The long strips with which the edge was bound were called the 'frame' (*Schildgestell*), the clasps introduced in the middle of the shield the 'buckle' or 'umbo' (see 28), from which frequently circularly arranged metal snaps reached the edge of the shield. This latter method of strengthening the shield was called the *Buckelrîs*, a figure which was afterwards frequently employed as a heraldic charge, and is known in Germany by the name of *Lilienhaspel* (Lily-staple) or *Glevenrad*, or, as we term it in England, the escarbuncle.

In the second half of the fourteenth century, when the tournament provided the chief occasion for the shield, the jousting-shield, called in Germany the *Tartsche* or *Tartscher*, came into use, and from this class of shield the most varied shapes were gradually developed. These *Tartschen* were decidedly smaller than the

30.

31.

32.

earlier Gothic shields, being only about one-fifth of a man's height. They were concave, and had on the side of the knight's right hand a circular indentation. This was the spear-rest, in which to place the tilting-spear. The later art of heraldic decoration symmetrically repeated the spear-rest on the sinister side of the shield, and, by so doing, transformed a useful fact into a matter of mere artistic design. Doubtless it was argued that if indentations were correct at one point in the outline they were correct at another, and when once the actual fact was departed from the imagination of designers knew no limits. But if the spear-rest as such is introduced into the outline of a shield it should be on the dexter side.

Reverting to the various shapes of shield, however, the degeneration is explained by a remark of Mr G. W. Eve in *Decorative Heraldry*. Alluding to heraldic art in general, he says (p. 235):

'With the Restoration heraldry naturally became again conspicuous, with the worst form of the Renaissance character in full sway, the last vestiges of the Gothic having disappeared. Indeed, the contempt with which the superseded style was regarded amounted to fanaticism, and explains, in a measure, how so much of good could be relinquished in favour of so weak a successor.'

Later came the era of gilded embellishments, of flowing palms, of borders decorated with grinning heads, festoons of ribbon, and fruit and flowers in abundance. The accompanying examples are reproduced from a book, Knight and Rumley's *Heraldry*. The book is not particularly well known to the public, inasmuch as its circulation was entirely confined to heraldic artists, coach-painters, engravers, and die-sinkers. Amongst these handicraftsmen its reputation was and is great. With the school of design it adopted, little or no sympathy now exists, but a short time ago (how short many of those who are now vigorous advocates of the Gothic and medieval styles would be startled to realise were they to recognise actual facts) no other style was known or considered by the public. As examples of that style the plates of Knight and Rumley were admittedly far in advance of any other book, and as specimens of copperplate engraving they are superb. 30, 31, and 32 show typical examples of escutcheons from Knight and

Rumley; and as the volume was in the hands of most of the heraldic handicraftsmen, it will be found that this type of design was constantly to be met with. The external decoration of the shield was carried to great lengths, and 31 found many admirers and users amongst the gallant 'sea-dogs' of the kingdom. In fact, so far was the idea carried that a trophy of military weapons was actually granted by patent as part of the supporters of the Earl of Bantry. 30, from the same source, is the military equivalent. These plates are interesting as being some of the examples from which most of the heraldic handicraft of a recent period was adapted. The official shield eventually stereotyped itself into a shape akin to that shown in 32, though nowadays considerable latitude is permitted. For paintings which are not upon patents the design of the shield rests with the individual taste of the different officers of arms, and recently some of the work for which they have been responsible has reached a high standard judged even by the strictest canons of art. In Scotland, until quite recently, the actual workmanship of the emblazonments which were issued from Lyon Office was so wretchedly poor that one is hardly justified in taking them into consideration as a type. With the advent into office of the former Lyon King of Arms, Sir James Balfour Paul, a complete change has been made, and both the workmanship and design of the paintings upon the patents of grant and matriculation, and also in the Lyon Register, have been examples of everything that could be desired.[21]

21. Sir James Balfour Paul demitted the office of Lyon in 1926. He was followed by Mr G. S. C. Swinton (1927–9). Sir Francis Grant was Lyon from 1929–45, when he resigned and the present Lyon, Sir Thomas Innes of Learney, G.C.V.O., was appointed. The standard of painting is still high; bold, vigorous work is produced which, though it lacks the finish and fine gold work which is a characteristic of the paintings of College of Arms artists, it makes up for this by its medieval masculinity. Somehow it is typically Scottish.

PLATE II

Arms of Carlos

Arms of Ross-of-Bladênsburg

Arms of Campbell

Arms of Lane of Kings Bromley

7 · The field of a shield and the heraldic tinctures

The shield itself and its importance in armory is due to its being the vehicle where-on are elaborated the pictured emblems and designs which constitute coat-armour. It should be borne in mind that theoretically all shields are of equal value, saving that a shield of more ancient date is more estimable than one of recent origin, and the shield of the head of the house takes precedence of the same arms when differenced for a younger member of the family. A shield crowded with quarterings is interesting inasmuch as each quartering in the ordinary event means the representation through a female of some other family or branch thereof. But the real value of such a shield should be judged rather by the age of the single quartering which represents the strict male descent male upon male, and a simple coat of arms without quarterings may be a great deal more ancient and illustrious than a shield crowded with coat upon coat. A fictitious and far too great estimation is placed upon the right to display a long string of quarterings. In reality quarterings are no more than accidents, because they are only inherited when the wife happens to be an heiress in blood. It is quite conceivable that there may be families, in fact there are such families, who are able to begin their pedigrees at the time of the Conquest, and who have married a long succession of noble women, all of the highest birth, but yet none of whom have happened to be heiresses. Consequently the arms, though dating from the earliest period at which arms are known, would remain in their simple form without the addition of a solitary quartering. On the other hand, I have a case in mind of a marriage which took place some years ago. The husband is the son of an alien whose original position, if report speaks truly, was that of a pauper immigrant. His wealth and other attributes have placed him in a good social position; but he has no arms, and, as far as the world is aware, no ancestry whatever.* Let us now consider his wife's family. Starting soon after the Conquest, its descendants obtained high position and married heiress after heiress, and before the commencement of this century had amassed a shield of quarterings which can readily be proved to be little short of a hundred in number. Probably the number is really much greater. A large family followed in one generation, and one of the younger sons is the ancestor of the aforesaid wife. But the father of this lady never had any sons, and though there are many males of the name to carry on the family in the senior line and also in several younger branches, the wife, by the absence of brothers, happens to be a coheir; and as such she transmits to her issue the right to all the quarterings she has

---

* Since this book was written I have become aware that he has obtained a grant of arms. But I leave it as it was written, because his case illustrates the point I wish to make.

inherited. If the husband ever obtains a grant of arms, the date of them will be subsequent to the present time; but supposing such a grant to be obtained, the children will inevitably inherit the scores of quarterings which belong to their mother. Now it would be ridiculous to suppose that such a shield is better or such a descent more enviable than the shield of a family such as I first described. Quarterings are all very well in their way, but their glorification has been carried too far.

A shield which displays an augmentation is of necessity more honourable than one without. At the same time no scale of precedence has ever been laid down below the rank of esquires; and if such precedence does really exist at all, it can only be according to the date of the grant. Here in England the possession of arms carries with it no style or title, and nothing in his designation can differentiate the position of Mr Scrope of Danby, the male descendant of one of the oldest families in this country, whose arms were upheld in the Scrope and Grosvenor controversy in 1390, or Mr Daubeney of Cote, from a Mr Smith, whose known history may have commenced at the Foundling Hospital twenty years ago. In this respect English usage stands apart, for whilst a German is 'Von' and a Frenchman was 'De', if of noble birth, there is no such apparent distinction in England, and never has been. The result has been that the technical nobility attaching to the possession of arms is overlooked in this country. On the Continent it is usual for a patent creating a title to contain a grant of the arms, because it is recognised that the two are inseparable. This is not now the case in England, where the grant of arms is one thing and the grant of the title another, and where it is possible to possess a peerage without ever having obtained the first step in rank, which is nobility or gentility.

The foregoing is in explanation of the fact that except in the matter of date all shields are equal in value.

So much being understood, it is possible to put that consideration on one side, and speaking from the artistically technical point of view, the remark one often hears becomes correct, that the simpler a coat of arms the better. The remark has added truth from the fact that most ancient coats of arms were simple, and many modern coats are far from being worthy of such a description.

A coat of arms must consist of at least one thing, to wit, the 'field'. This is equivalent in ordinary words to the colour of the ground of the shield. A great many writers have asserted that every coat of arms must consist of at least the field, and a charge, though most have mentioned as a solitary exception the arms of Brittany, which were simply 'ermine'. A plain shield of ermine (33) was borne by John of Brittany, Earl of Richmond (d. 1399), though some of his predecessors had relegated the arms of Brittany to a 'quarter ermine' upon more elaborate escutcheons (61). This idea as to arms of one tincture was, however, exploded in Woodward and Burnett's *Treatise on Heraldry*, where no less than forty different examples are quoted. The above-mentioned writers continue: 'There is another use of a plain red shield which must not be omitted. In the full quartered coat of some high sovereign princes of Germany—Saxony (duchies), Brandenburg (Prussia), Bavaria, Anhalt—appears a plain red quartering; this is known as the *Blut Fahne* or *Regalien* quarter, and is indicative of Royal prerogatives. It usually occupies the base of the shield, and is often diapered.'

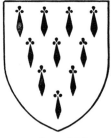

33 *Arms of John (de Montfort, otherwise de Bretagne), Duke of Brittany and Earl of Richmond. (From his seal.)*

But in spite of the lengthy list which is quoted in Woodward and Burnett, the fact remains that only one British instance is included. The family of Berington of Chester (on the authority of Harleian manuscript No. 1535)[22] is said to bear a plain shield of azure. Personally I doubt this coat of arms for the Berington family of Chester, which is probably connected with the neighbouring family in Shropshire, who in later times certainly used very different arms. The plain shield of ermine is sometimes to be found as a quartering for Brittany in the achievement of those English families who have the right to quarter the Royal arms; but I know of no other British case in which, either as a quartering or as a pronominal coat, arms of one tincture exist.

But there are many coats which have no charge, the distinctive device consisting of the partition of the shield in some recognised heraldic method into two or more divisions of different tinctures. Amongst such coats may be mentioned the arms of Waldegrave, which are simply: Party per pale argent and gules; Drummond of Megginch, whose arms are simply: Party per fess wavy or and gules; and the arms of Boyle, which are: Per bend embattled argent and gules. The arms of Berners—which are: Quarterly or and vert—are another example, as are the arms of Campbell (the first quarter in the Duke of Argyll's achievement), which are: Gyronny or and sable.

The coat bendy argent and gules, the ancient arms of Talbot, which are still borne as a quartering by the Earl of Shrewsbury, Waterford, and Talbot; and the coat chequy or and azure, a quartering for Warren, which is still borne by the House of Howard, all come within the same category. There are many other coats of this character which have no actual charge upon them.

The colour of the shield is termed the field when it consists of only one colour, and when it consists of more than one colour the two together compose the field. The field is usually of one or more of the recognised metals, colours, or furs.

The metals are gold and silver, these being termed 'or' and 'argent'. The colours, which are really the 'tinctures', if this word is to be used correctly, are: gules (red), azure (blue), vert (green), purpure (purple), and (in spite of the fact that it is not really a colour) black, which is known as sable.

The metal gold, otherwise 'or', is often represented in emblazonments by yellow: as a matter of fact yellow has always been used for gold in the Register Books of the College of Arms, and Lyon Office has recently reverted to this practice. In ancient paintings and emblazonments the use of yellow was rather more frequent than the use of gold, but gold at all times had its use, and was never discarded. Gold seems to have been usually used upon ancient patents, whilst yellow was used in the registrations of them retained in the Offices of Arms, but I know of no instance in British armory in which the word yellow has been used in a blazon to represent any tint distinct from gold. With regard to the other metal, silver, or, as it is always termed, 'argent', the same variation is found in the usage of silver and white in representing argent that we find in yellow and gold, though we find that the use of the actual metal (silver) in emblazonment does not

22. This manuscript is described in the catalogue of the Harleian manuscripts as: 'an heraldical book in folio written, tricked, or coloured (as it seemeth) by the hand of Mr Jacob Chaloner The Armes-Painter'. It is full of arms of Cheshire families and, in view of the absence of any official record, it is safe to assume that the plain azure coat of Berington is apocryphal.

occur to anything like the same extent as does the use of gold. Probably this is due to the practical difficulty that no one has yet discovered a silver medium which does not lose its colour. The use of aluminium was thought to have solved the difficulty, but even this loses its brilliancy, and probably its usage will never be universally adopted. This is a pity, for the use of gold in emblazonments gives a brilliancy in effect to a collection of coat-armour which it is a pity cannot be extended by an equivalent usage of silver. The use of silver upon the patents at the College of Arms has been discontinued some centuries, though aluminium is still in use in Lyon Office. Argent is therefore usually represented either by leaving the surface untouched, or by the use of Chinese white.

I believe I am the first heraldic writer to assert the existence of the heraldic colour of white in addition to the heraldic argent. Years ago I came across the statement that a white label belonged only to the Royal Family, and could be used by no one else. I am sorry to say that though I have searched high and low I cannot find the authority for the statement, nor can I learn from any officer of arms that the existence of such a rule is asserted; but there is this curious confirmation that in the warrants by which the various labels are assigned to the different members of the Royal Family, the labels are called white labels.[23] Now the label of the Prince of Wales is of three points and is plain. Heraldry knows nothing of the black lines which in drawing a coat of arms usually appear for the outline of a charge. In older work such lines are absent. In any case they are only mere accidents of draughtsmanship. Bearing this in mind, and bearing in mind that the sinister supporter of the Prince of Wales is a unicorn argent, how on earth is a plain label of argent to be depicted thereupon? Now it is necessary also that the label shall be placed upon the crest, which is a lion statant guardant or, crowned with the coronet of the Prince, and upon the dexter supporter, which is another golden lion; to place an argent label upon either is a flat violation of the rule which requires that metal shall not be placed upon metal, nor colour upon colour; but if the unicorn is considered argent, which it is, it would if really depicted in silver be quite possible to paint a white label upon it, for the distinction between white and silver is marked, and a white label upon a gold lion is not metal upon metal. Quite recently a still further and startling confirmation has come under my notice. In the grant of a crest to Thomas Mowbray, Earl of Nottingham, the coronet which is to encircle the neck of the leopard is distinctly blazoned argent, the label

23. It is true that there seems to be no evidence for the frequently repeated statement that a label argent, or a white label, is reserved for royalty. It is probably one of those fables perpetrated by an heraldic writer who thought the silver label *ought* to be reserved for royalty as it was so frequently used to difference royal arms. On the other hand, the warrants assigning arms to members of the Royal family do not blazon the labels 'white'. There are isolated instances of this, but in most cases the label is blazoned 'argent'. For example, it was so blazoned in the warrant assigning arms to William Augustus, Duke of Cumberland, in 1725, and also in recent assignments of arms to members of the Royal family.

It is possible that heralds have noticed the solecism of placing a silver label on a silver charge, and so have had recourse to the use of the colour and word white. Whether such use constitutes the invention of a new heraldic colour is questionable. Any colour may be used in heraldry so long as it is blazoned 'proper'. Thus the supporters of the arms of the London Borough of Richmond upon Thames each carry an oar, the blade of the dexter being dark blue, and that of the sinister light blue—variants in colour unknown to heraldry, but of paramount importance to Oxford and Cambridge.

to which he is previously said to have had a just hereditary right is as distinctly blazoned white, and the whole grant is so short that inadvertence could hardly be pleaded as an explanation for the distinction in blazon. Instances of an official exemplification of coats of arms with labels are not uncommon, because the label in some number of families, for example Courtenay and Prideaux-Brune and Barrington, has become stereotyped into a charge. In none of these cases, however, is it either argent or white, but instances of the exemplification of a coat of arms bearing a label as a mark of cadency are, outside the members of the Royal Family, distinctly rare; they are necessarily so, because outside the Royal Family the label is merely the temporary mark of the eldest son or grandson during the lifetime of the head of the house, and the necessity for the exemplification of the arms of an eldest son can seldom occur. The one circumstance which might provide us with the opportunity is the exemplification consequent upon a change of name and arms by an eldest son during the lifetime of his father; but this very circumstance fails to provide it, because the exemplification only follows a change of arms, and the arms being changed, there no longer exists the necessity for a mark of cadency; so that instances of the official use of a label for cadency are rare, but of such as occur I can learn of none which has received official sanction which blazons the label white. There is, however, one coat which is said to have a label argent as a charge, this is the coat of Fitz-Simon, which is quoted in Papworth, upon the authority of one of the Harleian Manuscripts, as follows: Sable, three crescents, in chief a label of two drops and in fess another of one drop argent; and the same coat of arms is recorded in a funeral entry in Ulster's Office. The label is not here termed white, and it is peculiar that we find it of another colour in another coat of Fitz-Simon (azure, a lion rampant ermine, a label of four points gules).

Of other colours may be mentioned purpure (purple). This in English heraldry is a perfectly well recognised colour, and though its use is extremely rare in comparison with the others, it will be found too frequently for it to be classed as an exception. The earliest instance of this tincture which I have met with is in the coat of De Lacy (34). The Roll of Caerlaverock speaks of his

34 *Armorial bearings of Henry de Lacy, Earl of Lincoln* (d. *1311*):
Or, a lion rampant purpure. (*From his seal.*)

> Baniere ot de un cendall saffrin,
> O un lion rampant porprin,

whilst MS. Cott. Calig. A. xviii quotes the arms: '*De or, a un lion rampaund de pourpre.*' The Burton coat of the well-known Shropshire family of Lingen-Burton is: Quarterly purpure and azure, a cross engrailed or between four roses argent. The Irish baronets of the name of Burton, who claimed descent from this family, bore a very similar coat, namely: Per pale azure and purpure, a cross engrailed or between four roses argent.

Two other colours will be found in nearly all text-books of English armory. These are murrey or sanguine, and orange or tenné. The exact tint of murrey is between gules and purpure; and tenné is an orange-tawny colour. They are both 'stains', and were perhaps invented by the old heralds for the perpetration of their preposterous system of abatements, which will be found set out in full in the old heraldry books, but which have yet to be found occurring in fact. The subject of abatements is one of those pleasant little insanities which have done so much to the detriment of heraldry. One, and one only, can be said to have had the slightest foundation in fact; that was the entire reversal of the escutcheon in the ceremony of degradation following upon attainder for high treason. Even this, however, was but temporary, for a man forfeited his arms entirely by attainder. They were torn down from his banner of knighthood; they were erased in the records of the College of Arms; but on that one single occasion when he was drawn upon a hurdle to the place of his execution, they are said to have been painted reversed upon paper, which paper was fastened to his breast. But the arms then came to an end, and his descendants possessed none at all. They certainly had not the right to depict their shield upside down (even if they had cared to display such a monstrosity). Unless and until the attainder was reversed, arms (like a title) were void; and the proof of this is to be found in the many regrants of arms made in cases where the attainder has remained, as in the instances of the Earl of Stafford and the ancestor of Lord Barnard. But that any person should have been supposed to have been willing to make use of arms carrying an abatement is preposterous, and no instance of such usage is known. Rather would a man decline to bear arms at all; and that any one should have imagined the existence of a person willing to advertise himself as a drunkard or an adulterer, with variations in the latter case according to the personality of his partner in guilt, is idiotic in the extreme. Consequently, as no example of an abatement has ever been found, one might almost discard the 'stains' of murrey and tenné were it not that they were largely made use of for the purposes of liveries, in which usage they had no such objectionable meaning. At the present day scarlet or gules being appropriated to the Royal Family for livery purposes, other people possessing a shield of gules are required to make use of a different red, and though it is now termed chocolate or claret colour by the utilitarian language of the day, it is in reality nothing more than the old sanguine or murrey. Of orange-tawny I can learn of but one livery at the present day. I refer to the orange-tawny coats used by the hunt servants of the Lords Fitzhardinge, and of the Old Berkeley country near London. *A propos* of this it is interesting to note the curious legend that the 'pink' of the hunting field is not due to any reasons of optical advantage, but to an entirely different reason. Formerly no man might hunt even on his own estate until he had had licence of free warren from the Crown. Consequently he merely hunted by the pleasure of the Crown, taking part in what was exclusively a Royal sport by Royal permission, and for this Royal sport he wore the King's livery of scarlet. This being the case, it is a curious anomaly that although the livery of the only Royal pack recently in existence, the Royal Buck Hounds, was scarlet and gold, the Master wore a green coat. The legend may be a fallacy, inasmuch as scarlet did not become the Royal livery until the accession of the Stuarts; but it is by no means clear to what date the scarlet hunting coat can be traced.

There is, however, one undoubted instance of the use of sanguine for the field of a coat of arms, namely, the arms of Clayhills of Invergowrie,* which are properly matriculated in Lyon Register.[24]

A *Arms of Goonetilleke.*

* The arms of Clayhills of Invergowrie: Parted per bend sanguine and vert, two greyhounds courant bendwise argent. Mantling gules doubled argent; and upon a wreath of the liveries is set for crest, an arm holding an Imperial crown proper; and in an escroll over the same, this motto, 'Corde et animo.' Matriculated in Lyon Office *circa* 1672.

24. Since Fox-Davies wrote, indeed since the end of World War II, sanguine, murrey and tenné have been used on several occasions. The arms of Sir Oliver Goonetilleke, G.C.M.G., K.C.V.O., K.C.B., sometime Governor-General of Ceylon are: sanguine, a lotus flower and a bordure or (A).

To these colours German heraldry has added brown, blood-red (this apparently is different from the English sanguine, as a different hatching has been invented for it), earth-colour, iron-grey, water-colour, flesh-colour, ashen-grey, orange (here also a separate hatching from the one to represent tenné has been invented), and the colour of nature, *i.e.* 'proper'. These doubtless are not intended to be added to the list of heraldic tinctures, but are noted because various hatchings have been invented in modern times to represent them.

Dr Woodward, in Woodward and Burnett's *Treatise on Heraldry*, alludes to various tinctures amongst Continental arms which he has come across.

'Besides the metals, tinctures, and furs which have been already described, other tinctures are occasionally found in the Heraldry of Continental nations; but are comparatively of such rarity as that they may be counted among the curiosities of blazon, which would require a separate volume. That of which I have collected instances is *Cendrée*, or ash colour, which is borne by (among others) the Bavarian family of Ashua, as its *armes parlantes*: *Cendrée, a mount of three coupeaux in base or.*

'*Brunâtre*, a brown colour, is even more rare as a tincture of the field; the Mieroszewsky in Silesia bear, "*de Brunâtre, A cross patée argent supporting a ravenrising sable, and holding in its beak a horseshoe proper, its points towards the chief.*"

'*Bleu-céleste*, or *bleu du ciel*, appears occasionally, apart from what we may term "landscape coats". That it differs from, and is a much lighter colour than, azure is shown by the following example. The Florentine Cinti (now Cini) bear a coat which would be numbered among the *armes fausses, or à enquérir: Per pale azure and bleu-céleste, an estoile counterchanged.*'

'*Amaranth* or *columbine* is the field of a coat (of which the blazon is too lengthy for insertion in this place) which was granted to a Bohemian knight in 1701.'

Carnation is the French term for the colour of naked flesh, and is often employed in the blazonry of that country.[25]

Perhaps mention should here be made of the English term 'proper'. Anything, alive or otherwise, which is depicted in its natural colours is termed 'proper', and

---

A good example of the use of murrey is to be found in the arms granted to Sir George Williams University, Ontario on 3 December 1964: murrey, a dove wings addorsed or, about the neck a wreath of olive proper and charged on each wing with a maple leaf murrey, on a chief or, between two roses murrey, barbed and seeded proper, an inverted triangle murrey, surmounted by an open book proper, edged or, bound azure (B). Tenné is less frequently found but the arms of Sir Ronald Prain afford an example: azure, a bend tenné, between two spurs the rowels upwards or.

25. The term 'carnation' is also used in English blazon. Today it is the exception rather than the rule, but in Tudor times it was frequently employed. The crest granted by Christopher Barker, Garter, to Thomas Knighte of Hoo on 8 April 1546 is blazoned: 'an arm with a hande holdenge a swourde under the hiltes charnois the sleeve bendy in bylleke of IIII peeces gole and gouls, the swourde silver the hilts goulde thereupon II spurres sables Buckells & rowells golden.' The hand in the crest granted to John Mardocks of Middlesex by William Dethick is blazoned 'carnation', following the English orthography. In modern times the crest granted to the Royal Over-Seas League on 7 January 1960 provides an example of the use of this term; two hands that to the dexter sable, that to the sinister carnation, supporting a terrestrial globe the sea or, the land gules.

B *Arms of Sir George Williams University.*

or

argent

gules

azure

sable

vert

purpose

35.

it should be depicted in its really correct tones or tints, without any attempt to assimilate these with any heraldic tincture. It will not be found in the very ancient coats of arms, and its use is not to be encouraged. When a natural animal is found existing in various colours it is usual to so describe it, for the term 'proper' alone would leave uncertainty. For instance, the crest of the Lane family, which was granted to commemorate the ride of King Charles II behind Mistress Jane Lane as her servant, in his perilous escape to the coast after the disastrous Battle of Worcester, is blazoned 'a strawberry roan horse, couped at the flanks proper, bridled sable, and holding between the feet an Imperial crown also proper'. Lord Cowper's supporters were, on either side of the escutcheon, 'a light dun horse proper, with a large blaze down the face, the mane close shorn except a tuft on the withers, a black list down the back, a bob tail, and the near fore-foot and both hind feet white'. Another instance that might be quoted are the supporters of Lord Newlands, which are: 'On either side a dapple-grey horse proper, gorged with a riband and suspended therefrom an escutcheon gules, charged with three bezants in chevron.' The crest of the family of Bewes, of St Neots, Cornwall, is: 'On a chapeau gules, turned up ermine, a pegasus rearing on his hind legs of a bay colour, the mane and tail sable, winged or, and holding in the mouth a sprig of laurel proper.'

There are and were always many occasions in which it was desired to represent armorial bearings in black and white, or where from the nature of the handicraft it was impossible to make use of actual colour. But it should always be pointedly remembered that unless the right colours of the arms could be used the tinctures were entirely ignored in all matters of handicraft until the seventeenth century. Various schemes of hatchings, however, were adopted for the purpose of indicating the real heraldic colours when arms were represented and the real colours could not be employed, the earliest being that of Francquart in Belgium, *circa* 1623. Woodward says this was succeeded by the systems of Butkens, 1626; Petra Sancta, 1638; Lobkowitz, 1639; Gelenius; and De Rouck, 1645; but all these systems differed from each other, and were for a time the cause of confusion and not of order. Eventually, however, the system of Petra Sancta (the author of *Tesseræ Gentilitia*) superseded all the others, and has remained in use up to the present time.

Upon this point Herr Ströhl in his *Heraldischer Atlas* remarks: 'The system of hatching used by Marcus Vulson de la Colombière, 1639, in the course of time found acceptance everywhere, and has maintained itself in use unaltered until the present day; these are shown in 35, only that later, hatchings have been invented for brown, grey, &c.; which, however, seems rather a superfluous enriching.' None of these later creations, by the way, have ever been used in this country. For the sake of completeness, however, let them be mentioned (see 36): *a*, brown; *b*, blood-red; *c*, earth-colour; *d*, iron-grey; *e*, water-colour; *f*, flesh-colour; *g*, ashen-grey; *h*, orange; and *i*, colour of nature. In English armory 'tenné' is represented by a combination of horizontal (as azure) lines with diagonal lines from sinister to dexter (as purpure), and sanguine or murrey by a combination of diagonal lines from dexter to sinister (as vert), and from sinister to dexter (as purpure).

The hatchings of the shield and its charges always accommodate themselves to the angle at which the shield is placed, those of the crest to the angle of the helmet. A curious difficulty, however, occurs when a shield, as is so often the case in this country, forms a part of the crest. Such a shield is seldom depicted quite upright upon the wreath. Are the tincture lines to follow the angle of the smaller shield in the crest or the angle of the helmet? Opinion is by no means agreed upon the point.

But though this system of representing colours by 'hatching' has been adopted and extensively made use of, it is questionable whether it has ever received official sanction, at any rate in Great Britain. It certainly has never been made use of in any *official* record or document in the College of Arms. Most of the records are in colour. The remainder are all without exception 'tricked', that is, drawn in outline, the colours being added in writing in the following contracted forms: 'O', or 'or', for or; 'A', 'ar', or 'arg', for argent; 'G', or 'gu', for gules; 'Az', or 'B' (for blue, owing to the likelihood of confusion between 'ar' and 'az', 'B' being almost universally used in old trickings), for azure; 'S', or 'sa', for sable; 'Vt' for vert, and 'Purp' for purpure. It is unlikely that any change will be made in the future, for the use of tincture lines is now very rapidly being discarded by all good heraldic artists in this country. With the reversion to older and better forms and methods these hatchings become an anachronism, and save that sable is represented by solid black they will probably be unused and forgotten before very long.

The plain, simple names of colours, such as red and green, seemed so unpoetical and unostentatious to the heralds and poets of the Middle Ages, that they substituted for gold, topaz; for silver, pearl or 'meergries'; for red, ruby; for blue, sapphire; for green, emerald; and for black, diamond or 'zobel' (sable, the animal, whence the word 'sable'). Let the following blazonment from the grant of arms to Mödling bei Wien in 1458 serve as example of the same: 'Mit namen ain Schilt gleich getailt in fasse, des ober und maister tail von Rubin auch mit ainer fasse von Berlein, der under thail von grunt des Schilts von Schamaragaden, darinnein Pantel von Silber in Rampannt'—(*lit.* 'Namely, a shield equally divided in fess, the upper and greater part of ruby, also with a fess of pearl, the under part of the field of the shield of emerald, therein a panther of silver, rampant'); that is, 'Per fess gules and vert, in chief a fess argent, in base a panther rampant of the last.'

Even the planets, and, as abbreviations, their astronomical signs, are occasionally employed: thus, the *sun* for gold, the *moon* for silver, *Mars* for red, *Jupiter* for blue, *Venus* for green, *Saturn* for black, and *Mercury* for purple. This aberration of intellect on the part of medieval heraldic writers, for it really amounted to little more, had very little, if indeed it had any, English official recognition. No one dreams of using such blazon at the present time, and it might have been entirely disregarded were it not that Guillim sanctions its use; and he being the high priest of English armory to so many, his example has given the system a certain currency. I am not myself aware of any instance of the use of these terms in an English patent of arms.

The furs known to heraldry are now many, but originally they were only two, 'ermine' and 'vair'. Ermine, as every one knows, is of white covered with black spots, intended to represent the tails of the animal. From ermine has been evolved the following variations, viz. ermines, erminois, pean, and erminites. 'Ermines' is

36.

a black field with white ermine spots (the French term for this is *contre-hermin*, the German, *gegen-hermelin*). A gold background with black ermine spots is styled erminois, and pean is a black ground with gold ermine spots. Planché mentions still another, as does Parker in his *Glossary of Heraldry*, namely, 'erminites', which is supposed to be white, with black ermine spots and a red hair on each side of the spot. I believe there is no instance known of any such fur in British armory. It is not mentioned in Ströhl's *Heraldischer Atlas*, nor can I find any foreign instance, so that who invented it, or for what purpose it was invented, I cannot say; and I think it should be relegated, with abatements and the *seize quartiers* of Jesus Christ, to the category of the silly inventions of former heraldic writers, not of former heralds, for I know of no official act which has recognised the existence of erminites. The German term for erminois is *gold-hermelin*, but there are no distinctive terms either in French or German heraldry for the other varieties. Thus, erminois would be in French blazon: d'or, semé d'hermines de sable; pean would be de sable, semé d'hermines d'or. Though ermine is always nowadays represented upon a white background, it was sometimes depicted with black ermine spots upon a field of silver, as in the case of some of the stall plates of the Knights of the Garter in St George's Chapel at Windsor. Ermine spots are frequently to be found as charges. For instance, in the well-known coat of Kay, which is: 'Argent, three ermine spots in bend between two bendlets sable, the whole between as many crescents azure.' As charges two ermine spots figure upon the arms recently granted to Sir Francis Laking, Bart., G.C.V.O. The ermine spot has also sometimes been used in British armory as the difference mark granted under a Royal Licence to assume name and arms when it is necessary to indicate the absence of blood relationship. Other instances of the use of an ermine spot as a charge are:

Or, on two bars azure, as many barrulets dancetté argent, a chief indented of the second charged with an ermine spot or (Sawbridge).

Argent, a chevron between three crows sable, in each beak an ermine spot (Lloyd, Bishop of St Asaph, 1680; Lichfield, 1692; and Worcester, 1700–17).

Argent, a fess gules between three ermine spots sable (Kilvington).

Argent, two bars sable, spotted ermine, in chief a lion passant gules (Hill, co. Wexford).

The earliest form in which ermine was depicted shows a nearer approach to the reality of the black tail, inasmuch as the spots above the tail to which we are now accustomed are a modern variant.

When a bend is ermine, the spots (like all other charges placed upon a bend) must be bendwise; but on a chevron, saltire, &c., they are drawn upright.

The other variety of fur is 'vair'. This originated from the fur of a kind of squirrel (the ver or vair, differently spelt; Latin *varus*), which was much used for the lining of cloaks. The animal was bluey-grey upon the back and white underneath, and the whole skin was used. It will be readily seen that by sewing a number of these skins together a result is obtained of a series of cup-shaped figures, alternating bluey-grey and white, and this is well shown in 28, which shows the effigy upon the tomb of Geoffrey Plantagenet, Count of Anjou, where the lining of vair to his cloak is plainly to be seen.

The word seems to have been used independently of heraldry for fur, and the

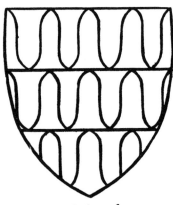

37 *Arms of*
William de Ferrers,
Earl of Derby (d. 1247):
'Scutum variatum
auro & gull.'
(From B.M. MS. Cott. Nero,
D. 1.)

38 *Arms of*
Robert de Ferrers,
Earl of Derby (1254–1265).
(From stained glass
in Dorchester Church.)

following curious error, which is pointed out in Parker's *Glossary of the Terms used in Heraldry*, may be noted in passing. The familiar fairy tale of Cinderella was brought to us from the French, and the slippers made of this costly fur, written, probably, *verre* for *vairé*, were erroneously translated 'glass' slippers. This was, of course, an impossible material, but the error has always been repeated in the nursery-tale books.

In the oldest records vair is represented by means of straight horizontal lines alternating with horizontal wavy or nebuly lines (see 37), but the cup-shaped divisions therefrom resulting having passed through various intermediate forms (see 38), have now been stereotyped into a fixed geometrical pattern, formed of rows of ear-shaped shields of alternate colours and alternately reversed, so depicted that each reversed shield fits into the space left by those on either side which are not reversed (see 39, *k*).[26] The accompanying illustration will show plainly what is intended. In some of the older designs it was similar to that shown in the arms of the Earl Ferrers, Earl of Derby, 1254–65, the sketch (38) being taken from almost contemporary stained glass in Dorchester Church, Oxon; whilst sometimes the division lines are drawn, after the same manner, as *nebuly*. There does not seem to have been any fixed proportion for the number of rows of vair, as 40 shows the arms of the same Earl as represented upon his seal. The palpable pun upon the name which a shield vairé supplied no doubt affords the origin of the arms of Ferrers. Some families of the name at a later date adopted the horseshoes, which are to be found upon many Farrer and Ferrers shields, the popular assumption being that they are a reference to the 'farrier' from whom some would derive the surname. Woodward, however, states that a horseshoe being the badge of the Marshalls, horseshoes were assumed as *armes parlantes* by their descendants the Ferrers, who appear to have borne: Sable, six horseshoes argent. As a matter of fact the only one of that family who bore the horseshoes seems to have been William de Ferrers, Earl of Derby (*d.* 1254), as will be seen from the arms as on his seal (41). His wife was Sybilla, daughter of William Marshall, Earl of Pembroke. His son reverted to the plain shield of vairé, or and gules. The arms of the Ferrers family at a later date are found to be: Gules, seven mascles conjoined or, in which form they are still borne by Ferrers of Baddesley Clinton; but whether

26. Happily the form which vair takes is no longer stereotyped, if indeed it ever were. Certainly there was a fashion, which persisted for an unconscionably long time, of representing vair with hard, ugly little shield-shapes. Various forms are in current use, but the most popular is not unlike that shown in 38, the cups, however, being drawn rather shallower.

It cannot be stressed sufficiently often that the 'rules' of heraldry are really conventions which act as guides to the kings of arms but which in no way bind them. As the basic conventions of heraldry are essentially functional, it is the spirit not the letter of the convention which an able herald will follow. It would be considered 'against the rule' to have a field 'argent, three bars or' as metal may not lie on metal. On the other hand, Fox-Davies would have us believe that a field 'barry of six argent and or' is perfectly in order. Yet the visual impact of these two coats is identical. The myope would never be able to tell how the shields were charged for, whilst one is 'right' and the other 'wrong' as far as text-book rules are concerned, both are bad heraldry because they are not distinctive, and no king of arms worth his salt would consider for one moment allowing the barry coat simply because of a technicality. In the same way a gold collar on a silver beast or a red crown on the head of a silver lion on a blue field do not defeat easy recognition and so may be acceptable. This is not so much 'an exception to the rule' as an intelligent interpretation of an ancient convention.

39.

40 *Arms of Robert de Ferrers, Earl of Derby (1254–1265). (From his seal.)*

63

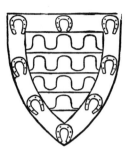

41 *Arms of William de Ferrers, Earl of Derby: Vairé, or, and gules, a bordure argent, charged with eight horseshoes sable. (From a drawing of his seal, B.M. MS. Cott. Julius, C. vii.)*

the mascles are corruptions of the horseshoes, or whether (as seems infinitely more probable) they are merely a corrupted form of the vairé, or and gules, it is difficult to say. Personally I rather doubt whether any Ferrers ever used the arms: Argent, six horseshoes sable.

The early manner of depicting vair is still occasionally met with in foreign heraldry, where it is blazoned as Vair ondé or Vair ancien. The family of MARGENS in Spain bears: Vair ondé, on a bend gules three griffins or; and TARRAGONE of Spain: Vair ondé, or and gules. German heraldry seems to distinguish between *wolkenfeh* (cloud vair) and *wogenfeh* (wave vair; see 39, *n*). The former is equivalent to vair ancient, the latter to vair en point.

The verbal blazon of vair nearly always commences with the metal, but in the arrangement of the panes there is a difference between French and English usage. In the former the white panes are generally (and one thinks more correctly) represented as forming the first, or upper, line; in British heraldry the reverse is more usually the case. It is usual to depict the white panes of ordinary vair with white rather than silver, though the use of the latter cannot be said to be incorrect, there being precedents in favour of that form. When an ordinary is of vair or vairy, the rows of vair may be depicted either horizontally or following the direction of the ordinary. There are accepted precedents for both methods.

Vair is always blue and white, but the same subdivision of the field is frequently found in other colours; and when this is the case, it is termed vairy of such and such colours. When it is vairy, it is usually of a colour and metal, as in the case of Ferrers, Earls of Derby, above referred to; though a fur is sometimes found to take the place of one or other, as in the arms of Gresley, which are: 'Vairé gules and ermine.' I know of no instance where vairé is found of either two metals or of two colours, nor at the same time do I know of any rule against such a combination. Probably it will be time enough to discuss the contingency when an instance comes to light. Gerard Leigh mentions vair of three of more tinctures, but instances are very rare. Parker, in his 'Glossary', refers to the coat of Roger Holthouse, which he blazons: 'Vairy argent, azure, gules, and or, en point.'

The *Vair* of commerce was formerly of three sizes, and the distinction is continued in foreign armory. The middle or ordinary size is known as *Vair*; a smaller size as *Menu-vair* (whence our word 'miniver'); the largest as *Beffroi* or *Gros vair*, a term which is used in armory when there are less than four rows. The word *Beffroi* is evidently derived from the bell-like shape of the *vair*, the word *Beffroi* being anciently used in the sense of the alarm-bell of a town. In French armory, *Beffroi* should consist of three horizontal rows; *Vair*, of four; *Menu-vair*, of six. This rule is not strictly observed, but in French blazon if the rows are more than four it is usual to specify the number; thus VARROUX bears: *de Vair de cinq traits*. *Menu-vair* is still the blazon of some families; BANVILLE DE TRUTEMNE bears: *de Menu-vair de six tires*; the Barons van HOUTHEM bore: *de Menu-vair, au franc quartier de gueules chargé de trois maillets d'or*. In British armory the foregoing distinctions are unknown, and *Vair* is only of one size, that being at the discretion of the artist.

When the Vair is so arranged that in two horizontal rows taken together, either the points or the bases of two panes of the same tincture are in apposition, the fur is known as COUNTER VAIR (*Contre Vair*) (see 39*l*). Another variation, but

64

an infrequent one, is termed VAIR IN PALE, known in German heraldry as *Pfahlfeh* (*Vair appointé* or *Vair en pal*; but if of other colours than the usual ones, *Vairé en pal*). In this all pànes of the same colour are arranged in vertical, or palar, rows (39, *m*). German heraldry apparently distinguishes between this and *Stūrzpfahlfeh*, or *reversed* vair in pale. VAIR IN BEND (or in bend-sinister) is occasionally met with in foreign coats; thus MIGNIANELLI in Italy bears: *Vairé d'or et d'azur en bande*; while *Vairé en barre* (that is, in bend-sinister) *d'or et de sable* is the coat of PICHON of Geneva.

'Vair en pointe' is a term applied by Nisbet to an arrangement by which the azure shield pointing downwards has beneath it an argent shield pointing downwards, and *vice versâ*, by which method the resulting effect is as shown in 39, *n*. The German term for this is *Wogenfeh*, or wave vair. 39, *o*, shows a purely German variety— *Wechselfeh*, or alternate vair; and 39, *p*, which is equivalent to the English vairé of four colours, is known in German armory as *Buntfeh*, *i.e.* gay-coloured or checked vair.

Ordinary vair in German heraldry is known as *Eisenhüt-feh*, or iron hat vair. On account of its similarity, when drawn, to the old iron hat of the fourteenth and fifteenth centuries (see 42), this skin has received the name of *Eisenhütlein* (little iron hat) from German heraldic students, a name which later gave rise to many incorrect interpretations. An old charter in the archives of the chapter-house of Lilienfield, in Lower Austria, under the seal (43) of one Chimrad Pellifex, 1329, proves that at that time vair was so styled. The name of Pellifex (in German *Wildwerker*, a worker in skins, or furrier) is expressed in a punning or canting form on the dexter side of the shield. This Conrad the Furrier was Burgomaster of Vienna 1340–3.

A considerable number of British and foreign families bear *Vair* only; such are FERRERS and GRESLEY, above mentioned; VARANO, Dukes de CAMERINO; VAIRIÈRE, in France; VERET, in Switzerland; GOUVIS, FRESNAY (Brittany); DE VERA in Spain; LOHEAC (Brittany); VARENCHON (Savoy); SOLDANIERI (Florence). *Counter vair* is borne by LOFFREDO of Naples; by BOUCHAGE, DU PLESSIS ANGERS, and BROTIN, of France. HELLEMMES of Tournay uses: *de Contre vair, à lac otice de gueules brochante sur le tout*.

Mr Woodward, in his *Treatise on Heraldry*, writes: 'Two curious forms of Vair occasionally met with in Italian or French coats are known as *Plumeté* and *Papelonné*.

'In *Plumeté* the field is apparently covered with feathers. *Plumeté d'argent et d'azur* is the coat of Ceba (note that these are the tinctures of *Vair*); SOLDONIERI of Udine, *Plumeté au natural* (but the SOLDONIERI of Florence bore: *Vairé argent and sable* with *a bordure chequy or and azure*); TENREMONDE of Brabant: *Plumeté or and sable*. In the arms of the SCALTENIGHI of Padua, the BENZONI of Milan, the GIOLFINI, CATANEI, and NUVOLONI of Verona, each feather of the *plumeté* is said to be charged with an ermine spot sable.

'The bearing of PAPELONNÉ is more frequently found; in it the field is covered with what appear to be scales, the heraldic term *papelonné* being derived from a supposed resemblance of these scales to the wings of butterflies; for example the coat of MONTI: *Gules, papelonné argent*. DONZEL at Besançon bears: Papelonné d'or et de sable. It is worthy of note that DONZÉ of Lorraine used: Gules, three bars

42.

43 *Seal of Chimrad Pellifex,* *1329.*

wavy or. The FRANCONIS of Lausanne are said to bear: *de Gueules papelonné d'argent*, and on *a chief of the last a rose of the first*, but the coat is otherwise blazoned: *Vaire gules and or*, &c. The coat of ARQUINVILLIERS, or HARGENVILLIERS, in Picardy, of *d'Hermine papelonné de gueules* (not being understood, this has been blazoned *'semé of caltraps'*). So also the coat of CHEMILLÉ appears in French books of blazon indifferently as: *d'Or papelonné de gueules*: and *d'Or semé de chausse-trapes de gueules*. GUÉTTEVILLE DE GUÉNONVILLE is said to bear: *d'Argent semé de chausse-trapes de sable*, but it is more probable that this is simply *d'Argent papelonné de sable*. The BARISONI of Padua bear: *Or, a bend of scales, bendwise argent, on each scale an ermine spot sable, the bend bordered sable*. The ALBERICI of Bologna bear: *Papelonné of seven rows, four of argent, three of or*; but the ALBERGHI of the same city: *Papelonné of six rows, three of argent, as many of gules*. The connection with *vairé* is much clearer in the latter than in the former. CAMBI (called FIGLIAMBUCHI), at Florence, carried: *d'Argent, papelonné de gueules*; MONTI of Florence and Sicily, and RONQUEROLLES of France the reverse.

'No one who is familiar with the licence given to themselves by armorial painters and sculptors in Italy, who were often quite ignorant of the meaning of the blazons they depicted, will doubt for a moment the statement that Papelonné was originally a corruption from or perhaps is simply ill-drawn Vair.'

POTENT, and its less common variant COUNTER POTENT, are usually ranked in British heraldic works as separate furs. This has arisen from the writers being ignorant that in early times *Vair* was frequently depicted in the form now known as *Potent* (see 39, *q*). (By many heraldic writers the ordinary *Potent* is styled *Potent-counter-potent*. When drawn in the ordinary way, *Potent* alone suffices.) An example of *Vair* in the form now known as *Potent* is afforded by the seal of JEANNE DE FLANDRE, wife of ENGUERRAND IV (De Courcy); here the well-known arms of COURCY, *Barry of six vair and gules*, are depicted as if the bars of *vair* were composed of bars of *potent* (VRÉE, *Généalogie des Comtes de Flandre*). In a *Roll of Arms at the time of Edward I* the *Vair* resembles *Potent* (-counter-potent), which Dr Perceval erroneously terms an 'invention of later date'. The name and the differentiation may be, but not the fact. In the First Nobility Roll of the year 1297, the arms of No. 8, ROBERT DE BRUIS, Baron of Brecknock, are: *Barry of six, Vaire ermine and gules, and azure*. Here the vair is potent; so is it also in No. 19, where the coat of INGELRAM DE GHISNES, or GYNES, is: *Gules, a chief vair*. The same coat is thus drawn in the Second Nobility Roll, 1299, No. 57. POTENT, like its original *Vair*, is always of *argent* and *azure*, unless other tinctures are specified in the blazon. The name *Potent* is the old English word for a crutch or walking-staff. Chaucer, in his description of 'Elde' (*i.e.* old age) writes:

> So olde she was, that she ne went
> A fote, but it were by potent.

And though a potent is a heraldic charge, and a cross potent a well-known variety of that ordinary, 'potent' is usually intended to indicate the fur of blue and white as in 39, *q*. It is not of frequent usage, but it undoubtedly has an accepted place in British armory, as also has 'counter-potent', which, following the same rules as counter-vair, results in a field as 39, *r*. The German terms for Potent and counter-potent are respectively *Sturzkrückenfeh* and *gegensturzkrückenfeh*. German heraldry has evolved yet another variant of Potent, viz. *Verschobenes Gegensturz-krückenfeh* (i.e. displaced potent-counter-potent), as in 39, *s*. There is still yet another German heraldic fur which is quite unknown in British armory. This is called *Kursch*, otherwise 'Vair bellies', and is usually shown to be hairy and represented brown. Possibly this is the same as the *Plumeté* to which Mr Woodward refers.

Some heraldic writers also speak of *varry* as meaning the pieces of which the vair is composed; they also use the terms *vairy cuppy* and *vairy tassy* for *potent-counter-potent*, perhaps from the drawings in some instances resembling *cups*; that is a possible meaning of *tassa*. It may be said that all these variations of the ancient *vair* arise from mere accident (generally bad drawing), supplemented by over refinement on the part of the heraldic writers who have described them. This generalisation may be extended in its application from vair to many other heraldic matters. To all intents and purposes British heraldry now or hitherto has only known vair and potent.

One of the earliest rules one learns in the study of armory is that colour cannot be placed upon colour, nor metal upon metal. Now this is a definite rule which must practically always be rigidly observed. Many writers have gone so far as to say that the only case of an infraction of this rule will be found in the arms of Jerusalem: Argent, a cross potent between four crosslets or. This was a favourite windmill at which the late Dr Woodward tilted vigorously, and in the appendix to his *Treatise on Heraldry* he enumerates some twenty-six instances of the violation of the rule. The whole of the instances he quoted, however, are taken from Continental armory, in which these exceptions—for even on the Continent such *armes fausses* are noticeable exceptions—occur much more frequently than in this country. Nevertheless such exceptions *do* occur in British armory, and the following instances of well-known coats which break the rule may be quoted.

The arms of Lloyd of Ffos-y-Bleiddied, co. Cardigan, and Danyrallt, co. Carmarthen, are: 'Sable, a spearhead imbrued proper between three scaling-ladders argent, on a chief *gules* a castle of the second.' Burke, in his *General Armory*, says this coat of arms was granted to Cadifor ap Dygnwal, ninth in descent from Roderick the Great, Prince of Wales, by his cousin the great Lord Rhys, for taking the castle of Cardigan by escalade from the Earl of Clare and the Flemings in 1164. Another instance is a coat of Meredith recorded in Ulster's Office and now inherited by the Hon. Richard Edmund Meredith, a judge of the Supreme Court of Judicature of Ireland and a Judicial Commissioner of the Irish Land Commission. These arms are: 'Gules, on a chevron *sable*, between three goats' heads erased, as many trefoils or.' An instance of comparatively recent date will be found in the grant of the arms of Thackeray. A little careful research, no doubt, would produce a large number of English instances, but one is bound to admit the possibility that the great bulk of these cases may really be instances of augmentation.

Furs may be placed upon either metal or colour, as may also any charge which is termed proper. German heralds describe furs and natural colours as amphibious. It is perfectly legitimate to place fur upon fur, and though not often found, numbers of examples can be quoted; probably one will suffice. The arms of

Richardson are: Sable, two hawks belled or, on a chief indented ermine, a pale ermines, and three lions' heads counterchanged. It is also correct to place ermine upon argent. But such coats are not very frequently found, and it is usual in designing a coat to endeavour to arrange that the fur shall be treated as metal or colour according to what may be its background. The reason for this is obvious. It is correct, though unusual, for a charge which is blazoned proper, and yet depicted in a recognised heraldic colour, to be placed upon colour; and where such cases occur, care should be taken that the charges are blazoned proper. A charge composed of more than one tincture, that is, of a metal and colour, may be placed upon a field of either; for example the well-known coat of Stewart, which is: Or, a fess chequy azure and argent; other examples being: Per pale ermine and azure, a fess wavy gules (Broadbent); and: Azure, a lion rampant argent, debruised by a fess per pale of the second and gules (Walsh); but in such coats it will usually be found that the first tincture of the composite charge should be in opposition to the field upon which it is superimposed. For instance, the arms of Stewart are: Or, a fess chequy azure and argent, and to blazon or depict them with a fess chequy argent and azure would be incorrect. When an ordinary is charged upon both metal and colour, it would be quite correct for it to be of either metal, colour, or fur, and in such cases it has never been considered either exceptional or an infraction of the rule that colour must not be placed upon colour, nor metal upon metal. There is one point, however, which is one of these little points one has to learn from actual experience, and which I believe has never yet been quoted in any handbook of heraldry, and that is, that this rule must be thrown overboard with regard to crests and supporters. I cannot call to mind an instance of colour upon colour, but a gold collar around the neck of an argent crest will constantly be met with. The sinister supporter of the Royal achievement is a case in point, and this rule, which forbids colour upon colour, and metal upon metal, only holds with regard to supporters and crests when the crest or supporter itself is treated as a field and *charged with* one or more objects. The Royal labels, as already stated, appear to be a standing infraction of the rule if white and argent are to be heraldically treated as identical. The rule is also disregarded entirely as regards augmentations and Scottish cadency bordures.

So long as the field is party, that is, divided into an equal number of pieces (for example, paly, barruly, or bendy, or party per bend or per chevron), it may be composed of two metals or two colours, because the pieces all being equal, and of equal number, they all are parts of the field lying in the same plane, none being charges.

Before leaving the subject of the field, one must not omit to mention certain exceptions which hardly fall within any of the before-mentioned categories. One of these can only be described by the word 'landscape'. It is not uncommon in British armory, though I know of but one instance where the actual field itself needs to be so described. This is the coat of the family of Franco, the paternal ancestors of Sir Massey Lopes, Bart., and Lord Ludlow. The name was changed from Franco to Lopes by Royal Licence dated 4 May 1831. Whether this coat of arms originated in an English grant, or whether the English grant of it amounts to no more than an attempt at the registration of a previously existing or greatly similar foreign coat of arms for the name of Franco, I am unaware, but the coat certainly is blazoned: 'In a landscape field, a fountain, therefrom issuing a palm-tree all proper.'[27]

But landscape has very extensively been made use of in the augmentations which were granted at the end of the eighteenth and beginning of the nineteenth centuries. In these cases the augmentation very generally consisted of a chief and thereon a representation either of some fort or ship or action, and though the field of the augmentation is officially blazoned argent in nearly every case, there is no doubt the artist was permitted, and perhaps intended, to depict clouds and other 'atmosphere' to add to the verisimilitude of the picture. These augmentations will be more especially considered in a later chapter, but here one may perhaps be permitted to remark that, execrable as we now consider such landscape heraldry, it ought not to be condemned in the wholesale manner in which it has been, because it was typical of the over elaboration to be found in all art and all artistic ideas of the period in which we find it originating. Heraldry and heraldic art have always been a mirror of the artistic ideas prevalent at equivalent periods, and unless heraldry is to be wholly relegated to consideration as a dead subject, it is an anachronism to depict an action the date of which is well known (and which date it is desired to advertise and not conceal) in a method of art belonging to a different period. In family arms the case is different, as with those the idea apparently is always the concealment of the date of nobility.

The 'landscape' variety of heraldry is more common in Germany than with us, and Ströhl writes: 'Of very little heraldic worth are the old house and home signs as they were used by landed proprietors, tradesmen, and artisans or workmen, as indicative of their possessions, wares, or productions. These signs, originally simply outline pictures, were later introduced into heraldic soil, inasmuch as bourgeois families raised to the nobility adopted their house signs as heraldic charges upon their shields.'

There are also many coats of arms which run: 'In base, a representation of water proper,' and one of the best instances of this will be found in the arms of Oxford, though for the sake of preserving the pun the coat in this case is blazoned: 'Argent, an ox gules passing over a ford proper.' Similar instances occur in the arms of Renfrew, Queensferry, Leith, Ryde, and scores of other towns. It has always been considered permissible to represent these either by an attempt to depict natural water, or else in the ancient heraldic way of representing water, namely 'barry wavy argent and azure'. There are many other coats of arms which are of a similar character though specifically blazoned 'barry wavy argent and azure'. Now this representation of water in base can hardly be properly said to be a charge, but perhaps it might be dismissed as such were it not that one coat of

27. An example of a landscape field in English heraldry is to be found in the arms granted to the Gardeners' Company of London on 8 September 1905: on a shield representing a landscape the figure of a man, habited about the body with a skin delving the ground with a spade all proper (C). The crest is: a basket of flowers and fruit proper and the supporters: on either side a female figure (proper), vested argent, wreathed about the temples with flowers and supporting on the exterior arm a cornucopia proper. These arms lend eloquent support to the theory that *anything* placed upon a shield becomes an heraldic bearing.

An earlier example of a landscape is to be found in the unauthentic and rather grim arms of Lichfield. In John Guillim's *A Display of Heraldry* these arms are blazoned: 'in an Escutcheon, a Landskip with divers Martyrs in several Manners massacred.'

C *Arms of The Gardeners' Company.*

44 *Arms of John,*
Lord de la Warr (d. 1398).
(From MS. Ashm. 804, iv.)

45 *Arms of John,*
Lord Beaumont, K.G.
(d. 1396).
From his Garter Plate:
1 and 4, Beaumont;
2 and 3, azure, three
garbs or (for Comyn).

46 *Arms of Gilbert*
Umfraville,
Earl of Kyme
(d. 1421).[30]
(From B.M. Harl. MS.
6163.)

arms exists in Scotland, the whole of the field of which is simply a representation of water. Unfortunately this coat of arms has never been matriculated in Lyon Register or received official sanction; but there is no doubt of its ancient usage, and were it to be now matriculated in conformity with the Act of 1672, there is very little doubt that the ancient characteristic would be retained. The arms are those of the town of Inveraray in Argyllshire, and the blazon of the coat, according to the form it is depicted upon the Corporate seal, would be for the field: 'The sea proper, there in a net suspended from the dexter chief and the sinister fess points to the base; and entangled in its meshes five herrings,' which is about the most remarkable coat of arms I have ever come across.[28]

Occasionally a 'field', or portion of a field, will be found to be a representation of masonry. This may be either proper or of some metal or colour. The arms of the city of Bath are: 'Party per fesse embattled azure and argent, the base masonry, in chief two bars wavy of the second; over all, a sword in pale gules, hilt and pommel or.'[29] The arms of Reynell are: 'Argent, masoned sable, a chief indented of the second.'

Semé

The use of the term 'semé' must be considered before we leave the subject of the field. It simply means 'powdered with' or 'strewed with' any objects, the number of the latter being unlimited, the purpose being to distribute them evenly over the shield. In depicting anything semé, care is usually taken that some of the charges (with which the field is semé), shall be partly defaced by the edges of the shield, or the ordinary upon which they are charged, or by the superior charge itself, to indicate that the field is not charged with a specific number of objects.

There are certain special terms which may be noted. A field or charge semé of fleurs-de-lis is termed 'semé-de-lis', but if semé of bezants it is bezanté, and is termed platé if semé of plates.

A field semé of billets is billetty or billetté, and when semé of cross crosslets it is termed crusilly. A field or charge semé of drops is termed goutté or gutty.

Instances of coats of which the field is semé will be found in the arms of De la Warr (see 44), which are: Gules, crusilly, and a lion rampant argent; Beaumont (see 45): Azure, semé-de-lis and a lion rampant or; and Umfraville (see 46): Gules, semé of crosses flory, and a cinquefoil or.

28. The arms were matriculated on 7 April 1927, and are blazoned: in the waves of the sea five herrings entering a herring net pendent from the sinister chief all proper. The motto is 'Semper tibi pendeat halec', and the arms are ensigned by a mural crown proper (i.e. of stone) masoned sable. The sea is represented as a field azure scored across with thin wavy lines argent.
29. The proper blazon of the arms of the City of Bath is in doubt. Although there are many examples of the arms as blazoned here, in the 1623 Visitation of Somerset, which is an official and relatively recent record, the following arms were allowed by the visiting heralds: per fess embattled gules and a representation of water proper, a sword erect argent, pommel and hilt or, charged with a key also erect ward uppermost and pointing to the sinister gold.
30. Gilbert Umfraville does not appear to have been created Earl of Kyme, although he was popularly known by this title. In official documents he is invariably described as 'knight' or 'chivaler'. Hardyng in his chronicle calls him 'Umfrevile erle of Kyme,' but he is probably not to be relied on in this instance, as he was in the service of the Umfravilles.

The goutte or drop occasionally figures (in a specified number) as a charge; but such cases are rare, its more frequent use being to show a field semé. British heraldry alone has evolved separate names for the different colours, all other nations simply using the term 'goutté' or 'gutté', and specifying the colour. The terms we have adopted are as follows: For drops of gold, 'gutté-d'or'; silver, 'gutté-d'eau'; for gules, 'gutté-de-sang'; azure, 'gutté-de-larmes'; vert, 'gutté-d'huile'; and sable, 'gutté-de-poix'.

The term semé must not be confused with diapering, for whilst the objects with which a field is semé are an integral part of the arms, diapering is a purely artistic and optional matter.

Diapering

The diapering of armorial emblazonments is a matter with which the *science* of armory has no concern. Diaper never forms any part of the blazon, and is never officially noticed, being considered, and very properly allowed to remain, a purely artistic detail. From the artistic point of view it has some importance, as in many of the earliest instances of handicraft in which armorial decoration appears, very elaborate diapering is introduced. The frequency with which diapering is met with in armorial handicraft is strangely at variance with its absence in heraldic paintings of the same periods, a point which may perhaps be urged upon the attention of some of the heraldic artists of the present day, who would rather seem to have failed to grasp the true purpose and origin and perhaps also the use of diaper. In stained glass and enamel work, where the use of diaper is most frequently met with, it was introduced for the express purpose of catching and breaking up the light, the result of which was to give an enormously increased effect of brilliance to the large and otherwise flat surfaces. These tricks of their art and craft the old handicraftsmen were past masters in the use of. But no such purpose could be served in a small painting upon vellum. For this reason early heraldic emblazonments are seldom if ever found to have been diapered. With the rise of heraldic engraving amongst the 'little masters' of German art, the opportunity left to their hands by the absence of colour naturally led to the renewed use of diaper to avoid the appearance of blanks in their work. The use of diaper at the present day needs to be the result of careful study and thought, and its haphazard employment is not recommended.

If, as Woodward states (an assertion one is rather inclined to doubt), there are some cases abroad in which the constant use of diapering has been stereotyped into an integral part of the arms, these cases must be exceedingly few in number, and they certainly have no counterpart in the armory of this country. Where for artistic reasons diapering is employed, care must always be taken that the decorative form employed cannot be mistaken for a field either charged or semé.

Partition lines

If there is one subject which the ordinary text-books of armory treat in the manner of classification adapted to an essay on natural history or grammar, with its attendant rigidity of rule, it is the subject of partition lines; and yet the whole

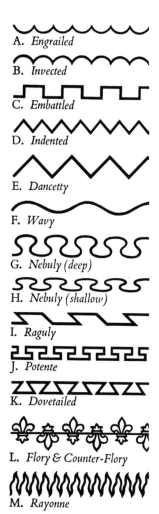

A. *Engrailed*

B. *Invected*

C. *Embattled*

D. *Indented*

E. *Dancetty*

F. *Wavy*

G. *Nebuly (deep)*

H. *Nebuly (shallow)*

I. *Raguly*

J. *Potente*

K. *Dovetailed*

L. *Flory & Counter-Flory*

M. *Rayonne*

47 *Lines of Partition.*

subject is more in the nature of a set of explanations which must each be learned on its own merits. The usual lines of partition are themselves well enough known; and it is hardly necessary to elaborate the different variations at any great length. They may, however, be enumerated as follows: Engrailed, embattled, indented, invecked or invected, wavy or undy, nebuly, dancetté, raguly, potenté, dovetailed, and urdy. These are the lines which are recognised by most modern heraldic text-books and generally recapitulated; but we shall have occasion later to refer to others which are very well known, though apparently they have never been included in the classification of partition lines (47). *Engrailed*, as every one knows, is formed by a continuous and concurrent series of small semicircles conjoined each to each, the sharp points formed by the conjunction of the two arcs being placed outwards. This partition line may be employed for the rectilinear charges known as 'ordinaries' or 'sub-ordinaries'. In the bend, pale, pile, cross, chief, and fess, when these are described as engrailed the enclosing lines of the ordinary, other than the edges of the shield, are all composed of these small semicircles with the points turned *outwards*, and the word 'outwards' must be construed as pointing away from the centre of the ordinary when it is depicted. In the case of a chief the points are turned downwards, but it is rather difficult to describe the use of the term when used as a partition line of the field. The only instance I can call to mind where it is so employed is the case of Baird of Ury, the arms of this family being: Per gale engrailed gules and or, a boar passant counterchanged. In this instance the points are turned towards the sinister side of the shield, which would seem to be correct, as, there being no ordinary, they must be outwards from the most important position affected, which in this case undoubtedly is the dexter side of the shield. In the same way 'per fess engrailed' would be presumably depicted with the points outwards from the chief line of the shield, that is, they would point downwards; and I should imagine that in 'per bend engrailed' the points of the semicircles would again be placed inclined towards the dexter base of the shield, but I may be wrong in these two latter cases, for they are only supposition. This point, however, which puzzled me much in depicting the arms of Baird of Ury, I could find explained in no text-book upon the subject.

The term *invected* or *invecked* is the precise opposite of engrailed. It is similarly composed of small semicircles, but the points are turned inwards instead of outwards, so that it is no more than the exact reverse of engrailed, and all the regulations concerning the one need to be observed concerning the other, with the proviso that they are reversed.

The partition line *embattled* has certain peculiarities of its own. When dividing the field there can be no difficulty about it, inasmuch as the crenellations are equally inwards and outwards from any point, and it should be noted that the term 'crenellé' is almost as often used as 'embattled'. When, however, the term describes an ordinary, certain points have to be borne in mind. The fess or the bar embattled is drawn with the crenellations *on the upper side* only, the under edge being plain unless the ordinary is described both as 'embattled and counter-embattled'. Similarly a chevron is only crenellated on the upper edge unless it is described as both embattled and counter-embattled, but a pale embattles is crenellated on both edges as is the cross or saltire. Strictly speaking, a bend embattled is crenellated upon the upper edge only, though with regard to this ordinary there is much laxity of practice. I have never come across a pile embattled; but it would naturally be embattled on both edges.[31] Some writers make a distinction between embattled and bretessed, giving to the former term the meaning that the embattlements on the one side are opposed to the indentations on the other, and using the term bretessed to signify that embattlements are opposite embattlements and indentations opposite indentations. I am doubtful as to the accuracy of this distinction, because the French term *bretessé* means only counter-embattled.[32]

The terms *indented* and *dancetté* need to be considered together, because they differ very little, and only in the fact that whilst indented may be drawn with any number of teeth, dancetté is drawn with a limited number, which is usually three complete teeth in the width of the field. But it should be observed that this rule is not so hard and fast that the necessity of artistic depicting may not modify it slightly. An ordinary which is indented would follow much the same rules as an ordinary which was engrailed, except that the teeth are made by small straight lines for the indentations instead of by small semicircles, and instances can doubtless be found of all the ordinaries qualified by the term indented. Dancetté, however, does not lend itself so readily to general application, and is usually to be found applied to either a fess or chief, or occasionally a bend. In the case of a fess dancetté the indentations on the top and bottom lines are made to fit into each other, so that instead of having a straight band with the edge merely toothed, one gets an up and down zig-zag band with three complete teeth at the top and three complete teeth at the bottom. Whilst a fess, a bar, a bend, and a chief can be found dancetté, I do not see how it would be possible to draw a saltire or a cross dancetté. At any rate the resulting figure would be most ugly, and would appear ill-balanced. A pile and a chevron seem equally impossible, though there does not seem to be the like objection to a pale dancetté. An instance of a bend dancetté is found in the arms of Cuffe (Lord Desart), which are: Argent, on a bend dancetté sable, plain cotised azure, three fleurs-de-lis, and on each cotise as many bezants.

Wavy or *undy*, which is supposed to have been taken from water, and *nebuly*, which is supposed to be derived from clouds, are of course lines which are well known. They are equally applicable to any ordinary and to any partition of the field; but in both cases it should be noticed by artists that there is no one definite or accepted method of depicting these lines, and one is quite at liberty, and might be recommended, to widen out the indentations, or to increase them in height, as the artistic requirements of the work in hand may seem to render advisable. It is only by bearing this in mind and treating these lines with freedom that really artistic work can sometimes be produced where they occur. There is no fixed rule either as to the width which these lines may occupy or as to the number of

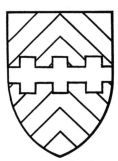

D *Arms of Llewelyn-Davies.*

31. The arms granted to Major-General Sir George Townshend Walker on 13 April 1815 provide an example of an embattled pile: or, on a pile embattled azure, three caltraps two and one and in chief point a mural crown of the field, inscribed 'Badajoz'. These arms were granted to Sir George, for him and his descendants, and also for the descendants of his two brothers Frederick Nathaniel Walker and Charles Montagu Walker and of his sister Mary Murthwaite Hobbs, but in their case the mural crown, which referred to Sir George's assault on and capture of Badajoz in 1812, was to be omitted.

32. I can find no ancient example in English blazon of this distinction between bretessed and embattled and counter-embattled, but there is a modern example. The arms of Lord Llewellyn-Davies, a life peer, are blazoned: chevronny of eight argent and azure, a fess bretessed gules (D).

indentations as compared with the width of the shield, and it is a pity to introduce or recognise any regulations of this character where none exist. There are writers who think it not unlikely that vairé and barry nebuly were one and the same thing. It is at any rate difficult in some old representations to draw any noticeable distinctions between the methods of depicting barry nebuly and vair.

The line *raguly* has been the subject of much discussion. It, and the two which follow, viz. potenté and dovetailed, are all comparatively modern introductions. It would be interesting if some enthusiast would go carefully through the ancient Rolls of Arms and find the earliest occurrences of these terms. My own impression is that they would all be found to be inventions of the medieval writers on heraldry. Raguly is the same as embattled, with the crenellations put upon the slant. Some writers say they should slant one way, others give them slanting the reverse. In a pale or a bend the teeth must point upwards; but in a fess I should hesitate to say whether it were more correct for them to point to the dexter or to the sinister, and I am inclined to consider that either is perfectly correct. At any rate, whilst they are usually drawn inclined to the dexter, in Woodward and Burnett they are to the sinister, and Guillim gives them turned to the dexter, saying, 'This form of line I never yet met with in use as a partition, though frequently in composing of ordinaries referring them like to the trunks of trees with the branches lopped off, and that (as I take it) it was intended to represent.' Modern heraldry supplies an instance which in the days of Mr Guillim, of course, did not exist to refer to. This instance occurs in the arms of the late Lord Leighton, which were: 'Quarterly per fesse raguly or and gules, in the second and third quarters a wyvern of the first.' It is curious that Guillim, even in the edition of 1724, does not mention any of the remaining terms. *Dovetailed* in modern armory is even yet but seldom made use of, though I can quote two instances of coats of arms in which it is to be found, namely, the arms of Kirk, which are: 'Gules, a chevron dovetailed ermine, on a chief argent, three dragons' heads couped of the field;' and Ambrose: 'Azure, two lions passant in pale argent, on a chief dovetailed of the last, a fleur-de-lis between two annulets of the first.' Other instances of dovetailed used as a line of partition will be found in the case of the arms of Farmer, which are: 'Per chevron dovetailed gules and argent, in chief two lions' heads erased of the last, and in base a salamander in flames proper;' and in the arms of Fenton namely: 'Per pale argent and sable, a cross dovetailed, in the first and fourth quarters a fleur-de-lis, and in the second and third a trefoil slipped all countercharged.' There are, of course, many others. The term *potenté*, as will be seen from a reference to 47, is used to indicate a line which follows the form of the division lines in the fur potent. As one of the partition lines potenté is very rare.[33]

As to the term *urdy*, which is given in Woodward and Burnett and also in Berry, I can only say I personally have never come across an instance of its use as a partition line. A cross or a billet urdy one knows, but urdy as a partition line I have yet to find. It is significant that it is omitted in Parker except as a term applicable to a cross, and the instances and variations given by Berry, 'urdy in point

33. The division line potenté, now always called potent, is probably rare, as it is not one of the more beautiful division lines; however it has a decent antiquity, for the arms of the old Counts of Champagne are azure, a bend argent, cottised potent and counter-potent or.

paleways' and 'contrary urdy', I should be much more inclined to consider as variations of vair; and, though it is always well to settle points which can be settled, I think urdy and its use as a partition line may be well left for further consideration when examples of it come to hand.

There is one term, however, which is to be met with at the present time, but which I have never seen quoted in any text-book under the heading of a partition line; that is, *flory counter-flory*, which is of course formed by a succession of fleurs-de-lis alternately reversed and counterchanged. They might of course be blazoned after the quotation of the field as 'per bend' or 'per chevron' as the case might be, simply as so many fleurs-de-lis counterchanged, and alternately reversed in a specified position; but this never appears to be the case, and consequently the fleurs-de-lis would appear to be essentially parts of the field and not charges. I have sometimes thought whether it would not be more correct to depict 'per something' flory and counter-flory without completing the fleurs-de-lis, simply leaving the alternate tops of the fleurs-de-lis to show. In the cases of the illustrations which have come under my notice, however, the whole fleur-de-lis is depicted, and as an instance of the use of the term may be mentioned the arms of Dumas, which are: 'Per chevron flory and counter-flory or and azure, in chief two lions' gambs erased, and in base a garb counterchanged.' But when the term flory and counter-flory is used in conjunction with an ordinary, *e.g.* a fess flory and counter-flory, the *half* fleurs-de-lis, only alternately reversed, are represented on the *outer* edges of the ordinary.

I think also that the word '*arched*' should now be included as a partition line. I confess that the only form in which I know of it is that it was frequently used by the late Garter King of Arms in designing coats of arms with chiefs arched. Recently Garter has granted a coat with a chief double arched.[34] But if a chief can be arched I see no reason why a fesse or a bar cannot equally be so altered, and in that case it undoubtedly becomes a recognised line of partition. Perhaps it should be stated that a chief arched is a chief with its base line one arc of a large circle. The diameter of the circle and the consequent acuteness of the arch do not appear to be fixed by any definite rule, and here again artistic requirements must be the controlling factor in any decision. Elvin in his *Dictionary of Heraldic Terms* gives a curious assortment of lines, the most curious of all, perhaps, being indented embowed, or hacked and hewed. Where such a term originated or in what coat of arms it is to be found I am ignorant, but the appearance is exactly what would be presented by a piece of wood hacked with an axe at regular intervals. Elvin again makes a difference between bretessed and embattled-counter-embattled, making the embattlement on either side of an ordinary identical in the former and alternated in the latter. He also makes a difference between raguly, which is the conventional form universally adopted, and raguled and trunked, where the ordinary takes the representation of the trunk of a tree with the branches lopped; but these and many others that he gives are refinements of idea which personally I should never expect to find in actual use, and of the instances of which I am unaware. I think, however, the term '*rayonné*', which is found in both the arms of

34. I cannot find the grant to which Fox-Davies refers, but the first such chief seems to be that granted on 18 December 1806 to William Proctor Smith of Plymouth Dock, Devon. His arms were simply, gules, on a chief double arched or, three trefoils slipped proper.

O'Hara and the arms of Colman, and which is formed by the addition of rays to the ordinary, should take a place amongst lines of partition, though I admit I know of no instance in which it is employed to divide the field.

Methods of partition

The field of any coat of arms is the surface colour of the shield, and is supposed to include the area within the limits formed by its outline. There are, as has been already stated, but few coats of a single colour minus a charge to be found in British heraldry. But there are many which consist of a field divided by partition lines only, of which some instances were given on page 55.

A shield may be divided by partition lines running in the direction of almost any 'ordinary', in which case the field will be described as 'per bend' or 'per chevron', &c. It may be:

Per fess 48, Per bend 49, Per bend sinister 50, Per pale 51, Per chevron 52, Per cross 53 (though it should be noted that more usual term employed for this is 'quarterly'), Per saltire 54.

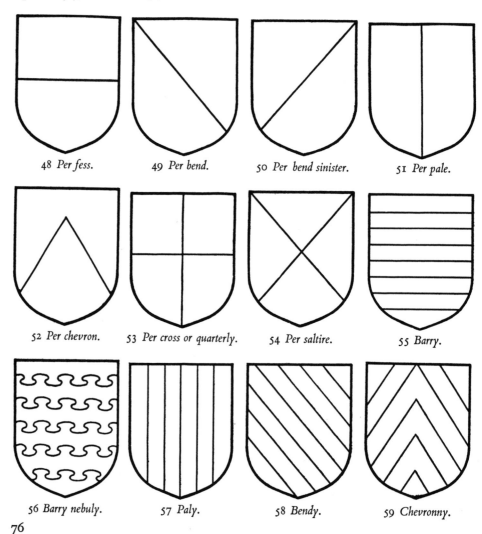

48 *Per fess.*   49 *Per bend.*   50 *Per bend sinister.*   51 *Per pale.*

52 *Per chevron.*   53 *Per cross or quarterly.*   54 *Per saltire.*   55 *Barry.*

56 *Barry nebuly.*   57 *Paly.*   58 *Bendy.*   59 *Chevronny.*

But a field cannot be 'per pile' or 'per chief', because there is no other way of representing these ordinaries.

A field can be composed of any number of pieces in the form of the ordinaries filling the area of the shield, in which case the field is said to be 'barry' (55 and 56), 'paly' (57), 'bendy' (58), 'chevronny' (59), &c., but the number of pieces must be specified.

Another method of partition will be found in the fields 'checky' (or 'chequy') and lozengy; but these divisions, as also the foregoing, will be treated more specifically under the different ordinaries. A field which is party need not necessarily have all its lines of partition the same. This peculiarity, however, seldom occurs except in the case of a field quarterly, the object in coats of this character being to prevent different quarters of one coat of arms being ranked as or taken to be quarterings representing different families.[35]

35. There are several types of field which Fox-Davies has not mentioned, and there have been one or two designs since he wrote. The principal omission is that there is no mention of masonry. A field or charge composed of bricks is blazoned as being masoned. A modern example is the coat granted to the Leeds and Moorlands Building Society on 20 May 1954: or, masoned sable, two flaunches of the last, each charged with a curlew facing to the centre proper. A modern variant of this type of field is one 'masoned of chequers'. One such field is blazoned, masoned of chequers or and azure, the tinctures bendwise.

A curious modern design consists of a field of cubes and is blazoned, a field of cubes conjoined in perspective the tops azure, the dexter and sinister sides or and argent respectively.

A field composed of feathers is to be found in B.M. Harleian MS. 2169, published under the title *A Tudor Book of Arms*, edited by Joseph Foster (1904). This is a book of arms tricked by Robert Cooke, who was Clarenceux King of Arms from 1567 until 1593. The coat is ascribed to Mydlam of Coverdale and is tricked plomte (i.e. plumettée) or and purpure. There is a recent example of a field 'plumettée of peacock's feathers'.

Spiders' webs are found in old text books, but I have not discovered a genuine ancient example in English heraldry. However there are several recent examples of a field composed of a spider's web throughout. The web starts in the centre of the shield and radiates outwards.

Another new and curious design is a field which is blazoned 'vert, a network of annulets interlaced or'.

8 · The rules of blazon

The word 'Blazon' is used with some number of meanings, but practically it may be confined to the verb 'to blazon', which is to describe in words a given coat of arms, and the noun 'blazon', which is such a description.

Care should be taken to differentiate between the employment of the term 'blazon' and the verb 'to emblazon', which latter means to depict in colour.

It may here be remarked, however, that to illustrate by the use of outline with written indications of colour is termed 'to trick', and a picture of arms of this character is termed 'a trick'.

The term *trick* has been extended (though one almost thinks improperly) to include representations of arms in which the colours are indicated by the specified tincture lines which have been already referred to.

The subject of blazon has acquired rather more importance than has hitherto been conceded to it, owing to an unofficial attempt to introduce a new system of blazoning under the guise of a supposed reversion to earlier forms of description. This it is not, but even if it were what it claims to be, merely the revival of ancient forms and methods, its reintroduction cannot be said to be either expedient or permissible, because the ancient practice does not permit of extension to the limits within which more modern armory has developed, and modern armory, though less ancient, is armory equally with the more ancient and simpler examples to be found in earlier times. To ignore modern armory is simply futile and absurd.

The rules to be employed in blazon are simple, and comparatively few in number.

The commencement of any blazon is of necessity a description of the *field*, the one word signifying its colour being employed if it be a simple field; or, if it be composite, such terms as are necessary. Thus, a coat divided 'per pale' or 'per chevron' is so described, and whilst the Scottish field of this character is officially termed 'Parted' [per pale, or per chevron], the English equivalent is 'Party', though this word in English usage is more often omitted than not in the blazon which commences 'per pale', or 'per chevron', as the case may be.

The description of the different colours and different divisions of the field have all been detailed in earlier chapters, but it may be added that in a 'party' coloured field, that colour or tincture is mentioned first which occupies the more important part of the escutcheon. Thus, in a field 'per bend', 'per chevron', or 'per fess', the upper portion of the field is first referred to; in a coat 'per pale', the dexter side is the more important; and in a coat 'quarterly', the tinctures of the 1st and 4th quarters are given precedence of the tinctures of the 2nd and 3rd. The only division upon which there has seemed any uncertainty is the curious one 'gyronny', but the correct method to be employed in this case can very easily be

78

recognised by taking the first quarter of the field, and therein considering the field as if it were simply 'per bend'.

After the field has been described, anything of which the field is semé must next be alluded to, *e.g.* gules, semé-de-lis or, &c.

The second thing to be mentioned in the blazon is the principal charge. We will consider first those cases in which it is an ordinary. Thus, one would speak of 'Or, a chevron gules', or, if there be other charges as well as the ordinary, 'Azure, a bend between two horses' heads or', or 'Gules, a chevron between three roses argent'.

The colour of the ordinary is not mentioned until after the charge, if it be the same as the latter, but if it be otherwise it must of course be specified, as in the coat: 'Or, a fess gules between three crescents sable.' If the ordinary is charged, the charges thereupon, being less important than the charges in the field, are mentioned subsequently, as in the coat: 'Gules, on a bend argent between two fountains proper, a rose gules between two mullets sable.'

The position of the charges need not be specified when they would naturally fall into a certain position with regard to the ordinaries. Thus, a chevron between three figures of necessity has two in chief and one in base. A bend between two figures of necessity has one above and one below. A fess has two above and one below. A cross between four has one in each angle. In none of these cases is it necessary to state the position. If, however, those positions or numbers do not come within the category mentioned, care must be taken to specify what the coat exactly is.

If a bend is accompanied only by one charge, the position of this charge must be stated. For example: 'Gules, a bend or, in chief a crescent argent.' A chevron with four figures would be described: 'Argent, a chevron between three escallops in chief and one in base sable,' though it would be equally correct to say: 'Argent, a chevron between four escallops, three in chief and one in base sable.' In the same way we should get: 'Vert, on a cross or, and in the 1st quarter a bezant, an estoile sable;' though, to avoid confusion, this coat would more probably be blazoned: 'Vert, a cross or, charged with an estoile sable, and in the first quarter a bezant.' This example will indicate the latitude which is permissible if, for the sake of avoiding confusion and making a blazon more readily understandable, some deviation from the strict formulas would appear to be desirable.

If there be no ordinary on a shield, the charge which occupies the chief position is mentioned first. For example: 'Or, a lion rampant sable between three boars' heads erased gules, two in chief and one in base.' Many people, however, would omit any reference to the position of the boars' heads, taking it for granted that, as there were only three, they would be 2 and 1, which is the normal position of three charges in any coat of arms. If, however, the coat of arms had the three boars' heads all above the lion, it would then be necessary to blazon it: 'Or, a lion rampant sable, in chief three boars' heads erased gules.'

When a field is *semé* of anything, this is taken to be a part of the field, and not a representation of a number of charges. Consequently the arms of Long are blazoned: 'Sable, semé of cross crosslets, a lion rampant argent.' As a matter of fact the semé of cross crosslets is always termed *crusilly*, as has been already explained.

60 *Arms of Aymer de Valence, Earl of Pembroke: ' Baruly argent and azure, an orle of martlets gules.' (From his seal.)*

61 *The arms of John de Bretagne, Earl of Richmond.*

When charges are placed around the shield in the position they would occupy if placed upon a bordure, these charges are said to be *in orle*, as in the arms of Hutchinson: 'Quarterly, azure and gules, a lion rampant erminois, within four cross crosslets argent, and as many bezants alternately in orle;' though it is equally permissible to term charges in such a position 'an orle of [*e.g.* cross crosslets argent and bezants alternately],' or so many charges 'in orle' (see 60).

If an ordinary be engrailed, or invected, this fact is at once stated, the term occurring before the colour of the ordinary. Thus: 'Argent, on a chevron nebuly between three crescents gules, as many roses of the field.' When a charge upon an ordinary is the same colour as the field, the name of the colour is not repeated, but those charges are said to be 'of the field'.

It is the constant endeavour, under the recognised system, to avoid the use of the name of the same colour a second time in the blazon. Thus: 'Quarterly, gules and or, a cross counterchanged between in the first quarter a sword erect proper, pommel and hilt of the second; in the second quarter a rose of the first, barbed and seeded of the third; in the third quarter a fleur-de-lis azure; and in the fourth quarter a mullet *gold*'—the use of the term 'gold' being alone permissible in such a case.

Any animal which needs to be described also needs its position to be specified. It may be rampant, segreant, passant, statant, or trippant, as the case may be. It may also sometimes be necessary to specify its position upon the shield, but the terms peculiarly appropriated to specific animals will be given in the chapters in which these animals are dealt with.

With the exception of the chief, the quarter, the canton, the flaunch, and the bordure, an ordinary or sub-ordinary is always of greater importance, and therefore should be mentioned before any other charge, but in the cases alluded to the remainder of the shield is first blazoned, before attention is paid to these figures. Thus we should get: 'Argent, a chevron between three mullets gules, on a chief of the last three crescents of the second;' or 'Sable, a lion rampant between three fleurs-de-lis or, on a canton argent a mascle of the field;' or 'Gules, two chevronels between three mullets pierced or, within a bordure engrailed argent charged with eight roses of the field.' The arms in 61 are an interesting example of this point. They are those of John de Bretagne, Earl of Richmond (*d.* 1334), and would properly be blazoned: 'Chequy or and azure, a bordure gules, charged with lions passant guardant or ("a bordure of England"), over all a canton (sometimes a quarter) ermine.'

If two ordinaries or sub-ordinaries appear in the same field, certain discretion needs to be exercised, but the arms of Fitzwalter, for example, are as follows: 'Or, a fess between two chevrons gules.'

When charges are placed in a series following the direction of any ordinary they are said to be 'in bend', 'in chevron', or 'in pale', as the case may be, and not only must their position on the shield as regards each other be specified, but their individual direction must also be noted.

A coat of arms in which three spears were placed side by side, but each erect, would be blazoned: 'Gules, three tilting-spears palewise in fess'; but if the spears were placed horizontally, one above the other, they would be blazoned: 'Three tilting-spears fesswise in pale,' because in the latter case each spear is placed fesswise, but the three occupy in relation to each other the position of a pale. Three tilting-spears fesswise which were not *in pale* would be depicted 2 and 1.

When one charge surmounts another, the undermost one is mentioned first, as in the arms of Beaumont (see 62). Here the lion rampant is the principal charge, and the bend which debruises it is consequently mentioned afterwards.

In the cases of a cross and of a saltire, the charges when all are alike would simply be described as between four objects, though the term 'cantonned by' four objects is sometimes met with. If the objects are not the same, they must be specified as being in the 1st, 2nd, or 3rd quarters, if the ordinary be a cross. If it be a saltire, it will be found that in Scotland the charges are mentioned as being in chief and base, and in the 'flanks'. In England they would be described as being *in pale* and *in fess* if the alternative charges are the same; if not, they would be described as *in chief*, on the dexter side, on the sinister side, and *in base*.

When a specified number of charges is immediately followed by the same number of charges elsewhere disposed, the number is not repeated, the words 'as many' being substituted instead. Thus: 'Argent, on a chevron between three roses gules, as many crescents of the field.' When any charge, ordinary, or mark of cadency surmounts a single object, that object is termed 'debruised' by that ordinary. If it surmounts *everything*, as, for instance, 'a bendlet sinister', this would be termed 'over all'. When a coat of arms is 'party' coloured in its field and the charges are alternately of the same colours transposed, the term *counterchanged* is used. For example, 'Party per pale argent and sable, three chevronels between as many mullets pierced all counterchanged.' In that case the coat is divided down the middle, the dexter field being argent, and the sinister sable; the charges on the sable being argent, whilst the charges on the argent are sable. A mark of cadency is mentioned last, and is termed 'for difference'; a mark of bastardy, or a mark denoting lack of blood descent, is termed 'for distinction'.

Certain practical hints, which, however, can hardly be termed *rules*, were suggested by the late Mr J. Gough Nicholls in 1863, when writing in the *Herald and Geneaolgist*, and subsequent practice has since conformed therewith, though it may be pointed out with advantage that these suggestions are practically, and to all intents and purposes, the same rules which have been observed officially over a long period. Amongst these suggestions he advises that the blazoning of every coat or quarter should begin with a capital letter, and that, save on the occurrence of proper names, no other capitals should be employed. He also suggests that punctuation marks should be avoided as much as possible, his own practice being to limit the use of the comma to its occurrence after each tincture. He suggests also that figures should be omitted in all cases except in the numbering of quarterings.

When one or more quarterings occur, each is treated separately on its own merits and blazoned entirely without reference to any other quartering.

In blazoning a coat in which some quarterings (grand quarterings) are composed of several coats placed sub-quarterly, sufficient distinction is afforded for English purposes of writing or printing if Roman numerals are employed to indicate the grant quarters, and Arabic figures the sub-quarters. But in *speaking* such a method would need to be somewhat modified in accordance with the Scottish practice, which describes grand quarterings as such, and so alludes to them.

62 *Arms of John de Beaumont, Lord Beaumont (d. 1369): Azure, semé-de-lis and a lion rampant or, over all a bend gobony argent and gules. (From his seal.)*

The extensive use of bordures, charged and uncharged, in Scotland, which figure sometimes round the sub-quarters, sometimes round the grand quarters, and sometimes round the entire escutcheon, causes so much confusion that for the purposes of blazoning it is essential that the difference between quarters and grand quarters should be clearly defined.

In order to simplify the blazoning of a shield, and so express the position of the charges, the *field* has been divided into *points*, of which those placed near the top, and to the dexter, are always considered the more important. In heraldry, dexter and sinister are determined, not from the point of view of the onlooker, but from that of the bearer of the shield. The diagram (63) will serve to explain the plan of a shield's surface.

If a second shield be placed upon the fess point, this is called an inescutcheon (in German, the 'heart-shield'). The enriching of the shield with an inescutcheon came into lively use in Germany in the course of the latter half of the fifteenth century. Later on, further points of honour were added, as the honour point (a, 64), and the nombril point (b, 64). These extra shields laid upon the others should correspond as much as possible in shape to the chief shield. If between the inescutcheon and the chief shield still another be inserted, it is called the 'middle shield', from its position, but except in Anglicised versions of Continental arms, these distinctions are quite foreign to British armory.

In conclusion, it may be stated that although the foregoing are the rules which are usually observed, and that every effort should be made to avoid unnecessary tautology, and to make the blazon as brief as possible, it is by no manner of means considered officially, or unofficially, that any one of these rules is so unchangeable that in actual practice it cannot be modified if it should seem advisable so to do. For the essential necessity of accuracy is of far greater importance than any desire to be brief, or to avoid tautology. This should be borne in mind, and also the fact that in official practice no such hide-bound character is given to these rules, as one is led to believe is the case when perusing some of the ordinary text-books of armory. They certainly are not laws, they are hardly 'rules', perhaps being better described as accepted methods of blazoning.[36]

63 *A to B, the chief;*
C to D, the base;
A to C, dexter side;
B to D, sinister side.
A, dexter chief;
B, sinister chief;
C, dexter base;
D, sinister base.
1, 2, 3, chief;
7, 8, 9, base;
2, 5, 8, pale;
4, 5, 6, fees;
5, fess point.

64.

36. There is much wisdom in the last paragraph of this chapter. Throughout the chapter Fox-Davies has laid down the rules of blazon in didactic and uncompromising terms; but finally he climbs down from his lofty peak of absolute blazon, and admits that his 'rules' are no more than 'accepted methods of blazoning'. Yet he should have gone further and mentioned that these methods were those accepted at the time of writing; for what really constitutes official blazon? Quite simply, it is the minds of the granting Kings of Arms. It is they who blazon arms and who must take the responsibility for good or bad blazon. The rest of us can write about what has been done in the past and what we think ought to have been done, but our opinions are chaff before the wind unless we can persuade the King of Arms of the day to adopt our ideas.

Today the official method of blazoning arms is to omit all punctuation, use capital letters for nouns and the names of the tinctures and to avoid, where possible, reference to tinctures by numbers: phrases such as 'of the second' and 'of the field' are generally eschewed. The use of 'gold' to avoid the repetition of 'or' is general. This and the use of 'silver' for 'argent' are ancient devices of blazon. The arms granted to John Aleyn of Buckinghamshire by Roger Leigh, Clarenceux, on 7 May 1454 are blazoned: 'quartley in the first quarter silvere and sinoble (the French term for vert) paled of iiij peeces iij Cressantes counterchaunged, in the second quarter Asure ii egles of golde membered of silue crowned of gowles (gules).' In this blazon Leigh appears to assume that the 3rd and 4th quarters will repeat the 2nd and 1st.

As it is impossible to predict how the Kings of Arms will blazon a given coat, a person naturally develops his own system of blazon; and if this is based on the principles laid down by Fox-Davies he will not go far wrong. The main point to bear in mind is that the blazon must be unequivocal, otherwise it is of no value to anyone but its author. In the second place it should if possible be euphonious, for everything to do with heraldry should be beautiful. This means that sometimes tautology is acceptable, at other times it should be avoided; there is no rule. What should always be avoided are the home-made blazons advocated by some writers, not because they are bad, though some are, but simply because they are not generally understood. 'A fess with three crescents' is a form of blazon favoured by some people; but does it mean 'a fess between three crescents' or 'on a fess three crescents'? Only the members of the exclusive sect who favour this method of blazon can say.

9 · The so-called ordinaries and sub-ordinaries

Arms, and the charges upon arms, have been divided into many fantastical divisions. There is a type of the precise mind much evident in the scientific writing of the last and the preceding centuries which is for ever unhappy unless it can be dividing the object of its consideration into classes and divisions, into sub-classes and sub-divisions. Heraldry has suffered in this way; for, oblivious of the fact that the rules enunciated are impossible as rigid guides for general observance, and that they never have been complied with, and that they never will be, a 'tabular' system has been evolved for heraldry as for most other sciences. The 'precise' mind has applied a system obviously derived from natural history classification to the principles of armory. It has selected a certain number of charges, and has been pleased to term them ordinaries. It has selected others which it has been pleased to term sub-ordinaries. The selection has been purely arbitrary, at the pleasure of the writer, and few writers have agreed in their classifications. One of the foremost rules which former heraldic writers have laid down is that an ordinary must contain the third part of the field. Now it is doubtful whether an ordinary has ever been drawn containing the third part of the field by rigid measurement, except in the solitary instance of the pale, when it is drawn 'per fess counterchanged', for the obvious *purpose* of dividing the shield into six equal portions, a practice which has been lately pursued very extensively owing to the ease with which, by its adoption, a new coat of arms can be designed bearing a distinct resemblance to one formerly in use without infringing the rights of the latter. Certainly, if the ordinary is the solitary charge upon the shield, it will be drawn about that specified proportion. But when an attempt is made to draw the Walpole coat (which cannot be said to be a modern one) so that it shall exhibit three ordinaries, to wit, one fess and two chevrons (which being interpreted as three-thirds of the shield, would fill it entirely), and yet leave a goodly proportion of the field still visible, the absurdity is apparent. And a very large proportion of the classification and rules which occupy such a large proportion of the space in the majority of heraldic text-books are equally unnecessary, confusing, and incorrect, and what is very much more important, such rules have never been recognised by the powers that have had the control of armory from the beginning of that control down to the present day. I shall not be surprised to find that many of my critics, bearing in mind how strenuously I have pleaded elsewhere for a right and proper observance of the laws of armory, may think that the foregoing has largely the nature of a recantation. It is nothing of the kind, and I advocate as strenuously as I have ever done, the compliance with and the observance of every rule which can be shown

PLATE III

Arms of the Duke of Argyll

to exist. But this is no argument whatever for the idle invention of rules which never have existed; or for the recognition of rules which have no other origin than the imagination of heraldic writers. Nor is it an argument for the deduction of unnecessary regulations from cases which can be shown to have been exceptions. Too little recognition is paid to the fact that in armory there are almost as many rules of exception as original rules. There are vastly more plain exceptions to the rules which should govern them.

On the subject of ordinaries, I cannot see wherein lies the difference between a bend and a lion rampant, save their difference in form, yet the one is said to be an ordinary, the other is merely a charge. Each has its special rules to be observed, and whilst a bend can be engrailed or invected, a lion can be guardant or regardant; and whilst the one can be placed between two objects, which objects will occupy a specified position, so can the other. Each can be charged, and each furnishes an excellent example of the futility of some of the ancient rules which have been coined concerning them. The ancient rules allow of but one lion and one bend upon a shield, requiring that two bends shall become bendlets, and two lions lioncels, whereas the instance we have already quoted—the coat of Walpole—has never been drawn in such form that either of the chevrons could have been considered chevronels, and it is rather late in the day to degrade the lions of England into unblooded whelps. To my mind the ordinaries and sub-ordinaries are no more than first charges, and though the bend, the fess, the pale, the pile, the chevron, the cross, and the saltire will always be found described as honourable ordinaries, whilst the chief seems also to be pretty universally considered as one of the honourable ordinaries, such hopeless confusion remains as to the others (scarcely any two writers giving similar classifications), that the utter absurdity of the necessity for any classification at all is amply demonstrated. Classification is only necessary or desirable when a certain set of rules can be applied identically to all the set of figures in that particular class. Even this will not hold with the ordinaries which have been quoted.

A pale embattled is embattled upon both its edges; a fess embattled is embattled only upon the upper edge; a chief is embattled necessarily only upon the lower; and the grave difficulty of distinguishing 'per pale engrailed' from 'per pale invected' shows that no rigid rules can be laid down. When we come to sub-ordinaries, the confusion is still more apparent, for as far as I can see the only reason for the classification is the tabulating of rules concerning the lines of partition. The bordure and the orle can be, and often are, engrailed or embattled; the fret, the lozenge, the fusil, the mascle, the rustre, the flanche, the roundel, the billet, the label, the pairle, it would be practically impossible to meddle with; and all these figures have at some time or another, and by some writer or other, been included amongst either the ordinaries or the sub-ordinaries. In fact there is no one quality which these charges possess in common which is not equally possessed by scores of other well-known charges, and there is no particular reason why a certain set should be selected and dignified by the name of ordinaries; nor are there any rules relating to ordinaries which require the selection of a certain number of figures, or of any figures to be controlled by those rules, with one exception. The exception is to be found not in the rules governing the ordinaries, but in the rules of blazon. After the field has been specified, the principal charge

65 Bend.

66 Bend engrailed.

67 Bend invecked.

68 Bend embattled.

*69 Bend embattled
counter-embattled.*

must be mentioned first, and no charge can take precedence of a bend, fess, pale, pile, chevron, cross, or saltire, except one of themselves. If there be any reason for a subdivision those charges must stand by themselves, and might be termed the honourable ordinaries, but I can see no reason for treating the chief, the quarter, the canton, gyron, flanche, label, orle, tressure, fret, inescutcheon, chaplet, bordure, lozenge, fusil, mascle, rustre, roundel, billet, label, shakefork, and pairle, as other than ordinary charges. They certainly are purely heraldic, and each has its own special rules, but so in heraldry have the lion, griffin, and deer. Here is the complete list of the so-called ordinaries, and sub-ordinaries: The bend; fess; bar; chief; pale; chevron; cross; saltire; pile; pairle, shakefork or pall; quarter; canton; gyron; bordure; orle; tressure; flanche; label, fret; inescutcheon; chaplet; lozenge; fusil; mascle; rustre; roundel; billet, together with the diminutives of such of these as are in use.

With reference to the origin of these ordinaries, by the use of which term is meant for the moment the rectilinear figures peculiar to armory, it may be worth the passing mention that the said origin is a matter of some mystery. Guillim and the old writers almost universally take them to be derived from the actual military scarf or a representation of it placed across the shield in various forms. Other writers, taking the surcoat and its decoration as the real origin of coats of arms, derive the ordinaries from the belt, scarf, and other articles of raiment. Planché, on the other hand, scouted such a derivation, putting forward upon very good and plausible grounds the simple argument that the origin of the ordinaries is to be found in the cross-pieces of wood placed across a shield for strengthening purposes. He instances cases in which shields, apparently charged with ordinaries but really strengthened with cross-pieces, can be taken back to a period long anterior to the existence of regularised armory. But then, on the other hand, shields can be found decorated with animals at an equally early or even an earlier period, and I am inclined myself to push Planché's own argument even farther than he himself took it, and assert unequivocally that the ordinaries had in themselves no particular symbolism and no definable origin whatever beyond that easy method of making some pattern upon a shield which was to be gained by using straight lines. That they ever had any military meaning, I cannot see the slightest foundation to believe; their suggested and asserted symbolism I totally deny. But when we can find, as Planché did, that shields were strengthened with cross-pieces in various directions, it is quite natural to suppose that these cross-pieces afforded a ready means of decoration in colour, and this would lead a good deal of other decoration to follow similar forms, even in the absence of cross-pieces upon the definite shield itself. The one curious point which rather seems to tell against Planché's theory is that in the earliest 'rolls' of arms but a comparatively small proportion of the arms are found to consist of these rectilinear figures, and if the ordinaries really originated in strengthening cross-pieces one would have expected a larger number of such coats of arms to be found; but at the same time such arms would, in many cases, in themselves be so palpably mere meaningless decoration of cross-pieces upon plain shields, that the resulting design would not carry with it such a compulsory remembrance as would a design, for example, derived from lines which had plainly had no connection with the construction of the shield. Nor could it have any such basis of continuity. Whilst a son would naturally paint a lion upon his

86

shield if his father had done the same, there certainly would not be a similar
inducement for a son to follow his father's example where the design upon a shield
were no more than different-coloured strengthening pieces, because if these were
gilt, for example, the son would naturally be no more inclined to perpetuate a
particular form of strengthening for his shield, which might not need it, than any
particular artistic division with which it was involved, so that the absence of arms
composed of ordinaries from the early rolls of arms may not amount to so very
much. Still further, it may well be concluded that the compilers of early rolls
of arms, or the collectors of the details from which early rolls were made at a
later date, may have been tempted to ignore, and may have been justified in
discarding from their lists of arms, those patterns and designs which palpably were
then no more than a meaningless colouring of the strengthening pieces, but which
patterns and designs by subsequent continuous usage and perpetuation became
accepted later by certain families as the 'arms' their ancestors had worn. It is easy
to see that such meaningless patterns would have less chance of survival by continuity of usage, and at the same time would require a longer continuity of usage,
before attaining to fixity as a definite design.

The undoubted symbolism of the cross in so many early coats of arms has
been urged strongly by those who argue either for a symbolism for all these
rectilinear figures or for an origin in articles of dress. But the figure of the cross
preceded Christianity and organised armory, and it had an obvious decorative
value which existed before, and which exists now outside any attribute it may have
of a symbolical nature. That it is an utterly fallacious argument must be admitted
when it is remembered that two lines at right angles make a cross—probably the
earliest of all forms of decoration—and that the cross existed before its symbolism.
Herein it differs from other forms of decoration (*e.g.* the Masonic emblems)
which cannot be traced beyond their symbolical existence. The cross, like the
other heraldic rectilinear figures, came into existence, meaningless as a decoration
for a shield, before armory as such existed, and probably before Christianity
began. Then being in existence the Crusading instinct doubtless caused its frequent selection with an added symbolical meaning. But the argument can truth-
fully be pushed no farther.

The bend

The bend is a broad band going from the dexter chief corner to the sinister base
(65). According to the old theorists this should contain the third part of the field.
As a matter of fact it hardly ever does, and seldom did even in the oldest examples.
Great latitude is allowed to the artist on this point, in accordance with whether
the bend be plain or charged, and more particularly according to the charges
which accompany it in the shield and their disposition thereupon.

'Azure, a bend or,' is the well-known coat concerning which the historic
controversy was waged between Scrope and Grosvenor. As every one knows, it
was finally adjudged to belong to the former, and a right to it has also been proved
by the Cornish family of Carminow.

A bend is, of course, subject to the usual variations of the lines of partition
(66–75).

70 *Bend raguly.*

71 *Bend dovetailed.*

72 *Bend indented.*

73 *Bend dancetté.*

74 *Bend wavy.*

87

75 Bend nebuly.

76 Bend compony.

77 Bend barry.

78 Bend within tressure.

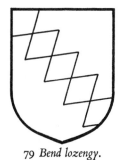

79 Bend lozengy.

A bend compony (76), will be found in the arms of Beaumont, and the difference between this (in which the panes run with the bend) and a bend barry (in which the panes are horizontal, 77), as in the arms of King,* should be noticed.

A bend wavy is not very usual, but will be found in the arms of Wallop, De Burton, and Conder. A bend raguly appears in the arms of Strangman.[37]

When a bend and a bordure appear upon the same arms, the bend is not continued over the bordure, and similarly it does not surmount a tressure (78), but stops within it.

A bend upon a bend is by no means unusual. An example of this will be found in a coat of Waller. Cases where this happens need to be carefully scrutinised to avoid error in blazoning.

A bend lozengy, or of lozenges (79), will be found in the arms of Bolding.

A bend flory and counterflory will be found in the arms of Fellows, a quartering of Tweedy.

A bend chequy will be found in the arms of Menteith, and it should be noticed that the checks run the way of the bend.

Ermine spots upon a bend are represented the way of the bend.

Occasionally two bends will be found, as in the arms of Lever: Argent, two bends sable, the upper one engrailed (*vide* Lyon Register—escutcheon of pretence on the arms of Goldie-Scot of Craigmore, 1868); or as in the arms of James Ford, of Montrose, 1804: Gules, two bends vairé argent and sable, on a chief or, a greyhound courant sable between two towers gules. A different form appears in the arms of Zorke or Yorke (see Papworth), which are blazoned: Azure, a bend argent, impaling argent, a bend azure. A solitary instance of *three* bends (which, however, effectually proves that a bend cannot occupy the third part of the field) occurs in the arms of Penrose, matriculated in Lyon Register in 1795 as a quartering of Cumming-Gordon of Altyre. These arms of Penrose are: Argent, three bends sable, each charged with as many roses of the field.[38]

* Armorial bearings of Sir Henry Seymour King, K.C.I.E.: Quarterly, argent and azure, in the second and third quarters a quatrefoil of the first, over all a bend barry of six of the second, charged with a quatrefoil also of the first, and gules.

37. The arms of the families of Wallop, Earls of Portsmouth and Burton of Surflete, Lincolnshire provide an instance of identical arms, namely argent, a bend wavy sable. The Burtons exhibited this coat at the 1634 Visitation of Lincolnshire, but it was respited for proof. The arms, however, were allowed to the family at a later date, and are recorded for them in the College of Arms, as are the Wallop arms for the Earls of Portsmouth.

Perhaps a better and more ancient example of a bend raguly than the coat of Strangman is to be found in the arms of the Penruddocks of Arkelby, Cumberland, and later of Compton Chamberlain, Wiltshire, Gules, a bend raguly argent.

38. The present fashion of blazon does not seem to favour the use of diminutive terms. Thus little lions are called lions not lioncels, and when there are three chevrons shown they are so blazoned and are not termed chevronels. This underlines the fact that there are no official dimensions in heraldry. The space occupied by a charge is determined by heraldic and artistic sensibility, and not by a ruler. Fox-Davies tended, as others had done before him, to rationalise heraldry, although he was constantly frustrated, and frequently had to climb down and admit defeat. The terms employed to describe diminutives are not, however, useless. If a man wanted one narrow diagonal strip across the field of his shield, it would have to be so blazoned; and there are examples of diminatives of the ordinaries being borne on their own. But the use of diminutive terms is very ancient, and there is certainly no reason why they should not be employed if the author of a blazon finds them attractive.

A charge half the width of a bend is a bendlet (80), and one half the width of a bendlet is a cottise (81), but a cottise cannot exist alone, inasmuch as it has of itself neither direction nor position, but is only found accompanying one of the ordinaries. The arms of Harley are an example of a bend cottised.

Bendlets will very seldom be found either in addition to a bend, or charged, but the arms of Vaile show both these peculiarities.[39]

A bend will usually be found between two charges. Occasionally it will be found between four, but more frequently between six. In none of these cases is it necessary to specify the position of the subsidiary charges. It is presumed that the bend separates them into even numbers, but their exact position (beyond this) upon the shield is left to the judgment of the artist, and their disposition is governed by the space left available by the shape of the shield. A further presumption is permitted in the case of a bend between *three* objects, which are presumed to be two in chief and one in base. But even in the case of three the position will be usually found to be specifically stated, as would be the case with any other uneven number.

Charges on a bend are placed in the direction of the bend. In such cases it is not necessary to specify that the charges are bendwise. When a charge or charges occupy the position which a bend would, they are said to be placed 'in bend'. This is not the same thing as a charge placed 'bendwise' (or bendways). In this case the charge itself is slanted into the angle at which the bend crosses the shield, but the position of the charge upon the shield is not governed thereby.

When a bend and chief occur together in the same arms, the chief will usually surmount the bend, the latter issuing from the angle between the base of the chief and the side of the shield. An instance to the contrary, however, will be found in the arms of Fitz-Herbert of Swynnerton, in which the bend is continued over the chief. This instance, however (as doubtless all others of the kind), is due to the use of the bend in early times as a mark of difference. The coat of arms, therefore, had an earlier and separate existence without the bend, which has been superimposed as a difference upon a previously existing coat. The use of the bend as a difference will be again referred to when considering more fully the marks and methods of indicating cadency.

A curious instance of the use of the sun's rays in bend will be found in the arms of Warde-Aldam.*

The bend sinister (82), is very frequently stated to be the mark of illegitimacy. It certainly has been so used upon some occasions, but these occasions are very few and far between, the charge more frequently made use of being the bendlet or its derivative the baton (83). These will be treated more fully in the chapter on the marks of illegitimacy. The bend sinister, which is a band running from the sinister chief corner through the centre of the escutcheon to the dexter base, need not necessarily indicate bastardy. Naturally the popular idea which has originated and

80 *Bendlets.*

81. *Bend cottised.*

82 *Bend sinister.*

83 *Baton sinister.*

39. The arms in question were granted to William Phelps Vaile of West Malling, Kent on 3 March 1827, and are blazoned: ermine, on a bend between two bendlets azure, each charged with three cross crosslets fitched or, three calves statant argent.

* Armorial bearings of William Warde-Aldam, Esq.: Quarterly, 1 and 4, partly per fesse azure and ermine, in the sinister chief and dexter base an eagle displayed or, in the dexter canton issuant towards the sinister base seven rays, the centre one gold, the others argent (for Aldam); 2 and 3 (for Warde).

84 *Bendlets enhanced.*

E *Arms of London County Council.*

F *Arms of Greater London Council.*

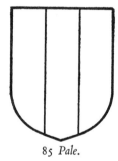

85 *Pale.*

become stereotyped concerning it renders its appearance extremely rare, but in at least two cases it occurs without, as far as I am aware, carrying any such meaning. At any rate, in neither case are the coats 'bastardised' versions of older arms. These cases are the arms of Shiffner: 'Azure, a bend sinister, in chief two estoiles, in like bend or; in base the end and stock of an anchor gold, issuing from waves of the sea proper'; and Burne-Jones: 'Azure, on a bend sinister argent, between seven mullets, four in chief and three in base or, three pairs of wings addorsed purpure.'

No coat with the chief charge a single bendlet occurs in Papworth. A single case, however, is to be found in the Lyon Register in the duly matriculated arms of Porterfield of that Ilk: 'Or, a bendlet between a stag's head erased in chief and a hunting-horn in base sable, garnished gules.' Single bendlets, however, both dexter and sinister, occur as ancient difference marks, and are then sometimes known as ribands. So described, it occurs in blazon of the arms of Abernethy: 'Or, a lion rampant gules, debruised of a ribbon sable,' quartered by Lindsay, Earl of Crawford and Balcarres; but here again the bendlet is a mark of cadency. In the *Gelre Armorial*, in this particular coat the ribbon is made 'engrailed', which is most unusual, and which does not appear to be the accepted form. In many of the Scottish matriculations of this Abernethy coat in which this riband occurs it is termed a 'cost', doubtless another form of the word cottise.

When a bend or bendlets (or, in fact, any other charge) are raised above their natural position in the shield they are termed 'enhanced' (84). An instance of this occurs in the well-known coat of Byron, viz.: 'Argent, three bendlets enhanced gules,' and in the arms of Manchester, which were based upon this coat.

When the field is composed of an even number of equal pieces divided by lines following the angle of a bend the field is blazoned 'bendy' of so many (58). In most cases it will be composed of six or eight pieces, but as there is no diminutive of 'bendy', the number must always be stated.[40]

40. There has recently been a return to the practice of not ennumerating the bends, bars, chevrons and so forth in a parted field. This reversion to a former convention is eloquently illustrated in the grants of arms to the London County Council (19 August 1914) and the Greater London Council (1 September 1965). The former is blazoned: barry wavy of six azure and argent, on a chief of the last, a St George's cross charged with a Lion of England (E); whilst the latter is simply blazoned: barry wavy argent and azure, on a chief gules, a Saxon crown or (F).

The pale

The pale is a broad perpendicular band passing from the top of the escutcheon to the bottom (85). Like all the other ordinaries, it is stated to contain ·the third part of the area of the field, and it is the only one which is at all frequently drawn in that proportion. But even with the pale, the most frequent occasion upon which this proportion is definitely given, this exaggerated width will be presently explained. The artistic latitude, however, permits the pale to be drawn of this proportion if this be convenient to the charges upon it.

Like the other ordinaries, the pale will be found varied by the different lines of partition (86–94).

86 *Pale engrailed.*

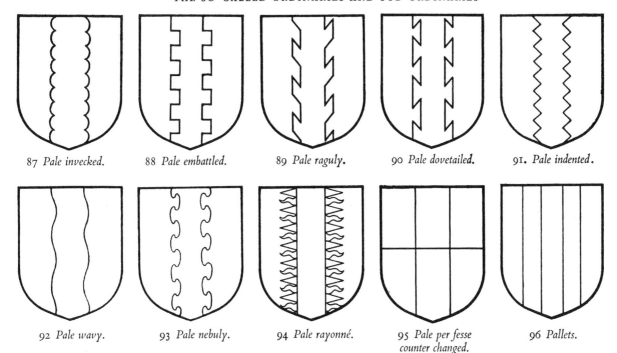

87 *Pale invecked.* 88 *Pale embattled.* 89 *Pale raguly.* 90 *Pale dovetailed.* 91. *Pale indented.*

92 *Pale wavy.* 93 *Pale nebuly.* 94 *Pale rayonné.* 95 *Pale per fesse counter changed.* 96 *Pallets.*

The single circumstance in which the pale is regularly drawn to contain a full third of the field by measurement is when the coat is 'per fess and a pale counterchanged'. This, it will be noticed, divides the shield into six equal portions (95). The ease with which, by the employment of these conditions, a new coat can be based upon an old one which shall leave three original charges in the same position, and upon a field of the original tincture, and yet shall produce an entirely different and distinct coat of arms, has led to this particular form being constantly repeated in modern grants.

The diminutive of the pale is the pallet (96), and the pale cottised is sometimes termed 'endorsed'.

Except when it is used as a mark of difference or distinction (then usually wavy), the pallet is not found singly; but two pallets, or three, are not exceptional. Charged upon other ordinaries, particularly on the chief and the chevron, pallets are of constant occurrence.

When the field is striped vertically it is said to be 'paly' of so many (57).

The arms shown in 97 are interesting inasmuch as they are doubtless an early form of the coat per pale indented argent and gules, which is generally described as a banner borne for the honour of Hinckley, by the Simons de Montfort, Earls of Leicester, father and son. In a Roll *temp.* Henry III, to Simon the younger is ascribed 'Le Banner party endentee dargent & de goules', although the arms of both father and son are known to have been as 98: 'Gules, a lion rampant queue-fourchée argent.' More probably the indented coat gives the original Montfort arms.[41]

97 *The arms of Amaury de Montfort, Earl of Gloucester; died before 1214. (From his seal.)*

98 *Arms of Simon de Montfort, Earl of Leicester; died 1265. (From MS. Cott., Nero, D. 1.)*

41. In *Historic Heraldry of Britain* by A. R. (now Sir Anthony) Wagner, the author notes that the party coat of the Montforts was borne for the Honour of Hinckley, and cites the Great Coucher Book of the Duchy of Lancaster as his authority.

The fess

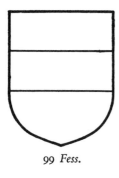

99 *Fess.*

The fess is a broad horizontal band crossing the escutcheon in the centre (99). It is seldom drawn to contain a full third of the area of the shield. It is subject to the lines of partition (100–9).

A curious variety of the fess dancetté is borne by the Shropshire family Plowden of Plowden. They bear: Azure, a fess dancetté, the upper points terminating in fleurs-de-lis (110). A fess couped (111) is found in the arms of Lee.[42]

The 'fess embattled' is only crenellated upon the upper edge; but when both edges are embattled it is a fess embattled and counter-embattled. The term *bretessé* (which is said to indicate that the battlements on the upper edge are opposite the battlements on the lower edge, and the indentations likewise corresponding) is a term and a distinction neither of which are regarded in British armory.

A fess wreathed (112) is a bearing which seems to be almost peculiar to the Carmichael family, but the arms of Waye of Devon are an additional example, being: Sable, two bars wreathed argent and gules. I know of no other ordinary borne in a wreathed form, but there seems no reason why this peculiarity should be confined to the fess.

It is a fixed rule of British armory that there can be only *one* fess upon a shield. If two figures of this character are found they are termed *bars* (113). But it is hardly correct to speak of the bar as a diminutive of the fess, because if two bars only appear on the shield there would be little, if any, diminution made from the width of the fess when depicting the bars. As is the case with other ordinaries, there is much latitude allowed to the artist in deciding the dimensions, it being usually permitted for these to be governed by the charges upon the fess or bars, and the charges between which these are placed.

Bars, like the fess, are of course equally subject to all the varying lines of partition (114–18).

The diminutive of the bar is the barrulet, which is half its width and double the width of the cottise. But the barrulet will *almost invariably* be found borne in *pairs*, when such a pair is usually known as a 'bar gemel' and not as two barrulets. Thus a coat with four barrulets would have these placed at equal distances from each other; but a coat with two bars gemel would be depicted with two of its barrulets placed closely together in chief and two placed closely together in base, the disposition being governed by the fact that the two barrulets comprising the 'bar gemel' are only *one charge*. 119 shows three bars gemel. There is theoretically no limit to the number of bars or bars gemel which can be placed upon the shield. In practical use, however, four will be found the maximum.

A field composed of four, six, eight, or ten horizontal pieces of equal width is 'barry of such and such a number of pieces', the number being always specified (55 and 56). A field composed of an equal number of horizontally shaped pieces, when these exceed ten in number, is termed 'barruly' of such and such a number.

42. What we now call a fess dancetty was termed a dance in the old rolls of arms, and there are one or two modern examples of a reversion to this blazon. On the other hand, the current trend is to blazon this charge even more pedantically than before; thus, the arms of the Maidenhead Building Society contain what is blazoned as 'a Fess dancetée of two points': in the arms of Market Bosworth Rural District Council there is 'a Fess dancetée of two *pieces*' (my italics), whilst yet another recent grant has a coat containing 'a Fess dancetty of two downward points'.

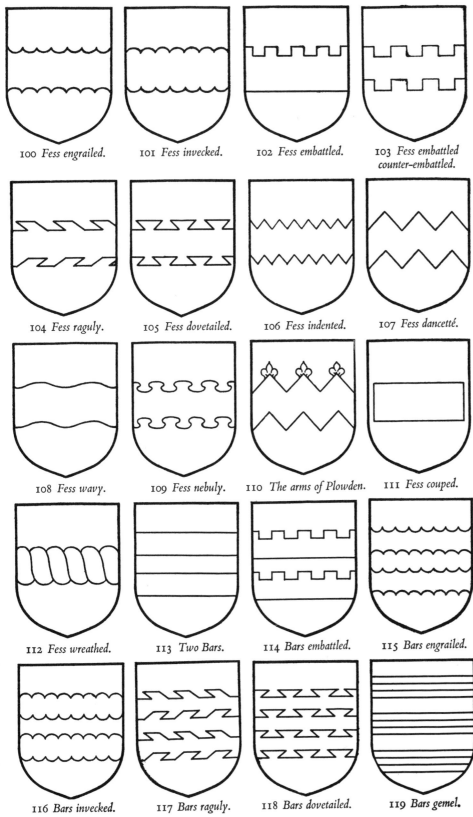

100 *Fess engrailed.*

101 *Fess invecked.*

102 *Fess embattled.*

103 *Fess embattled counter-embattled.*

104 *Fess raguly.*

105 *Fess dovetailed.*

106 *Fess indented.*

107 *Fess dancetté.*

108 *Fess wavy.*

109 *Fess nebuly.*

110 *The arms of Plowden.*

111 *Fess couped.*

112 *Fess wreathed.*

113 *Two Bars.*

114 *Bars embattled.*

115 *Bars engrailed.*

116 *Bars invecked.*

117 *Bars raguly.*

118 *Bars dovetailed.*

119 *Bars gemel.*

120 *Arms of William de Valence, Earl of Pembroke (d. 1296); Barruly azure and argent, a label of five points gules, the files depending from the chief line of the shield, and each file charged with three lions passant guardant or. (From MS. Reg. 14, C. vii.)*

121 *Arms of Laurence de Hastings, Earl of Pembroke (d. 1348); Quarterly, 1 and 4, or, a maunch gules (for Hastings); 2 and 3, barruly argent and azure, an orle of martlets (for Valence). (From his seal.)*

122 *Arms of Edmund Grey, Earl of Kent (d. 1489): Quarterly, 1 and 4, barry of six, argent and azure, in chief three torteaux (for Grey); 2 and 3, Hastings and Valence sub-quarterly. (From his seal, 1442.)*

The term barruly is also sometimes used for ten pieces. If the number is omitted 'barry' will usually be of six pieces, though sometimes of eight. On the other hand a field composed of five, seven, or nine pieces is not barry, but (*e.g.*) two bars, three bars, and four bars respectively. This distinction in modern coats needs to be carefully noted, but in ancient coats it is not of equal importance. Anciently also a shield 'barry' was drawn of a great number of pieces (see 120, 121 and 122) than would nowadays be employed. In modern armory a field so depicted would more correctly be termed 'barruly'.[43]

Whilst a field can be and often is barry of two colours or two metals, an uneven number of pieces must of necessity be of metal and colour or fur. Consequently in a shield *e.g.* divided into seven equal horizontal divisions, alternately gules and sable, there must be a mistake somewhere.

Although these distinctions require to be carefully noted as regards modern arms, it should be remembered that they are distinctions evolved by the intricacies and requirements of modern armory, and ancient arms were not so trammelled.

A field divided horizontally into three equal divisions of *e.g.* gules, sable, and argent is theoretically blazoned by British rules 'party per fess gules and argent, a fess sable'. This, however, gives an exaggerated width to the fess which it does not really possess with us, and the German rules, which would blazon it 'tierced per fess gules, sable, and argent', would seem preferable.

A field which is barry may also be counterchanged, as in the arms of Ballingall, where it is counterchanged per pale; but it can also be counterchanged per chevron (123), or per bend dexter or sinister. Such counterchanging should be carefully distinguished from fields which are 'barry-bendy' (124), or 'paly-bendy' (125). In these latter cases the field is divided first by lines horizontal (for barry) or perpendicular (for paly), and subsequently by lines bendy (dexter or sinister).

43. In the grant of arms made to Nyasaland Railways Ltd, on 12 June 1957 a barry wavy field of many pieces is shown, but it is simply blazoned: barry wavy argent and azure, two pallets or, in the centre chief point a railway wheel also or, over all a fess enarched gold fretty sable (note the term 'enarched' for an arched fess, in contradistinction to 'arched', which is generally used in connection with the chief). As the visual impact of a field containing many bars, such as the above or that of de Valence, is quite different from that of a field of say six bars, there would seem a good case to distinguish between them in blazon. It is perhaps pertinent to remark here that pendantries in blazon are not peculiar to the Victorians, nor indeed to the early writers such as Gerard Leigh and John Guillim. One has only to turn to the Caerlaverock poem (*c.* 1300) to find the same inconsistencies that face us today. There the de Valence coat is blazoned 'burlee' but that of Pointz 'barre de Viiij'. John de Grey's six bars are blazoned 'barree' as are those of Roger Mortimer.

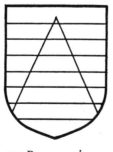

123 *Barry, per chevron counter-changed.*

124 *Barry-bendy.*

125 *Paly-bendy.*

126 *Lozengy.*

The result produced is very similar to 'lozengy' (126), and care should be taken to distinguish the two.

Barry-bendy is sometimes blazoned 'fusilly in bend', whilst paly-bendy is sometimes blazoned 'fusilly in bend sinister'; but the other terms are the more accurate and acceptable.

'Lozengy' is made by use of lines in bend crossed by lines in bend sinister (126), and 'fusilly' the same, only drawn at a more acute angle.

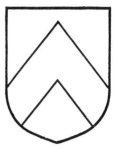

127 *Chevron.*

The chevron

Probably the ordinary of most frequent occurrence in British, as also in French armory, is the chevron (127). It is comparatively rare in German heraldry. The term is derived from the French word *chevron*, meaning a rafter, and the heraldic chevron is the same shape as a gable rafter. In early examples of heraldic art the chevron will be found depicted reaching very nearly to the top of the shield, the angle contained within the chevron being necessarily more acute. The chevron then attained very much more nearly to its full area of one-third of the field than is now given to it. As the chevron became accompanied by charges, it was natur-ally drawn so that it would allow of these charges being more easily represented, and its height became less whilst the angle it enclosed was increased. But now, as then, it is perfectly at the pleasure of the artist to design his chevron at the height and angle which will best allow the proper representation of the charges which accompany it.

The chevron, of course, is subject to the usual lines of partition (128–36), and can be cottised and doubly cottised (137).

It is usually found between three charges, but the necessity of modern differenti-ation has recently introduced the disposition of four charges, three in chief and one in base, which is by no means a happy invention. An even worse disposition occurs in the arms of a certain family of Mitchell, where the four escallops which are the principal charges are arranged two in chief and two in base.[44]

Ermine spots upon a chevron do not follow the direction of it, but in the cases of chevrons vair, and chevrons chequy, authoritative examples can be found in which the chequers and rows of vair both do, and do not, conform to the direction of the chevron.[45] My own preference is to make the rows horizontal.

A chevron quarterly is divided by a line chevronwise, apparently dividing the chevron into two chevronels, and then by a vertical line in the centre (138).

A chevron in point embowed will be found in the arms of Trapaud quartered by Adlercron (139).

A field per chevron (52) is often met with, and the division line in this case (like the enclosing lines of a real chevron) is subject to the usual partition lines, but

128 *Chevron engrailed.*

129 *Chevron invecked.*

130 *Chevron embattled.*

131 *Chevron embattled and counter-embattled.*

44. The reference is to a grant made on 15 March 1894 to Frank Johnstone Mitchell of Llanfrechfa Grange, Monmouthshire, of: sable, a chevron raguly plain cotised or, between four escallops two in chief and as many in base argent, a wool-pack proper.

45. A scrutiny of chevrons from the beginning of heraldry to the present day shows that objects charged on a chevron are almost always shown palewise, that vair and potent are invariably drawn in horizontal rows, but that in chevrons chequy, compony or composed of masonry the horizontal lines are nearly always made to follow the direction of the chevron.

132 *Chevron indented.*

133 *Chevron wavy.*

134 *Chevron nebuly.*

135 *Chevron raguly.*

136 *Chevron dovetailed.*

137 *Chevron doubly cotised.*

139 *Armorial bearings of Rodolph Ladeveze Adlercron, Esq.: Quarterly, 1 and 4, argent, an eagle displayed, wings inverted sable, langued gules, membered and ducally crowned or (for Adlercron): 2 and 3, argent, a chevron in point embowed between in chief two mullets and in base a lion rampant all gules (for Trapaud). Mantling sable and argent. Crest: on a wreath of the colours, a demi-eagle displayed sable, langued gules, ducally crowned or, the dexter wing per fess argent and azure, the sinister per fess of the last and or. Motto: 'Quo fata vocant.'*

138 *Chevron quarterly.*

140 *Chevronels.*

141 *Chevronels braced.*

142 *Chevron rompu.*

G *Arms of Vickers Limited.*

how one is to determine the differentiation between per chevron engrained and per chevron invecked I am uncertain, but think the points should be upwards for engrailed.

The field when entirely composed of an even number of chevrons is termed 'chevronny' (59).

The diminutive of the chevron is the chevronel (140).

Chevronels 'interlaced' or 'braced' (141), will be found in the arms of Sirr. The chevronel is very seldom met with singly, but a case of this will be found in the arms of Spry.

A chevron 'rompu' or broken is depicted as in 142.[46]

46. The chevron reversed has been used in several recent grants. The County Borough of Newport, Monmouthshire, used: or, a chevron reversed gules, without authority and in allusion to the Staffords who once held Newport. This coat was confirmed and granted on 17 April 1929, and on 7 May 1958 supporters were added. The arms of Vickers Ltd, granted on 5 March 1963, contain a reversed chevron to represent the first letter of the firm's name (azure, a chevron reversed between a lion's head caboshed affronty in chief, and two mullets in base or [G]), and a chevronel reversed is included for a similar reason in the arms granted to the Victory Insurance Co. Ltd on 23 October 1944. This coat is interesting as it affords an example of a diminutive of an ordinary being borne singly. The arms are simply barry wavy of six argent and azure, a chevronel reversed gules.

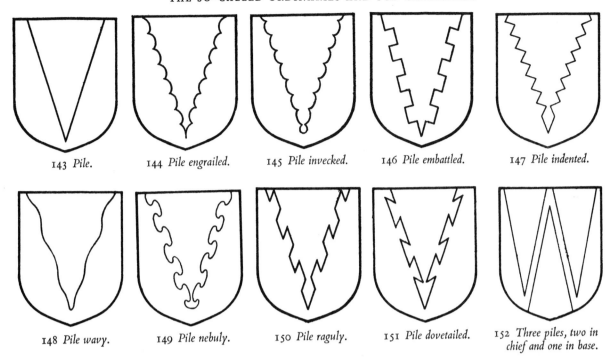

143 *Pile.*   144 *Pile engrailed.*   145 *Pile invecked.*   146 *Pile embattled.*   147 *Pile indented.*

148 *Pile wavy.*   149 *Pile nebuly.*   150 *Pile raguly.*   151 *Pile dovetailed.*   152 *Three piles, two in chief and one in base.*

The pile

The pile (143) is a triangular wedge usually (and unless otherwise specified) issuing from the chief. The pile is subject to the usual lines of partition (144–51).

The early representation of the pile (when coats of arms had no secondary charges and were nice and simple) made the point nearly reach to the base of the escutcheon, and as a consequence it naturally was not so wide. It is now usually drawn so that its upper edge occupies very nearly the whole of the top line of the escutcheon; but the angles and proportions of the pile are very much at the discretion of the artist, and governed by the charges which need to be introduced in the field of the escutcheon or upon the pile.

A single pile may issue from any point of the escutcheon except the base; the arms of Darbishire showing a pile issuing from the dexter chief point.

A single pile cannot issue in base if it be unaccompanied by other piles, as the field would then be blazoned per chevron.[47]

Two piles issuing in chief will be found in the arms of Holles, Earl of Clare.

When three piles, instead of pointing directly at right angles to the line of the chief, all point to the same point, touching or nearly touching at the tips, as in the

H *Arms of Dr. William's School.*

47. Examples of a single pile issuing from the base can be found; but where a wide pile, in contradistinction to the long, narrow medieval pile, is used, the blazon could well be per chevron. The arms granted to Dr William's School, Merioneth, on 27 October 1932 are: or, a pile reversed sable ensigned on the top with a fire-beacon proper, on a chief of the second, three mullets of six points of the first (H). Although this coat is drawn as if per chevron, possibly the device of calling it a reversed pile was resorted to so as to make it easy to blazon the fire-beacon.

An unusual disposition of piles is to be found in the arms granted to the Milk Marketing Board on 6 September 1954: vert issuant from the sinister base three piles wavy bendwise conjoined at the dexter chief point argent (I). This is a most distinctive coat, but one is tempted to wonder why three rather than four piles should have been chosen.

I *Arms of The Milk Marketing Board.*

arms of the Earl of Huntingdon and Chester or in the arms of Isham,* they are described as three piles in point. This term and its differentiation probably are modern refinements, as with the early long-pointed shield any other position was impossible. The arms of Henderson show three piles issuing from the sinister side of the escutcheon.

A disposition of three piles which will very frequently be found in modern British heraldry is two issuing in chief and one in base (152).

Piles terminating in fleurs-de-lis or crosses patée are to be met with, and reference may be made to the arms of Poynter and Dickson-Poynder. Each of these coats has the field pily counter-pily, the points ending in crosses formée.

An unusual instance of a pile in which it issues from a chevron will be found in the arms of Wright, which are: 'Sable, on a chevron argent, three spear-heads gules, in chief two unicorns' heads erased argent, armed and maned or, in base on a pile of the last, issuant from the chevron, a unicorn's head erased of the field.'

153 *Shakefork.*

154 *Ecclesiastical pallium.*

J *Arms of Wylie-Harris.*

K *Arms of Hillsborough R.D.C.*

The shakefork

The pall, pairle, or shakefork (153), is almost unknown in English heraldry, but in Scotland its constant occurrence in the arms of the Cunninghame and allied families has given it a recognised position among the ordinaries.[48]

48. Since Fox-Davies wrote the pall has increased in popularity, and it would seem that it can be subject to the lines of partition. A pall wavy is found in the arms of the Grand Union Canal Company granted on 24 June 1935: or, a pall wavy azure, in chief a fountain. The arms of Mr William Harold Wylie-Harris provide an example of a pall chequy: Paly of twelve vert and argent, a pall chequy or and gules, the chequers pallwise, within a bordure of the last charged with alternate cross crosslets argent and bezants, on a chief also gules, three hares' heads erased silver (J). In this coat the arrangement of the chequers is specified in the blazon, but there are examples of palls charged where the position of the charges is not mentioned in the blazon; sometimes they are shown palewise and sometimes pallwise.

Where the ecclesiastical pallium is intended, it is so blazoned. The arms granted to the Archbishopric of East Africa on 20 November 1962 are: azure, a pallium argent, fimbriated and fringed or, charged with four crosses formy fitchy sable, between in chief a cross urdy and in fess an anchor and cross raguly gold. The Pallium should perhaps be blazoned as 'couped', for the top ends do not extend to the corners of the shield, as they do in the arms of the see of Canterbury.

Just as there has been a revival in the use of the pall, so has there been in dividing a shield per pall, generally blazoned as: tierced in pairle, or when turned upside down: tierced in pairle reversed. Generally the partition lines are not used, as they do not lend themselves to this particular division of the shield; however I have lighted on one example of the use of a partition line, namely in the arms granted to Hillsborough (Co. Down) Rural District Council on 20 April 1964: tierced in pairle reversed wavy gules, vert and azure divided argent, in chief a shuttle erect and an ear of wheat erect and in base a representation of the Round Tower of Drumbo or, charged with a sinister hand appaumy couped gules (K). The expression 'divided argent' is new to armory, and means that the dividing line is silver. As the line is held to be non-existent in heraldry, this seems a curious solecism and, if taken as a precedent, could be unfortunate, as it certainly does not make for the bold visual impact which is the essence of true heraldry. It would be well if the clumsy, foreign term 'tierced in pairle' could be superseded by the terse yet adequate 'per pall'.

* Armorial bearings of Isham: Gules, a fesse wavy, and in chief three piles in point also wavy, the points meeting in fesse argent.

As usually borne by the Cunninghame family the ends are couped and pointed, but in some cases it is borne throughout.

The pall in its proper ecclesiastical form appears in the arms of the Archiepiscopal Sees of Canterbury, Armagh, and Dublin. Though in these cases the pall or pallium (154), is now considered to have no other heraldic status than that of an appropriately ecclesiastical charge upon an official coat of arms, there can be very little doubt that originally the pall of itself was the heraldic symbol in this country of an archbishop, and borne for that reason by all archbishops, including the Archbishop of York, although his official archiepiscopal coat is now changed to: 'Gules, two keys in saltire argent, in chief a royal crown or.'

The necessity of displaying this device of rank—the pallium—upon a field of some tincture has led to its corruption into a usual and stereotyped 'charge'.

The cross

The heraldic cross (155), the huge preponderance of which in armory we of course owe to the Crusades, like all other armorial charges, has strangely developed. There are nearly four hundred varieties known to armory, or rather to heraldic text-books, and doubtless authenticated examples could be found of most if not of them all. But some dozen or twenty forms are about as many as will be found regularly or constantly occurring. Some but not all of the varieties of the cross are subject to the lines of partition (156–61).

When the heraldic cross was first assumed with any reason beyond geometrical convenience, there can be no doubt that it was intended to represent the Sacred Cross itself. The symbolism of the cross is older than our present system of armory, but the cross itself is more ancient than its symbolism. A cross depicted upon the long, pointed shields of those who fought for the Cross would be of that shape, with the elongated arm in base.

But the contemporary shortening of the shield, together with the introduction of charges in its angles, led naturally to the arms of the cross being so disposed that the parts of the field left visible were as nearly as possible equal. The Sacred Cross, therefore, in heraldry is now known as a 'Passion Cross' (162) (or sometimes as a 'long cross'), or, if upon steps or 'grieces', the number of which needs to be specified, as a 'Cross Calvary' (163). The crucifix (164), under that description is sometimes met with as a charge.

The ordinary heraldic cross (155) is always continued throughout the shield unless stated to be couped (165).

Of the crosses more regularly in use may be mentioned the cross botonny (166), the cross flory (167), which must be distinguished from the cross fleuretté (168); the cross moline, (169), the cross potent (170), the cross patée, or formée (171), the cross patonce (172), and the cross crosslet (173).

Of other but much more uncommon varieties examples will be found of the cross parted and fretty (174), of the cross patée quadrate (175), of a cross pointed and voided in the arms of Dukinfield (quartered by Darbishire), and of a cross cleché voided and pometté as in the arms of Cawston. A cross quarter-pierced

155 *Cross.*

156 *Cross engrailed.*

157 *Cross invecked.*

158 *Cross embattled.*

99

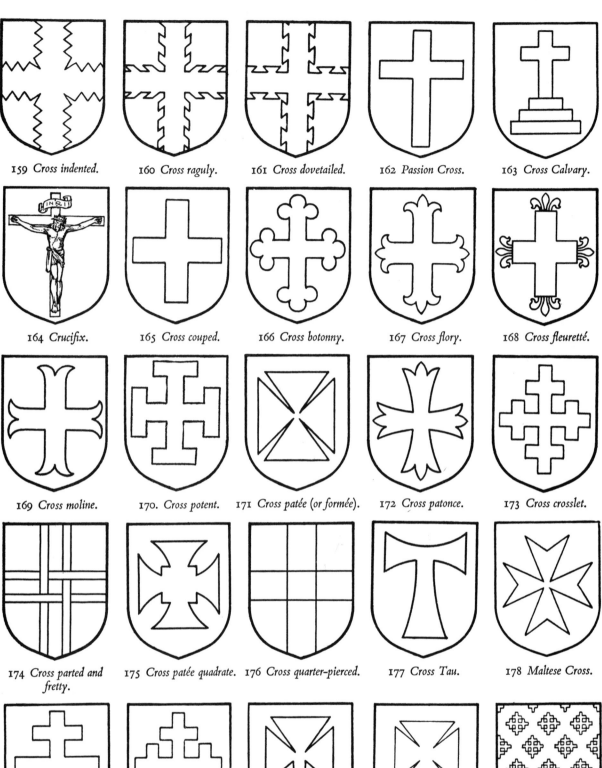

159 Cross indented.

160 Cross raguly.

161 Cross dovetailed.

162 Passion Cross.

163 Cross Calvary.

164 Crucifix.

165 Cross couped.

166 Cross botonny.

167 Cross flory.

168 Cross fleuretté.

169 Cross moline.

170. Cross potent.

171 Cross patée (or formée).

172 Cross patonce.

173 Cross crosslet.

174 Cross parted and fretty.

175 Cross patée quadrate.

176 Cross quarter-pierced.

177 Cross Tau.

178 Maltese Cross.

179 Patriarchal Cross.

180 Cross crosslet fitched.

181 Cross patée fitched.

182 Cross patée fitched at foot.

183 Crusilly.

(176) has the field visible at the centre. A cross tau or St Anthony's Cross is shown in 177, the real Maltese Cross in 178, and the Patriarchal Cross in 179.

Whenever a cross or cross crosslet has the bottom arm elongated and pointed it is said to be 'fitched' (180 and 181), but when a point is added at the foot, *e.g.* of a cross patée, it is then termed 'fitched at the foot' (182).

Of the hundreds of other varieties it may confidently be said that a large proportion originated in misunderstandings of the crude drawings of early armorists, added to the varying and alternating descriptions applied at a more pliable and fluent period of heraldic blazon. A striking illustration of this will be found in the cross botonny, which is now, and has been for a long time past, regularised with us as a distinct variety of constant occurrence. From early illustrations there is now no doubt that this was the original form, or one of the earliest forms, of the cross crosslet. It is foolish to ignore these varieties, reducing all crosses to a few original forms, for they are now mostly stereotyped and accepted; but at the same time it is useless to attempt to learn them, for in a lifetime they will mostly be met with but once each or thereabouts. A field semé of cross crosslets (183) is termed crusilly.

The saltire

The saltire or saltier (184) is more frequently to be met with in Scottish than in English heraldry. This is not surprising, inasmuch as the saltire is known as the Cross of St Andrew, the Patron Saint of Scotland. Its form is too well known to need description. It is of course subject to the usual partition lines (185–92).

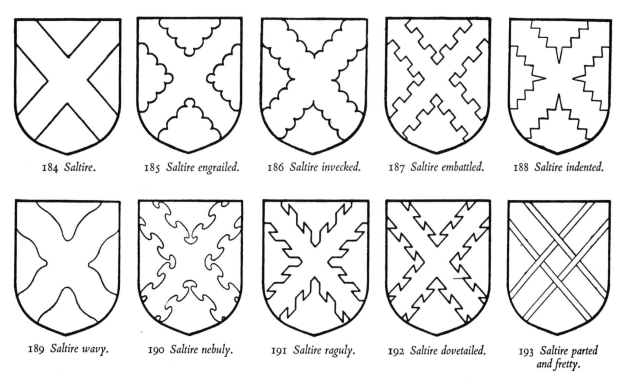

184 *Saltire.*   185 *Saltire engrailed.*   186 *Saltire invecked.*   187 *Saltire embattled.*   188 *Saltire indented.*

189 *Saltire wavy.*   190 *Saltire nebuly.*   191 *Saltire raguly.*   192 *Saltire dovetailed.*   193 *Saltire parted and fretty.*

When a saltire is charged the charges are usually placed conformably therewith.[49]

The field of a coat of arms is often per saltire.

When one saltire couped is the principal charge it will usually be found that it is couped conformably to the outline of the shield; but if the couped saltire be one of a number or a subsidiary charge it will be found couped by horizontal lines, or by lines at right angles. The saltire has not developed into so many varieties of form as the cross, and (*e.g.*) a saltire botonny is assumed to be a cross botonny placed saltireways, but a saltire parted and fretty is to be met with (193).

The chief

The chief (194), which is a broad band across the top of the shield containing (theoretically, but not in fact) the uppermost third of the area of the field, is a very favourite ordinary. It is of course subject to the variations of the usual partition lines (195–203). It is usually drawn to contain about one-fifth of the area of the field, though in cases where it is used for a landscape augmentation it will usually be found of a rather greater area.

The chief especially lent itself to the purposes of honourable augmentation,

49. An examination of charged saltires shows that the reverse is true. The only examples I have been able to find of charges on a saltire following the direction of the ordinary are in certain coats of Scottish families of Dalrymple. The quartering for Dalrymple (an English grant) in the arms of Dalrymple-Champneys, baronets, is blazoned: or, on a saltire couped azure, between two cinquefoils ermine in pale and as many water bougets sable in fess, nine lozenges of the first. The lozenges are depicted, but not blazoned, saltirewise. On the other hand, in the Dalrymple quartering (also an English grant) in the arms of Dalrymple-White, baronets, there is a saltire charged with nine lozenges, but here they are shown, though not blazoned, erect.

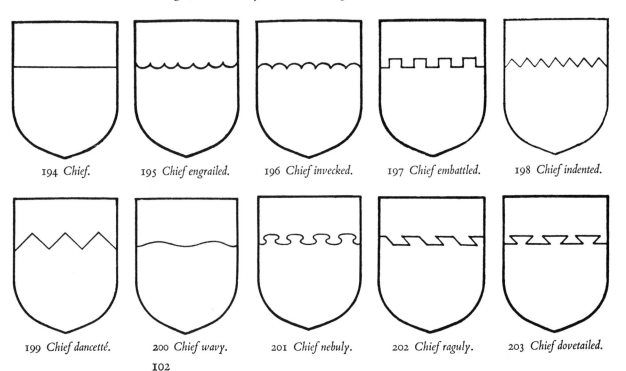

194 *Chief.*   195 *Chief engrailed.*   196 *Chief invecked.*   197 *Chief embattled.*   198 *Chief indented.*

199 *Chief dancetté.*   200 *Chief wavy.*   201 *Chief nebuly.*   202 *Chief raguly.*   203 *Chief dovetailed.*

and is constantly found so employed. As such it will be referred to in the chapter upon augmentations, but a chief of this character may perhaps be here referred to with advantage, as this will indicate the greater area often given to it under these conditions, as in the arms of Ross-of-Bladensburg (Plate II).

Knights of the old Order of St John of Jerusalem and also of the modern Order of the Hospital of St John of Jerusalem in England display above their personal arms a chief of the order, but this will be dealt with more fully in the chapter relating to the insignia of knighthood.

Save in exceptional circumstances, the chief is never debruised or surmounted by any ordinary.

The chief is ordinarily superimposed over the tressure and over the bordure, partly defacing them by the elimination of the upper part thereof. This happens with the bordure when it is a part of the original coat of arms. If, however, the chief were in existence at an earlier period and the bordure is added later as a mark of difference, the bordure surrounds the chief. On the other hand, if a bordure exists, even as a mark of difference, and a chief of augmentation is *subsequently* added, or a canton for distinction, the chief or the canton in these cases would surmount the bordure.

Similarly a bend when added later as a mark of difference surmounts the chief. Such a case is very unusual, as the use of the bend for differencing has long been obsolete.

A chief is never couped or cotised, and it has no diminutive in British armory.

204 *Arms of Peter de Dreux, Earl of Richmond (c. 1230): Chequy or and azure, a quarter ermine. (From his seal.)*

205 *Arms of De Vere, Earls of Oxford: Quarterly gules and or, in the first quarter a mullet argent.*

The quarter

The quarter is not often met with in English armory, the best-known instance being the well-known coat of Shirley, Earl Ferrers, viz.: Paly of six or and azure, a quarter ermine. The arms of the Earls of Richmond (204) supply another instance. Of course as a division of the field under the blazon of 'quarterly' (*e.g.* or and azure) it is constantly to be met with, but a single quarter is rare.

Originally a single quarter was drawn to contain the full fourth part of the shield, but with the more modern tendency to reduce the size of all charges, its area has been somewhat diminished. Whilst a quarter will only be found within a plain partition line, a field divided quarterly (occasionally, but I think hardly so correctly, termed 'per cross') is not so limited. Examples of quarterly fields will be found in the historic shield of De Vere (205) and De Mandeville. An irregular partition line is often introduced in a new grant to conjoin quarterings borne without authority into one single coat. The diminutive of the quarter is the canton (206), and the diminutive of that the chequer of a chequy field (207).[50]

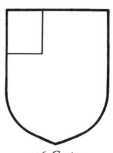

206 *Canton.*

50. I find no example of a single chequer being borne alone, and would not have thought that it could reasonably be called a diminutive of a canton. Cantons of all sizes seem to be blazoned as such except when one whole quarter of the field is shown. Then and then only is it blazoned a quarter (e.g. Gules, fretty or a quarter azure, charged with two ears of wheat slipped gold [Wishaw of Hungerford]). A canton normally occupies just under a quarter of the field, but it can be much smaller, as in the case of the canton of augmentation in the arms of baronets of the United Kingdom. This is usually shown not much larger than a single chequer, but is blazoned as a canton in the original letters patent of James I.

207 *Chequy.*

The canton

The canton is supposed to occupy one-third of the chief, and that being supposed to occupy one-third of the field, a simple arithmetical sum gives us one-ninth of the field as the theoretical area of the canton. Curiously enough, the canton to a certain extent gives us a confirmation of these ancient proportions, inasmuch as all ancient drawings containing both a fess and a canton depict these conjoined. This will be seen in the Garter plate of Earl Rivers. In modern days, however, it is very seldom that the canton will be depicted of such a size, though in cases where, as in the arms of Boothby, it forms the only charge, it is even nowadays drawn to closely approximate to its theoretical area of one-ninth of the field. It may be remarked here perhaps that, owing to the fact that there are but few instances in which the quarter or the canton have been used as the sole or principal charge, a coat of arms in which these are employed would be granted with fewer of the modern bedevilments than would a coat with a chevron for example. I know of no instance in modern times in which a quarter, when figuring as a charge, or a canton have been subject to the usual lines of partition.

The canton (with the single exception of the bordure, when used as a mark of cadency or distinction) is superimposed *over* every other charge or ordinary, no matter what this may be. Theoretically the canton is supposed to be always a later addition to the coat, and even though a charge may be altogether hidden or 'absconded' by the canton, the charge is always presumed to be there, and is mentioned in the blazon.

Both a cross and a saltire are sometimes described as 'cantonned' by such-and-such charges, when they are placed in the blank spaces left by these ordinaries. In addition, the spaces left by a cross (but not by a saltire) are frequently spoken of, *e.g.* as the dexter chief canton or the sinister base canton.

The canton is frequently used to carry an augmentation, and these cantons of augmentation will be referred to under that heading, though it may be here stated that a 'canton of England' is a canton gules, charged with three lions passant guardant or, as in the arms of Lane (Plate II).

The canton, *unless it is an original charge*, need not conform to the rule forbidding colour on colour, or metal on metal; otherwise the canton of Ulster would often be an impossibility.

The canton, with rare exceptions, is always placed in the dexter chief corner. The canton of augmentation in the arms of Clerke, Bart.—'Argent, on a bend gules, between three pellets as many swans of the field; on a sinister canton azure, a demi-ram salient of the first, and in chief two fleurs-de-lis, or debruised by a baton'—is, however, a sinister one, as is the canton upon the arms of Charlton. In this latter case the sinister canton is used to signify illegitimacy. This will be more fully dealt with in the chapter upon marks of illegitimacy.

A curious use of the canton for the purposes of marshalling occurs in the case of a woman who, being an heiress herself, has a daughter or daughters only, whilst her husband has sons and heirs by another marriage. In such an event, the daughter being heir (or in the case of daughters these being coheirs) of the mother, but not heir of the father, cannot transmit as quarterings the arms of the father whom she does not represent, whilst she ought to transmit the arms of the mother whom she *does* represent. The husband of the daughter, therefore, places upon an escutcheon of pretence the arms of her mother, with those of her father on a canton thereupon. The children of the marriage quarter this combined coat, the arms of the father always remaining upon a canton. This will be more fully dealt with under the subject of marshalling.

The canton has yet another use as a 'mark of distinction'. When, under a Royal Licence, the name and arms of a family are assumed where there is no blood descent from the family, the arms have some mark of distinction added. This is usually a plain canton. This point will be treated more fully under 'Marks of Cadency'.

Woodward mentions three instances in which the lower edge of the canton is 'indented', one taken from the Calais Roll, viz. the arms of Sir William de la Zouche—'Gules, bezantée, a canton indented at the bottom'—and adds that the canton has been sometimes thought to indicate the square banner of a knight-baronet, and he suggests that the lower edge being indented may give some weight to the idea. As the canton does not appear to have either previously or subsequently formed any part of the arms of Zouche, it is possible that in this instance some such meaning may have been intended, but it can have no such application generally.

The 'Canton of Ulster'—*i.e.* 'Argent, a sinister hand couped at the wrist gules'—is the badge of a baronet of England, Ireland, Great Britain, or the United Kingdom. This badge may be borne upon a canton, dexter or sinister, or upon an inescutcheon, at the pleasure of the wearer. There is some little authority and more precedent for similarly treating the badge of a Nova Scotian Baronet, but as such Baronets *wear* their badges it is more usually depicted below the shield, depending by the orange tawny ribbon of their order.

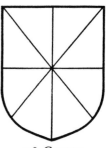

208 *Gyronny.*

The gyron

As a charge, the gyron (sometimes termed an esquire) is very seldom found, but as a subdivision of the field, a coat 'gyronny' (208) is constantly met with, all arms for the name of Campbell being gyronny. Save in rare cases, a field gyronny is divided quarterly and then per saltire, making eight divisions, but it may be gyronny of six, ten, twelve, or more pieces, though such cases are seldom met with and always need to be specified. The arms of Campbell of Succoth are gyronny of eight *engrailed*, a most unusual circumstance. I know of no other instance of the use of lines of partition in a gyronny field. The arms of Lanyon afford an example of the gyron as a charge, as does also the well-known shield of Mortimer (209).

209 *The arms of Roger Mortimer, Earl of March and Ulster (d. 1398): Quarterly, 1 and 4, azure, three bars or (sometimes but not so correctly quoted barry of six), on a chief of the first two pallets between two base esquires of the second, over all an inescutcheon argent (for Mortimer); 2 and 3, or, a cross gules (for Ulster). (From his seal.)*

The inescutcheon

The inescutcheon is a shield appearing as a charge upon the coat of arms. Certain writers state that it is termed an inescutcheon if only one appears as the charge, but that when more than one is present they are merely termed escutcheons. This is an unnecessary refinement not officially recognised or adhered to, though

105

unconsciously one often is led to make this distinction, which seems to spring naturally to one's mind.[51]

When one inescutcheon appears, it is sometimes difficult to tell whether to blazon the arms as charged with a bordure or an inescutcheon. Some coats of arms, for example the arms of Molesworth, will always remain more or less a matter of uncertainty.

But as a matter of fact a bordure should not be wide enough to fill up the field left by an inescutcheon, nor an inescutcheon large enough to occupy the field left by a bordure.

The inescutcheon in German armory (or, as they term it, the heart escutcheon), when superimposed upon other quarterings, is usually the paternal or most important coat of arms. The same method of marshalling has sometimes been adopted in Scotland, and the arms of Hay are an instance. It usually in British heraldry is used to carry the arms of an heiress wife, but both these points will be dealt with later under the subject of marshalling. The inescutcheon, no matter what its position, should never be termed an escutcheon of pretence if it forms a charge upon the original arms. A curious instance of the use of an inescutcheon will be found in the arms of Gordon-Cumming (Plate IV).

When an inescutcheon appears on a shield it should conform in its outline to the shape of the shield upon which it is placed.[52]

210 Bordure.

211 Bordure engrailed.

212 Bordure invecked.

The bordure

The bordure (210) occurs both as a charge and as a mark of difference. As may be presumed from its likeness to our word border, the bordure is simply a border round the shield. Except in modern grants in which the bordure forms a part of the original design of the arms, there can be very little doubt that the bordure has always been a mark of difference to indicate either cadency or bastardy, but its stereotyped continuance without further alteration in so many coats of arms in which it originally was introduced as a difference, and also its appearance in new grants, leave one no alternative but to treat of it in the ordinary way as a charge, leaving the consideration of it as a mark of difference to a future chapter.

There is no stereotyped or official size for the bordure, the width of which has at all times varied, though it will almost invariably be found that a Scottish bordure is depicted rather wider than is an English one; and naturally a bordure

51. It may be an unnecessary refinement (indeed I think it is) to term a single shield an inescutcheon and several shields simply escutcheons, but in practice this has often been done. The arms granted to Henry Parker of Fryth Hall, Essex on 21 February 1537 are blazoned: 'gold three escocheons sable upon eche scochen a brode arrowe hedde of the felde.' The arms of Sir James Hays of Great Badgbury, Kent, were confirmed on 8 May 1689 and blazoned: ermine, three escutcheons gules. He claimed descent from the earls of Erroll, and his claim was allowed by the then Earl. A single shield occurs in the arms granted to Captain John Weddall on 3 May 1627; this coat is blazoned: argent, an inescutcheon baruly wavy of ten or and gules an orle of fireballs proper. A more recent example of the use of the term inescutcheon for a single shield can be found in the arms granted to Sir Robert Williams, baronet (the title is now extinct), on 1 August 1928, namely; gules, a saltire or on an inescutcheon argent, a representation of the Continent of Africa sable, charged with a cross of the third.

52. This is purely an aesthetic canon, and is not a rule or convention of arms.

which is charged is a little wider than an entirely plain one. The bordure of course is subject to all the lines of partition (211–18). Bordures may also be per fesse, per pale (219), quarterly (220), gyronny (221), or tierced in pairle (222), &c.

The bordure has long since ceased to be a mark of cadency in England, but as a mark of distinction the bordure wavy (215) is still used to indicate bastardy. A bordure of England was granted by Royal warrant as an augmentation to H.M. Queen Victoria Eugenie of Spain, on the occasion of her marriage.[53] The use of the bordure is, however, the recognised method of differencing in Scotland, but it is curious that with the Scots the bordure wavy is in no way a mark of illegitimacy. The Scottish bordure for indicating this fact is the bordure compony (223), which has been used occasionally for the same purpose in England, but the bordures added to indicate cadency and the various marks to indicate illegitimacy will be discussed in later chapters. The difference should here be observed between the bordure compony (223), which means illegitimacy; the bordure counter compony (224), which may or may not have that meaning; and the bordure chequy (225), which certainly has no relation to bastardy. In the two former the panes run with the shield, in the latter the chequers do not. Whilst the bordure as a mark of cadency or illegitimacy surrounds the whole shield, being superimposed upon even the chief and canton, a bordure when merely a charge gives way to both.

A certain rule regarding the bordure is the sole remaining instance in modern

53. This bordure was only an augmentation inasmuch as it was an addition to the paternal arms of Princess Victoria Eugenie. In the Royal Warrant of 1 March 1906 it is not described as an augmentation. The Warrant simply 'gives and assigns' arms, coronet and supporters. The arms are those of Prince Maurice of Battenburg within a bordure of England borne on a lozenge. The supporters are two lions guard   double queued gold, each supporting a flag-staff erect proper, flowing therefrom a banner c   ed with the royal arms with an inescutcheon of the arms of 'the August House of Saxony'.

213 *Bordure embattled.*

214 *Bordure indented.*

215 *Bordure wavy.*

216 *Bordure nebuly.*

217 *Bordure dovetailed.*

218 *Bordure potenté.*

219 *Bordure per pale.*

220 *Bordure quarterly.*

221 *Bordure gyronny.*

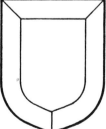

222 *Bordure tierced in pairle.*

223 *Bordure compony.*

224 *Bordure counter compony.*

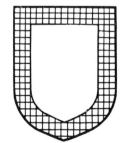

225 *Bordure chequy.*

heraldry of the formerly recognised practice of conjoining two coats of arms (which it might be necessary to marshal together) by 'dimidiation' instead of using our present-day method of impalement. To dimidiate two coats of arms, the dexter half of one shield was conjoined to the sinister half of the other. The objections to such a practice, however, soon made themselves apparent (*e.g.* a dimidiated chevron was scarcely distinguishable from a bend), and the 'dimidiation' of arms was quickly abandoned in favour of 'impalement', in which the entire designs of both coats of arms are depicted. But in impaling a coat of arms which is surrounded by a bordure, the bordure is not continued down the centre between the two coats, but stops short top and bottom at the palar line. The same rule, by the way, applies to the tressure, but not to the orle.[54] The curious fact, however, remains that this rule as to the dimidiation of the bordure in cases of impalement is often found to have been ignored in ancient seals and other examples. The charges upon the bordure are often three, but more usually eight in number, in the latter case being arranged three along the top of the shield, one at the base point, and two on either side. The number should, however, always be specified, unless (as in a bordure bezantée, &c.) it is immaterial; in which case the number eight must be *exceeded* in emblazoning the shield. The rule as to colour upon colour does not hold and seems often to be ignored in the cases of bordures, noticeably when these occur as marks of Scottish cadency.

The orle

226 *Orle.*

227 *An inescutcheon within a bordure.*

The orle (226), or, as it was originally termed in ancient British rolls of arms, 'un faux ecusson', is a narrow bordure following the exact outline of the shield, but within it, showing the field (for at least the width usually occupied by a bordure) between the outer edge of the orle and the edge of the escutcheon. An orle is about half the width of a bordure, rather less than more, but the proportion is never very exactly maintained. The difference may be noted between this figure and the next (227), which shows an inescutcheon within a bordure.

Though both forms are very seldom so met with, an orle may be subject to the usual lines of partition, and may also be charged. Examples of both these variations are met with in the arms of Yeatman-Biggs, and the arms of Gladstone afford an instance of an orle 'flory'. The arms of Knox, Earl of Ranfurly, are: Gules, a falcon volant or, within an orle wavy on the outer and engrailed on the inner edge argent.

When a series of charges are placed round the edges of the escutcheon (*theoretically* in the position occupied by the orle, but as a matter of actual fact usually more in the position occupied by the bordure), they are said to be 'in orle', which is the correct term, but they will often be found blazoned 'an orle of (*e.g.*) martlets or mounds'.

54. Although I have come across examples of an impaled orle being discontinued down the palar line, such examples are rare. Possibly the reason why it has been treated differently from the bordure and tressure is that it is frequently depicted as a voided escutcheon. In other words, when it is impaled or placed upon a banner it does not, like the bordure, follow the line of the edge of the field, but retains its shield shape.

The tressure

The tressure is really an orle gemel, *i.e.* an orle divided into two narrow ones set closely together, the one inside the other. It is, however, usually depicted a trifle nearer the edge of the escutcheon than the orle is generally placed.

228 *Tressure flory and counter-flory.*

The tressure cannot be borne singly, as it would then be an orle, but plain tressures under the name of 'concentric orles' will be found mentioned in Papworth. In that Ordinary eight instances are given of arms containing more than a single orle, though the eight instances are plainly varieties of only four coats. Two concentric orles would certainly be a tressure, save that perhaps they would be drawn of rather too great a width for the term 'tressure' to be properly applied to them.

If these instances be disregarded, and I am inclined to doubt them as genuine coats, there certainly is no example of a plain tressure in British heraldry, and one's attention must be directed to the tressure flory and counterflory (228), so general in Scottish heraldry.[55]

Originating entirely in the Royal escutcheon, one cannot do better than reproduce the remarks of a Lyon King of Arms[56] upon the subject from his work *Heraldry in relation to Scottish History and Art*:

'William the Lion has popularly got the credit of being the first to introduce heraldic bearings into Scotland, and to have assumed the lion as his personal cognisance. The latter statement may or may not be true, but we have no trace of hereditary arms in Scotland so early as his reign (1165–1214). Certainly the lion does not appear on his seal, but it does on that of his son and successor Alexander II, with apparent remains of the double tressure flory counterflory, a device which is clearly seen on the seals of Alexander III (1249–85). We are unable to say what the reason was **for** the adoption of such a distinctive coat; of course, if you turn to the older writers you will find all sorts of fables on the subject. Even the sober and sensible Nisbet states that "the lion has been carried on the armorial ensign of Scotland since the first founding of the monarchy by King Fergus I"—a very mythical personage, who is said to have flourished about 300 B.C.—though he is careful to say that he does not believe arms are as old as that period. He says, however, that it is "without doubt" that Charlemagne entered into an alliance with Achaius, King of Scotland, and for the services of the Scots the French king added to the Scottish lion the double tressure fleur-de-lisée to show that the former had defended the French lilies, and that therefore the latter would surround the lion and be a defence to him.'

All this is very pretty, but it is not history. Chalmers remarks in his *Caledonia* that the lion may possibly have been derived from the arms of the old Earls of Northumberland and Huntingdon, from whom some of the Scottish kings were descended; and he mentions an old roll of arms preserved by Leland,★ which is certainly not later than 1272, in which the arms of Scotland are blazoned as: *Or,*

---

55. Since Fox-Davies wrote, a single tressure flory has been granted on several occasions, the first being that granted to the Heraldry Society on 10 August 1957: quarterly azure and gules, a lion's face crowned with an ancient crown or, within a tressure flory on the outer edge of the same.

56. The author of this book, published in 1900, was Sir James Balfour Paul, Lyon King of Arms.

★ *Collectanea*, ed. 1774, ii. 611.

a lion gules within a bordure or fleuretté gules, which we may reasonably interpret as an early indication of what may be considered as a foreign rendering of the double tressure. Sylvanus Morgan, one of the very maddest of the seventeenth-century heraldic writers, says that the tressure was added to the shield of Scotland, in testimony of a league between Scotland and France, by Charles V; but that king did not ascend the throne of France till 1364, at which time we have clear proof that the tressure was a firmly established part of the Scottish arms. One of the earliest instances of anything approaching the tressure in the Scottish arms which I have met with is in an armorial of Matthew Paris, which is now in the Cottonian MSS. in the British Museum, and at one time belonged to St Alban's Monastery. Here the arms of the King of Scotland are given as: 'Or, a lion rampant flory gules in a bordure of the same.' The drawing represents a lion within a bordure, the latter being pierced by ten fleurs-de-lis, their heads all looking inwards, the other end not being free, but attached to the inner margin of the shield. This, you will observe, is very like the arms I mentioned as described by Chalmers, and it may possibly be the same volume which may have been acquired by Sir Robert Cotton. In 1471 there was a curious attempt of the Scottish Parliament to displace the tressure. An Act was passed in that year, for some hitherto unexplained reason, by which it was ordained 'that in tyme to cum thar suld be na double tresor about his (the king's) armys, but that he suld ber hale armys of the lyoun without ony mair'. Seeing that at the time of this enactment the Scottish kings had borne the tressure for upwards of 220 years, it is difficult to understand the cause of this procedure. Like many other Acts, however, it never seems to have been carried into effect; at least I am not aware of even a solitary instance of the Scottish arms without the tressure either at or after this period.

★   ★   ★   ★   ★

There are other two representations of the Scottish arms in foreign armorials, to which I may briefly allude. One is in the *Armorial de Gelre,* a beautiful MS. in the Royal Library at Brussels, the Scottish shields in which have been figured by Mr Stodart in his book on Scottish arms, and, more accurately, by Sir Archibald Dunbar in a paper read to the Society of Antiquaries of Scotland in 1890. The armorial is believed to be the work of Claes Heynen, Gelre Herald to the Duke of Gueldres between 1334 and 1372, with later additions by another hand. The coat assigned in it to the King of Scotland is the lion and double tressure; the lion is uncrowned, and is armed and langued azure; above the shield is a helmet argent adorned behind with a short capelin or plain mantling, on which is emblazoned the saltire and chief of the Bruces, from which we may gather that the arms of David II are here represented; the lining is blue, which is unusual, as mantlings are usually lined or doubled with a metal, if not with ermine. The helmet is surmounted by an Imperial crown, with a dark green bonnet spotted with red.★ On the crown there is the crest of a lion sejant guardant gules, imperially crowned or, holding in his paw a sword upright; the tail is coué or placed between the hind-legs of the lion, but it then rises up and flourishes high above his back in a sufficiently defiant fashion. This shows that the Scottish arms were well known on the Continent of Europe nearly a hundred years before the date of the Grunenberg

★ In M. Victor Bouton's edition of the *Armorial de Gelre* (Paris, 1881) the bonnet is described as a mount.

MS., while Virgil de Solis (*c.* 1555) gives a sufficiently accurate representation of the Royal shield, though the fleur-de-lis all project outwards as in the case of Grunenberg; he gives the crest as a lion rampant holding a sword in bend over his shoulder. Another ancient representation of the Scottish arms occurs in a MS. treatise on heraldry of the sixteenth century, containing the coats of some foreign sovereigns and other personages, bound up with a Scottish armorial, probably by David Lindsay, Lyon in 1568.'

The tressure, like the bordure, in the case of an impalement stops at the line of impalement, as will be seen by a reference to the arms of Queen Anne after the union of the crowns of England and Scotland.

It is now held, both in England and Scotland, that the tressure flory and counter-flory is, as a part of the Royal Arms, protected, and cannot be granted to any person without the express licence of the Sovereign.[57] This, however, does not interfere with the matriculation or exemplification of it in the case of existing arms in which it occurs.

Many Scottish families bear or claim to bear the Royal tressure by reason of female descent from the Royal House, but it would seem much more probable that in most if not in all cases where it is so borne by right its origin is due rather to a gift by way of augmentation than to any supposed right of inheritance. The apparently conflicting statements of origin are not really antagonistic, inasmuch as it will be seen from many analogous English instances (*e.g.* Mowbray, Manners, and Seymour) that near relationship is often the only reason to account for the grant of a Royal augmentation. As an ordinary augmentation of honour it has been frequently granted.

The towns of Aberdeen and Perth obtained early the right of honouring their arms with the addition of the Royal tressure. It appears on the still existing matrix of the burgh seal of Aberdeen, which was engraved in 1430.

James V in 1542 granted a warrant to Lyon to surround the arms of John Scot, of Thirlestane, with the Royal tressure, in respect of his ready services at Soutra Edge with three score and ten lances on horseback, when other nobles refused to follow their Sovereign. The grant was put on record by the grantee's descendant, Patrick, Lord NAPIER, and is tressured coat borne in the second and third quarters of the NAPIER arms.

When the Royal tressure is granted to the bearer of a quartered coat it is usually placed upon a bordure surrounding the quartered shield, as in the case of the arms of the Marquess of QUEENSBERRY, to whom, in 1682, the Royal tressure was granted upon a *bordure or.* A like arrangement is borne by the Earls of EGLINTON, occurring as far back as a seal of Earl HUGH, appended to a charter of 1598.

The Royal tressure had at least twice been granted as an augmentation to the arms of foreigners. James V granted it to NICOLAS CANIVET of Dieppe, secretary to JOHN, Duke of ALBANY (Reg. Mag. Sig., xxiv 263, 24 Oct. 1529). James VI

---

57. The double tressure flory counterflory has been granted in England without a Royal Licence. The arms granted to the Cambridgeshire and Isle of Ely County Council on 1 September 1965 provide an example: or, a double tressure flory counterflory gules, over all on a bend wavy azure three crowns or. Here the tressure refers to the fact that King David I of Scotland held the Earldom of Cambridge, which was united with that of Huntingdon, in the twelfth century. The arms of the former Cambridgeshire County Council also contained the double tressure.

gave it to Sir Jacob Van Eiden, a Dutchman on whom he conferred the honour of knighthood.

On 12 March 1762, a Royal Warrant was granted directing Lyon to add a 'double tressure counterflowered as in the Royal arms of Scotland' to the arms of

229 *Armorial bearings of Sir Archibald Kennedy, Marquess of Ailsa: Argent, a chevron gules between three cross crosslets fitchée sable, all within a double tressure flory and counter-flory of the second. Mantling gules, doubled ermine. Crest: upon a wreath of his liveries, a dolphin naiant proper. Supporters: two swans proper, beaked and membered gules. Motto: 'Avise la fin.' (From the painting by Mr Graham Johnston in the Lyon Register.)*

ARCHIBALD, Viscount PRIMROSE. Here the tressure was *gules*, as in the Royal arms, although the field on which it was placed was *vert*. In a later record of the arms of ARCHIBALD, Earl of ROSEBERY, in 1823, this heraldic anomaly was brought to an end, and the blazon of the arms of Primrose is now: 'Vert, three primroses within a double tressure flory counterflory or.' (See Stodart, *Scottish Arms*, vol. i, pp. 262, 263, where mention is also made of an older use of the Royal tressure or, by 'ARCHBALD PRIMROSE of Dalmenie, Knight and baronet, be his majesty CHARLES ii create, *Vert, three primroses within a double tressure flowered counter-flowered or.*') Another well-known Scottish instance in which the tressure occurs will be found in the arms of the Marquess of Ailsa (229).

Two instances are known in which the decoration of the tressure has differed from the usual conventional fleurs-de-lis. The tressure granted to Charles, Earl of Aboyne, has crescents without and demi-fleurs-de-lis within, and the tressure round the Gordon arms in the case of the Earls of Aberdeen is of thistles, roses, and fleurs-de-lis alternately.

The tressure gives way to the chief and canton, but all other ordinaries are enclosed by the tressure, as will be seen from the arms of Lord Ailsa.

230 *Lozenge.*

The lozenge, the fusil, the mascle, and the rustre

Why these, which are simply varying forms of one charge, should ever have been included amongst the list of ordinaries is difficult to understand, as they do not seem to be 'ordinaries' any more than say the mullet or the crescent. My own opinion is that they are no more than distinctively heraldic charges. The *lozenge* (230), which is the original form, is the same shape as the 'diamond' in a pack of cards, and will constantly be found as a charge. In addition to this, the arms of a lady as maid, or as widow, are always displayed upon a lozenge. Upon this point reference should be made to the chapter upon marshalling. The arms of Kyrke show a single lozenge as the charge, but a single lozenge is very rarely met with. The arms of Guise show seven lozenges conjoined. The arms of Barnes show four lozenges conjoined in cross, and the arms of Bartlett show five lozenges conjoined in fess. Although the lozenge is very seldom found in English armory as a single charge, nevertheless as a lozenge throughout (that is, with its four points touching the borders of the escutcheon) it will be found in some number of instances in Continental heraldry, for instance in the family of Eubing of Bavaria. An indefinite number of lozenges conjoined as a bend or a pale are known as a bend lozengy, or a pale lozengy, but care should be taken in using this term, as it is possible for these ordinaries to be plain ordinaries tinctured 'lozengy of two colours'. The arms of Bolding are an example of a bend lozengy.

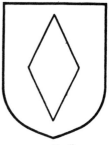

231 *Fusil.*

The *fusil* is supposed to be, and is generally depicted, of a greater height and less width than a lozenge, being an altogether narrower figure (231). Though this distinction is generally observed, it is not always easy to decide which figure any emblazonment is intended to represent, unless the blazon of the arms in question is known. In many cases the variations of different coats of arms, to suit or to fit the varying shapes of shields, have resulted in the use of lozenges and fusils indifferently. Fusils occur in the historic arms of Daubeney, from which family

232 *Mascle.*

233 *Rustre.*

234 *Arms of Roger de Quincy, Earl of Winchester (d. 1264): Gules, seven mascles conjoined, three, three and one or. (From his seal.)*

235 *Arms of Seiher de Quincy, Earl of Winchester (d. 1219): Or, a fess gules, a label of seven points azure. (From his seal.)*

236 *Arms of Louis de Bruges, Earl of Winchester (d. 1492.)*

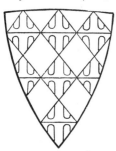

237 *Arms of Hubert de Burgh, Earl of Kent (d. 1243). (From his seal.)*

Daubeney of Cote, near Bristol, is descended, being one of the few families who have an undoubted male descent from a companion of William the Conqueror. In the ordinary way five or more lozenges in fess would be fusils, as in the arms of Percy, Duke of Northumberland, who bears in the first quarter: Azure, five fusils conjoined in fess or. The charges in the arms of Montagu, though only three in number, are always termed fusils. But obviously in early times there could have been no distinction between the lozenge and the fusil.

The *mascle* is a lozenge voided, *i.e.* only the outer framework is left, the inner portion being removed (232). Mascles have no particular or special meaning, but are frequently to be met with.[58]

The blazon of the arms of De Quincy in Charles's Roll is: 'De goules poudré ā fause losengez dor', and in another Roll (MS. Brit. Mus. 29,796) the arms are described: 'De gules a set fauses lozenges de or' (234). The great Seiher de Quincy, Earl of Winchester, father of Roger, bore quite different arms (235). In 1472 Louis de Bruges, Lord of Gruthuyse, was created Earl of Winchester, having no relation to the De Quincy line. The arms of De Bruges, or rather of Gruthuyse, were very different, yet nevertheless, we find upon the Patent Roll (12 Edward IV pt. 1, m. 11) a grant of the following arms: 'Azure, dix mascles d'Or, enormé d'une canton de nostre propre Armes de Angleterre; cest a savoir de Gules a une Lipard passant d'Or, armée d'Azure,' to Louis, Earl of Winchester (236). The recurrence of the mascles in the arms of the successive Earls of Winchester, whilst each had other family arms, and in the arms of Ferrers, whilst not being the original Ferrers coat, suggests the thought that there may be hidden some reference to a common saintly patronage which all enjoyed, or some territorial honour common to the three of which the knowledge no longer remains with us.

There are some number of coats which are said to have had a field masculy. Of course this is quite possible, and the difference between a field masculy and a field fretty is that in the latter the separate pieces of which it is composed interlace each other; but when the field is masculy it is all one fretwork surface, the field being visible through the voided apertures. Nevertheless it seems by no means certain that in every case in which the field masculy occurs it may not be found in other, and possibly earlier, examples as fretty. At any rate, very few such coats of arms are even supposed to exist. The arms of De Burgh (237) are blazoned in the Grimaldi Roll: 'Masclee de vêre and de goules,' but whether the inference is that

58. For better or for worse, the mascle now has a very special meaning. It is added as a mark of distinction (although perhaps this is the wrong word) to the arms of a divorced woman. When a woman is divorced, she reverts to using her maiden arms, but with the addition of a mascle. If one of the purposes of heraldry is to identify, then this ruling is rather misleading. When a woman divorces, she normally retains her husband's name and the marital prefix 'Mrs'. If she has been married to a peer, the Lord Chamberlain has laid down that she shall be styled as a widowed peeress, using her christian name before her title. It therefore seems slightly misleading if a woman is properly called Ann, Lady Blank and is perhaps the mother of the living Lord Blank, that she should use her maiden arms. I submit it would illustrate her position more clearly if the mascle were added to her marital arms, which should be borne in a lozenge.

When a divorced woman remarries, she takes the name of her new husband and, if her former husband were a peer, must cease to enjoy the use of a consort's title. Thus it is not unreasonable for her to marshal her arms with those of her new husband in whatever way is appropriate (see the chapter on Marshalling).

this blazon is wrong or that lozenge and mascle were identical terms I am not aware.

The *rustre* is comparatively rare (233). It is a lozenge pierced in the centre with a circular hole. It occurs in the arms of J.D.G. Dalrymple, Esq., F.S.A. Some few coats of arms are mentioned in Papworth in which the rustre appears; for example the arms of Pery, which are: 'Or, three rustres sable'; and Goodchief, which are: 'Per fess or and sable, three rustres counterchanged';[59] but so seldom is the figure met with that it may be almost dropped out of consideration. How it ever reached the position of being considered one of the ordinaries has always been to me a profound mystery.

The fret

The fret (238), which is very frequently found occurring in British armory, is no doubt derived from earlier coats of arms, the whole field of which was covered by an interlacing of alternate bendlets and bendlets sinister, because many of the families who now bear a simple fret are found in earlier representations and in the early rolls of arms bearing coats which were fretty (239). Instances of this kind will be found in the arms of Maltravers, Verdon, Tollemache, and other families.

'Sable fretty or' was the original form of the arms of the ancient and historic family of Maltravers. At a later date the arms of Maltravers are found simply 'sable, a fret or', but, like the arms of so many other families which we now find blazoned simply as charged with a fret, their original form was undoubtedly 'fretty'. They appear fretty as late as in the year 1421, which is the date at which the Garter plate of Sir William Arundel, K.G. (1395–1400), was set up in St George's Chapel at Windsor. His arms as there displayed are in the first and fourth quarters, 'gules, a lion rampant or', and in the second and third, 'purpure[60] fretty or' for Maltravers. Probably the seal of John Fitz Alan, Earl of Arundel (d. 1435), roughly marks the period, and shows the source of the confusion (240). But it should be noted that Sir Richard Arundel, Lord Maltravers, bore at the siege of Rouen, in the year 1418, gules a lion rampant or, quarterly with 'sable a fret or' (for Maltravers). This would seem to indicate that those who treat the fret and fretty as interchangeable have good grounds for so doing. A Sir John Maltravers bore 'sable fretty or' at the siege of Calais, and another Sir John Maltravers, a knight banneret, bore at the first Dunstable tournament 'sable fretty or, a label of three points argent'. As he is there described as Le Fitz, the label was probably a purely temporary mark of difference. In a roll of arms which is believed to belong to the latter part of the reign of Henry III, a Sir William Maltravers is credited with 'sable fretty or, on a quarter argent, three lions passant in pale gules'. The palpable origin of the fret or fretty in the case of the arms of Maltravers is simply the canting similarity between a traverse and the name Maltravers. Another case, which starting fretty has ended in a fret, occurs in the arms of the family of Harington.

59. I have not been able to substantiate the authenticity of these coats quoted in Papworth. Indeed, I have been unable to locate a genuine example of a rustre so blazoned, and even several of the early text books omit any mention of such a charge. This would seem to make the rustre a classic example of a 'textbook' charge.

60. This is clearly an error for sable.

238 *The Fret.*

239 *Fretty.*

240 *Arms of John Fitz Alan, Earl of Arundel (d. 1435): Quarterly, 1 and 4, gules, a lion rampant or (for Fitz Alan); 2 and 3, sable, fretty or (for Maltravers). (From his seal, c. 1432.)*

Sir John de Haverington, or Sir John de Harington, is found at the first Dunstable tournament in 1308 being 'sable fretty argent', and this coat of arms variously differenced appears in some number of the other early rolls of arms. The Harington family, as may be seen from the current baronetages, now bear 'sable a fret argent', but there can be little doubt that in this case the origin of the fretty is to be found in a representation of a herring-net.

The fret is usually depicted *throughout* when borne singly, and is then composed of a bendlet dexter and a bendlet sinister, interlaced in the centre by a mascle. Occasionally it will be found couped, but it is then, as a rule, only occupying the position of a subsidiary charge. A coat which is *fretty* is entirely covered by the interlacing bendlets and bendlets sinister, no mascles being introduced.

The Flaunch

241 *Flaunches.*

The flaunch, which is never borne singly, and for which the additional names of 'flasks' and 'voiders' are sometimes found, is the segment of a circle of large diameter projecting into the field from either side of the escutcheon, of a different colour from the field. It is by no means an unusual charge to be met with, and, like the majority of other ordinaries, is subject to the usual lines of partition, but so subject is, however, of rather rare occurrence.[61]

Planché, in his *Pursuivant of Arms*, mentions the old idea, which is repeated by Woodward, 'that the base son of a noble woman, if he doe gev armes, must give upon the same a surcoat, but unless you do well mark such coat you may take it for a coat flanchette'. The surcoat is much the same figure that would remain after flaunches had been taken from the field of a shield, with this exception, that the flaunches would be wider and the intervening space necessarily much narrower. In spite of the fact that this is supposed to be one of the recognised rules of armory, one instance only appears to be known of its employment, which, however, considering the circumstances, is not very much to be wondered at. One exceptional case surely cannot make a rule. I know of no modern case of a mother's coat bastardised—but I assume it would fall under the ordinary practice of the bordure wavy.

The roundel (or roundle)

The roundel is a generic name which comprises all charges which are plain circular figures of colour or metal. Foreign heraldry merely terms them roundels

61. I have only been able to find three examples of a flaunch drawn with one of the partition lines. All occur in one of the sixteenth century copies of Sir George Calveley's book (*c.* 1350–1450), namely in the Cheshire section of College of Arms manuscript MjD14. Sir Hugh de Lym bore: argent two flaunches dancetty gules. The same arms, but debruised by a bendlet sable, are given for Stathum and Sir John and Sir Thomas Danyell both bore: sable, two flaunches dancetty argent, the latter having a fleur-de-lis for difference. One is tempted to think that this unusual variant of the flaunch may have been an artistic error for a pale of fusils, especially as the arms of Daniel of Cheshire are given in the Visitations of that county as argent, fusils fesswise conjoined in pale sable. On the other hand where such a pale occurs in Calveley's book it is so drawn. Whatever the origin of these curious Cheshire coats, there certainly seems to be no reason why a flaunch drawn with one of the partition lines should not make its appearance in armory.

PLATE IV

Arms of Sir William Gordon Cumming, Bt.

of such and such a colour, but in England we have special terms for each tincture.

When the roundel is gold it is termed a 'bezant', when silver a 'plate', when gules a 'torteau', when azure a 'hurt', when sable an 'ogress', 'pellet', or 'gunstone', when vert a 'pomeis', when purpure a 'golpe', when tenné an 'orange', when sanguine a 'guze'. The golpes, oranges, and guzes are seldom, if ever, met with, but the others are of constant occurrence, and roundels of fur are by no means unknown. A roundel of more than one colour is described as a roundel 'per pale', for examples of gules and azure, or whatever it may be. The plates and bezants are naturally flat, and must be so represented. They should never be shaded up into a globular form. The torteau is sometimes found shaded, but is more correctly flat, but probably the pellet or ogress and the pomeis are intended to be globular. Roundels of fur are always flat. One curious roundel is a very common charge in British armory, that is, the 'fountain', which is a roundel barry wavy argent and azure (242). This is the conventional heraldic representation of water, of course. A fountain will be found termed a 'syke' when occurring in the arms of any family of the name of Sykes. It typifies naturally anything in the nature of a well, in which meaning it occurs on the arms of Stourton (243).

242 *Fountain.*

The arms of Stourton are one of the few really ancient coats concerning which a genuine explanation exists. The blazon of them is: Sable a bend or, between six fountains proper. Concerning this coat of arms Aubrey says: 'I believe anciently 'twas only Sable a bend or.' With all deference to Aubrey, I personally neither think he was right, nor do I pay much attention to his *opinions*, particularly in this case, inasmuch as every known record of the Stourton arms introduces the six fountains. The name Stourton, originally 'de Stourton', is emphatically a territorial name, and there is little opportunity for this being gainsaid, inasmuch as the lordship and manor of Stourton, in the counties of Wilts and Somerset, remained in the possession of the Lords Stourton until the year 1714. Consequently there is no doubt whatever that the Lords Stourton derived their surname from this manor of Stourton. Equally is it certain that the manor of Stourton obtained its name from the river Stour, which rises within the manor. The sources of the river Stour are six wells, which exist in a tiny valley in Stourton Park, which to this day is known by the name of 'The Six Wells Bottom'. In the present year of grace only one of the six wells remains visible. When Sir Richard Colt Hoare wrote, there were four visible. Of these four, three were outside and one inside the park wall. The other two within the park had been then closed up. When Leland wrote in 1540 to 1542, the six wells were in existence and visible; for he wrote: 'The ryver of Stoure risith ther of six fountaynes or springes, whereof 3 be on the northe side of the Parke, harde withyn the Pale, the other 3 be north also, but withoute the Parke. The Lorde Stourton giveth these 6 fountaynes yn his Armes.' Guillim says the same thing: 'These six Fountains are borne in signification of six Springs, whereof the River of Sture in Wiltshire hath his beginning, and passeth along to Sturton, the seat of that Barony.' Here, then, is the origin of the six fountains upon the coat of arms; but Aubrey remarks that three of the six springs in the park are in the county of Wilts, whereas Mr Camden has put them all in Somersetshire. However, the fact is that three of the springs were inside the park and three outside, and that three were in Wiltshire and three in Somersetshire. Here, then, is to be found the division upon the coat of arms of

243 *The Arms of Stourton.*

the six fountains in the two sets of three each, and it is by no means an improbable suggestion that the bend which separates the three from the three is typical of, or was suggested by, either the park wall or pale, or by the line of division between the two counties, and the more probable of the two seems to be the park wall. The coat of arms is just a map of the property. Now, with regard to the arms, as far as is known there has not been at any time the slightest deviation by the family of the Lords Stourton from the coat quoted and illustrated. But before leaving the subject it may be well to point out that in the few cases in which an ancient coat of arms carries with it an explanation, such explanation is usually to be found either in some such manner as that in which these arms of Stourton have been explained, or else in some palpable pun, and not in the mythical accounts and legends of supernatural occurrences which have been handed down, and seldom indeed in any explanation of personal nobility which the tinctures or charges are sometimes said to represent.

What is now considered quite a different charge from the fountain is the whirlpool or gurges, which is likewise intended to represent water, and is borne by a family of the name of Gorges, the design occupying the whole of the field. This is represented by a spiral line of azure commencing in the centre of an argent field, continuing round and round until the edges of the shield are reached; but there can be very little doubt that this was an early form of representing the watery roundle which happens to have been perpetuated in the instance of that one coat. The fountains upon the seal of the first Lord Stourton are represented in this manner.

Examples of a field semé of roundels are very usual, these being termed bezanté or platé if semé of bezants or plates; but in the cases of roundles of other colours the words 'semé of' need to be used.

The annulet

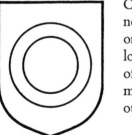

244 Annulet.

Closely akin to the roundel is the annulet (244) and though, as far as I am aware, no text-book has as yet included this in its list of ordinaries and sub-ordinaries, one can see no reason, as the annulet is a regularly used heraldic figure, why the lozenge should have been included and the annulet excluded, when the annulet is of quite as frequent occurrence. It is, as its name implies, simply a plain ring of metal or colour, as will be found in the arms of Lowther, Hutton, and many other families. Annulets appear anciently to have been termed false roundles.

Annulets will frequently be found interlaced.

Care should be taken to distinguish them from gem-rings, which are always drawn in a very natural manner with stones, which, however, in real life would approach an impossible size.

The label

The label (245) as a charge must be distinguished from the label as a mark of difference for the eldest son, though there is no doubt that in those cases in which it now exists as a charge, the origin must be traced to its earlier use as a difference.

Concerning its use as a mark of difference it will be treated of further in the chapter upon marks of difference and cadency, but as a charge it will seldom be found in any position except in chief, and not often of other than three points, and it will always be found drawn throughout, that is, with the upper line extended to the size of the field. It consists of a narrow band straight across the shield, from which depend at right angles three short bands. These shorter arms have each of late years been drawn more in the shape of a dovetail, but this was not the case until a comparatively recent period, and now-a-days we are quite as inclined to revert to the old forms as to perpetuate this modern variety. Other names for the label are the 'lambel' and the 'file'. The label is the only mark of difference now borne by the Royal Family. Every member of the Royal Family has the Royal arms assigned to him for use presumably during life, and in these warrants, which are separate and personal for each individual, both the coronet and the difference marks which are to be borne upon the label are quoted and assigned. This use of the label, however, will be subsequently fully dealt with. As a charge, the label occurs in the arms of Barrington: 'Argent, three chevronels gules, a label azure'; and Babington: 'Argent, ten torteaux, four, three, two, and one, in chief a label of three points azure'; also in the earlier form of the arms of De Quincy (235) and Courtenay (246). As a charge on the cross of St David it appears in the arms of Davidson. Various curious coats of arms in which the label appears are given in Papworth as follows:

245 *The Label.*

246 *Arms of Hugh Courtenay, Earl of Devon (d. 1422): Or, three torteaux, a label azure.
(From his seal.)*

. . . a label of four points in bend sinister . . . Wm. de Curli, 20th Hen. III. (Cotton, Julius F., vii. 175.)

Argent, a label of five points azure. Henlington, co. Gloucester. (Harl. MS. 1404, fo. 109.)

Or, a file gules, with three bells pendent azure, clappers sable. (Belfile.)

Sable, three crescents, in chief a label of two drops and in fess another of one drop argent. Fitz-Simons. (Harl. MSS. 1441 and 5866.)

Or, three files borne barways gules, the first having five points, the second four, and the last three. Liskirke, Holland. (Guillim.)

A curious label will have been noticed in the arms of De Valence (120).

The billet

The billet (247), though not often met with as a charge, does sometimes occur, as for example, in the arms of Alington and Ambrose.

Its more frequent appearance is as an object with which a field or superior charge is semé, in which case these are termed billetté (248). The best known instance of this is probably the coat borne on an inescutcheon over the arms of England during the joint reign of William and Mary. The arms of Gasceline afford another example of a field billetté. These are 'or, billetté azure, and a label gules'. Though not many instances are given under each subdivision, Papworth affords examples of coats with every number of billets from 1 to 20, but many of them, particularly some of those from 10 to 20 in number, are merely mistaken renderings of fields which should have been termed billetté. The billet, slightly widened, is sometimes known as a block, and as such will be found in the arms of Paynter. Other instances are to be found where the billets are termed delves or

247 *The Billet.*

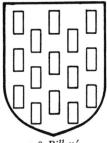

248 *Billetté.*

gads. The billet will sometimes be found pointed at the bottom, in which case it is termed 'urdy at the foot'.[62] But neither as a form of semé, nor as a charge, is the billet of sufficiently frequent use to warrant its inclusion as one of the ordinaries or sub-ordinaries.

249 Armorial bearings of R. E. Yerburgh, Esq.: Per pale argent and azure, on a chevron between three chaplets all counterchanged, an annulet for difference. Mantling azure and argent. Crest: on a wreath of the colours, a falcon close or, belled of the last preying upon a mallard proper. (LEFT)

250 Armorial bearings of Robert Berry, Esq.: Quarterly, 1 and 4, vert, a cross crosslet argent (for Berry); 2 and 3, parted per pale argent and sable, on a chaplet four mullets counterchanged (for Nairne), in the centre of the quarters a crescent or, for difference. Mantling vert, doubled argent. Crest: upon a wreath of his liveries, a demi-lion rampant gules, armed and langued, holding in his dexter paw a cross crosslet fitchée azure; and in an escroll over the same this motto, 'In hoc signo vinces,' and in another under the shield, 'L'espérance me comforte.' (RIGHT)

62. I have found no example of a billet 'urdy at the foot', but see no reason why one should not make its appearance. Likewise I have found no examples of billets drawn with any of the partition lines. The gad, which Fox-Davies equates with the billet, is really a wedge-shaped bar of steel; it occurs in the arms granted to the Ironmongers' Company of London on 1 September 1455: 'Silver a cheveron of gowles sette bytwene three gaddes of stele of Asure on the cheveron three swevells of golde.' Billets fimbriated are to be found in the arms granted to Stroud Urban District Council on 1 June 1960: vert, a bendlet wavy argent, between six billets gules, each fimbriated or. It will be noticed that the principal charge is a diminutive of an ordinary borne singly, another example that this is accepted practice.

The only example of a single billet that I have come upon is in the arms of Bostock quoted in a sixteenth-century list of arms of Herefordshire and Shropshire families; the arms are: azure, a billet fesswise argent.

The chaplet

Why the chaplet was ever included amongst the ordinaries and sub-ordinaries passes my comprehension. It is not of frequent occurrence, and I have yet to ascertain in which form it has acquired this status. The chaplet which is usually meant when the term is employed is the garland of oak, laurel, or other leaves or flowers (249), which is found more frequently as part of a crest. There is also the chaplet, which it is difficult to describe, save as a large broad annulet such as the one which figures in the arms of Nairne (250), and which is charged at four regular intervals with roses, mullets, or some other objects.

The chaplet of oak and acorns is sometimes known as a civic crown, but the term chaplet will more frequently be found giving place to the use of the word wreath, and a chaplet of laurel or roses, unless completely conjoined and figuring as a charge upon the shield, will be far more likely to be termed a wreath or garland of laurel or roses than a chaplet.

There are many other charges which have no great distinction from some of these which have been enumerated, but as nobody hitherto has classed them as ordinaries I suppose there could be no excuse for so introducing them, but the division of any heraldic charges into ordinaries and sub-ordinaries, and their separation from other figures, seems to a certain extent incomprehensible and very unnecessary.

10 · The human figure in heraldry

If we include the many instances of the human head and the human figure which exist as crests, and also the human figure as a supporter, probably it or its parts will be nearly as frequently met with in armory as the lion; but if crests and supporters be disregarded, and the human figure be simply considered as a charge upon the shield, it is by no means often to be met with.

English (but not Scottish) official heraldry now and for a long time past has set its face against the representation of any specific saint or other person in armorial bearings.[63] In many cases, however, particularly in the arms of ecclesiastical sees and towns, the armorial bearings registered are simply the conventionalised heraldic representation of seal designs dating from a very much earlier period.

Seal engravers laboured under no such limitations, and their representations were usually of some specific saint or person readily recognisable from accompanying objects. Consequently, if it be desirable, the identity of a figure in a coat of arms can often be traced in such cases by reference to a seal of early date, whilst all the time the official coat of arms goes no further than to term the figure that of a saint.

The only representation which will be found in British heraldry of the Deity is in the arms of the See of Chichester, which certainly originally represented our Lord seated in glory. Whether by intention or carelessness, this, however, is now represented and blazoned as: 'Azure, a Prester [Presbyter] John sitting on a tombstone, in his left hand a mound, his right hand extended all or, with a linen mitre on his head, and in his mouth a sword proper.' Possibly it is a corruption, but I am inclined to think it is an intentional alteration to avoid the necessity of any attempt to pictorially represent the Deity.

Christ upon the Cross, however, will be found represented in the arms of Inverness (251). The shield used by the town of Halifax has the canting 'Holy Face' upon a chequy field. This coat, however, is without authority, though it is sufficiently remarkable to quote the blazon in full: 'Chequy or and azure, a man's face with long hair and bearded and dropping blood, and surmounted by a

63. This convention was not universally adhered to, and had been broken even before Fox-Davies wrote, for on 17 August 1906 the following arms were granted to the Borough of Merthyr Tydfil: azure, a figure representing St Tydvil the Martyr, in chief two crosses paty fitchy all or. This is not an isolated example, as the arms of Christopherson of Kent are blazoned (quite inadequately, I maintain): azure, a figure representing St Christopher proper, on a chief arched argent, two crosses couped gules. In fact St Christopher is represented up to his waist in water, with the Holy Child on his shoulder carrying a red pennant charged with a silver lamb.

251 Armorial bearings of the Royal Burgh of Inverness: Gules, our Lord upon the Cross proper. Mantling gules, doubled or. Crest: upon a wreath of the proper liveries a cornucopia proper. Supporters: dexter, a dromedary; sinister, an elephant, both proper. (From a painting by Mr. Graham Johnston in Lyon Register.)

halo, all proper; in chief the letters HALEZ, and in base the letters FAX.'[64]

No other instance is known, but, on the other hand, representations of the Virgin Mary with her Babe are not uncommon. She will be found so described in the arms of the Royal Burgh of Banff. The Virgin Mary and Child appear also in the arms of the town of Leith, viz.: 'Argent, in a sea proper, an ancient galley with two masts, sails furled sable, flagged gules, seated therein the Virgin Mary with the Infant Saviour in her arms, and a cloud resting over their heads, all also proper.'

The Virgin and Child appear in the crest of Marylebone (252),[65] but in this

64. Arms have now been granted to the Corporation of Halifax. The arms, granted on 12 April 1948, are blazoned: chequy or and azure, a man's face affronty bearded and surrounded by a halo proper. Crest: issuant from a Saxon crown or, a mount vert, thereon a pascal lamb proper, holding a staff gold, flying therefrom a forked pennant also argent, charged with a cross gules. Supporters: on either side a lion or, holding with the interior paw a rose argent, barbed and seeded proper. Motto: Except the Lord keep the City.

65. The Metropolitan Borough of St Marylebone was absorbed into the City of Westminster under the terms of the London Government Act 1963, but the Virgin and Child were preserved as the principal charge in the arms granted on 2 September 1964 to the new City of Westminster. However, in spite of the change of heart regarding blazoning actual persons, they retained their anonymity. This is particularly strange, as the arms granted on 6 December 1955 to the Maria Assumpta Training College, Kensington, are blazoned: per fess or and argent, on a pale purpure, a representation of Our Lady also argent, the nimbus gold (L). This followed the precedent set in the grant to the Collegiate Church of St Mary the Virgin, Port Elizabeth, South Africa, on 24 August 1951, namely: azure, a representation of the Virgin Mary and the Holy Infant proper. It is curious that 'proper' in this case means that the Virgin is clothed in red, with a short white cloak and a blue veil. The Holy Child is naked, and the haloes are identical, that of the child not having the customary cross on it.

L Arms of Maria Assumpta Training College.

252 *Arms of Marylebone: Per chevron sable and barry wavy of six, argent and azure in chief, in the dexter a fleur-de-lis, and in the sinister a rose, both or. Crest: on a wreath of the colours, upon two bars wavy argent and azure, between as many lilies of the first, stalked and leaved vert, a female figure affronté proper, vested of the first, mantled of the second, on the left arm a child also proper, vested or, around the head of each a halo of the last. Motto: 'Fiat secundum verbum tuum.'*

case, in accordance with the modern English practice, the identity is not alluded to. The true derivation of the name from 'St Mary le Bourne' (and not 'le bon') is perpetuated in the design of the arms.

A demi-figure of the Virgin is the crest of Rutherglen;★ and the Virgin and Child figure, amongst other ecclesiastical arms, on the shields of the Sees of Lincoln ['Gules, two lions passant-guardant or; on a chief azure, the Holy Virgin and Child, sitting crowned, and bearing a sceptre of the second'], Salisbury ['Azure, the Holy Virgin and Child, with sceptre in her left hand all or'], Sodor and Man ['Argent, upon three ascents the Holy Virgin standing with her arms extended between two pillars, on the dexter whereof is a church; in base the ancient arms of Man upon an inescutcheon'], Southwell ['Sable, three fountains proper, a chief paly of three, on the first or, a stag couchant proper, on the second gules, the Virgin holding in her arms the infant Jesus, on the third also or, two staves raguly couped in cross vert'], and Tuam ['Azure, three figures erect under as many canopies or stalls of Gothic work or, their faces, hands, and legs proper; the first representing an archbishop in his pontificals; the second the Holy Virgin Mary, a circle of glory over her head, holding in her left arm the infant Jesus; and the third an angel having his dexter arm elevated, and under the sinister arm a lamb, all of the second'].

Various saints figure in different Scottish coats of arms, and amongst them will be found the following:

St Andrew, in the arms of the National Bank of Scotland, granted in 1826

★ Arms of Rutherglen: Argent, in a sea proper an ancient galley sable, flagged gules, therein two men proper, one rowing, the other furling the sail. Above the shield is placed a suitable helmet, with a mantling gules, doubled argent; and on a wreath of the proper liveries is set for crest, a demi-figure of the Virgin Mary with the Infant Saviour in her arms proper; and on a compartment below the shield, on which is an escroll containing this motto 'Ex fumo fama,' are placed for supporters, two angels proper, winged or.

['Or, the image of St Andrew with vesture vert and surcoat purpure bearing before him the cross of his martyrdom argent, all resting on the base of the second, in the dexter flank a garb gules, in the sinister a ship in full sail sable, the shield surrounded with two thistles proper, disposed in orle']; St Britius, in the arms of the Royal Burgh of Kirkcaldy ['Azur, ane abbay of three pyramids argent, each ensigned with a cross patée or. And on the reverse of the seal is insculped in a field azure the figure of St Bryse with long garments, on his head a mytre, in the dexter a fleur-de-lis, the sinister laid upon his breast all proper. Standing in ye porch of the church or abbay. Ensigned on the top as before all betwixt a descrescent and a star in fess or. The motto is "Vigilando Munio". And round the escutcheon of both sydes these words— "Sigillum civitatus Kirkaldie"']; St Columba, in the arms of the College of the Holy Spirit at Cumbræ ['Quarterly, 1 and 4 grand quarters, azure, St Columba in a boat at sea, in his sinister hand a dove, and in the dexter chief a blazing star all proper; 2 and 3 grand quarters, quarterly, i and iv, argent, an eagle displayed with two heads gules; ii and iii, parted per bend embattled gules and argent; over the second and third grand quarters an escutcheon of the arms of Boyle of Kelburne, viz. or, three stags' horns gules']; St Duthacus, in the arms of the Royal Burgh of Tain ['Gules, St Duthacus in long garments argent, holding in his dexter hand a staff garnished with ivy, in the sinister laid on his breast a book expanded proper']; St Ægidius (St Giles), in the arms of the Royal Burgh of Elgin ['Argent, Sanctus Ægidius habited in his robes and mitred, holding in his dexter hand a pastoral staff, and in his left hand a clasped book, all proper. Supporters; two angels proper, winged or volant upwards. Motto: "Sic itur ad astra," upon ane compartment suitabil to a Burgh Royal, and for their colours red and white']; St Ninian, in the arms of the Episcopal See of Galloway ['Argent, St Ninian standing and full-faced proper, clothed with a pontifical robe purple, on his head a mitre, and in his dexter hand a crosier or']; and St Adrian, in the arms of the town of Pittenweem ['Azur, in the sea a gallie with her oars in action argent, and therein standing the figure of St Adrian, with long garments close girt, and a mytre on his head proper, holding in his sinister hand a crosier or. On the stern a flag developed argent, charged with the Royall Armes of Scotland, with this word, "Deo Duce"'].

Biblical characters of the Old Testament have found favour upon the Continent, and the instances quoted by Woodward are too amusing to omit:

'The families who bear the names of saints, such as ST ANDREW, ST GEORGE, ST MICHAEL, have (perhaps not unnaturally) included in their arms representation of their family patrons.

'The Bavarian family of REIDER include in their shield the mounted effigy of the good knight ST MARTIN dividing his cloak with a beggar (date of diploma 1760). The figure of the great Apostle of the Gentiles appears in the arms of VON PAULI JOERG, and JORGER, of Austria, similarly make use of St George.

'Continental Heraldry affords not a few examples of the use of the personages of Holy Writ. The ADAMOLI of Lombardy bear: "Azure, the Tree of Life entwined with the Serpent, and accosted with our first parents, all proper" (i.e. in a state of nature). The addition of a chief of the Empire to this coat makes it somewhat incongruous.

'The family of ADAM in Bavaria improve on Sacred History by eliminating

EVE, and by representing ADAM as holding the apple in one hand, and the serpent wriggling in the other. On the other hand, the Spanish family of EVA apparently consider there is a sufficiently transparent allusion to their own name, and to the mother of mankind, in the simple bearings: "Or, on a mount in base an apple-tree vert, fructed of the field, and encircled by a serpent of the second."

'The family of ABEL in Bavaria make the patriarch in the attitude of prayer to serve as their crest; while the coat itself is: "Sable, on a square altar argent, a lamb lying surrounded by fire and smoke proper."

'SAMSON slaying the lion is the subject of the arms of the VESENTINA family of Verona. The field is gules, and on a terrace in base vert the strong man naked bestrides a golden lion and forces its jaws apart. The Polish family of SAMSON naturally use the same device, but the field is azure and the patriarch is decently habited. The STARCKENS of the Island of OESEL also use the like as *armes parlantes*; the field in this case is or. After these we are hardly surprised to find that Daniel in the lions' den is the subject of the arms of the Rhenish family of DANIELS, granted late in the eighteenth century; the field is azure. The Bolognese DANIELS are content to make a less evident allusion to the prophet; their arms are: 'per fess azure and vert, in chief "the lion of the tribe of Judah" naissant or, holding an open book with the words "LIBRI APERTI SUNT" (Daniel vii, 10).

'The Archangel ST MICHAEL in full armour, as conventionally represented, treading beneath his feet the great adversary, sable, is the charge on an azure field of the VAN SCHOREL of Antwerp.'

Other instances will be found, as St Kentigern (who is sometimes said to be the same as St Mungo), and who occurs as the crest of Glasgow: 'The half-length figure of St Kentigern affronté, vested and mitred, his right hand raised in the act of benediction, and having in his left hand a crosier, all proper'; St Michael, in the arms of Linlithgow: 'Azure, the figure of the Archangel Michael, with wings expanded, treading on the belly of a serpent lying with its tail nowed fesswise in base, all argent, the head of which he is piercing through with a spear in his dexter hand, and grasping with his sinister an escutcheon charged with the Royal Arms of Scotland. The same saint also figures in the arms of the city of Brussels; while the family of MITCHELL-CARRUTHERS bears as a crest: 'St Michael in armour, holding a spear in his dexter hand, the face, neck, arms and legs bare, all proper, the wings argent, and hair auburn.'

St Martin occurs in the arms of Dover, and he also figures, as has been already stated, on the shield of the Bavarian family of REIDER, whilst St Paul occurs as a charge in the arms of the Dutch family of VON PAULI.

The arms of the See of Clogher are: 'A Bishop in pontifical robes seated on his chair of state, and learning towards the sinister, his left hand supporting a crosier, his right pointing to the dexter chief, all or, the feet upon a cushion gules, tasselled or.'

'A curious crest will be found belonging to the arms of a family of Stewart, which is: 'A king in his robes, crowned.' The arms of the Episcopal See of Ross afford another instance of a bishop, together with St Boniface.

The arms of the town of Queensferry, in Scotland, show an instance of a queen. 'A king in his robes, and crowned,' will be found in the arms of Dartmouth ['Gules, the base barry wavy, argent and azure, thereon the hulk of a ship, in the centre of which is a king robed and crowned, and holding in his sinister hand a sceptre, at each end of the ship a lion sejant guardant all or].'

Allegorical figures, though numerous as supporters, are comparatively rare as charges upon a shield; but the arms of the University of Melbourne show a representation of the figure of Victory ['Azure, a figure intended to represent Victory, robed and attired proper, the dexter hand extended holding a wreath of laurel or, between four stars of eight points, two in pale and two in fess argent'], which also appears in other coats of arms.

The figure of Truth will be found in the coats of arms for various members of the family of Sandeman.

The bust of Queen Elizabeth was granted by that Queen, as a special mark of her Royal favour, to Sir Anthony Weldon, her Clerk of the Spicery.

Apollo is represented in the arms of the Apothecaries' Company: 'Azure, Apollo, the inventor of physic, proper, with his head radiant, holding in his left hand a bow and in his right hand an arrow or, supplanting a serpent argent.'

The figure of Justice appears in the arms of Wiergman [or Wergman].

Neptune appears in the arms granted to Sir Isaac Heard, Lancaster Herald, afterwards Garter King of Arms, and is again to be found in the crest of the arms of Monneypenny ['On a dolphin embowed, a bridled Neptune astride, holding with his sinister hand a trident over his shoulder'].

The figure of Temperance occurs in the crest of Goodfellow.

The head of St John the Baptist in a charger figures in the crest of the Tallow Chandlers' Livery Company and in the arms of Ayr, whilst the head of St Denis is the charge upon the arms of a family of that name.

Angels, though very frequently met with as supporters, are far from being usual, either as a charge upon a shield or as a crest. The crest of Leslie, however, is an angel.

The crest of Lord Kintore is an angel in a praying posture or, within an orle of laurel proper.

Cherubs are far more frequently to be met with. They are represented in various forms, and will be found in the arms of Chaloner, Thackeray, Maddocks, and in the crest of Carruthers.[66]

The nude figure is perhaps the most usual form in which the human being is made use of as a charge, and examples will be found in the arms of Wood (Lord Halifax), and in the arms of Oswald.

The arms of Dalziell show an example—practically unique in British heraldry

66. The various forms of the cherub are worth noting. Usually the cherub is depicted as a child's face between two wings displayed. Sometimes these wings are inverted, as in the arms confirmed to John Ade of Doddington, Co. Kent, on 20 May 11 James I; here the arms are blazoned: azure, a fess indented between three 'cherubyns' or, their faces argent. On the other hand, a very different sort of cherub occurs in the arms of the United Grand Lodge of Ancient Free and Accepted Masons of England granted by Royal Warrant on 13 June 1919. Here the crest is blazoned: a representation of an ark, supported on either side by a cherub, with the motto over in Hebrew characters, 'Holiness to the Lord', and the supporters of the arms consist of a cherub on either side. In this case the cherubim are shown as humans of indeterminate sex with wings in place of arms and the lower parts of an ox-like creature. Cherubim are variously described in the Bible and equally diversely depicted in Jewish and Christian art; it is therefore a little confusing that one term of blazon should be used to describe such very different creatures.

—of a naked man, the earliest entry (1685) of the arms of Dalziell of Binns (a cadet of the family) in the Lyon Register, having them then blazoned: 'Sable, a naked man with his arms extended *au naturel*, on a canton argent, a sword and pistol disposed in saltire proper.'

This curious coat of arms has been the subject of much speculation. The fact that in some early examples the body is swinging from a gibbet has led some to suppose the arms to be an allusion to the fact, or legend, that one of the family recovered the body of Kenneth III, who had suffered death by hanging at the hands of the Picts. But it seems more likely that if the gibbet is found in any authoritative versions of the arms possibly the coat may owe its origin to a similar reason to that which is said, and probably correctly, to account for the curious crest of the Davenport family, viz.: 'A man's head in profile couped at the shoulders proper, about the neck a rope or,' or as it is sometimes termed, 'a felon's head proper, about the neck a halter or'. There was in the possession of the Capesthorne branch of the Davenport family a long and very ancient roll, containing the names of the master robbers captured and beheaded in the times of Koran, Roger, and Thomas de Davenport, and probably the Davenport family held some office or Royal Commission which empowered them to deal in a summary way with the outlaws which infested the Peak country. It is more than probable that the crest of Davenport should be traced to some such source as this, and I suggest the possibility of a similar origin for the arms of Dalziell.

As a crest the savage and demi-savage are constantly occurring. They are in heraldry distinguished by the garlands of leaves about either or both loins and temples.

Men in armour are sometimes met with. The arms of O'Loghlen are an instance in point, as are the crests of Marshall, Morse, Bannerman, and Seton of Mounie.

Figures of all nationalities and in all costumes will be found in the form of supporters, and occasionally as crests, but it is difficult to classify them, and it must suffice to mention a few curious examples. The human figure as a supporter is fully dealt with in the chapter devoted to that subject.

The arms of Jedburgh have a mounted warrior, and the same device occurs in the crest of the Earls and Duke of Fife, and in the arms of Lanigen-O'Keefe.

The arms of Londonderry afford an instance of a skeleton.

The emblematical figure of Fortune is a very favourite charge in foreign heraldry.

A family of the name of Rodd use the Colossus of Rhodes as a crest: and the arms of Sir William Dunn, Bart., are worth the passing mention ['Azure, on a mount in base a bale of wool proper, thereon seated a female figure representing Commerce, vested argent, resting the dexter hand on a stock of an anchor, and in the sinister a caduceus, both or, on the chief of the last a tree eradicated, thereon hanging a hunting-horn between a thistle slipped proper on the dexter and a fleur-de-lis azure on the sinister. Crest: a cornucopia fesswise, surmounted by a dexter hand couped proper, holding a key in bend sinister or. Motto: "Vigilans et audax".'].

The crests of Vivian ['A demi-hussar of the 18th Regiment, holding in his right hand a sabre, and in his left a pennon flying to the sinister gules, and inscribed in gold letters, "Croix d'Orade", issuant from a bridge of one arch, embattled, and at each end a tower'], and Macgregor ['two brass guns in saltire in front of a demi-Highlander armed with his broadsword, pistols, and with a target, thereon the family arms of Macgregor', viz.: 'Argent: a sword in bend dexter azure, and an oak-tree eradicated in bend sinister proper, in the dexter chief an antique crown gules, and upon an escroll surmounting the crest the motto, "E'en do and spare not"'] are typical of many crests of augmentation and quasi-augmentation granted in the early part of the nineteenth century.

The crest of the Devonshire family of Arscot ['A demi-man affronté in a Turkish habit, brandishing in his dexter hand a scimitar, and his sinister hand resting on a tiger's head issuing from the wreath'] is curious, as is the crest granted by Sir William Le Neve in 1642 to Sir Robert Minshull, viz.: 'A Turk kneeling on one knee, habited gules, legs and arms in mail proper, at the side a scymitar sable, hilted or, on the head a turban with a crescent and feather argent, holding in the dexter hand a crescent of the last.'

The crest of Pilkington ['a mower with his scythe in front habited as follows: a high-crowned hat with flap, the crown party per pale, flap the same, counterchanged; coat buttoned to the middle, with his scythe in bend proper, habited through quarterly and counterchanged argent and gules'], and the very similar crest of De Trafford, in which the man holds a flail, are curious, and are the subjects of appropriate legends.

The crest of Clerk of Pennycuick (a demi-man winding a horn) refers to the curious tenure by which the Pennycuick estate is supposed to be held, namely, that whenever the sovereign sets foot thereupon, the proprietor must blow a horn from a certain rocky point. The motto, 'Free for a blast', has reference to the same.

The arms of the College of Surgeons in Edinburgh, I fancy, afford the only instance of what is presumably a corpse, the blazon being: 'Azure, a man (human body) fesswise between a dexter hand having an eye on the palm issuing out of a cloud downward and a castle situate on a rock proper, within a bordure or charged with several instruments peculiar to the art (sic); on a canton of the first a saltire argent surmounted of a thistle vert, crowned of the third.'

When we come to parts of the human body instances of heads, arms, and legs are legion.

There are certain well-known heraldic heads, and though many instances occur where the blazon is simply a 'man's head', it will be most frequently found that it is more specifically described.

Sloane Evans in his *Grammar of Heraldry* specifies eight different varieties, namely: 1. The wild man's; 2. The Moor's; 3. The Saracen's; 4. The Saxon's; 5. The Englishman's; 6. The old man's; 7. The woman's; 8. The child's.

The wild man's or savages' head is usually represented with a wreath of leaves about the temples, but not necessarily so (253).

The head of the Moor, or 'blackamoor', as it is more usually described, is almost always in profile, and very frequently adorned with a twisted wreath (torse) about the temples (254).

The head of the Saracen is also usually found with wreaths about the temples (255).

The head of the Saxon is borne by several Welsh families, and is supposed to be known by the absence of a beard.

253 A savage's head.

254 A blackamoor's head.

255 A Saracen's head.

256 A woman's head and bust.

The Englishman's head, which is borne by the Welsh family of Lloyd of Plymog, has no very distinctive features, except that whilst the hair and beard of the savage are generally represented brown, they are black in the case of the Moor and Saracen, and fair for the Saxon and Englishman.

The old man's head, which, like that of the Saxon and Englishman, is seldom met with, is bald and grey-haired and bearded.

But for all practical purposes these varieties may be all disregarded except the savage's (253), the blackamoor's (254), and the Saracen's (255). Examples of the savage's head will be found in the arms of Eddington of Balbartan ['Azure, three savages' heads couped argent'], in the arms of Gladstone, and in the canting coat of Rochead of Whitsonhill ['Argent, a savage's head erased, distilling drops of blood proper, between three combs azure']. Moir of Otterburn bears the Moors' heads ['Argent, three negroes' heads couped proper within a bordure counter-indented sable and or'], and Moir of Stonniwood matriculated a somewhat similar coat in which the heads are termed Mauritanian ['Argent, three Mauritanian negroes' heads couped and distilling guttés-de-sang']. Alderson of Homerton, Middlesex, bears Saracens' heads ['Argent, three Saracens' heads affronté, couped at the shoulders proper, wreathed about the temples of the first and sable'].

The woman's head (256) in heraldry is always represented young and beautiful (that is, if the artist is capable of so drawing it), and it is almost invariably found with golden hair. The colour, however, should be blazoned, the term 'crined' being used. Five maidens' heads appear upon the arms of the town of Reading, and the crest of Thornhill shows the same figure. The arms of the Mercers' Livery Company ['Gules, a demi-virgin couped below the shoulders, issuing from clouds all proper, vested or, crowned with an Eastern crown of the last, her hair dishevelled, and wreathed round the temples with roses of the second, all within an orle of clouds proper'[67]] and of the Master of the Revels in Scotland ['Argent, a lady rising out of a cloud in the nombril point, richly apparelled, on her head a garland of ivy, holding in her right hand a poinziard crowned, in her left a vizard all proper, standing under a veil or canopy azure, garnished or, in base a thistle vert'] are worthy of quotation.

The boy's head will seldom be found except in Welsh coats, of which the arms of Vaughan and Price are examples.

Another case in which the heads of children appear are the arms of Fauntleroy ['Gules, three infants' heads couped at the shoulders proper, crined or'], which are a very telling instance of a canting device upon the original form of the name, which was 'Enfantleroy'.

M Arms of Mercers' Company.

67. As there was no extant patent granting arms to the Mercers' Company, Fox-Davies' blazon is only an attempt to describe a popular version of the arms used by the Company and entered in several of the Visitations of London. However, on 2 April 1911, the arms of the Company were blazoned in a confirmation which also embodied the grant of a crest. The arms should now properly be blazoned: gules, issuant from a bank of clouds a figure of the Virgin couped at the shoulders proper, vested in a crimson robe adorned with gold, the neck encircled by a jewelled necklace, crined or and wreathed about the temples with a chaplet of roses alternately argent and of the first, and crowned with a celestial crown, the whole within a bordure of clouds also proper (M). The crest is: on a wreath of the colours, issuant from a bank of clouds proper, a figure of the Virgin as in the arms.

257 *A dexter hand.*

258 *A sinister hand.*

259 *A hand 'in benediction'.*

260 *A cubit arm.*

261 *An arm couped at the elbow.*

262 *An arm embowed.*

263 *An arm embowed to the dexter.*

264 *An arm embowed fesseways.*

265 *An arm embowed the upper part in fesse.*

266 *Two arms counter-embowed.*

Children, it may be here noted, are seldom met with in armory, but instances will be found in the arms of Davies, of Marsh, co. Salop ['Sable, a goat argent, attired or, standing on a child proper swaddled gules, and feeding on a tree vert'], of the Foundling Hospital ['Per fesse azure and vert, in chief a crescent argent, between two mullets of six points or, in base an infant exposed, stretching out its arms for help proper'], and in the familiar 'bird and bantling' crest of Stanley, Earls of Derby.[68] Arms and hands are constantly met with, and have certain terms of their own. A hand should be stated to be either dexter (257), or sinister (258), and is usually blazoned and always understood to be couped at the wrist. If the hand is open and the palm visible it 'apaumé' (257 and 258), but this being by far the most usual position in which the hand is met with, unless represented to be holding anything, the term 'apaumé' is not often used in blazon, that position being presumed unless anything contrary is stated.

The hand is occasionally represented 'clenched', as in the arms and crest of Fraser-Mackintosh. When the thumb and first two fingers are raised, they are said to be 'raised in benediction' (259).

68. A curious instance of a naked child appearing in arms occurs in the grant made to William Sitlington on 2 December 1748. The arms are blazoned: azure, on the ecliptic circle (shown as a fess enarched) or, the sign libra sable, in chief a terrestrial globe in a stand all proper and in base on a mount vert, a male child extended in bend sinister (proper) (N). This grant is unusual, inasmuch as it recites the reasons why the charges were selected. The grant, referring to the original petition, states: 'That your petitioner's father John Sitlington lived at Wigton and that his mother, coming thro' the Forest of Westwood to Wigton aforesaid, fell in Labour, and was there On the Twenty first Day of July One Thousand Seven Hundred and Twenty two, at Six of the Clock in the Afternoon, delivered of the said William Sitlington . . . and that in regard to such an Accident he is desirous to have some Mark in his Arms to commemorate the same to Posterity as likewise to denote his Travels, having been round the greatest part of the Globe. Whereby he hath acquired a sufficient Competency to support the Condition of a Gentleman.'

N *Arms of Sitlington.*

131

267 *Two arms counter-embowed and interlaced.*

268 *A cubit arm habited.*

269 *An arm embowed in armour.*

270 *A cubit arm in armour, the hand in a gauntlet.*

The cubit arm (260), should be carefully distinguished from the arm couped at the elbow (261). The former includes only about two-thirds of the entire arm from the elbow. The form 'couped at the elbow' is not frequently met with.

When the whole arm from the shoulder is used, it is always bent at the elbow, and this is signified by the term 'embowed', and an arm embowed necessarily includes the whole arm. 262 shows the usual position of an arm embowed, but it is sometimes placed embowed to the dexter (263), upon the point of the elbow, that is, 'embowed fesseways' (264), and also, but still more infrequently, resting on the upper arm (265). Either of the latter positions must be specified in the blazon. Two arms 'counter-embowed' occur in many crests (266 and 267).

When the arm is bare it is termed 'proper'. When clothed it is termed either 'vested' or 'habited' (268). The cuff is very frequently of a different colour, and the crest is then also termed 'cuffed'. The hand is nearly always bare, but if not represented of flesh colour it will be presumed and termed to be 'gloved' of such and such a tincture. When it is represented in armour it is termed 'in armour' or 'vambraced' (269). Even when in armour the hand is usually bare, but if in a gauntlet this must be specifically so stated (270). The armour is always represented as riveted *plate* armour unless it is specifically stated to be *chain armour*, as in the crest of Bathurst, or *scale armour*. Armour is sometimes decorated with gold, when the usual term employed will be 'garnished or', though occasionally the word 'purfled' is used.[69]

Gloves are occasionally met with as charges, *e.g.* in the arms of Barttelot. Gauntlets will be found in the arms of Vane.

Legs are not so frequently met with as arms. They will be found, however, in the arms of the Isle of Man and the families Gillman, Bower, Legg, and as the crest of Eyre. Boots will be found in the crests of various families of the name of Hussey.[70]

Bones occur in the arms of Scott-Gatty and Baines.

A skull occurs in the crest of Græme ['Two arms issuing from a cloud erected and lighting up a man's skull encircled with two branches of palm, over the head a marquess's coronet, all proper'].

A woman's breast occurs in the canting arms of Dodge (Plate VI) ['Barry of six or and sable, on a pale gules, a woman's breast distilling drops of milk proper. Crest: upon a wreath of the colours, a demi sea-dog azure, collared, maned, and finned or'].

An eye occurs in the crest of Blount of Maple-Durham ['On a wreath of the colours, the sun in splendour charged in the centre with an eye all proper'].

The man-lion, the merman, mermaid, melusine, satyr, satyral, harpy, sphinx, centaur, sagittarius, and werewolf are included in the chapter upon mythical animals.

69. The term 'purfled' is more frequently, and perhaps more accurately, used in connection with borders, trimmings and embroidery on cloth, particularly sleeves.

70. Not unexpectedly, boots also occur in the arms of the founder of Boot's Pure Drug Company, Sir Jesse Boot, later Lord Trent (title extinct 1956). The original arms were: argent, a chevron between three boots sable, soles, heels and tops gules. Crest: a boot as in the arms. These arms were later altered to: argent, on a chevron between three boots sable, soles and heels gules, spurred proper, a lion passant or. Crest: a boot as in the arms.

11 · The heraldic lion

Heraldic art without the lion would not amount to very much, for no figure plays such an important or such an extensive part in armory as the lion, in one or other of its various positions. These present-day positions are the results of modern differentiation, arising from the necessity of a larger number of varying coats of arms; but there can be little doubt that in early times the majority of these positions did not exist, having been gradually evolved, and that originally the heraldic animal was just 'a lion'. The shape of the shield was largely a governing factor in the manner in which we find it depicted; the old artists, with a keener artistic sense than is evidenced in so many later examples of heraldic design, endeavoured to fill up as large a proportion of the space available as was possible, and consequently when only one lion was to be depicted upon the shield they very naturally drew the animal in an upright position, this being the one most convenient and adaptable for their purpose. Probably their knowledge of natural history was very limited, and this upright position would seem to them the most natural, and probably was the only one they knew; at any rate, at first it is almost the only position to be found. A curious commentary upon this may be deduced from the head-covering of Geoffrey of Anjou (28), which shows a lion. This lion is identically of the form and shape of the lions rampant upon the shield, but from the nature of the space it occupies, is what would now be termed statant; but there is at the same time no such alteration in the relative position of the limbs as would now be required. This would seem to indicate very clearly that there was but the one stereotyped pattern of a lion, which answered all their purposes, and that our forerunners applied that one pattern to the spaces they desired to decorate.

Early heraldry, however, when the various positions came into recognised use, soon sought to impose this definite distinction, that the *lion* could only be depicted erect in the *rampant* position, and that an animal represented to be walking must therefore be a *leopard* from the very position which it occupied. This, however, was a distinction known only to the more pedantic heralds, and found greatest favour amongst the French; but we find in Glover's Roll, which is a copy of a roll originally drawn up about the year 1250, that whilst he gives lions to six of the English earls, he commences with 'le Roy d'Angleterre porte, Gules, trois lupards d'or'. On the other hand, the monkish chronicler John of Harmoustier in Touraine (a contemporary writer) relates that when Henry I chose Geoffrey, son of Foulk, Earl of Anjou, Touraine, and Main, to be his son-in-law, by marrying him to his only daughter and heir, Maud the Empress, and made him knight; after the bathing and other solemnities (pedes ejus solutaribus in superficie Leonculos aureos habentibus muniuntur), boots embroidered with golden lions were drawn on his legs, and also that (Clypeus Leonculos aureos imaginarios habens collo ejus suspenditur) a shield with lions of gold therein was hung about his neck.

271 *Shield, helmet and crest of Edward the Black Prince, suspended over his tomb in Canterbury Cathedral.*

It is, therefore, evident that the refinement of distinction between a lion and a leopard was not of the beginning; it is a later addition to the earlier simple term of lion. This distinction having been invented by French heralds, and we taking so much of our heraldry, our language, and our customs from France, adopted, and to a certain extent used, this description of lions passant as 'leopards'. There can be no doubt, however, that the lions passant guardant upon the English shield have always been represented as *lions*, no matter what they may have been called, and the use of the term leopard in heraldry to signify a certain position for the lion never received any extensive sanction, and has long since become obsolete in British armory. In French blazon, however, the old distinction is still observed,

134

and it is curious to observe that on the coins of the Channel Islands the shield of arms distinctly showed three leopards. The French lion is our lion rampant, the French leopard is our lion passant guardant, whilst they term our lion passant a *léopard-lionné*, and our lion rampant guardant is their *lion-léopardé*.

A lion rampant and any other beast of prey is usually represented in heraldry with the tongue and claws of a different colour from the animal. If it is not itself gules, its tongue and claws are usually represented as of that colour, unless the lion be on a field of gules. They are then represented azure, the term being 'armed and langued' of such and such a colour. It is not necessary to mention that a lion is 'armed and langued' in the blazon when tongue and claws are emblazoned in gules, but whenever any other colour is introduced for the purpose it is better that it should be specified. Outside British heraldry a lion is always supposed to be rampant unless otherwise specifically described. The earliest appearance of the lions in the arms of any member of the Royal Family in England would appear to be the seal of King John when he was Prince and before he ascended the throne. This seal shows his arms to be two lions passant.[71] The English Royal crest, which originated with Richard I, is now always depicted as a lion statant guardant. There can be no doubt, however, that this guardant attitude is a subsequent derivation from the position of the lions on the shield, when heraldry was ceasing to be actual and becoming solely pictorial. We find in the case of the crest of Edward the Black Prince, now suspended over his tomb in Canterbury Cathedral, that the lion upon the chapeau looks straight forward over the front of the helm (see 271).

Another ancient rule belonging to the same period as the controversy between leopards and lions was that there cannot be more than *one lion* upon a shield, and this was one of the great arguments used to determine that the charges on the Royal Arms of England must be leopards and not lions. It was admitted as a rule of British armory to a limited extent, viz., that when two or more lions rampant appeared upon the same shield, unless combatant, they were always formerly described as lioncels. Thus the arms of Bohun are: 'Azure, a bend argent, cottised between six lioncels rampant or.' British heraldry has, however, long since disregarded any such rule (if any definite rule ever really existed upon the point), though curiously enough in the recent grant of arms to the town of Warrington the animals are there blazoned six 'lioncels'.

The artistic evolution of the lion rampant can be readily traced in the examples and explanations which follow, but, as will be understood, the employment in the case of some of these models cannot strictly be said to be confined within a certain number of years, though the details and periods given are roughly accurate, and sufficiently so to typify the changes which have occurred.

Until perhaps the second half of the thirteenth century the body of the lion appears straight upright, so that the head, the trunk, and the left hind-paw fall into the angle of the shield. The left fore-paw is horizontal, the right fore- and the right hind-paw are placed diagonally (or obliquely) upwards (272). The paws each end in three knobs, similar to a clover-leaf, out of which the claws come

272.

273.

274.

71. The reference would seem to be to John's seal as 'Comes Moritonie' (i.e. Count of Mortiagne). In Samuel Stebbing's edition of Francis Sandford's *A Genealogical History of the Kings and Queens of England*, etc. there is a mention of this seal affixed to three grants made by John as Count of Mortaigne.

276.

275 *Arms of Strange and Talbot. (From a design for a banner.)*

277 *Lions. (Drawn by Mr J. Forbes Nixon.)*

278 *Lion passant guardant.*
(By Mr G. Scruby.)

279 *Lion rampant. (By Mr G. Scruby.)*

forth. The fourth or inferior toes appeared in heraldry somewhat later. The jaws are closed or only very slightly opened, without the tongue being visible. The tail is thickened in the middle with a bunch of longer hair and is turned down towards the body.

In the course of the period lasting from the second half of the thirteenth to the second half of the fourteenth centuries, the right hind-paw sinks lower until it forms a right angle with the left. The mouth grows pointed, and in the second half of the period the tongue becomes visible. The tail also shows a knot near its root (273).

In examples taken from the second half of the fourteenth century and the fifteenth century the lion's body is no longer placed like a pillar, but lays its head back to the left so that the right fore-paw falls into an oblique upward line with the trunk. The toes are lengthened, appearing almost as fingers, and spread out from one another; the tail, adorned with flame-like bunches of hair, strikes outwards and loses the before-mentioned knot, which only remains visible in a forked tail (*queue-fourché*). The jaws grow deep and are widely opened, and the breast rises and expands under the lower jaw (274).

280 *Lion rampant.
and lion statant guardant,
by Mr G. W. Eve.
(From Decorative
Heraldry.)*

Lions of peculiar virility and beauty appear upon a fourteenth-century banner which shows the arms of the family of Talbot, Earls of Shrewsbury: Gules, a lion rampant within a bordure engrailed or, quartered with the arms of *Strange*: Argent, two pions passant in pale gules, armed and langued azure. 275 gives the lower half of the banner, which was published in colours in the Catalogue of the Heraldic Exhibition in London, 1894.

276 is an Italian coat of arms of the fourteenth century, and shows a lion of almost exactly the same design, except the paws are here rendered somewhat more heraldically. The painting (azure, a lion rampant argent) served as an 'Ex libris', and bears the inscription 'Libe accusacionum mey p. he . . .' (The remainder has been cut away. It is reproduced from Warnecke's *German Bookplates*, 1890.)

When we come to modern examples of lions, it is evident that the artists of the present day very largely copy lions which are really the creations of, or adaptations from, the work of their predecessors. The lions of the late Mr Forbes Nixon, as shown in 277, which were specially drawn by him at my request as typical of his style, are respectively as follows:

A winged lion passant coward. A lion rampant regardant. A lion rampant queue-fourché. A lion passant crowned. A lion passant. A lion rampant. A lion rampant to the sinister. A lion passant guardant, ducally gorged. A lion statant guardant, ducally crowned. A lion rampant. A lion statant guardant. A lion sejant guardant erect. Lions drawn by Mr Scruby will be found in 278 and 279, which are respectively: 'Argent, a lion rampant sable', 'Sable, a lion passant guardant argent', and 'Sable, a lion rampant argent'. These again were specially drawn by Mr Scruby as typical of his style.

The lions of the late Mr Eve would seem to be entirely original. Their singularly graceful form and proportions are perhaps best shown by 280 and 281, which are taken from his book *Decorative Heraldry*.

The lions of Mr Graham Johnston can be appreciated from the examples in 284–9.

Examples of lions drawn by Miss Helard will be found in 282, 283.

281 *Lion statant,
lion passant guardant,
and lion passant regardant,
by Mr G. W. Eve. (From
Decorative Heraldry.)*

282 *A lion rampant.*
(By Miss Helard.)

283 *A lion rampant.*
(By Miss Helard.)

284 *Lion rampant.*

285 *Lion rampant*
guardant.

The various positions which modern heraldry has evolved for the lions, together with the terms of blazon used to describe these positions, are as follows, and the differences can best be appreciated from a series drawn by the same artist, in this case Mr Graham Johnston:

Lion rampant. The animal is here depicted in profile, and erect, resting upon its sinister hind-paw (see 284).

Lion rampant guardant. In this case the head of the lion is turned to face the spectator (285).

Lion rampant regardant. In this case the head is turned completely round, looking backwards (286).

Lion rampant double-queued. In this case the lion is represented as having two tails (287). These must both be apparent from the base of the tail, otherwise confusion will arise with the next example.

Lion rampant queue-fourché. In this case one tail springs from the base, which is divided or 'forked' in the centre (288). There is no doubt that whilst in modern times and with regard to modern arms this distinction must be adhered to, anciently queue-fourché and double-queued were interchangeable terms.

Lion rampant tail nowed. The tail is here tied in a knot (289). It is not a term very frequently met with.

Lion rampant tail elevated and turned over its head. The only instances of the existence of this curious variation (290) which have come under my own notice occur in the coats of two families of the name of Buxton, the one being obviously a modern grant founded upon the other.

Lion rampant with two heads. This occurs (291) in the coat of arms, probably founded on an earlier instance, granted in 1739 to Mason of Greenwich, the arms being: 'Per fess ermine and azure, a lion rampant with two heads counterchanged.' This curious charge had been adopted by Mason's College in Birmingham, and on the foundation of Birmingham University it was incorporated in its arms.

Lion rampant guardant bicorporated. In this case the lion has one head and two bodies. An instance of this curious creature occurs in the arms of Attewater, but I am not aware of any modern instance of its use.

Lion rampant tricorporate. In this case three bodies are united in one head (292). Both this and the preceding variety are most unusual, but the tricorporate lion occurs in a coat of arms (*temp.* Car. II) registered in Ulster's Office: 'Or, a tricorporate lion rampant, the bodies disposed in the dexter and sinister chief points and in base, all meeting in one head guardant in the fess point sable.'

Lion coward. In this case the tail of the lion is depressed, passing between its hind legs (293). The exactitude of this term is to some extent modern. Though a lion cowarded was known in ancient days, there can be no doubt that formerly an artist felt himself quite at liberty to put the tail between the legs if this seemed artistically desirable, without necessarily having interfered with the arms by so doing.

Lion couped in all its joints is a charge which seems peculiar to the family of Maitland, and it would be interesting to learn to what source its origin can be traced. It is represented with each of its four paws, its head and its tail severed from the body, and removed slightly away therefrom. A Maitland coat of arms exhibiting this peculiarity will be found in 294.

286 *Lion rampant regardant.*

287 *Lion rampant doubled queued.*

288 *Lion rampant queue-fourché.*

289 *Lion rampant, tail nowed.*

290 *Lion rampant, tail elevated and turned over its head.*

291 *Lion rampant, with two heads.*

292 *Tricorporate lion.*

293 *Lion coward.*

295 *Two lions rampant combatant.*

294 *Armorial bearings of Alexander Charles Richards Maitland, Esq.: Or, a lion rampant gules, coupled in all his joints of the field, within a double tressure flory and counterflory azure, a bordure engrailed ermine. Mantling gules and or. Crest: upon a wreath of his liveries, a lion sejant erect and affronté gules, holding in his dexter paw a sword proper, hilted and pommelled gold, and in his sinister a fleur-de-lis argent. Motto: 'Consilio et animis.'*

296 *Lion passant.*

Lions rampant combatant are so termed when two are depicted in one shield facing each other in the attitude of fighting (295).

A very curious and unique instance of a lion rampant occurs in the arms of Williams (matriculated in Lyon Register in 1862, as the second and third quarterings of the arms of Sir James Williams Drummond of Hawthornden, Bt.), the coat in question being: Argent, a lion rampant, the body sable, the head, paws, and tuft of the tail of the field.

Lion passant. A lion in this position (296) is represented in the act of walking, the dexter forepaw being raised, but all three others being upon the ground.

Lion passant guardant. This (297) is the same as the previous position, except that the head is turned to face the spectator. The lions in the quartering for England in the Royal coat of arms are 'three lions passant guardant in pale'.

Lion of England. This is 'a lion passant guardant or', and the term is only employed for a lion of this description when it occurs as or in an honourable

139

297 Lion passant guardant.

298 Lion passant regardant.

299 Lion passant guardant, dimidiated with the hulk of a ship.

300 Lion statant.

301 Lion statant tail extended.

augmentation, then being usually represented on a field of gules. A lion passant guardant or is now never granted to any applicant except under a specific Royal Warrant to that effect.[72] It occurs in many augmentations, *e.g.* Wolfe, Camperdown, and many others; and when three lions passant guardant in pale or upon a canton gules are granted, as in the arms of Lane (Plate II), the augmentation is termed a 'canton of England'.

Lion passant regardant is as the lion passant, but with the head turned right round looking behind (298). A lion is not often met with in this position.

Lions passant dimidiated. A curious survival of the ancient but now obsolete practice of dimidiation is found in the arms of several English seaport towns. Doubtless all can be traced to the 'so-called' arms of the 'Cinque Ports', which show three lions passant guardant dimidiated with the hulks of three ships. There can be no doubt whatever that this originally came from the dimidiation of two separate coats, viz. the Royal Arms of England (the three lions passant guardant), and the other 'azure, three ships argent', typical of the Cinque Ports, referring perhaps to the protection of the coasts for which they were liable, or possibly merely to their seaboard position. Whilst Sandwich* uses the two separate coats simply dimidiated upon one shield, the arms of Hastings vary slightly, being: 'Party per pale gules and azure, a lion passant guardant or, between in chief and in base a lion passant guardant of the last dimidiated with the hulk of a ship argent.' From long usage we have grown accustomed to consider these two conjoined and dimidiated figures as one figure (299), and in the grant of arms to Ramsgate† a figure of this kind was granted as a simple charge.

The arms of Yarmouth‡ afford another instance of a resulting figure of this class, the three lions passant guardant of England being here dimidiated with as many herrings naiant.

Lion statant. The distinction between a lion passant and a lion statant is that the lion statant has all four paws resting upon the ground. The two forepaws are usually placed together (300). Whilst but seldom met with as a charge upon a shield, the lion statant is by no means rare as a crest.

Lion statant tail extended. This term is a curious and, seemingly, a purposeless refinement, resulting from the perpetuation in certain cases of one particular method of depicting the crest—originally when a crest a lion was always so drawn—but it cannot be overlooked, because in the crests of both Talbot, Earl of Shrewsbury, and Percy, Duke of Northumberland, the crest is now stereotyped as a lion in this form (301) upon a chapeau.

72. This may have been true at the time Fox-Davies wrote, but recent grants show that the lion passant guardant or is now granted without a Royal Licence. It occurs in the arms of Ampthill Rural District Council (1957), Bridgnorth (1958), Llandudno Urban District Council (1959), where it is on a red field, and other local authorities.

* Arms of Sandwich: Party per pale gules and azure, three demi-lions passant guardant or, conjoined to the hulks of as many ships argent.

† Arms of Ramsgate: Quarterly gules and azure, a cross parted and fretty argent between a horse rampant of the last in the first quarter, a demi-lion passant guardant of the third conjoined to the hulk of a ship or in the second, a dolphin naiant proper in the third, and a lymphad also or in the fourth. Crest: a naval crown or, a pier-head, thereon a lighthouse, both proper. Motto: 'Salus naufragis salus ægris.'

‡ Arms of Yarmouth: Party per pale gules and azure, three demi-lions passant guardant or, conjoined to the bodies of as many herrings argent. Motto: 'Rex et nostra jura.'

Lion statant guardant (302). This (crowned) is of course the Royal crest of England, and examples of it will be found in the arms of the Sovereign and other descendants, legitimate and illegitimate, of Sovereigns of this country. An exceptionally fine rendering of it occurs in the Windsor Castle bookplates executed by Mr G. W. Eve.

Lion salient. This, which is a very rare position for a lion, represents it in the act of springing, the *two* hind legs being on the ground, the others in the air (303).

Lion salient guardant. There is no reason why the lion salient may not be guardant or regardant, though an instance of the use of either does not come readily to mind.[73]

Lion sejant. Very great laxity is found in the terms applied to lions sejant, consequently care is necessary to distinguish the various forms. The true lion sejant is represented in profile, seated on its haunches, with the forepaws resting on the ground (304).

Lion sejant guardant. This is as the foregoing, but with the face (only) turned to the spectator (305).

Lion sejant regardant. In this the head is turned right back to gaze behind (306).

Lion sejant erect (or, as it is sometimes not very happily termed, *sejant-rampant*). In this position the lion is sitting upon its haunches, but the body is erect, and it has its forepaws raised in the air (307).

Lion sejant guardant erect is as the last figure, but the head faces the spectator (308).

Lion sejant regardant erect is as the foregoing, but with the head turned right round to look backwards (309).

Lion sejant affronté. In this case the lion is seated on its haunches, but *the whole body* is turned to face the spectator, the forepaws resting upon the ground in front of its body. Ugly as this position is, and impossible as it might seem, it certainly is to be found in some of the early rolls.

Lion sejant erect affronté (294). This position is by no means unusual in Scotland. A lion sejant erect and affronté, &c., is the Royal crest of Scotland, and it will also be found in the arms of Lyon Office.

A good representation of the lion sejant affronté and erect is shown in 310, which is taken from Jost Amman's *Wappen und Stammbuch* (1589). It represents the arms of the celebrated Lansquenet Captain Sebastian Schärtlin (Schertel) von Burtenbach ['Gules, a lion sejant affronté erect, double-queued, holding in its dexter paw a key argent and in its sinister a fleur-de-lis]. His victorious assault on Rome in 1527, and his striking successes against France in 1532, are strikingly typified in these arms, which were granted in 1534.

Lion couchant. In this position the lion is represented lying down, but the head is erect and alert (311).

Lion dormant. A lion dormant is in much the same position as a lion couchant, except that the eyes are closed, and the head rests upon the extended forepaws (312). Lions dormant are seldom met with, but they occur in the arms of Lloyd, of Stockton Hall, near York.

73. The only example that I have found is contained in a grant made to Benjamin Inglish, formerly Benjamin Hanson on 25 June 1800. He was granted for Inglish: azure, a lion salient guardant argent, in chief three mullets or.

302 *Lion statant guardant.*

303 *Lion salient.*

304 *Lion sejant.*

305 *Lion sejant guardant.*

306 *Lion sejant regardant.*

307 *Lion sejant erect.*

308 *Lion sejant guardant erect.*

309 *Lion sejant regardant erect.*

O *Crest of Metcalfe.*

P *Crest of Blunte.*

Lion morné. This is a lion without teeth and claws, but no instance of the use of the term would appear to exist in British armory. Woodward mentions amongst other Continental examples the arms of the old French family of De Mornay ['Fascé d'argent et de gueules au lion morné de sable, couronné d'or brochant sur le tout'].

Lions as supporters. Refer to the chapter on Supporters.

Winged lion. The winged lion—usually known as the lion of St Mark—is not infrequently met with. It will be found both passant and sejant, but more frequently the latter (313). The true lion of St Mark (that is, when used as a badge for sacred purposes to typify St Mark) has a halo. Winged lions are the supporters of Lord Braye.

Sea lion (or, to use another name for it, a *morse*) is the head, fore-paws, and upper part of a lion conjoined to the tail of a fish. The most frequent form in which sea lions appear are as supporters, but they are also met with as crests and charges. When placed horizontally they are termed naiant. Sea lions, however, will also be found 'sejant' and 'sejant-erect' (314). When issuing from waves of the sea they are termed 'assurgeant'.[74]

Lion-dragon. One hesitates to believe that this creature has any existence outside heraldry books, where it is stated to be of similar form and construction to the sea lion, the difference being that the lower half is the body and tail of a wyvern. I know of no actual arms or crest in which it figures.[75]

Man-lion or *man-tiger.* This is as a lion but with a human face. Two of these are the supporters of Lord Huntingdon, and one was granted to Lord Donington as a supporter, whilst as charges they also occur in the arms of Radford. This semi-human animal is sometimes termed a 'lympago' (315).

Other terms relating to lions occur in many heraldic works—both old and new—but their use is very limited, if indeed of some, any example at all could be found in British armory. In addition to this, whilst the fact may sometimes exist, the *term* has never been adopted or officially recognised. Personally I believe most of the terms which follow may for all practical purposes be entirely disregarded. Amongst such terms are *contourné*, applied to a lion passant or rampant to the sinister. It would, however, be found blazoned in these words and not as contourné. 'Dismembered', 'Demembré', 'Dechaussée', and 'Trononnée' are all 'heraldry-book' terms specified to mean the same as 'couped in all its joints', but the uselessness and uncertainty concerning these terms is exemplified by the fact that the same books state 'dismembered' or 'demembré' to mean (when applied to a lion) that the animal is shown without legs or tail. The term 'embrued' is sometimes applied to a lion to signify that its mouth is bloody and dropping blood; and 'vulned' signifies wounded, heraldically represented by a blotch of gules,

74. The sea lion can also be winged. A winged sea lion or, the nether parts proper, finned gold, is the dexter supporter of the arms of Newport, Monmouthshire. Almost any creature can be made into a sea creature by the substitution of a fish's tail and fins for its lower parts. In the same way, it can be winged by the addition of a pair of eagle's wings. The Tudor heralds were very alive to the possibilities of finning and winging. A typical example is the crest granted to Thomas Metcalfe, citizen and goldsmith of London, on 25 March, 1 and 2 Philip and Mary: on a wreath argent and azure, a demi-sea calf sable, scaled and finned gold (O).

75. In fact, this monster does exist. The crest granted to William Blunte on 16 November 1572 is blazoned: on a wreath or and azure, a lion 'dregoney' ermine, crowned or (P).

from which drops of blood are falling. A lion 'disarmed' is without teeth, tongue, or claws.

A term often found in relation to lions rampant, but by no means peculiar thereto, is 'debruised'. This is used when it is partly defaced by another charge (usually an ordinary) being placed over it.

Another of these guide-book terms is 'decollated', which is said to be employed in the case of a lion which has its head cut off. A lion 'defamed' or 'diffamed' is supposed to be rampant to the sinister but looking backwards, the supposition being that the animal is being (against his will) chased off the field with infamy. A lion 'evire' is supposed to be emasculated and without signs of sex. In this respect it is interesting to note that in earlier days, before mock modesty and prudery had become such prominent features of our national life, the genital organ was always represented of a pronounced size in a prominent position, and it was as much a matter of course to paint it gules as it now is to depict the tongue of that colour. To prevent error I had better add that this is not now the usual practice.

Lions placed back to back are termed 'endorsed' or 'addorsed', but when two lions passant in pale are represented, one passing to the dexter and one to the sinister, they are termed 'counter-passant'. This term is, however, also used sometimes when they are merely passant towards each other. A more correct description in such cases would be passant 'respecting' or 'regarding' each other.

The term *lionné* is one stated to be used with animals other than lions when placed in a rampant position. Whilst doubtless of regular acceptation in French heraldry as applied to a leopard, it is unknown in English, and the term rampant is indifferently applied; *e.g.* in the case of a leopard, wolf, or tiger when in the rampant position.

Lionced is a term seldom met with, but it is said to be applied (for example to a cross) when the arms end in lions' heads. I have yet to find an authentic example of the use of such a cross.

When a bend or other ordinary issues from the mouths of lions (or other animals), the heads issuing from the edges or angles of the escutcheon, the ordinary is said to be 'engouled'.

A curious term, of the use of which I know only one example, is 'fleshed' or 'flayed'. This, as doubtless will be readily surmised, means that the skin is removed, leaving the flesh gules. This was the method by which the supporters of Wurtemburg were 'differenced' for the Duke of Teck, the forepaws being 'fleshed'.

Woodward gives the following very curious instances of the lion in heraldry:

'Only a single example of the use of the lioness as a heraldic charge is known to me. The family of COING, in Lorraine, bears: d'Azure, à une lionne arrêtée d'or.

'The following fourteenth-century examples of the use of the lion as a heraldic charge are taken from the oft-quoted *Wappenrolle von Zurich*, and should be of interest to the student of early armory:

'51: END: Azure, a lion rampant-guardant argent, its feet or.

'305. WILDENVELS: Per pale argent and sable, in the first a demi-lion statant-guardant issuant from the dividing line.

310 *Arms of Sebastian Schärtlin von Burtenbach.*

311 *Lion couchant.*

312 *Lion dormant.*

313 *Winged lion.*

314 *Sea lion.*

143

315 *Man-Lion.*

316 *Arms of*
Richard of Conisburgh,
Earl of Cambridge.
(From B.M. MS. Cott.,
Julius C. vii.)

317 *Arms of Bohemia.*
From the Pulver Turme in
Prague. (Latter half of
15th century).

318 *A demi-lion rampant.*

'408. TANNENVELS: Azure, a lion rampant or, queué argent.
'489. RINACH: Or, a lion rampant gules, headed azure.

'A curious use of the lion as a charge occurs in several ancient coats of the Low Countries, *e.g.* in that of TRASEGNIES, whose arms are: Bandé d'or et d'azur, a l'ombre du lion brochant sur le tout, à la bordure engrêlée d'or. Here the ombre du lion is properly represented by a darker shade of the tincture (either of or or of azure), but often the artist contents himself with simply drawing the outline of the animal in a neutral tint.

'Among other curiosities of the use of the lion are the following foreign coats:
'BOISSIAU, in France, bears: De gueules, semé de lions d'argent.
'MINUTOLI, of Naples: Gules, a lion rampant vair, the head and feet or.
'LOEN, of Holland: Azure, a decapitated lion rampant argent, three jets of blood spurting from the neck proper.
'PAPACODA, of Naples: Sables, a lion rampant or, its tail turned over its head and held by its teeth.
'The Counts REINACH, of Franconia: Or, a lion rampant gules, hooded and masked azure (see above).'

To these instances the arms of Westbury[76] may well be added, these being: Quarterly, or an azure, a cross patonce, on a bordure twenty lions rampant all counter-changed. No doubt the origin of such a curious bordure is to be found in the 'bordure of England', which, either as a mark of cadency or as an indication of affinity or augmentation, can be found in some number of instances. Probably one will suffice as an example. This is forthcoming in 61, which shows the arms of John de Bretagne, Earl of Richmond. Of a similar nature is the bordure of Spain (indicative of his maternal descent) borne by Richard of Conisburgh, Earl of Cambridge, who bore: Quarterly France and England, a label of three points argent, each charged with as many torteaux, on a bordure of the same twelve lions rampant purpure (316).

Before leaving the lion, the hint may perhaps be usefully conveyed that the temptation to over-elaborate the lion when depicting it heraldically should be carefully avoided. The only result is confusion — the very contrary of the essence of heraldic emblazonment, which was, is, and should be, the method of clear advertisement of identity. Examples of over-elaboration can, however, be found in the past, as will be seen from 317. This example belongs to the latter half of the fifteenth century, and represents the arms of Bohemia. It is taken from a shield on the 'Pulver Turme' at Prague.

Parts of lions are very frequently to be met with, particularly as crests. In fact the most common crest in existence is the *demi-lion rampant* (318). This is the upper half of a lion rampant. It is comparatively seldom found other than rampant and couped, so that the term 'a demi-lion', unless otherwise qualified, may always be assumed to be a demi-lion rampant couped. As charges upon the shield three will be found in the arms of Bennet, Earl of Tankerville: 'Gules, a bezant between three demi-lions rampant argent.'

The demi-lion may be both guardant and regardant.

76. The reference is to the town of Westbury in Wiltshire, which uses the arms quoted without authority.

Demi-lions rampant and erased are more common as charges than as crests. They are to be found in several Harrison coats of arms.

Demi-lions passant (319) are rather unusual, but in addition to the seeming cases in which they occur by dimidiation they are sometimes found, as in the case of the arms of Newman.[77]

Demi-lion affronté. The only case which has come under notice would appear to be the crest of Campbell of Aberuchill.

Demi-lion issuant. This term is applied to a demi-lion when it issues from an ordinary, *e.g.* from the base line of the chief, as in the arms of Dormer, Markham, and Abney; or from behind a fesse, as in the arms of Chalmers.

Demi-lion naissant issues from the centre of an ordinary, and not from behind it.

Lion's heads, both couped (320) and erased, are very frequently met with both as charges on the shield and as crests.

Lion's gamb. Many writers make a distinction between the *gamb* (which is stated to be the lower part only, couped or erased half-way up the leg) and the *paw*, but this distinction cannot be said to be always rigidly observed. In fact some authorities quote the exact reverse as the definition of the terms. As charges the gamb or paw will be found to occur in the arms of Lord Lilford ['Or, a lion's gamb erased in bend dexter between two crosslets fitchée in bend sinister gules'], and in the arms of Newdigate. This last is a curious example, inasmuch as, without being so specified in the blazon, the gambs are represented in the position occupied by the sinister foreleg of a lion passant.

The crest upon the Garter Plate of Edward Cherleton, Lord Cherleton of Powis, must surely be unique. It consists of two lions' paws embowed, the outer edge of each being adorned with fleurs-de-lis issuant therefrom.

A *lion's tail* will sometimes be found as a crest, and it also occurs as a charge in the arms of Corke, viz.: 'Sable, three lions' tails erect and erased argent.'[78]

A *lion's face* (321) should be carefully distinguished from a lion's head. In the latter case the neck, either couped or erased, must be shown; but a lion's face is affronté and cut off closely behind the ears. The distinction between the head and the face can be more appropriately considered in the case of the leopard.

319 *A demi-lion passant.*

320 *A lion's head couped.*

321 *A lion's face.*

77. I cannot trace the Newman coat referred to; most families of Newman bear demi-lions rampant. However, in the arms granted to Powles Harrison-Powles of Darlington, co. Durham, on 28 January 1808 three demi-lions passant guardant are shown. The blazon is: per pale indented vert and gules, a fess vair, between three demi-lions passant guardant couped or. Unlike the lion in 319, the Powles' lions have demi-tails.

78. This coat is given in Burke's *General Armory* for a family of Corke of Cornwall, but the arms appear to have been borne without authority.

12 · Beasts

322 *Heraldic tyger rampant.*

323 *Heraldic tyger passant.*

324 *Bengal tiger passant.*

Next after the lion should be considered the tiger, but it must distinctly be borne in mind that heraldry knows two kinds of tigers—the heraldic tyger (322 and 323) and the Bengal tiger[79] (324 and 325). Doubtless the heraldic tyger, which was the only one found in British armory until a comparatively recent date, is the attempt of artists to depict their idea of a tiger. The animal was unknown to them, except by repute, and consequently the creature they depicted bears little relation to the animal of real life; but there can be no doubt that their intention was to depict an animal which they knew to exist. The heraldic tyger had a body much like the natural tiger; it had a lion's tufted tail and mane, and the curious head which it is so difficult to describe, but which appears to be more like the wolf than any other animal we know. This, however, will be again dealt with in the chapter on fictitious animals, and is here only introduced to demonstrate the difference which heraldry makes between the heraldic tyger and the real animal. A curious conceit is that the heraldic tiger will anciently be often found spelt 'tyger', but this peculiar spelling does not seem ever to have been applied to the tiger of nature.

When it became desirable to introduce the real tiger into British armory as typical of India and our Eastern Empire, something of course was necessary to distinguish it from the tyger which had previously usurped the name in armory, and for this reason the natural tiger is always heraldically known as the Bengal tiger. This armorial variety appears towards the end of the eighteenth century in this country, though in foreign heraldry it appears to have been recognised somewhat earlier. There are, however, but few cases in which the Bengal tiger has appeared in armory, and in the majority of these cases as a supporter, as in the supporters of Outram, which are two tigers rampant guardant gorged with wreaths of laurel and crowned with Eastern crowns all proper. Another instance of the tiger as a supporter will be found in the arms of Bombay. An instance in which it appears as a charge upon a shield will be found in the arms granted to the University of Madras.

Another coat is that granted in 1874 to Augustus Beaty Bradbury of Edinburgh, which was: 'Argent, on a mount in base vert, a Bengal tiger passant proper, on a chief of the second two other tigers dormant also proper.' A *tigress* is said to be occasionally met with, and, when so, is sometimes represented with a mirror, in relation to the legend that ascribes to her such personal vanity that her young ones might be taken from under her charge if she had the counter attraction of a hand-glass! At least so say the heraldry books, but I have not yet come across such a case.

79. The Bengal tiger is still in general use where the beast of nature is required, but, as might be expected, a Malayan tiger occurs in the arms granted to the University of Malaya on 27 August 1953: argent, a Malayan tiger passant reguardant proper on a chief azure an open book bound, edged and clasped or.

The *leopard* (326, 327, and 328) has to a certain extent been referred to already. Doubtless it is the peculiar cat-like and stealthy walk which is so characteristic of the leopard which led to any animal in that position being considered a leopard; but the leopard in its natural state was of course known to Europeans in the early days of heraldry, and appears amongst the lists of heraldic animals apart from its existence as 'a lion passant'. The animal, however, except as a supporter or crest, is by no means common in English heraldry. It will be found, however, in the crests of some number of families; for example, Taylor and Potts.

A very similar animal is the ounce, which for heraldic purposes is in no way altered from the leopard. Parts of the latter will be found in use as in the case of the lion. As a crest the demi-leopard, the leopard's head (329), and the leopard's head affronté (330) are often to be met with. In both cases it should be noticed that *the neck is visible*, and this should be borne in mind, because this constitutes the difference between the leopard's head and the leopard's face (331). The leopard's face is by far the most usual form in which the leopard will be found in armory, and can be traced back to quite an early period in heraldry. The leopard's face shows no neck at all, the head being removed close behind the ears. It is then represented affronté. For some unfathomable reason these charges when they occur in the arms of Shrewsbury are usually referred to locally as 'loggerheads'. They were perpetuated in the arms of the county in its present grant.[80] A curious de-

325 *Bengal tiger rampant.*

326 *Leopard passant.*

80. It should be pointed out that the leopard's faces of Shrewsbury are not officially referred to as 'loggerheads'. In the grant to Shropshire County Council made on 18 June 1896 the arms are blazoned: erminois, three piles azure, two issuant from the chief and one in base, each charged with a leopard's face. The leopard's faces first appear on the Shrewsbury town seal of 1425, and they were allowed at the 1623 Visitation of Shropshire. No satisfactory explanation as to why they are called loggerheads has been put forward, but the word 'logger' or 'lubbar' may be a dialectal form of leopard. (See J. L. Hobbs's article in *The Coat of Arms*, vol. VII, no. 29, p. 12.)

327 *Leopard passant guardant.*

328 *Leopard rampant.*

329 *Leopard's head erased.*

330 *Leopard's head erased and affronté.*

331 *Leopard's face.*

332 *Leopard's face jessant-de-lis.*

333 *Arms of Styria. (Drawn by Hans Burgkmair, 1523.)*

velopment or use of the leopard's face occurs when it is jessant-de-lis (332). This will be found referred to at greater length under the heading of the Fleur-de-lis.

The *panther* is an animal which in its relation to heraldry it is difficult to know whether to place amongst the mythical or actual animals. No instance occurs to me in which the panther figures as a charge in British heraldry, and the panther as a supporter, in the few cases in which it is met with, is certainly not the actual animal, inasmuch as it is invariably found flammant, *i.e.* with flames issuing from the mouth and ears. In this character it will be found as a supporter of the Duke of Beaufort, and derived therefrom as a supporter of Lord Raglan. Foreign heraldry carries the panther to a most curious result. It is frequently represented with the tail of a lion, horns, and for its fore-legs the claws of an eagle. Even in England it is usually represented vomiting flames, but the usual method of depicting it on the Continent is greatly at variance with our own. 333 represents the same arms of Styria [Vert, a panther argent, armed close, vomiting flames of fire] from the title-page of the *Land-bond* of Styria in the year 1523, drawn by Hans Burgkmair. In *Physiologus*, a Greek writing of early Christian times of about the date 140, which in the course of time has been translated into every tongue, mention is made of the panther, to which is there ascribed the gaily spotted coat and the pleasant, sweet-smelling breath which induces all other animals to approach it; the dragon alone retreats into its hole from the smell, and consequently the panther appears to have sometimes been used as a symbol of Christ. The earliest armorial representations of this animal show the form not greatly dissimilar to nature; but very soon the similarity disappears in Continental representations, and the fancy of the artist transferred the animal into the fabulous creature which is now represented. The sweet-smelling breath, *suozzon-stanch* as it is called in the early German translation of the *Physiologus*, was expressed by the flames issuing from the mouth, but later in the sixteenth century flames issued from every open-ing in the head. The head was in old times similar to that of a horse, occasionally horned (as in the seal of Count Heinrich von Lechsgemünd, 1197); the fore-feet were well developed. In the second half of the fourteenth century the fore-feet assume the character of eagles' claws, and the horns of the animal were a settled matter. In the neighbourhood of Lake Constance we find the panther with divided hoofs on his hind-feet; perhaps with a reference to the panther's 'cleanness'. According to the Mosaic law, of course, a four-footed animal, to be considered clean, must not have paws, and a ruminant must not have an undivided hoof. Italian heraldry is likewise acquainted with the panther, but under another name (*La Dolce*, the sweet one) and another form. The dolce has a head like a hare, and in unhorned. (See A. Anthony v. Siegenfeld, *The Territorial Arms of Styria*, Graz, 1898.)

The panther is given by Segar, Garter King of Arms 1603–63, as one of the badges of King Henry VI, where it is silver, spotted of various colours, and with flames issuing from its mouth and ears. No doubt this Royal badge is the origin of the supporter of the Duke of Beaufort.

English armory knows an animal which it terms the male griffin, which has no wings, but which has gold rays issuing from its body in all directions. Ströhl terms the badge of the Earls of Ormonde, which from his description are plainly male griffins, *keythongs*, which he classes with the panther; and probably he is correct in looking upon our male griffin as merely one form of the heraldic panther.

The *cat*, under the name of the cat, the wild cat, the cat-a-mountain, or the cat-a-mount (334, 335, and 336), is by no means infrequent in British armory, though it will usually be found in Scottish or Irish examples. The arms of Keates and Scott-Gatty in which it figures are English examples, however.[81]

The *wolf* (337–41) is a very frequent charge in English armory. Apart from its use as a supporter, in which position it is found in conjunction with the shields of Lord Welby, Lord Rendell, and Viscount Wolseley, it will be found in the arms of Lovett and in by far the larger proportion of the coats for the name of Wilson and in the arms of Low.

The wolf, however, in earlier representations has a less distinctly wolf-like character, it being sometimes difficult to distinguish the wolf from some other heraldic animals. This is one of these cases in which, owing to insufficient know-ledge and crude draughtsmanship, ancient heraldry is not to be preferred to more realistic treatment. The demi-wolf is a very frequent crest, occurring not only in the arms and crests of members of the Wilson and many other families, but also as the crest of Wolfe. The latter crest is worthy of remark, inasmuch as the Royal crown which is held within its paws typifies the assistance given to King Charles II, after the battle of Worcester, by Mr Francis Wolfe of Madeley, to whom the crest was granted. King Charles, it may be noted, also gave to Mr. Wolfe a silver tankard, upon the lid of which was a representation of this crest. Wolves' heads are particularly common, especially in Scottish heraldry. An ex-ample of them will be found in the arms of 'Struan' Robertson, and in the coats used by all other members of the Robertson Clan having or claiming descent from, or relationship with, the house of Struan. The wolf's head also appears in the arms of Skeen. Woodward states that the wolf is the most common of all heraldic animals in Spanish heraldry, where it is frequently represented as *ravissant*, *i.e.* carrying the body of a lamb in its mouth or across its back.[82]

Much akin to the wolf is the *lynx*; in fact the heraldic representation of the two animals is not greatly different. The lynx does not often occur in heraldry except as a supporter, but it will be found as the crest of the family of Lynch. The

334 *Cat-a-mountain sejant guardant.*

335 *Cat-a-mountain sejant guardant erect.*

336 *Cat-a-mountain passant guardant.*

81. Siamese cats have recently made their heraldic debut as the supporters of Lord Snow.
82. A strange version of the wolf occurs in the arms granted to John Fennor of Sussex on 10 November 1557. The arms are blazoned: argent, a chevron sable, between three wolves marine passant sable finned, 'ventred' (an obscure term which presumably refers to the abdominal fins) and dented argent, langued and eyed gules. The representation of this sea wolf is akin to that of the sea dog rather than the sea lion. (See note 108.)

337 *Wolf rampant.*

338 *Wolf salient.*

339 *Wolf courant.*

340 *Wolf passant.*

341 *Wolf statant.*

342 *A lynx coward.*

343 *Fox passant.*

344 *Fox sejant.*

345 *A fox's mask.*

346 *Bear rampant.*

lynx is nearly always depicted and blazoned 'coward', *i.e.* with its tail between its legs (342). Another instance of this particular animal is found in the crest of Comber.[83]

A *fox* (343 and 344) which from the similarity of its representation is often confused with a wolf, is said by Woodward to be very seldom met with in British heraldry. This is hardly a correct statement, inasmuch as countless instances can be produced in which a fox figures as a charge, a crest, or a supporter. The fox is found on the arms and as the crest, and two are the supporters of Lord Ilchester, and instances of its appearance will be found amongst others in the arms or crests, for example, of Fox, Colfox, and Ashworth. Probably the most curious example of the heraldic fox will be found in the arms of Sir Watkin Williams Wynn, who for the arms of Williams quarters: 'Argent, two foxes counter-salient gules, the dexter surmounted of the sinister.' The face of a fox is termed its mask (345).

The *bear* (346–9) is frequently found figuring largely in coats of arms for the names of Barnard, Baring, Barnes, and Bearsley, and for other names which can be considered to bear canting relation to the charge. In fact the arms, crest, and motto of Barnard together form such an excellent example of the little jokes which characterise heraldry that I quote the blazon in full. The coat is 'argent, a bear rampant sable', and the motto 'Bear and forbear'.

The bear is generally muzzled, but this must not be presumed unless mentioned in the blazon. Bears' paws are often found both in crests and as charges upon shields, but as they differ little if anything in appearance from the lion's gamb, they need not be further particularised. To the bear's head, however, considerable attention should be paid, inasmuch as the manner of depicting it in England and Scotland differs. The bear's head, according to English ideas of heraldry, would be depicted down to the shoulders, and would show the neck couped or erased (350). In Scottish heraldry, bears' heads are almost invariably found couped or erased close behind the ears without any of the neck being visible (351 and 352); they are not, however, represented as caboshed or affronté.

The *boar* is an animal which, with its parts, will constantly be met with in British armory (353–5). Theoretically there is a difference between the boar, which is the male of the domestic animal, and the wild boar, which is the untamed creature of the woods. Whilst the latter is usually blazoned as a wild boar or sanglier, the former is just a boar; but for all practical purposes no difference whatever is made in heraldic representations of these varieties, though it may be noted that the crest of Swinton is often described as a sanglier, as invariably is also the crest of Douglas, Earl of Morton ['A sanglier sticking between the cleft of an oak-tree fructed, with a lock holding the clefts together all proper']. The boar, like the lion, is usually described as armed and langued, but this is not necessary when the tusks are represented in their own colour and when the tongue is gules. It will, however, be very frequently found that the tusks are or. The 'armed',

83. The crest of the South African Broadcasting Association, granted on 20 October 1959, is a South African lynx's head proper. Here it is a symbol of television, for the keen eyesight of the lynx gave rise to the fable that it could see through walls.

347 *Bear passant.*

348 *Bear statant.*

349 *Bear sejant erect.*

350 *Bear's head couped (English).*

355 *Boar statant.*

351 *Bear's head couped (Scottish).*

352 *Bear's head erased and muzzled (Scottish).*

353 *Boar rampant.*

354 *Boar passant.*

356 *Boar's head erased (English).*

however, does not include the hoofs, and if these are to be of any colour different from that of the animal, it must be blazoned 'unguled' of such and such a tincture. Precisely the same distinction occurs in the heads of boars (356–8) that was referred to in bears. The real difference is this, that whilst the English boar's head has the neck attached to the head and is couped or erased at the shoulders, the Scottish boar's head is separated close behind the ears. No one ever troubled to draw any distinction between the two for the purposes of blazon, because the English boars' heads were more usually drawn with the neck, and the boars' heads in Scotland were drawn couped or erased close. But the boar's head in Welsh heraldry followed the Scottish and not the English type. Matters armorial, however, are now cosmopolitan, and one can no longer ascertain that the crest of Campbell must be Scottish, or that the crest of any other family must be English; and consequently, though the terms will not be found employed officially, it is just as well to distinguish them, because armory can provide means of such distinction—the true description of an English boar's head being couped or erased 'at the neck', the Scottish term being a boar's head couped or erased 'close'.

Occasionally a boar's head will be stated to be borne erect; this is then shown with the mouth pointing upwards. A curious example of this is found in the crest of Tyrrell: 'A boar's head erect argent, in the mouth a peacock's tail proper.'

Woodward mentions three very strange coats of arms in which the charge, whilst not being a boar, bears very close connection with it. He states that among the curiosities of heraldry we may place the canting arms of Ham, of Holland: 'Gules, five hams proper, 2, 1, 2.' The Verhammes also bear: 'Or, three hams sable.' These commonplace charges assume almost a poetical savour when placed beside the matter-of-fact coat of the family of Bacquere: 'd'Azur, à un ecusson

357 *Boar's head coupled (Scottish).*

358 *Boar's head erased (Scottish).*

151

359 *A chevalier on horseback.*

360 *Horse rampant.*

361 *Horse courant.*

362 *Horse passant.*

363 *Horse-shoe.*

d'or en abîme, accompagné de trois groins de porc d'argent,' and that of the Wursters of Switzerland: 'Or, two sausages gules on a gridiron sable, the handle in chief.'

Horses

It is not a matter of surprise that the horse is frequently met with in armory. It will be found, as in the arms of Jedburgh, carrying a mounted warrior (359), and the same combination appears as the crest of the Duke of Fife.[84]

The horse will be found rampant (or forcene, or salient) (360),[85] and will be found courant (361), passant (362), and trotting.

When it is 'caparisoned' or 'furnished' it is shown with saddle and bridle and all appurtenances; but if the saddle is not present it would only be blazoned 'bridled'.

'Gules, a horse argent', really the arms of Westphalia, is popularly known in this country as the coat of Hanover, inasmuch as it was the most prominent charge upon the inescutcheon or quartering of Hanover formerly borne with the Royal Arms. Every one in this country is familiar with the expression, 'the white horse of Hanover'.

Horses will also be found in many cases as supporters, and these will be referred to in the chapter upon that subject, but reference should be particularly made here to the crest of the family of Lane, of King's Bromley, which is a strawberry roan horse, couped at the flanks, bridled, saddled, and holding in its feet the Imperial crown proper. This commemorates the heroic action of Mistress Jane Lane, afterwards Lady Fisher, and the sister of Sir Thomas Lane, of King's Bromley, who, after the battle of Worcester and when King Charles was in hiding, rode from Staffordshire to the south coast upon a strawberry roan horse, with King Charles as her serving-man. For this the Lane family were first of all granted the canton of England as an augmentation to their arms, and shortly afterwards this crest of the demi-horse (Plate II).

The arms of Trevelyan afford an interesting example of a horse, being: 'Gules, issuant out of water in base proper, a demi-horse argent, hoofed and maned or.'

The heads of horses are either so described or (and more usually) termed

84. This crest denotes the ancient Macduff, and is borne for the dukedom of Fife by the present Duke, the third of the 1900 creation. He also bears two other crests, namely his patronymic crest of Carnegie and the crest of Bannerman. Alexander William George Duff, first Duke of Fife married Princess Louise, the Princess Royal, daughter of King Edward VII. When he died in 1912 he was succeeded, under special remainder, by his elder daughter. She died in 1959 and, still under special remainder, her nephew James, son of her sister Maud by Charles Alexander (Carnegie), 11th Earl of Southesk, succeeded. The mother of the 11th Earl was Ethel, only daughter and heiress of Sir Alexander Bannerman, 9th baronet.

85. Confusion reigns about the terms rampant, forcene and salient when applied to a horse. I have found examples of a salient horse being blazoned salient (Cox) or forcene (Butler). I have also found examples of a rampant horse being blazoned forcene (Men of Kent) or rampant (Dartford Grammar School). The textbooks are equally uncertain about this term but, as it derives from the French word meaning furious, it would seem that it might properly be applied to the salient position. On the other hand, what is wrong with 'salient'? The only justification for forcene is when the horse is accorded three rearing positions: rampant, salient (hind legs apart, fore legs together) and forcene (hind legs together, fore legs apart). It is to be found depicted in these three different ways but is blazoned capriciously.

'nag's heads', though what the difference may be is beyond the comprehension of most people; at any rate heraldry knows of none.

The crest of the family of Duncombe is curious, and is as follows: 'Out of a ducan coronet or, a horse's hind-leg sable, the shoe argent.'

Though they can hardly be termed animate charges, perhaps one may be justified in here mentioning the horse-shoe (363), which is far from being an uncommon charge. It will be found in various arms for the name of Ferrar, Ferrers, Farrer, and Marshall; and, in the arms of one Scottish family of Smith, three horse-shoes interlaced together form an unusual and rather a curious charge.

Other instances in which it occurs will be found in the arms of Burlton, and in the arms used by the town of Oakham.[86] In the latter case it doubtless has reference to the toll of a horse-shoe, which the town collects from every peer or member of the Royal Family who passes through its limits. The collection of these, which are usually of silver, and are carefully preserved, is one of the features of the town.

The sea-horse, the unicorn, and the pegasus may perhaps be more properly considered as mythical animals, and the unicorn will, of course, be treated under that heading; but the sea-horse and the pegasus are so closely allied in form to the natural animal that perhaps it will be simpler to treat of them in this chapter. The *sea-horse* (364) is composed of the head and neck of a horse and the tail of a fish, but in place of the fore-feet, webbed paws are usually substituted. Two sea-horses respecting each other will be found in the coat of arms of Pirrie, and sea-horses naiant will be found in the arms of M'Cammond. It is a matter largely left to the discretion of the artist, but the sea-horse will be found as often as not depicted with a fin at the back of its neck in place of a mane. A sea-horse as a crest will be found in the case of Belfast and in the crests of Clippingdale and Jenkinson. The sea-horse is sometimes represented winged, but I know of no officially sanctioned example. When represented rising from the sea the animal is said to be 'assurgeant'.[87]

The *pegasus* (365 and 366), though often met with as a crest or found in use as a supporter, is very unusual as a charge upon an escutcheon. It will be found, however, in the arms of the Society of the Inner Temple and in the arms of Richardson, which afford an example of a pegasus rampant and also an example

---

86. The arms used by Oakham (or, a horse shoe sable, nailed argent) are of no authority. The arms reflect the story that, when Queen Elizabeth was passing through the town, her horse lost a shoe; since which time the burghers have claimed, and have been given, a horse shoe from any royal person visiting the town. Oakham Rural District Council was granted arms which reflect the legend on 6 November 1958, namely: vert, semé of acorns and fretty or, on a chief gules, a pegasus currant argent, between two horseshoes or.

In passing it should be noted that the heraldic horseshoe is always shown inverted, with the luck running out, unless otherwise blazoned.

87. Recently there have been several grants containing the sea-horse of nature, and on these occasions it has been blazoned 'a sea-horse (hippocampus)' to distinguish it from the mythological creature. An attractive 'hippocampus' coat is that granted on 15 December 1950 to Mr William Edward Cartwright of Hawaii. The arms are blazoned: barry wavy of eight argent and azure, a sea-horse (hippocampus) or; for a crest, on a wreath of the colours, a demi sea-horse (hippocampus) or (Q). Badge: within an oval garland of kelp or, set at intervals with pearls proper, a sea-horse (hippocampus) or.

In Tudor times the sea-horse was usually blazoned 'a horse marine'.

364 *Sea-horse.*

365 *Pegasus rampant.*

366 *Pegasus passant.*

367 *Arms of Herr von Frouberg.*

Q *Arms of Cartwright.*

368 *Talbot passant.*

369 *Talbot statant.*

370 *Talbot rampant.*

371 *Talbot sejant.*

372 *Greyhound passant.*

in the crest of a pegasus sejant, which at present is the only one which exists in British heraldry.[88]

367 gives a solitary instance of a mare. The arms, which are from Grünenberg's *Wappenbuch* (1483), are attributed to 'Herr von Frouberg from the Forest in Bavaria', and are: Gules, a mare rampant argent, bridled sable. The *ass* is not a popular charge, but the family of Mainwaring have an ass's head for a crest. A mule occurs in the arms of the family of Mole.

Dogs

Dogs will be found of various kinds in many English and Scottish coats of arms, though more frequently in the former than in the latter. The original English dog, the hound of early days, is, of course, the *talbot* (368, 369, 370, and 371). Under the heading of supporters certain instances will be quoted in which dogs of various kinds and breeds figure in heraldry, but the talbot as a charge will be found in the arms of the old Staffordshire family, Wolseley of Wolseley, whose arms are: 'Argent, a talbot passant gules.' Other instances of the talbot will be found in the arms or crests of the families of Grosvenor, Talbot, and Gooch. The arms: 'Azure, three talbots statant or' were granted by Cooke to Edward Peke of Heldchurchgate, Kent. A sleuth-hound treading gingerly upon the points of a coronet ['On a ducal coronet, a sleuth-hound proper, collared and leashed gules'] was the crest of the Earl of Perth and Melfort, and one wonders whether the motto, 'Gang warily', may not really have as much relation to the perambulations of the crest as to the dangerous foothold amongst the galtraps which is provided for the supporters.

Greyhounds (372 and 373) are, of course, very frequently met with, and amongst the instances which can be mentioned are the arms of Clayhills, Hughes-Hunter of Plas Coch, and Hunter of Hunterston. A curious coat of arms will be found under the name of Udney of that Ilk, registered in the Lyon Office, namely: 'Gules, two greyhounds counter-salient argent, collared of the field, in the inner point a stag's head couped and attired with ten tynes, all between the three fleurs-de-lis, two in chief and one in base, or.' Another very curious coat of arms is registered as the design of the reverse of the seal of the Royal Burgh of Linlithgow, and is: 'Or, a greyhound bitch sable, chained to an oak-tree within a loch proper.' This curious coat of arms, however, being the reverse of the seal, is seldom if ever made use of.

Two *bloodhounds* are the supporters to the arms of Campbell of Aberuchill.

The dog may be salient, that is, springing, its hind-feet on the ground; passant, when it is sometimes known as trippant, otherwise walking; and courant when it is at full speed. It will be found occasionally couchant or lying down, but if depicted chasing another animal (as in the arms of Echlin) it is described as 'in full chase', or 'in full course'.

A *mastiff* will be found in the crest of Crawshay, and there is a well-known crest of a family named Phillips which is 'a dog sejant regardant surmounted by

88. The arms of the Inner Temple are not officially recorded. Those of the Middle Temple, however, were confirmed in 1949 as being: argent on a cross gules, a Paschal Lamb supporting a banner or.

a bezant charged with a representation of a dog saving a man from drowning'. Whether this crest has any official authority or not I do not know, but I should imagine it is highly doubtful.

Foxhounds appear as the supporters of Lord Hindlip; and when depicted with its nose to the ground a dog is termed 'a hound on scent'.

A winged greyhound is stated to be the crest of a family of Benwell. A greyhound 'courant' will be found in the crests of Daly and Watney; and a curious crest is that of Biscoe, which is a greyhound seizing a hare. The crest of Anderson, formerly borne by the Earl of Yarborough, is a water spaniel, and a recent grant included a fox-terrier as a crest.

373 *Greyhound courant.*

The *sea-dog* (374) is a most curious animal. It is represented much as the talbot, but with scales, webbed feet, and a broad scaly tail like a beaver. In my mind there is very little doubt that the sea-dog is really the early heraldic attempt to represent a beaver, and I am confirmed in that opinion by the arms of the city of Oxford. There has been considerable uncertainty as to what the sinister supporter was intended to represent. A reference to the original record shows that a beaver is the real supporter, but the representation of the animal, which in form has varied little, is very similar to that of a sea-dog. The only instances I am aware of in British heraldry in which it occurs under the name of a sea-dog are the supporters of the Barony of Stourton and the crest of Dodge★ (Plate IX).

374 *A sea-dog.*

Bulls

The bull (375 and 376), and also the calf, and very occasionally the cow and the buffalo, have their allotted place in heraldry. They are amongst the few animals which can never be represented proper, inasmuch as in its natural state the bull is of very various colours. And yet there is an exception to even this apparently obvious fact, for the bulls connected with or used either as crests, badges, or supporters by the various branches of the Nevill family are all pied bulls ['Arms of the Marquis of Abergavenny: Gules, on a saltire argent, a rose of the field, barbed and seeded proper. Crest: a bull statant argent, pied sable, collared and chain reflexed over the back or. Supporters; two bulls argent, pied sable, armed, unguled, collared and chained, and at the end of the chain two staples or. Badges: on the dexter a rose gules, seeded or, barbed vert; on the sinister a portcullis or. Motto: "Ne vile velis."'] The bull in the arms of the town of Abergavenny, which are obviously based upon the arms and crest of the Marquess of Abergavenny, is the same.

375 *Bull rampant.*

Examples of the bull will be found in the arms of Verelst, Blyth, and Ffinden. A bull salient occurs in the arms of De Hasting ['Per pale vert and or, a bull salient counterchanged']. The arms of the Earl of Shaftesbury show three bulls, which happen to be the quartering for Ashley. This coat of arms affords an instance, and a striking one, of the manner in which arms have been improperly assumed in England. The surname of the Earl of Shaftesbury is Ashley-Cooper. It may be mentioned here in passing, though the subject is properly dealt with elsewhere in

★ Armorial bearings of Dodge: Barry of six or sable, on a pale gules, a woman's breast distilling drops of milk proper. Crest: upon a wreath of the colours, a demi sea-dog azure, collared, maned, and finned or.

376 *Bull passant.*

377 Bull's head caboshed.

the volume, that in an English sub-quarterly coat for a double name the arms for the last and most important name are the first and fourth quarterings. But Lord Shaftesbury himself is the only person who bears the name of Cooper, all other members of the family except his lordship being known by the name of Ashley only. Possibly this may be the reason which accounts for the fact that by a rare exception Lord Shaftesbury bears the arms of Ashley in the first and fourth quarters, and Cooper in the second and third. But by a very general mistake these arms of Ashley ['Argent, three bulls passant sable, armed and unguled or'] were until recently almost invariably described as the arms of Cooper. The result has been that during the last century they were 'jumped' right and left by people of the name of Cooper, entirely in ignorance of the fact that the arms of Cooper (if it were, as one can only presume, the popular desire to indicate a false relationship to his lordship) are: 'Gules, a bend engrailed between six lions rampant or.' The ludicrous result has been that to those who know, the arms have stood self-condemned, and in the course of time, as it has become necessary for these Messrs. Cooper to legalise these usurped insignia, the new grants, differentiated versions of arms previously in use, have nearly all been founded upon this Ashley coat. At any rate there must be a score or more Cooper grants with bulls as the principal charges, and innumerable people of the name of Cooper are still using without authority the old Ashley coat pure and simple.[89]

The bull as a crest is not uncommon, belonging amongst other families to Ridley, Sykes, and De Hoghton; and the demi-bull, and more frequently the bull's head, are often met with. A bull's leg is the crest of De la Vache, and as such appears upon two of the early Garter plates. Winged bulls are the supporters of the Butchers' Livery Company. A bull's scalp occurs upon a canton over the arms of Cheney, a coat quartered by Johnston and Cure.

The ox seldom occurs, except that, in order sometimes to preserve a pun, a bovine animal is sometimes so blazoned, as in the case of the arms of the City of Oxford. Cows also are equally rare, but occur in the arms of Cowell ['Ermine, a cow statant gules, within a bordure sable, bezantée'] and in the modern grants to the towns of Rawtenstall and Cowbridge. Cows' heads appear on the arms of Veitch ['Argent, three cows' heads erased sable'], and these were transferred to the cadency bordure of the Haig arms when these were rematriculated for Mr H. Veitch Haig.[90]

378 Armorial bearings of John Henry Metcalfe, Esq.: Argent, three calves passant sable, a canton gules.

Calves are of much more frequent occurrence than cows, appearing in many coats of arms in which they are a pun upon the name. They will be found in the arms of Vaile and Metcalfe (378). Special attention may well be drawn to the last-mentioned illustration, inasmuch as it is by Mr J. H. Metcalfe, whose heraldic

89. It does seem reasonable that a coat showing three bulls should belong to a family of Cooper or Cowper, but in fact this is not the case, and Fox-Davies' assessment of the situation is correct. Sir John Cowper, baronet, married Anne, daughter and sole heir of Sir Anthony Ashley of Wimborne, Dorset, and their son Anthony, born in 1621, was created Lord Ashley in 1661 and Earl of Shaftesbury in 1672.

90. The coat of arms granted on 27 November 1950 to the Prebendal Foundation of St Endellion affords an example of both the cow and the heifer. The arms are blazoned: per chevron wavy azure and vert, in chief a crown vallary between two heifer's heads caboshed, and in base a cow couchant guardant or. Particular breeds of cattle are not unknown; Lord Lambury's sinister supporter is a Hereford bull.

379 *Stag lodged.*

380 *Stag trippant.*

381 *Stag courant.*

382 *Stag springing.*

383 *Stag at gaze.*

work has obtained a well-deserved reputation. A bull or cow is termed 'armed' if the horns are of a different tincture from the head. The term 'unguled' applies to the hoofs, and 'ringed' is used when, as is sometimes the case, a ring passes through the nostrils. A bull's head is sometimes found caboshed (377), as in the crest of Macleod, or as in the arms of Walrond. The position of the tail is one of those matters which are left to the artist, and unless the blazon contains any statement to the contrary, it may be placed in any convenient position.

Stags

The stag, using the term in its generic sense, under the various names of stag, deer, buck, roebuck, hart, doe, hind, reindeer, springbok, and other varieties, is constantly met with in British armory, as well as in that of other countries.

In the specialised varieties, such as the springbok and the reindeer, naturally an attempt is made to follow the natural animal in its salient peculiarities, but as to the remainder, heraldry knows little if any distinction after the following has been properly observed. The stag, which is really the male red deer, has horns which are branched with pointed branches from the bottom to the top; but a buck, which is the fallow deer, has broad and flat palmated horns. Anything in the nature of a stag must be subject to the following terms. If lying down it is termed 'lodged' (379), if walking it is termed 'trippant' (380), if running it is termed 'courant' (381), or 'at speed' or 'in full chase'. It is termed 'salient' when springing (382), though the term 'springing' is sometimes employed, and it is said to be 'at gaze' when statant with the head turned to face the spectator (383); but it should be noted that a stag may also be 'statant' (384); and it is not 'at gaze' unless the head is turned round. When it is necessary owing to a difference of tincture or for other reasons to refer to the horns, a stag or buck is described as 'attired' of such and such a colour, whereas bulls, rams, and goats are said to be 'armed'.

When the stag is said to be attired of ten or any other number of tynes, it means that there are so many points to its horns. Like other cloven-footed animals, the stag can be unguled of a different colour.

The stag's head is very frequently met with, but it will be almost more frequently found as a stag's head caboshed (385). In these cases the head is represented affronté and removed close behind the ears, so that no part of the neck is visible. The stag's head caboshed occurs in the arms of Cavendish and Stanley, and also in the arms of Legge, Earl of Dartmouth. 386 and 387 are examples of other heads.

384 *Stag statant.*

385 *Stag's head caboshed.*

386 *Stag's head erased.*

387 *Buck's head couped.*

388 *Hind.*

389 *Reindeer.*

390 *Winged stag rampant.*

394 *Armorial bearings of Marindin.*

391 *Heraldic antelope statant.*

392 *The heraldic antelope rampant.*

393 *Heraldic antelope passant.*

The attires of a stag are to be found either singly (as in the arms of Boyle) or in the form of a pair attached to the scalp. The crest of Jeune[91] affords an instance of a scalp. The hind or doe (388) is sometimes met with, as in the crest of Hatton, whilst a hind's head is the crest of Conran.

The *reindeer* (389) is less usual, but reindeer heads will be found in the arms of Fellows. It, however, appears as a supporter for several English peers. Winged stags (390) were the supporters of De Carteret, Earls of Granville, and 'a demi-winged stag gules, collared argent', is the crest of Fox of Coalbrookdale, co. Salop.

Much akin to the stag is the antelope, which, unless specified to be an *heraldic* antelope, or found in a very old coat, is usually represented in the natural form of the animal, and subject to the foregoing rules.

Heraldic Antelope. This animal (391, 392, and 393) is found in English heraldry more frequently as a supporter than as a charge. As an instance, however, of the latter from may be mentioned the family of Dighton (Lincolnshire): 'Per pale argent and gules, an heraldic antelope passant counterchanged.' It bears little if any relation to the real animal, though there can be but small doubt that the earliest forms originated in an attempt to represent an antelope or an ibex. Since,

91. The reference is to the crest granted to Francis Jeune, Bishop of Peterborough, on 26 October 1878 for the use of his descendants. As he was a bishop he would not himself use a crest. In fact, the crest is blazoned: between a stags' attires an estoil all argent. No mention is made of a scalp. However, an example of the scalp is found in the arms and crest allowed to a family of Buck of London at the 1634 Visitation of Middlesex, namely: per fess nebuly, three pairs of attires on a scalp, and for a crest a like pair of attires.

158

however, heraldry has found a use for the real antelope, it has been necessary to distinguish it from the creations of the early armorists, which are now known as heraldic antelopes. Examples will be found in the supporters of Lord Carew, in the crest of Moresby, and of Bagnall.

The difference chiefly consists in the curious head and horns and in the tail, the heraldic antelope being an heraldic tyger, with the feet and legs similar to those of a deer, and with two straight serrated horns.

Ibex. This is another form of the natural antelope, but with two saw-edged horns projecting from the forehead.

A curious animal, namely the *sea-stag*, is often met with in German heraldry. This is the head, antlers, fore-legs, and the upper part of the body of a stag conjoined to the fish-tail end of a mermaid. The only instance I am aware of in which it occurs in British armory is the case of the arms of Marindin, which have been matriculated in Lyon Register (394). This coat, however, it should be observed, is really of German or perhaps of Swiss origin.[92]

The ram and goat

The ram (395 and 396), the consideration of which must of necessity include the sheep (397), the Paschal lamb (398), and the fleece (399), plays no unimportant part in armory. The chief heraldic difference between the ram and the sheep, to some extent, in opposition to the agricultural distinctions, lies in the fact that the ram is always represented with horns and the sheep without. The lamb and the ram are always represented with the natural tail, but the sheep is deprived of it. A ram can of course be 'armed' (*i.e.* with the horns of a different colour) and 'unguled', but the latter will seldom be found to be the case. The ram, the sheep, and the lamb will nearly always be found either passant or statant, but a demi-ram is naturally represented in a rampant posture, though in such a case the word 'rampant' is not necessary in the blazon.

Occasionally, as in the crest of Marwood, the ram will be found couchant. As a charge upon a shield the ram will be found in the arms of Sydenham ['Argent, three rams passant sable'], and a ram couchant occurs in the arms of Pujolas (granted 1762) ['Per fess wavy azure and argent, in base on a mount vert, a ram couchant sable, armed and unguled or, in chief three doves proper']. The arms of Ramsey ['Azure, a chevron between three rams passant or'] and the arms of Harman ['Sable, a chevron between six rams counter-passant two and two argent, armed and unguled or'] are other instances in which rams occur. A sheep occurs in the arms of Sheepshanks ['Azure, a chevron erminois between in chief three roses and in base a sheep passant argent. Crest: on a mount vert, a sheep passant argent'].

The lamb, which is by no means an unusual charge in Welsh coats of arms, is most usually found in the form of a 'paschal lamb' (398), or some variation evidently founded thereupon.

92. There is a recent example of a sea stag, namely in the arms of Mr Michael Desmond Seiflow Hubble, which are blazoned: or, a chief indented sable, over all a sea stag proper, attired of the first.

395 *Ram statant.*

396 *Ram rampant.*

397 *Sheep passant.*

398 *Paschal lamb.*

399 *Fleece.*

400 Ram's head caboshed.

401 Goat passant.

402 Goat rampant.

403 Goat salient.

404 Elephant and castle.

The fleece—of course originally of great repute as the badge of the Order of the Golden Fleece—has been frequently employed in the grants of arms to towns or individuals connected with the woollen industry.

The demi-ram and the demi-lamb are to be found as crests, but far more usual are rams' heads, which figure, for example, in the arms of Ramsden, and in the arms of the towns of Huddersfield, and Barrow-in-Furness. The ram's head will sometimes be found caboshed, as in the arms of Ritchie and Roberts.

Perhaps here reference may fittingly be made to the arms granted by Lyon Office in 1812 to Thomas Bonar, co. Kent ['Argent, a saltire and chief azure, the last charged with a dexter hand proper, vested with a shirt-sleeve argent, issuing from the dexter chief point, holding a shoulder of mutton proper to a lion passant or, all within a bordure gules'].

The Goat (401–3) is very frequently met with in armory. Its positions are passant, statant, rampant, and salient. When the horns are of a different colour it is said to be 'armed'.

Other animals

The Elephant is by no means unusual in heraldry, appearing as a crest, as a charge, and also as a supporter. Nor, strange to say, is its appearance exclusively modern. The elephant's head, however, is much more frequently met with than the entire animal. Heraldry generally finds some way of stereotyping one of its creations as peculiarly its own, and in regard to the elephant, the curious 'elephant and castle' (404) is an example, this latter object being, of course, simply a derivative of the howdah of Indian life. Few early examples of the elephant omit the castle. The elephant and castle is seen in the arms of Dumbarton and in the crest of Corbet.

A curious practice, the result of pure ignorance, has manifested itself in British armory. As will be explained in the chapter upon crests, a large proportion of German crests are derivatives of the stock basis of two bull's horns, which formed a recognised ornament for a helmet in Viking and other pre-heraldic days. As heraldry found its footing it did not in Germany displace those horns, which in many cases continued alone as the crest or remained as a part of it in the form of additions to other objects. The craze for decoration at an early period seized upon the horns, which carried repetitions of the arms or their tinctures. As time went on the decoration was carried further, and the horns were made with bell-shaped open ends to receive other objects, usually bunches of feathers or flowers. So universal did this custom become that even when nothing was inserted the horns came to be always depicted with these open mouths at their points. But German heraldry now, as has always been the case, simply terms the figures 'horns'. In course of time German immigrants made application for grants of arms in this country, which, doubtless, were based upon other German arms previously in use, but which, evidence of right not being forthcoming, could not be recorded as borne of right, and needed to be granted with alteration as a new coat. The curious result has been that these horns have been incorporated in some number of English grants, but they have universally been described as elephants' proboscides, and are now always so represented in this country. A case in point is the crest of Verelst, and another is the crest of Allhusen.

Elephants' tusks have also been introduced into grants, as in the arms of Liebreich (borne in pretence by Cock) and Randles ['Or, a chevron wavy azure between three pairs of elephants' tusks in saltire proper'].[93]

The Hare (405) is but rarely met with in British armory. It appears in the arms of Cleland, and also in the crest of Shakerley, Bart. ['A hare proper resting her forefeet on a grab or']. A very curious coat ['Argent, three hares playing bagpipes gules'] belongs to an ancient Derbyshire family FitzErcald, now represented (through the Sacheverell family) by Coke of Trussley, who quarter the FitzErcald shield.

405 *Hare salient.*

The Rabbit (406), or, as it is more frequently termed heraldically, the *Coney*, appears more frequently in heraldry than the hare, being the canting charge on the arms of Coningsby, Cunliffe ['Sable, three conies courant argent'], and figuring also as the supporters of Montgomery Cunningham ['Two conies proper'].

The Squirrel (407) occurs in many English coats of arms. It is always sejant, and very frequently cracking a nut.

406 *Coney.*

The Ape is not often met with, except in the cases of the different families of the great Fitz Gerald clan. It is usually the crest, though the Duke of Leinster also has apes as supporters. One family of Fitzgerald, however, bear it as a charge upon the shield ['Gules, a saltire invected per pale argent and or, between four monkeys statant of the second, environed with a plain collar and chained of the second. Mantling gules and argent. Crest: on a wreath of the colours, a monkey as in the arms, charged on the body with two roses, and resting the dexter fore-leg on a saltire gules. Motto: "Crom-a-boo"'], and the family of Yorke bear an ape's head for a crest.

407 *Squirrel.*

The ape is usually met with 'collared and chained' (408), though, unlike any other animal, the collar of an ape environs its loins and not its neck. A winged ape is included in Elvin's *Dictionary of Heraldry* as a heraldic animal, but I am not aware to whom it is assigned.

The Brock or *Badger* (409) figures in some number of English arms. It is most frequently met with as the crest of Brooke, but will be also found in the arms or crests of Brocklebank and Motion.

The Otter (410) is not often met with except in Scottish coats, but an English example is that of Sir George Newnes, and a demi-otter issuant from a fess wavy will be found quartered by Seton of Mounie.

408 *Ape collared and chained.*

93. Elephants' tusks are popular among the new African states, several of which bear their arms on the oval African war shield. An elephant's tusk held by a supporter follows the shape of the shield, and so is both symbolic and artistically pleasing. The supporters of the arms adopted by Mid-Western Nigeria by proclamation of the Governor in 1964 are: dexter, a lion guardant; sinister, a horse, each supporting an elephant's tusk argent. The supporters of the arms granted to Tanganyika on 6 September 1961, and shown on an African war shield, are: dexter, a Tanganyikan man proper, habited vert, supporting in the exterior hand an elephant's tusk, and at the feet a cotton bush leaved and fructed also proper; sinister, a Tanganyikan woman likewise proper, habited vert, and with a head cloth gold, supporting with the exterior hand an elephant's tusk, and at the feet a coffee bush leaved and fructed also proper. These arms passed rapidly into history, for Tanganyika became a republic in 1962, one year after becoming an independent state, and on 25 April 1964 Tanganyika and Zanzibar united to form the Republic of Tanzania.

409 *Brock.*

410 Otter.

411 Urcheon.

bibrach

412 Arms of
the town of Biberach.
(From Ulrich Reichenthal's
Concilium von Constanz,
Augsburg, 1483.)

An otter's head, sometimes called a seal's head, for it is impossible to distinguish the heraldic representations of the one or the other, appears in many coats of arms of different families of the name of Balfour, and two otters are the supporters belonging to the head of the Scottish house of Balfour.

The Ermine, the Stoat, and *the Weasel, &c.,* are not very often met with, but the ermine appears as the crest of Crawford and the marten as the crest of a family of that name.

The Hedgehog, or, as it is usually heraldically termed, the *Urcheon* (411), occurs in some number of coats. For example, in the arms of Maxwell ['Argent, an eagle with two heads displayed sable, beaked and membered gules, on the breast an escutcheon of the first, charged with a saltire of the second, surcharged in the centre with a hurcheon (hedgehog) or, all within a bordure gules'], Harris, and as the crest of Money-Kyrle.[94]

The Beaver has been introduced into many coats of late years for those connected in any way with Canada. It figures in the arms of Lord Strathcona and Mount Royal, and in the arms of Christopher.

The beaver is one of the supporters of the city of Oxford, and is the sole charge in the arms of the town of Biberach (412). Originally the arms were: 'Argent, a beaver azure, crowned and armed gules', but the arms authorised by the Emperor Frederick IV, 18 July 1448, were: 'Azure, a beaver or.'[95]

It is quite impossible, or at any rate very unnecessary, to turn a work on armory into an Illustrated Guide to Natural History, which would be the result if under the description of heraldic charges the attempt were made to deal with all the various animals which have by now been brought to the armorial fold, owing to the inclusion of each for special and sufficient reasons in one or two isolated grants.

Far be it from me, however, to make any remark which should seem to indicate the raising of any objection to such use. In my opinion it is highly admirable, providing there is some definite reason in each case for the introduction of these strange animals other than mere caprice. They add to the interest of heraldry, and they give to modern arms and armory a definite status and meaning, which is a relief from the endless monotony of meaningless lions, bends, chevrons, mullets, and martlets.

But at the same time the isolated use in a modern grant of such an animal as the kangaroo does not make it one of the peculiarly heraldic menagerie, and consequently such instances must be dismissed herein with brief mention, particularly as many of these creatures heraldically exist only as supporters, in which chapter some are more fully discussed. Save as a supporter, the only instances I know of the *Kangaroo* are in the coat of Moore and in the arms of Arthur, Bart.[96]

94. In pursuance of a Royal licence this family bears two crests. The hedgehog is, in fact, the crest of the Kyrle family: on a mount vert, a hedgehog or.

95. The beaver, under its archaic name of castor and not looking like the natural beaver so frequently granted to those with Canadian connections, was granted as a crest to William Partriche of Cirencester, Gloucestershire, on 22 April 1561. The crest is blazoned: a castor argent pelletty, langued gules.

96. The great increase of interest in heraldry in Australia has led to a like increase in the number of kangaroos to be found in arms. However, these are seldom shown in the actual arms although frequently in the crest, either whole or demi, as in the crest of the city of Melbourne, and as supporters, as in the achievement of the Australian Medical Association.

The Zebra will be found as the crest of Kemsley.

The Camel, which will be dealt with later as a supporter, in which form it appears in the arms of Viscount Kitchener, the town of Inverness (251), and some of the Livery Companies, also figures in the reputed but unrecorded arms of Camelford, and in the arms of Cammell of Sheffield and various other families of a similar name.[97]

The fretful *Porcupine* was borne ['Gules, a porcupine erect argent, tusked, collared, and chained or'] by Simon Eyre, Lord Mayor of London in 1445: and the creature also figures as one of the supporters and the crest of Sidney, Lord De L'Isle and Dudley.[98]

The Bat (413) will be found in the arms of Heyworth and as the crest of a Dublin family named Wakefield.

The Tortoise occurs in the arms of a Norfolk family named Gandy, and is also stated by Papworth to occur in the arms of a Scottish family named Goldie. This coat, however, is not matriculated. It also occurs in the crests of Deane and Hayne.

The Springbok, which is one of the supporters of Cape Colony, and two of which are the supporters of Viscount Milner, is also the crest of Randles ['On a wreath of the colours, a springbok or South African antelope statant in front of an assegai erect all proper'].

The Rhinoceros occurs as one of the supporters of Viscount Colville of Culross, and also of the crest of Wade, and the *Hippopotamus* is one of the supporters of Speke.

The Crocodile, which is the crest and one of the supporters of Speke, is also the crest of Westcar ['A crocodile proper, collared and chained or'].

The Alpaca, and also two *Angora Goats'* heads figure in the arms of Benn.[99]

The Rat occurs in the arms of Ratton,⋆ which is a peculiarly good example of a canting coat.

The Mole, sometimes termed a moldiwarp, occurs in the arms of Mitford ['Argent, a fess sable between three moles displayed sable'].

413 *Bat.*

97. The Livery Companies referred to are the Merchant Taylors', Coopers' and Grocers' Companies. The former two were both granted supporters by Robert Cooke, Clarenceux. In 1574 he granted the Coopers' Company the following supporters: on either side a camel gules, semy of annulets and bridled or. Twelve years later, on 23 December 1586, he granted two gold camels as supporters to the arms of the Merchant Taylors' Company. A camel statant or, bridled sable, on his back two bags of pepper argent, powdered with cloves and corded sable, was granted to the Grocers' Company as a crest on 14 October 1562. In all these cases the camels were not the Bactrian or common camel with two humps but the one-humped variety. The common camel, however, is not unknown, and it appears in the arms granted to Charles Cammell of Derbyshire on 10 December 1877. The blazon does not refer to the humps, but simply describes the arms thus: sable, on a chevron argent, cottised or, between three camels statant of the second, as many trefoils slipped of the first.

98. William Philip Sidney, 6th Baron De L'Isle and Dudley, was created Viscount De L'Isle in 1956. There was no alteration in the supporters.

99. These are the arms granted to Joseph Benn of Bradford, Yorks, on 20 July 1887. They are blazoned: per chevron or and azure on a mount in base vert, an Alpaca statant, and two angora goats heads affronty in chief all proper.

⋆ Armorial bearings of James Joseph Louis Ratton, Esq.: Azure, in base the sea argent, and thereon a tunny sable, on a chief of the second a rat passant of the third. Upon the escutcheon is placed a helmet befitting his degree, with a mantling azure and argent; and for his crest, upon a wreath of the colours, an ibex statant guardant proper, charged on the body with two fleurs-de-lis fesswise azure, and resting the dexter foreleg on a shield argent charged with a passion cross sable. Motto: 'In Deo spero.'

13 · Monsters

The heraldic catalogue of beasts runs riot when we reach those mythical or legendary creatures which can only be summarised under the generic term of monsters. Most mythical animals, however, can be traced back to some comparable counterpart in natural history.

The fauna of the New World was of course unknown to those early heraldic artists in whose knowledge and imagination, no less than in their skill (or lack of it) in draughtsmanship, lay the nativity of so much of our heraldry. They certainly thought they were representing animals in existence in most if not in all cases, though one gathers that they considered many of the animals they used to be misbegotten hybrids. Doubtless, working on the assumption of the mule as the hybrid of the horse and the ass, they jumped to the conclusion that animals which contained salient characteristics of two other animals which they knew were likewise hybrids. A striking example of their theories is to be found in the heraldic *Camelopard*, which was anciently devoutly believed to be begotten by the leopard upon the camel. A leopard they would be familiar with, also the camel, for both belong to that corner of the world where the north-east of the African Continent, the south-east of Europe, and the west of Asia join, where were fought out the wars of the Cross, and where heraldry took on itself a definite being. There the known civilisations of the world met, taking one from the other knowledge, more or less distorted, ideas and wild imaginings. A stray giraffe was probably seen by some journeyer up the Nile, who, unable to otherwise account for it, considered and stated the animal to be the hybrid offspring of the leopard and camel. Another points needs to be borne in mind. Earlier artists were in no way fettered by any supposed necessity for making their pictures realistic representations. Realism is a modernity. Their pictures were decoration, and they thought far more of making their subject fit the space to be decorated than of making it a 'speaking likeness'.

Nevertheless, their work was not all imagination. In the *Crocodile* we get the basis of the dragon, if indeed the heraldic dragon be not a perpetuation of ancient legends, or even perhaps of then existing representations of those winged antediluvian animals, the fossilised remains of which are now available. Wings, however, need never be considered a difficulty. It has ever been the custom (from the angels of Christianity to the personalities of Mercury and Pegasus) to add wings to any figure held in veneration. Why, it would be difficult to say, but nevertheless the fact remains.

The Unicorn, however, it is not easy to resolve into an original basis, because until the seventeenth century every one fondly believed in the existence of the animal. Mr Beckles Wilson appears to have paid considerable attention to the subject, and was responsible for the article 'The Rise of the Unicorn' which once appeared in *Cassell's Magazine*. That writer traces the matter to a certain extent from non-heraldic sources, and the following remarks, which are taken from the above article, are of considerable interest:

'The real genesis of the unicorn was probably this: at a time when armorial bearings were becoming an indispensable part of a noble's equipment, the attention of those knights who were fighting under the banner of the Cross was attracted to the wild antelopes of Syria and Palestine. These animals are armed with long, straight, spiral horns set close together, so that at a side view they appeared to be but a single horn. To confirm this, there are some old illuminations and drawings extant which endow the early unicorn with many of the attributes of the deer and goat kind. The sort of horn supposed to be carried by these Eastern antelopes had long been a curiosity, and was occasionally brought back as a trophy by travellers from the remote parts of the earth. There is a fine one to be seen today at the abbey of St Denis, and others in various collections in Europe. We now know these so-called unicorn's horns, usually carved, to belong to that marine monster the narwhal, or sea-unicorn. But the fable of a breed of horned horses is at least as old as Pliny' [Had the 'gnu' anything to do with this?], 'and centuries later the Crusaders, or the monkish artists who accompanied them, attempted to delineate the marvel. From their first rude sketches other artists copied; and so each presentment was passed along, until at length the present form of the unicorn was attained. There was a time—not so long ago—when the existence of the unicorn was as implicitly believed in as the camel or any other animal not seen in these latitudes; and the translators of the Bible set their seal upon the legend by translating the Hebrew word *reem* (which probably meant a rhinoceros) as "unicorn". Thus the worthy Thomas Fuller came to consider the existence of the unicorn clearly proved by the mention of it in Scripture! Describing the horn of the animal, he writes, "Some are plain, as that of St Mark's in Venice; others wreathed about it, which probably is the effect of age, those wreaths being but the wrinkles of most vivacious unicorns. The same may be said of the colour: white when newly taken from the head; yellow, like that lately in the Tower, of some hundred years' seniority; but whether or no it will soon turn black, as that of Plinie's description, let others decide."

'All the books on natural history so late as the seventeenth century describe at length the unicorn; several of them carefully depict him as though the artist had drawn straight from the life.

'If art had stopped here, the wonder of the unicorn would have remained but a paltry thing after all. His finer qualities would have been unrecorded, and all his virtues hidden. But, happily, instead of this, about the animal first conceived in the brain of a Greek (as Pegasus also was), and embodied through the fertile fancy of the Crusader, the monks and heraldists of the Middle Ages devised a host of spiritual legends. They told of his pride, his purity, his endurance, his matchless spirit.

'"The greatnesse of his mynde is such that he chooseth rather to dye than be taken alive." Indeed, he was only conquerable by a beautiful maiden. One fifteenth-century writer gives a recipe for catching a unicorn. "A maid is set where he hunteth; and she openeth her lap, to whom the unicorn, as seeking rescue from the force of the hunter, yieldeth his head and leaveth all his fierceness, and resteth himself under her protection, sleepeth until he is taken and slain." But although many were reported to be thus enticed to their destruction, only their horns, strange to say, ever reached Europe. There is one in King Edward's collection at Buckingham Palace.

'Naturally, the horn of such an animal was held a sovereign specific against poison, and "ground unicorn's horn" often figures in medieval books of medicine.

'There was in Shakespeare's time at Windsor Castle the "horn of a unicorn of above eight spans and a half in length, valued at above £10,000." This may have been the one now at Buckingham Palace. One writer, describing it, says:

'"I doe also know that horn the King of England possesseth to be wreathed in spires, even as that is accounted in the Church of St Dennis, than which they suppose none greater in the world, and I never saw anything in any creature more worthy praise than this horne. It is of soe great a length that the tallest man can scarcely touch the top thereof, for it doth fully equal seven great feet. It weigheth thirteen pounds, with their assize, being only weighed by the gesse of the hands it seemeth much heavier."

'Spenser, in the *Færie Queen*, thus describes a contest between the unicorn and the lion:

> Like as the lyon, whose imperial powre
> A proud rebellious unicorn defyes,
> T'avoide the rash assault and wrathful stowre
> Of his fiers foe, him to a tree applies.
> And when him running in full course he spyes
> He slips aside; the whiles that furious beast
> His precious horne, sought of his enimyes,
> Strikes in the stroke, ne thence can be released,
> But to the victor yields a bounteous feast.

414 *Unicorn rampant.*

'"It hath," remarked Guillim, in 1600, "been much questioned among naturalists which it is that is properly called the unicorn; and some have made doubt whether there be such a beast or no. But the great esteem of his horn in many places to be seen may take away that needless scruple."

'Another old writer, Topsell, says:

'"These beasts are very swift, and their legs have not articles. They keep for the most part in the deserts, and live solitary in the tops of the mountaines. There was nothing more horrible than the voice or braying of it, for the voice is strained above measure. It fighteth both with the mouth and with the heeles, with the mouth biting like a lyon, and with the heeles kicking like a horse."

415 *Unicorn passant.*

'Nor is belief in the unicorn confined to Europe. By Chinese writers it is characterised as a "spiritual beast". The existence of the unicorn is firmly credited by the most intelligent natives and by not a few Europeans. A very trustworthy observer, the Abbé Huc, speaks very positively on the subject: "The unicorn really exists in Tibet. . . . We had for a long time a small Mongol treatise on Natural History, for the use of children, in which a unicorn formed one of the pictorial illustrations."'

The unicorn, however, as it has heraldically developed, is drawn with the body of a horse, the tail of the heraldic lion, the legs and feet of the deer, the head and mane of a horse, to which is added the long twisted horn from which the animal is named, and a beard (414, 415, and 416). A good representation of the unicorn will be found in the figure of the Royal Arms herein, and in 417, which is as fine a piece of heraldic design as could be wished.

416 *Unicorn statant.*

The crest of Yonge of Colbrooke, Devonshire, is 'a demi-sea-unicorn argent, armed gules, finned or,' and the crest of Tynte (Kemeys-Tynte of Cefn Mably and Halswell) is 'on a mount vert, a unicorn sejant argent, armed and crined or.'[100]

The unicorn will be found in the arms of Styleman, quartered by Le Strange, and Swanzy.

The Griffin or *Gryphon*. Though in the popular mind any heraldic monster is generically termed a griffin, the griffin has, nevertheless, very marked and distinct peculiarities. It is one of the hybrid monstrosities which heraldry is so fond of, and is formed by the body, hind-legs, and a tail of a lion conjoined to the head and claws of an eagle, the latter acting as its forepaws (418–20). It has the wings of the eagle, which are never represented close, but it also has ears, and this, by the way, should be noted, because herein is the only distinction between a griffin's head and an eagle's head when the rest of the body is not represented (421). Though but very seldom so met with, it is occasionally found proper, by which description is meant that the plumage is of the brown colour of the eagle, the rest of the body being the natural colour of the lion. The griffin is frequently found with its beak and fore-legs of a different colour from its body, and is then termed 'armed', though another term, 'beaked and fore-legged', is almost as frequently used. A very popular idea is that the origin of the griffin was the dimidiation of two coats of arms, one having an eagle and the other a lion as charges, but taking the origin of armory to belong to about the end of the eleventh century, or thereabouts, the griffin can be found as a distinct creation, not necessarily heraldic, at a very much earlier date. An exceedingly good and an early representation of the griffin will be found in 422. It is a representation of the great seal of the town of Schweidnitz

417 *Unicorn rampant.*

100. A winged sea-unicorn is to be found as one of the supporters of the arms of the Royal Overseas League.

418 *Gryphon segreant.*

419 *Gryphon passant.*

420 *Gryphon statant.*

421 *Gryphon's head erased.*

422 *Seal of the Town of Schweidnitz.*

in the jurisdiction of Breslau, and belongs to the year 1315. The inscription is '+S universitatis civium de Swidnitz'. In the grant of arms to the town in the year 1452, the griffin is gules on a field of argent.[101]

The griffin will be found in all sorts of positions, and the terms applied to it are the same as would be applied to a lion, except in the single instance of the rampant position. A griffin is then termed 'segreant' (418). The wings are usually represented as endorsed and erect, but this is not compulsory, as will be noticed by reference to the supporters of the Earl of Mar and Kellie, in which the wings are inverted.

There is a certain curiosity in English heraldry, wholly peculiar to it, which may be here referred to. A griffin in the ordinary way is merely so termed, but a male griffin by some curious reasoning has no wings, but is adorned with spikes showing at some number of points on its body (423). I have, under my remarks upon the panther, hazarded the supposition that the male griffin of English heraldry is nothing more than a British development and form of the Continental heraldic panther which is unknown to us. The origin of the clusters and spikes, unless they are to be found in the flames of fire associated with the panther, must remain a mystery. The male griffin is very seldom met with, but two of these creatures were the supporters of Sir George John Egerton Dashwood, Bart. Whilst we consider the griffin a purely mythical animal, there is no doubt whatever that earlier writers devoutly believed that such animals existed. Sir John Maundeville tells us in his *Travels* that they abound in Bacharia. 'Sum men seyn that thei han the body upward as an egle, and benethe as a lyoun; and treuly thei seyn sothe that thei ben of that schapp. But a Griffoun hathe the body more gret and more strong than eight lyouns of such lyouns as ben o' this half [of the world], and more gret and stronger than an 100 egles such as we han amonges us . . .,' and other writers, whilst not considering them an original type of animal, undoubtedly believed in their existence as hybrid of the eagle and the lion. It is of course a well-known fact that the mule, the most popular hybrid, does not breed. This fact would be accepted as accounting for the rarity of animals which were considered to be hybrids.

Though there are examples of griffins in some of the earliest rolls of arms, the animal cannot be said to have come into general use until a somewhat later period. Nowadays, however, it is probably next in popularity to the lion.

The demi-griffin is very frequently found as a crest.

A griffin's head (421) is still yet more frequently met with, and as a charge upon the shields it will be found in the arms of Raikes, Kay, and many other families.

A variety of the griffin is found in the gryphon-marine, or sea-griffin. In it the fore part of the creature is that of the eagle, but the wings are sometimes omitted; and the lower half of the animal is that of a fish, or rather of a mermaid. Such a creature is the charge in the arms of the Silesian family of Mestich: 'Argent, a sea-griffin proper' (Siebmacher, *Wappenbuch*, i, 69). 'Azure, a (winged) sea-griffin per fess gules and argent crowned or', is the coat of the Barons von Puttkammer. One of two other Pomeranian families have the like charge without wings.

423 *Male gryphon.*

424 *Dragon rampant.*

101. In this illustration it will be noted that the griffin sports a short beard. Medieval representations of this monster almost always show a beard, and the current artistic trend is to give the griffin its ancient tuft.

The Dragon. Much akin to the griffin is the dragon, but the similarity of appearance is more superficial than real, inasmuch as in all details it differs, except in the broad similarity that it has four legs, a pair of wings, and is a terrible creature. The much referred to 'griffin' opposite the Law Courts in the Strand is really a dragon. The head of a dragon is like nothing else in heraldry, and from what source it originated or what basis existed for ancient heraldic artists to imagine it from must remain a mystery, unless it has developed from the crocodile or some antediluvian animal much akin. It is like nothing else in heaven or on earth. Its neck is covered with scales not unlike those of a fish. All four legs are scaled and have claws, the back is scaled, the tongue is barbed, and the under part of the body is likewise scaled, but here, in rolls of a much larger size. Great differences will be found in the shape of the ears, but the wings of the dragon are always represented as the wings of a bat, with the long ribs or bones carried to the base (424–6). The dragon is one of the most artistic of heraldic creations, and lends itself very readily to the genius of any artist. In nearly all modern representations the tail, like the tongue, will be found ending in a barb, but it should be observed that this is a comparatively recent addition. All dragons of the Tudor period were invariably represented without any such additions to their tails. The tail was long and smooth, ending in a blunt point.[102]

425 *Dragon passant.*

426 *Dragon statant.*

Whilst we have separate and distinct names for many varieties of dragon-like creatures, other countries in their use of the word 'dragon' include the wyvern, basilisk, cockatrice, and other similar creatures, but the distinct name in German heraldry for our foot-footed dragon is the *Lindwurm*, and 427 is a representation of the dragon according to German ideas, which nevertheless might form an example for English artists to copy, except that we very seldom represent ours as coward.

The red dragon upon a mount vert, which forms a part of the Royal achievement as the badge of Wales, is known as the red dragon of Cadwallader, and in deference to a loudly expressed sentiment on the subject, His Majesty King George V added the Welsh dragon differenced by a label of three points argent as an additional badge to the achievement of His Royal Highness the Prince of Wales.[103] The red dragon was one of the supporters of the Tudor kings, being used by Henry VII, Henry VIII, and Edward VI. Queen Elizabeth I, however, whose liking for gold is evidenced by her changing the Royal mantle from gules and ermine to gold and ermine, also changed the colour of the dragon as her supporter to gold, and many Welsh scholars hold that the ruddy dragon of Wales was and should be of ruddy gold and not of gules. There is some room for doubt whether the dragon in the Royal Arms was really of Welsh origin. The

427 *A German dragon.*

R *Augmented Royal Badge for Wales.*

102. The barbed tail is to be found in the early seventeenth century. I have in my possession an exemplification of the quarterings of Sir Thomas Monke of Powderham, Devon, by Sir William Segar, Garter, painted *c.* 1620, in which the wyvern crest has an almost ostentatiously barbed tail. The barbed tongue is to be found at a much earlier period.

103. The Royal Badge for Wales was augmented by Royal Warrant dated 11 March 1953. The Warrant recites that, 'for the greater honour and distinction of Wales', the Royal Badge for Wales, namely the Red dragon passant, shall be augmented as follows: 'Within a circular riband argent, fimbriated or, bearing the motto Y. DDRAIG. GOCH. DDYRYO. CYCHWYN. in letters vert and ensigned with a representation of the Crown proper, an escutcheon per fess argent and vert and thereon the red dragon passant' (R).

428 *Wyvern.*

429 *Wyvern with wings displayed.*

430 *Wyvern erect.*

431 *Cockatrice.*

S *Crest of Elderkor.*

point was discussed at some length by the present writer in the *Genealogical Magazine* (October 1902). It was certainly in use by King Henry III.

A dragon may be statant (426), rampant (424), or passant (425), and the crests of Bicknell and of Sir Charles Young, Garter King of Arms, are examples of dragons couchant.

A sea-dragon, whatever that creature may be, occurs in one of the crests of Mr Mainwaring-Ellerker-Onslow.[104]

Variations such as that attributed to the family of Raynor ['Argent, a dragon volant in bend sable'], the dragon overthrown on the arms of Langridge as quartered by Lowdell, and the sinister supporter of the arms of Viscount Gough ['The dragon of China or gorged with a mural crown and chained sable'] may be noted. The Chinese dragon, which is also the dexter supporter of Sir Robert Hart, Bart., follows closely the Chinese model, and is without wings.

The Wyvern. There is no difference whatever between a wyvern's head and a dragon's, but there is considerable difference between a wyvern and a dragon, at any rate in English heraldry, though the wyvern appears to be the form more frequently met with under the name of a dragon in other countries. The wyvern has only two legs, the body curling away into the tail, and it is usually represented as resting upon its legs and tail (428 and 429). On the other hand, it will occasionally be found sitting erect upon its tail with its claws in the air (430), and the supporters of the Duke of Marlborough are generally so represented. As a charge or crest, however, probably the only instance of a wyvern sejant erect is the crest of Mansergh. A curious crest also is that of Langton, namely: 'On a wreath of the colours, an eagle or and a wyvern vert, interwoven and erect on their tails,' and an equally curious one is the crest of Maule, *i.e.* 'A wyvern vert, with two heads vomiting fire at both ends proper, charged with a crescent argent.'

Occasionally the wyvern is represented without wings and with the tail nowed. Both these peculiarities occur in the case of the crest of a Lancashire family named Farington.

The Cockatrice. The next variety is the cockatrice (431), which is, however, comparatively rare. Two cockatrices are the supporters to the arms of the Earl of Westmeath, and also to the arms of Sir Edmund Charles Nugent, Bart. But the animal is not common as a charge. The difference between a wyvern and a cockatrice is that the latter has the head of a cock substituted for the dragon's head with which the wyvern is decorated. Like the cock, the beak, comb, and wattles are often of another tincture, and the animal is then termed 'armed, combed, and wattled'.

104. Fox-Davies' perplexity is understandable. When the arms and crest of Ellerker of Risby, Yorkshire were exemplified to Mr G. J. H. Onslow by virtue of a Royal Licence (he having succeeded to the estates of Ellerker) in 1861, the crest was blazoned: a dolphin haurient azure and a sea dragon or, emitting flames of fire proper, embowed and addorsed and enfiled by a ducal coronet per pale or and azure, charged with a roundel counterchanged for difference. In fact the patent granting this crest to Sir Raufe Elderkor of Risby on 20 March 1545 was discovered after the exemplification had been made and the true blazon of the crest was found to be: 'a dollphyn asure tusked golde a salamanders hed rased of the same castenge flames of fyre indosant (addorsed) within a croun counterchaunged' (S).

The sea dragon, like other sea creatures (except the sea wolf and sea dog), is half dragon, half fish. The sinister supporter of the arms of Newport, Monmouthshire, is a sea dragon gules, the nether parts proper finned gold.

The cockatrice is sometimes termed a *basilisk*, and according to ancient writers the basilisk is produced from an egg laid by a nine-year old cock and hatched by a toad on a dunghill. Probably this is merely the expression of the intensified loathing which it was desired to typify. But the heraldic basilisk is stated to have is tail terminating in a dragon's head. In English heraldry, at any rate, I know of no such example.

432 *Camelopard.*

The Hydra, or *Seven-headed Dragon*, as the crest, is ascribed to the families of Barret, Crespine, and Lownes.

The Camelopard (432), which is nothing more or less than an ordinary giraffe, must be properly included amongst mythical animals, because the form and semblance of the giraffe was used to represent a mythical hybrid creation which the ancients believed to be begotten between a leopard and a camel. Possibly they represented the real giraffe (which they may have known), taking that to be a hybrid between the two animals stated. It occurs as the crest of several coats of arms for the name of Crisp.

The Camelopardel, which is another mythical animal fathered upon armory, is stated to be the same as the camelopard, but with the addition of two long horns curved backwards. I know of no instance in which it occurs.

The human face or figure conjoined to some other animal's body gives us a number of heraldic creatures, some of which play no inconsiderable part in armory.

The human figure (male) conjoined to the tail of a fish is known as the *Triton* or *Merman* (433). Though there are some number of instances in which it occurs as a supporter, it is seldom met with as a charge upon a shield. It is, however, to be found in the arms of Otway, and is assigned as a crest to the family of Tregent, and a family of Robertson, of London.

433 *Merman.*

The Mermaid (434), is much more frequently met with. It is generally represented with the traditional mirror and comb in the hands. It will be found appearing, for example, in the arms of Ellis, of Glasfryn, co. Monmouth. The crest of Mason, used without authority by the founder of Mason's College, led to its inclusion in the arms of the University of Birmingham. It will also be found as the crest of Rutherford and many other families.

434 *Mermaid.*

The Melusine, i.e. a mermaid with two tails disposed on either side, though not unknown in British heraldry, is more frequent in German.[105]

The Sphinx, of course originally derived from the Egyptian figure, has the body, legs, and tail of a lion conjoined to the breasts, head, and face of a woman (435). As a charge it occurs in the arms of Cochrane and Cameron of Fassiefern. This last-mentioned coat affords a striking example of the over-elaboration to be found in so many of the grants which owe their origin to the Peninsular War and the other 'fightings' in which England was engaged at the period. A winged sphinx is the crest of a family of the name of Asgile. Two sphinxes were granted as supporters to Sir Edward Malet, G.C.B.[106]

435 *Sphinx.*

105. The only example that I can find of the Melusine in English heraldry occurs in the arms of the late Sir Hans Vischer: sable, issuant from water barry in base a mermaid with two tails reflexed and grasped in her hands proper, crined and ducally crowned or.

106. These supporters, granted on 14 September 1885, are not the sphinxes shown in the illustration, but are rampant. They are blazoned: on either side a sphinx ermine, hooded or, charged on the shoulder with an escallop of the last.

436 Centaur.

The Centaur (436)— the familiar fabulous animal, half man, half horse—is sometimes represented carrying a bow and arrow, when it is called a 'sagittarius'. It is not infrequently met with in heraldry, though it is to be found more often in Continental than in English blazonry. In its 'sagittarius' form it is sculptured on a column in the Romanesque cloister of St Aubin at Angers. It will be found as the crest of most families named Lambert, and it was one of the supporters of Lord Hood of Avelon. It is also the crest of a family of Fletcher. A very curious crest was borne by a family of Lambert, and is to be seen on their monuments. They could establish no official authority for their arms as used, and consequently obtained official authorisation in the early part of the eighteenth century, when the crest then granted was a regulation sagittarius, but up to that time, however, they had always used a 'female centaur' holding a rose in its dexter hand.

Chimera. This legendary animal happily does not figure in English heraldry, and but rarely abroad. It is described as having the head and breast of a woman, the forepaws of a lion, the body of a goat, the hind-legs of a griffin, and the tail of a dragon, and would be about as ugly and misbegotten a creature as can readily be imagined.

The Man-Lion will be found referred to under the heading of lions, and Elvin mentions in addition the *Werewolf*, *i.e.* the wolf with a human face and horns. Probably this creature has strayed into heraldic company by mistake. I know of no armorial use of it.

The Satyr, which has a well-established existence in other than heraldic sources of imagination, is composed of a demi-savage united to the hind-legs of a goat.

The Satyral is a hybrid animal having the body of a lion and the face of an old man, with the horns of an antelope. I know of no instance of its use.

The Harpy— which is a curious creature consisting of the head, neck, and breasts of a woman conjoined to the wings and body of a vulture— is peculiarly German, though it does exist in the heraldry of this country. The German name for it is the *Jungfraunadler*. The shield of the Rietbergs, Princes of Ost-Friesland, is: 'Sable, a harpy crowned, and with wings displayed all proper, between four stars, two in chief and as many in base or.' The harpy will be found as a crest in this country.[107]

The Devil is not, as may be imagined, a favourite heraldic charge. The arms of Sissinks of Groningen, however, are: 'Or, a horned devil having six paws, the body terminating in the tail of a fish all gules.' The family of Bawde have for a crest: 'A satyr's head in profile sable, with wings to the side of the head or, the tongue hanging out of his mouth gules.' Though so blazoned, I feel sure it is really intended to represent a fiend. On the Garter Stall-plate of John de Grailly, Captal de Buch, the crest is a man's head with ass's ears. This is, however, usually termed a Midas' head. A certain coat of arms which is given in the *General Armory* under the name of Dannecourt, and also under the name of Morfyn or Murfyn, has for a crest: 'A blackamoor's head couped at the shoulders, habited paly of six ermine and ermines, pendents in his ears or, wreathed about the forehead, with bat's wings to the head sable, expanded on each side.'

107. The harpy also occurs in the arms of Moody of Worcestershire and Wiltshire, as recorded in the 1624 Visitation of the latter county. The arms are: vert, on a fess engrailed between three harpies argent, another fess gules. Later grants to families of Moody generally contain harpies.

Many mythical animals can be more conveniently considered under their natural counterparts. Of these the notes upon the heraldic antelope and the heraldic ibex accompany those upon the natural antelope, and the heraldic panther is included with the real animal. The heraldic tyger, likewise, is referred to concurrently with the Bengal or natural tiger. The pegasus, the sea-horse, and the winged sea-horse are mentioned with other examples of the horse, and the sea-dog is included with other breeds and varieties of that useful animal. The winged bull, of which only one instance is known to me, occurs as the supporters of the Butchers' Livery Company, and has been already alluded to, as also the winged stag. The sea-stag is referred to under the sub-heading of stags. The two-headed lion, the double-queued lion, the lion queue-fourché, the sea-lion (which is sometimes found winged) are all included in the chapter upon lions, as are also the winged lion and the lion-dragon. The winged ape was mentioned when considering the natural animal, and perhaps it may be as well to allude to the asserted heraldic existence of the sea-monkey, though I am not aware of any instance in which it is borne.

The arms of Challoner afford an instance of the *Sea-Wolf*, the crest of that family being: 'A demi-sea-wolf rampant or.' Guillim, however (p. 271), in quoting the arms of Fennor, would seem to assert the sea-wolf and sea-dog to be one and the same.[108] They certainly look rather like each other.

The Phœnix and the *Double-headed Eagle* will naturally be more conveniently dealt with in the chapter upon the eagle.

The Salamander has been represented in various ways, and is usually described as a dragon in flames of fire. It is sometimes so represented but without wings, though it more usually follows the shape of a lizard.

437 *Salamander.*

The salamander is, however, best known as the personal device of Francis I, King of France. It is to this origin that the arms of the city of Paris can be traced.

The remainder of the list of heraldic monsters can be very briefly dismissed. In many cases a good deal of research has failed to discover an instance of their use, and one is almost inclined to believe that they were invented by those medieval writers of prolific imagination for their treatises, without ever having been borne or emblazoned upon helmet or shield.

The Allocamelus is supposed to have the head of an ass conjoined to the body of a camel. I cannot call to mind any British instance of its use.

The Amphiptère is the term applied to a 'winged serpent', a charge of but rare occurrence in either English or foreign heraldry. It is found in the arms of the French family of Potier, viz.: 'Azure, a bendlet purpure between two amphiptères or,' while they figure as supporters also in that family, and in those of the Ducs de Tresmes and De Gevres.

The Apres is an animal with the body similar to that of a bull, but with a bear's tail. It is seldom met with outside heraldic text-books.

The Amphisbæna is usually described as a winged serpent (with two legs) having a head at each end of its body, but in the crest of Gwilt ['On a saltire or, interlaced by two amphisbænæ azure, langued gules, a rose of the last, barbed and seeded proper'] the creatures certain do not answer to the

108. See note 82. This shows that Guillim was wrong in his assertion, and that the heralds distinguished both in blazon and pictorial representation between these two monsters.

foregoing description. They must be seen to be duly appreciated.[109]

The Cockfish is a very unusual charge, but it is to be met with in the arms of the family of Geyss, in Bavaria, *i.e.*: 'Or, a cock sable, beaked of the first, crested and armed gules, its body ending in that of a fish curved upwards, proper.'

The Enfield (438) is a purely fanciful animal, having the head of a fox, chest of a greyhound, talons of an eagle, body of a lion, and hind legs and tail of a wolf. It occurs as the crest of most Irish families of the name of Kelly.

The Bagwyn is an imaginary animal with the head of and much like the heraldic antelope, but with the body and tail of a horse, and the horns long and curved backwards. It is difficult to say what it is intended to represent, and I can give no instance in which it occurs.[110]

The Musimon is a fabulous animal with the body and feet of a goat and the head of a ram, with four horns. It is supposed to be the hybrid between the ram and the goat, the four horns being the two straight ones of the goat and the two curled ones of the ram. Though no heraldic instance is known to me, one cannot definitely say such an animal never existed. Another name for it is the tityron.

The Opinicus (439) is another monster seldom met with in armory. When it does occur it is represented as a winged gryphon, with a lion's legs and short tail. Another description of it gives it the body and forelegs of a lion, the head, neck, and wings of an eagle, and the tail of a camel. It is the crest of the Livery Company of Barbers in London, which doubtless gives us the origin of it in the grant of arms to Sir Frederick Treves, Bart. Sometimes the wings are omitted.

The Manticora, *Mantegre*, or *Man-Tiger* is the same as the man-lion, but has horns attached to its forehead.

The Hippogriff has the head, wings and foreclaws of the griffin united to the hinder part of the body of a horse.

The Calopus or *Chatloup* is a curious horned animal difficult to describe, but which appears to have been at one time the badge of the Foljambe family. No doubt, as the name would seem to indicate, it is a variant of the wolf.[111]

Many of the foregoing animals, particularly those which are or are supposed to be hybrids, are, however well they may be depicted, ugly, inartistic, and unnecessary. Their representation leaves one with a disappointed feeling of crudity of draughtmanship. No such objection applies to the pegasus, the griffin, the sea-

438 *Enfield.*

439 *Opinicus.*

T *Crest of Cathorne.*

109. This crest, granted to Joseph Gwilt of Westminster on 11 January 1728, is here blazoned that it may be duly appreciated. The etymology of the word amphisbæna ($\dot{\alpha}\mu\varphi\acute{\iota}\varsigma$ = both ways, plus $\beta\alpha\acute{\iota}\nu\epsilon\iota\nu$ = to go) suggests that it should have two heads; but in fact amphisbæna is the name given to a group of lizards which can move backwards and forwards with equal facility; it is this that has given rise to the legend that they have two heads. The Gwilt amphisbænæ should perhaps be in the section devoted to reptiles, as they are not the fabulous variety. The two-headed monster, which is illustrated in Elvin's *Dictionary of Heraldry*, does not, in fact, seem to have found its way into armory.

110. The bagwyn is an Arundel beast, and is so designated in *Prince Arthur's Book*, an early Tudor armorial in the possession of the College of Arms.

111. This monster, also called the calippus or calypus, predominates in the heraldry of a family of Cathorne. The following arms were granted to Thomas Cathorne of Pembrokeshire on 1 December 1553: gules, on a fess engrailed between three calypus' heads erased argent, horned or, as many hawthorn branches proper. Crest: on a wreath or and azure a calypus statant proper, horned or, holding in the dexter paw a hawthorn branch leaved vert, budded argent, stalked sable (T). The calypus is painted a brownish colour.

horse, the dragon, or the unicorn, and in these modern days, when the differentiation of well-worn animals is producing singularly inept results, one would urge that the sea-griffin, the sea-stag, the winged bull, the winged stag, the winged lion, and winged heraldic antelope might produce (if the necessity of differentiation continue) very much happier results.[112]

112. Fox-Davies has described various weird monsters, some of which are never found in heraldy. Curiously, he has omitted to describe or even note a number of equally strange monsters who are more or less well known in armory. Some of the more important omissions are:

The Yale. The principal characteristic of this monster is its ability to swivel its long horns about at will. Apart from this it is shown in a variety of ways. Generally it has tushes and tufts of hair on its body, which is sometimes goat-like and sometimes more like that of a boar, whilst the tail is either short and stumpy, or similar to that of the heraldic lion. The yale first appears in heraldry as a supporter of the arms of John, Duke of Bedford (died 1435), and is illustrated in *The Bedford Book of Hours.* Perhaps the best known yale is that which formed one of the ten Queen's Beasts and stood outside Westminster Abbey at the Coronation in 1953. This silver yale spattered with bezants is that used by various members of the Beaufort family, from some of whom the Queen descends. Splendid examples of this yale can be seen on the gatehouses of Christ's and St John's Colleges at Cambridge.

U *Crest of Hollinsyde.*

The Bonacon. The bonacon or bonasus appears in ancient beastiaries, and is a bull-like creature but with a mane and serrated horns which curve in towards each other. It has the unlovely habit of ejecting its excrements in the direction of its enemies, whereby they are burnt up as if with fire. It appears to have been introduced into heraldry by Sir Gilbert Dethick, Garter. On 22 June 1560 he granted Richard Chandelor, of Walsingham, Norfolk, this crest: a bonacon's head couped sable, horned and maned azure; and on 1 July following he granted Hugh Hollinsyde alias Hollenshed of Bosley, Cheshire, a bonacon's head erased gules, horned, maned and about the neck a coronet or, for his crest (U).

The Pantheon. Like the yale, the pantheon can be found in various forms, but its principal characteristic is that it is spattered with stars and has cloven hooves. Usually it is represented like a hind, and it is in this guise that it makes an early appearance in heraldry as a Paulet beast in *Prince Arthur's Book* (c. 1539). Pantheons still support the arms of the Marquesses of Winchester, although they are generally blazoned as hinds semy of estoils. On 10 July 1556 Sir Gilbert Dethick granted the following arms to Henry Northey of Bocking, Essex: or, on a fess azure, between three pantheons proper, a pansy of the field between two lilies argent. Here the pantheons look more like donkeys, but it is interesting to note that Dethick considered the 'proper' colour for a pantheon to be purpure and in this way it is usually depicted. Pantheons have recently been granted as supporters to the arms of the United Kingdom Atomic Energy Authority.

The Calygreyhound and others. This and the monsters which follow are usually peculiar to one family. Thus the calygreyhound is a de Vere beast, and was used as a supporter and badge by the de Veres, Earls of Oxford. It is frequently referred to in the inventory to the will of John de Vere, 13th Earl of Oxford, who died in 1513. It appears to have the body of a cat, but tufted and with eagle's claws in place of the fore-paws; it has sprouting antler-like horns and a long tufted tail. The *Theow* or *Thoye* is a Cheyne beast, and is so described in *Prince Arthur's Book.* It is rather like a wolf or mastiff, but with a cows tail and cloven hooves. West, Lords de la Warr, had a beast referred to in Tudor books as an *Alphyn.* It was rather like the heraldic tyger, but with eagle's claws for fore-legs and a knotted tail. Another version gives it an unknotted tail and cloven hooves. In *Sir John Fenn's Book of Badges* (c. 1470) (B.M. Add. MS. 40742), an *Ypotryll* is given as the badge of 'Worcestre', probably of John Tiptoft, Earl of Worcester 1449–71. It has a face like that of a boar with tushes, the body of a camel with two hairy humps a long tapering tail and ox-like legs, hooves and mane.

The horned demi-eagle granted to Robert Laward, or Lord, of London (early sixteenth century) has been identified by the late Mr H. S. London, Norfolk Herald Extraordinary, as the *Tragopan* mentioned in Pliny's *Natural History.* Details of this and the other monsters mentioned above can be found in a series of articles entitled 'Minor Monsters' by H. S. London, illustrated by A. Colin Cole (now Windsor Herald), and published in *The Coat of Arms,* volumes 3 and 4 (1954–8).

14 · Birds

440.

441.

442.

443 *Arms of Duke of Calabria.*

Birds of course play a large and prominent part in heraldry. Those which have been impressed into the service of heraldic emblazonment comprise almost every species known to the zoological world.

Though the earliest rolls of arms give us instances of various other birds, the bird which makes the most prominent appearance is the *Eagle*, and in all early representations this will invariably be found 'displayed'. A double-headed eagle displayed, from a Byzantine silk of the tenth century, is illustrated by Mr Eve in his *Decorative Heraldry*, so that it is evident that neither the eagle displayed nor the the double-headed eagle originated with the science of armory, which appropriated them ready-made, together with their symbolism. An eagle displayed as a symbolical device was certainly in use by Charlemagne.

It may perhaps here be advantageous to treat of the artistic development of the eagle displayed. Of this, of course, the earliest prototype is the Roman eagle of the Cæsars, and it will be to English eyes, accustomed to our conventional spread-eagle, doubtless rather startling to observe that the German type of the eagle, which follows the Roman disposition of the wings (which so many of our heraldic artists at the present day appear inclined to adopt either in the accepted German or in a slightly modified form as an eagle displayed) is certainly not a true displayed eagle according to our English ideas and requirements, inasmuch as the wings are inverted. It should be observed that in German heraldry it is simply termed an eagle, and not an eagle displayed. Considering, however, its very close resemblance to our eagle displayed, and also its very artistic appearance, there is every excuse for its employment in this country, and I for one should be sorry to observe its slowly increasing favour checked in this country. It is quite possible, however, to transfer the salient and striking points of beauty to the more orthodox position of the wings. The eagle (compared with the lion and the ordinaries) had no such predominance in early British heraldry that it enjoyed in Continental armory, and therefore it may be better to trace the artistic development of the German eagle.

In the twelfth and thirteenth centuries the eagle appears with the head raised and the beak closed. The *sachsen* (bones of the wings) are rolled up at the ends like a snail, and the pinions (like the talons) take a vertical downward direction. The tail, composed of a number of stiff feathers, frequently issues from a knob or ball. Compare 440 herewith.

With the end of the fourteenth century the head straightens itself, the beak opens and the tongue becomes visible. The rolling up of the wing-bones gradually disappears, and the claws form an acute angle with the direction of the body; and at this period the claws occasionally receive the 'hose' covering the upper part of the leg. The feathers of the tail spread out sicklewise (441).

444 *Eagle of Tyrol.*

445 *Arms of the Prussian Province of Brandenburg.*
(*From Ströhl's* Deutsche Wappenrolle.)

The fifteenth century shows the eagle with *sachsen* forming a half circle, the pinions spread out and radiating therefrom, and the claws more at a right angle (442). The sixteenth century draws the eagle in a more ferocious aspect, and depicts it in as ornamental and ornate a manner as possible.

From Konrad Grünenberg's *Wappenbuch* (Constance, 1483) is reproduced the shield (443) with the boldly sketched *Alderflügel mit Schwerthand* (eagle's wing with the sword hand), the supposed arms of the Duke of Calabria.

Quite in the same style is the eagle of Tyrol on a corporate flag of the Society of the Schwazer Bergbute (444), which belongs to the last quarter of the fifteenth century. This is reproduced from the impression in the Bavarian National Museum given in Hefner-Alteneck's *Book of Costumes*.

A modern German eagle drawn by H. G. Ströhl is shown in 445. The illustration is of the arms of the Prussian province of Brandenburg.

The double eagle has, of course, undergone a somewhat similar development.

The double eagle occurs in the East as well as in the West in very early times. Since about 1335 the double eagle has appeared sporadically as a symbol of the Roman-German Empire, and under the Emperor Sigismund (*d.* 1447) became the settled armorial device of the Roman Empire. King Sigismund, before his coronation as Emperor, bore the single-headed eagle.

It may perhaps be as well to point out, with the exception of the two positions 'displayed' (451) and 'close' (446), very little if any agreement at all exists amongst authorities either as to the terms to be employed or as to the position intended for the wings when a given term is used in a blazon. Practically every other single position is simply blazoned 'rising', this term being employed without any additional distinctive terms of variation in official blazons and emblazonments. Nor can one obtain any certain information from a reference to the real eagle, for the result of careful observation would seem to show that in the first stroke of the wings, when rising from the ground, the wings pass through every position from

177

446 *Eagle close.*

447 *Eagle rising, wings elevated and addorsed.*

448 *Eagle rising, wings addorsed and inverted.*

449 *Eagle rising, wings displayed and inverted.*

450 *Eagle rising, wings elevated and displayed.*

the wide outstretched form, which I term 'rising with wings elevated and displayed' (450), to a position practically 'close'. As a consequence, therefore, no one form can be said to be more correct than any other, either from the point of view of nature or from the point of view of ancient precedent. This state of affairs is eminently unsatisfactory, because in these days of necessary differentiation no heraldic artist of any appreciable knowledge or ability has claimed the liberty (which certainly has not been officially conceded) to depict an eagle rising with wings elevated and displayed, when it has been granted with the wings in the position addorsed and inverted. Such a liberty when the wings happen to be charged, as they so frequently are in modern English crests, must clearly be an impossibility.

Until some agreement has been arrived at, I can only recommend my readers to follow the same plan which I have long adopted in blazoning arms of which the official blazon has not been available to me. That is, to use the term 'rising', followed by the necessary description of the position of the wings (447–50). This obviates both mistake and uncertainty. Originally with us, as still in Germany, an eagle was always displayed, and in the days when coats of arms were few in number and simple in character the artist may well have been permitted to draw an eagle as he chose, providing it was an eagle. But arms and their elaboration in the last four hundred years have made this impossible. It is foolish to overlook this and idle in the face of existing facts to attempt to revert to former ways. Although now the English eagle displayed has the tip of its wings pointed upwards (451), and the contrary needs now to be mentioned in the blazon (452), this even with us was not so in the beginning. A reference to 453 and 454 will show how the eagle was formerly depicted.

The earliest instance of the eagle as a definitely heraldic charge upon a shield would appear to be its appearance upon the Great Seal of the Markgrave Leopold of Austria in 1136, where the equestrian figure of the Markgrave carries a shield so charged. More or less regularly, subsequently to the reign of Frederick Barbarossa, elected King of Romans in 1152, and crowned as Emperor in 1155, the eagle with one or two heads (there seems originally to have been little unanimity upon the point) seems to have become the recognised heraldic symbol of the Holy Roman Empire; and the seal of Richard, Earl of Cornwall, elected King of the Romans in 1257, shows his arms ['Argent, a lion rampant gules, within a bordure sable, bezanté'] displayed upon the breast of an eagle; but no properly authenticated contemporary instance of the use of this eagle by the Earl of Cornwall is found in this country. The origin of the double-headed eagle (455) has been the subject of endless controversy, the tale one is usually taught to believe being that it originated in the dimidiation upon one shield of two separate coats of arms. Nisbet states that the Imperial eagle was 'not one eagle with two heads, but two eagles, the one laid upon the other, and their heads separate, looking different ways, which represent the two heads of the Empire after it was divided into East and West'. The whole discussion is an apt example of the habit of earlier writers to find or provide hidden meanings and symbolisms when no such meanings existed. The real truth undoubtedly is that the double-headed eagle was an accepted figure long before heraldry came into existence, and that when the displayed eagle was usurped by armory as one of its peculiarly heraldic figures, the single-headed and double-headed varieties were used indifferently, until the double-headed eagle became stereotyped as the Imperial emblem. Napoleon, however, reverted to the single-headed eagle, and the former German Imperial eagle had likewise only one head.

451 *Eagle displayed.*

The Imperial eagle of Napoleon had little in keeping with then existing armorial types of the bird. There can be little doubt that the model upon which it was based was the Roman Eagle of the Cæsars as it figured upon the head of the Roman standards. In English terms of blazon the Napoleonic eagle would be: 'An eagle displayed with wings inverted, the head to the sinister, standing upon a thunderbolt or' (456).

The then existing double-headed eagles of Austria and Russia probably supply the reason why, when the German Empire was created, the Prussian eagle in a modified form was preferred to the resuscitation of the older double-headed eagle, which had theretofore been more usually accepted as the symbol of Empire.

452 *Eagle displayed with wings inverted.*

By the same curious idea which was noticed in the earlier chapter upon lions, and which ruled that the mere fact of the appearance of two or more lions rampant in the same coat of arms made them into lioncels, so more than one eagle upon a shield resulted sometimes in the birds becoming eaglets. Such a rule has never had official recognition, and no artistic difference is made between the eagle and the eaglet. The charges on the arms of Piers Gaveston, Earl of Cornwall, are blazoned as eagles (454). In the blazon of a few coats of arms, the term eaglet, however, still survives, *e.g.* in the arms of Child ['Gules a chevron ermine, between three eaglets close argent'], and in the arms of Smitheman ['Vert, three eaglets statant with wings displayed argent, collared or'].

When an eagle has its beak of another colour, it is termed 'armed' of that colour, and when the legs differ it is termed 'membered'.

453 *Arms of Ralph de Monthermer, Earl of Gloucester and Hereford: Or, an eagle vert. (From his seal, 1301.)*

An eagle volant occurs in the crest of Jessel ['On a wreath of the colours, a torch fesswise, fired proper, surmounted by an eagle volant argent, holding in the beak a pearl also argent. Motto: "Persevere"'].

Parts of an eagle are almost as frequently met with as the entire bird. Eagles' heads (457) abound as crests (they can be distinguished from the head of a griffin by the fact that the latter has always upstanding ears).

Unless otherwise specified (*e.g.* the crest of the late Sir Noel Paton was between the two wings of a dove), wings occurring in armory are always presumed to be the wings of an eagle. This, however, in English heraldry has little effect upon their design, for probably any well-conducted eagle (as any other bird) would disown the English heraldic wing, as it certainly would never recognise the German heraldic variety. A pair of wings when displayed and conjoined at the base is termed 'conjoined in leure' (458), from the palpable similarity of the figure in its appearance to the lure with which, thrown into the air, the falconer brought back his hawk to hand. The best known, and most frequently quoted instance, is the well-known coat of Seymour or St Maur ['Gules, two wings conjoined in leure the tips downwards or']. It should always be stated if the wings (as in the arms of Seymour) are inverted. Otherwise the tips are naturally presumed to be in chief.

Pairs of wings not conjoined can be met with in the arms and crest of Burne-Jones ['Azure, on a bend sinister argent between seven mullets, four in chief and

454 *Arms of Piers de Gaveston, Earl of Cornwall* (d. *1312*): *Vert, six eagles or.*

455 *Double-headed eagle displayed.*

456 *Napoleonic Eagle.*

457 *Eagle's head couped.*

458 *A pair of wings conjoined in leure.*

459 *An eagle's leg erased à la quise.*

three in base or, three pairs of wings addorsed purpure, charged with a mullet or. Crest: in front of fire proper two wings elevated and addorsed purpure, charged with a mullet or']; but two wings, unless conjoined or addorsed, will not usually be described as a pair. Occasionally, however, a pair of wings will be found in saltire, but such a disposition is most unusual. Single wings, unless specified to be the contrary, are presumed to be dexter wings.

Care needs to be exercised in some crests to observe the difference between (*a*) a bird's head between two wings, (*b*) a bird's head winged (a form not often met with, but in which rather more of the neck is shown, and the wings are conjoined thereto), and (*c*) a bird's head between two wings addorsed. The latter form, which of course is really no more than a representation of a crest between two wings turned to be represented upon a profile helmet, is one of the painful results of our absurd position rules for the helmet.

A pair of wings conjoined is sometimes termed a *vol*, and one wing a demivol. Though doubtless it is desirable to know these terms, they are but seldom found in use, and are really entirely French.

Eagles' legs are by no means an infrequent charge. They will usually be found erased at the thigh, for which there is a recognised term 'erased à la quise' (459), which, however, is by no means a compulsory one. An eagle's leg so erased was a badge of the house of Stanley. The eagle's leg will sometimes be met with couped below the feathers, but would then be more properly described as a claw.

A curious form of the eagle is found in the *alerion*, which is represented without beak or legs. It is difficult to conjecture what may have been the origin of the bird in this debased form, unless its first beginnings may be taken as a result of the unthinking perpetuation of some crudely drawn example. Its best-known appearance is, of course, in the arms of Loraine; and, as Planché has pointed out, this is as perfect an example of a canting anagram as can be met with in armory.

The Phœnix (460), one of the few mythical birds which heraldry has familiarized us with, is another, and perhaps the most patent example of all, of the appropriation by heraldic art of an ancient symbol, with its symbolism ready made. It belongs to the period of Grecian mythology. As a charge upon a shield it is comparatively rare, though it so occurs in the arms of Samuelson. On the other hand, it is frequently to be found as a crest. It is always represented as a demieagle issuing from flames of fire, and though the flames of fire will generally be found mentioned in the verbal blazon, this is not essential. Without its fiery surroundings it would cease to be a phœnix. On the other hand, though it is always depicted as a *demi*-bird (no instance to the contrary exists), it is never considered necessary to so specify it. It occurs as the crest of the Seymour family ['Out of a ducal coronet a phœnix issuant from flames of fire'].[113]

113. There is in fact a well-known instance of a whole phœnix being depicted. In the grant of arms to the Painters' Company of London made in 1486 the crest is blazoned: 'a Fenyx in his propre nature and coloure set with a wrethe gold and gowles,' and the illustration in the margin of the patent clearly shows the legs of the bird. The patent is exhibited at Painters' Hall in London. This phœnix is a distinctive bird emblazoned in many colours, indeed this presumably is why it was chosen as a symbol for the Painters. It is so frequently drawn as to be indistinguishable from a demi-eagle that it is forgotten that the phœnix is a mythical bird in no way related to the eagle.

The Osprey may perhaps be here mentioned, because its heraldic representation always shows it as a white eagle. It is however seldom met with, though it figures in the crests of Roche (Lord Fermoy) and Trist. The osprey is sometimes known as the sea-eagle, and heraldically so termed.

The Vulture (probably from its repulsive appearance in nature and its equally repulsive habits) is not a heraldic favourite. Two of these birds occur, however, as the supporters of Lord Graves.

The Falcon (461) naturally falls next to the eagle for consideration. Considering the very important part this bird played in the social life of earlier centuries, this cannot be a matter of any surprise. Heraldry, in its emblazonment, makes no distinction between the appearance of the hawk and the falcon, but for canting and other reasons the bird will be found described by all its different names, *e.g.* in the arms of Hobson, to preserve the obvious pun, the two birds are blazoned as hobbies.

460 *Phœnix.*

461 *Falcon.*

The falcon is frequently (more often than not) found belled. With the slovenliness (or some may exalt it into the virtue of freedom from irritating restriction) characteristic of many matters in heraldic blazon, the simple term 'belled' is found used indiscriminately to signify that the falcon is belled on one leg or belled on both, and if it is belled the bell must of necessity be on a jess. Others state that every falcon must of necessity (whether so blazoned or not) be belled upon at least one leg, and that when the term 'belled' is used it signifies that it is belled upon both legs. There is still yet another alternative, viz. that when 'belled' it has the bell on only one leg, but that when 'jessed and belled' it is belled on both legs. The jess is the leather thong with which the bells are attached to the leg, and it is generally considered, and this may be accepted, that when the term 'jessed' is included in the wording of the blazon the jesses are represented with the ends flying loose, unless the use of the term is necessitated by the jesses being of a different colour. When the term 'vervelled' is also employed it signifies that the jesses have small rings attached to the floating ends. In actual practice, however, it should be remembered that if the bells and jesses are of a different colour, the use of the terms 'jessed' and 'belled' is essential. A falcon is seldom drawn without at least one bell, and when it is found described as 'belled', in most cases it will be found that the intention is that it shall have two bells.

Like all other birds of prey the falcon may be 'armed', a technical term which theoretically should include the beak and legs, but in actual practice a falcon will be far more usually found described as 'beaked and legged' when these differ in tincture from its plumage.

When a falcon is blindfolded it is termed 'hooded'. It was always so carried on the wrist until it was flown.

The position of the wings and the confusion in the terms applied thereto is even more marked in the case of the falcon than the eagle.

Demi-falcons are not very frequently met with, but an example occurs in the crest of Jerningham.

A falcon's head is constantly met with as a crest.

When a falcon is represented preying upon anything it is termed 'trussing' its prey, though sometimes the description 'preying upon' is (perhaps less accurately) employed. Examples of this will be found in the arms of Madden ['Sable, a hawk

or, trussing a mallard proper, on a chief of the second a cross botonny gules'],
and in the crests of Graham, Cawston, and Yerburgh.

A falcon's leg appears in the crest of Joscelin.

The Pelican, with its curious heraldic representation and its strange terms, may
almost be considered an instance of the application of the existing name of a
bird to an entirely fanciful creation. Mr G. W. Eve, in his *Decorative Heraldry*,
states that in early representations of the bird it was depicted in a more naturalistic
form, but I confess I have not myself met with such an ancient representation.

462 Pelican in her piety.

Heraldically, it has been practically always depicted with the head and body
of an eagle, with wings elevated and with the neck embowed, pecking with its
beak at its breast. The term for this is 'vulning itself', and although it appears to
be necessary always to describe it in the blazon as 'vulning itself', it will never be
met with save in this position; a pelican's head even, when erased at the neck,
being always so represented. It is supposed to be pecking at its breast to provide
drops of blood as nourishment for its young, and it is termed 'in its piety' when
depicted standing in its nest and with its brood of young (462). It is difficult to
imagine how the pelican came to be considered as always existing in this position,
because there is nothing in the nature of a natural habit from which this could be
derived. There are, however, other birds which, during the brooding season, lose
their feathers upon the breast, and some which grow red feathers there, and it is
doubtless from this that the idea originated.[114]

In heraldic and ecclesiastical symbolism the pelican has acquired a somewhat
sacred character as typical of maternal solicitude. It will never be found 'close', or
in any other positions than with the wings endorsed and either elevated or
inverted.

When blazoned 'proper', it is always given the colour and plumage of the
eagle, and not its natural colour of white. In recent years, however, a tendency has
rather made itself manifest to give the pelican its natural and more ungainly appearance, and its curious pouched beak.

The Ostrich (463) is doubtless the bird which is most frequently met with as a
crest after the falcon, unless it be the dove or martlet. The ostrich is heraldically
emblazoned in a very natural manner, and it is difficult to understand why in the
case of such a bird heraldic artists of earlier days should have remained so true to
the natural form of the bird, whilst in other cases, in which they could have had
no less intimate acquaintance with the bird, greater variation is to be found.

463 Ostrich.

As a charge upon a shield it is not very common, although instances are to be
found in the arms of MacMahon ['Argent, an ostrich sable, in its beak a horse-
shoe or'], and in the arms of Mahon ['Per fess sable and argent, an ostrich counterchanged, holding in its beak a horse-shoe or'].

It is curious that, until quite recent times, the ostrich is never met with heraldically, unless holding a horse-shoe, a key, or some other piece of old iron in its
beak. The digestive capacity of the ostrich, though somewhat exaggerated, is by
no means fabulous, and in the earliest forms of its representation in all the old
natural history books it is depicted feeding upon this unnatural food. If this were

114. In fact, there is considerable doubt that this is the origin of the legend. It is more likely that
the pelican's habit of resting the pouched bill on its breast is responsible for this belief.

the popular idea of the bird, small wonder is it that heraldic artists perpetuated the idea, and even now the heraldic ostrich is seldom seen without a key or a horse-shoe in its beak.

The ostrich's head alone is sometimes met with, as in the crest of the Earl of Carysfort.

The wing of an ostrich charged with a bend sable is the crest of a family of Gulston, but an ostrich wing is by no means a usual heraldic charge.

Ostrich feathers, of course, play a large part in armory, but the consideration of these may be postponed for the moment until the feathers of cocks and pea-cocks can be added thereto.

The Dove—at least the heraldic bird—has one curious peculiarity. It is always represented with a slight tuft on its head. Mr Eve considers this to be merely the perpetuation of some case in which the crude draughtsman has added a tuft to its head. Possibly he is correct, but I think it may be an attempt to distinguish between the domestic dove and the wood-pigeon—both of which varieties would be known to the early heraldic artists.

464 *Dove.*

The dove with an olive branch in its beak is constantly and continually met with. When blazoned 'proper' it is quite correct to make the legs and feet of the natural pinky colour, but it will be more usually found that a dove is specifically described as 'legged gules'.

The ordinary heraldic dove will be found most frequently represented with its wings close and holding a branch of laurel in its beak, but it also occurs volant and with outstretched wings. It is then frequently termed a 'dove rising'.

The doves in the arms of the College of Arms are always represented with the sinister wing close, and the dexter wing extended and inverted. This has given rise to much curious speculation; but whatever may be the reason of the curious position of the wings, there can be very little doubt that the coat of arms itself is based upon the coat of St Edward the Confessor. The so-called coat of St Edward the Confessor is a cross patonce between five martlets, but it is pretty generally agreed that these martlets are a corruption of the doves which figure upon his coins, and one of which surmounts the sceptre which is known as St Edward's staff, or 'the sceptre with the dove'.[115]

The Wood-Pigeon is not often met with, but it does occur, as in the crest of the arms of Bradbury ['On a wreath of the colours, in front of a demi-wood-pigeon, wings displayed and elevated argent, each wing charged with a round

115. This is a curious speculation. It is true that the attributed arms of St Edward the Confessor appear to have been based on a cross between four birds, which is to be found on a penny minted in his reign. It is also true that the four birds are certainly not martlets, whatever else they may be, as they have legs. In the attributed arms the birds are generally shown as martlets, as in the Wilton Diptych. However, the suggestion that the arms of the College of Arms are based on those of St Edward seems unlikely. In a manuscript at the College of Arms (L.5, L.6, L.8) the following arms are described as 'Les Armes de l'office Au Temptz du Roy H. le V iem': argent, a cross gules, a chief quarterly azure and gules, the first and fourth charged with a fleur-de-lis or, and the second and third with a lion of England. After the incorporation of the heralds in 1483/4 a common seal was required, and the arms on it show the red cross as previously used but with four doves, symbolic of a herald's functions, in the quarters. Garter Writhe (1478–85) used azure, a cross or, between four doves close argent, beaked and legged gules and it is likely that he based these arms on those of the College, although the converse could be true.

buckle tongue pendent sable, and holding in the beak a sprig of barberry, the trunk of a tree fesswise eradicated, and sprouting to the dexter, both proper'].

465 Martlet.

The Martlet is another example of the curious perpetuation in heraldry of the popular errors of natural history. Even at the present day, in many parts of the country, it is popularly believed that a swallow has no feet, or, at any rate, cannot perch upon the ground, or raise itself therefrom. The fact that one never does see a swallow upon the ground supports the foundation of the idea. At any rate the heraldic swallow, which is known as the martlet, is never represented with feet, the legs terminating in the feathers which cover the upper parts of the leg (465).[116] It is curious that the same idea is perpetuated in the little legend of the explanation, which may or may not be wholly untrue, that the reason the martlet has been adopted as the mark of cadency for the fourth son is to typify the fact that whilst the eldest son succeeds to his father's lands, and whilst the second son may succeed, perhaps, to the mother's, there can be very little doubt that by the time the fourth son is reached, there is no land remaining upon which he can settle, and that he must, perforce, fly away from the homestead to gather him means elsewhere. At any rate, whether this be true or false, the martlet certainly is never represented in heraldry with feet. If the feet are shown, the bird becomes a swallow.

Most heraldry books state also that the martlet has no beak. How such an idea originated I am at a loss to understand, because I have never yet come across an official instance in which the martlet is so depicted.

Perhaps the confusion between the foreign merlette—which is drawn like a duck without wings, feet, or forked tail—and the martlet may account for the idea that the martlet should be depicted without a beak.

It is very seldom that the martlet occurs except close, and consequently it is never so specified in blazon. An instance, however, in which it occurs 'rising' will be found in the crest of a family of Smith, and there are a number of instances in which it is volant (466).

466 Martlet volant.

The Swallow, as distinct from the martlet, is sometimes met with.

A swallow 'volant' appears upon the arms usually ascribed to the town of Arundel. These, however, are not recorded as arms in the Visitation books, the design being merely noted as a seal device, and one hesitates to assert definitely what the status of the design in question may be.[117] The pun upon 'l'hirondelle' was too good for ancient heralds to pass by.

The Swan (467) is a very favourite charge, and will be found both as a crest and as a charge upon a shield, and in all varieties of position. It is usually, however, when appearing as a charge, to be found 'close'. A swan couchant appears as the crest of Barttelot, a swan regardant as the crest of Swaby, and a swan

116. Fox-Davies equates the martlet with the swallow without argument, but other writers believe the martlet represents either the martin or the swift. I incline to the latter belief, for swifts are found in great numbers in the Holy Land, and Crusaders may well have come to associate the sturdy and apparently legless migrants with their own exploits in the near East, and so adopted them as symbols of speed and endurance.

117. A grant was made on 14 January 1938 of the following arms to the borough of Arundel: or, three martlets sable, on a chief embattled gules, a lion rampant of the first between two cross crosslets fitched argent. Crest: upon a fleur-de-lis or, a swallow rising to the sinister proper.

'rising' will be found as a crest of Guise and as a charge upon the arms of Muntz. Swimming in water it occurs in the crest of Stilwell, and a swan to which the unusual term of 'rousant' is sometimes applied figures as the crest of Stafford: 'Out of a ducal coronet per pale gules and sable, a demi-swan rousant, wings elevated and displayed argent, beaked gules.' It is, however, more usually blazoned as :'A demi-swan issuant (from the coronet, per pale gules and sable).'

467 *Swan.*

Swans' heads and necks are not often met with as a charge, though they occur in the arms of Baker. As a crest they are very common, and will be found in the cases of Lindsay and Bates.

The Duck—with its varieties of the moorhen and eider-duck—is sometimes met with, and appears in the arms of Duckworth and Billiat. Few better canting examples can be found than the latter coat, in which the duck is holding the billet in its bill.

The other domestic bird—the *Cock*—is often met with, though it more often figures as a crest than upon a shield. A cock 'proper' is generally represented of the kind which in farmyard phraseology is known as a gamecock (468). Nevertheless the gamecock—as such—does occur; though in these cases, when so blazoned, it is usually depicted in the artificial form—deprived of its comb and wattles, as was the case when it was prepared for cock-fighting. Birds of this class are usually met with, with a comb and wattles, &c., of a different colour, and are then termed 'combed (or crested), wattled, and jelopped'—if it is desired to be strictly accurate —though it will be generally found that the term is dropped to 'combed and jelopped'.[118] If the bird is termed 'armed', the beak and spurs are thereby referred to. It occurs in the arms of Handcock (Lord Castlemaine) ['Ermine, on a chief sable, a dexter hand between two cocks argent'] and in the arms of Cokayne ['Argent, three cocks gules, armed, crested, and jelopped sable'], and also in that of Law. It likewise occurs in the arms of Aitken.

468 *Cock.*

The Sheldrake appears occasionally under another name, *i.e.* that of the *Shoveller*, and as such will be found in the arms of Jackson, of Doncaster.[119]

The gorgeous plumage of the *Peacock* has of course resulted in its frequent employment. It has a special term of its own, being stated to be 'in his pride' when shown affronté, and with the tail displayed (469). It is seldom met with except in this position, though the well-known crest of Harcourt is an example to the contrary, as is the crest of Sir Jamsetjee Jejeebhoy, Bart., viz. 'A mount vert, thereon a peacock amidst wheat, and in the beak an ear of wheat all proper.' With the tail closed it also figures as one of the supporters of Sir Robert Hart, Bart. ['Sinister, a peacock close proper']: its only appearance in such a position that I am aware of.[120]

A peacock's tail is not a familiar figure in British armory, though the exact contrary is the case in German practices. 'Issuant from the mouth of a boar's head

469 *Peacock in his pride.*

118. Current practice is to use the terms 'combed' and 'wattled'. 'Jelloped' does not appear to have been used for some thirty or more years.
119. It should be noted that the Sheldrake, although belonging to the same family as Shoveller (*Anserini*) is not identical to it. The former belongs to the tribe *Tadorini*, the latter to *Anatini*.
120. Since Fox-Davies wrote, the peacock close has once again done service as a supporter, namely in the achievement of Lord Cadman, where it is blazoned, a peacock argent, beaked gules, gorged with a collar azure, charged with a fleur-de-lis also argent.

470 *Crane in its vigilance.*

471 *Stork holding in its beak a snake.*

472 *Heron.*

473 *Raven.*

erect' it occurs as the crest of Tyrell, and 'A plume of peacock's feathers'— which perhaps is the same thing— 'issuant from the side of a chapeau' is the crest of Lord Sefton.

Another bird for which heraldry has created a term of its own is the *Crane*. It is seldom met with except holding a stone in its claw, the term for which stone is its 'vigilance', a curious old fable, which explains the whole matter, being that the crane held the stone in its foot so that if by any chance it fell asleep, the stone, by dropping, would awaken it, and thus act as its 'vigilance' (470). It is a pity that the truth of such a charming example of the old world should be dissipated by the fact that the crest of Cranstoun is the crane *asleep*— or rather dormant— with its head under its wing, but nevertheless holding its 'vigilance' in its foot! The crane is not often met with, but it occurs in the arms of Cranstoun, with the curious and rather perplexing motto, 'Thou shalt want ere I want.' Before leaving the crane, it may be of interest to observe that the derivation of the word 'pedigree' is from *pied de grue*, the appearance of a crane's foot and the branching lines indicative of issue being similar in shape.

Heraldic representation makes little if any difference when depicting a crane, a stork, or a heron, except that the tuft on the head of the latter is never omitted when a heron is intended.

Instances of the *Stork* are of fairly frequent occurrence, the usual heraldic method of depicting the bird being with the wings close.

More often than not the stork is met with a snake in its beak (471); and the fact that a heron is also generally provided with an eel to play with adds to the confusion.

The Heron— or, as it was anciently more frequently termed heraldically, the *Herne* (472)— will naturally be found in the arms of Hearne and some number of other coats and crests.

The Raven (473) occurs almost as early as any other heraldic bird. It is said to have been a Danish device. The powerful Norman family of Corbet, one of the few remaining families which can show an unbroken male descent from the time of the Conquest to the present day, have always remained faithful to the raven, though they have added to it sometimes a *bordure* or additional numbers of its kind. 'Or, a raven sable', the well-known Corbet coat, is, of course, a canting allusion to their Norman name, or nickname, 'Le Corbeau'. Their name, like their pedigree, is unique, inasmuch as it is one of the few names of undoubted Norman origin which are not territorial, and possibly the fact that their lands of Moreton Corbett, one of their chief seats, were known by their name has assisted in the perpetuation of what was, originally, undoubtedly a personal nickname.

474 is a striking example of the virility which can be imparted to the raven. It is reproduced from Grünenberg's *Book of Arms* (1483). Ströhl suggests it may be of 'Corbie' in Picardy, but the identity of the arms leads one to fancy the name attached may be a misdescription of the English family of Corbet.

Heraldically, no difference is made in depicting the raven, the rook, and the crow; and examples of the *Crow* will be found in the arms of Crawhall, and of the *Rook* in the crest of Abraham. The arms of the Yorkshire family of Creyke are always blazoned as rooks, but I am inclined to think they may possibly have been originally *creykes*, or corn-crakes.

186

The Cornish Chough is very much more frequently met with than either the crow, rook, or raven, and it occurs in the arms of Bewley, the town of Canterbury, and (as a crest) of Cornwall.

It can only be distinguished from the raven in heraldic representations by the fact that the Cornish chough is always depicted and frequently blazoned as 'beaked and legged gules', as it is found in its natural state.

The Owl (475), too, is a very favourite bird. It is always depicted with the face affronté, though the body is not usually so placed. It occurs in the arms of Leeds—which, by the way, are an example of colour upon colour[121]— Oldham, and Dewsbury. In the crest of Brimacombe the wings are open, a most unusual position.

The Lark will be found in many cases of arms or crests for families of the name of Clarke.

The Parrot, or, as it is more frequently termed heraldically, the *Popinjay* (476), will be found in the arms of Lumley and other families. It also occurs in the arms of Curzon: 'Argent, on a bend sable three popinjays or, collared gules.'

There is nothing about the bird, or its representations, which needs special remark, and its usual heraldic form follows nature pretty closely.

The Moorcock or *Heathcock* is curious, inasmuch as there are two distinct forms in which it is depicted. Neither of them are correct from the natural point of view, and they seem to be pretty well interchangeable from the heraldic point of view. The bird is always represented with the head and body of an ordinary cock, but sometimes it is given the wide flat tail of black game, and sometimes a curious tail of two or more erect feathers at right angles to its body (477).

Though usually represented close, it occurs sometimes with open wings, as in the crest of a certain family of Moore.

Many other birds are to be met with in heraldry, but they have nothing at all especial in their bearing, and no special rules govern them.

The Lapwing, under its alternative names of *Peewhit*, *Plover*, and *Tyrwhitt*, will be found in the arms of Downes, Tyrwhitt, and Tweedy.

The Pheasant will be found in the crest of Scott-Gatty, and the *Kingfisher* in many cases of arms of the name of Fisher.

The Magpie occurs in the arms of Dusgate, and in those of Finch.

Woodward mentions an instance in which the *Bird of Paradise* occurs (p. 267); 'Argent, on a terrace vert, a cannon mounted or, supporting a Bird of Paradise proper' [Rjevski and Yeropkin]; and the arms of Thornton show upon a canton the Swedish bird *tjader*: 'Ermine, a chevron sable between three hawthorn trees eradicated proper, a canton or, thereon the Swedish bird tjader, or cock of the wood, also proper.' Two similar birds were granted to the first Sir Edward Thornton, G.C.B., as supporters, he being a Knight Grand Cross.

Single feathers as charges upon a shield are sometimes met with, as in the

475 *Owl.*

476 *Popinjay.*

477 *Moorcock.*

121. The arms of Leeds, as recorded in the 1666 Visitation of Yorkshire, are: azure, a fleece or, on a chief sable, three mullets argent. Now the chief is generally regarded as an ordinary, so that technically the colour-on-colour rule has been broken; but, in fact, the chief looks just like a division of the field, so that, from a purely practical point of view, if a coloured chief on a coloured shield is wrong, then so is per fess, per pale, quarterly and so forth, of two colours. Many kings of arms have approached the problem of the chief in this way. There is a number of examples of coloured chiefs on coloured fields, so although adjacent colours and metals are not ideal, they appear to be permitted.

478 The 'Shield for Peace'
of Edward the Black Prince
(d. 1376):
Sable, three ostrich
feathers with scrolls argent.
(From his tomb in
Canterbury Cathedral.)

'shield for peace' of Edward the Black Prince (478) and in the arms of Clarendon. These two examples are however, derivatives from the historic ostrich-feather badges of the English Royal Family, and will be more conveniently dealt with later when considering the subject of badges. The single feather enfiled by the circlet of crosses patée and fleurs-de-lis, which is borne upon a canton of augmentation upon the arms of Gull, Bart., is likewise a derivative, but feathers as a charge occur in the arms of Jervis ['Argent, six ostrich feathers, three, two, and one sable']. A modern coat founded upon this, in which the ostrich feathers are placed upon a pile, between two bombshells fracted in base, belongs to a family of a very similar name, and the crest granted therewith is a single ostrich feather between two bombs fired. Cock's feathers occur as charges in the arms of Galpin.

In relation to the crest, feathers are constantly to be found, which is not to be wondered at, inasmuch as fighting and tournament helmets, when actually in use, frequently did not carry the actual crests of the owners, but were simply adorned with the plume of ostrich feathers. A curious instance of this will be found in the case of the family of Dymoke of Scrivelsby, the Honourable the King's Champions. The crest is really: 'Upon a wreath of the colours, the two ears of an ass sable,' though other crests ['1. a sword erect proper; 2. a lion as in the arms'] are sometimes made use of. When the Champion performs his service at a Coronation the shield which is carried by his esquire is not that of his sovereign, but is emblazoned with his personal arms of Dymoke ['Sable, two lions passant in pale argent, ducally crowned or']. The helmet of the Champion is decorated with a triple plume of ostrich feathers and not with the Dymoke crest. In old representations of tournaments and warfare the helmet will far oftener be found simply adorned with a plume of ostrich feathers than with a heritable crest, and consequently such a plume has remained in use as the crest of a very large number of families. This point is, however, more fully dealt with in the chapter upon crests.

The plume of ostrich feathers is, moreover, attributed to a crest to a far greater number of families than it really belongs to, because if a family possessed no crest the helmet was generally ornamented with a plume of ostrich feathers, which later generations have accepted and adopted as their heritable crest, when it never possessed such a character. A notable instance of this will be found in the crest of Astley, as given in the Peerage Books.

The number of feathers in a plume requires to be stated; it will usually be found to be three, five, or seven, though sometimes a larger number are met with. When it is termed a double plume they are arranged in two rows, the one issuing above the other, and a triple plume is arranged in three rows; and though it is correct to speak of any number of feathers as a plume, it will usually be found that the word is reserved for five or more, whilst a plume of three feathers would more frequently be termed three ostrich feathers. Whilst they are usually white, they are also found of varied colours, and there is even an instance to be met with of ostrich feathers of ermine. When the feathers are of different colours they need to be carefully blazoned; if alternately, it is enough to use the word 'alternately', the feather at the extreme dexter side being depicted of the colour first mentioned. In a plume which is of three colours, care must be used in noting the arrangement of the colours, the colours first mentioned being that of the dexter feather; the others then follow from dexter to sinister, the fourth feather commencing the series of colours again. If any other arrangement of the colours occurs it must be specifically detailed. The rainbow-hued plume from which the crest of Sir Reginald Barnewall★ issues is the most variegated instance I have met with.

Two peacock's feathers in saltire will be found in the crest of a family of Gatehouse, and also occur in the crest of Crisp-Molineux-Montgomerie.[122] The pen in heraldry is always of course of the quill variety, and consequently should not be mistaken for a single feather. The term 'penned' is used when the quill of a feather is of a different colour from the remainder of it. Ostrich and other feathers are very frequently found on either side of a crest, both in British and Continental armory; but though often met with in this position, there is nothing peculiar about this use in such character. German heraldry has evolved one use of the peacock's feather, or rather for the eye from the peacock's feather, which happily has not yet reached this country. It will be found adorning the outer edges of every kind of object, and it even occurs on occasion as a kind of dorsal fin down the back of animals. Bunches of cock's feathers are also frequently made use of for the same purpose. There has been considerable diversity in the method of depicting the ostrich feather. In its earliest form it was stiff and erect as if cut from a piece of board (478), but gradually, as the realistic type of heraldic art came into vogue, it was represented more naturally and with flowing and drooping curves. Of later years, however, we have followed the example of His Majesty King Edward VII when Prince of Wales and reverted to the earlier form, and it is now very general to give the ostrich feather the stiff and straight appearance which it originally possessed when heraldically depicted. Occasionally a plume of ostrich feathers is found enclosed in a 'case', that is, wrapped about the lower part as if it were a bouquet, and this form is the more usual in Germany. In German heraldry these plumes are constantly met with in the colours of the arms, or charged with the whole or a part of the device upon the shield. It is not a common practice in this country, but an instance of it will be found in the arms of Lord Waldegrave: 'Per pale argent and gules. Crest: out of a ducal coronet or a plume of five ostrich feathers, the first two argent, the third per pale argent and gules, and the last two gules.'[123]

122. Thomas Tomlinson Crisp-Molineux-Montgomerie had arms granted for Crisp and Molineux, under the terms of a Royal Licence, on 9 October 1813. The crest granted for Molineux is that referred to by Fox-Davies.

123. Almost every variety of bird has either made an appearance, or doubtless will in the future, in the heraldic aviary. It would be impracticable and indeed almost impossible to list them all. However, Fox-Davies has omitted one classic example, the *turkey*. This bird forms the crest granted to William Strickland of Yorkshire in 1550, and it was granted to him because he was supposed to have introduced the turkey into England from North America.

★ Upon a wreath of the colours, from a plume of five ostrich feathers or, gules, azure, vert, and argent, a falcon rising of the last; with the motto, 'Malo mori quam fœdari.'

15 · Fish

479 *Dolphin naiant.*

480 *Dolphin hauriant.*

481 *Arms of the Grauff von Dälffin lett och in Dalffinat (Count von Dälffin), which also lies in Dauphiné (from Grünenberg's* Book of Arms)*: Argent, a dolphin azure within a bordure compony of the first and second.*

Heraldry has a system of 'natural' history all its very own, and included in the comprehensive heraldic term of fish are dolphins, whales, and other creatures. There are certain terms which apply to heraldic fish which should be noted. A fish in a horizontal position is termed 'naiant', whether it is in or upon water or merely depicted as a charge upon a shield. A fish is termed 'hauriant' if it is in a perpendicular position, but though it will usually be represented with the head upwards in default of any specific direction to the contrary, it by no means follows that this is always the case, and it is more correct to state whether the head is upwards or downwards, a practice which it is usually found will be conformed to. When the charges upon a shield are simply blazoned as 'fish', no particular care need be taken to represent any particular variety, but on the other hand it is not in such cases usual to add any distinctive signs by which a charge which is merely a fish might become identified as any particular kind of fish.

The heraldic representations of the *Dolphin* are strangely dissimilar from the real creature, and also show amongst themselves a wide variety and latitude. It is early found in heraldry, and no doubt its great importance in that science is derived from its usage by the Dauphins of France. Concerning its use by these Princes there are all sorts of curious legends told, the most usual being that recited by Berry.

Woodward refers to this legend, but states that 'in 1343 King Philip of France *purchased* the domains of Humbert III, Dauphin de Viennois', and further remarks that the legend in question 'seems to be without solid foundation'. But neither Woodward nor any other writer seems to have previously suggested what is doubtless the true explanation, that the title of Dauphin and the province of Viennois were a separate dignity of a sovereign character, to which were attached certain territorial and sovereign arms ['Or, a dolphin embowed azure, finned and langued gules']. The assumption of these sovereign arms with the sovereignty and territory to which they belonged, was as much a matter of course as the use of separate arms for the Duchy of Lancaster by His Majesty King Edward VII, or the use of separate arms for his Duchy of Cornwall by H.R.H. the Prince of Wales.

Berry is wrong in asserting that no other family were permitted to display the dolphin in France, because a very similar coat (but with the dolphin lifeless) to that of the Dauphin was quartered by the family of La Tour du Pin, who claimed descent from the Dauphins d'Auvergne, another ancient House which originally bore the sovereign title of Dauphin. A dolphin was the charge upon the arms of the Grauff von Dälffin (481).

The dolphin upon this shield, as also that in the coat of the Dauphin of France, is neither naiant nor hauriant, but is 'embowed', that is, with the tail curved towards the head. But the term 'embowed' really signifies nothing further than 'bent' in some way, and as a dolphin is never heraldically depicted straight, it is always understood to be and usually is termed 'embowed', though it will generally be 'naiant embowed' (479), or 'hauriant embowed' (480). The dolphin occurs in the arms of many British families, *e.g.* in the arms of Ellis, Monypenny, Loder-Symonds, Symonds-Taylor, Fletcher, and Stuart-French.

Woodward states that the dolphin is used as a supporter by the Trevelyans, Burnabys, &c. In this statement he is clearly incorrect, for neither of those families are entitled to or use supporters. But his statement probably originates in the practice which in accordance with the debased ideas of artistic decoration at one period added all sorts of fantastic objects to the edges of a shield for purely decorative (!) purposes. The only instance within my knowledge in which a dolphin figures as a heraldic supporter will be found in the case of the arms of Waterford.[124]

The Whale is seldom met with in British armory, one of its few appearances being in the arms of Whalley, viz.: 'Argent, three whales' heads erased sable,' and another in the arms of Lord Jellicoe.

The crest of an Irish family named Yeates is said to be: 'A shark issuant regardant swallowing a man all proper,' and the same device is also attributed to some number of other families.

Another curious piscine coat of arms is that borne, but still unmatriculated, by the burgh of Inveraray, namely: 'The field is the sea proper, a net argent suspended to the base from the dexter chief and the sinister fess points, and in chief two and in base three herrings entangled in the net.'[125]

Salmon are not infrequently met with, but they need no specific description. They occur in the arms of Peebles,* a coat of arms which in an alternative blazon introduces to one's notice the term 'contra-naiant'. The explanation of the quaint and happy conceit of these arms and motto is that for every fish which goes up the river to spawn two return to the sea. A salmon on its back figures in the arms of the city of Glasgow, and also in the arms of Lumsden and Finlay, whilst other instances of salmon occur in the arms of Blackett-Ord, Sprot, and Winlaw.

The Herring occurs in the arms of Maconochie, the *Roach* in the arms of Roche ['Gules, three roaches naiant within a bordure engrailed argent. Crest: a rock, thereon a stork close, charged on the breast with a torteau, and holding in his dexter claw a roach proper'], and *Trout* in the arms of Troutbeck ['Azure, three trout fretted tête à la queue argent']. The same arrangement of three fish occurs upon the seal of Anstruther Wester, but this design unfortunately has never been matriculated as a coat of arms.

The arms of Iceland present a curious charge, which is included upon the Royal

124. More recently the dolphin has gained in popularity as a supporter, although there is an English example of decent antiquity: the sinister supporter of the Merchant Venturers' Company of Exeter is a dolphin argent, finned or. When Malta achieved independence in 1964, new arms were assigned and these are supported by: on either side a dolphin, the dexter supporting with the fins an olive branch, the sinister likewise supporting a palm branch all proper. The arms granted are worthy of note, as they are those of the family of Waldegrave (per pale argent and gules) differenced only by a representation of the George Cross proper fimbriated gules.

125. See note 28.

* Armorial bearings of Peebles (official blazon): Gules, three salmon naiant in pale, the centre towards the dexter, the other towards the sinister. Motto: 'Contra nando incrementum.'

shield of Denmark. The coat in question is: 'Gules, a stockfish argent, crowned with an open crown or.' The *Stockfish* is a dried and cured cod, split open and with the head removed.[126]

A *Pike* or *Jack* is more often termed a 'lucy' in English heraldry and a 'ged' in Scottish. Under its various names it occurs in the arms of Lucy, Lucas, Geddes, and Pyke.

The Eel is sometimes met with, as in the arms of Ellis, and though, as Woodward states, it is always given a wavy form, the term 'ondoyant', which he uses to express this, has, I believe, no place in an English armorist's dictionary.

The Lobster and *Crab* are not unknown to English armory, being respectively the crests of the families of Dykes and Bridger. The arms of Bridger are: 'Argent, a chevron engrailed sable, between three crabs gules.' Lobster claws are a charge upon the arms of Platt-Higgins.

The arms of Birt are given in Papworth as: 'Azure, a birthfish proper,' and of Bersich as: 'Argent, a perch azure.' The arms of Cobbe (Bart., extinct) were: 'Per chevron gules and sable, in chief two swans respecting and in base a herring cob naiant proper.' The arms of Bishop Robinson of Carlisle were: 'Azure, a flying fish in bend argent, on a chief of the second, a rose gules between two torteaux,' and the crest of Sir Philip Oakley Fysh was 'On a wreath of the colours, issuant from a wreath of red coral, a cubit arm vested azure, cuffed argent, holding in the hand a flying fish proper.' The coat of arms of Colston of Essex is: 'Azure, two barbels hauriant respecting each other argent,' and a barbel occurs in the crest of Binney. 'Vert, three sea-breams or hakes hauriant argent' is the coat of arms attributed to a family of Dox or Doxey, and 'Or, three chabots gules' is that of a French family of the name of Chabot. 'Barry wavy of six argent and gules, three crevices (crayfish) two and one or' is the coat of Atwater. Codfish occur in the arms of Beck, dogfish in the arms of Dodds (which may, however, be merely the sea-dog of the Dodge achievement), flounders or flukes in the arms of Arbutt, garvinfishes in the arms of Garvey, and gudgeon in the arms of Gobion. Papworth also includes instances of mackerel, prawns, shrimps, soles, sparlings, sturgeon, sea-urchins, turbots, whales, and whelks. The whelk shell (482) appears in the arms of Storey and Wilkinson.

482 Whelk shell.

126. Iceland became an independent republic in 1944, and as from 6 July 1948 the stockfish was dropped from the dexter base of the third quarter of the Danish royal arms. It was replaced by the ram of the Faroes, which previously shared the sinister base with the bear of Greenland. The bear now has a quarter to himself. By Royal Decree dated 15 December 1959 the royal arms with quarterings are reserved to the King, royal house and Court. Other departments must use the first grand quartering only surmounted by the crown, unless the Prime Minister's office makes exceptions.

16 · Reptiles

If armorial zoology is 'shaky' in its classification of and dealings with fish, it is most wonderful when its laws and selections are considered under the heading of reptiles. But with the exception of serpents (of various kinds), the remainder must have no more than a passing mention.

The usual heraldic *Serpent* is most frequently found 'nowed', that is, interlaced in a knot (483). There is a certain well-understood form for the interlacing which is always officially adhered to, but of late there has manifested itself amongst heraldic artists a desire to break loose to a certain extent from the stereotyped form. A serpent will sometimes be found 'erect' and occasionally gliding or 'glissant', and sometimes it will be met with in a circle with its tail in its mouth—the ancient symbol of eternity. Its constant appearance in British armory is due to the fact that it is symbolically accepted as the sign of medicine, and many grants of arms made to doctors and physicians introduce in some way either the serpent or the rod of Æsculapius, or a serpent entwined round a staff.[127] A serpent embowed biting its tail occurs in the arms of Falconer, and a serpent on its back in the crest of Backhouse. Save for the matter of position, the serpent of British armory is always drawn in a very naturalistic manner. It is otherwise, however, in Continental armory, where the serpent takes up a position closely allied to that of our dragon. It is even sometimes found winged, and the arms of the family of Visconti, which subsequently came into use as the arms of the Duchy of Milan (484), have familiarised us as far as Continental armory is concerned with a form of serpent which is very different from the real animal or from our own heraldic variety. Another instance of a serpent will be found in the arms of the Irish family of Cotter, which are: 'Argent, a chevron gules between three serpents proper,' and the family of Lanigan O'Keefe bear in one quarter of their shield: 'Vert, three lizards in pale or.' The family of Cole bear: 'Argent, a chevron gules between three scorpions reversed sable,' a coat of arms which is sometimes quoted with the chevron and the scorpions both gules or both sable.[128] The family of

483 *Serpent nowed.*

127. The use of the rod of Æsculapius has done yeoman service since Fox-Davies wrote and it appears not only in the arms of doctors of medicine but in those of medical bodies, such as hospitals and professional medical associations.

It is sometimes confused with the rod of Hermes, the caduceus. This was originally a magic wand, symbol of power and prosperity. It consisted of a rod with two shoots entwined together and forming a knot on the top. Later these shoots were represented as two serpents, and the caduceus took the form in which it now appears in heraldry. Because Hermes was herald to the gods, so the caduceus came to be regarded as the attribute of a herald and is found in the arms of at least two newspaper publishing companies. The arms granted to the Times Publishing Co. Ltd have the caduceus as the principal charge, viz: argent, eight barrulets sable, over all a caduceus in pale or.

128. In fact, various families of Cole bear scorpions in their arms. That quoted by Fox-Davies, with the scorpions sable, is recorded; Segar granted to Ralph Cole or Colle, mayor of Newcastle-on-Tyne: argent, a chevron engrailed between three scorpions sable, on a chief azure, three fleurs-de-lis or. This was later altered to: argent, a fess engrailed between three scorpions sable.

484 *Arms of the Visconti, Dukes of Milan: Argent, a serpent azure, devouring a child gules, (A wood-carving from the castle of Passau at the turn of the fifteenth century.)*

Preed of Shropshire bear: 'Azure, three horse-leeches'; and the family of Whitby bear: 'Gules, three snakes coiled or; on a chief of the second, as many pheons sable.' A family of Sutton bears: 'Or, a newt vert, in chief a lion rampant gules all within a bordure of the last, and Papworth mentions a coat of arms for the name of Ory: 'Azure, a chameleon on a shady ground proper, in chief a sun or.' Another coat mentioned by Papworth is the arms of Bume: 'Gules, a stellion serpent proper,' though what the creature may be it is impossible to imagine. Unfortunately, when one comes to examine so many of these curious coats of arms, one finds no evidence that such families existed, or that there is no official authority or record of the arms to which reference can be made. There can be no doubt that they largely consist of misreadings or misinterpretations of both names and charges, and I am sorely afraid this remark is the true explanation of what otherwise would be most strange and interesting curiosities of arms. Sir Walter Scott's little story in *Quentin Durward* of Toison d'Or, who depicted the 'cat looking through the dairy window' as the arms of Childebert, and blazoned it 'sable a musion passant or, oppressed with a trellis gules, cloué of the second', gives in very truth the real origin of many quaint coats of arms and heraldic terms. Ancient heraldic writers seem to have amused themselves by inventing 'appropriate' arms for mythological or historical personages, and I verily believe that when so doing they never intended these arms to stand for more than examples of their own wit. Their credulous successors incorporated these little witticisms in the rolls of arms they collected, and one can only hope that in the distant future the charming drawings of Mr E. T. Reed which in recent years have appeared in *Punch* may not be used in like manner.

There are but few instances in English armory in which the *Toad* or *Frog* is met with. In fact, the only instance which one can recollect is the coat of arms attributed to a family of Botreaux, who are said to have borne: 'Argent, three

194

toads erect sable.' I am confident, however, that this coat of arms, if it ever existed, and if it could be traced to its earliest sources, would be found to be really three buckets of water, a canting allusion to the name. Toads of course are the charges on the mythical arms of Pharamond.

Amongst the few instances I have come across of a snail in British armory are the crest of Slack of Derwent Hill ('in front of a crescent or, a snail proper') and the coat attributed by Papworth to the family of Bartan or Bertane, who are mentioned as bearing, 'Gules, three snails argent in their shells or.' This coat, however, is not matriculated in Scotland, so that one cannot be certain that it was ever borne. The snail occurs, however, as the crest of a family named Billers, and is also attributed to several other families as a crest.

Lizards appear occasionally in heraldry, though more frequently in Irish than English or Scottish coats of arms. A lizard forms part of the crest of Sillifant, and a hand grasping a lizard is the crest of M'Carthy, and 'Azure, three lizards or' the first quarter of the arms of an Irish family of the name of Cotter, who, however, blazon these charges upon their shield as evetts. The family of Enys, who bear: 'Argent, three wyverns volant in pale vert,' probably derive their arms from some such source.

17 · Insects

The insect which is most usually met with in heraldry is undoubtedly the *Bee*. Being considered, as it is, the symbol of industry, small wonder that it has been so frequently adopted. It is usually represented as if displayed upon the shield, and it is then termed 'volant', though of course the real term which will sometimes be found used is 'volant *en arrière*' (485). It occurs in the arms of Dore, Beatson, Abercromby, Samuel, and Sewell, either as a charge or as a crest. Its use, however, as a crest is slightly more varied, inasmuch as it is found walking in profile, and with its wings elevated, and also perched upon a thistle as in the arms of Ferguson. A bee-hive 'with bees diversely volant' occurs in the arms of Rowe, and the popularity of the bee in British armory is doubtless due to the frequent desire to perpetuate the fact that the foundation of a house has been laid by business industry. The fact that the bee was adopted as a badge by the Emperor Napoleon gave it considerable importance in French armory, inasmuch as he assumed it for his own badge, and the mantle and pavilion around the armorial bearings of the Empire sere semé of these insects. They also appeared upon his own coronation mantle. He adopted them under the impression, which may or may not be correct, that they had at one time been the badge of Childeric, father of Clovis. The

485 *Bee volant.*

whole story connected with their assumption by Napoleon has been a matter of much controversy, and little purpose would be served by going into the matter here, but it may be added that Napoleon changed the fleur-de-lis upon the chief in the arms of Paris to golden bees upon a chief of gules, and a chief azure, semé of bees or, was added as indicative of their rank to the arms of 'Princes-Grand-Dignitaries of the Empire'. A bee-hive occurs as the crest of a family named Gwatkin, and also upon the arms of the family of Kettle of Wolverhampton.[129]

The Grasshopper is most familiar as the crest of the family of Gresham, and this is the origin of the golden grasshoppers which are so constantly met with in the city of London. 'Argent, a chevron sable between three grasshoppers vert' is the coat of arms of Woodward of Kent. Two of them figure in the arms of Treacher, which arms are now quartered by Bowles.

Ants are but seldom met with. 'Argent, six ants, three, two, and one sable', is a coat given by Papworth to a family of the name of Tregent; 'Vert, an ant argent', to Kendiffe; and 'Argent, a chevron vert between three beetles proper' are the arms attributed by the same authority to a family named Muschamp. There can be little doubt, however, that these 'beetles' should be described as flies.

Butterflies figure in the arms of Papillon ['Azure, a chevron between three butterflies volant argent'] and in the arms of Penhellicke ['Sable, three butterflies volant argent'].

Gadflies are to be found in a coat of arms for the name of Adams ['Per pale argent and gules, a chevron between three gadflies counterchanged'], and also in the arms of Somerscales, quartered by Skeet of Bishop Stortford. 'Sable, a hornet argent' is one blazon for the arms of Bollord or Bolloure, but elsewhere the same coat is blazoned: 'Sable, a harvest-fly in pale volant *en arrière* argent.' Harvest flies were the charges on the arms of the late Sir Edward Watkin, Bart.

Crickets appear in the arms ['azure, a fire chest argent, flames proper, between three crickets or'] granted to Sir George Anderson Critchett, Bart.

The arms of Bassano (really of foreign origin and not an English coat) are: 'Per chevron vert and argent, in chief three silkworm flies palewise *en arrière*, and in base a mulberry branch all counterchanged.' 'Per pale gules and azure, three stag-beetles, wings extended or,' is assigned by Papworth to the Cornish family of Dore, but elsewhere these charges (under the same family name) are quoted as bees, gadflies, and flies. 'Or, three spiders azure' is quoted as a coat for Chettle. A spider also figures as a charge on the arms of Macara. The crest of Thorndyke of Great Carleton, Lincolnshire, is: 'On a wreath of the colours a damask rose proper, leaves and thorns vert, at the bottom of the shield a beetle or scarabæus proper.'

Woodward, in concluding his chapter upon insects, quotes the arms of the family of Pullici of Verona, viz.: 'Or, semé of fleas sable, two bends gules, surmounted by two bends sinister of the same.'

---

129. One of the crests of Lord Lansdowne is a beehive beset by bees volant. When it became necessary to make a crest for the 5th marquess to place over his stall at Windsor, as he was a Knight of the Garter, the wood carver gave up the unequal struggle of keeping bees in suspended animation, and so left them out. New grantees should heed the moral of this tale, which is: if you want any of your family to become Knights of the Garter, choose a crest which can be modelled in the round.

18 · Trees, leaves, fruits, and flowers

The vegetable kingdom plays an important part in heraldry. Trees will be found of all varieties and in all numbers, and though little difference is made in the appearance of many varieties when they are heraldically depicted, for canting purposes the various names are carefully preserved. When, however, no name is specified, they are generally drawn after the fashion of oak-trees.

When a tree issues from the ground it will usually be blazoned 'issuant from a mount vert', but when the roots are shown it is termed 'eradicated'.

A Hurst of Trees figures both on the shield and in the crest of France-Hayhurst, and in the arms of Lord Lismore ['Argent, in base a mount vert, on the dexter side a hurst of oak-trees, therefrom issuing a wolf passant towards the sinister, all proper']. A hurst of elm-trees very properly is the crest of the family of Elmhurst. Under the description of a forest, a number of trees figure in the arms of Forrest.

The arms of Walkinshaw of that Ilk are: 'Argent, a grove of fir-trees proper,' and Walkinshaw of Barrowfield and Walkinshaw of London have matriculated more or less similar arms.

The Oak-tree (486) is of course the tree most frequently met with. Perhaps the most famous coat in which it occurs will be found in the arms granted to Colonel Carlos, to commemorate his risky sojourn with King Charles in the oak-tree at Boscobel, after the King's flight subsequent to the ill-fated battle of Worcester. The coat was: 'Or, on a mount in base vert, an oak-tree proper, fructed or, surmounted by a fess gules, charged with three imperial crowns of the third' (Plate II).

Fir-Trees will be found in the arms of Greg, Melles, De la Ferté, and Farquharson.

A Cedar-Tree occurs in the arms of Montefiore ['Argent, a cedar-tree, between two mounts of flowers proper, on a chief azure, a dagger erect proper, pommel and hilt or, between two mullets of six points gold'], and a *hawthorn-tree* in the arms of MacMurrogh-Murphy, Thornton, and in the crest of Kynnersley.

A Maple-Tree figures in the arms of Lord Mount-Stephen ['Or, on a mount vert, a maple-tree proper, in chief two fleurs-de-lis azure'], and in the crest of Lord Strathcona ['On a mount vert, a maple-tree, at the base thereof a beaver gnawing the trunk all proper'].

A Cocoanut-Tree is the principal charge in the arms of Glasgow (Robertson-Glasgow) of Montgrennan, matriculated in 1807 ['Argent, a cocoanut-tree fructed proper, growing out of a mount in base vert, on a chief azure, a shake-fork

486 *An oak-tree eradicated.*

197

between a martlet on the dexter and a salmon on the sinister argent, the last holding in the mouth a ring or'].

The arms of Clifford afford an instance of a *Coffee-Tree*, and the coat of Chambers has a negro cutting down a *Sugar-Cane*.

A *Palm-Tree* occurs in the arms of Besant and in the armorials of many other families. The crest of Grimké-Drayton affords an instance of the use of *palmetto-trees*. An *Olive-Tree* is the crest of Tancred, and a *Laurel-Tree* occurs in the crest of Somers.

Cypress-Trees are quoted by Papworth in the arms of Birkin, probably an error for birch-trees, but the cypress does occur in the arms of Tardy, Comte de Montravel ['Argent, three cypress-trees eradicated vert, on a chief gules, as many bezants'], and 'Or, a willow (salix) proper' is the coat of the Counts de Salis (now Fane-de-Salis).

The arms of Sweetland, granted in 1808, are: 'Argent, on a mount vert, an orange-tree fructed proper, on a chief embattled gules, three roses of the field, barbed and seeded also proper.'

A *Mountain-Ash* figures in the shield and crest of Wigan,[130] and a *Walnut-Tree* is the crest of Waller of Groombridge ['On a mount vert, a walnut-tree proper, on the sinister side an escutcheon pendent, charged with the arms of France, and thereupon a label of three points argent'].

The arms of Arkwright afford an example of a *Cotton-Tree*.

The curious crest of Sir John Leman, Lord Mayor of London, affords an instance of a *Lemon-Tree* ['In a lemon-tree proper, a pelican in her piety proper'].

The arms of a family whose name appears to have been variously spelled Estwere, Estwrey, Estewer, Estower, and Esture, have: 'Upon an argent field a tree proper', variously described as an apple-tree, an ash-tree, and a cherry-tree. The probabilities largely point to its being an ash-tree. 'Or, on a mount in base vert, a pear-tree fructed proper' is the coat of arms of Pyrton or Peryton, and the arms granted in 1591 to Dr Lopus, a physician to Queen Elizabeth, were: 'Or, a pomegranate-tree eradicated vert, fructed gold, supported by a hart rampant proper, crowned and attired of the first.'

A *Poplar Tree* occurs in the arms of Gandolfi, but probably the prime curiosity must be the coat of Abank, which Papworth gives as: 'Argent, a China-cokar tree vert.' Its botanical identity remains a mystery.

Trunks of Trees for some curious reason play a prominent part in heraldry. The arms of Borough, of Chetwynd Park, granted in 1702, are: 'Argent, on a mount in base, in base the trunk of an oak-tree sprouting out two branches proper, with the shield of Pallas hanging thereon or, fastened by a belt gules,' and the arms of Houldsworth (1868) of Gonaldston, co. Notts, are: 'Ermine, the trunk of a tree in bend raguly eradicated at the base proper, between three foxes' heads, two in chief and one in base erased gules.'

But it is as a crest that this figure of the withered trunk sprouting again is most often met with, it being assigned to no less than forty-three families.[131]

---

130. This was an unauthorised coat. A proper grant was obtained in 1922. The mountain ash, or 'wiggin tree', is retained inasmuch as the lion supporters each grasp a branch.
131. This crest may be 'assigned to' many families; but it is in fact fairly unusual, being borne, with various differences, by about a dozen families.

In England again, by one of those curious fads by which certain objects were repeated over and over again in the wretched designs granted by Sir Albert Woods, Garter; notwithstanding their unsuitability, tree-trunks fesswise eradicated and sprouting are constantly met with either as the basis of the crest or placed 'in front of it' to help in providing the differences and distinctions which he insisted upon in a new grant. An example of such use of it will be found in the arms of the town of Abergavenny.

Stocks of Trees 'couped and eradicated' are by no means uncommon. They figure in the arms of the Borough of Woodstock: 'Gules, the stump of a tree couped and eradicated argent, and in chief three stags' heads caboshed of the same, all within a bordure of the last charged with eight oak-leaves vert.' They also occur in the arms of Grove, of Shenston Park, co. Stafford, and in the arms of Stubbs.

The arms matriculated in Lyon Register by Capt. Peter Winchester (*c.* 1672–7) are: 'Argent, a vine growing out of the base, leaved and fructed, between two papingoes endorsed feeding upon the clusters all proper.' The vine also appears in the arms of Ruspoli, and the family of Archer-Houblon bear for the latter name: 'Argent, on a mount in base, three hop-poles erect with hop-vines all proper.'

The town of St Ives (Cornwall) has no authorised arms, but those usually attributed to the town are: 'Argent, an ivy branch overspreading the whole field vert.'

'Gules, a flaming bush on the top of a mount proper, between three lions rampant argent, in the flanks two roses of the last' is the coat of Brander (now Dunbar-Brander) of Pitgavenny. Holly-bushes are also met with, as in the crests of Daubeney and Crackanthorpe, and a rose-bush as in the crest of Inverarity.

The arms of Owen, co. Pembroke, are: 'Gules, a boar argent, armed, bristled, collared, and chained or to a holly-bush on a mount in base both proper.'

A Fern-Brake is another stock object used in designing modern crests, and will be found in the cases of Harter, Scott-Gatty, and Lloyd.

Branches are constantly occurring, but they are usually oak, laurel, palm, or holly. They need to be distinguished from 'slips', which are much smaller and with fewer leaves. Definite rules of distinction between, *e.g.* an acorn 'slipped', a slip of oak, and an oak-branch have been laid down by purists, but no such minute detail is officially observed, and it seems better to leave the point to general artistic discretion, the colloquial difference between a slip and a branch being quite a sufficient guide upon the point.

An example of an *Oak-Branch* occurs in the arms of Aikman, and another, which is rather curious, is the crest of Accrington.★

Oak-Slips, on the other hand, occur in the arms of Baldwin.

A Palm-Branch occurs in the crests of Innes, Chafy, and Corfield.

Laurel-Branches occur in the arms of Cooper, and sprigs of laurel in the arms of Meeking.

Holly-Branches are chiefly found in the arms of families named Irvine or Irwin,

★ Arms of Accrington: Gules, on a fess argent, a shuttle fesswise proper, in base two printing cylinders, issuant therefrom a piece of calico (parsley pattern) also proper, on a chief per pale or and vert, a lion rampant purpure and a stag current or; and for the crest, an oak-branch bent chevronwise, sprouting and leaved proper, fructed or. Motto: 'Industry and prudence conquer.'

but they are invariably blazoned as 'sheaves' of holly or as holly-branches of three leaves. To a certain extent this is a misnomer, because the so-called 'branch' is merely three holly-leaves tied together.

'Argent, an almond-slip proper' is the coat of arms attributed to a family of Almond, and Papworth assigns 'Argent, a barberry-branch fructed proper' to Berry.

'Argent, three sprigs of balm flowered proper' is stated to be the coat of a family named Balme, and 'Argent, three teasels slipped proper' the coat of Bowden, whilst Boden of the Friary bears, 'Argent, a chevron sable between three teasels proper, a bordure of the second.' A teasle on a canton figures in the arms of Chichester-Constable.

The Company of Tobacco-Pipe Makers in London, incorporated in the year 1663, bore: 'Argent, on a mount in base vert, three plants of tobacco growing and flowering all proper.' The crest of Sir Thomas Lipton, Bart. ['On a wreath of the colours, two arms in saltire, the dexter surmounted by the sinister holding a sprig of the tea-plant erect, and the other a like sprig of the coffee-plant both slipped and leaved proper, vested above the elbow argent'] affords an example of both the coffee-plant and the tea-plant, both of which assisted him so materially in piling up his immense fortune. 'Or, three birch-twigs sable' is the coat of Birches, and 'Or, a bunch of nettles vert' is the coat of Mallerby of Devonshire. The pun in the last case is apparent.

The Cotton-Plant figures in the arms of the towns of Darwen, Rochdale, and Nelson, and two culms of the papyrus plant occur in the arms of the town of Bury.[132]

The Coffee-Plant also figures in the arms of Yockney: 'Azure, a chevron or, between a ship under sail in chief proper, and a sprig of the coffee-plant slipped in base of the second.'

A branch, slip, bush, or tree is termed 'fructed' when the fruit is shown, though the term is usually disregarded unless 'fructed' of a different colour. When represented as 'fructed', the fruit is usually drawn out of all proportion to its relative size.

Leaves are not infrequent in their appearance. Holly-leaves occur in the various coats for most people of the name of Irwin and Irvine, as already mentioned. Laurel-leaves occur in the arms of Leveson-Gower, Foulis, and Foulds.

Oak-Leaves occur in the arms of Trelawney ['Argent, a chevron sable, between three oak-leaves slipped proper']; and *hazel-leaves* in the arms of Hesilrige or Hazlerigg ['Argent, a chevron sable, between three hazel-leaves vert].

'Argent, three edock (dock or burdock) leaves vert' is the coat of Hepburn. Papworth assigns 'Argent, an aspen leaf proper' to Aspinal, and 'Or, a betony-leaf proper' to Betty. 'Argent, three aspen-leaves' is an unauthorised coat used by Espin, and the same coat with varying tinctures is assigned to Cogan. Killach is stated to bear: 'Azure, three bay-leaves argent,' and to Woodward, of Little Walsingham, Norfolk, was granted in 1806: 'Vert, three mulberry-leaves or.'

---

132. Since Fox-Davies wrote, the use of the cotton plant has grown in popularity in the municipal heraldry of Lancashire, and it also occurs in the arms of many individuals connected with the cotton trade and industry.

The Maple-Leaf has been generally adopted as a Canadian emblem, and consequently figures upon the arms of that Dominion, and in the arms of many families which have or have had Canadian associations.[133]

'Vert, three vine-leaves or' is assigned by Papworth to Wortford, and the same authority mentions coats in which woodbine-leaves occur for Browne, Theme, and Gamboa. Rose-leaves occur in the arms of Utermarck, and walnut-leaves figure in the arms of Waller.

A curious leaf—usually called the 'sea-leaf', which is properly the 'nenuphar-leaf', is often met with in German heraldry, as are *Linden leaves.*

Although theoretically leaves, the trefoil, quatrefoil, and cinquefoil are a class by themselves, having a recognised heraldic status as exclusively heraldic charges, and the quatrefoil and cinquefoil, in spite of the derivation of their names, are as likely to have been originally flowers as leaves.

The heraldic Trefoil (487), though frequently specifically described as 'slipped', is nevertheless always so depicted, and it is not necessary to so describe it. Of late a tendency has been noticeable in paintings from Ulster's Office to represent the trefoil in a way more nearly approaching the Irish shamrock, from which it has undoubtedly been derived. Instances of the trefoil occur in the arms of Rodd, Dobrée, MacDermott, and Gilmour. The crowned trefoil is one of the national badges of Ireland.

A four-leaved 'lucky' shamrock has been introduced into the arms of Sir Robert Hart, Bart.

The Quatrefoil (488) is not often met with, but it occurs in the arms of Eyre, King, and Dreyer.

The Cinquefoil (489) is of frequent appearance, but, save in exceedingly rare instances, neither the quatrefoil nor the cinquefoil will be met with 'slipped'. The constant occurrence of the cinquefoil in early rolls of arms is out of all proportion to its distinctiveness or artistic beauty, and the frequency with which it is met with in conjunction with the cross crosslet points clearly to the fact that there is some allusion behind, if this could only be fathomed. Many a man might adopt a lion through independent choice, but one would not expect independent choice to lead so many to pitch upon a combination of cross crosslets and cinquefoils. The cross crosslets, I am confident, are a later addition in many cases, for the original arms of D'Arcy, for example, were simply: 'Argent, three cinquefoils gules.' The arms of the town of Leicester are: 'Gules, a cinquefoil ermine,' and this is the coat attributed to the family of the De Beaumonts or De Bellomonts, Earls of Leicester. Simon de Montfort, the great Earl of Leicester, was the son or grandson of Amicia, a coheir of the former Earls, and as such entitled to quarter the arms of the De Bellomonts. As stated on page 91 (*vide* 97 and 98), there are two coats attributed to De Montfort. His only status in this country depended solely upon the De Bellomont inheritance, and, conformably with the custom of the period, we are far more likely to find him using arms of De Bellomont or De

487 *Trefoil.*

488 *Quatrefoil.*

489 *Cinquefoil.*

133. On 8 February 1965 a new Canadian Flag was proclaimed. It is blazoned: gules, on a Canadian pale argent, a maple leaf of the first. A 'Canadian pale' is about half as wide again as an ordinary pale. The use of a single red maple leaf has given this emblem a rather special character, and the kings of arms will not now normally include it in a new coat of arms, whether English or Canadian. Before 1965 the red maple leaf was very frequently found in Canadian arms.

490 *From the seal of Robert Fitz-Pernell, Earl of Leicester, d. 1206.*

Beaumont than of Montfort. From the similarity of the charge to the better-known Beaumont arms, I am inclined to think the lion rampant to be the real De Bellomont coat. The origin of the cinquefoil has yet to be accounted for. The earliest De Bellomont for whom I can find proof of user thereof is Robert 'Fitz-Pernell', otherwise De Bellomont, who died in 1206, and whose seal (490) shows it. Be it noted it is not on a shield, and though of course this is not proof in any way, it is in accord with my suggestion that it is nothing more than a pimpernel flower adopted as a device or badge to typify his own name and his mother's name, she being Pernelle or Petronilla, the heiress of Grantmesnil. The cinquefoil was not the coat of Grantmesnil but a quaint little conceit, and is not therefore likely to have been used as a coat of arms by the De Bellomonts, though no doubt they used it as a badge and device, as no doubt did Simon de Montfort. Simon de Montfort split England into two parties. Men were for Montfort or the king, and those that were for De Montfort very probably took and used his badge of a cinquefoil as a party badge.

The cinquefoil in its ordinary heraldic form also occurs in the arms of Umfraville, Bardolph, Hamilton, and D'Arcy, and sprigs of cinquefoil will be found in the arms of Hill, and in the crest of Kersey. The cinquefoil is sometimes found pierced. The five-foiled flower being the blossom of so many plants, what are to all intents and purposes cinquefoils, occur in the arms of Fraser, where they are termed 'fraises', of Primrose, where they are blazoned 'primroses', and of Lambert, where they are called 'narcissus flowers'.

The double Quatrefoil is cited as the English difference mark for the ninth son, but as these difference marks are but seldom used, and as ninth sons are somewhat of a rarity, it is seldom indeed that this particular mark is seen in use. Personally I have never seen it.

The Turnip makes an early appearance in armory, and occurs in the coat of Dammant ['Sable, a turnip leaved proper, a chief or, butté-de-poix'].[134]

The curious crest of Lingen, which is 'Seven leeks root upwards issuing from a ducal coronet all proper', is worthy of especial mention.

In considering flowers as a charge, a start must naturally be made with the rose, which figures so prominently in the heraldry of England.

The heraldic Rose until a much later date than its first appearance in armory—it occurs, however, at the earliest period—was always represented in what we now term the 'conventional' form, with five displayed petals (491). Accustomed as we are to the more ornate form of the cultivated rose of the garden, those who speak of the 'conventional' heraldic rose rather seem to overlook that it is an exact reproduction of the wild rose of the hedgerow, which, moreover, has a tendency to show itself 'displayed' and not in the more profile attitude we are perhaps accustomed to. It should also be observed that the earliest representations of the heraldic rose depict the intervening spaces between the petals which are noticeable in the wild rose. Under the Tudor sovereigns, the heraldic rose often shows a double row of petals, a fact which is doubtless accounted for by the then

491 *Rose.*

134. This coat appears to have been borne without authority. This means, as far as I can discover, that heraldry is happily free of root vegetables. So far the potato, carrot, turnip, parsnip, artichoke, beetroot, swede and mangel-wurzel do not appear to have been planted in the heraldic field.

increasing familiarity with the cultivated variety, and also by the attempt to con-join the rival emblems of the warring factions of York and Lancaster.

Though the heraldic rose is seldom, if ever, otherwise depicted, it should be described as 'barbed vert' and 'seeded or' (or 'barbed and seeded proper') when the centre seeds and the small intervening green leaves (the calyx) between the petals are represented in their natural colours. In the reign of the later Tudor sovereigns the conventionality of earlier heraldic art was slowly beginning to give way to the pure naturalism towards which heraldic art thereafter steadily degenerated, and we find that the rose then begins (both as a Royal badge and elsewhere) to be met with 'slipped and leaved' (492). The Royal fleurs-de-lis are turned into natural lilies in the grant of arms to Eton College, and in the grant to William Cope, Cofferer to Henry VII, the roses are slipped ['Argent, on a chevron azure, between three roses gules, slipped and leaved vert, as many fleurs-de-lis or. Crest: out of a fleur-de-lis or, a dragon's head gules']. A rose when 'slipped' theoretically has only a stalk added, but in practice it will always have at least one leaf added to the slip, and a rose 'slipped and leaved' would have a leaf on either side. A rose 'stalked and leaved' is not so limited, and will usually be found with a slightly longer stalk and several leaves; but these technical refinements of blazon, which are really unnecessary, are not greatly observed or taken into account. The arms of the Burgh of Montrose afford an example of a single rose as the only charge, although other instances will be met with in the arms of Boscawen, Viscount Falmouth ['Ermine, a rose gules, barbed and seeded proper'], and of Nightingale, Bart. ['Per pale ermine and gules, a rose counterchanged'].

492 *Rose slipped and leaved.*

Amongst the scores of English arms in which the rose figures, it will be found in the original heraldic form in the case of the arms of Southampton (Plate X); and either stalked or slipped in the arms of Brodribb and White-Thomson. A curious instance of the use of the rose will be found in the crest of Bewley, and the 'cultivated' rose was depicted in the emblazonment of the crest of Inverarity, which is a rose-bush proper.

Heraldry, with its roses, has accomplished what horticulture has not. There is an old legend that when Henry VII succeeded to the English throne some enter-prising individual produced a natural parti-coloured rose which answered to the conjoined heraldic rose of gules and argent. Our roses 'or' may really find their natural counterpart in the primrose, but the arms of Rochefort ['Quarterly or and azure, four roses counterchanged'] give us the *blue* rose, the arms of Berendon ['Argent, three roses sable'] give us the *black* rose, and the coat of Smallshaw ['Argent, a rose vert, between three shakeforks sable'] is the long-desired *green* rose.

The Thistle (493) ranks next to the rose in British heraldic importance. Like the rose, the reason of its assumption as a national badge remains largely a matter of mystery, though it is of nothing like so ancient an origin. Of course one knows the time-honoured and wholly impossible legend that its adoption as a national symbol dates from the battle of Largs, when one of the Danish invaders gave away an attempted surprise by his cry of agony caused by stepping bare-footed upon a thistle.

The fact, however, remains that its earliest appearance is on the silver coinage of 1474, in the reign of James III, but during that reign there can be no doubt

493 *Thistle.*

that it was accepted either as a national badge or else as the personal badge of the sovereign. The period in question was that in which badges were so largely used, and it is not unlikely that, desiring to vie with his brother of England, and fired by the example of the broom badge and the rose badge, the Scottish king, remembering the ancient legend, chose the thistle as his own badge. In 1540, when the thistle had become recognised as one of the national emblems of the kingdom, the foundation of the Order of the Thistle stereotyped the fact for all future time. The conventional heraldic representation of the thistle is as it appears upon the star of that Order, that is, the flowered head upon a short stalk with a leaf on either side. Though sometimes represented of gold, it is nearly always proper. It has frequently been granted as an augmentation, though in such a meaning it will usually be found crowned. The coat of augmentation carried in the first quarter of his arms by Lord Torphichen is: 'Argent, a thistle vert, flowered gules' (really a thistle proper), 'on a chief azure an imperial crown or.' 'Sable, a thistle' (possibly really a teasel) 'or, between three pheons argent' is the coat of Teesdale, and 'Gules, three thistles or' is attributed in Papworth to Hawkey. A curious use of the thistle occurs in the arms of the National Bank of Scotland (granted 1826), which are: 'Or, the image of St Andrew with vesture vert, and surcoat purpure, bearing before him the cross of his martyrdom argent, all resting on a base of the second, in the dexter flank a garb gules, in the sinister a ship in full sail sable, *the shield surrounded with two thistles proper disposed in orle.*'

The Lily in its natural form sometimes occurs, though of course it generally figures as the fleur-de-lis, which will presently be considered. The natural lily will be found in the arms of Aberdeen University, of Dundee, and in the crests of various families of the name of Chadwick. It also occurs in the arms of the College of St Mary the Virgin, at Eton ['Sable, three lilies argent, on a chief per pale azure and gules a fleur-de-lis on the dexter side, and a lion passant guardant or on the sinister']. Here they doubtless typify the Virgin, to whom they have reference; as also in the case of Marylebone (252).

The arms of Lilly, of Stoke Prior, are: 'Gules, three lilies slipped argent'; and the arms of J. E. Lilley, Esq., of Harrow, are: 'Azure, on a pile between two fleurs-de-lis argent, a lily of the valley eradicated proper. Crest: on a wreath of the colours, a cubit arm erect proper, charged with a fleur-de-lis argent and holding in the hand two lilies of the valley, leaved and slipped in saltire, also proper.'

Columbine Flowers occur in the arms of Cadman, and *Gillyflowers* in the arms of Livingstone. *Fraises*— really the flowers of the strawberry-plant— occur, as has been already mentioned, in the arms of Fraser, and *Narcissus Flowers* in the arms of Lambeth. 'Gules, three poppy bolles on their stalks in fess or' are the arms of Boller.

The Lotus-Flower, which is now very generally becoming the recognised emblem of India, is constantly met with in the arms granted to those who have won fortune or reputation in that country. Instances in which it occurs are the arms of Sir Roper Lethbridge, K.C.I.E., Sir Thomas Seccombe, G.C.I.E., and the University of Madras.[135]

The *Sylphium-Plant* occurs in the arms of General Sir Henry Augustus Smyth,

135. The lotus flower is usually shown in the natural way, but like the rose, it can be shown in stylized form, as in the arms of Sir Oliver Goonetilleke illustrated on page 58.

K.C.M.G., which are: Vert, a chevron erminois, charged with a chevron gules, between three Saracens' heads habited in profile couped at the neck proper, and for augmentation a chief argent, thereon a mount vert inscribed with the Greek letters K Y P A gold and issuant therefrom a representation of the plant Silphium proper. Crests: 1. (of augmentation) on a wreath of the colours, a mount vert inscribed with the aforesaid Greek letters and issuant therefrom the Silphium as in the arms; 2. on a wreath of the colours, an anchor fesswise sable, thereon an ostrich erminois holding in the beak a horse-shoe or. Motto: 'Vincere est vivere.'

The arms granted to Sir Richard Quain were: 'Argent, a chevron engrailed azure, in chief two fers-de-moline gules, and issuant from the base a rock covered with daisies proper.

Primroses occur (as was only to be expected) in the arms of the Earl of Rose-bery ['Vert, three primroses within a double tressure flory counterflory or'].[136]

The Sunflower or *Marigold* occurs in the crest of Buchan ['A sunflower in full bloom towards the sun in the dexter chief'], and also in the arms granted in 1614 to Florio. Here, however, the flower is termed a heliotrope. The arms in question are: 'Azure, a heliotrope or, issuing from a stalk sprouting from two leaves vert, in chief the sun in splendour proper.'

Tulips occur in the arms of Raphael, and the *Cornflower* or *Bluebottle* in the arms of Chorley of Chorley, Lancs. ['Argent, a chevron gules between three bluebottles slipped proper'], and also in the more modern arms of that town.

Saffron-Flowers are a charge upon the arms of Player of Nottingham. The arms granted to Sir Edgar Boehm, Bart., were: 'Azure, in the sinister canton a sun issuant therefrom eleven rays, over all a clover-plant eradicated proper.'

The Fleur-de-Lis. Few figures have puzzled the antiquary so much as the fleur-de-lis. Countless origins have been suggested for it; we have even lately had the height of absurdity urged in a suggested phallic origin, which only rivals in ridiculousness the long since exploded legend that the fleurs-de-lis in the arms of France were a corrupted form of an earlier coat, 'Azure, three toads or', the reputed coat of arms of Pharamond!

494 *Fleur-de-lis.*

To France and the arms of France one must turn for the origin of the heraldic use of the fleur-de-lis. To begin with, the form of the fleur-de-lis as a mere pre-sumably meaningless form of decoration is found long before the days of armory, in fact from the earliest period of decoration. It is such an essentially natural development of decoration that it may be accepted as such without any attempt to give it a meaning or any symbolism. Its earliest heraldic appearances as the finial of a sceptre or the decoration of a coronet need not have had any symbolical character.

We then find the 'lily' accepted as having some symbolical reference to France, and it should be remembered that the iris was known by the name of a lily until comparatively modern times.

It is curious—though possibly in this case it may be only a coincidence—that, on a coin of the Emperor Hadrian, Gaul is typified by a female figure holding in the hand a lily, the legend being, 'Restutori Galliæ'. The fleur-de-lis as the finial of a sceptre and as an ornament of a crown can be taken back to the fifth century.

136. The point of this remark is lost unless the reader appreciates that the family name of the Earl of Rosebery is Primrose.

Fleurs-de-lis upon crowns and coronets in France are at least as old as the reign of King Robert (son of Hugh Capet), whose seal represents him crowned in this manner.

We have, moreover, the ancient legendary tradition that at the baptism of Clovis, King of the Franks, the Virgin (whose emblem the lily has always been) sent a lily by an angel as a mark of her special favour. It is difficult to determine the exact date at which this tradition was invented, but its accepted character may be judged from the fact that it was solemnly advanced by the French bishops at the Council of Trent in a dispute as to the precedence of their sovereign. The old legend as to Clovis would naturally identify the flower with him, and it should be noted that the names Clovis, Lois, Loys, and Louis are identical. 'Loys' was the signature of the kings of France until the time of Louis XIII. It is worth the passing conjecture that what are sometimes termed 'Cleves lilies' may be a corrupted form of Clovis lilies. There can be little doubt that the term 'fleur-de-lis' is quite as likely to be a corruption of 'fleur-de-lois' as flower of the lily. The chief point is that the desire was to represent a *flower* in allusion to the old legend, without perhaps any very definite certainty of the flower intended to be represented. Philip I on his seal (A.D. 1060) holds a short staff terminating in a fleur-de-lis. The same object occurs in the great seal of Louis VII. In the seal of his wife, Queen Constance, we find her represented as holding in either hand a similar object, though in these last cases it is by no means certain that the objects are not attempts to represent the natural flower. A signet of Louis VII bears a single fleur-de-lis 'florencée' (or flowered), and in his reign the heraldic fleur-de-lis undoubtedly became stereotyped as a symbolical device, for we find that when in the lifetime of Louis VII his son Philip was crowned, the king prescribed that the prince should wear 'ses chausses appelées sandales ou bottines de soye, couleur bleu azuré sémée en moult endroits de fleurs-de-lys or, puis aussi sa dalmatique de même couleur at œuvre.' On the oval counterseal of Philip II (*d.* 1223) appears a heraldic fleur-de-lis. His great seal, as also that of Louis VIII, shows a seated figure crowned with an open crown of 'fleurons', and holding in his right hand a flower, and in his left a sceptre surmounted by a heraldic fleur-de-lis enclosed within a lozenge-shaped frame. On the seal of Louis VIII the conjunction of the essentially heraldic fleur-de-lis (within the lozenge-shaped head of the sceptre), and the more natural flower held in the hand, should leave little if any doubt of the intention to represent flowers in the French fleurs-de-lis. The figure held in the hand represents a flower of five petals. The upper pair turned inwards to touch the centre one, and the lower pair curved downwards, leave the figure with a marked resemblance both to the iris and to the conventional fleur-de-lis. The counter-seal of Louis VIII shows a Norman-shaped shield semé of fleurs-de-lis of the conventional heraldic pattern. By then, of course, 'Azure, semé-de-lis or' had become the fixed and determined arms of France. By an edict dated 1376, Charles V reduced the number of fleurs-de-lis in his shield to three: 'Pour symboliser la Sainte-Trinité.'

The claim of Edward III to the throne of France was made on the death of Charles IV of France in 1328, but the decision being against him, he apparently acquiesced, and did homage to Philip of Valois (Philip VI) for Guienne. Philip, however, lent assistance to David II of Scotland against King Edward, who

206

immediately renewed his claim to France, assumed the arms and the title of king of that country, and prepared for war. He commenced hostilities in 1339, and upon his new Great Seal (made in the early part of 1340) we find his arms represented upon shield, surcoat, and housings as: 'Quarterly, 1 and 4, azure, semé-de-lis or (for France); 2 and 3, gules, three lions passant guardant in pale or (for England).' The Royal Arms thus remained until 1411,[137] when upon the second Great Seal of Henry IV the fleurs-de-lis in England (as in France) were reduced to three in number, and so remained as part of the Royal Arms of this country until the latter part of the reign of George III.

Fleurs-de-lis (probably intended as badges only) had figured upon all the Great Seals of Edward III. On the first seal (which with slight alterations had also served for both Edward I and II), a small fleur-de-lis appears over each of the castles which had previously figured on either side of the throne. In the second Great Seal, fleurs-de-lis took the places of the castles.

The similarity of the Montgomery arms to the Royal Arms of France has led to all kinds of wild genealogical conjectures, but at a time when the arms of France were hardly determinate, the seal of John de Mundegumbri is met with, bearing a single fleur-de-lis, the original from which the arms of Montgomery were developed. Letters of nobility and the name of Du Lis were granted by Charles VII in December 1429 to the brothers of Joan of Arc, and the following arms were then assigned to them: 'Azure, a sword in pale proper, hilted and supporting on its point an open crown or, between two fleurs-de-lis of the last.'

The fleur-de-lis 'florencée', or the 'fleur-de-lis flowered', as it is termed in England, is officially considered a distinct charge from the simple fleur-de-lis. Eve employs the term 'seeded', and remarks of it: 'This being one of the numerous instances of pedantic, because unnecessary distinction, which showed marks of decadence; for both forms occur at the same period, and adorn the same object, evidently with the same intention.' The difference between these forms really is that the fleur-de-lis is 'seeded' when a stalk having seeds at the end issues in the upper interstices. In a fleur-de-lis 'florencée', the natural flower of a lily issues instead of the seeded stalk. This figure formed the arms of the city of Florence.[138]

Fleurs-de-lis, like all other Royal emblems, are frequently to be met with in the arms of towns, e.g. in the arms of Lancaster, Maryborough, Wakefield, and Great Torrington. The arms of Wareham afford an instance of fleurs-de-lis reversed, and the Corporate Seals of Liskeard and Tamworth merit reproduction, did space permit, from the designs of the fleurs-de-lis which there appear. One cannot leave the fleur-de-lis without referring to one curious development of it, viz. the leopard's face jessant-de-lis (332), a curious charge which undoubtedly originated in the arms of the family of Cantelupe. This charge is not uncommon, though by no means so usual as the leopard's face. Planché considers that it was originally derived from the fleur-de-lis, the circular boss which in early repre-

137. There is evidence that other members of the Royal family used France Modern (three fleurs-de-lis or) before the new Great Seal was struck. Henry of Monmouth, Prince of Wales, sealed a document in 1404 with a seal showing France Modern, and Edward Duke of York's seal, affixed to a charter of 1403, likewise shows three fleurs-de-lis.
138. A new version of the fleur-de-lis has appeared in heraldry in recent years; it is the fleur-de-lis burgeonée. It is shown with the outer petals closed, but just about to burst open.

sentations so often figures as the centre of the fleur-de-lis, being merely *decorated* with the leopard's face. One can follow Planché a bit further by imagining that this face need not necessarily be that of a leopard, for at a certain period all decorative art was crowded with grotesque masks whenever opportunity offered. The leopard's face jessant-de-lis is now represented as a leopard's face with the lower part of a fleur-de-lis issuing from the mouth, and the upper part rising from behind the head. Instances of this charge occur as early as the thirteenth century as the arms of the Cantelupe family, and Thomas de Cantelupe having been Bishop of Hereford 1275 to 1282, the arms of that See have since been three leopards' faces jessant-de-lis, the distinction being that in the arms of the See of Hereford the leopards' faces are reversed.

The origin may perhaps make itself apparent when we remember that the earliest form of the name was Cantelowe. Is it not probable that 'lions'' faces (*i.e.* head *de leo*) may have been suggested by the name? Possibly, however, wolf-heads may have been meant, suggested by *lupus*, or by the same analogy which gives us wolf-heads or wolves upon the arms of Low and Lowe.

Fruit—the remaining division of those charges which can be classed as belonging to the vegetable kingdom—must of necessity be but briefly dealt with.

Grapes perhaps cannot be easily distinguished from vines (to which refer, page 199), but the arms of Bradway of Potscliff, co. Gloucester ['Argent, a chevron gules between three bunches of grapes proper'] and of Viscountess Beaconsfield, the daughter of Captain John Viney Evans ['Argent, a bunch of grapes stalked and leaved proper, between two flaunches sable, each charged with a boar's head argent'] are instances in point.

Apples occur in the arms of Robert Applegarth (Edward III Roll) ['Argent, three apples slipped gules'] and 'Or, a chevron between three apples gules' is the coat of a family named Southbey.

Pears occur in the arms of Allcroft, of Stokesay Castle, Perrins, Perry, Perryman, and Pirie.

Oranges are but seldom met with in British heraldry, but an instance occurs in the arms of Lord Polwarth, who bears over the Hepburn quarterings an inescutcheon azure, an orange slipped and surmounted by an imperial crown all proper. This was an augmentation conferred by King William III, and a very similar augmentation [in the 1st and 4th quarters, azure, three oranges slipped proper within an orle of thistles or] was granted to Livingstone, Viscount Teviot.[139]

The Pomegranate (495), which dimidiated with a rose was one of the badges of Queen Mary, is not infrequently met with.

The Pineapple in heraldry is nearly always the fir-cone. In the arms of Perring, Bart. ['Argent, on a chevron engrailed sable between three pineapples (fir-cones) pendent vert, as many leopards' faces of the first. Crest: on a mount a pineapple (fir-cone) vert'], and in the crest of Parkyns, Bart. ['Out of a ducal coronet or, a pineapple proper'], and also in the arms of Pyne ['Gules, a chevron ermine

495 *Pomegranate.*

139. The natural orange seems to be always blazoned as an orange. It might be thought that confusion could arise between the fruit and the roundel tenné, which Fox-Davies and others state is termed an orange. I have only ever found one such roundel in English heraldry, and it is blazoned a roundel tenné, not an orange. If this may be regarded as a firm precedent, there never need be confusion.

between three pineapples or'] and Parkin-Moore, the fruit is the fir or pine cone. Latterly the likelihood of confusion has led to the general use of the term 'pine-cone' in such cases, but the ancient description was certainly 'pineapple'. The arms of John Apperley, as given in the Edward III Roll, are: 'Argent, a chevron gules between three pineapples (fir-cones) vert, slipped or.'

The real pineapple of the present day does, however, occur, *e.g.* in the arms of Benson, of Lutwyche, Shropshire ['Argent, on waves of the sea, an old English galley all proper, on a chief wavy azure a hand couped at the wrist, supporting on a dagger the scales of Justice between two pineapples erect or, leaved vert. Mantling azure and argent. Crest: upon a wreath of the colours, a horse caparisoned, passant, proper, on the breast a shield argent, charged with a pineapple proper. Motto: "Leges arma tenent sanctas"'].

Bean-Pods occur in the arms of Rise of Trewardreva, co. Cornwall ['Argent, a chevron gules between three bean-pods vert'], and Papworth mentions in the arms of Messarney an instance of cherries ['Or, a chevron per pale gules and vert between three cherries of the second slipped of the third']. Elsewhere, however, the charges on the shield of this family are termed apples. Strawberries occur in the arms and crest of Hollist, and the arms of Duffield are: 'Sable, a chevron between three cloves or.' The arms of the Grocers' Livery Company, granted in 1531–2, are: 'Argent, a chevron gules between nine cloves, three, three and three.' The arms of Garwynton are stated to be: 'Sable, a chevron between three heads of garlick pendent argent,' but another version gives the charges as pomegranates. 'Azure, a chevron between three gourds pendent, slipped or' is a coat attributed to Stukele, but here again there is uncertainty, as the charges are sometimes quoted as pears. The arms of Bonefeld are: 'Azure, a chevron between three quinces or.' The arms of Alderberry are naturally: 'Argent, three branches of alder-berries proper.' The arms of Haseley of Suffolk are: 'Argent, a fess gules, between three hazel-nuts or, stalks and leaves vert.' Papworth also mentions the arms of Tarsell, viz.: 'Or, a chevron sable, between three hazel-nuts erect, slipped gules.' It would, however, seem more probable that these charges are really teazles.

The fruit of the oak—the *Acorn* (496)—has already been incidentally referred to, but other instances occur in the arms of Baldwin, Stable, and Huth.

Wheat and other grain is constantly met with in British armory. The arms of Bigland ['Azure, two ears of big wheat erect in fess and bladed or] and of Cheape are examples, and others occur in the arms of Layland-Barratt, Cross, and Rye ['Gules, on a bend argent, between two ears of rye, stalked, leaved, and slipped or, three crosses cramponné sable'].

Garbs, as they are invariably termed heraldically, are sheaves, and are of very frequent occurrence. The earliest appearance of the garb (497) in English heraldry is on the seal of Ranulph, Earl of Chester, who died in 1232. Garbs therefrom became identified with the Earldom of Chester, and subsequently 'Azure, three garbs or' became and still remain the territorial or possibly the sovereign coat of that earldom. Garbs naturally figure, therefore, in the arms of many families who originally held land by feudal tenure under the Earls of Chester, *e.g.* the families of Cholmondeley ['Gules, in chief two helmets in profile argent, and in base a garb vert'] and Kevilioc ['Azure, six garbs, three, two, and one or']. Grosvenor ['Azure, a garb or'] is usually quoted as another example, and possibly correctly, but a

496 *Acorn slipped and leaved.*

497 *Garb.*

very interesting origin has been suggested by Mr W. G. Taunton in his work *The Tauntons of Oxford, by One of Them*:

'I merely wish to make a few remarks of my own that seem to have escaped other writers on genealogical matters.

'In the first place, Sir Gilbert le Grosvenor, who is stated to have come over with William of Normandy at the Conquest, is described as nephew to Hugh Lupus, Earl of Chester; but Hugh Lupus was himself nephew to King William. Now, William could not have been very old when he overthrew Harold at Hastings. It seems, therefore, rather improbable that Sir Gilbert le Grosvenor, who was his nephew's nephew, could actually have fought with him at Hastings, especially when William lived to reign for twenty-one years after, and was not very old when he died.

'The name Grosvenor does not occur in any of the versions of the Roll of Battle Abbey. Not that any of these versions of this celebrated Roll are considered authentic by modern critics, who say that many names were subsequently added by the monks to please ambitious parvenus. The name Venour is on the Roll, however, and it is just possible that this Venour was the Grosvenor of our quest. The addition of "Gros" would then be subsequent to his fattening on the spoils of the Saxon and cultivating a corporation. "Venour" means hunter, and 'Gros' means fat. Gilbert's uncle, Hugh Lupus, was, we know, a fat man; in fact, he was nicknamed "Hugh the Fat". The Grosvenors of that period probably inherited obesity from their relative, Hugh Lupus, therefore, and the fable that they were called Grosvenor on account of their office of "Great Huntsman" to the Dukes of Normandy is not to be relied on.

'We are further on told by the old family historians that when Sir Robert Grosvenor lost the day in that ever-memorable controversy with Sir Richard le Scrope, Baron of Bolton, concerning the coat of arms—"Azure, a bend or"— borne by both families, Sir Robert Grosvenor took for his arms one of the garbs of his kinsman, the Earl of Chester.

'It did not seem to occur to these worthies that the Earl of Chester, who was their ancestor's uncle, never bore the garbs in his arms, but a wolf's head.

'It is true that one or two subsequent Earls of Chester bore garbs, but these Earls were far too distantly connected with the Grosvenors to render it likely that the latter would borrow their new arms from this source.

'It is curious that there should have been in this same county of Chester a family of almost identical name also bearing a garb in their arms, though their garb was surrounded by three bezants.

'The name of this family was Grasvenor, or Gravenor, and, moreover, the tinctures of their arms were identical with those of Grosvenor. It is far more likely, therefore, that the coat assumed by Sir Robert after the adverse decision of the Court of Chivalry was taken from that of Grasvenor, or Gravenor, and that the two families were known at that time to be of common origin, although their connection with each other has subsequently been lost.

'In French both *gros* and *gras* mean fat, and we have both forms in Grosvenor and Grasvenor.

'A chief huntsman to Royalty would have been Grandvenor, not Grosvenor or Grasvenor.

'All these criticisms of mine, however, only affect the origin of the arms, and not the ancient and almost Royal descent of this illustrious race. Hugh Lupus, Earl of Chester, was a son of the Duke of Brittany, as is plainly stated in his epitaph.

'This connection of uncle and nephew, then, between "Hugh the Fat" and Gilbert Grosvenor implies a maternal descent from the Dukes of Brittany for the first ancestor of the Grosvenor family.

'In virtue of their descent from an heiress of the house of Grosvenor, it is only necessary to add the Tauntons of Oxford are Grosvenors, heraldically speaking, and that quartering so many ancient coats through the Tanners and the Grosvenors with our brand-new grant is like putting old wine into new bottles.

'Hugh Lupus left no son to succeed him, and the subsequent descent of the Earldom of Chester was somewhat erratic. So I think there is some point in my arguments regarding the coat assumed by Sir Robert Grosvenor of Hulme."

Though a garb, unless quoted otherwise, is presumed to be a sheaf of wheat, the term is not so confined. The garbs in the arms of Comyn, which figure as a quartering in so many Scottish coats, are really of cummin, as presumably are the garbs in the arms of Cummins. When a garb is 'banded' of a different colour this should be stated, and Elvin states that it may be 'eared' of a different colour, though I confess I am aware of no such instance.

'Argent, two bundles of reeds in fess vert,' is the coat of Janssen of Wimbledon, Surrey (Bart., extinct), and a bundle of rods occurs in the arms of Evans, and the crest of Harris, though in this latter case it is termed a faggot.

Reeds also occur in the crest of Reade, and the crest of Middlemore ['On a wreath of colours, a moorcock amidst grass and reeds proper'] furnishes another example.

Bulrushes occur in the crest of Billiat, and in the arms of Scott ['Argent, on a mount of bulrushes in base proper, a bull passant sable, a chief pean, billetté or'].

Grass is naturally presumed on the mounts vert which are so constantly met with, but more definite instances can be found in the arms of Sykes, Hulley, and Hill.

19 · Inanimate objects

In dealing with those charges which may be classed under the above description one can safely say that there is scarcely an object under the sun which has not at some time or other been introduced into a coat of arms or crest. One cannot usefully make a book on armory assume the character of a general encyclopædia of useful knowledge, and reference will only be made in this chapter to a limited number, including those which from frequent usage have obtained a recognised heraldic character. Mention may, at the outset, be made of certain letters of the *alphabet*. Instances of these are scarcely common, but the family of Kekitmore may be adduced as bearing 'Gules, three S's or', while Bridlington Priory had for arms: 'Per pale, sable and argent, three B's counterchanged.' The arms of Rashleigh are: 'Sable, a cross or, between in the first quarter a Cornish chough argent, beaked and legged gules; in the second a text 𝕿; in the third and fourth a crescent all argent.'' Corporate arms (in England) afford an instance of alphabetical letters in the case of the B's on the shield of Bermondsey.[140]

498 Anchor.

The Anchor (498). This charge figures very largely in English armory, as may, perhaps, be looked for when it is remembered that maritime devices occur more frequently in sea-board lands than in continents. The arms of the town of Musselburgh are: 'Azure, three anchors in pale, one in the chief and two in the flanks or, accompanied with as many mussels, one in the dexter and one in the sinister chief points, and the third in base proper.' The Comtes de St Cricq, with 'Argent, two anchors in saltire sable, on a chief three mullets or,' will be an instance in point as to France.

Anvils. These are occasionally met with, as in the case of the arms of a family of the name of Walker, who bear: 'Argent, on a chevron gules, between two anvils in chief and an anchor in base sable, a bee between two crescents or.

V *Arms of the Bishopric of Trinidad and Tobago.*

140. In ecclesiastical heraldry the sacred monograms I.H.S. and I.X.P. are frequently used. For example, the arms granted to the Vicar Apostolic of Salisbury, Southern Rhodesia are blazoned: azure the emblem of the Society of Jesus (the letters I.H.S. irradiated between in chief a long cross formy, and in base three nails pilewise) and in dexter chief a representation of the Southern Cross all or.

A very wordy coat is that granted to the Bishopric of Trinidad and Tobago on 12 October 1951. It is blazoned: azure, a long cross flory or, surmounted of a representation of the emblem of the Holy and Undivided Trinity argent, the lettering sable, between the two Greek letters alpha and omega gold. The illustration (V) is more impressive than a verbal description.

Numerals are also found. The borough of Aberystwyth has the date of its first charter, granted by Edward I in 1277, inscribed on a book in its arms. The British Bank of the Middle East has its name inscribed on an enarched chief, but as it is written in Kufic Arabic letters the effect is not, at least to western eyes, as startlingly commercial as it might have been.

PLATE V

Arms of Swinton of that Ilk

Mantling gules and argent. Crest: upon a wreath of the colours, on a mount within a wreathed serpent a dove statant all proper.'[141]

Arches, castles, towers, and turrets may be exemplified, amongst others, by the following.

Instances of *Castles* and *Towers* will be found in the arms of Carlyon and Kelly, and of the former fractured castles will be found in the shield of Willoughby quartered by Bertie; while an example of a quadrangular castle may be seen in the arms of Rawson. The difference between a Castle (499) and a Tower (500) should be carefully noticed, and though it is a distinction but little observed in ancient days it is now always adhered to. When either castle or tower is surmounted by smaller towers (as 501) it is termed 'triple-towered'.

An instance of a *Fortification* as a charge occurs in the shield of Sconce: 'Azure, a fortification (sconce) argent, masoned sable, in the dexter chief point a mullet of six points of the second.'

Gabions were hampers filled with earth, and were used in the construction of fortifications and earthworks. They are of occasional occurrence in English armory at any rate, and may be seen in the shields of Christie and of Goodfellow.

The arms of Banks supply an instance of *Arches*. Mention may here perhaps be made of William Arches, who bore at the siege of Rouen: 'Gules, three double arches argent.' The family of Lethbridge bear a bridge, and this charge figures in a number of other coats.

An Abbey occurs in the arms of Maitland of Dundrennan ['Argent, the ruins of an old abbey on a piece of ground all proper'], and a monastery in that of McLarty ['Azure, the front of an ancient monastery argent']. A somewhat isolated instance of a *Temple* occurs in the shield of Templer.

A curious canting grant of arms may be seen in that to the town of Eccles, in which the charge is an *Ecclesiastical Building*, and similar though somewhat unusual charges figure also in the quartering for Chappel ['Per chevron or and azure, in chief a mullet of six points between two crosses patée of the last, and in base the front elevation of a chapel argent'], borne by Brown-Westhead.

Arrows are very frequently found, and the arms of Hales supply one of the many examples of this charge, while a bow—without the arrows—may be instanced in the shield of Bowes: 'Ermine, three bows bent and stringed palewise in fess proper.'

Arrow-Heads and *Pheons* are of common usage, and occur in the arms of Foster and many other families. Pheons, it may be noticed in passing, are arrow-heads with an inner engrailed edge (502), while when depicted without this peculiarity they are termed 'broad arrows' (503). This is not a distinction very stringently adhered to.

Charges associated with warfare and military defences are frequently to be found both in English and foreign heraldry.

Battle-Axes (504), for example, may be seen in the shield of Firth and in that of Renty in Artois, which has: 'Argent, three doloires, or broad-axes, gules, those in

499 *Castle.*

500 *Tower.*

501 *Tower triple-towered.*

502 *Pheon.*

503 *Broad arrow.*

141. This grant was made on 13 December 1778 to Samuel Walker of Rotherham, Co. York, with limitation to him and his descendents and to the other descendents of his father Joseph Walker of Ecclesfield, Co. York.

C.G.H.—8   213

504 Battle-axe.

505 Caltrap.

506 Portcullis.

507 Beacon.

508 Grenade.

chief addorsed.' In blazoning a battle-axe care should be taken to specify the fact if the head is of a different colour, as is frequently the case.[142]

The somewhat infrequent device of a *Battering-Ram* is seen in the arms of Bertie, who bore: 'Argent, three battering-rams fesswise in pale proper, armed and garnished azure.'

An instrument of military defence consisting of an iron frame of four points, and called a *Caltrap* (505) or *Galtrap* (and sometimes a Cheval trap, from its use of impending the approach of cavalry), is found in the arms of Trappe ['Argent, three caltraps sable'], Gilstrap and other families; while French armory supplies us with another example in the case of the family of Guetteville de Guénonville,who bore for arms: 'D'argent, semée de chausse-trapes de sable.' Caltraps are also strewn upon the compartment upon which the supporters to the arms of the Earl of Perth are placed.

As the well-known badge of the Royal House of Tudor, the *Portcullis* (506) is familiar to any one conversant with Henry VII's Chapel at Westminster Abbey, but it also appears as a charge in the arms of the family of Wingate ['Gules, a portcullis and a chief embattled or'], where it forms an obvious pun on the earliest form of the name, viz. Windygate, whilst it figures also as the crest of the Dukes of Beaufort ['A portcullis or, nailed azure, chained of the first']. The disposition of the chains is a matter always left to the discretion of the artist.

Examples of *Beacons* (507) are furnished by the achievements of the family of Compton and of the town of Wolverhampton. A *fire chest* occurs in the arms of Critchett (*vide* p. 196).

Chains are singularly scarce in armory, and indeed nearly wholly absent as *charges*, usually occurring where they do as part of the crest. The English shield of Anderton, it is true, bears: 'Sable, three chains argent;' while another one (Duppa de Uphaugh) has: Quarterly, 1 and 4, a lion's paw couped in fess between two chains or, a chief nebuly of the last, thereon two roses of the first, barbed and seeded proper (for Duppa); 2 and 3, party fess azure and sable, a trident fesswise or, between three turbots argent (for Turbutt).' In Continental heraldry, however, chains are more frequently met with. Principal amongst these cases may be cited the arms of Navarre ('Gules, a cross saltire and double orle of chains, linked together or'), while many other instances are found in the armories of Southern France and of Spain.

Bombs or *Grenades* (508), for Heraldry does not distinguish, figure in the shields of Vavasseur, Jervoise, Boycott, and many other families.

Among the more recent grants *Cannon* have figured, as in the case of the Pilter arms and in those of the burgh of Portobello; while an earlier counterpart, in the form of a culverin, forms the charge of the Leigh family: 'Argent, a culverin in fess sable.' The arms of the late Admiral Sir Percy Scott are interesting.

The *Column* appears as a crest in the achievement of Coles. Between two cross crosslets it occurs in the arms of Adam of Maryburgh ['Vert, a Corinthian column with capital and base in pale proper, between two cross crosslets fitchée in fess or'], while the arms of the See of Sodor and Man are blazoned: 'Argent, upon a

142. The arms of Hatcher of Dorset contain a hatchet: per bend gules and sable, three roses in bend sinister or, over all a hatchet blade to the dexter argent. There are also examples of the kris and various other eastern knives.

pedestal the Virgin Mary with her arms extended between two pillars, in the dexter hand a church proper, in base the arms of Man in an escutcheon.' Major, of Suffolk, bears: 'Azure, three Corinthian columns, each surmounted by a ball, two and one argent.' It is necessary to specify the kind of column in the blazon.

Scaling-Ladders (509) (viz. ordinary-shaped ladders with grapnels affixed to the tops) to be seen in the English coats of D'Urban and Lloyd, while the Veronese Princes della Scala bore the ordinary ladder: 'Gules, a ladder of four steps in pale argent.' A further instance of this form of the charge occurs in the Swiss shield of Laiterberg: 'Argent, two ladders in saltire gules.'

Spears and *Spear-Heads* are to be found in the arms of many families both in England, Wales, and abroad; for example, in the arms of Amherst and Edwards. Distinction must be drawn between the lance or javelin (510) and the heraldic tilting-spear (511), particularly as the latter is always depicted with the sharp point for warfare instead of the blunted point which was actually used in the tournament. The Shakespeare arms (512) are: 'Or, on a bend sable a tilting-spear of the field,' while 'Azure, a lance or enfiled at its point by an annulet argent' represents the French family of Danby.

Spurs (513) occur in coat armour as such in the arms of Knight and Harben, and also occasionally 'winged' (514), as in the crest of Johnston.

Spur-Rowels, or *Spur-Revels*, are to be met with under that name, but they are, and are more often termed, 'mullets of five points pierced.'

Examples of *Stirrups* are but infrequent, and the best-known one (as regards English armory) is that of Scudamore, while the Polish Counts Brzostowski bore: 'Gules, a stirrup argent, within a bordure or.'

Stones are even more rare, though a solitary example may be quoted in the arms of Staniland: Per pale or and vert, a pale counter-changed, three eagles displayed two and one, and as many flint-stones one and two all proper. The 'vigilance' of the crane has been already alluded to on page 186. The mention of stones brings one to the kindred subject of *Catapults*. These engines of war, needless to say on a very much larger scale than the object which is nowadays associated with the term, were also known by the name *balistæ*, and also by that of *swepe*. Their occurrence is very infrequent, but for that very reason one may, perhaps, draw attention to the arms of the (English) family of Magnall: 'Argent, a swepe azure, charged with a stone or.'[143]

Swords, differing in number, position, and kind are, perhaps, of this class of charge the most numerous. A single sword as a charge may be seen in the shield of Dick of Wicklow, and Macfie, and a sword entwined by a serpent in that of Mackesy. A flaming sword occurs in the arms of Maddocks and Lewis. Swords frequently figure, too, in the hands or paws of supporters, accordingly as the latter are human figures or animals, whilst they figure as the 'supporters' themselves in the unique case of the French family of Bastard, whose shield is cottised

143. This coat appears to have been borne without authority, for on 19 February 1765 Thomas Magnall was granted the following arms, having deposed that his family had long used arms without authority: argent on a mount vert, a balista azure, charged with a stone proper, a chief per fess embattled or and gules. The grantee's father called himself Mangnall and the grant has this curious limitation. The arms are granted to Thomas Magnall and his descendents and 'by such of the Descendents of his said Father who shall write their Names Magnall and by no Others'.

509 *Scaling ladder.*

510 *Lance or javelin.*

511 *Tilting-spear.*

512 *Arms of William Shakespeare the poet (d. 1616): Or, on a bend sable, a tilting-spear of the field.*

513 *Spur.*

514 *Winged spur.*

515 *Sword.*

516 *Scimitar.*

517 *Seax.*

518 *Church-bell.*

519 *Hawk's bell.*

520 *Oval buckle.*

521 *Circular buckle.*

522 *Square buckle.*

by 'two swords, point in base.' The heraldic sword is represented as 515, the blade of the *dagger* being shorter and more pointed. The *scimitar* follows the form depicted in 516.

A *Seax* is the term employed to denote a curved scimitar, or falchion, having a notch at the back of the blade (517). In heraldry the use of this last is fairly frequent, though generally, it must be added, in shields of arms of doubtful authority. As such they were to be seen, amongst others, in the formerly reputed arms of Middlesex. That county, however, has them now included in their grant of arms.[144] They are also included in the grant of arms to the town of Ealing. The sabre and the cutlass when so blazoned follow their utilitarian patterns.

Torches or *Firebrands* are depicted in the arms and crest of Gillman and Tyson.

Barnacles (or *Breys*)—horse curbs—occur in some of the earlier coats, as in the arms of Wyatt ['Gules, a barnacle argent'], while another family of the same name (or, possibly, Wyot) bore: 'Per fess gules and azure (one or) three barnacles argent'.[145]

Bells are well instanced in the shield of Porter, and the poet Wordsworth bore: 'Argent, three bells azure.' It may be noted in passing that in Continental armory the clapper is frequently of a different tincture to that of the bell, as, for instance, 'D'Azure, à la cloche d'argent, butaillé [viz., with the clapper] de sable'—the arms of the Comtes de Bellegrade. A bell is assumed to be a church-bell (518) unless blazoned as a hawk's bell (519).

Bridle-Bits are of very infrequent use, though they may be seen in the achievement of the family of Milner.

The *Torse* (or wreath surmounting the helm) occasionally figures as a charge, for example, in the arms of Jocelyn and Joslin.

The Buckle is a charge which is of much more general use than some of the foregoing. It appears very frequently both in English and foreign heraldry—sometimes oval-shaped (520), circular (521), or square (522), but more generally

144. The county of Middlesex, now no longer an administrative county, was granted the following arms on 7 November 1910: gules, three seaxes fesswise proper, pomelled and hilted or, points to the sinister and cutting edges upwards, in chief a Saxon crown of the last.

145. 'Per fess gules and azure, a barnacle argent' are the arms recorded for the Wyatts of Kent in the 1619 Visitation of that county. The pedigree begins with William Wyatt of Yorkshire who must have lived at the beginning of the fifteenth century. Sir Thomas Wyatt the poet was a member of this family, but he bore a different coat granted to his father Sir Henry in 17 Henry VII. In the Kent Visitation the barnacle coat is in the first quarter and the later coat in the second quarter of the arms. The same arms were allowed to the descendents of Thomas Wiat of Banton, Co. Devon (*floruit circa* 1500) in the 1620 Visitation of Devon.

lozenge-shaped (523), especially in the case of Continental arms. A somewhat curious variation occurs in the arms of the Prussian Counts Wallenrodt, which are: 'Gules, a lozenge-shaped buckle argent, the tongue broken in the middle.' It is, of course, purely an artistic detail in all these buckles whether the tongue is attached to a crossbar, as in 520 and 521, or not, as in 522 and 523. As a badge the buckle is used by the Pelhams, Earls of Chichester and Earls of Yarborough, and a lozenge-shaped arming buckle is the badge of Jerningham.

523 *Lozenge-shaped buckle.*

Cups (covered) appear in the Butler arms, and derived therefrom in the arms of the town of Warrington. Laurie, of Maxwelltown, bears: 'Sable, a cup argent, issuing therefrom a garland between two laurel-branches all proper,' and similar arms are registered in Ireland for Lowry. The Veronese family of Bicchieri bear: 'Argent, a fess gules between three drinking-glasses half-filled with red wine proper.' An uncovered cup occurs in the arms of Fox, derived by them from the crest of Croker, and another instance occurs in the arms of a family of Smith. In this connection we may note in passing the rare use of the device of a *Vase*, which forms a charge in the coat of the town of Burslem, whilst it is also to be met with in the crest of the family of Doulton: 'On a wreath of the colours, a demi-lion sable, holding in the dexter paw a cross crosslet or, and resting the sinister upon an escutcheon charged with a vase proper.' The motto is perhaps well worth recording; 'Le beau est la splendeur de vrai.'

524 *Chess-rook.*

The arms of both the city of Dundee and the University of Aberdeen afford instances of a *Pot of Lilies*, and *Bowls* occur in the arms of Bolding.

Though blazoned as a *Cauldron*, the device occurring in the crest of De la Rue may be perhaps as fittingly described as an open bowl, and as such may find a place in this classification: 'Between two olive-branches vert a cauldron gules, fired and issuant therefrom a snake nowed proper.' The use of a *Pitcher* occurs in the arms of Bertrand de Monbocher, who bore at the siege of Carlaverock: 'Argent, three pitchers sable (sometimes found gules) within a bordure sable bezanté;' and the arms of Standish are: 'Sable, three standing dishes argent.' *Fleshpots* occur in the arms of Darling.

525 *Crescent.*

The somewhat singular charge of a *Chart* appears in the arms of Christopher,[146] and also as the crest of a Scottish family of Cook.

Chess-Rooks (524) are somewhat favourite heraldic devices, and are to be met with in a shield of Smith and the arms of Rocke of Clungunford.

The *Crescent* (525) figures largely in all armories, both as a charge and (in English heraldry) as a difference.

526 *Increscent.*

Variations, too, of the form of the crescent occur, such as when the horns are turned to the dexter (526), when it is termed 'a crescent increscent,' or simply 'an increscent,' or when they are turned to the sinister—when it is styled 'decrescent' (527). An instance of the crescent 'reversed' may be seen in the shield of the Austrian family of Puchberg, whose blazon was: 'Azure, three crescents, those in chief addorsed, that in base reversed.' In English 'difference marks' the

146. There was a somewhat singular reason for this. George Christopher, the grantee in 1824, was the son of Commodore William Christopher who, in 1761 and 1762, surveyed Chesterfield's Inlet for the Hudson's Bay Company. The arms are blazoned: per chevron wavy azure and erminois, a chart of Chesterfield's Inlet between two estoils in chief argent and on a mount in base vert, a beaver passant proper.

527 *Decrescent.*

*528 Crosier,
or pastoral staff.*

529 Palmer's staff.

530 Shuttle.

531 Woolpack.

532 Escarbuncle.

crescent is used to denote the second son, but under this character it will be discussed later.

Independently of its use in conjunction with ecclesiastical armory, the *Crosier* (528) is not widely used in ordinary achievements. It does occur, however, as a principal charge, as in the arms of the Irish family of Crozier and in the arms of Benoit (in Dauphiny) ['Gules, a pastoral staff argent'], while it forms part of the crest of Alfrod. The term 'crosier' is synonymous with the pastoral or episcopal staff, and is independent of the cross which is borne *before* (and not *by*) Archbishops and Metropolitans. The use of pastoral staves as charges is also to be seen in the shield of Were, while MacLaurin of Dreghorn bears: 'Argent, a shepherd's crook sable.' The *Palmer's Staff* (529) has been introduced into many coats of arms for families having the surname of Palmer, as has also the palmer's wallet.[147]

Cushions, somewhat strangely, form the charges in a number of British shields, occurring, for example, in the arms of Brisbane, and on the shield of the Johnstone family. In Scottish heraldry, indeed, cushions appear to have been of very ancient (and general) use, and are frequently to be met with. The Earls of Moray bore: 'Argent, three cushions lozengewise within a double tressure flory-counterflory gules,' but an English example occurs in the arms of Hutton.

The Distaff, which is supposed to be the origin of the lozenge upon which a lady bears her arms, is seldom seen in heraldry, but the family of Body, for instance, bear one in chief, and three occur in the arms of a family of Lees.

The Shuttle (530) occurs in the arms of Shuttleworth, and in those of the town of Leigh, while the shield of the borough of Pudsey affords an illustration of shuttles in conjunction with a woolpack (531).[148]

The Escarbuncle (532) is an instance of a charge having so developed by the evolution of an integral part of the shield itself. In ancient warfare shields were sometimes strengthened by being bound with iron bands radiating from the centre, and these bands, from the shape they assumed, became in course of time a charge in themselves under the term escarbuncle.

The crest of the Fanmakers' Company is: 'A hand couped proper holding a *fan* displayed,' while the chief charge in the arms is '. . . a fan displayed . . . the sticks gules.' This, however, is the only case I can cite of this object.[149]

The *Fasces* (533), emblematic of the Roman magisterial office, are very frequently introduced in grants of arms to Mayors and Lord Mayors, which no doubt accounts for its appearance in the arms of Durning-Lawrence, Knill, Evans, and Spokes.[150]

147. The palmer's wallet is usually termed a palmer's script; blazoned in this way, it is found in the arms granted to Banjamin Tathwell, formerly Barber, in 1804. The same charge was granted in 1770 to Micajah Towgood but was blazoned an open wallet.
148. The shuttle, like the cotton plant, has become an increasingly popular charge in both the personal and corporate heraldry of the palatine county of Lancaster. Accrington, Blackburn, Bury, Darwen Farnworth, Hashingden begin the alphabet of Lancashire towns bearing shuttles.
149. It is sad to record that this attractive coat, although it has been used for over two hundred years, is of no authority.
150. The fasces are also found in the arms of lawyers. The arms of Lord Carson afford an example: argent, on a chevron couped gules, between three crescents sable, two fasces chevronwise or. This symbol has, not unnaturally, declined in popularity since it was adopted as the symbol of the Italian Fascist Party.

An instance of *Fetterlocks* (534) occurs in the arms of Kirkwood, and also in the coat of Lockhart and the crest of Wyndham. A chain is often substituted for the bow of the lock. The modern padlock has been introduced into the grant of arms to the town of Wolverhampton.

Keys, the emblem of St Peter, and, as such, part of the insignia of His Holiness the Pope, occur in many ecclesiastical coats, the arms of the Fishmongers' Livery Company, and many families.

533 *Fasces.*

Flames of Fire are not frequently met with, but they are to be found in the arms of Baikie, and as crests they figure in the achievements of Graham-Wigan, and also in conjunction with keys in that of Flavel. In connection with certain other objects flames are common enough. The phœnix always issues from flames, and a salamander is always in the midst of flames (437). The flaming sword, a device, by the way, included in the grant to Sir George Lewis, Bart, has been already alluded to, as has also the flaming brand. A notable example of the torch occurs in the crest of Sir William Gull, Bart, no doubt an allusion (as is his augmentation) to the skill by which he kept the torch of life burning in the then Prince of Wales during his serious illness in 1871. A flaming mountain occurs as the crest of several families of the name of Grant.[151]

534 *Fetterlock.*

A curious instrument now known nearly exclusively in connection with its use by farriers, and termed a *Fleam* (535), occurs on the chief of the shield of Moore. A fleam, however, is the ancient form and name of a surgeon's lancet, and some connection with surgery may be presumed when it occurs. It is one of the charges in the arms granted to Sir Frederick Treves, Bart.

Furison. This singular charge occurs in the shield of Black, and also in that of Steel. Furisons were apparently the instruments by which fire was struck from flint stones.

535 *Fleam.*

Charges in connection with music and musical instruments do not occur very frequently, though the heraldic use of the *Clarion* (536) and the *Harp* may perhaps be mentioned. The *Bugle-Horn* (537) also occurs 'stringed' (538), and when the bands round it are of a different colour it is termed 'veruled' or 'virolled' of that colour.[152]

536 *Clarion.*

151. Flames of fire have become more popular during recent years. Sometimes they are shown spurting upwards from a single point, whilst at other times the flames radiate outward from a central point, as if from an unseen coal. An unusual use of flames is to be found in the arms granted to the Northern Ireland Fire Authority on 15 May 1952: purpure, three tongues of flame issuant from the base, a chief of water barry wavy proper.

With so many schools and colleges receiving grants of arms in the post-war years, it is not surprising that the torch has gained in popularity. An attractive variant of this charge is the winged torch; one is to be found as the principal charge in the arms of the Marine and General Life Assurance Society granted in 1955.

152. Presumably this term 'veruled' or 'virolled' comes from the Latin *viriola*, meaning a small bracelet, but I have never found it used in an official blazon. The term 'garnished' is invariably employed.

The real problem about the bugle-horn is, which way should it face? Although it is a rare charge in medieval heraldry, such examples as I have found show the horn to the dexter and the mouthpiece to the sinister, which I would have thought the logical way of drawing it. However, later examples, even up to the present day, generally, though by no means universally, depict the bugle-horn as shown in the illustration. I have never found an instance where the position of the horn is mentioned in the blazon, so presumably this is still a matter of caprice.

537 *Bugle-horn.*

538 *Bugle-horn stringed.*

539 *Maunch.*

540 *Gauntlet.*

541 *Morion.*

542 *Mill-rind.*

The Human Heart, which should perhaps have been more correctly referred to in an earlier chapter, is a charge which is well known in heraldry, both English and foreign. Perhaps the best known examples of the heart ensigned with a crown is seen in the shields of Douglas and Johnstone. The legend which accounts for the appearance of this charge in the arms of Douglas is too well known to need repetition.

Ingots of silver occur in the shield of the borough of St Helens, whilst the family of Woollan go one better by bearing ingots of gold.

A Maunch (539), which is a well-known heraldic term for the sleeve, is, as it is drawn, scarcely recognisable as such. Nevertheless its evolution can be clearly traced. The maunch—which, of course, as a heraldic charge, originated in the knightly 'favour' of a lady's sleeve—was borne from the earliest periods in different tinctures by the three historic families of Conyers, Hastings, and Wharton. Other garments have been used as heraldic charges; gloves in the arms of Fletcher and Bartelot; stockings in the arms of Hose; a boot in the crest of Hussy, and a hat in the arms of Huth. Armour is frequently met with, a cuirass appearing in the crest of Somers, helmets in the arms of Salvesen, Trayner, Roberton, and many other families, gauntlets (540), which need to be specified as dexter or sinister, in the arms of Vane and the crest of Burton, and a morion (541) in the crest of Pixley. The Garter is, of course, due to that Order of knighthood; and the Blue Mantle of the same Order, besides giving his title to one of the Pursuivants of Arms, who uses it as his badge, has also been used as a charge.

The *Mill-rind* or *Fer-de-moline* is, of course, as its name implies, the iron from the centre of a grindstone. It is depicted in varying forms, more or less recognisable as the real thing (542).

Mirrors occur almost exclusively in crests and in connection with mermaids, who, as a general rule, are represented as holding one in the dexter hand with a comb in the sinister. Very occasionally, however, mirrors appear as charges, an example being that of the Counts Spiegel zum Desenberg, who bore: 'Gules, three round mirrors argent in square frames or.'

Symbols connected with the Sacred Passion—other than the cross itself—are not of very general use in armory, though there are instances of the *Passion-Nails* being used, as, for example, in the shield of Proctor viz.: 'Or, three passion-nails sable.'

Pelts, or Hides, occur in the shield of Pilter, and the Fleece has been mentioned under the division of Rams and Sheep.

Plummets (or *Sinkers* used by masons) form the charges in the arms of Jennings.

An instance of a *Pyramid* is met with in the crest of Malcolm, Bart, and an *Obelisk* in that of the town of Todmorden.

The shield of Crookes affords an example of two devices of very rare occurrence, viz. a *Prism* and a *Radiometer*.[153]

Water, lakes, ships, &c., are constantly met with in armory, but a few instances

---

153. It is not surprising that the radiometer is of rare occurrence, as the blazon of this coat, granted to Sir William Crookes, F.R.S. demonstrates: or, on a chevron vert, between two crosses paty in chief of the last and a representation of a radiometer in base, invented by the grantee, three prisms proper.

must suffice. The various methods of heraldically depicting water have been already referred to (p. 69 and 117).

Three Wells figure in the arms of Hodsoll, and a masoned well in that of Camberwell. The shields of Stourton and Mansergh supply instances of heraldic *Fountains*, whilst the arms of Brunner and of Franco contain Fountains of the ordinary kind. A *Tarn*, or *Loch*, occurs in the shield of the family of Tarn, while Lord Loch bears: 'Or, a saltire engrailed sable, between in fess two swans in water proper, all within a bordure vert.'

The use of *Ships* may be instanced by the arms of many families, while a *Galley* or *Lymphad* (543) occurs in the arms of Campbell, Macdonald, Galbraith, Macfie, and numerous other families, and also in the arms of the town of Oban. Another instance of a coat of arms in which a galley appears will be found in the arms recently granted to the burgh of Alloa, while the towns of Wandsworth and Lerwick each afford instances of a *Dragon Ship*. The *Prow of a Galley* appears in the arms of Pitcher.

A modern form of ship in the shape of a *Yacht* may be seen in the arms of Ryde; while two Scottish families afford instances of the use of the *Ark*. 'Argent, an ark on the waters proper, surmounted of a dove azure, bearing in her beak an olive-branch vert,' are the arms borne by Gellie of Blackford; and 'Argent, an ark in the sea proper, in chief a dove azure, in her beak a branch of olive of the second, within a bordure of the third' are quoted as the arms of Primrose Gailliez of Chorleywood. Lastly, we may note the appropriate use of a *Steamer* in the arms of Barrow-in-Furness. The curious figure of the lion dimidiated with the hulk of a ship which is met with in the arms of several of the towns of the Cinque Ports has been referred to on page 140.[154]

Clouds form part of the arms of Leeson, which are: 'Gules, a chief nebuly argent, the rays of the sun issuing therefrom or.'

The *Rainbow* (544), though not in itself a distinctly modern charge, for it occurs in the crest of Hope, has been of late very frequently granted as part of a crest. Instances occur in the crest of the family of Pontifex, and again in that of Thurston, and of Wigan. Its use as a part of a crest is to be deprecated, but in these days of complicated armory it might very advantageously be introduced as a charge upon a shield.

An unusual device, the *Thunderbolt*, is the crest of Carnegy. The arms of the German family of Donnersperg very appropriately are: 'Sable, three thunderbolts or issuing from a chief nebuly argent, in base a mount of three coupeaux of the second.' The arms of the town of Blackpool furnish an instance of a thunderbolt in dangerous conjunction with windmill sails.

Stars, a very common charge, may be instanced as borne under that name in the Scottish shield of Alston. There has, owing to their similarity, been much confusion between *stars, estoiles, and mullets*. The difficulty is increased by the fact that no very definite lines have ever been followed officially. In England stars

154. Almost every type of ship has, or doubtless will some day, appear on a shield. I have come across an oil tanker, an Arab dhow, several Chinese junks, a Norfolk wherry, a caique, a caravel and even a representation of the ship 'Argonaut'.

543 *Lymphad, sail furled.*

544 *Rainbow.*

545 *Estoile.*

546 *Mullet (Scottish star).*

547 *Mullet pierced (Scottish spur-revel).*

548 *Mullet of six points.*

549 *Mullet of eight points.*

550 *Sun in splendour.*

under that name are practically unknown.[155] When the rays are wavy the charge is termed an estoile, but when they are straight the term mullet is used. That being so, these rules follow: that the estoile is never pierced (and from the accepted method of depicting the estoile this would hardly seem very feasible), and that unless the number of points is specified there will be six (see 545). Other numbers are quite permissible, but the number of points (more usually in an estoile termed 'rays') must be stated. The arm of Hobart, for example, are: 'Sable, an estoile of eight rays or, between two flaunches ermine.' An estoile of sixteen rays is used by the town of Ilchester, but the arms are not of any authority. Everything with straight points being in England a mullet, it naturally follows that the English practice permits a mullet to be plain (546) or pierced (547). Mullets are occasionally met with pierced of a colour other than the field they are charged upon. According to the English practice, therefore, the mullet is not represented as pierced unless it is expressly stated to be so. The mullet both in England and Scotland is of five points unless a greater number are specified. But mullets pierced and unpierced of six (548) or eight points (549) are frequent enough in English armory.

The Scottish practice differs, and it must be admitted that it is more correct than the English, though, strange to say, more complicated. In Scottish armory they have the estoile, the star, and the mullet or the spur-revel. As to the estoile, of course, their practice is similar to the English. But in Scotland a straight-pointed charge is a mullet if it be pierced, and a star if it be not. As a mullet is really the 'molette' or rowel of a spur, it certainly could not exist as a fact unpierced. Nevertheless it is by no means stringently adhered to in that country, and they make confusion worse confounded by the frequent use of the additional name of 'spur-rowel', or 'spur-revel' for the pierced mullet. The mullet occurs in the arms of Vere, and was also the badge of that family. The part this badge once played in history is well known. Had the De Veres worn another badge on that fatal day the course of English history might have been changed.

The six-pointed mullet pierced occurs in the arms of De Clinton.

The *Sun in Splendour*—(550), always so blazoned—is never represented without the surrounding rays, but the human face is not essential though usual to its heraldic use. The rays are alternately straight and wavy, indicative of the light and heat we derive therefrom, a typical piece of genuine symbolism. It is a charge in the arms of Hurst, Pearson, and many other families; and a demi-sun issuing in base occurs in the arms of Davies (Plate IX) and of Westworth. The coat of Warde-Aldam affords an example of the *Rays* of the sun alone.

A Scottish coat, that of Baillie of Walstoun, has 'Azure, the moon in her complement, between nine mullets argent, three, two, three and one.' The term 'in her complement' signifies that the moon is full, but with the moon no rays are shown, in this of course differing from the sun in splendour. The face is usually represented in the full moon, and sometimes in the crescent moon, but

155. There used to be much confusion in English blazons. The charges in the arms granted by Robert Cooke to Sir Francis Drake are estoils irradiated, but are blazoned 'stars'. In 1580 the same king of arms granted a six-pointed mullet to Thomas Wesley and so blazoned it. Yet in 44 Elizabeth I Sir William Segar confirmed arms to Humphrey Westwood and blazoned the seven pointed mullets therein as 'stars'. Later, in 1626, Segar granted plain estoils to Richard Colchester, but also called them 'stars'.

the crescent moon must not be confused with the ordinary heraldic crescent.

In concluding this class of charges, we may fitly do so by an allusion to the shield of Sir William Herschel, with its appropriate though clumsy device of a *Telescope*.

As may be naturally expected, the insignia of sovereignty are of very frequent occurrence in all armories, both English and foreign. Long before the days of heraldry, some form of decoration for the head to indicate rank and power had been in vogue amongst, it is hardly too much to say, all nations on the earth. As in most things, Western nations have borrowed both ideas, and added developments of those ideas, from the East, and in traversing the range of armory, where crowns and coronets appear in modern Western heraldry, we find a large proportion of these devices are studiously and of purpose delineated as being Eastern.

With crowns and coronets as symbols of rank I am not now, of course, concerned, but only with those cases which may be cited as supplying examples where the different kinds of crowns appear either as charges on shields, or as forming parts of crests.

Crowns, in heraldry, may be differentiated under the Royal or the Imperial, the Eastern or antique, the Naval, and the Mural, which with the Crowns Celestial, Vallery and Palisado are all known as charges. Modern grants of crowns of Eastern character in connection with valuable service performed in the East by the recipient may be instanced; *e.g.* by the Eastern Crown in the grant to Sir Abraham Roberts, G.C.B., the father of Field-Marshal Earl Roberts, K.G.

In order of antiquity one may best perhaps at the outset allude to the arms borne by the seaport towns of Boston, and of Kingston-on-Hull (or Hull, as the town is usually called), inasmuch as a tradition has it that the three crowns which figure on the shield of each of these towns originate from a recognised device of merchantmen, who, travelling in and trading with the East and likening themselves to the Magi, in their Bethlehem visit, adopted these crowns as the device or badge of their business. The same remarks may apply to the arms of Cologne: 'Argent, on a chief gules, three crowns or.'

From this fact (if the tradition be one) to the adoption of the same device by the towns to which these merchants traded is not a far step.

One may notice in passing that, unlike what from the legend one would expect, these crowns are not of Eastern design, but of a class wholly connected with heraldry itself. The legend and device, however, are both much older than these modern minutiæ of detail.

The Archbishopric of York has the well-known coat: 'Gules, two keys in saltire argent, in chief a regal crown proper.'

The reputed arms of St Etheldreda, who was both Queen, and also Abbess of Ely, find their perpetuation in the arms of that See, which are: 'Gules, three ducal (an early form of the Royal) crowns or'; while the recently-created See of St Alban's affords an example of a celestial crown: 'Azure, a saltire or, a sword in pale proper; in chief a celestial crown of the second.' The *Celestial Crown* is to be observed in the arms of the borough of Kensington and as a part of the crest of Dunbar. The See of Bristol bears: 'Sable, three open crowns in pale or.' The Royal or Imperial Crown occurs in the crest of Eye, while an *Imperial Crown* occurs in the crests of Robertson, Wolfe, and Lane.

223

The family of Douglas affords an instance of a crown ensigning a human heart. The arms of Toledo afford another case in point, being: 'Azure, a Royal crown or' (the cap being gules).

Antique Crowns— as such— appear in the arms of Fraser and also in the arms of Grant.

The crest of the Marquess of Ripon supplies an unusual variation, inasmuch as it issues from a coronet composed of fleurs-de-lis.[156]

The other chief emblem of sovereignty— the *Sceptre*— is occasionally met with, as in the Whitgreave crest of augmentation.

The Marquises of Mun bear the Imperial orb: 'Azure, an orb argent, banded, and surmounted by the cross or.' The reason for the selection of this particular charge in the grant of arms [Azure, on a fess or, a horse courant gules, between three orbs gold, banded of the third] to Sir H. E. Moss, of the Empire Theatre in Edinburgh and the London Hippodrome, will be readily guessed.

Under the classification of tools and implements the *Pick* may be noted, this being depicted in the arms of Mawdsley, Moseley, and Pigott, and a pick and shovel in the arms of Hales.

The arms of Crawshay supply an instance of a *Plough*— a charge which also occurs in the arms of Waterlow and the crest of Provand, but is otherwise of very infrequent occurrence.

In English armory the use of *Scythes*, or, as they are sometimes termed, *Sneds*, is but occasional, though, as was only to be expected, this device appears in the Sneyd coat, as follows: 'Argent, a scythe, the blade in chief, the sned in bend sinister sable, in the fess point a fleur-de-lis of the second.' In Poland the Counts Jezierski bore: 'Gules, two scythe-blades in oval, the points crossing each other argent, and the ends in base tied together or, the whole surmounted in chief by a cross-patriarchal-patée, of which the lower arm on the sinister side is wanting.'

Two sickles appear in the arms of Shearer, while the Hungerford crest in the case of the Holdich-Hungerford family is blazoned: 'Out of a ducal coronet or, a pepper garb of the first between two sickles erect proper.' The sickle was the badge of the Hungerfords.

A *Balance* forms one of the charges of the Scottish Corporation of the Dean and Faculty of Advocates: 'Gules, a balance or, and a sword argent in saltire, surmounted of an escutcheon of the second, charged with a lion rampant within a double tressure flory counterflory of the first,' but it is a charge of infrequent appearance. It also figures in the arms of the Institute of Chartered Accountants.[157]

Bannerman of Elsick bears a *Banner* for arms: 'Gules, a banner displayed argent and thereon on a canton azure a saltire argent as the badge of Scotland.'

156. This coronet of fleurs-de-lis is very ancient. A beautiful example of it, used as a crest coronet, is to be found in the garter stall plate of Richard Beauchamp, Earl of Warwick (*d.* 1439). It has recently enjoyed a revival, and is quite frequently used as a crest coronet especially in personal arms. As an example of its use in corporate heraldry the crest of the borough of Bexley may be cited.

157. The balance has become a very popular charge, particularly with lawyers and accountants. Over sixty coats granted in the past forty years contain a balance. Sometimes this is shown on a stand and sometimes the hanging variety is depicted. These are blazoned indifferently as scales or a balance, but as they are so very differently portrayed there would seem to be a case for recognising this graphic difference in blazon.

Books are frequently made use of. The arms of Rylands, the family to whose generosity Manchester owes the Rylands Library, afford a case in point, and such charges occur in the arms of the Universities of both Oxford and Cambridge, and in many other university and collegiate achievements.

Buckets and *Water-bougets* (551) can claim a wide use. In English armory Pemberton has three buckets, and water-bougets appear in the well-known arms of Bourchier (552). Water-bougets, which are really the old form of water-bucket, were leather bags or bottles, two of which were carried on a stick over the shoulder. The heraldic water-bouget represents the pair.

For an instance of the heraldic usage of the *Comb* the case of the arms of Ponsonby, Earls of Bessborough, may be cited. Combs also figure in the delightfully punning Scottish coat for Rocheid.

Generally, however, when they do occur in heraldry they represent combs for carding wool, as in the shield of Tunstall: 'Sable, three wool-combs argent,' while the Russian Counts Anrep-Elmpt use: 'Or, a comb in bend azure, the teeth downwards.'

Escallops (553) rank as one of the most widely used heraldic charges in all countries. They figured in early days outside the limits of heraldry as the badge of pilgrims going to the Holy Land, and may be seen on the shields of many families at the period of the Crusades. Many other families have adopted them, in the hope of a similar interpretation being applied to the appearance of them in their own arms. Indeed, so numerous are the cases in which they occur that a few representative ones must suffice.

They will be found in the arms of the Lords Dacre, who bore: 'Gules, three escallops argent'; and an escallop argent was used by the same family as a badge. The Scottish family of Pringle, of Greenknowe, supplies an instance in: 'Azure, three escallops or within a bordure engrailed of the last'; while the Irish Earls of Bandon bore: 'Argent, on a bend azure three escallops of the field.'[159]

Hammers figure in the crests of Hammersmith (554) and of Swindon (Plate IX), and a hammer is held in the claw of the demi-dragon which is the crest of Fox-Davies of Coalbrookdale, co. Salop (Plate IX).

A *Lantern* is a charge on the shield of Cowper, and the arms of the town of Hove afford an absolutely unique instance of the use of *Leg-Irons*.

Three towns—Eccles, Bootle, and Ramsgate—supply cases in their arms in which a *Lighthouse* is depicted, and this charge would appear, so far as can be ascertained, not only to be restricted to English armory, but to the three towns now named.[160]

551 *Water-bouget.*

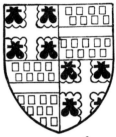

552 *Arms of Henry Bourchier, Earl of Essex, K.G.: Quarterly, 1 and 4, argent, a cross engrailed gules, between four water-bougets sable (for Bourchier); 2 and 3, gules, billetté or, a fess argent (for Louvain). (From his seal.)*

553 *Escallop.*

158. These arms were granted on 23 December 1897 to an incorporated body called the Vestry of the Parish of Hammersmith. When the Metropolitan Borough of Hammersmith was formed, it continued, although without any authority, to use the arms. Death may be said to have purged this sin, for the Metropolitan Borough is no more. The new Greater London Borough of Hammersmith was granted new arms on 1 March 1965.

159. This remark suggests that the Earldom of Bandon is extinct; such is not the case. The arms blazoned are those of Barnard, and are borne by the Earls of Bandon of the 1800 Irish creation.

160. Two further grants of lighthouses bring the score up to five. A family of Christopher bears a representation of the Godrevy Lighthouse with a beam of light issuant to the dexter from the lantern, and the Beachy Head Lighthouse is the principal charge in the arms of the Eastbourne Mutual Building Society.

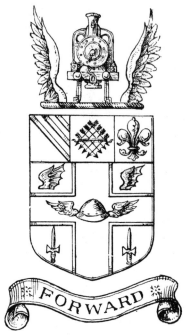

554 *Arms of Hammersmith: Party per pale azure and gules, on a chevron between two cross crosslets in chief and an escallop in base argent, three horseshoes of the first. Crest: on a wreath of the colours, upon the battlements of a tower, two hammers in saltire all proper. Motto: 'Spectemur agendo.'*

555 *Arms of the Great Central Railway: Argent, on a cross gules, voided of the field, between two wings in chief sable and as many daggers erect in base of the second, in the fess point a morion winged of the third, on a chief also of the second a pale of the first, thereon eight arrows saltirewise banded also of the third, between on the dexter side three bendlets enhanced and on the sinister a fleur-de-lis or. Crest: on a wreath of the colours, a representation of the front of a locomotive engine proper, between two wings or. [The grant is dated February 25, 1898.]*

Locomotives appear in the arms of Swindon (Plate IX) and the Great Central Railway (555).[161]

Of a similar industrial character is the curious coat of arms granted at his express wish to the late Mr Samson Fox of Leeds and Harrogate, which contains a representation of the *Corrugated Boiler-Flue* which formed the basis of his fortune.

An instance of the use of a *Sand-Glass* occurs in the arms of the Scottish family of Joass of Collinwort, which are thus blazoned: 'Vert, a sand-glass running argent, and in chief the Holy Bible expanded proper.'

A Scottish corporation, too, supplies a somewhat unusual charge, that of *Scissors*: 'Azure, a pair of scissors or' (Incorporation of Tailors of Aberdeen);

161. A locomotive has also found its way into personal heraldry. On 1 August 1907 the following arms were granted to Sir Adamjee Peerbhoy of Bombay: per fess azure and argent, in chief a tent with two poles of the last and in base the front of a locomotive engine between four bees volant, two and two, in pale proper.

226

though a Swabian family (by name Jungingen) has for its arms: 'Azure, a pair of scissors open, blades upwards argent.'

Barrels and *Casks*, which in heraldry are always known as *tuns*, naturally figure in many shields where the name lends itself to a pun, as in the arms of Bolton.

Wheels occur in the shields of Turner ['Argent, gutté-de-sang, a wheel of eight spokes sable, on a chief wavy azure, a dolphin naiant of the first'] and Carter, and also in the arms of Gooch. The *Catherine Wheel* (556), however, is the most usual heraldic form. The *Staple* (557) and the *Hawk's Lure* (558) deserve mention, and I will wind up the list of examples with the *Fylfot* (559), which no one knows the meaning or origin of.[162]

The list of heraldic charges is very far, indeed, from being exhausted. The foregoing must, however, suffice; but those who are curious to pursue this branch of the subject further should examine the arms, both ancient and modern, of towns and trade corporations.

162. Under its early name *swastika*, this charge has become all too familiar since its adoption as the symbol of the Nazi party in Germany. Whilst it is not surprising that it is no longer popular in heraldry, there are some pre-war examples. The quartering for Cox in the arms of Hippisley-Cox contains three fylfots. It was given the name fylfot as it was frequently used to 'fill the foot' of a window. The swastika was almost certainly a sun symbol, not unlike the triskeles. It originated in India but also, like the triskeles, spread widely and was everywhere regarded as a symbol of good fortune. Another name for the swastika is *cross gammadion*, as it can be made by joining four capital gammas.

   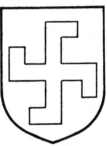

556 *Catherine wheel.*   557 *Staple.*   558 *Hawk's Lure.*   559 *Fylfot.*

227

20 · The heraldic helmet

Since one's earliest lessons in the rules of heraldry, we have been taught, as one of the fundamental laws of the achievement, that the helmet by its shape and position is indicative of rank; and we early learnt by rote that the esquire's helmet was of steel, and was placed in profile, with the visor closed: the helmet of the knight and baronet was to be open and affronté; that the helmet of the peer must be of silver, guarded by grilles and placed in profile; and that the royal helmet was of gold, with grilles, and affronté. Until recent years certain stereotyped forms of the helmet for these varying circumstances were in use, hideous alike both in the regularity of their usage and the atrocious shapes into which they had been evolved. These regulations, like some other adjuncts of heraldic art, are comparatively speaking of modern origin. Heraldry in its earlier and better days knew them not, and they came into vogue about the Stuart times, when heraldic art was distinctly on the wane. It is puzzling to conceive a desire to stereotype these particular forms, and we take it that the fact, which is undoubted, arose from the lack of heraldic knowledge on the part of the artists, who, having one form before them, which they were assured was correct, under the circumstances simply reproduced this particular form in facsimile time after time, not knowing how far they might deviate and still remain correct. The knowledge of heraldry by the heraldic artist was the real point underlying the excellence of medieval heraldic art, and underlying the excellence of much of the heraldic art in the revival of the last few years. As it has been often pointed out, in olden times they 'played' with heraldry, and therein lay the excellence of that period. The old men knew the lines within which they could 'play', and knew the laws which they could not transgress. Their successors, ignorant of the laws of arms, and afraid of the hidden meanings of armory, had none but the stereotyped lines to follow. The result was bad. Let us first consider the development of the actual helmet, and then its application to heraldic purposes will be more readily followed.

To the modern mind, which grumbles at the weight of present-day head coverings, it is often a matter of great wonder how the knights of ancient days managed to put up with the heavy weight of the great iron helmet, with its wooden or leather crest. A careful study of ancient descriptions of tournaments and warfare will supply the clue to the explanation, which is simply that the helmet was very seldom worn. For ceremonial purposes and occasions it was carried by a page, and in actual use it was carried slung at the saddle-bow, until the last moment, when it was donned for action as blows and close contact became imminent. Then, by the nature of its construction, the weight was carried by the shoulders, the head and neck moving freely within necessary limits inside. All this will be more readily apparent, when the helmet itself is considered. Our present-day ideas of helmets—their shape, their size, and their proportions—are largely taken from the specimens manufactured (not necessarily in modern times) for ceremonial purposes; *e.g.* for exhibition as insignia of knighthood. By far the larger proportion of the genuine helmets now to be seen were purposely made (certainly at remote dates) not for actual use in battle or tournament, but for ceremonial use, chiefly at funerals. Few, indeed, are the examples still existing of helmets which have been actually used in battle or tournament. Why there are so few remaining to us, when every person of position must necessarily have possessed one throughout the Plantagenet period, and probably at any rate to the end of the reign of Henry VII, is a mystery which has puzzled many people—for helmets are not, like glass and china, subject to the vicissitudes of breakage. The reason is doubtless to be found in the fact that at that period they were so general, and so little out of the common, that they possessed no greater value than any other article of clothing; and whilst the real helmet, lacking a ceremonial value, was not preserved, the sham ceremonial helmet of a later period, possessing none but a ceremonial value, was preserved from ceremonial to ceremonial, and has been passed on to the present day. But a glance at so many of these helmets which exist will plainly show that it was quite impossible for any man's head to have gone inside them, and the sculptured helmets of what may seem to us uncouth shape and exaggerated size, which are occasionally to be found as part of a monumental effigy, are the size and shape of the helmets that were worn in battle. This accounts for the much larger-sized helmets in proportion to the size of shield which will be found in heraldic emblazonments of the Plantagenet and Tudor periods. The artists of those periods were accustomed to the sight of real helmets, and knew and drew the real proportion which existed between the fighting helmet and the fighting shield. Artists of Stuart and Georgian days knew only the ceremonial helmet, and consequently adopted and stereotyped its impossible shape, and equally impossible size. Victorian heraldic artists, ignorant alike of the actual and the ceremonial, reduced the size even further, and until the recent revulsion in heraldic art, with its reversion to older types, and its copying of older examples, the helmets of heraldry had reached the uttermost limits of absurdity.

The recent revival of heraldry is due to men with accurate and extensive knowledge, and many recent examples of heraldic art well compare with ancient types. One happy result of this revival is a return to older and better types of the helmet. But it is little use discarding the 'heraldic' helmet of the stationer's shop unless a better and more accurate result can be shown, so that it will be well to trace in detail the progress of the real helmet from earliest times.

In the Anglo-Saxon period the common helmet was merely a cap of leather, often four-cornered, and with a serrated comb (560 and 561), but men of rank had a conical one of metal (562), which was frequently richly gilt. About the time of Edward the Confessor a small piece, of varying breadth, called a 'nasal', was added (563), which, with a quilted or gamboised hood, or one of mail, well protected the face, leaving little more than the eyes exposed; and in this form the helmet continued in general use until towards the end of the twelfth century, when we find it merged into or supplanted by the 'chapelle-de-fer', which is first mentioned in documents at this period, and was shaped like a flat-topped, cylindrical cap. This, however, was soon enlarged so as to cover the whole head (564), an opening being left for the features, which were sometimes protected by a

560.

561.

562.

563.

564.

movable 'ventaille', or a visor, instead of the 'nasal'. This helmet (which was adopted by Richard I, who is also sometimes represented with a conical one) was the earliest form of the large war and tilting 'heaume' (or helm), which was of great weight and strength, and often had only small openings or slits for the eyes (565 and 566). These eyepieces were either one wide slit or two, one on either

565.

566.

567.

568.

569 Painted 'Pot-Helmet,' c. 1241.

570. 'Pot-Helmet,' from the Eneit of Heinrich von Veldeke.

571 Helmet of Hamelin, Earl of Surrey and Warenne (d. 1202). (From MS. Cott., Julius, C. vii).

572 From the seal of Richard de Clare, Earl of Gloucester and Hertford (d. 1262).

573 From the seal of John de Warenne, Earl of Surrey (d.1305).

574 From the seal (1315) of John de Bretagne, Earl of Richmond.

side. The former was, however, sometimes divided into two by an ornamental bar or buckle placed across. It was afterwards pointed at the top, and otherwise slightly varied in shape, but its general form appears to have been the same until the end of the fourteenth century (567, 568). This type of helmet is usually known as the 'pot-shaped'. The helmets themselves were sometimes painted, and 569 represents an instance which is painted in green and white diagonal stripes. The illustration is from a parchment MS. of about 1241 now in the Town Library of Leipzic. 570 shows another German example of this type, being taken from the *Eneit* of Heinrich von Veldeke, a MS. now in the Royal Library in Berlin, belonging to the end of the twelfth century. The crest depicted in this case, a red lion, must be one of the earliest instances of a crest. These are the helmets which we find on early seals and effigies, as will be seen from 571-4.

575.

576.

The cylindrical or 'pot-shaped' helmet of the Plantagenets, however, disappears in the latter part of the thirteenth century, when we first find mention of the 'bascinet' (from Old French for a basin), 575-9. This was at first merely a hemispherical steel cap, put over the coif of mail to protect the top of the head, when the knight wished to be relieved from the weight of his large helm (which he then slung at his back or carried on his saddlebow), but still did not consider the mail coif sufficient protection. It soon became pointed at the top, and gradually lower at the back, though not so much as to protect the neck. In the fourteenth century the mail, instead of being carried over the top of the head, was hung to the bottom rim of the helmet, and spread out over the shoulders, overlapping the cuirass. This was called the 'camail', or 'curtain of mail'. It is shown in 576 and 577 fastened to the bascinet by a lace or thong passing through staples.

577.

The large helm, which throughout the fourteenth century was still worn over the bascinet, did not fit down closely to the cuirass (though it may have been fastened to it with a leather strap), its bottom curve not being sufficiently arched for that purpose; nor did it wholly rest on the shoulders, but was probably wadded inside so as to fit closely to the bascinet.

578.

It is doubtful if any actual helm previous to the fourteenth century exists, and there are very few of that period remaining. In that of the Black Prince at Canterbury (271) the lower, or cylindrical, portion is composed of a front and back piece, riveted together at the sides, and this was most likely the usual form of construction; but in the helm of Sir Richard Pembridge (580 and 581) the three pieces (cylinder, conical piece, and top piece) of which it is formed are fixed with nails, and are so welded together that no trace of a join is visible. The edges of the metal, turned outwards round the ocularium, are very thick, and the bottom edge is rolled inwards over a thick wire, so as not to cut the surcoat. There are many twin holes in the helmet for the aiglets, by which the crest and lambrequin were attached, and in front, near the bottom, are two + shaped holes for the T bolt, which was fixed by a chain to the cuirass.

579.

The helm of Sir Richard Hawberk (582 and 583), who died in 1417, is made of five pieces, and is very thick and heavy. It is much more like the later form adapted for jousting, and was probably only for use in the tilt-yard; but, although more firmly fixed to the cuirass than the earlier helm, it did not fit closely down to it, as all later helms did.

Singularly few examples of the pot-helmet actually exist. The 'Linz' example

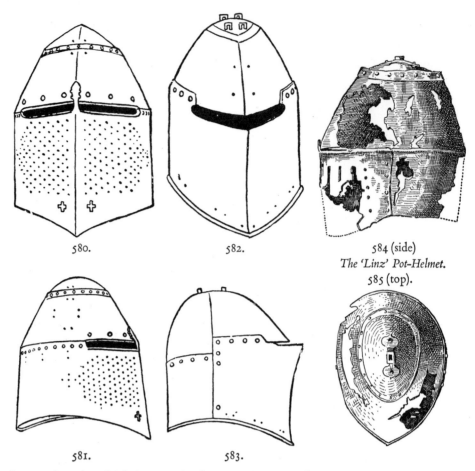

580.

582.

584 (side)
The 'Linz' Pot-Helmet.
585 (top).

581.

583.

(584 and 585), which is now in the Francisco-Carolinum Museum at Linz, was dredged out of the Traun, and is unfortunately very much corroded by rust. The fastening-place for the crest, however, is well preserved. The example belongs to the first half of the fourteenth century.

The so-called 'Pranker-Helm' (586), from the chapter of Seckau, now in the collection of armour in the Historical Court Museum at Vienna, and belonging to the middle of the fourteenth century, could only have been used for tournaments. It is made of four strong hammered sheets of iron 1–2 millimetres thick, with other strengthening plates laid on. The helmet by itself weighs 5 kilogrammes 357 grammes.

The custom of wearing the large helm over the bascinet being clumsy and troublesome, many kinds of visor were invented, so as to dispense with the large helm, except for jousting, two of which are represented in 575 and 579. In the first a plate shaped somewhat to the nose was attached to the part of the camail which covered the mouth. This plate, and the mail mouth-guard, when not in use, hung downwards towards the breast; but when in use it was drawn up and attached to a staple or locket on the front of the bascinet. This fashion, however, does not appear to have been adopted in England, but was peculiar to Germany, Austria, &c. None of these contrivances seem to have been very satisfactory, but towards the end of the fourteenth century the large and salient beaked visor was invented (587). It was fixed to hinges at the sides of the bascinet with pins and was removable at will. A high collar of steel was next added as a substitute for the

586.

587.

588.

camail. This form of helmet remained in use during the first half of the fifteenth century, and the large helm, which was only used for jousting, took a different form, or rather several different forms, which may be divided into three kinds. In this connection it should be remembered that the heavy jousting helmet to which the crest had relation was probably never used in actual warfare. The first was called a bascinet, and was used for combats on foot. It had an almost spherical crown-piece, and came right down to the cuirass, to which it was firmly fixed, and was, like all large helms of the fifteenth century, large enough for the wearer to move his head about freely inside. The helm of Sir Giles Capel (588) is a good specimen of this class; it has a visor of great thickness, in which are a great number of holes, thus enabling the wearer to see in every direction. The 'barbute', or ovoid bascinet, with a chin-piece riveted to it, was somewhat like this helm, and is often seen on the brasses of 1430–50; the chin-piece retaining the name of 'barbute', after the bascinet had gone out of fashion.

The second kind of large helm used in the fifteenth century was the 'jousting-helm', which was of great strength, and firmly fixed to the cuirass. One from the Brocas Collection (589 and 590, date about 1500) is perhaps the grandest helm in existence. It is formed of three pieces of different thicknesses (the front piece being the thickest), which are fixed together with strong iron rivets with salient heads and thin brass caps soldered to them. The arrangements for fixing it in front and behind are very complete and curious.

The manner in which the helmet was connected with the rest of the armour is shown in 591, which is a representation of a German suit of tilting armour of the period about 1480, now in the collection of armour at the Royal Museum in Vienna.

Of the same character, but of a somewhat different shape, is the helmet (592) of Sir John Gostwick, who died in 1541, which is now in Willington Church, Bedfordshire. The illustration here given is taken from the *Portfolio*, No. 33. The visor opening on the right side of the helmet is evidently taken from an Italian model.

The third and last kind of helm was the 'tournament helm', and was similar to the first kind, and also called a 'bascinet'; but the visor was generally barred, or, instead of a movable visor, the bars were riveted on the helm, and sometimes the face was only protected by a sort of wire-work, like a fencing-mask. It was only used for the tourney or mêlée, when the weapons were the sword and mace.

The 'chapelle-de-fer', which was in use in the thirteenth, fourteenth, and fifteenth centuries, was a light iron head-piece, with a broad, flat brim, somewhat

589.

590.

233

591 *German Tilting Armour, 1480, from the Collection in the Museum at Vienna.*

592 *Tilting-Helmet of Sir John Gostwick, 1541.*

593.

594.

595.

596.

597.

turned down. 593 represents one belonging to the end of the fifteenth century, which is one of the few remaining, and is delicately forged in one piece of thin, hard steel.

During the fourteenth century a new kind of helmet arose, called in England the 'sallad', or 'sallet'. The word appears to have two derivations, each of which was applied to a different form of head-piece. First, the Italian 'celata' (594), which seems originally to have been a modification of the bascinet. Second, the German 'schallern', the form of which was probably suggested by the chapelle-de-fer. Both of these were called by the French 'salade', whence our English 'sallad'. The celata came lower down than the bascinet, protected the back and sides of the neck, and, closing round the cheeks, often left only the eyes, nose, and mouth exposed. A standard of mail protected the neck if required. In the fifteenth century the celata ceased to be pointed at the summit, and was curved outwards at the nape of the neck, as in 595.

The 'schallern' (from *shale*, a shell, or bowl), was really a helmet and visor in one piece; it had a slit for the eyes, a projecting brim, and a long tail, and was completed by a chin-piece, or 'bavier' (Eng. 'beaver'), which was strapped round the neck. 596 shows a German sallad and a Spanish beaver. The sallad was much used in the fifteenth century, during the latter half of which it often had a visor, as in one from Rhodes (597), which has a spring catch on the right side to hold the visor in place when down. The rivets for its lining-cap have large, hollow, twisted heads, which are seldom found on existing sallads, though often seen in sculpture.

The schale, schallern (*schêlern*), or sallad, either with or without a visor, is very seldom seen in heraldic use. An instance, however, in which it has been made use of heraldically will be found in 598, which is from a pen and ink drawing in the *Fest-Buch* of Paulus Kel, a MS. now in the Royal Library at Munich. This shows the schallern with the slit for seeing through, and the fixed neck-guard. The 'bart', 'bavière', or beaver, for the protection of the under part of the face, is also visible. It is not joined to the helmet. The helmet bears the crest of Bavaria, the red-

*598 Schallern, with Crest of Bavaria
(Duke of Ludwig of Bavaria, 1449).*

599 Schallern (end of fifteenth century).

600.

601.

602.

603.

crowned golden lion of the Palatinate within the wings of the curiously disposed Bavarian tinctures. 599 is a very good representation of a schallern dating from the latter part of the fifteenth century, with a sliding neck-guard. It is reproduced from the *Deutscher Herald*, 1892, No. 2.

Until almost the middle of the fifteenth century all helmets fitted on the top of the head, or were put right over; but about 1440 the Italians made a great improvement by inventing the 'armet', the lower part of which opened out with hinges, so that when put on it enclosed the head, fitting closely round the lower part of it, while its weight was borne by the steel collar, or 'gorget'. The Italian armet had a roundel or disc to protect the opening at the back of the neck, and a bavier strapped on in front to cover the joining of the two cheek-pieces. The earlier armets, like the beaked bascinet, had a camail attached by a row of staples (600), which was continued later, but then fixed either to a metal band or leather strap and riveted to the base of the armet. This form of helmet was not in common use in England until about 1500.

600 shows the earliest form of Italian armet, with a reinforcing-piece on the forehead, and a removable visor. Date 1450–80. 601 represents an armet of very fine form (probably Italian), which is a nearer approach to the close-helmet of the sixteenth century, as the visor cannot be removed, and the eye-slit is *in* the visor, instead of being formed by the space between it and the crown-piece, and there is also no reinforcing-piece in the crown. Date 1480–1500. 602 is still more like the sixteenth-century helmet, for it opens down the sides instead of down the chin and back, and the same pivot which secures the visor also serves as a hinge for the crown and chin-piece. The small mentonnière, or bavier, is equal on both sides, but it was often of less extent on the right. Date about 1500.

603 shows a German fluted helmet, of magnificent form and workmanship, which is partly engraved and gilded. Date 1510–25. It opens down the chin, like the early armets, but the tail-piece of the crown is much broader. The skill shown

235

604.

605.

606 'Grid-iron' Helmet
(*fifteenth century*).

607.

in the forging of the crown and the fluting of the twisted comb is most remarkable, and each rivet for the lining-strap of the cheek-pieces forms the centre of an engraved six-leaved rose. A grooved rim ruond the bottom of the helmet fitted closely on a salient rim at the top of the steel gorget or hause col, so that when placed on its gorget and closed, it could not be wrenched off, but could yet be moved round freely in a horizontal direction. The gorget being articulated, the head could also be raised or lowered a little, but not enough to make this form of joint very desirable, and a looser kind was soon substituted.

604 shows what is perhaps the most perfect type of close helmet. The comb is much larger than was the custom at an earlier date, and much resembles those of the morions of this period. The visor is formed of two separate parts; the upper fits inside the lower, and could be raised to facilitate seeing without unfixing the lower portion. It is engraved with arabesques, and is probably Italian. Date 1550–70. 605 is an English helmet, half-way between a close helmet and a 'burgonet'. It is really a 'casque', with cheek-pieces to meet in front. The crown-piece is joined down the middle of the comb. This helmet was probably made for the Earl of Leicester. Date about 1590.

The word 'burgonet' first appeared about the beginning of the fifteenth century, and described a form of helmet like the 'celata', and called by that name in Italy. It was completed by a 'buffe', or chin-piece, similar to the bavier.

During this century the 'morion', really an improved 'chapelle-de-fer', was much in use. It had a curved top, surmounted by a comb, and a broad, turned-up brim, and was often elaborately engraved and gilt. The 'cabasset' was a similar head-piece, but had a peaked top, surmounted by a small spike turned backwards, and generally a flatter, narrower brim than the morion. These three forms of helmet were all called casques.

The barred or grilled helmet owed its introduction to tournaments with swords and clubs, which necessitated better opportunities of vision than the earlier tilting-helm afforded, sufficient though that was for encounters with the tilting-spear. The earliest form of this type of helmet will be seen in 606, which is termed a 'grid-iron' helmet, developing shortly afterwards into the form of 607, which has a lattice-work visor. The former figure, the 'grid-iron' helmet, is a representation taken from an original now in the possession of Count Hans Wilczek, of Vienna. 607, the helmet with the latticed visor, is from an example in the German National Museum at Nürnberg. Neither of these types of helmet appears to have been regularly adopted into heraldic art. Indeed they are seldom, if ever, to be found in heraldic emblazonment. For pictorial and artistic purposes they seem to be entirely supplanted in paintings, in seals, and in sculpture by the 'grilled' helmet or 'buckler.' Whether this helmet, as we find it depicted in paintings or on seals, was ever really worn in battle or tournament seems very doubtful, and no actual instance appears to have been preserved. On the other hand, the so-called 'Prankhelme' (pageant helmet) bucklers, frequently made of gilded leather and other materials, are extant in some number. It is evident from their nature, however, that they can only have been used for ceremonial or decorative purposes.

608 shows one of these buckled 'pageant' helmets surmounted by the crest of the Margraviate of Burgau. 609 shows another of these pageant helmets, with the

608 *Pageant Helmet, with the Crest of Burgau.*

609 *Pageant Helmet with the Crest of Austria (ancient) or Tyrol.*

crest of Austria (ancient) or of Tyrol. These were borne, with many others of the same character, in the pageant of the funeral procession of the Emperor Frederick III (IV) in 1493. The helmets were made of leather, and gilded, the two crests being carved out of boards and painted. The Burgau wings, which are inclined very far forward, are: 'Bendy of six argent and gules, charged with a pale or.' In their normal position the wings are borne upright. The second crest, which is 86 cm. in height, is black, and adorned on the outside with eared pegs 4 cm. long, from which gold linden-leaves hang. These helmets and crests, which were formerly in St Stephen's Cathedral, are now in the Vienna Historical Museum.

At the beginning of the seventeenth century the workmanship became inferior, and beauty of line was no longer sought after. Shortly afterwards helmets ceased to be worn outside the regular army, and with the subsequent evolution of military head coverings heraldry has no concern.

As part of a heraldic achievement the helmet is not so old as the shield. It was not until the introduction of the crest that any one thought of depicting a helmet with a shield.

A careful and attentive examination of the early 'Rolls of Arms,' and of seals and other ancient examples of heraldic art and handicraft, will at once make it plainly apparent that the helmets then heraldically depicted were in close keeping and of the style actually in use for warfare, joust, or tournament at the period. This is particularly noticeable in the helmets on the stall plates of the Knights of the Garter in St George's Chapel at Windsor. The helms on the early stall plates,

237

though far from being identical in shape, all appear to be of the same class or type of tilting-helm drawn in profile. Amongst the early plates only one instance (Richard, Duke of Gloucester, elected 1475) can be found of the barred helmet. This is the period when helmets actually existed in fact, and were actually used, but at the end of the sixteenth and the beginning of the seventeenth centuries, when the helmet was being fast relegated to ceremonial usage and pictorial emblazonment, ingenious heralds began to evolve the system by which rank and degree were indicated by the helmet.

Before proceeding to consider British rules concerning the heraldic helmet, it may be well to note those which have been accepted abroad. In Germany heraldry has known but two classes of helmet, the open helmet guarded by bars (otherwise buckles or grilles), and the closed or 'visored' helmet. The latter was the helmet used by the newly ennobled, the former by the older families of higher position, it being originally held that only those families whose birth qualified them to tilt were permitted to use this buckled helmet. Tournaments were of course always conducted on very strict lines. Woodward reprints in his *Treatise on Heraldry* the 'Tourney Regulations for the Exposure of Arms and Crest, drawn up by René, Duke of Anjou, King of Sicily and Jerusalem,' from Menêtrier's *L'Origin des Armoiries*. The rules to be complied with are there set out. 12 (p. 23) is a representation of a 'Helmschau', where the examination of the crests is being carried on. It is interesting to notice therein that the whole of the helmets without exception have the grilles. Germany was perhaps the earliest country to fall from grace in the matter, for towards the end of the fifteenth century the buckled helmet is found with the arms of the lower Briefadels (those ennobled by patent), and the practice continued despite the violent protests of the tournament families, who considered their prerogative had been infringed. The closed helmet consequently sank gradually in Germany to the grade of a mere burgess's helmet, and as such became of little account, although in former times it had been borne by the proudest houses.

Similarly in France the 'buckled' helmet was considered to be reserved for the military noblesse, and newly ennobled families were denied its use until the third generation, when they became *bons gentil-hommes*. Woodward states that when 'in 1372 Charles V conferred on the bourgeoisie of Paris the right to use armorial bearings, it was strenuously denied that they could use the timbred helm. In 1568 an edict of Charles IX prohibited the use of *armoiries timbrées* to any who were not noble by birth.' The grilles of the helmet produced with the old French heralds the opportunity of a minutia of rule which, considering the multitude of rules fathered, rightly or wrongly, upon British heraldry, we may be devoutly happy never reached our shores. They assigned different numbers of grilles to different ranks, but as the writers differ as to the varying numbers, it is probable that such rules were never officially accepted even in that country. In France the rule was much as in this country, a gold helmet for the Sovereign, silver for princes and great nobles, steel for the remainder. It is curious that though the timbred helm was of course known in England whilst the controversy as to its heraldic use was raging in France and Germany, no heraldic use of it whatever occurs till the beginning of the seventeenth century. From Royalty to the humblest gentleman, all used for heraldic purposes the closed or visored helms.

The present rules concerning helmets which hold in Great Britain are that the helmet of the Sovereign and the Royal princes of this country shall be of gold, placed in an affronté position, and shall have grilles. The helmet of a peer shall be of silver, shall be placed in profile, and shall have golden grilles, frequently stated to be five in number, a detail not stringently adhered to. The helmet of a knight or baronet shall be of steel, placed full-faced, and shall be open; whilst the helmet of an esquire or gentleman shall be of steel and in profile, with the visor closed. Within these limits considerable latitude is allowed, and even in official grants of arms, which, as far as emblazonment goes, are very much of a stereotyped style, actual unvarying adherence to a particular pattern is not insisted upon.

The earliest instance amongst the Garter plates in which a helmet with grilles is used to denote the rank of a peer is the stall plate of Lord Knollys in 1615. In the Visitations but few instances can be found in which the arms of peers are included. Peers were not compelled to attend and enter their arms and pedigrees at Visitations, doubtless owing to the fact that no Garter King of Arms ever made a Visitation, whilst it has been the long-asserted prerogative of Garter to deal with peers and their arms by himself. At the same time, however, there are some number of instances of peers' arms and pedigrees in the Visitation Books, several occurring in the 1587 Visitation of Yorkshire. In these cases the arms of peers are set out with supporters and mottoes, but there is no difference between their helmets and what we should now term the helmet of an esquire or gentleman. This is all the more curious because neither helmet nor motto is found in the tricks given of the arms of commoners. Consequently one may with certainty date the introduction of the helmet with grilles as the distinguishing mark of a peer in this country between the years 1587 and 1615.[163] The introduction of the open full-faced helmet as indicative of knight or baronet is known to date from about the period of the Restoration.

Whilst these fixed rules as to helmets are still scrupulously adhered to by English heralds, Lyon King of Arms would seem to be inclined to let them quietly lapse into desuetude, and the emblazonment of the arms of Sir George Duff-Sutherland-Dunbar, Bart, in the Lyon Register at the rematriculation of his arms, affords an instance in which the rules have been ignored.

Some of the objections one hears raised to official heraldry will not hold water when all facts are known; but one certainly thinks that those who object to the present helmet and its methods of usage have ample reason for such remarks as one frequently sees in print upon the subject. To put it mildly, it is absolutely ridiculous to see a helmet placed affronté, and a lion passant looking out over the side of it; or to see a helmet in profile with the crest of a man's head affronté placed above it, and as a consequence also peeping over the side. The necessity for providing a resting-place for the crest other than unoccupied space has also led to the ridiculous practice of depicting the wreath or torse in the form of a straight bar balanced upon the apex of the helmet. The rule itself as to the positions of helmets for the varying ranks is officially recognised, and the elaboration of the rule with regard to the differing metals of the Royal helmet and the helmets

---

163. This helmet distinction was introduced by Sir William Segar, who was Garter from 1606 (nominated 1604) until his death in 1633.

of peers and knights and baronets is officially followed; though the supposed regulation, which requires that the helmet of an esquire or gentleman shall be of steel alone is not, inasmuch as the helmet painted upon a grant is *always* ornamented with gold.[164]

These rules in England only date from the times of the Stuarts, and they cannot be said to be advantageous from any point of view; they are certainly distinctly harmful from the artistic standpoint. It is plainly utterly impossible to depict some crests upon a profile helmet, and equally impossible to display others upon an affronté helmet. In Scotland the crests do not afford quite such a regular succession of glaring examples for ridicule as is the case in England. No need is recognised in Scotland for necessarily distinguishing the crest of one family from that of another, though proper differences are rigidly adhered to with regard to the coat of arms. Nevertheless, Scotland provides us with many crests which it is utterly impossible actually to carry on an actual helmet, and examples of this kind can be found in the rainbow which floats above the broken globe of the Hopes, and the coronets in space to which the hand points in the crest of the family of Dunbar of Boath, with many other similar absurdities.

In England an equal necessity for difference is insisted upon in the crest as is everywhere insisted upon with regard to the coat of arms; and in the time of the late Sir Albert Woods, Garter King of Arms, it was rapidly becoming almost impossible to obtain a new crest which has not got a row of small objects in front of it, or else two somethings, one on either side. (Things, however, have now considerably improved.) If a crest is to be depicted between two ostrich feathers, for example, it stands to reason that the central object should be placed upon the centre of the helmet, whilst the ostrich feathers would be one on either side— that is, placed in a position slightly above the ears. Yet, if a helmet is to be rigidly depicted in profile, with such a crest, it is by no means inconceivable that the one ostrich feather at the one side would hide both the other ostrich feather and the central object, leaving the crest to appear when properly depicted (for example, if photographed from a profile view of an actual helmet) as a single ostrich feather. Take, for instance, the Sievier crest, which is an estoile between two ostrich feathers. If that crest were properly depicted upon a profile helmet, the one ostrich feather would undoubtedly hide everything else, for it is hardly likely that the estoile would be placed edge-forwards upon an actual helmet; and to properly display it, it ought to take its place upon an affronté helmet. Under the present rules it would be officially depicted with the estoile facing the side, one ostrich feather in front over the nose, and the other at the back of the head, which of course reduces it to an absurdity. To take another example, one might instance the crest of Sir William Crookes. It is hardly to be supposed that a helmet would ever have been borne into a tournament surmounted by an elephant looking out over the side; it would most certainly have had its

164. This remark, which is repeated a few paragraphs further on, does not now apply. The painting of grants of arms at the turn of the century was very stereotyped, and helmets were invariably ornamented with gold; this was not a rule, but simply an artistic custom which found favour with, or at least did not displease, the kings of arms. Today helms are seldom garnished with gold, although a small amount of gold decoration on the helms of those below peerage rank is not objected to.

240

head placed to the front; and yet, because Sir William Crookes was a knight, he was required to use an affronté helmet, with a crest which most palpably was designed for use in profile. The absurd position which has resulted is chiefly due to the position rules and largely a consequence of the hideous British practice (for no other nation has ever adopted it) of depicting, as is so often done, a coat of arms and crest without the intervening helmet and mantling; though perhaps another cause may have had its influence. I allude to the fact that an animal's head, for example, in profile, is considered quite a different crest to the same animal's head when placed affronté; and so long as this idea holds, and so long as the rules concerning the position of the helmet exist, for so long shall we have these glaring and ridiculous anomalies. And whilst one generation of a family has an affronté helmet and another using the same crest may have a profile one, it is useless to design crests specifically to fit the one or the other.

Mr G. W. Eve, who was certainly one of the most accomplished heraldic artists of recent years, adopted a plan in his work which, whilst conforming with the rules to which I have referred, has reduced the peculiarities resulting from their observance to a minimum. His plan is simple, inasmuch as, with a crest which is plainly affronté and has to be depicted upon a profile helmet, he slightly alters the perspective of each, twisting round the helmet, which, whilst remaining slightly in profile, more nearly approaches the affronté position, and bringing the crest slightly round to meet it. In this way he has obtained some very good results from awkward predicaments. Mr Joseph Foster, in his *Peerage and Baronetage*, absolutely discarded all rules affecting the position of the helmet; and though the artistic results may be excellent, his plan cannot be commended, because whilst rules exist they ought to be adhered to. At the same time, it must be frankly admitted that the laws of position seem utterly unnecessary. No other country has them—they are, as has been shown, impracticable from the artistic standpoint; and there can be very little doubt that it is highly desirable that they should be wholly abolished.[165]

It is quite proper that there should be some means of distinction, and it would seem well that the helmet with grilles should be reserved for peers. In this we should be following or closely approximating to the rules observed formerly upon the Continent, and if all questions of position are waived the only difficulty which remains is the helmet of baronets and knights. The full-faced open helmet is ugly in the extreme—anything would be preferable (except an open helmet in profile),

---

165. Most people would agree that the helmet rule is absurd and that, as the crest was originally modelled in the round, it should always be considered as being in the round, and so capable of being displayed with the helm pointing in any direction. A moment's reflection, however, will show how difficult it would be to put the clock back, because, for many centuries, difference in direction has been considered an adequate distinction between two identical crests. For example, one man is granted a stag's head couped (that is facing dexter) and another a stag's head couped affronty (facing outwards); the moment you abolish the rule these two men will find themselves with identical crests. I think the sad fact must be faced that generations of heralds have considered the crest as two-dimensional, and have built up a system based on that assumption. It is now too late to do anything about this. The best one can do is to use a little artistic licence. Where the crest looks to the dexter and the helm forward, twist the one slightly to the front and the other a little to the dexter; the blatant absurdity of the relation of crest to helm will not now be nearly so apparent.

and probably it would be better to wipe out the rule on this point as well. Knights of any Order have the circle of that order within which to place their shields, and baronets have the augmentations of their rank and degree. The knight bachelor would be the only one to suffer. The gift of a plain circlet around the shield or (following the precedent of a baronet), a spur upon a canton or ines-cutcheon, could easily remove any cause of complaint.

But whilst one may think it well to urge strongly the alteration of existing rules, it should not be considered permissible to ignore rules which undoubtedly do exist whilst those rules remain in force.

The helmets of knights and baronets and of esquires and gentlemen, in accord-ance with present official practice, are usually ornamented with gold, though this would not appear to be a fixed and unalterable rule.

When two or more crests need to be depicted, various expedients are adopted. The English official practice is to paint one helmet only, and both the crests are detached from it. The same plan was formerly adopted in Scotland. The dexter crest is naturally the more important and the principal one in each case. By using one helmet only the necessity of turning the dexter crest to face the sinister is obviated.

The present official method adopted in England of depicting three crests is to use one helmet only, and all three crests face to the dexter. The centre one, which is placed on the helmet, is the principal or first crest, that on the dexter side the second, and the one on the sinister the third.

In Germany, the land of many crests (no less than thirteen were borne above the shield of the Margraves of Brandenburg-Anspach), there has from the earliest times been a fixed invariable practice of never dissociating a crest from the helmet which supported it, and consequently one helmet to every crest has long been the only recognised procedure. In the United Kingdom duplication of crests is quite a modern practice. Amongst the Plantagenet Garter plates there is not a single example to be found of a coat of arms with more than a single crest, and there is no ancient British example of more than one helmet which can be referred to for guidance. The custom originated in the sixteenth and seventeenth centuries in Germany. This point is more fully dealt with in the chapter devoted to the con-sideration of crests, but it may be here noted that in Austria a knight may place two and a baron three helmets over his shield. The Continental practice is as follows: 'When the number of the helms is even, they are arranged so that all look inwards towards the centre line of the escutcheon, half being turned to the dexter, half to the sinister. If the number be uneven, the principal helm is placed in the centre affronté, the others with their crests being turned towards it; thus some face to the dexter, some to the sinister. The crests are always turned with the helmets. In Scandinavia the centre helm is affronté; the others, with their crests, are often turned outwards.

English officialism, whilst confining its own emblazonments to one helmet only, has never sought to assert that the use of two or more was either incorrect or faulty heraldry, and particularly in these later days of the revival of heraldic art in this country, all heraldic artists, following the German example, are inclined to give each crest its own helmet. This practice has been adopted by Lyon King of Arms, and now all paintings of arms in Lyon Register which have two crests have the same number of helmets. Some of the Bath stall plates in Henry VII's chapel in Westminster Abbey also display two helmets.

When two helmets are used, it has been customary, still following the German model, to turn them to face each other, except in the cases of the full-faced helmets of a knight or baronet, and (with the same exception) when three helmets have been employed the outer ones have been placed to face the centre, whilst the centre one has been placed in profile, as would be the case were it standing alone. But the multiplication of English crests in number, all of which as granted are required to differ, has naturally resulted in the stereotyping of points of difference in attitude, &c., and the inevitable consequence is unfortunately that without sacrificing this character of differentiation it is impossible to allow the English heraldic artist the same latitude and freedom of disposition with regard to crests that his German confrère enjoys. These remarks apply solely to English and Irish crests, for Scottish practices, requiring no differentiation in the crests, have left Scottish crests simple and unspoiled. In England the result is that to 'play' with the position of a crest frequently results in an entire alteration of its character, and consequently, as there is nothing whatever in the nature of a law or of a rule to the contrary, it is quite as usual to now find that two profile helmets are both placed to face the dexter, as placed to face each other. Another point seems also in England to have been lost sight of in borrowing our methods from Germany. They hold themselves at liberty to, and usually *do*, make all their *charges on the shield* face to the centre. This is never done in England, where all face to the dexter. It seems therefore to me an anomaly to apply one rule to the shield and another to the helmet, and personally I prefer that both helmets and all charges should face the dexter.

In British heraldry (and in fact the rule is universal) no woman other than a reigning Sovereign is permitted to surmount her arms by a helmet. Woodward states that 'Many writers have denied the right of ecclesiastics (and, of course, of women) to the use of helmet and crest. Spener, the great German herald, defends their use by ecclesiastics, and says that, in Germany at any rate, universal custom is opposed to the restriction. There the prelates, abbots, and abbesses, who held princely fiefs by military tenure, naturally retained the full knightly insignia.'

In official English heraldry, there is a certain amount of confirmation and a certain amount of contradiction of this supposed rule which denies a helmet to an ecclesiastic. A grant of arms to a clergyman at the present day, and at all times previously, after the granting of crests had become usual, contains the grant of the crest and the emblazonment shows the helmet. But the grant of arms to a bishop is different. The emblazonment of the arms is surmounted by a mitre, and the crest is depicted in the body of the patent away from and distinct from the emblazonment proper in the margin. But the fact that a crest is granted proves that there is not any disability inherent in the ecclesiastic which debars him from the possession of the helmet and crest, and the rule which must be deduced, and which really is the definite and accepted rule, is that a mitre cannot be displayed together with a helmet or crest. It must be one or other, and as the mitre is indicative of the higher rank, it is the crest and helmet which are discarded.[166]

166. In Scotland, crests are not now granted to clergymen of any denomination. The arms are ensigned by the appropriate ecclesiastical hat and, if a crest is granted, it is contained in the body of the patent and limited to the lay heirs of the grantee.

There are few rules in heraldry to which exceptions cannot be found, and there is a painting now preserved in the College of Arms which depicts the arms of the Bishop of Durham surmounted by a helmet, that in its turn being surmounted by the mitre of episcopal rank. But the Bishopric of Durham was, in addition to its episcopal character, a temporal Palatinate, and the arms of the Bishops of that See therefore logically present many differences and exceptions from established heraldic rules.

The rules with regard to the use of helmets for the coats of arms of corporate bodies are somewhat vague and vary considerably. All counties, cities, and towns, and all corporate bodies to whom crests have been granted in England, have the ordinary closed profile helmet of an esquire or gentleman.

For some reason the arms of the City of London are always depicted with the helmet of a peer, but as the crest is not officially recorded, the privilege necessarily has no official sanction or authority.[167]

In Scotland the helmet painted upon a grant of arms to town or city is always the open full-faced helmet of a knight or baronet. But in the grant of arms to a county, where it includes a crest, the helmet is that of an esquire, which is certainly curious.[168]

In Ireland no helmet at all was painted upon the patent granting arms to the city of Belfast, in spite of the fact that a crest was included in the grant, and the late Ulster King of Arms informed me he would not allow a helmet to any impersonal arms.

Care should be taken to avoid errors of anachronism when depicting helmet and shield. The shapes of these should bear some approximate relation to each other in point of date. It is preferable that the helmet should be so placed that its lower extremity reaches somewhat over the edge of the shield. The inclined position of the shield in emblazonment is borrowed from the natural order of things, because the shield hanging by its chain or shield-strap (the guige), which was so balanced that the shield should most readily fall into a convenient position when slung on the rider's shoulders, would naturally retain its equilibrium only in a slanting direction.

167. The self-assumed privilege of using a peer's helm was confirmed to the City of London when crest and supporters were granted on 30 April 1957.

Recently it has become customary for independent countries within the Commonwealth to be assigned royal helms when granted arms. The first instance of such a use seems to be on the seal struck for Jamaica in 1661 and entered in one of the books of Sir Edward Walker, Garter King of Arms, at the College of Arms.

168. A glance at the official registers shows that practice has varied regarding the marshalling of impersonal arms in Scotland. However, the rules now observed are unequivocal; they are as follows: crests are not granted to towns; instead, the arms are ensigned by mural crowns of varying tinctures. A police burgh has a mural crown azure masoned argent; the crown is gules masoned argent in the case of a burgh of barony, and a Royal burgh has a mural crown of eight battlements proper (i.e. grey stone) masoned sable and a compartment beneath the arms which consists of a wall with a round uncrenellated tower at either end proper, masoned sable.

Helmets are not considered appropriate insignia for any corporate body and, where a helmet is required (as in arms of English provenance, matriculated in Scotland), a salade is used.

A special crown has been invented for use by County Councils; it consists of a circlet on which are eight spikes alternating with eight garbs (W).

W *Scottish County Councils' Crown.*

PLATE VI

Arms of Speke of Jordans

21 · The crest

If uncertainty exists as to the origin of arms, it is as nothing to the huge uncertainty that exists concerning the beginnings of the crest. Most wonderful stories are told concerning it; that it meant this and meant the other, that the right to bear a crest was confined to this person or the other person. But practically the whole of the stories of this kind are either wild imagination or conjecture founded upon in-sufficient facts.

The real facts—which one may as well state first as a basis to work upon—are very few and singularly unconvincing, and are useless as original data from which to draw conclusions.

First of all we have the definite, assured, and certain fact that the earliest known instance of a crest is in 1198, and we find evidence of the use of arms before that date.

The next fact is that we find infinitely more variation in the crests used by given families than in the arms, and that whilst the variations in the arms are as a rule trivial, and not affecting the general design of the shield, the changes in the crest are frequently radical, the crest borne by a family at one period having no earthly relation to that borne by the same family at another.

Again, we find that though the occasional use of a crest can (by isolated in-stances) be taken back, as already stated, to a fairly early period, the use of crests did not become general until very much later.

Another fact is that, except perhaps in the persons of sovereigns, there is no official instance, nor any other authentic instance of importance, in which a crest appears ever to have been used by a woman until these recent and unfortunate days when unofficial examples can be found of the wildest ignorance of all armorial rules.

The foregoing may be taken as general principles which no authentic instance known can be said to refute.

Bearing these in mind, let us now see what other results can be obtained by deduction from specific instances.

The earliest form in which anything can be found in the nature of a crest is the lion upon the head-dress of Geoffrey, Count of Anjou (28). This has been already referred to.

The helmet of Philippe D'Alsace, Count of Flanders (c. 1181), has painted upon the side the same figure of a lion which appears upon his shield.

What is usually accepted as the earliest authenticated instance of a regular crest is that afforded by the Great Seal of King Richard I of England, which shows over the helmet a lion passant painted upon the fan-shaped ornament which surmounts the helmet.

If one accepts—as most people nowadays are inclined to do—the Darwinian theory of evolution, the presumption is that the development of the human being, through various intermediate links including the ape, can be traced back to those cell-like formations which are the most 'original' types of life which are known to us. At the same time one is hardly disposed to assert that some antediluvian jellyfish away back in past ages was the first human being. By a similar, but naturally more restricted argument, one cannot accept these paintings upon helmets, nor possibly can one accept paintings upon the fan-like ornaments which surmounted the helmet, as examples of crests. The rudiments and origin of crests doubtless they were. Crests they were not.

We must go back, once again, to the bed-rock of the peacock-popinjay vanity ingrained in human nature. The same impulse which nowadays leads to the decoration of the helmets of the Life Guards with horsehair plumes and regimental badges, the cocked hats of field-marshals and other officers with waving plumes, the képis of commissionaires, and the smasher hats of Colonial irregulars with cocks' feathers, the hat of the poacher and gamekeeper with a pheasant's feather, led unquestionably to the 'decoration' of the helmets of the armoured knights of old. The matter was just a combination of decoration and vanity. At first (569) they frequently painted their helmets, and as with the gradual evolution and crystallisation of armory a certain form of decoration (the device upon his shield) became identified with a certain person, that particular device was used for the decoration of the helmet and painted thereupon.

Then it was found that a fan-shaped erection upon the helmet improved its appearance, and, without adding greatly to its weight, advantaged it as a head protection by attracting the blow of an opponent's sword, and lessening or nullifying its force ere the blow reached the actual crown-plates of the helmet. Possibly in this we see the true origin (as in the case of the scalloped edges of the mantling) of the serrated border which appears upon these fan-shaped erections. But this last suggestion is no more than a conjecture of my own, and may not be correct, for human nature has always had a weakness for decoration, and ever has been agreeable to pay the extra penny in the 'tuppence' for the coloured or decorated variety. The many instances which can be found of these fan-shaped ornaments upon helmets in a perfectly undecorated form leads me to unhesitatingly assert that they originated *not* as crests, nor as a vehicle for the display of crests, but as an integral and protective part of the *helmet* itself. The origin of the crest is due to the decoration of the fan. The derivation of the word 'crest', from the Latin *crista*, a cock's comb, should put the supposition beyond any doubt.

Disregarding crests of later grant or assumption, one can assert with confidence that a large proportion of those—particularly in German armory, where they are so frequent—which we now find blazoned or depicted as wings or plumes, carrying a device, are nothing more than developments of or derivatives from these fan-shaped ornaments.

These fans being (from other reasons) in existence, of course, and very naturally, were painted and decorated, and equally of course such decoration took the form of the particular decoration associated with the owner, namely, the device upon the shield. It seems to me, and for long has so seemed, essentially strange that no specialist authority, writing upon armory, has noticed that these 'fans' (as I will call them) are really a part, though possibly only a decorative part, of the

610 *From the seal (1301) of Richard Fitz Alan, Earl of Arundel.*

611 *From the seal (1301) of Humphrey de Bohun, Earl of Hereford.*

612 *From the seal (1305) of Edward of Caernarvon, Prince of Wales.*

246

helmet itself. There has always in these matters been far too great a tendency on the part of writers to accept conclusions of earlier authorities ready made, and to simply treat these fans as selected and chosen crests. 610–12 are instances of helmets having these fans. All are taken from seals, and it is quite possible that the actual fans upon the seal helmets had some device painted upon them which it was impossible by reason of the size to represent upon the seal. As has been already stated, the great seal of Richard I does show a lion painted on the fan.

There are many examples of the heraldic development of these fans—for their use obtained even in this country long after the real heraldic crest had an assured footing—and a typical example occurs in 613, but probably the best-known instance, one which has been often illustrated, is that from the effigy of Sir Geoffrey de Luttrell (c. 1340), which shows a fan of this character upon which the entire Luttrell arms are depicted.

613 *Arms of the family of Schaler (Basle): Gules, a bend of lozenges argent. (From the Zürich Roll of Arms.)*

A much later instance in this country will be found in the seal (dated 1539) of the City of London, which shows upon the helmet one of these fan-shaped ornaments, charged with the cross of the City arms (614).

The arms of the City of London are recorded in the College of Arms (Vincent) without a crest (and by the way without supporters) and this seal affords a curious but a very striking and authentic instance of the extreme accuracy of the records of the College of Arms. There being no crest for the City of London at the time of the preparation of this seal, recourse was had to the ancient practice of depicting the whole or a part (in this case a part) of the device of the shield upon a fan surmounting the helmet. In course of time this fan, in the case of London, as in so many other cases, has through ignorance been converted or developed into a wing, but the 'rays' of the fan in this instance are preserved in the 'rays' of the dragon's wing (charged with a cross) which the crest is now supposed to be.

Whilst dealing with the arms of London, one of the favourite 'flaring' examples of ancient but unrecorded arms often mentioned as an instance in which the Records of the College of Arms are at fault, perhaps I may be pardoned for adding that the shield *is* recorded. The crest and supporters are not. The seeming omission as to the crest is explained above. The real supporters of the City of London, to which a claim by user *could* (even now) be established (they are two lions, not dragons), had, with the single exception of their use upon the Mayor's seal, which use is continued to the present day, been practically discarded. Consequently the lions as supporters remained unclaimed, and therefore are not recorded.

614 *Modern reverse of the Common Seal of the City of London (1539).*

The supporters now used (two dragons) are *raw new* adornments, of which no example can be found before the seventeenth century. Those naturally, being 'assumed' without authority at so recent a date, are not recorded, which is yet another testimony to the impartial accuracy of the Heralds' College Records.

The use of the fan-crest has long been obsolete in British armory, in which it can hardly ever be said to have had a very great footing, unless such use was prevalent in the thirteenth century; but it still survives in Germany at the present day, where, in spite of the fact that many of these fans have now degenerated into reduplications of the arms upon wings or plumes of feathers, other crests to a considerable number are still displayed upon 'fans'.

Many of the current practices in British armory are the culmination of long-continued ignorance. Some, mayhap, can be allowed to pass without comment, but others deserve at any rate their share of criticism and remark. Amongst such may be included the objectionable practice, in the grants of so many modern crests, of making the crest itself a *shield* carrying a repetition of the arms or some other device, or of introducing in the crest an escutcheon. To the resuscitation of these 'fan' repetitions of the shield device there is not, and cannot be, any objection. One would even, in these days of the multiplication of differentiated crests, recommend this as a relief from the abominable rows of assorted objects nowadays placed (for the purposes of differentiation) in front of so many modern crests. One would gladly see a reversion to the German development (from this source) of wings charged with the arms or a part of the armorial device; but one of the things a new grantee should pray to be delivered from is an escutcheon of any sort, shape, or form in the crest assigned to him.[169]

To return, however, to the 'fans' upon the early helmets. Many of the examples which have come down to us show the fan of a rather diminutive height, but (in the form of an arc of a much enlarged circle) projected far forward beyond the front of the helmet, and carried far back, apparently as a safeguard from blows which would otherwise descend upon the neck. (A survival of the fan, by the way, may perhaps be found in the dragoon helmets of the time of the Peninsular War, in the firemen's helmets of today, and in the helmets now worn by different regiments in the Italian army.) The very shape of these fans should prove they were originally a protective part of the helmet. The long low shape, however, did not, as a general circumstance, lend itself to its decoration by a duplication thereupon of the whole of the arms. Consequently these fans will nearly always be found simply adorned with one figure from the shield. It should not be forgotten that we are now dealing with a period in armory when the charges upon the shield itself were very much, as far as number and position are concerned, of an indeterminate character. If they were indeterminate for the shield, it evidences that there cannot have been any idea of a necessity to repeat the whole of the device upon the fan. As there was seldom room or opportunity for the display of the whole device, we invariably find that these fan decorations were a duplication of a distinctive part, but not necessarily the whole of the device; and this device was disposed in the most suitable position which the shape of the fan would accommodate. Herein is the explanation of the fact that whilst the arms of Percy, Talbot, and Mowbray were all, in varying tinctures, a lion rampant, the crest in each case was a lion passant or statant. In short, the fan did not lend itself to the representation of a lion rampant, and consequently there is no early instance of such a crest. Perhaps the insecurity of a large and heavy crest balanced upon one leg may be an added reason.

The next step in the evolution of the crest, there can be little doubt, was the cutting of the fan into the outline of the crest, and, though I know of no instance of such a crest on any effigy, there can be no reasonable doubt on the point, if a little thought is given to the matter. Until a very much later period, we never find

169. Why Fox-Davies takes such a stand against the use of escutcheons in crests is not clear; but his spirit may rest easy, for these are no longer granted unless charged with the actual arms of the grantee. The theory is that the inclusion of a shield, or a tabard or a banner for that matter, in either arms or crest, charged with anything other than the grantee's arms, creates a new coat.

in any heraldic representation that the helmet or crest are represented in an affronté position. Why? Simply because crests at that period were merely profile representations.

In later days, when tournament crests were made of leather, the weight even of these was very considerable, but for tournament purposes that weight could be endured. Half-a-dozen courses down the *barrière* would be a vastly different matter to a whole day under arms in actual battle. Now a crest cut out from a thin plate of metal set on edge would weigh but little. But perhaps the strongest proof of all is to be found in the construction of so many German crests, which are adorned down the back with a fan.

Now it is hardly likely, if the demi-lion in relief had been the earliest form, that the fan would have been subsequently added to it. The fan is nothing more than the remains of the original fan-shaped ornament left when the crest, or most likely only the front outline of it, had been cut out in profile from the fan. We have no instance until a very much later period of a crest which could not be depicted in profile, and in the representations of crests upon seals we have no means of forming a certain judgment that these representations are not of profile crests, for the very nature of the craft of seal-engraving would lead the engraver to add a certain amount of relief, even if this did not actually exist. It is out of the question to suppose, by reason of their weight, that crests were made in metal. But if made of leather, as were the tournament crests, what protection did the crest add to the helmet? The fact that wreaths and coronets did not come into use at the earliest advent of crests is confirmatory evidence of the fact that modelled crests did not exist, inasmuch as the fan prolonged in front and prolonged behind was narrowed at its point of contact with the helmet into such a diminished length that it was comparatively easy to slip the mantling by means of a slit over the fan, or even drape it round it.

Many of the old illustrations of tournaments and battles which have come down to us show no crests on the helmets, but merely plumes of feathers or some fan-shaped erection. Consequently it is a fairly safe conclusion that for the actual purposes of warfare modelled crests never had any real existence, or, if they had any such existence, that it was most limited. Modelled crests were tournament crests. The crests that were used in battle must have been merely cut out in profile from the fan. Then came the era, in Plantagenet times, of the tournament. We talk glibly about tournaments, but few indeed really know much about them. Trial by combat and the real tournament *à l'outrance* seldom occurred, and though trial by combat remained upon the statute-book until the 59 Geo. III, it was seldom invoked. Tournaments were chiefly in the nature of athletic displays, taking the place of our games and sports, and inasmuch as they contributed to the training of the soldier, were held in the high repute that polo, for example, now enjoys amongst the upper and military classes. Added to this, the tournament was the essential climax of ceremony and ceremonial, and in all its details was ordered by such strict regulations, rules, and supervision that its importance and its position in the public and official estimate was far in advance of its present-day equivalents.

The joust was fought with tilting-spears, the 'tourney' with swords. The rules and regulations for jousts and tournaments drawn up by the High Constable of

England in the reign of Edward IV show clearly that in neither was contemplated any risk of life.

In the tourney the swords were blunted and without points, but the principal item was always the joust, which was fought with tilting-spears and shields. Many representations of the tourney show the participants without shields. The general ignorance as to the manner in which the tilt was run is very widespread. A strong barrier was erected straight down the centre of the lists, and the knights were placed one on either side, so that by no possible chance could the two horses come into contact. Those who will read Mallory's *Morte d'Arthur* carefully— bearing in mind that Mallory described legendary events of an earlier period clothed in the manners and customs of his own day (time of Edward IV), and made no attempt to reproduce the manners and customs and real atmosphere of the Arthurian times, which could have had no relation to the manners and proceedings which Sir Thomas Mallory employs in telling his legends— will notice that, when it came to jousting, some half-dozen courses would be all that were run between contending knights. In fact the tournament rules above referred to say, for the tourney, that two blows at passage and ten at the joining ought to suffice. The time which this would occupy would not exceed the period for which any man could easily sustain the weight of a modelled crest.

Another point needs to be borne in mind. The result of a joust depended upon the points scored, the highest number being gained for the absolute unhorsing of an opponent. This, however, happened comparatively seldom, and points or 'spears' were scored for the lances broken upon an opponent's helmet, shield, or body, and the points so scored were subject to deduction if the opponent's horse were touched, and under other circumstances. The head of the tilting-spear which was used was a kind of rosette, and heraldic representations are really incorrect in adding a point when the weapon is described as a tilting-spear. Whilst a fine point meeting a wooden shield or metal armour would stick in the one or glance off the other, and neither result in the breaking of the lance nor in the unhorsing of the opponent, a broad rosette would convey a heavy shock. But to effect the desired object the tilting-spear would need to meet resistance, and little would be gained by knocking off an opponent's ornamental crest. Certainly no prize appears to have been allotted for the performance of this feat (which always attracts the imagination of the novelist), whilst there was for striking the 'sight' of the helmet. Consequently there was nothing to be gained from the protection to the helmet which the fan of earlier date afforded, and the tendency of ceremonial led to the use in tournaments of helmets and elaborate crests which were not those used in battle. The result is that we find these tournament or ceremonial crests were of large and prominent size, and were carved in wood, or built up of leather. But I firmly believe that these crests were used only for ceremonial and tournament purposes, and were never actually worn in battle. That these modelled crests in relief are the ones that we find upon effigies is only natural, and what one would expect, inasmuch as a man's effigy displayed his garments and accoutrements in the most ornate and honourable form. The same idea exists at the present day. The subjects of modern effigies and modern portraits are represented in robes, and with insignia which are seldom if ever worn, and which sometimes even have no existence in fact. In the same way the ancient effigies are the repre-

615 Crest of
Roger de Quincey,
Earl of Winchester (d. 1264).
(From his seal.)

sentations of the ceremonial dress and not the everyday garb of those for whom they stand. But even allowing all the foregoing, it must be admitted that it is from these ceremonial or tournament helmets and crests that the heraldic crest has obtained its importance, and herein lies the reason of the exaggerated size of early heraldic crests, and also the unsuitability of some few for actual use. Tournaments were flourishing in the Plantagenet, Yorkist, and Lancastrian periods, and ended with the days of the Tudor dynasty; and the Plantagenet period witnessed the rise of the ceremonial and heraldic crest. But in the days when crests had any actual existence they were made to fit the helmet, and the crests in 615–18 show crests very much more naturally disposed than those of later periods. Crests appear to have come into wider and more general use in Germany at an earlier period than is the case in this country, for in the early part of the thirteenth century seals are there to be met with having only the device of helmet and crest thereupon, a proof that the 'oberwappen' (helmet and crest) was then considered of equal or greater value than the shield.

616 Crest of
Thomas, Earl of Lancaster.
(From his seal, 1301.)

The actual tournament crests were made of light material, paste-board, cloth, or a leather shell over a wood or wire framework filled with tow, sponge, or sawdust. 271, which shows the shield, helmet, and crest of the Black Prince undoubtedly contemporary, dating from 1376, and now remaining in Canterbury Cathedral, is made of leather and is a good example of an actual crest, but even this, there can be little doubt, was never carried in battle or tournament, and is no more than a ceremonial crest made for the funeral pageant.

The heraldic wings which are so frequently met with in crests are not the natural wings of a bird, but are a development from the fan, and in actual crests were made of wooden or basket-work strips, and probably at an earlier date were not intended to represent wings, but were mere pieces of wood painted and existing for the display of a certain device. Their shape and position led to their transition into 'wings', and then they were covered with dyed or natural-coloured feathers. It was the art of heraldic emblazonment which ignored the practical details, that first copied the wing from nature.

617 Crest of
William de Montagu,
Earl of Salisbury
(d. 1344). (From his seal.)

Actual crests were fastened to the helmets they surmounted by means of ribbons, straps, laces (which developed later into the fillet and torse), or rivets, and in Germany they were ornamented with hanging and tinkling metal leaves, tiny bells, buffalo horns, feathers, and projecting pieces of wood, which formed vehicles for still further decorative appendages.

Then comes the question, what did the crest signify? Many have asserted that no one below the rank of a knight had the right to use a crest; in fact some writers have asserted, and doubtless correctly as regards a certain period, that only those who were of tournament rank might assume the distinction, and herein lies another confirmation of the supposition that crests had a closer relation to the tournament than to the battlefield.

Doubts as to a man's social position might disqualify him from participation in a tournament—hence the 'helme-schau' previously referred to—but they certainly never relieved him from the obligations of warfare imposed by the tenure under which he held his lands. There is no doubt, however, that whatever the regulation may have been—and there seems little chance of our ever obtaining any real knowledge upon the point—the right to display a crest was an additional

618 Crest of
Thomas de Mowbray,
Earl of Nottingham,
and Earl Marshal.
(From a drawing of his seal, 1389:
B.M. MS Cott., Julius, C. vii.)

251

privilege and honour, something extra and beyond the right to a shield of arms. For how long any such supposition held good it is difficult to say, for whilst we find in the latter part of the fourteenth century that all the great nobles had assumed and were using crests, and whilst there is but one amongst the Plantagenet Garter plates without a crest where a helmet has been represented above the shield, we also find that the great bulk of the lesser landed gentry bore arms, but made no pretension to a crest. The lesser gentry were bound to fight in war, but not necessarily in the tournament. Arms were a necessity of warfare, crests were not. This continued to be the case till the end of the sixteenth century, for we find that at one of the Visitations no crests whatever are inserted with the arms and pedigrees of the families set out in the Visitation Book, and one is probably justified in assuming that whilst this state of feeling and this idea existed, the crest was highly thought of, and valued possibly beyond the shield of arms, for with those of that rank of life which aspired to the display of a crest the right to arms would be a matter of course. In the latter part of the reign of Queen Elizabeth I and in Stuart days the granting of crests to ancient arms became a widespread practice. Scores upon scores of such grants can be referred to, and I have myself been led to the irresistble conclusion that the opportunity afforded by the grant of a crest was urged by the heralds and officers of arms, in order to give them the opportunity of confirming and recording arms which they knew needed such confirmation to be rendered legal, without giving offence to those who had borne these arms merely by strength of user for some prolonged but at the same time insufficient period to confer an unquestioned right. That has always seemed to me the obvious reason which accounts for these numberless grants of crests to apparently existing arms, which arms are recited and emblazoned in the patents, because there are other grants of crests which can be referred to, though these are singularly few in number, in which the arms are entirely ignored. But as none of these grants, which are of a crest only, appear to have been made to families whose right to arms was not absolutely beyond question or dispute, the conclusion above recited appears to be irresistible. The result of these numerous grants of crests, which I look upon as carrying greater importance in the sense that they were also con-firmations of the arms, resulted in the fact that the value and dignity of the crest slowly but steadily declined, and the cessation of tournaments and, shortly after-wards, the marked decline in funereal pageantry no doubt contributed largely to the same result. Throughout the Stuart period instances can be found, though not very frequently, of grants of arms without the grant of a crest being included in the patent; but the practice was soon to entirely cease, and roughly speaking one may assert that since the beginning of the Hanoverian dynasty no person has ever been granted arms without the corresponding grant of a crest, if a crest could be properly borne with the arms. Now no crest has ever been granted where the right to arms has not existed or been simultaneously conferred, and therefore, whilst there are still many coats of arms legally in existence without a crest, a crest cannot exist without a coat of arms, so that those people, and they are many, who vehemently assert a right to the 'crest of their family', whilst admitting they have no right to arms, stand self-convicted heraldically both of having spoken unutterable rubbish, and of using a crest to which they can have no possible right. One exception, and one only, have I ever come across to the contrary, and very careful inquiry can bring me knowledge of no other. That crest is the crest of a family of Buckworth, now represented by Sir Charles Buckworth-Herne-Soame, Bart. This family at the time of the Visitations exhibited a certain coat of arms and crest. The coat of arms, which doubtless interfered with the rights of some other family, was respited for further proof; but the crest, which did not, appears to have been allowed, and as nothing further was done with regard to the arms, the crest stood, whilst the arms were bad. But even this one exception has long since been rectified, for when the additional name and arms of Soame were assumed by Royal License, the arms which had been exhibited and respited were (with the addition of an ermine spot as a charge upon the chevron) granted as the arms of Buckworth to be borne quarterly with the arms of Soame.

With the cessation of tournaments, we get to the period which some writers have stigmatised as that of 'paper' heraldry. That is a reference to the fact that arms and crests ceased to be painted upon shields or erected upon helmets that enjoyed actual use in battle and tournament. Those who are so ready to decry modern heraldry forget that from its very earliest existence heraldry has always had the *same* significance as a symbol of rank and social position which it now enjoys and which remains undiminished in extent, though doubtless less potent in effect. They forget also that from the very earliest period armory had three uses— viz. its martial use, its decorative use, and its use as a symbol of ownership. The two latter uses still remain in their entirety, and whilst that is the case, armory cannot be treated as a dead science.

But with the cessation of tournaments the decorative became the chief use of arms, and the crest soon ceased to have that distinctive adaptability to the purpose of a helmet ornament. Up to the end of the Tudor period crests had retained their original simplicity. Animals' heads and animals passant, human heads and demi-animals, comprised the large majority of the early crests. Scottish heraldry in a marked degree has retained the early simplicity of crests, though at the expense of lack of distinction between the crests of different families. German heraldry has to a large extent retained the same character as has Scottish armory, and though many of the crests are decidedly elaborated, it is noticeable that this elaboration is never such as to render the crest unsuitable for its true position upon a helmet.

In England this aspect of the crest has been almost entirely lost sight of, and a large proportion of the crests in modern English grants are utterly unsuitable for use in relief upon an actual helmet. Our present rules of position for a helmet, and our unfortunate stereotyped form of wreath, are largely to blame, but the chief reason is the definite English rule that the crests of separate English families must be differentiated as are the arms. No such rule holds good in Scotland, hence their simple crests.

Whether the rule is good or bad it is difficult to say. When all the pros and cons have been taken into consideration, the whole discussion remains a matter of opinion, and whilst one dislikes the Scottish idea under which the same identical crest can be and regularly is granted to half-a-dozen people of as many different surnames, one objects very considerably to the typical present-day crest of an English grant of arms. Whilst a collar can be put round an animal's neck, and whilst it can hold objects in its mouth or paws, it does seem ridiculous to put a string of varied and selected objects 'in front' of it, when these plainly would only be visible from one side, or to put a crest 'between' objects if these are to be represented 'fore and aft', one toppling over the brow of the wearer of the helmet and the other hanging down behind.

The crests granted by the late Sir Albert Woods, Garter, are the crying grievance of modern English heraldry, and though a large proportion are far greater abortions than they need be, and though careful thought and research even yet will under the present régime result in the grant of at any rate a quite unobjectionable crest, nevertheless we shall not obtain a real reform, or attain to any appreciable improvement, until the 'position' rule as to helmets is abolished. Some of the crests mentioned hereunder are typical and awful examples of modern crests.

Crest of Bellasis of Marton, Westmoreland: A mount vert, thereon a lion couchant guardant azure, in front of a tent proper, lined gules.

Crest of Hermon of Preston, Lancashire, and Wyfold Court, Checkendon, Oxon.: In front of two palm-trees proper, a lion couchant guardant erminois, resting the dexter claw upon a bale of cotton proper. Motto: 'Fido non timeo.'

Crest of James Harrison, Esq., M.A., Barrister-at-Law: In front of a demi-lion rampant erased or, gorged with a collar gemelle azure, and holding between the paws a wreath of oak proper, three mascles interlaced also azure. Motto: 'Pro rege et patria.'

Crest of Colonel John Davis, F.S.A., of Bifrons, Hants: A lion's head erased sable, charged with a caltrap or, upon two swords in saltire proper, hilted and pommelled also or. Motto: 'Ne tentes, aut perfice.'

Crest of Sir Saul Samuel, Bart., K.C.M.G.: Upon a rock in front of three spears, one in pale and two in saltire, a wolf current sable, pierced in the breast by an arrow argent, flighted or. Motto: 'A pledge of better times.'

Crest of Johnson of Kennal Manor, Chislehurst, Kent: In front of a dexter arm embowed in armour proper, the hand also proper, grasping a javelin in bend sinister, pheoned or, and enfiled with a chaplet of roses gules, two branches of oak in saltire vert.

Crest of C. E. Lamplugh, Esq.: In front of a cubit arm erect proper, encircled about the wrist with a wreath of oak and holding in the hand a sword also proper, pommel and hilt or, an escutcheon argent, charged with a goat's head couped sable. Mottoes: 'Through,' and 'Providentia Dei stabiliuntur familiæ.'

Crest of Glasford, Scotland: 'Issuing from clouds two hands conjoined grasping a caduceus ensigned with a cap of liberty, all between two cornucopiæ all proper. Motto: 'Prisca fides.'

We now come to the subject of the inheritance of crests, concerning which there has been much difference of opinion.

It is very usually asserted that until a comparatively recent date crests were not hereditary, but were assumed, discarded, and changed at pleasure. Like many other incorrect statements, there is a certain modicum of truth in the statement, for no doubt whilst arms themselves had a more or less shifting character, crests were certainly not 'fixed' to any greater extent.

But I think no one has as yet discovered, or at any rate brought into notice, the true facts of the case, or the real position of the matter, and I think I am the first to put into print what actually were the rules which governed the matter. The rules, I believe, were undoubtedly these:

Crests were, save in the remote beginning of things heraldic, definitely hereditary. They were hereditary even to the extent (and herein lies the point which has not hitherto been observed) that they were transmitted by an heiress.

Perhaps this heritability was limited to those cases in which the heiress transmitted the *de facto* headship of her house. We, judging by present laws, look upon the crest as a part of the *one* heraldic achievement inseparable from the shield. What proof have we that in early times any necessary connection between arms and crest existed? We have none. The shield of arms was one inheritance, descending by known rules. The crest was another, but a separate inheritance, descending equally through an heir or coheir-general. The crest was, as an inheritance, as separate from the shield as were the estates then. The social conditions of life prevented the possibility of the existence or inheritance of a crest where arms did not exist. But a man inheriting several coats of arms from different heiress ancestresses could marshal them all upon one shield, and though we find the heir often made selection at his pleasure, and marshalled the arms in various methods, the determination of which was a mere matter of arbitrary choice, he could, if he wished, use them all upon one shield. But he had but one helmet, and could use and display but one crest. So that, if he had inherited two, he was forced to choose which he would use, though he sometimes tried to combine two into one device. It is questionable if an instance can be found in England of the regular display of two helmets and crests together, surmounting one shield, before the eighteenth century, but there are countless instances of the contemporary but separate display of two different crests, and the Visitation Records afford us some number of instances of this tacit acknowledgment of the inheritance of more than one crest.

The patent altering or granting the Mowbray crest seems to me clear recognition of the right of inheritance of a crest passing through an heir female. This, however, it must be admitted, may be really no more than a grant, and is not in itself actual evidence that any crest had been previously borne. My own opinion, however, is that it is fair presumptive evidence upon the point, and conveys an alteration and not a grant.

The translation of this Patent (Patent Roll 339, 17 Ric. II pt 1, memb. 2) is as follows: 'The King to all to whom, &c., Greeting, Know that whereas our well-beloved and faithful kinsman, Thomas, Earl Marshal and Earl of Nottingham has a just hereditary title to bear for his crest a leopard or with a white label, which should be of right the crest of our eldest son if we had begotten a son. We, for this consideration, have granted for us and our heirs to the said Thomas and his heirs that for a difference in this crest they shall and may bear a leopard, and in place of a label a crown argent, without hindrance from us or our heirs aforesaid. In witness, &c. Witness the King at Westminster, the 12th day of January [17 Ric. II]. By writ of Privy Seal.'

Cases will constantly be found in which the crests have been changed. I necessarily totally exclude from consideration crests which have been changed owing to specific grants, and also changes due to the discarding of crests which can be shown to have been borne without right. Changes in crests must also be disregarded where the differences in emblazonment are merely differences in varying designs of the same crest. Necessarily from none of these instances can a law of inheritance be deduced. But if other changes in the crests of important families be considered, I think it will be very evident that practically the whole of these are due to the inheritance through heiresses or ancestresses of an alternative crest. It can be readily shown that selection played an important part in the marshalling of quarterings upon an escutcheon, and where important quarterings were inherited they are as often as not found depicted in the first quarter. Thus the Howards have borne at different periods the wings of Howard; the horse of Fitzalan; and the Royal crest granted to the Mowbrays with remainder to the heir general; and these crests have been borne, as will be seen from the Garter plates, quite irrespective of what the surname in use may have been. Consequently it is very evident the crests were considered to be inherited with the representation of the different families. The Stourton crest was originally a stag's head, and is to be seen recorded in one of the Visitations, and upon the earliest seal in existence of any member of the family. But after the inheritance through the heiress of Le Moyne, the Le Moyne crest of the demi-monk was adopted. The Stanleys, Earls of Derby, whatever their original crest may have been, inherited the well-known bird and bantling of the family of Lathom. The Talbot crest was originally a talbot, and this is still so borne by Lord Talbot of Malahide: it was recorded at the Visitation of Dublin; but the crest at present borne by the Earls of Shrewsbury is derived from the arms inherited by descent from Gwendolin, daughter of Rhys ap Griffith. The Nevill crest was a bull's head as it is now borne by the Marquess of Abergavenny, and as it will be seen on the Garter plate of William Nevill, Lord Fauconberg. An elder brother of Lord Fauconberg had married the heiress of the Earl of Salisbury, and was summoned to Parliament in her earldom. He quartered her arms, which appear upon his Garter plate and seal, in the first and fourth quarters of his shield, and adopted her crest. A younger son of Sir Richard Nevill, Earl of Salisbury, bore the same crest differenced by two annulets conjoined, which was the difference mark added to the shield. The crest of Bourchier was a soldan's head crowned, and with a pointed cap issuing from the crown, but when the barony of Bourchier passed to the family of Robsart, as will be seen from the Garter plate of Sir Lewis Robsart, Lord Bourchier, the crest of Bourchier was adopted with the inheritance of the arms and Barony of Bourchier.

I am aware of no important case in English heraldry where the change has been due to mere caprice, and it would seem therefore an almost incontrovertible assertion that changes were due to inheritance, and if that can be established it follows even more strongly that until the days when armory was brought under rigid and official control, and even until a much later date, say up to the beginning of the Stuart period, crests were heritable through heiresses equally with quarterings. The fact that we find comparatively few changes considering the number of crests in existence is by no means a refutation of this theory, because a man had but one helmet, and was forced therefore to make a selection. Unless, therefore, he had a very strong inclination it would be more likely that he would select the crest he was used to than a fresh one. I am by no means certain that to a limited extent the German idea did not hold in England. This was, and is, that the crest had not the same personal character that was the case with the arms, but was rather attached to or an appanage of the territorial fief or lordship. By the time of the Restoration any idea of the transmission of crests through heiresses had been abandoned. We then find a Royal License necessary for the assumption of arms and crests. Since that date it has been and at the present time it is stringently held, and is the official rule, that no woman can bear or inherit a crest, and that no woman can transmit a right to one. Whilst that is the official and accepted interpretation of heraldic law upon the point, and whilst it cannot now be gainsaid, it cannot, however, be stated that the one assertion is the logical deduction of the other, for whilst a woman cannot inherit a lordship of Parliament, she undoubtedly can transmit one, together with the titular honours, the enjoyment of which is not denied to her.[170]

In Scotland crests have always had a very much less important position than in England. There has been little if any continuity with regard to them, and instances of changes for which caprice would appear to be the only reason are met with in the cases of a large proportion of the chief families in that kingdom. To such a widespread extent has the permissive character been allowed to the crest, that many cases will be found in which each successive matriculation for the head of the house, or for a cadet, has produced a change in the crest, and instances are to be found where the different crests are the only existing differences in the achievements of a number of cadets of the same family. At the present time, little if any objection is ever made to an entire and radical change in the crest—if this is wished at the time of a rematriculation—and as far as I can gather such changes appear to have always been permitted. Perhaps it may be well here to point out that this is not equivalent to permission to change the crest at pleasure, because the patent of matriculation until it is superseded by another is the authority, and the compulsory authority, for the crest which is to be borne. In Germany the crest has an infinitely greater importance than is the case with ourselves, but it is there considered in a large degree a territorial appanage, and it is by no means unusual in a German achievement to see several crests surmounting a single coat of arms. In England the Royal coat of arms has really three crests, although the crests of Scotland and Ireland are seldom used, which, it may be noted, are all in a manner territorial; but the difference of idea with which crests are regarded in Germany may be gathered from the fact that the King of Saxony had five, the Grand Duke of Meckenlenburg-Schwerin five, the Duke of Saxe-Meiningen six, the Grand Duke of Saxe-Altenburg seven, the Duke of Anhalt seven, the Duke of Saxe-Coburg and Gotha six, the Prince of Schwarzburg-Sondershausen six, the Prince of Schwarzburg-Rudolstadt six, the Prince of Waldeck-Pyrmont five, the Prince of Lippe five, the Duke of Brunswick five, and instances can be quoted of sixteen and seventeen. Probably Woodward is correct when he says that each crest formerly denoted a noble fief, for which the proprietor had a right to vote in the 'circles' of the Empire, and he instances the Margraves of Brandenburg-Anspach, who were entitled to no less than thirteen crests. In France the use of crests is not nearly so general as in England or Germany. In Spain and Portugal it is less frequent still, and in Italy the use of a crest is the exception.

The German practice of using horns on either side of the crest, which the ignorance of English heralds has transformed into the proboscides of elephants, is dealt with at some length on page 160. The horns, which are termed buffalo's or bull's horns until the middle of the thirteenth century, were short and thick-set. It is difficult to say at what date these figures came to be considered as heraldic

170. This is now no longer the case for, under section 6 of the Peerage Act 1963 (1963 chapter 48), any woman holding an hereditary peerage in the peerage of England, Scotland, Great Britain or the United Kingdom has the same right to receive a writ of summons to attend, sit and vote in the House of Lords as an hereditary peer. Life peeresses have the same privileges as life peers.

crests, for as mere helmet ornaments they probably can be traced back very far beyond any proof of the existence of armory. In the fourteenth century we find the horns curved inwards like a sickle, but later the horns are found more erect, the points turning outwards, slimmer in shape, and finally they exhibit a decidedly marked double curve. Then the ends of the horns are met with open, like a trumpet, the fact which gave rise to the erroneous idea that they represented elephants' trunks. The horns became ornamented with feathers, banners, branches of leaves, balls, &c., and the orifices garnished with similar adornments.

In England, crests are theoretically subject to marks of cadency and difference. This is not the case, however, in any other country. In Germany, in cases where the crests reproduce the arms, any mark of cadency with which the arms are distinguished will of course be repeated; but in German heraldry, doubtless owing to the territorial nature of the crest, a change in the crest itself is often the only mark of distinction between different branches of the same family, and in Siebmacher's *Wappenbuch* thirty-one different branches of the Zorn family have different crests, which are the sole marks of difference in the achievements.

But though British crests are presumed to be subject to the recognised marks of cadency, as a matter of fact it is very seldom indeed that they are ever so marked, with the exception that the mark used (usually a cross crosslet) to signify the lack of blood relationship when arms are assumed under a Royal License, is compulsory. Marks of distinction added to signify illegitimacy are also compulsory and perpetual. What these marks are will be dealt with in a subsequent chapter upon the subject. How very seldom a mark of difference is added to a crest may be gathered from the fact that with the exception of labels, chiefly upon the Royal crest, one crest only amongst the Plantagenet Garter plates is differenced, that one being the crest of John Neville, Lord Montague. Several crests, however, which are not Royal, are differenced by similar labels to those which appear upon the shields; but when we find that the difference marks have very much of a permissive character, even upon the shield, it is not likely that they are perpetuated upon the crest, where they are even less desirable. The arms of Cokayne, as given in the funeral certificate of Sir William Cokayne, Lord Mayor of London, show upon the shield three crescents, sable, or, and gules, charged one upon the other, the Lord Mayor being the second son of a second son of Cokayne of Sturston, descending from William, second son of Sir John Cokayne of Ashborne. But, in spite of the fact that three difference marks are charged upon the shield (one of the quarterings of which, by the way, has an additional mark), the crest itself is only differenced by one crescent. These difference marks, as applied to arms, are in England (the rules in Scotland are utterly distinct) practically permissive, and are never enforced against the wish of the bearer except in one circumstance. If, owing to the grant of a crest or supporters, or a Royal License, or any similar opportunity, a formal exemplification of the arms is entered on the books of the College of Arms, the opportunity is generally taken to add such mark of cadency as may be necessary; and no certificate would be officially issued to any one claiming arms through that exemplification except subject to the mark of cadency therein depicted. In such cases as these the crest is usually differenced, because the necessity for an exemplification does not often occur, except owing to the establishment of an important branch of the family, which is likely to continue as a separate house in the future, and possibly to rival the importance of the chief of the name. Two examples will show my meaning. The crest of the Duke of Bedford is a goat statant argent, armed or. When Earl Russell, the third son of the sixth Duke of Bedford, was so created, the arms, crest, and supporters were charged with a mullet argent. When the first Lord Ampthill, who was the third son of the father of the ninth Duke of Bedford, was so created, the arms of Russell, with the crest and supporters, were also charged with mullets, these being of different tinctures from those granted to Earl Russell. The crest of the Duke of Westminster is a talbot statant or. The first Lord Stalbridge was the second son of the Marquess of Westminster. His arms, crest, and supporters were charged with a crescent. Lord Ebury was the third son of the first Marquess of Westminster. His arms, crest, and supporters were charged with a mullet. In cases of this kind the mark of difference upon the crest would be considered permanent; but for ordinary purposes, and in ordinary circumstances, the rule may be taken to be that it is not necessary to add the mark of cadency to a crest, even when it is added to the shield, but that, at the same time, it is not incorrect to do so.

Crests must nowadays always be depicted upon either a wreath, coronet, or chapeau; but these, and the rules concerning them, will be considered in a more definite and detailed manner in the separate chapters in which those objects are discussed.

Crests are nowadays very frequently used upon livery buttons. Such a usage is discussed at some length in the chapter on badges.

When two or more crests are depicted together, and when, as is often the case in England, the wreaths are depicted in space, and without the intervening helmets, the crests always all face to the dexter side, and the stereotyped character of English crests perhaps more than any other reason, has led of late to the depicting of English helmets all placed to face in the same direction to the dexter side. But if, as will often be found, the two helmets are turned to face each other, the crests also must be turned.

Where there are two crests, the one on the dexter side is the first and the one on the sinister side is the second. When there are three, the centre one comes first, then the one on the dexter side, then the one on the sinister. When there are four crests, the first one is the dexter of the two inner ones; the second is the sinister inner one; the third is the dexter outer, and the fourth the sinister outer. When there are five (and I know of no greater number in this country), they run as follows: (1) centre, (2) dexter inner, (3) sinister inner, (4) dexter outer, (5) sinister outer.

A very usual practice in official emblazonments in cases of three crests is to paint the centre one of a larger size, and at a slightly lower level, than the others. In the case of four, Nos. 1 and 2 would be of the same size, Nos. 3 and 4 slightly smaller, and slightly raised.

It is a very usual circumstance to see two or more crests displayed in England, but this practice is of comparatively recent date. How recent may be gathered from the fact that in Scotland no single instance can be found before the year 1809 in which two crests are placed above the same shield. Scottish heraldry, however, has always been purer than English, and the practice in England is much more ancient, though I question if in England any authentic official exemplification can be found before 1700.[171] There are, however, many cases in the Visitation Books in which two crests are allowed to the same family, but this fact does not prove the point, because a Visitation record is merely an official record of inheritance and possession, and not necessarily evidence of a regulation permitting the simultaneous display of more than one. It is of course impossible to use two sets of supporters with a single shield, but there are many peers who are entitled to two sets; Lord Ancaster, I believe, is entitled to three sets. But an official record in such a case would probably emblazon both sets as evidence of right, by painting the shield twice over.

During the eighteenth century we find many instances of the grant of additional crests of augmentation, and many exemplifications under Royal License for the use of two and three crests. Since that day the correctness of duplicate crests has never been questioned, where the right of inheritance to them has been established. The right of inheritance to two or more crests at the present time is only officially allowed in the following cases.

If a family at the time of the Visitations had two crests recorded to them, these would be now allowed. If descent can be proved from a family to whom a certain crest was allowed, and also from ancestors at an earlier date who are recorded as entitled to bear a different crest, the two would be allowed unless it was evident that the later crest had been granted, assigned, or exemplified *in lieu* of the earlier one. Two crests are allowed in the few cases which exist where a family has obtained a grant of arms in ignorance of the fact that they were then entitled to bear arms and crest of an earlier date to which the right has been subsequently proved, but on this point it should be remarked that if a right to arms is known to exist a second grant in England is point-blank refused unless the petition asks for it to be borne instead of, and in lieu of, the earlier one: it is then granted in those terms.[172]

To those who think that the Heralds' College is a mere fee-grabbing institution, the following experience of an intimate friend of mine may be of interest. In placing his pedigree upon record it became evident that his descent was not legitimate, and he therefore petitioned for and obtained a Royal License to bear

---

171. It is true that in some of the Visitations, notably the 1633–4 Visitation of London, two crests are shown; but in nearly every case one is that of a wife's family, and is shown in connection with an impaled coat. I have, however, come across one case where quartered arms with two crests were allowed, although the accompanying pedigree does not indicate how the quartering was acquired. The arms allowed to Samuel and John Langham of London, descended from a Northamptonshire family, at the 1633–4 Visitation of London may be blazoned: quarterly, 1 and 4: argent, three bear's heads erased sable, muzzled or; 2 and 3: ermine, a chevron gules and a bordure engrailed sable (for Revel). Crests: 1. A bear's head erased sable muzzled or. 2. A heath-cock sable.

172. This is not true today. There are several examples where a new coat has been granted without any reference to the extant arms and in some of these cases it must have been known that arms already existed. There is one school of thought which argues, and with some conviction, that arms cannot be granted *in lieu* of existing arms; that the acts of the kings of arms cannot be set aside and reversed by their successors, and that an incorporeal hereditament, legally granted to a man and his descendants, cannot be so easily extinguished. Whilst there is no reason why a man entitled to two patronymic coats should use both, it is held that he cannot be inhibited from doing so even if the second coat was granted *in lieu* of the first for, if one subscribes to this argument, one must regard the use of the phrase *'in lieu of'* as being *ultra vires*.

the name and arms of the family from which he had sprung. But the illegitimacy was not modern, and no one would have questioned his right to the name which all the other members of the family bear, if he had not himself raised the point in order to obtain the ancient arms in the necessarily differenced form. The arms had always been borne with some four or five quarterings and with two crests, and he was rather annoyed that he had to go back to a simple coat of arms and single crest. He obtained a grant for his wife, who was an heiress, and then, with the idea of obtaining an additional quartering and a second crest, he conceived the brilliant idea—for money was of no object to him—of putting his brother forward as a petitioner for arms to be granted to him and his descendants and to the other descendants of his father, a grant which would of course have brought in my friend. He moved heaven and earth to bring this about, but he was met with the direct statement that two grants of arms could not be made to the same man to be borne simultaneously, and that if he persisted in the grant of arms to his brother, his own name, as being then entitled to bear arms, would be specifically exempted from the later grant, and the result was that this second grant was never made.

In Scotland, where re-matriculation is constantly going on, two separate matriculations *to the same line* would not confer the right to two crests, inasmuch as the last matriculation supersedes everything which has preceded it. But if a cadet matriculates a different crest, *and subsequently* succeeds to the representation under an earlier matriculation, he legally succeeds to both crests, and incidentally to both coats of arms. As a matter of ordinary practice, the cadet matriculation is discarded. A curious case, however, occurs when after matriculation by a cadet there is a *later* matriculation behind it, by some one nearer the head of the house to which the first-mentioned cadet succeeds; in which event selection must be brought into play, when succession to both occurs. But the selection lies only between the two patients, and not from varied constituent parts.

Where as an augmentation an additional crest is granted, as has been the case in many instances, of course a right to the double crest is thereby conferred, and a crest of augmentation is not granted in lieu, but in addition.

A large number of these additional crests have been granted under specific warrants from the Crown, and in the case of Lord Gough, two additional crests were granted as separate augmentations and under separate patents. Lord Kitchener twice received a grant of an additional crest of augmentation.[173] There are also a number of grants on record, not officially ranking as augmentations, in which a second crest has been granted as a memorial of descent or office, &c.

The other cases in which double and treble crests occur are the results of exemplifications following upon Royal Licenses to assume name and arms. As a rule, when an additional surname is adopted by Royal License, the rule is that the arms adopted are to be borne in addition to those previously in existence; and where one name is adopted instead of another the warrant very frequently permits this, and at the same time permits or requires the new arms to be borne quarterly with those previously possessed, and gives the right to two crests. But in cases where names and arms are assumed by Royal License the arms and crest or crests are in

173. The grant of a pile of augmentation to the arms of Lord Kitchener and of an additional crest was dated 7 April 1900. A further augmentation, this time a chief, was granted to him on 8 July 1904.

accordance with the patent of exemplification, which, no matter what its terms (for some do not expressly exclude any prior rights), is always presumed to supersede everything which has gone before, and to be the authority by which the subsequent bearing of arms is regularised and controlled. Roughly speaking, under a Royal License one generally gets the right to one crest for every surname, and if the original surname be discarded, in addition a crest for every previous surname. Thus Mainwaring-Ellerker-Onslow has three crests, Wyndham-Campbell-Pleydell-Bouverie has four, and the last Duke of Buckingham and Chandos, who held the record, had one for each of his surnames, namely, Temple-Nugent-Brydges-Chandos-Grenville. In addition to the foregoing, there are one or two exceptions which it is difficult to explain. The Marquess of Bute for some reason or other obtained a grant, in the year 1822, of the crest of Herbert. The original Lord Liverpool obtained a grant of an additional crest, possibly an augmentation, and his representative, Lord Hawkesbury, afterwards created Earl of Liverpool, for some reason or other which I am quite at a loss to understand, obtained a grant of a crest very similar to that of Lord Liverpool to commemorate the representation which had devolved upon him.[174] He subsequently obtained a grant of a third crest, this last being of augmentation. Sir Charles Young, Garter King of Arms, obtained the grant of a second crest, and a former Marquess of Camden did the same thing; Lord Swansea is another recent case, and though the right of any person to obtain the grant of a second crest is not officially admitted, and is in fact strenuously denied, I cannot for the life of me see how in the face of the foregoing precedents any such privilege can be denied. Sir William Woods also obtained the grant of a second crest when he was Garter, oblivious of the fact that he had not really established a right to arms. Those he used were certainly granted in Lyon Office to a relative, but no matriculation of them in his own name was ever registered.

174. In fact the first Lord Liverpool was not granted a crest of augmentation. On 27 July 1796 Charles Jenkinson, 1st Earl of Liverpool, received a Royal Warrant for him and the heirs male of his body, being Earls of Liverpool, to quarter, at the request of the Mayor and Corporation of Liverpool, the arms of that town with his own arms. But Liverpool had no arms. So it came about that on 22 March 1797 arms were granted to Liverpool (argent, a cormorant in the beak a branch of sea weed called laver proper; the crest being a like bird but with wings elevated). The following day supporters were granted, and the day after that Lord Liverpool was granted an augmentation to his arms consisting of the arms of Liverpool shown on a chief wavy. Why the arms were not quartered as directed in the Royal Warrant I do not know.

An heiress of the last Lord Liverpool married George Savile Foljambe, and their son was successfully created Lord Hawkesbury and Earl of Liverpool. On 10 October 1893 he was granted an extra crest to commemorate his descent from and his representation of the 1st Earl of the first creation. Later, on 19 September 1906, he was granted, by virtue of a Royal Warrant, an augmentation to his arms and also a quite awful crest of augmentation which, if I have counted correctly, contains no less than sixteen charges.

22 · Crowns and coronets

The origin of the crown or coronet is, of course, to be met with in the diadem and fillet. In one of the Cantor Lectures delivered by Mr Cyril Davenport, F.S.A., in February 1902, on 'The History of Personal Jewellery from Prehistoric Times', he devoted considerable attention to the development of the diadem, and the following extracts are from the printed report of his lecture:

'The bandeau or fillet tied round the head was probably first used to keep long hair from getting into the eyes of primitive man. Presently it became specialised, priests wearing one pattern and fighting men another.

'The soft band which can be seen figured on the heads of kings in early coins, is no doubt a mark of chieftainship. This use of a band, of special colour, to indicate authority, probably originated in the East. It was adopted by Alexander the Great, who also used the diadem of the King of Persia. Justinian says that Alexander's predecessors did not wear any diadem. Justinian also tells us that the diadems then worn were of some soft material, as in describing the accidental wounding of Lysimachus by Alexander, he says that the hurt was bound up by Alexander *with his own diadem*. This was considered a lucky omen for Lysimachus, who actually did shortly afterwards become King of Thrace.

'In Egypt diadems of particular shape are of very ancient use. There were crowns for Upper and Lower Egypt, and a combination of both for the whole country. They were also distinguished by colour. The Uraeus or snake worn in the crowns and head-dresses of the Pharaohs was a symbol of royalty. Representations of the Egyptian gods always show them as wearing crowns.

'In Assyrian sculptures deities and kings are shown wearing diadems, apparently bands of stuff or leather studded with discs of *repoussé* work. Some of these discs, detached, have actually been found. Similar discs were plentifully found at Mycenæ, which were very likely used in a similar way. Some of the larger ornamental head-dresses worn by Assyrian kings appear to have been conical-shaped helmets, or perhaps crowns; it is now difficult to say which, because the material of which they were made cannot be ascertained. If they were of gold, they were probably crowns, like the wonderful openwork golden Scythian head-dress found at Kertch, but if of an inferior metal they may have been only helmets.

'At St Petersburg there is a beautiful ancient Greek diadem representing a crown of olive. An Etruscan ivy wreath of thin gold, still encircling a bronze helmet, is in the British Museum.

'Justinian says that Morimus tried to hang himself with the diadem, evidently a ribbon-like bandeau, sent to him by Mithridates. The Roman royal diadem was originally a white ribbon, a wreath of laurel was the reward of distinguished citizens, while a circlet of golden leaves was given to successful generals.

'Cæsar consistently refused the royal white diadem which Antony offered him, preferring to remain perpetual dictator. One of his partisans ventured to crown Cæsar's bust with a coronet of laurel tied with royal white ribbon, but the tribunes quickly removed it and heavily punished the perpetrator of the offence.

'During the Roman Empire the prejudice against the white bandeau remained strong. The emperors dared not wear it. Caligula wished to do so, but was dissuaded on being told that such a proceeding might cost his life. Eliogabalus used to wear a diadem studded with precious stones, but it is not supposed to have indicated rank, but only to have been a rich lady's parure, this emperor being fond of dressing himself up as a woman. Caracalla, who took Alexander the Great as his model as far as possible, is shown on some of his coins wearing a diadem of a double row of pearls, a similar design to which was used by the kings of Parthia. On coins of Diocletian, there shows a double row of pearls, sewn on a double band and tied in a knot at the back.

'Diadems gradually closed in and became crowns, and on Byzantine coins highly ornate diadems can be recognised, and there are many beautiful representations of them in enamels and mosaics, as well as a few actual specimens. At Ravenna, in mosaic work in the church of San Vitale, are crowned portraits of Justinian and his Empress Theodosia; in the enamel portrait of the Empress Irene in the Pal d'Oro at Venice, can be seen a beautiful jewelled crown with hinged plaques, and the same construction is used on the iron crown of Lombardy, the sacred crown of Hungary, and the crown of Charlemagne, all most beautiful specimens of jewellers' work.

'On the plaques of the crown of Constantine Monomachos are also fine enamel portraits of himself and his queen Zoë, wearing similar crowns. The cataseistas, or jewelled chains, one over each ear and one at the back, which occur on all these crowns, may be the survival of the loose ends of the tie of the original fillet.

'In later times of Greece and Rome, owing to the growth of republican feeling the diadem lost its political significance, and was relegated to the ladies.

'In the Middle Ages the diadem regained much of its earlier significance, and ceased to be only the simple head ornament it had become. Now it became specialised in form, reserved as an emblem of rank. The forms of royal crowns and diadems is a large and fascinating study, and where original examples do not now exist, the development can often be followed in sculpture, coins, or seals. Heraldry now plays an important part. Diadems or circlets gradually give way to closed crowns, in the case of sovereigns possessing independent authority.'

But to pass to the crown proper, there is no doubt that from the earliest times of recorded history crowns have been a sign and emblem of sovereignty. It equally admits of no doubt that the use of a crown or coronet was by no means exclusive to a sovereign, but whilst our knowledge is somewhat curtailed as to the exact relation in which great overlords and nobles stood to their sovereign, it is difficult to draw with any certainty or exactitude definitive conclusions of the symbolism a crown or coronet conveyed. Throughout Europe in the eleventh, twelfth, and thirteenth, and well into the fourteenth centuries, the great territorial lords enjoyed and exercised many—in fact most—of the attributes of sovereignty, and in England especially, where the king was no more than the first amongst his peers, the territorial earls were in much the position of petty sovereigns. It is only natural, therefore, that we should find them using this emblem of sovereignty. But what we do find in England is that a coronet or fillet was used, apparently without let or hindrance, even by knights. Many of these fillets were possibly simply the turban folded into the shape of a fillet, but capable of being unrolled. What the object of the wholesale wearing of crowns and coronets was, it is difficult to conjecture.

The development of the crown of the English sovereigns has been best told by Mr Cyril Davenport in his work *The English Regalia*. Mr Davenport, whose knowledge on these matters is probably unequalled, may best be allowed to tell the story in his own words, he and his publishers having very kindly permitted this course to be taken:

The crown of Great Britain

By Cyril Davenport, F.S.A.

'Crowns appear to have been at an early period worn by kings in battle, in order that they might be easily recognised; and although it is quite possible that this outward sign of sovereignty may have marked the wearer as being entitled to special protection by his own men, it is also likely that it was often a dangerous sign of importance. Upon the authority of their coins, the heads of the early British kings were adorned with variously formed fillets and ornamental wreaths. Helmets are also evidently intended to be shown, and on some of the coins of Athelstan the helmet bears upon it a crown of three raised points, with a single pearl at the top of each (619). Other coins bear the crown with the three raised points without the helmet (620). This crown of three points, bearing sometimes one and sometimes three pearls at the top of each, continued to be used by all the sole monarchs until Canute, on whose head a crown is shown in which the three points develop into three clearly-marked trefoils (621). On the great seal of Edward the Confessor the king is wearing an ornamental cap, which is described by Mr Wyon in his book about the Great Seals as bearing a crown with three points trefoiled; but the impressions of this Great Seal that I have been able to see are so indistinct in this particular that I do not feel justified in corroborating his opinion. On some of the coins, however, of Edward the Confessor, an arched crown is very clearly shown, and this crown has depending from it, on each side, tassels with ornamental ends (622).

'In the list of the English regalia which were destroyed under the Commonwealth in 1649 is found an item of great interest, viz. "a gold wyer work crown with little bells", which is there stated to have belonged to King Alfred, who appears to have been the first English king for whom the ceremony of coronation was used; and it is remarkable that on several of the crowns on coins and seals, from the time of Edward the Confessor until Henry I, little tassels or tags are shown which may indeed represent little bells suspended by a ribbon.

'On King Alfred's own coins there is unfortunately nothing which can be recognised as a crown.

'On the coins of Henry II a crown is shown with arches, apparently intended to be jewelled, as is also the rim. There are also tassels with ornamental ends at the back of the crown (623).

'William I on his Great Seal wears a crown with three points, at the top of

619.

620.

621.

622.

623.

624.

625.

626.

627.

628.

629.

630.

631.

632.

633.

634.

635.

636.

each of which are three pearls (624), and on some of his coins a more ornamental form of crown occurs having a broad jewelled rim and two arches, also apparently jewelled, and at each side are two pendants with pearl ends (625). William II on his Great Seal has a crown with five points (626), the centre one being slightly bigger than the others, and at the top of each a single pearl. At each side of the crown are pendants having three pearls at the ends.

'On some of the coins of Stephen a pretty form of crown is seen. It has three fleurs-de-lis and two jewelled arches (627). The arches disappear from this time until the reign of Edward IV. On the Great Seal of Henry I the king wears a simple crown with three fleurs-de-lis points, and two pendants each with three pearls at the ends (628), and after this the pendants seem to have been discontinued.

'On the first Great Seal of Henry III a crown with three fleurs-de-lis is shown surmounting a barred helmet (629), and Edward I wore a similar crown with three fleurs-de-lis, but having supplementary pearls between each (630), and this form lasted for a long time, as modifications of it are found on the coins of all the kings till Henry VII. On the third Great Seal of Edward IV the king wears a crown with five fleurs-de-lis, the centre one being larger than the others, and the crown is arched and has at the top an orb and cross (631). Henry VI on his first seal for foreign affairs, on which occurs the English shield, uses above it a crown with three crosses-patée and between each a pearl (632), this being the first distinct use of the cross-patée on the English crown; and it probably was used here in place of the fleurs-de-lis hitherto worn in order to make a clear distinction between it and the French crown, which has the fleurs-de-lis only and surmounts the coat of arms of that country. The king himself wears an arched crown, but the impressions are so bad that the details of it cannot be followed.

'Henry VII on his Great Seal uses as ornaments for the crown, crosses-patée alternatively with fleurs-de-lis, and also arches with an orb and cross at the top (633) and, on some of his coins, he reverts to the three fleurs-de-lis with points between them, arches being still used, with the orb and cross at the top (634). An ornamental form of crown bearing five ornamental leaves alternately large and small, with arches, orb, and cross at the top (635), occurs on the shillings of Henry VII. On the crowns of Henry VIII, as well as upon his Great Seals, the alternate crosses-patée and fleurs-de-lis are found on the rim of the crown, which is arched, and has an orb and cross at the top, and this is the form that has remained ever since (636). So we may consider that the growth of the ornament on the rim of the crown has followed a regular sequence from the points with one pearl at the top, of Æthelstan, to the trefoil of Canute; the arches began with Edward the Confessor, and the centre trefoil turned into the cross-patée of Henry VI. The fact that the remaining trefoils turned eventually into fleurs-de-lis is only, I think, a natural expansion of form, and does not appear to have had anything to do with the French fleur-de-lis, which was adopted as an heraldic bearing for an entirely different reason. The Royal coat of arms of England did bear for a long time in one of its quarterings the actual fleurs-de-lis of France, and this, no doubt, has given some reason to the idea that the fleurs-de-lis on the crown had also something to do with France; but as a matter of fact they had existed on the crown of England long anterior to our use of them on the coat of arms, as well as remaining there subsequently to their discontinuance on our Royal escutcheon.

'The cross-patée itself may possibly have been evolved in a somewhat similar way from the three pearls of William I, as we often find the centre trefoil, into which, as we have seen, these three points eventually turned, has a tendency to become larger than the others, and this difference has been easily made more apparent by squaring the ends of the triple leaf. At the same time it must not be forgotten that the cross-patée was actually used on the sceptre of Edward the Confessor, so it is just possible it may have had some specially English significance.

637.

'I have already mentioned that as well as the official crown of England, which alone I have just been describing, there has often been a second or State crown, and this, although it has in general design followed the pattern of the official crown, has been much more elaborately ornamented, and in it has been set and reset the few historic gems possessed by our nation. The fact that these State crowns have in turn been denuded of their jewels accounts for the fact that the old settings of some of them still exist.

638.

'Charles II's State Crown is figured in Sir Edward Walker's account of his coronation, but the illustration of it is of such an elementary character that little reliance can be placed on it; the actual setting of this crown, however—which was the one stolen by Colonel Blood on May 13, 1671—is now the property of Lord Amherst of Hackney, and the spaces from which the great ruby and the large sapphire—both of which are now in King Edward's State crown—have been taken are clearly seen (637). James II's State Crown, which is very accurately figured in Sandford's account of his coronation, and pieces of which are still in the Tower, also had this great ruby as its centre ornament (638). In Sir George Nayler's account of the coronation of George IV there is a figure of his so-called "new crown", the arches of which are composed of oak-leaf sprays with acorns, and the rim adorned with laurel sprays (639). The setting of this crown also belongs to Lord Amherst of Hackney, and so does another setting of a small State queen's crown, the ownership of which is doubtful. William IV appears to have had a very beautiful State crown, with arches of laurel sprays and a cross at the top with large diamonds. It is figured in Robson's *British Herald*, published in 1830 (640).

639.

640.

'There is one other crown of great interest, which, since the time of James Sixth of Scotland and First of England, forms part of our regalia. This is the crown of Scotland, and is the most ancient piece of State jewellery of which we can boast.

'Edward I, after his defeat of John Baliol in 1296, carried off the crown of Scotland to England, and Robert Bruce had another made for himself. This in its turn, after Bruce's defeat at Methven, fell into Edward's hands. Another crown seems to have been made for Bruce in 1314, when he was established in the sovereignty of Scotland after Bannockburn, and the present crown probably consists largely of the material of the old one, and most likely follows its general design. It has, however, much French work about it, as well as the rougher gold work made by Scottish jewellers, and it seems probable that the crown, as it now is, is a reconstruction by French workmen, made under the care and by order of James V about 1540. It was with this crown that Queen Mary was crowned when she was nine months old.

'In 1661 the Scottish regalia were considered to be in danger from the English, and were sent to Dunnottar Castle for safety. From 1707 until 1818 they were locked up in a strong chest in the Crown-Room of Edinburgh Castle, and Sir Walter Scott, in whose presence the box was opened, wrote an account of them in 1810. The crown consists of a fillet of gold bordered with flat wire. Upon it are twenty-two large stones set at equal distances, *i.e.* nine carbuncles, four jacinths, four amethysts, two white topazes, two crystals with green foil behind them, and one topaz with yellow foil. Behind each of these gems is a gold plate, with bands above and below of white enamel with black spots, and between each stone is a pearl. Above the band are ten jewelled rosettes and ten fleurs-de-lis alternately, and between each a pearl. Under the rosettes and fleurs-de-lis are jewels of blue enamel and pearls alternately. The arches have enamelled leaves of French work in red and gold upon them, and the mount at the top is of blue enamel studded with gold stars. The cross at the top is black enamel with gold arabesque patterns; in the centre is an amethyst, and in this cross and in the corners are Oriental pearls set in gold. At the back of the cross are the letters I. R. V. in enamel-work. On the velvet cap are four large pearls in settings of gold and enamel (641).

641.

'Generally, the Scottish work in gold is cast solid and chased, the foreign work being thinner and *repoussé*. Several of the diamonds are undoubtedly old, and are cut in the ancient Oriental fashion; and many of the pearls are Scottish. It is kept in Edinburgh Castle with the rest of the Scottish regalia. None of the other pieces at all equal it in interest, as with the exception of the coronation ring of Charles I they are of foreign workmanship, or, at all events, have been so altered that there is little or no original work left upon them.'

Very few people are aware, when they speak of the crown of England, that there are two crowns. The one is the official crown, the sign and symbol of the sovereigns of England. This is known by the name of St Edward's Crown, and is never altered or changed. As to this Mr Cyril Davenport writes:

'St Edward's crown was made for the coronation of Charles II in 1662, by Sir Robert Vyner. It was ordered to be made as nearly as possible after the old pattern, and the designs of it that have been already mentioned as existing in the works of Sir Edward Walker and Francis Sandford show that in a sensual form it was the same as now; indeed, the existing crown is in all probability mainly composed of the same materials as that made by Sir Robert. The crown consists of a rim or circlet of gold, adorned with rosettes of precious stones surrounded with diamonds, and set upon enamel arabesques of white and red. The centre gems of these rosettes are rubies, emeralds, and sapphires. Rows of large pearls mark the upper and lower edges of the rim, from which rise the four crosses-patée and four fleurs-de-lis alternately, adorned with diamonds and other gems. The gem clusters upon the crosses are set upon enamel arabesques in white and red, of similar workmanship to that upon the rim. From the tops of the crosses rise two complete arches of gold crossing each other, and curving deeply downwards at the point of intersection. The arches are considered to be the mark of independent sovereignty. They are edged with rows of large pearls, and have gems and clusters of gems upon them set in arabesques of red and white, like those upon the crosses. From the intersection of the arches springs a mound of gold, encircled by a fillet from which rises a single arch, both of which are ornamented with pearls and gems. On the top of the arch is a cross-patée of gold, set in which are coloured gems and diamonds. At the top of the cross is a large

268

spheroidal pearl, and from each of the side arms, depending from a little gold bracelet, is a beautifully formed pear-shaped pearl. The crown is shown in the Tower with the crimson velvet cap, turned up with miniver, which would be worn with it.

'This crown is very large, but whether it is actually worn or not it would always be present at the coronation, as it is the "official" crown of England.'

St Edward's crown is the crown supposed to be heraldically represented when for State or official purposes the crown is represented over the Royal Arms or other insignia. In this the fleurs-de-lis upon the rim are only half fleurs-de-lis. This detail is scrupulously adhered to, but during the reign of Queen Victoria many of the other details were very much 'at the mercy' of the artist. Soon after the accession of King Edward VII the matter was brought under consideration, and the opportunity afforded by the issue of a War Office Sealed Pattern of the Royal Crown and Cypher for use in the army was taken advantage of to notify his Majesty's pleasure, that for official purposes the Royal Crown should be as shown in 642, which is a reproduction of the War Office Sealed Pattern already mentioned.[175] It should be noted that whilst the cap of the real crown is of *purple* velvet, the cap of the *heraldic* crown is *always* represented as of crimson.

642 *Royal Crown.*

The second crown is what is known as the 'Imperial State Crown'. This is the one which is actually worn, and which the Sovereign after the ceremony of his coronation wears in the procession from the Abbey. It is also carrried before the Sovereign at the opening of Parliament.[176] Whilst the gems which are set in it are national property, the crown is usually remade for each successive sovereign. The following is Mr Davenport's description of Queen Victoria's State Crown:

'This beautiful piece of jewellery was made by Roundell & Bridge in 1838. Many of the gems in it are old ones reset, and many of them are new. The entire weight of the crown is 39 ozs. 5 dwts. It consists of a circlet of open work in silver, bearing in the front the great sapphire from the crown of Charles II which was bequeathed to George III by Cardinal York, with other Stuart treasure. At one end this gem is partly pierced. It is not a thick stone, but it is a fine colour. Opposite to the large sapphire is one of smaller size. The remainder of the rim is filled in with rich jewel clusters having alternately sapphires and emeralds in their centres, enclosed in ornamental borders thickly set with diamonds. These clusters are separated from each other by trefoil designs also thickly set with diamonds. The rim is bordered above and below with bands of large pearls, 129 in the lower row, and 112 in the upper. [The crown as remade for King Edward VII included 139 pearls in the lower row, and 122 in the upper.] Above the rim are shallow festoons of diamonds caught up between the larger ornaments by points of emeralds encircled with diamonds, and a large pearl above each. On these festoons

175. The present Queen has adopted a new design for the heraldic crown. This first appeared in conjunction with the Royal Cypher in May 1952; later it was shown in the approved representations of the royal arms. It has depressed arches, and more closely resembles St Edward's crown than that used in the three previous reigns (X). A feature of this crown which designers often miss is that there should be nine pearls on each of the outer arches and five showing on the front arch.
176. In fact the Sovereign wears the crown at the opening of Parliament. It arrives at the Palace of Westminster in a guarded coach, but spot-lit so that all can see it. It is then placed on a table in the Royal Gallery by the Lord Great Chamberlain, where it is guarded by the Yeomen of the Guard until it is taken to the robing room for the Sovereign to wear.

X *Royal Crown.*

are set alternately eight crosses-patée, and eight fleurs-de-lis of silver set with gems. The crosses-patée are thickly set with brilliants, and have each an emerald in the centre, except that in front of the crown, which contains the most remarkable jewel belonging to the regalia. This is a large spinal ruby of irregular drop-like form, measuring about 2 ins in length, and is highly polished on what is probably its natural surface, or nearly so. Its irregular outline makes it possible to recognise the place that it has formerly occupied in the older State crowns, and it seems always to have been given the place of honour. It is pierced after an Oriental fashion, and the top of the piercing is filled with a supplementary ruby set in gold. Don Pedro, King of Castille in 1367, murdered the King of Granada for the sake of his jewels, one of which was this stone, and Don Pedro is said to have given it to Edward the Black Prince after the battle of Najera, near Vittoria, in the same year. After this, it is said to have been worn by Henry V in his crown at Agincourt in 1415, when it is recorded that the King's life was saved from the attack of the Duc D'Alençon, because of the protection afforded him by his crown, a portion of which, however, was broken off. It may be confidently predicted that such a risk of destruction is not very likely to happen again to the great ruby.

'In the centre of each of the very ornamental fleurs-de-lis is a ruby, and all the rest of the ornamentation on them is composed of rose diamonds, large and small. From each of the crosses-patée, the upper corners of which have each a large pearl upon them, rises an arch of silver worked into a design of oak-leaves and acorn-cups. These leaves and cups are all closely encrusted with a mass of large and small diamonds, rose brilliant, and table-cut; the acorns themselves formed of beautiful drop-shaped pearls of large size. From the four points of intersection of the arches at the top of the crown depend large egg-shaped pearls. From the centre of the arches, which slope slightly downwards, springs a mound with a cross-patée above it. The mound is ornamented all over with close lines of brilliant diamonds, and the fillet which encircles it, and the arch which crosses over it, are both ornamented with one line of large rose-cut diamonds set closely together. The cross-patée at the top has in the centre a large sapphire of magnificent colour set openly. The outer lines of the arms of the cross are marked by a row of small diamonds close together and in the centre of each arm is a large diamond, the remaining spaces being filled with more small diamonds. The large sapphire in the centre of this cross is said to have come out of the ring of Edward the Confessor, which was buried with him in his shrine at Westminster, and the possession of it is supposed to give to the owner the power of curing the cramp. If this be indeed the stone which belonged to St Edward, it was probably recut in its present form of a "rose" for Charles II, even if not since his time.

'Not counting the large ruby or the large sapphire, this crown contains: Four rubies, eleven emeralds, sixteen sapphires, 277 pearls, 2783 diamonds. [As remade for King Edward VII the crown included 297 pearls and 2818 diamonds.]

'The large ruby has been valued at £110,000.

'When this crown has to take a journey it is provided with a little casket, lined with white velvet, and having a sliding drawer at the bottom, with a boss on which the crown fits closely, so that it is safe from slipping. The velvet cap turned up with miniver, with which it is worn, is kept with it.'

This crown was last remade for King George VI, but has not been altered in any essential details. The cap of the *real* crown is of purple velvet.

643 represents the crown of the Queen Consort with which Queen Alexandra was crowned on 9 August, 1902. It will be noticed that, unlike the King's crowns, this has eight arches. The circlet which forms the base is 1½ inches in height. The crown is entirely composed of diamonds, of which there are 3972, and these are placed so closely together that no metal remains visible. The large diamond visible in the illustration is the famous Koh-i-noor. Resting upon the rim are four crosses-patée, and as many fleurs-de-lis, from each of which springs an arch. As a matter of actual fact the crown was made for use on this one occasion and has since been broken up.

643 *Queen Alexandra's Coronation Crown.*

There is yet another crown, probably the one with which we are most familiar. This is a small crown entirely composed of diamonds: and the earliest heraldic use which can be found of it is in the design by Sir Edgar Boehm for the 1887 Jubilee coinage. Though effective enough when worn, it does not, from its small size, lend itself effectively to pictorial representation, and as will be remembered, the design of the 1887 coinage was soon abandoned. This crown was made at the personal expense of Queen Victoria, and under her instructions, owing to the fact that the Queen felt that her 'State' crown was uncomfortable to wear, and too heavy for prolonged or general use. It is understood, also, that the Queen found the regulations concerning its custody both inconvenient and irritating. During the later part of her reign this smaller crown was the only one Queen Victoria ever wore. By her will the crown was settled as an heirloom upon Queen Alexandra, to devolve upon future Queens Consort for the time being. This being the case, it is not unlikely that in the future this crown may come to be regarded as a part of the national regalia, and it is as well, therefore, to reiterate the remark, that it was made at the personal expense of her late Majesty, and is to no extent and in no way the property of the nation.

644 *Coronet of Thomas Fitz Alan, Earl of Arundel. (From his monument in Arundel Church, 1415.)*

Coronets of rank

In spite of various Continental edicts, the heraldic use of coronets of rank, as also their actual use, seems elsewhere than in Great Britain to be governed by no such strict regulations as are laid down and conformed to in this country. For this reason, no less than for the greater interest these must necessarily possess for readers in this country, English coronets will first claim our attention. It has been already observed that coronets or jewelled fillets are to be found upon the helmets even of simple knights from the earliest periods. They probably served no more than decorative purposes, unless these fillets be merely turbans, or suggestions thereof. As late as the fifteenth century there appears to have been no regularised form, as will be seen from 644, which represents the coronet as shown upon the effigy of Thomas FitzAlan, Earl of Arundel, in Arundel Church (1415). A very similar coronet surmounts the head-dress of the effigy of Beatrice, Countess of Arundel, at the same period. In his will, Lionel, Duke of Clarence (1368), bequeaths 'two golden circles', with one of which he was created Duke. It is of interest to compare this with 645, which represents the crown of King Henry IV as represented on his effigy. Richard, Earl of Arundel, in his will (December 5

645 *Crown of King Henry IV (1399–1413). (From his monument in Trinity Chapel, Canterbury Cathedral.)*

271

1375), leaves his 'melieure coronne' to his eldest son Richard, his 'second melieure coronne' to his daughter Alice. Though not definite proof of the point, the fact that the earl distributes his coronets amongst his family, irrespective of the fact that the earldom (of which one would presume the coronets to be a sign) would pass to his son, would seem to show that the wearing of a coronet even at that date was merely indicative of high nobility of birth, and not of the possession of a substantive Parliamentary peerage. In spite of the variations in form, coronets were, however, a necessity. When both dukes and earls were created they were invested with a coronet in open Parliament. As time went on the coronet, however, gradually came to be considered the sign of the possession of a peerage, and was so borne; but it was not until the reign of Charles II that coronets were definitely assigned by Royal Warrant (19 February, 1660) to peers not of the Blood Royal.[177] Before this date a coronet had not (as has been already stated) been used heraldically or in fact by barons, who, both in armorial paintings and in Parliament, had used a plain crimson cap turned up with white fur.

The former coronet of the Prince of Wales is exactly like the official (St Edward's) crown, except that instead of two intersecting arches it has only one. An illustration of this is given in 646 (this being the usual form in which it is heraldically depicted). It should be noticed, however, that this coronet belongs to the prince as eldest son of the Sovereign and heir-apparent to the Throne, and not as Prince of Wales. It was assigned by Royal Warrant 9 February, 13 Charles II. The coronet of the Princess of Wales, as such, is heraldically the same as that of her husband.

The coronet of the sons and daughters or brothers and sisters of a sovereign of Great Britain (other than a Prince of Wales) is as in 647, that is, the circlet being identical with that of the Royal Crown, and of the Prince of Wales' coronet, but without the arch. This was also assigned in the warrant of 9 February, 13 Charles II. Officially this coronet is described as being composed of crosses-patée and fleurs-de-lis alternately.

The grandchildren of a sovereign being sons and daughters of the Prince of Wales, or of other sons of the sovereign, have a coronet in which strawberry leaves are substituted for the two outer crosses-patée appearing at the edges of the coronet, which is officially described as composed of crosses-patée, fleurs-de-lis, and strawberry leaves.

Princes of the English Royal Family, being sons of younger sons of a sovereign, or else nephews of a sovereign being sons of brothers of a sovereign, and having the rank and title of a duke of the United Kingdom, have a coronet composed alternately of crosses-patée and strawberry leaves, the latter taking the place of the fleurs-de-lis upon the circlet of the Royal Crown. This coronet was also assigned in the warrant of 9 February, 13 Charles II.

It will be observed by those who compare one heraldic book with another that I have quoted these rules differently from any other work upon the subject. A moment's thought, however, must convince any one of the accuracy of my

646 *Former coronet of the Prince of Wales.*

647 *Coronet of the younger children of the Sovereign.*

177. I cannot locate this warrant, but a late Elizabethan manuscript in the Vincent Collection at the College of Arms (Vincent 172) details the coronets of dukes, marquesses, earls and viscounts. These are in most respects the same as today. Barons had no coronets until a Royal Warrant of King Charles II dated 7 August 1660 assigned the coronet at present used by barons to 'Barons of England'.

version. It is a cardinal rule of armory that save for the single circumstance of attainder no man's armorial insignia shall be degraded. Whilst any man's status may be increased, it cannot be lessened. Most heraldic books quote the coronet of crosses-patée, fleurs-de-lis, and strawberry leaves as the coronet of the 'grandsons' of the sovereign, whilst the coronet of crosses-patée and strawberry leaves is stated to be the coronet of 'nephews' or cousins of the sovereign. Such a state of affairs would be intolerable, because it would mean the liability at any moment to be degraded to the use of a less honourable coronet. Take, for example, the case of Prince Arthur of Connaught. During the lifetime of Queen Victoria, as a grandson of the sovereign he would be entitled to the former, whereas as soon as King Edward ascended the throne he would have been forced to relinquish it in favour of the more remote form.

The real truth is that the members of the Royal Family do not inherit these coronets as a matter of course. They technically and in fact have no coronets until these have been assigned by Royal Warrant with the arms. When such warrants are issued, the coronets assigned have up to the present time conformed to the above rules. I am not sure that the 'rules' now exist in any more potent form than that up to the present time those particular patterns happen to have been assigned in the circumstances stated. But the warrants (though they contain no hereditary limitation) certainly contain no clause limiting their operation to the lifetime of the then sovereign, which they certainly would do if the coronet only existed whilst the particular relationship continued.

The coronets only apply to the children of princes. The children of princesses are not technically members of the Royal Family, nor do they inherit either rank or coronet from their mothers.

By a curious fatality there has never, since these Royal coronets were differentiated, been any male descendant of an English sovereign more remotely related than a nephew, with the exception of the Dukes of Cumberland. Their succession to the throne of Hanover rendered them useless as a precedent, inasmuch as their right to arms and coronet must be derived from Hanover and its laws, and not from this country. The Princess Frederica of Hanover, however, used an English coronet and the Royal Arms of England, presumably preferring her status as a princess of this country to whatever *de jure* Hanoverian status might be claimed. It is much to be wished that a Royal Warrant should be issued which would decide the point—at present in doubt—as to what degree of relationship the coronet of the crosses-patée and strawberry leaves is available for, or failing that coronet what the coronet of prince or princess of this country might be, he or she not being child, grandchild, or nephew or niece of a sovereign.[178]

178. By a royal warrant dated 19 November 1917 the following royal coronets were assigned. The use of the coronet appropriate to sons and brothers of the sovereign (four crosses patée and four fleurs-de-lis) was extended to include daughters and sisters of the sovereign. A coronet composed of two strawberry leaves, two crosses patée and four fleurs-de-lis was assigned to the sons and daughters of the son and heir apparent (Y). A coronet composed for four crosses patée and four strawberry leaves, which heretofore had been used by sons of sons and brothers of the sovereign being dukes, was further assigned to sons (not being dukes) and daughters of sons (other than the heir apparent) and brothers of the sovereign (Z). Sons and daughters of daughters of the sovereign were assigned a coronet composed of four fleur-de-lis and four strawberry leaves (AA). Apart from the above there have also been one or two warrants conferring an *ad hoc* coronet.

Y *Coronet of Sons and Daughters of the Heir-Apparent.*

Z *Coronet of Sons and Daughters of Sons and Brothers (other than the Heir-Apparent) of the Sovereign.*

AA *Coronet of Sons and Daughters of Daughters of the Sovereign.*

The unique use of actual coronets in England at the occasion of each coronation ceremony has prevented them becoming (as in so many other countries) mere pictured heraldic details. Consequently the instructions concerning them which are issued prior to each coronation will be of interest. The following is from the *London Gazette* of October 1, 1901:

'EARL MARSHAL'S OFFICE,
NORFOLK HOUSE, ST JAMES'S SQUARE, S.W.,
October 1, 1901.

'The Earl Marshal's Order concerning the Robes, Coronets, &c., which are to be worn by the Peers at the Coronation of Their Most Sacred Majesties King Edward the Seventh and Queen Alexandra.

'These are to give notice to all Peers who attend at the Coronation of Their Majesties, that the robe or mantle of the Peers be of crimson velvet, edged with miniver, the cape furred with miniver pure, and powdered with bars or rows of ermine (*i.e.* narrow pieces of black fur), according to their degree, viz.:

'Barons, two rows.

'Viscounts, two rows and a half.

'Earls, three rows.

'Marquesses, three rows and a half.

'Dukes, four rows.

'The said mantles or robes to be worn over full Court dress, uniform, or regimentals.

'The coronets to be of silver-gilt; the caps of crimson velvet turned up with ermine, with a gold tassel on the top; and no jewels or precious stones are to be set or used in the coronets, or counterfeit pearls instead of silver balls.

'The coronet of a Baron to have, on the circle or rim, six silver balls at equal distances.

'The coronet of a Viscount to have, on the circle, sixteen silver balls.

'The coronet of an Earl to have, on the circle, eight silver balls, raised upon points, with gold strawberry leaves between the points.

'The coronet of a Marquess to have, on the circle, four gold strawberry leaves and four silver balls alternately, the latter a little raised on points above the rim.

'The coronet of a Duke to have, on the circle, eight gold strawberry leaves.

'By His Majesty's Command,
'NORFOLK, *Earl Marshal.*'

'EARL MARSHAL'S OFFICE,
NORFOLK HOUSE, ST JAMES'S SQUARE, S.W.,
October 1, 1901.

'The Earl Marshal's Order concerning the Robes, Coronets, &c., which are to be worn by the Peeresses at the Coronation of Their Most Sacred Majesties King Edward the Seventh and Queen Alexandra.

'These are to give notice to all Peeresses who attend at the Coronation of Their Majesties, that the robes or mantles appertaining to their respective ranks are to be worn over the usual full Court dress.

'That the robe or mantle of a Baroness be of crimson velvet, the cape whereof to be furred with miniver pure, and powdered with two bars or rows of ermine (*i.e.* narrow pieces of black fur); the said mantle to be edged round with miniver pure 2 inches in breadth, and the train to be 3 feet on the ground; the coronet to be according to her degree—viz. a rim or circle with six pearls (represented by silver balls) upon the same, not raised upon points.

'That the robe or mantle of a Viscountess be like that of a Baroness, only the cape powdered with two rows and a half of ermine, the edging of the mantle 2 inches as before, and the train 1¼ yards; the coronet to be according to her degree—viz. a rim or circle with pearls (represented by silver balls) thereon, sixteen in number, and not raised upon points.

'That the robe or mantle of a Countess be as before, only the cape powdered with three rows of ermine, the edging 3 inches in breadth, and the train 1½ yards; the coronet to be composed of eight pearls (represented by silver balls) raised upon points or rays, with small strawberry leaves between, above the rim.

'That the robe or mantle of a Marchioness be as before, only the cape powdered with three rows and a half of ermine, the edging 4 inches in breadth, the train 1¾ yards; the coronet to be composed of four strawberry leaves and four pearls (represented by silver balls) raised upon points of the same height as the leaves, alternately, above the rim.

'That the robe or mantle of a Duchess be as before, only the cape powdered with four rows of ermine, the edging 5 inches broad, the train 2 yards; the coronet to be composed of eight strawberry leaves, all of equal height, above the rim.

'And that the caps of all the said coronets be of crimson velvet, turned up with ermine, with a tassel of gold on the top.

'By His Majesty's Command,

'NORFOLK, *Earl Marshal.*'

648.

The Coronation Robe of a peer is not identical with his Parliamentary Robe of Estate. This latter is of fine scarlet cloth, lined with taffeta. The distinction between the degrees of rank is effected by the guards or bands of fur. The robe of a duke has four guards of *ermine* at equal distances, with gold lace above each guard and tied up to the left shoulder by a white riband. The robe of a marquess has four guards of *ermine* on the right side, and three on the left, with gold lace above each guard and tied up to the left shoulder by a white riband. An earl's robe has three guards of *ermine and gold lace.* The robes of a viscount and baron are identical, each having two guards of plain *white fur.*

649.

By virtue of various warrants of Earls Marshal, duly recorded in the College of Arms, the use or display of a coronet of rank by any person other than a peer is stringently forbidden. This rule, unfortunately, is too often ignored by many eldest sons of peers, who use peerage titles by courtesy.

The heraldic representations of these coronets of rank are as follows:

The coronet of a duke shows five strawberry leaves (648). This coronet should not be confused with the ducal *crest* coronet.

The coronet of a marquess shows two balls of silver technically known as 'pearls', and three strawberry leaves (649).

The coronet of an earl shows five 'pearls' raised on tall spikes, alternating with four strawberry leaves (650).

650.

275

651.

652.

653 *The Crown
of a King of Arms.*

654 *Mauerkrone.*

655 *Naval crown.*

The coronet of a viscount shows nine 'pearls', all set closely together, directly upon the circlet (651).

The coronet of a baron shows four 'pearls' upon the circlet (652). This coronet was assigned by Royal Warrant, dated 7 August 12 Charles II, to Barons of England, and to Barons of Ireland by warrant, 16 May 5 James II.

All coronets of degree actually, and are usually represented to, enclose a cap of crimson velvet, turned up with ermine. None of them are permitted to be jewelled, but the coronet of a duke, marquess, earl, or viscount is chased in the form of jewels. In recent times, however, it has become very usual for peers to use, heraldically, for more informal purposes a representation of the circlet only, omitting the cap and the ermine edging.

The crown or coronet of a king of arms (653) is of silver-gilt formed of a circlet, upon which is inscribed part of the first verse of the 51st Psalm, viz.: 'Miserere mei Deus secundum magnam misericordiam tuam.' The rim is surmounted with sixteen leaves, in shape resembling the oak-leaf, every alternate one being somewhat higher than the rest, nine of which appear in the profile view of it or in heraldic representations. The cap is of crimson satin, closed at the top by a gold tassel and turned up with ermine.

Anciently, the crown of Lyon King of Arms was, in shape, an exact replica of the crown of the King of Scotland, the only difference being that it was not jewelled.

Coronets of rank are used very indiscriminately on the Continent, particularly in France and the Low Countries. Their use by no means implies the same as with us, and frequently indicates little if anything beyond mere 'noble' birth.

The *Mauerkrone* [mural crown] (654) is used in Germany principally as an adornment to the arms of towns. It is borne with three, four, or five battlemented towers. The tincture, likewise, is not always the same: gold, silver, red, or the natural colour of a wall being variously employed. Residential [*i.e.* having a *royal* residence] and capital towns usually bear a Mauerkrone with five towers, large towns one with four towers, smaller towns one with three. Strict regulations in the matter do not yet exist. It should be carefully noted that this practice is peculiar to Germany and is quite incorrect in Great Britain.

The *Naval Crown* [Schiffskrone] (655), on the circlet of which sails and sterns of ships are alternately introduced, is very rarely used on the Continent. With us it appears as a charge in the arms of the towns of Chatham, Ramsgate, Devonport, &c. The Naval Coronet, however, is more properly a crest coronet, and as such will be more fully considered in the next chapter. It had, however, a limited use as a coronet of rank at one time, inasmuch as the admirals of the United Provinces of the Netherlands placed a crown composed of prows of ships above their escutcheons, as may be seen from various monuments.

PLATE VII

The Arms of Edinburgh

23 · Crest coronets and chapeaux

The present official rules are that crests must be upon, or must issue from, a wreath (or torse), a coronet, or a chapeau. It is not at the pleasure of the wearer to choose which he will, one or other being specified and included in the terms of the grant. If the crest have a lawful existence, one or other of them will unchangeably belong to the crest, of which it now is considered to be an integral part.

In Scotland and Ireland, Lyon King of Arms and Ulster King of Arms have always been considered to have, and still retain, the right to grant crests upon a chapeau or issuing from a coronet. But the power is (very properly) exceedingly sparingly used; and, except in the cases of arms and crests matriculated in Lyon Register as of ancient origin and in use before 1672, or 'confirmed' on the strength of user by Ulster King of Arms, the ordinary ducal crest coronet and the chapeau are not now considered proper to be granted in ordinary cases.

Since about the beginning of the nineteenth century the rules which follow have been very definite, and have been very rigidly adhered to in the English College of Arms.

Crests issuing from the ordinary 'ducal crest coronet' are not now granted under any circumstances. The chapeau is only granted in the case of a grant of arms to a peer, a mural coronet is only granted to officers in the army of the rank of general or above, and the naval coronet is only granted to officers in his Majesty's Royal Navy of the rank of admiral and above. An Eastern coronet is now only granted in the case of those of high position in one or other of the Imperial Services, who have served in India and the East.

The granting of crests issuing from the other forms of crest coronets, the 'Crown Vallary' and the 'Palisado Crown', is always discouraged, but no rule exists denying them to applicants, and they are to be obtained if the expectant grantee is sufficiently patient, importunate, and pertinacious. Neither form is, however, particularly ornamental, and both are of modern origin.[179]

There is still yet another coronet, the 'celestial coronet'. This is not unusual as a charge, but as a coronet from which a crest issues I know of no instance, nor am I aware of what rules, if any, govern the granting of it.[180]

179. This is a curious remark in view of the fact that the badge granted to Fox-Davies includes the 'not particularly ornamental' crown vallary.
180. I know of no rules governing the use of what is usually termed a 'celestial crown' rather than a 'celestial coronet'. An example of a crest issuing from such a crown is afforded by the crest of Stockton-on-Tees granted in 1951: within a celestial crown gules, a wheatsheaf or.

Definite rank coronets have been in times past granted for use as crest coronets, but this practice, the propriety of which cannot be considered as other than highly questionable, has only been pursued, even in the more lax days which are past, on rare and very exceptional occasions, and has long since been definitely abandoned as improper.

In considering the question of crest coronets, the presumption that they originated from coronets of rank at once jumps to the mind. This is by no means a foregone conclusion. It is difficult to say what is the earliest instance of the use of a coronet in this country as a coronet of rank. When it is remembered that the coronet of a baron had no existence whatever until it was called into being by a warrant of Charles II after the Restoration, and that differentiated coronets for the several ranks in the Peerage are not greatly anterior in date, the question becomes distinctly complicated. From certainly the reign of Edward the Confessor the kings of England had worn crowns, and the great territorial earls, who it must be remembered occupied a position akin to that of a petty sovereign (far beyond the mere high dignity of a great noble at the present day), from an early period wore crowns or coronets not greatly differing in appearance from the crown of the king. But the Peerage as such certainly neither had nor claimed the technical right to a coronet as a mark of their rank, in the thirteenth and fourteenth centuries. But coronets of a kind were used, as can be seen from early effigies, long before the use of crests became general. But these coronets were merely in the nature of a species of decoration for the helmet, many of them far more closely resembling a jewelled torse than a coronet. Parker in his *Glossary of Terms used in Heraldry* probably correctly represents the case when he states: 'From the reign of Edward III coronets of various forms were worn (as it seems indiscriminately) by princes, dukes, earls, and even knights, but apparently rather by way of ornament than distinction, or if for distinction, only (like the collar of SS) as a mark of gentility. The helmet of Edward the Black Prince, upon his effigy at Canterbury, is surrounded with a coronet totally different from that subsequently assigned to his rank.'

The instance quoted by Parker might be amplified by countless others, but it may here with advantage be pointed out that the great helmet (or, as this probably is, the ceremonial representation of it) suspended above the Prince's tomb (271) has no coronet, and the crest is upon a chapeau. Of the fourteen instances in the Plantagenet Garter plates in which the *torse* appears, twelve were peers of England, one was a foreign count, and one only a commoner. On the other hand, of twenty-nine whose Garter plates show crests issuing from coronets, four are foreigners, seven are commoners, and eighteen were peers. The coronets show very great variations in form and design, but such variations appear quite capricious, and to carry no meaning, nor does it seem probable that a coronet of gules or of azure, of which there are ten, could represent a coronet of rank. The Garter plate of Sir William De la Pole, Earl of (afterwards Duke of) Suffolk, shows his crest upon a narrow black fillet. Consequently, whatever may be the conclusion as to the wearing of coronets alone, it would seem to be a very certain conclusion that the heraldic crest coronet bore no relation to any coronet of rank or to the right to wear one. Its adoption must have been in the original instance, and probably even in subsequent generations, a matter of pure fancy and inclination. This is borne out by the fact that whilst the Garter plate of Sir Henry Bourchier, Earl of Essex, shows his crest upon a torse, his effigy represents it issuing from a coronet.

Until the reign of Henry VIII, the Royal crest, both in the case of the sovereign and all the other members of the Royal Family, is always represented upon a chapeau or cap of dignity. The Great Seal of Edward VI shows the crest upon a coronet, though the present form of crown and crest were originated by Queen Elizabeth. In depicting the Royal Arms, it is usual to omit one of the crowns, and this is always done in the official warrants controlling the arms. One crown is placed upon the helmet, and upon this crown is placed the crest, but theoretically the Royal achievement has two crowns, inasmuch as one of the crowns is an inseparable part of the crest. Probably the finest representation of the Royal crest which has ever been done is the design for one of the smaller bookplates for the Windsor Castle Library. This was executed by Mr Eve, and it would be impossible to imagine anything finer.[181] Like the rest of the Royal achievement, the Royal crest is of course not hereditary, and consequently it is assigned by a *separate* Royal Warrant to each male member of the Royal Family, and the opportunity is then taken to substitute for the Royal crown, which is a part of the sovereign's crest, a coronet identical with whatever may be assigned in that particular instance as the coronet of rank. In the case of Royal bastards the crest has always been assigned upon a chapeau.

The only case which comes to one's mind in which the Royal crown has (outside the sovereign) been allowed as a crest coronet is the case of the town of Eye.

The Royal crown of Scotland is the crest coronet of the sovereign's crest for the kingdom of Scotland. This crest, together with the crest of Ireland, is never assigned to any member of the Royal Family except the sovereign. The crest of Ireland (which is on a wreath or and azure) is by the way confirmatory evidence that the crowns in the crests of Scotland and England have a duplicate and separate existence apart from the crown denoting the sovereignty of the realm.

The ordinary crest coronet or, as it is usually termed in British heraldry, the 'ducal coronet' (Ulster, however, describes it officially as 'a ducal crest coronet'), is quite a separate matter from a duke's coronet of rank. Whilst the coronet of a duke has upon the rim five strawberry leaves visible when depicted, a ducal coronet has only three. The 'ducal coronet' (656) is the conventional 'regularised' development of the crest coronets employed in early times.

656 *Ducal coronet.*

Unfortunately it has in many instances been depicted of a much greater and very unnecessary width, the result being inartistic and allowing unnecessary space between the leaves, and at the same time leaving the crest and coronet with little circumferential relation. It should be noted that it is quite incorrect for the rim of the coronet to be jewelled in colour though the outline of jewelling is indicated.

Though ducal crest coronets are no longer granted (of course they are still exemplified and their use permitted where they have been previously granted), they are of very frequent occurrence in older grants and confirmations.

181. Whilst the excellence of Mr Eve's work is beyond question, there have been several fine heraldic artists since his time, the most noted of the elder generation today being Mr Gerald Cobb, M.V.O., F.S.A.

It is quite incorrect to depict a cap (as in a coronet of rank) in a crest coronet, which is never more than the metal circlet, and consequently it is equally incorrect to add the band of ermine below it which will sometimes be seen.

The coronet of a duke has in one or two isolated cases been granted as a crest coronet. In such a case it is not described as a duke's coronet, but as a 'ducal coronet of five leaves'. It so occurs in the case of Ormsby-Hamilton.

The colour of the crest coronet must be stated in the blazon. Crest coronets are of all colours, and will be sometimes found bearing charges upon the rim (particularly in the cases of mural and naval coronets). An instance of this will be seen in the case of Sir John W. Moore, and of Mansergh, the label in this latter case being an unalterable charge and not the difference mark of an eldest son. Though the tincture of the coronet ought to appear in the blazon, nevertheless it is always a fair presumption (when it is not specified) that it is of gold, coronets of colours being very much less frequently met with. On this point it is interesting to note that in some of the cases where the crest coronet is figured upon an early Garter plate as of colour, it is now borne gold by the present descendants of the family. For example on the Garter plate of Sir Walter Hungerford, Lord Hungerford, the crest ['A garb or, between two silver sickles'] issues from a coronet azure. The various Hungerford families now bear it 'or'. The crest upon the Garter plate of Sir Humphrey Stafford, Duke of Buckingham ['A demi-swan argent, beaked gules'], issues from a coronet gules. This crest as it is now borne by the present Lord Stafford is: 'Out of a ducal coronet per pale gules and sable,' &c.

Another instance of coloured coronets will be found in the crest of Nicholson, now borne by Shaw.★

Probably, however, the most curious instance of all will be found in the case of a crest coronet of ermine, of which an example occurs in the Gelre 'Armorial'.

A very general misconception—which will be found stated in practically every text-book of armory—is that when a crest issues from a coronet the wreath must be omitted. There is not and never has been any such rule. The rule is rather to the contrary. Instances where both occur are certainly now uncommon, and the presence of a wreath is not in present-day practice considered to be essential if a coronet occurs, but the use or absence of a wreath when the crest issues from a coronet really depends entirely upon the original grant. If no wreath is specified with the coronet, none will be used or needed, but if both are granted both should be used. An instance of the use of both will be found on the Garter Stall plate of Sir Walter Devereux, Lord Ferrers. The crest (a talbot's head silver) issues from a coronet or, which is placed upon a torse argent and sable. Another instance will be found in the case of the grant of the crest of Hanbury.[182]

A quite recent case was the grant by Sir Bernard Burke, Ulster King of Arms, of a crest to Sir Richard Quain, Bart, the blazon of which was: 'On a wreath argent and azure, and out of a mural coronet proper a demi-lion rampant or, charged on the shoulder with a trefoil slipped vert, and holding between the paws a battle-axe also proper, the blade gold.'

Other instances are the crests of Hamilton of Sunningdale and Tarleton.

182. It is now usual practice to include a torse, if for some particular reason a crest coronet is allowed.

★ Out of a ducal coronet gules, a lion's head ermine (Nicholson).

Another instance will be found in the grant to Ross-of-Bladensburg. Possibly this blazon may be a clerical error in the engrossment, because it will be noticed that the wreath does not appear in the emblazonment (Plate II).

I wonder how many of the officers of arms are aware of the existence of a warrant, dated in 1682, issued by the Deputy Earl-Marshal to the Companies of Painters, Stainers, and Coachmakers, forbidding them to paint crests which issue out of ducal coronets without putting them upon 'wreaths of their colours'. The wording of the warrant very plainly shows that at that date a wreath was always painted below a crest coronet. The warrant, however, is not so worded that it can be accepted as determining the point for the future, or that it would override a subsequent grant of a crest in contrary form. But it is evidence of what the law then was.

No crest is now granted without either wreath, coronet, or chapeau.

An instance of the use of the coronet of a marquess as a crest coronet will be found in the case of the Bentinck crest.*

There are some number of instances of the use of an earl's coronet as a crest coronet. Amongst these may be mentioned the crests of Sir Alan Seton Steuart, Bart. ['Out of an earl's coronet a dexter hand grasping a thistle all proper'], that granted to Cassan of Sheffield House, Ireland ['Issuant from an earl's coronet proper, a boar's head and neck erased or, langued gules'], James Christopher Fitzgerald Kenney, Esq., Dublin ['Out of an earl's coronet or, the pearls argent, a cubit arm erect vested gules, cuffed also argent, the hand grasping a roll of parchment proper'], and Davidson ['Out of an earl's coronet or, a dove rising argent, holding in the beak a wheat-stalk bladed and eared all proper'].

I know of no crest which issues from the coronet of a viscount, but a baron's coronet occurs in the case of Forbes of Pitsligo and the cadets of that branch of the family: 'Issuing out of a baron's coronet a dexter hand holding a scimitar all proper.'

Foreign coronets of rank have sometimes been granted as crest coronets in this country, as in the cases of the crests of Sir Francis George Manningham Boileau, Bart, Norfolk ['In a nest or, a pelican in her piety proper, charged on the breast with a saltire couped gules, the nest resting in a foreign coronet'], Henry Chamier, Esq., Dublin ['Out of a French noble coronet proper, a cubit arm in bend vested azure, charged with five fleurs-de-lis in saltire or, cuffed ermine, holding in the hand a scroll, and thereon an open book proper, garnished gold'], John Francis Charles Fane De Salis, Count of the Holy Roman Empire ['1. Out of a marquis' coronet or, a demi-woman proper, crowned or, hair flowing down the back, winged in place of arms and from the armpits azure; 2. out of a ducal coronet or, an eagle displayed sable, ducally crowned also or; 3. out of a ducal coronet a demi-lion rampant double-queued and crowned with a like coronet all or, brandishing a sword proper, hilt and pommel of the first, the lion cottised by two tilting-spears of the same, from each a banner paly of six argent and gules, fringed also or'], and Mahony, Ireland ['Out of the coronet of a Count of France a dexter arm in armour embowed grasping in the hand a sword all proper, hilt and pommel or, the blade piercing a fleur-de-lis of the last'].

* Crest of Bentinck: Out of a marquess's coronet proper, two arms counter-embowed, vested gules, on the hands gloves or, and in each hand an ostrich feather argent.

A curious crest coronet will be found with the Sackville crest. This is composed of fleurs-de-lis only, the blazon of the crest being: 'Out of a coronet composed of eight fleurs-de-lis or, an estoile of eight points argent.'[183]

A curious use of coronets in a crest will be found in the crest of Sir Archibald Dunbar, Bart ['A dexter hand apaumée reaching at an astral crown proper'] and Sir Alexander James Dunbar, Bart ['A dexter hand apaumée proper reaching to two earls' coronets tied together'].

657 Mural coronet.

Next after the ordinary 'ducal coronet' the one most usually employed is the mural coronet (657), which is composed of masonry. Though it may be and often is of an ordinary heraldic tincture, it will usually be found 'proper'. An exception occurs in the case of the crest of Every-Halstead ['Out of a mural coronet chequy or and azure, a demi-eagle ermine beaked or'].[184]

Care should be taken to distinguish the mural crown from the 'battlements of a tower'. This originated as a modern 'fakement' and is often granted to those who have been using a mural coronet, and desire to continue within its halo, but are not qualified to obtain in their own persons a grant of it. It should be noticed that the battlements of a tower must always be represented upon a wreath. Its facility for adding a noticeable distinction to a crest has, however, in these days, when it is becoming somewhat difficult to introduce differences in a stock pattern kind of crest, led to its very frequent use in grants during the last hundred years.

Care should also be taken to distinguish between the 'battlements of a tower' and a crest issuing from 'a castle', as in the case of Harley: 'a tower', as in that of Boyce; and upon the 'capital of a column', as in the crests of Cowper-Essex and Pease.

Abroad, *e.g.* in the arms of Paris, it is very usual to place a mural crown over the shield of a town, and some remarks upon the point will be found on page 275. This at first sight may seem an appropriate practice to pursue, and several heraldic artists have followed it and advocate it in this country. But the correctness of such a practice was, for British purposes, strongly and emphatically denied officially until first Lyon King of Arms fell and granted it to St Andrews, and Garter granted it to the London County Council. Whilst we reserve this privilege for grants to certain army officers of high rank, it does not seem proper that it should be available for casual and haphazard assumption by a town or city. That being the case, it should be borne in mind that the practice is not permissible in British armory.

The naval coronet (658), though but seldom granted now, was very popular at one time. In the latter part of the eighteenth and the early part of the nine-

183. This is a particularly attractive coronet of ancient provenance and is frequently granted today. It is generally composed of six rather than eight fleurs-de-lis, which is an improvement aesthetically.

184. The use of the mural crown (the word 'coronet' has been used but 'crown' is the more usual term) has increased greatly during the past sixty years. It is frequently employed as a crest coronet, either with or without a wreath beneath it. Examples of it without a wreath include the boroughs of Maidstone, Radcliffe, Taunton and Burton-upon-Trent; whilst Gainsborough, Birmingham and Carshalton are among the many local authorities which bear the mural crown on a wreath. Many individuals, whether or not ex-soldiers, have also been granted the mural crown in this way. County Councils, such as Oxfordshire and Pembrokeshire have mural crowns as crest coronets whilst others have been granted arms 'ensigned by a mural crown' *in lieu* of a crest; amongst such are Cambridgeshire and Isle of Ely, Durham and Monmouth County Councils.

teenth centuries, naval actions were constantly being fought, and in a large number of cases where the action of the officer in command was worthy of high praise and reward, part of such reward was usually an augmentation of arms. Very frequently it is found that the crest of augmentation issued from a naval coronet. This is, as will be seen, a curious figure composed of the sail and stern of a ship repeated and alternating on the rim of a circlet. Sometimes it is entirely gold, but usually the sails are argent. An instance of such a grant of augmentation will be found in the crest of augmentation for Brisbane, and in a crest of augmentation granted to Sir Philip Bowes Broke to commemorate his glorious victory in the *Shannon* over the American ship *Chesapeake*.

Any future naval grant of a crest of augmentation would probably mean that it would be granted issuing out of a naval coronet, but otherwise the privilege is now confined to those grants of arms in which the patentee is of the rank of admiral. Instances of its use will be found in the crests of Schomberg and Farquhar, and in the crest of Dakyns of Derbyshire: 'Out of a naval coronet or, a dexter arm embowed proper, holding in the hand a battle-axe argent, round the wrist a ribbon azure.' The crest of Dakyns is chiefly memorable for the curious motto which accompanies it: 'Strike, Dakyns, the devil's in the hempe,' of which no one knows the explanation.

Why a naval crown was granted as a badge to a family named Vickers (Plate XI) I am still wondering. The inexplicable action of the Admiralty in assigning the naval crown to the Mercantile Marine uniform leaves one puzzled as to the next absurdity they will perpetrate.

The crest of Lord St Vincent ['Out of a naval coronet or, encircled by a wreath of oak proper, a demi-pegasus argent, maned and hoofed of the first, winged azure, charged on the wing with a fleur-de-lis gold'] is worthy of notice owing to the encircling of the coronet, and in some number of cases the circlet of the coronet has been made use of to carry the name of a captured ship or of a naval engagement.

658 *Naval crown.*

The Eastern Coronet (659) is a plain rim heightened with spikes. Formerly it was granted without restriction, but now, as has been already stated, it is reserved for those of high rank who have served in India or the East. An instance occurs, for example, in the crest of Rawlinson, Bart ['Sable, three swords in pale proper, pommels and hilts or, two erect, points upwards, between them one, point downwards, on a chief embattled of the third an antique crown gules. Crest: out of an Eastern crown or, a cubit arm erect in armour, the hand grasping a sword in bend sinister, and the wrist encircled by a laurel wreath proper'].

659 *Eastern crown.*

Of *identically* the same shape is what is known as the 'Antique Coronet'. It has no particular meaning, and though no objection is made to granting it in Scotland and Ireland, it is not granted in England. Instances in which it occurs under such a description will be found in the cases of Lanigan O'Keefe and Matheson.

660 *Crown vallary.*

The Crown Vallary or Vallary Coronet (660) and the Palisado Crown (661) were undoubtedly originally the same, but now the two forms in which it has been depicted are considered to be different coronets. Each has the rim, but the vallary coronet is now heightened only by pieces of the shape of vair, whilst the Palisado Crown is formed by high 'palasadoes' affixed to the rim. These two are

661 *Palisado crown.*

the only forms of coronet granted to ordinary and undistinguished applicants in England.

The circlet from the crown of a king of arms has once at least been granted as a crest coronet, this being in the case of Rogers Harrison.

In a recent grant of arms to Gee, the crest has no wreath, but issues from 'a circlet or, charged with a fleur-de-lis gules'. The circlet is emblazoned as a plain gold band. This has also been done in several other cases.[185]

The chapeau

Some number of crests will be found to have been granted to be borne upon a 'chapeau' in lieu of wreath or coronet. Other names for the chapeau, under which it is equally well known, are the 'cap of maintenance' or 'cap of dignity'.

There can be very little doubt that the heraldic chapeau combines two distinct origins or earlier prototypes. The one is the real cap of dignity, and the other is the hat or 'capelot' which covered the top of the helm before the mantling was introduced, but from which the lambrequin developed. The curious evolution of the chapeau from the 'capelot', which is so marked and usual in Germany, is the tall conical hat, often surmounted by a tuft or larger plume of feathers, and usually employed in German heraldry as an opportunity for the repetition of the livery colours, or a part of, and often the whole design of, the arms. But it should at the

BB *Coronet of Ears of Wheat and Acorns.*

CC *Saxon Crown.*

DD *Astral Crown.*

EE *Ancient Crown.*

185. Mention must be made here of a device much used since the Second World War, namely encircling the crest with a 'made up' coronet—that is, a circlet having about the rim a diversity of likely and unlikely objects. Generally speaking, these quasi-coronets were employed either as a method of differencing an otherwise common crest or else as a means of cramming more symbolism into an achievement of arms which could not normally, either for æsthetic or purely physical reasons, take more. For some years now the kings of arms have refused to grant such coronets, but the heraldry of crests for the past forty years has groaned with them. A few examples culled from municipal heraldry will suffice. The crest of the borough of Clitheroe granted in 1952 contains a coronet consisting of four pierced mollets sable and four crescents or, set about a golden circlet. A circlet with six or more roses on the rim was popular in the 1930s, and can be found in the crests of the borough of Stretford, Chorley R.D.C., Thornton Cleveleys U.D.C. and Merioneth County Council, among many other local authorities. Whitley Bay, whose arms were granted in 1954, has a crest coronet consisting of four lily flowers set upon a rim argent. A coronet devised by Mr H. Ellis Tomlinson for use as a crest coronet in the arms of Rural District Councils has been much used in recent years. It is composed of four ears of wheat and as many acorns leaved alternatively set upon a rim of gold (BB) Amongst many other authorities, Lydney R.D.C. bears this coronet in its crest, which, with the arms, was granted in 1965.

Three other new coronets should be noted. The first is the Saxon Crown (CC). This is often used as a charge, as in the arms of the former Middlesex County Council, but it is also frequently used as a crest coronet, particularly to symbolise Saxon associations, in the arms of local authorities. The crests of Yeovil (1954), Halifax (1948) and the former borough of Wembley (1938) are among several which issue from Saxon crowns.

The second is the Astral Crown (DD). This is composed of wings and stars set on a rim, and is used in connection with aviation in much the same way as the Naval Crown is used to symbolise naval achievements and marine associations. It features as a charge in the arms and as a crest coronet in the achievement of Marshal of the Royal Air Force Viscount Portal of Hungerford, K.G., and also in the arms of both British European and British Overseas Airways Corporations.

The third is termed an Ancient Crown (EE). It is really an elaboration of the ducal coronet, and is based on a fine early example of a crest coronet. It was first granted in 1956 in the arms and badge of The Heraldry Society, and has since been used frequently.

same time be noticed that this tall, conical hat is much more closely allied to the real cap of maintenance than our present crest 'chapeau'.

Exactly what purpose the real cap of maintenance served, or of what it was a symbol, remains to a certain extent a matter of mystery. The 'Cap of Maintenance' —a part of the regalia borne before the sovereign at the State opening of Parliament (but *not* at a coronation) by the Marquesses of Winchester,[186] the hereditary bearers of the cap of maintenance—bears, in its shape, no relation to the heraldic chapeau. The only similarity is its crimson colour and its lining of ermine. It is a tall, conical cap, and is carried on a short staff.

Whilst crest coronets in early days appear to have had little or no relation to titular rank, there is no doubt whatever that caps of dignity had. Long before, a coronet was assigned to the rank of baron in the reign of Charles II; all barons had their caps of dignity, of scarlet lined with white fur; and in the old pedigrees a scarlet cap with a gold tuft or tassel on top and a lining of fur will be found painted above the arms of a baron. This fact, the fact that until after Stuart days the chapeau does not appear to have been allowed or granted to others than peers, the fact that it is now reserved for the crests granted to peers, the fact that the velvet cap is a later addition both to the sovereign's crown and to the coronet of a peer, and finally the fact that the cap of maintenance is borne before the sovereign only in the precincts of Parliament, would seem to indubitably indicate that the cap of maintenance was inseparably connected with the lordship and overlordship of Parliament vested in peers and in the sovereign. In the crumpled and tasselled top of the velvet cap, and in the ermine border visible below the rim, the high conical form of the cap of maintenance proper can be still traced in the cap of a peer's coronet, and that the velvet cap contained in the crown of the sovereign and in the coronet of a peer is the survival of the old cap of dignity there can be no doubt. This is perhaps even more apparent in 662, which shows the crown of King Charles II, than in the representations of the Royal crown which we are more accustomed to see. The present form of a peer's coronet is undoubtedly the conjoining of two separate emblems of his rank. The cap of maintenance or dignity, however, as represented above the arms of a baron, as above referred to, was not of this high, conical shape. It was much flatter.

662 The Crown of King Charles II.

The high, conical, original shape is, however, preserved in many of the early heraldic representations of the chapeau, as will be noticed from an examination of the ancient Garter plates or from a reference to 271, which shows the helmet with its chapeau-borne crest of Edward the Black Prince.

Of the chapeaux upon which crests are represented in the early Garter plates following facts may be observed. They are twenty in number of the eighty-six plates reproduced in Mr St John Hope's book. It should be noticed that until the end of the reign of Henry VIII the Royal crest of the sovereign was always depicted upon a chapeau gules, lined with ermine. Of the twenty instances in which the chapeau appears, no less than twelve are representations of the Royal crest, borne by closely allied relatives of the sovereign, so that we have only eight examples from which to draw deductions. But of the twenty it should be pointed out that

186. It is now customary for the Sovereign to nominate some member of the Government to carry the Cap of Maintenance. For example, in 1966 the Earl of Longford and in 1967 Lord Shackleton carried it.

nineteen are peers, and the only remaining instance (Sir John Grey, K.G.) is that of the eldest son and heir apparent of a peer, both shield and crest being in this case boldly marked with the 'label' of an eldest son. Consequently it is a safe deduction that whatever may have been the regulations and customs concerning the use of coronets, there can be no doubt that down to the end of the fifteenth century the use of a chapeau marked a crest as that of a peer. Of the eight non-Royal examples one has been repainted, and is valueless as a contemporary record. Of the remaining seven, four are of the conventional gules and ermine. One only has not the ermine lining, that being the crest of Lord Fanhope. It is plainly the Royal crest 'differenced' (he being of Royal but illegitimate descent), and probably the argent in lieu of ermine lining is one of the intentional marks of distinction. The chapeau of Lord Beaumont is azure, semé-de-lis, lined ermine, and that of the Earl of Douglas is azure lined ermine, this being in each case in conformity with the mantling. Whilst the Beaumont family still use this curiously coloured chapeau with their crest, the Douglas crest is now borne (by the Duke of Hamilton) upon one of ordinary tinctures. Chapeaux, other than of gules lined ermine, are but rarely met with, and unless specifically blazoned to the contrary a cap of maintenance is always presumed to be gules and ermine.[187]

About the Stuart period the granting of crests upon chapeaux to others than peers became far from unusual, and the practice appears to have been frequently adopted prior to the beginning of the nineteenth century. Some of these crest chapeaux, however, were not of gules. An instance of this kind will be found in the grant in 1667 to Sir Thomas Davies, then one of the sheriffs of the City of London, but afterwards (in 1677) Lord Mayor. The crest granted was: 'On a chapeau sable, turned up or, a demi-lion rampant of the last.' The reason for the grant at that date of such a simple crest and the even more astonishingly simple coat of arms ['Or, a chevron between three mullets pierced sable'] has always been a mystery to me.

The arms of Lord Lurgan (granted or confirmed 1840) afford another instance of a chapeau of unusual colour, his crest being: 'Upon a chapeau azure turned up ermine, a greyhound statant gules, collared or.'

There are some number of cases in which peers whose ancestors originally bore their crests upon a wreath have subsequently placed them upon a chapeau. The Stanleys, Earls of Derby, are a case in point, as are also the Marquesses of Exeter. The latter case is curious, because although they have for long enough so depicted their crest, they only comparatively recently obtained the necessary authorisation by the Crown.

At the present time the official form of the chapeau is as in 663, with the turn up split at the back into two tails. No such form can be found in any early representation, and most heraldic artists have now reverted to an earlier type.

663 *The Chapeau.*

Before leaving the subject of the cap of maintenance, reference should be made to another instance of a curious heraldic headgear often, but *quite incorrectly*, styled a 'cap of maintenance'. This is the fur cap invariably used over the shields of the cities of London, Dublin, and Norwich. There is no English official authority

---

187. In Scotland the chapeau gules turned up ermine is now reserved for peers and feudal barons who are in actual possession of the *caput baronum*. A feudal baron who is not in possession but who is the representer is accorded a chapeau azure turned up ermine.

whatever for such an addition to the arms, but there does appear to be some little official recognition of it in Ulster's Office in the case of the city of Dublin. The late Ulster King of Arms, however, informed me that he would, in the case of Dublin, have no hesitation whatever in certifying the right of the city arms to be so displayed (Plate X).

In the utter absence of anything in the nature of a precedent, it is quite unlikely that the practice will be sanctioned in England. The hat used is a flat-topped, brown fur hat of the shape depicted with the arms of the City of Dublin. It is merely (in London) a part of the official uniform or livery of the City sword-bearer. It does not even appear to have been a part of the costume of the Lord Mayor, and it must always remain a mystery why it was ever adopted for heraldic use. But then the chain of the Lord Mayor of London is generally called a Collar of SS. Besides this the City of London uses a Peer's helmet, a bogus modern crest, and even more modern bogus supporters, so a few other eccentricities need not in that particular instance cause surprise.[188]

24 · The mantling or lambrequin

The mantling is the ornamental design which in a representation of an armorial achievement depends from the helmet, falling away on either side of the escutcheon. Many authorities have considered it to have been no more than a fantastic series of flourishes, devised by artistic minds for the purpose of assisting ornamentation and affording an artistic opportunity of filling up unoccupied spaces in heraldic design. There is no doubt that its readily apparent advantages in that character have greatly led to the importance now attached to the mantling in heraldic art. But equally is it certain that its real origin is to be traced elsewhere.

The development of the heraldry of today was in the East during the period of the Crusades, and the burning heat of the Eastern sun upon the metal helmet led to the introduction and adoption of a textile covering, which would act in some way as a barrier between the two. It was simply in fact and effect a primeval prototype of the 'puggaree' of Margate and Hindustan. It is plain from all early representations that originally it was short, simply hanging from the apex of the helmet to the level of the shoulders, overlapping the textile tunic or 'coat of arms', but probably enveloping a greater part of the helmet, neck, and shoulders than we are at present (judging from pictorial representations) inclined to believe.

188. See note 167.

Adopted first as a protection against the heat, and perhaps also the rust which would follow damp, the lambrequin soon made evident another of its advantages, an advantage to which we doubtless owe its perpetuation outside Eastern warfare in the more temperate climates of Northern Europe and England. Textile fabrics are peculiarly and remarkably deadening to a sword-cut, to which fact must be added the facility with which such a weapon would become entangled in the hanging folds of cloth. The hacking and hewing of battle would show itself plainly upon the lambrequin of one accustomed to a prominent position in the forefront of a fight, and the honourable record implied by a ragged and slashed lambrequin accounts for the fact that we find at an early period after their introduction into heraldic art, that mantlings are depicted cut and 'torn to ribbons'. This opportunity was quickly seized by the heraldic artist, who has always, from those very earliest times of absolute armorial freedom down to the point of greatest and most regularised control, been allowed an entire and absolute discretion in the design to be adopted for the mantling. Hence it is that we find so much importance is given to it by heraldic artists, for it is in the design of the mantling, and almost entirely in that opportunity, that the personal character and abilities of the artist have their greatest scope. Some authorities have, however derived the mantling from the robe of estate, and there certainly has been a period in British armory when most lambrequins found in heraldic art are represented by an unmutilated cloth, suspended from and displayed behind the armorial bearings and tied at the upper corners. In all probability the robes of estate of the higher nobility, no less than the then existing and peremptorily enforced sumptuary laws, may have led to the desire and to the attempt, at a period when the actual lambrequin was fast disappearing from general knowledge, to display arms upon something which should represent either the parliamentary robes of estate of a peer, or the garments of rich fabric which the sumptuary laws forbade to those of humble degree. To this period undoubtedly belongs the term 'mantling', which is so much more frequently employed than the word lambrequin, which is really—from the armorial point of view—the older term.

The heraldic mantling was, of course, originally the representation of the actual 'capeline' or textile covering worn upon the helmet, but many early heraldic representations are of mantlings which are of skin, fur, or feathers, being in such cases invariably a continuation of the crest drawn out and represented as the lambrequin. When the crest was a part of the human figure, the habit in which that figure was arrayed is almost invariably found to have been so employed. The Garter plate of Sir Ralph Bassett, one of the Founder Knights, shows the crest as a black boar's head, the skin being continued as the sable mantling.

Some Slavonic families have mantlings of fur only; that of the Hungarian family of Chorinski is a bear skin, and countless other instances can be found of the use of German families of a continuation of the crest for a mantling. This practice affords instances of many curious mantlings, this in one case in the Zurich *Wappenrolle* being the scaly skin of a salmon. The mane of the lion, the crest of Mertz, and the hair and beard of the crests of Bohn and Landschaden, are similarly continued to do duty for the mantling. This practice has never found great favour in England, the cases amongst the early Garter plates where it has been followed standing almost alone. In a manuscript (M. 3, 67*b*) of the reign of Henry VII,

664 The Crest of Stourton.

now in the College of Arms, probably dating from about 1506, an instance of this character can be found, however. It is a representation of the crest of Stourton (664) as it was borne at that date, and was a black Benedictine demi-monk proper holding erect in his dexter hand a scourge. Here the proper black Benedictine habit (it has of later years been corrupted into the russet habit of a friar) is continued to form the mantling.

By what rules the colours of the mantlings were decided in early times it is impossible to say. No rules have been handed down to us—the old heraldic books are silent on the point—and it seems equally hopeless to attempt to deduce any from ancient armorial examples. The one fact that can be stated with certainty is that the rules of early days, if there were any, are not the rules presently observed. Some hold that the colours of the mantling were decided by the colours of the actual livery in use as distinct from the 'livery colours' of the arms. It is difficult to check this rule, because our knowledge of the liveries in use in early days is so meagre and limited; but in the few instances of which we now have knowledge we look in vain for a repetition of the colours worn by the retainers as liveries in the mantlings used. The fact that the livery colours are represented in the background of some of the early Garter plates, and that in such instances in no single case do they agree with the colours of the mantling, must certainly dissipate once and for all any such supposition as far as it relates to that period.

A careful study and analysis of early heraldic emblazonment, however, reveals one point as a dominating characteristic. That is, that where the crest, by its nature, lent itself to a continuation into the mantling it generally was so continued. This practice, which was almost universal upon the Continent, and is particularly to be met with in German heraldry, though seldom adopted in England, certainly had some weight in English heraldry. In the reproductions of the Plantagenet Garter plates published in 1901 eighty-seven armorial achievements are included. Of these, in ten instances the mantlings are plainly continuations of the crests, being 'feathered' or in unison. Fifteen of the mantlings have both the outside and the inside of the principal colour and of the principal metal of the arms they accompany, though in a few cases, contrary to the present practice, the metal is outside, the lining being of the colour. Nineteen more of the mantlings are of the principal colour of the arms, the majority (eighteen) of these being lined with ermine. No less than forty-nine are of some colour lined with ermine, but thirty-four of these are of gules lined ermine, and in the large majority of cases in these thirty-four instances neither the gules nor the ermine are in conformity with the principal colour and metal (what we now term the 'livery colours') of the arms. In some cases the colours of the mantling agree with the colours of the crest, a rule which will usually be found to hold good in German heraldry. The constant occurrence of gules and ermine incline one much to believe that the colours of the mantling were not decided by haphazard fancy, but that there was some law—possibly in some way connected with the sumptuary laws of the period—which governed the matter, or, at any rate, which greatly limited the range of selection. Of the eighty-seven mantlings, excluding those which are gules lined ermine, there are four only the colours of which apparently bear no relation whatever to the colours of the arms or the crests appearing upon the same Stall plate. In some number of the plates the colours certainly are taken from a quartering other than the first one, and in one at least of the four exceptions the mantling (one of the most curious examples) is plainly derived from a quartering inherited by the knight in question though not shown upon the Stall plate. Probably a closer examination of the remaining three instances would reveal a similar reason in each case. That any law concerning the colours of their mantlings was enforced upon those concerned would be an unwarrantable deduction not justified by the instances under examination, but one is clearly justified in drawing from these cases some deductions as to the practice pursued. It is evident that unless one was authorised by the rule or reason governing the matter—whatever such rule or reason may have been—in using a mantling of gules and ermine, the dominating *colour* (not as a rule the metal) of the coat of arms (or of one of the quarterings), or sometimes of the crest if the tinctures of arms and crest were not in unison, decided the colour of the mantling. That there was some meaning behind the mantlings of gules lined with ermine there can be little doubt, for it is noticeable that in a case in which the colours of the arms themselves are gules and ermine, the mantling is of gules and argent, as by the way in this particular case is the chapeau upon which the crest is placed. But probably the reason which governed these mantlings of gules lined with ermine, as also the ermine linings of other mantlings, must be sought outside the strict limits of armory. That the colours of mantlings are repeated in different generations, and in the plates of members of the same family, clearly demonstrates that selection was not haphazard.

Certain of these early Garter plates exhibit interesting curiosities in the mantlings:

1. Sir William Latimer, Lord Latimer, K.G., *c.* 1361–1381. Arms: gules a cross patonce or. Crest: a plume of feathers sable, the tips or. Mantling gules with silver vertical stripes, lined with ermine.

2. Sir Bermond Arnaud de Presac, Soudan de la Tran, K.G., 1380–*post* 1384. Arms: or, a lion rampant double-queued gules. Crest: a Midas' head argent. Mantling sable, lined gules, the latter veined or.

3. Sir Simon Felbrigge, K.G., 1397–1442. Arms: or, a lion rampant gules.

Crest: out of a coronet gules, a plume of feathers ermine. Mantling ermine, lined gules (evidently a continuation of the crest).

4. Sir Reginald Cobham, Lord Cobham, K.G., 1352–1361. Arms: gules, on a chevron or, three estoiles sable. Crest: a soldan's head sable, the brow encircled by a torse or. Mantling sable (evidently a continuation of the crest), lined gules.

5. Sir Edward Cherleton, Lord Cherleton of Powis, K.G., 1406–7 to 1420–1. Arms: or, a lion rampant gules. Crest: on a wreath gules and sable, two lions' gambs also gules, each adorned on the exterior side with three demi-fleurs-de-lis issuing argent, the centres thereof or. Mantling: on the dexter side, sable; on the sinister side, gules; both lined ermine.

6. Sir Hertong von Clux, K.G., 1421–45 or 6. Arms: argent, a vine branch couped at either end in bend sable. Crest: out of a coronet or, a plume of feathers sable and argent. Mantling: on the dexter side, azure; on the sinister, gules; both lined ermine.

7. Sir Miles Stapleton, K.G. (Founder Knight, died 1364). Arms: argent, a lion rampant sable. Crest: a soldan's head sable, around the temples a torse azure, tied in a knot, the ends flowing. Mantling sable (probably a continuation of the crest), lined gules.

8. Sir Walter Hungerford, Lord Hungerford and Heytesbury, K.G., 1421–49. Arms: sable, two bars argent, and in chief three plates. Crest: out of a coronet azure a garb or, enclosed by two sickles argent. Mantling (within and without): dexter, barry of six ermine and gules; sinister, barry of six gules and ermine. (The reason for this is plain. The mother of Lord Hungerford was a daughter and coheir of Hussey. The arms of Hussey are variously given: 'Barry of six ermine and gules,' or 'Ermine, three bars gules.')

9. Sir Humphrey Stafford, Earl of Stafford, 1429–60. Arms: or, a chevron gules. Crest: out of a coronet gules, a swan's head and neck proper, beaked gules, between two wings also proper. Mantling: the dexter side, sable; the sinister side, gules; both lined ermine. Black and gules, it may be noted, were the livery colours of Buckingham, an earldom which had devolved upon the Earls of Stafford.

10. Sir John Grey of Ruthin, K.G., 1436–9. Arms: quarterly, 1 and 4, barry of six argent and azure, in chief three torteaux; 2 and 3, quarterly i and iiii, or, a maunch gules; ii and iii, barry of eight argent and azure, an orle of ten martlets gules; over all a label of three points argent. Crest: on a chapeau gules, turned up ermine, a wyvern or, gorged with a label argent. Mantling or, lined ermine.

11. Sir Richard Nevill, Earl of Salisbury, K.G., 1436–60. Arms: quarterly, 1 and 4, quarterly i and iiii, argent, three lozenges conjoined in fess gules; ii and iii, or, an eagle displayed vert; 2 and 3, gules, a saltire argent, a label of three points compony argent and azure. Crest: on a coronet, a griffin sejant, with wings displayed or. Mantling: dexter side, gules; the sinister, sable; both lined ermine.

12. Sir Gaston de Foix, Count de Longueville, &c., K.G., 1438–58. Arms: quarterly, 1 and 4, or, three pallets gules; 2 and 3, or, two cows passant in pale gules, over all a label of three points, each point or, on a cross sable five escallops argent. Crest: on a wreath or and gules, a blackamoor's bust with ass's ears sable, vested paly or and gules, all between two wings, each of the arms as in the first quarter. Mantling paly of or and gules, lined vert.

13. Sir Walter Blount, Lord Mountjoye, K.G., 1472–4. Arms: quarterly, 1. argent, two wolves passant in pale sable, on a bordure also argent eight saltires couped gules (for Ayala); 2. or, a tower (? gules) (for Mountjoy); 3. barry nebuly or and sable (for Blount); 4. vairé argent and gules (for Gresley). Crest: out of a coronet two ibex horns or. Mantling sable, lined on the dexter side with argent, and on the sinister with or.

14. Frederick, Duke of Urbino. Mantling or, lined ermine.

In Continental heraldry it is by no means uncommon to find the device of the arms repeated either wholly or in part upon the mantling. In reference to this the 'Tournament Rules' of René, Duke of Anjou, throw some light on the point. These it may be of interest to quote:

Vous tous Princes, Seigneurs, Barons, Cheualiers, et Escuyers, qui auez intention de tournoyer, vous estes tenus vous rendre és heberges le quartrième jour deuan le jour du Tournoy, pour faire de vos Blasons fenestres, sur payne de non estre receus audit Tournoy. Les armes seront celles-cy. Le tymbre doit estre sur vne piece de cuir boüilly, la quelle doit estre bien faultrée d'vn doigt d'espez, ou plus, par le dedans: et doit contenir la dite pièce de cuir tout le sommet du heaulme, et sera couuerte la dite piece du lambrequin armoyé des armes de celuy qui le portera, et sur le dit lambrequin au plus haut du sommet, sera assis le dit Tymbre, et autour d'iceluy aura vn tortil des couleurs que voudra le Tournoyeur.

Item, et quand tous les heaulmes seront ainsi mis et ordonnez pour les departir, viendront toutes Dames et Damoiselles et tous Seigneurs, Cheualiers, et Escuyers, en les visitant d'vn bout à autre, la present les Juges, qui meneront trois ou quatre tours les Dames pour bien voir et visiter les Tymbres, et y aura vu Heraut ou poursuiuant, qui dira aux Dames selon l'endroit où elles seront, le nom de ceux à qui sont les Tymbres, afin que s'il en a qui ait des Dames médit, et elles touchent son Tymbre, qu'il soit le lendemain pour recommandé. (Menêtrier, *L'Origine des Armoiries*, pp. 79–81.)

Whilst one can call to mind no instance of importance of ancient date where this practice has been followed in this country, there are one or two instances in the Garter plates which approximate closely to it. The mantling of John, Lord Beaumont, is azure, semé-de-lis (as the field of his arms), lined ermine. Those of Sir John Bourchier, Lord Berners, and of Sir Henry Bourchier, Earl of Essex, are of gules, billetté or, evidently derived from the quartering for Louvaine upon the arms, this quartering being: 'Gules, billetté and a fess or.'

According to a MS. of Vincent, in the College of Arms, the Warrens used a mantling chequy of azure and or with their arms.

A somewhat similar result is obtained by the mantling, 'Gules, semé of lozenges or,' upon the small plate of Sir Sanchet Dabrichecourt. The mantling of Sir Lewis Robessart, Lord Bourchier, is: 'Azure, bezanté, lined argent.'

'The azure mantling on the Garter Plate of Henry V, as Prince of Wales, is "semé of the French golden fleurs-de-lis".... The Daubeny mantling is "semé of mullets". On the brass of Sir John Wylcote, at Tew, the lambrequins are chequy.... On the seals of Sir John Bussy, in 1391 and 1407, the mantlings are barry, the coat being "argent, three bars sable".'

There are a few cases amongst the Garter plates in which badges are plainly and unmistakably depicted upon the mantlings. Thus, on the linings of the mantling on the plate of Sir Henry Bourchier (elected 1452) will be found waterbougets, which are repeated on a fillet round the head of the crest. The Stall plate of Sir John Bourchier, Lord Berners, above referred to (elected 1459), is lined with silver on the dexter side, semé in the upper part with water-bougets, and in the lower part with Bourchier knots. On the opposite side of the mantling the knots are in the upper part, and the water-bougets below. That these badges upon the mantling are not haphazard artistic decoration is proved by a reference to the monumental effigy of the Earl of Essex, in Little Easton Church, Essex. The differing shapes of the helmet, and of the coronet and the mantling, and the different representation of the crest, show that, although depicted in his Garter robes, upon his effigy the helmet, crest, and mantling upon which the earl's head there rests, and the representations of the same upon the Garter plate, are not slavish copies of the same original model. Nevertheless upon the effigy, as on the Garter plate, we find the outside of the mantling 'semé of billets', and the inside 'semé of water-bougets'. Another instance amongst the Garter plates will befound in the case of Viscount Lovell, whose mantling is strewn with gold padlocks

Nearly all the mantlings on the Garter Stall plates are more or less heavily 'veined' with gold, and many are heavily diapered and decorated with floral devices. So prominent is some of this floral diapering that one is inclined to think that in a few cases it may possibly be a diapering with floral badges. In other cases it is equally evidently no more than a mere accessory of design, though between these two classes of diapering it would be by no means easy to draw a line of distinction. The veining and 'heightening' of a mantling with gold is at the present day nearly always to be seen in elaborate heraldic painting.

From the Garter plates of the fourteenth century it has been shown that the colours of a large proportion of the mantlings approximated in early days to the colours of the arms. The popularity of gules, however, was then fast encroaching upon the frequency of appearance which other colours should have enjoyed; and in the sixteenth century, in grants and other paintings of arms, the use of a mantling of gules had become practically universal. In most cases the mantling of 'gules, doubled argent' forms an integral part of the terms of the grant itself, as sometimes do the 'gold tassels' which are so frequently found terminating the mantlings of that and an earlier period. This custom continued through the Stuart period, and though dropped officially in England during the eighteenth century (when the mantling reverted to the livery colours of the arms, and became in this form a matter of course and so understood, not being expressed in the wording of the patent), it continued in force in Lyon Office in Scotland until the year 1890, when Sir James Balfour Paul altered the practice, and, as had earlier been done in England, ordered that all future Scottish mantlings should be depicted in the livery colours of the arms, but in Scotland the mantlings, though now following the livery colours, are still included in the terms of the grant, and thereby stereotyped. In England, in an official 'exemplification' at the present day of an ancient coat of arms (e.g. in an exemplification following the assumption of name and arms by Royal License), the mantling is painted in the livery colours, irrespective of any ancient patent in which 'gules and argent' may have been *granted* as the colour of the mantling. Though probably most people will agree as to the expediency of such a practice, it is at any rate open to criticism on the score of propriety, unless the new mantling is expressed in terms in the new patent. This would of course amount to a grant overriding the earlier one, and would do all that was necessary; but failing this, there appears to be a distinct hiatus in the continuity of authority.

Ermine linings to the mantling were soon denied to the undistinguished commoner, and with the exception of the early Garter plates, it would be difficult to point to an instance of their use. The mantlings of peers, however, continued to be lined with ermine, and English instances under official sanction can be found in the Visitation Books and in the Garter plates until a comparatively recent period. In fact the relegation of peers to the ordinary livery colours for their mantlings is, in England, quite a modern practice. In Scotland, however, the mantlings of peers have always been lined with ermine, and the present Lyon continues this whilst usually making the colours of the outside of the mantlings agree with the principal colour of the arms. This, as regards the outer colour of the mantling, is not a fixed or stereotyped rule, and in some cases Lyon has preferred to adopt a mantling of gules lined with ermine as more comfortable to a peer's Parliamentary Robe of Estate.[189]

In the Deputy Earl-Marshal's warrant referred to on page 281 are some interesting points as to the mantling. It is recited that 'some persons under yᵉ degree of yᵉ Nobilitie of this Realme doe cause Ermins to be Depicted upon ye Lineings of those Mantles which are used with their Armes, and also that there are some that have lately caused the Mantles of their Armes to be painted like Ostrich feathers as tho' they were of some peculiar and superior degree of Honor', and the warrant commands that these points are to be rectified.

The Royal mantling is of cloth of gold. In the case of the sovereign and the Prince of Wales it is lined with ermine, and for other members of the Royal Family it is lined with argent. Queen Elizabeth I was the first sovereign to adopt the golden mantling, the Royal tinctures before that date (for the mantling) being gules lined ermine. The mantling of or and ermine has, of course, since that date been rigidly denied to all outside the Royal Family. Two instances, however, occur amongst the early Garter plates, viz. Sir John Grey de Ruthyn and Frederick, Duke of Urbino. It is sometimes stated that a mantling of or and ermine is a sign of sovereignty, but the mantling of our own sovereign is really the only case in which it is presently so used.

In Sweden, as in Scotland, the colours of the mantling are specified in the patent, and, unlike our own, are often curiously varied.

The present rules for the colour of a mantling are as follows in England and Ireland:[190]

   1. That with ancient arms of which the grant specified the colour, where this has not been altered by a subsequent exemplification, the colours must be stated in the grant, *i.e.* usually gules, lined argent.

189. Lyon King of Arms now gives all peers a red mantling doubled ermine, or else uses the Robe of Estate itself. This device is adopted in the case of peeresses in their own right, where their uncrested arms are displayed on the Robe of Estate in much the same way as was frequently done, as an unauthorised conceit, on coach panels in the nineteenth century (665).

190. The English kings of arms have now reverted to the pre-Elizabethan practice of granting mantlings of diverse colours. The only rule is that colours form the outside and metals the lining of the mantling. Mantlings may be parti-coloured and, if the grantee has a badge, this can be strewn over the mantling, although this is not specified in the grant.

2. That the mantling of the sovereign and Prince of Wales of cloth is of gold, lined with ermine.

3. That the mantling of other members of the Royal Family is of cloth of gold lined with argent.

4. That the mantlings of all other people shall be of the livery colours.

The rules in Scotland are now as follows:

1. That in the cases of peers whose arms were matriculated before 1890 the mantling is of gules lined with ermine (the Scottish term for 'lined' is 'doubled').

2. That the mantlings of all other arms matriculated before 1890 shall be of gules and argent.

3. That the mantlings of peers whose arms have been matriculated since 1890 shall be either of the principal colour of the arms, lined with ermine, or of gules lined ermine (conformably to the Parliamentary Robe of Estate of a peer) as may happen to have been matriculated.[191]

4. That the mantlings of all other persons whose arms have been matriculated since 1890 shall be of the livery colours, unless other colours are, as is occasionally the case, specified in the patent of matriculation.

Whether in Scotland a person is entitled to assume of his own motion an ermine lining to his mantling upon his elevation to the peerage, without a re-matriculation in cases where the arms and mantling have been otherwise matriculated at an earlier date, or whether in England any peer may still line his mantling with ermine, are points on which one hesitates to express an opinion.

When the mantling is of the livery colours the following rules must be observed. The outside must be of some colour and the lining of some metal. The colour must be the principal colour of the arms, *i.e.* the colour of the field if it be of colour, or if it is of metal, then the colour of the principal ordinary or charge upon the shield. The metal will be as the field, if the field is of metal, or if not, it will be as the metal of the principal ordinary or charge. In other words, it should be the same tinctures as the wreath.

If the field is party of colour and metal (*i.e.* per pale barry, quarterly, &c.), then that colour and that metal are 'the livery colours'. If the field is party of two *colours* the principal colour (*i.e.* the one first mentioned in the blazon) is taken as the colour and the other is ignored. The mantling is *not* made party to agree with the field in British heraldry, as would be the case in Germany. If the field is of a fur, then the dominant metal or colour of the fur is taken as one component part of the 'livery colours', the other metal or colour required being taken from the next most important tincture of the field. For example, 'ermine, a fess gules' has a mantling of gules and argent, whilst 'or, a chevron ermines' would need a mantling of sable and or. The mantling for 'azure, a lion rampant erminois' would be azure and or. But in a coat showing fur, metal, and colour, sometimes the fur is ignored. A field of vair has a mantling argent and azure, but if the charge be vair the field will supply the one, *i.e.* either colour or metal, whilst the vair

---

191. In Scotland peers invariably have mantlings gules doubled ermine, but they may also have a representation of their Robe of Estate, not their Parliament Robe; this is also used for peeresses who, of course, have no crest nor ordinary mantling. The arms of Baroness Elliot of Harwood are shown in this way.

supplies whichever is lacking. Except in the cases of Scotsmen who are peers and of the Sovereign and Prince of Wales, no fur is ever used nowadays in Great Britain for a mantling.

In cases where the principal charge is 'proper', a certain discretion must be used. Usually the heraldic colour to which the charge approximates is used. For example, 'argent, issuing from a mount in base a tree proper', &c., would have a mantling vert and argent. The arms 'or, three Cornish choughs proper', or 'argent, three negroes' heads couped proper', would have mantlings respectively sable and or and sable and argent. Occasionally one comes across a coat which supplies an 'impossible' mantling, or which does not supply one at all. Such a coat would be 'per bend sinister ermine and erminois, a lion rampant counterchanged'. Here there is no colour at all, so the mantling would be gules and argent. 'Argent, three stags trippant proper' would have a mantling gules and argent. A coat of arms with a landscape field would also probably be supplied (in default of a chief, e.g. supplying other colours and tinctures) with a mantling gules and argent. It is quite permissible to 'vein' a mantling with gold lines, this being always done in official paintings.[192]

In English official heraldry, where, no matter how great the number of crests, one helmet only is painted, it naturally follows that one mantling only can be depicted. This is always taken from the livery colours of the chief (i.e. the first) quartering or sub-quartering. In Scottish patents at the present day in which a helmet is painted for each crest the mantlings frequently vary, being in each case in accordance with the livery colours of the quartering to which the crest belongs. Consequently this must be accepted as the rule in cases where more than one helmet is shown.

In considering the fashionings of mantlings it must be remembered that styles and fashions much overlap, and there has always been the tendency in armory to repeat earlier styles. Whilst one willingly concedes the immense gain in beauty by the present reversion in heraldic art to older and better, and certainly more artistic types, there is distinctly another side to the question which is strangely overlooked by those who would have the present-day heraldic art slavishly copied in all minutiæ of detail, and even (according to some) in all the crudity of draughtmanship from examples of the earliest periods.

Hitherto each period of heraldic art has had its own peculiar style and type, each within limits readily recognisable. Whether that style and type can be considered when judged by the canons of art to be good or bad, there can be no doubt that each style in its turn has approximated to, and has been in keeping with, the concurrent decorative art outside and beyond heraldry, though it has always exhibited a tendency to rather lag behind. When all has been said and done that can be, heraldry, in spite of its symbolism and its many other meanings, remains but a form of decorative art; and therefore it is natural that it should be influenced by other artistic ideas and other manifestations of art and accepted forms of design current at the period to which it belongs. For, from the artistic point of view, the part played in art by heraldry is so limited in extent compared

192. This 'veining' with gold was no more than a passing artistic fashion. It is seldom employed today, but if it were I doubt whether any serious objection would be raised, so long as there were no question of the gold looking as if it were one of the tinctures of the mantling.

with the part occupied by other forms of decoration, that one would naturally expect heraldry to show the influence of outside decorative art to a greater extent than decorative art as a whole would be likely to show the influence of heraldry. In our present revulsion of mind in favour of older heraldic types, we are apt to speak of 'good' or 'bad' heraldic art. But art itself cannot so be divided, for after all allowances have been made for crude workmanship, and when bad or imperfect examples have been eliminated from consideration (and given always necessarily the essential basis of the relation of line to curve and such technical details of art), who on earth is to judge, or who is competent to say, whether any particular style of art is good or bad? No one from preference executes speculative art which he knows whilst executing it to be bad. Most manifestations of art, and peculiarly of decorative art, are commercial matters executed with the frank idea of subsequent sale, and consequently with the subconscious idea, true though but seldom acknowledged, of pleasing that public which will have to buy. Consequently the ultimate appeal is to the taste of the public, for art, if it be not the desire to give pleasure by the representation of beauty, is nothing. Beauty, of course, must not necessarily be confounded with prettiness; it may be beauty of character. The result is, therefore, that the decorative art of any period is an indication of that which gives pleasure at the moment, and an absolute reflex of the artistic wishes, desires, and tastes of the cultivated classes to whom executive art must appeal. At every period it has been found that this taste is constantly changing, and as a consequence the examples of decorative art of any period are a reflex only of the artistic ideas current at the time the work was done.

At all periods, therefore, even during the early Victorian period, which we are now taught and believe to be the most ghastly period through which English art has passed, the art in vogue has been what the public have admired, and have been ready to pay for, and most emphatically what they have been taught and brought up to consider good art. In early Victorian days there was no lack of educated people, and because they liked the particular form of decoration associated with their period, who is justified in saying that, because that peculiar style of decoration is not acceptable now to ourselves, their art was bad, and worse than our own? If throughout the ages there had been one dominating style of decoration equally accepted at all periods and by all authorities as the highest type of decorative art, then we should have some standard to judge by. Such is not the case, and we have no such standard, and any attempt to arbitrarily create and control ideas between given parallel lines of arbitrary thought, when the ideas are constantly changing, is impossible and undesirable. Who dreams of questioning the art of Benvenuto Cellini, or of describing his craftsmanship as other than one of the most vivid examples of his period, and yet what had it in keeping with the art of the Louis XVI period, or the later art of William Morris and his followers? Widely divergent as are these types, they are nevertheless all accepted as the highest expressions of three separate types of decorative art. Any one attempting to compare them, or to rank these schools of artistic thought in order of superiority, would simply be laying themselves open to ridicule unspeakable, for they would be ranked by the highest authorities of different periods in different orders, and it is as impossible to create a permanent standarad of art as it is impossible to ensure a permanence of any particular public taste. The fact that taste changes, and as a consequence that artistic styles and types vary, is simply due to the everlasting desire on the part of the public for some new thing, and their equally permanent appreciation of novelty of idea or sensation. That master-minds have arisen to teach, and that they have taught with some success their own particular brand of art to the public, would seem rather to argue against the foregoing ideas were it not that, when the master-mind and the dominating influence are gone, the public desiring as always change and novelty, are ready to fly to any new teacher and master who can again afford them artistic pleasure. The influence of William Morris in household decoration is possibly the most far-reaching modern example of the influence of a single man upon the art of his period; but master-mind as was his, and master-craftsman as he was, it has needed but a few years since his death to start the undoing of much that he taught. After the movement initiated by Morris and carried further by the Arts and Crafts Society, which made for simplicity in structural design as well as in the decoration of furniture, we have now fallen back upon the flowery patterns of the early Victorian period, and there is hardly a drawing-room in fashionable London where the chairs and settees are not covered with early Victorian chintzes.

Artistic authorities may shout themselves hoarse, but the fashion having been set in Mayfair will be inevitably followed in Suburbia, and we are doubtless again at the beginning of the cycle of that curious manifestation of domestic decorative art which was current in the early part of the nineteenth century. It is, therefore, evident that it is futile to describe varying types of art of varying periods as good or bad, or to differentiate between them, unless some such permanent basis of comparison or standard of excellence be conceded. The differing types must be accepted as no more than the expression of the artistic period to which they belong. That being so, one cannot help thinking that the abuse which has been heaped of late (by unthinking votaries of Platagenet and Tudor heraldry) upon heraldic art in the seventeenth, eighteenth, and nineteenth centuries has very greatly overstepped the true proportion of the matter. Much that has been said is true, but what has been said too often lacks proportion. There is consequently much to be said in favour of allowing each period to create its own style and type of heraldic design, in conformity with the ideas concerning decorative art which are current outside heraldic thought. This is precisely what is not happening at the present time, even with all our boasted revival of armory and armorial art. The tendency at the present time is to slavishly copy examples of other periods. There is another point which is usually overlooked by the most blatant followers of this school of thought. What are the ancient models which remain to us? The early Rolls of Arms of which we hear so much are not, and were never intended to be, examples of artistic execution. They are merely memoranda of *fact*. It is absurd to suppose that an actual shield was painted with the crudity to be met with in the Rolls of Arms. It is equally absurd to accept as unimpeachable models Garter plates, seals, or architectural examples unless the purpose and medium—wax, enamel, or stone—in which they are executed is borne in mind, and the knowledge used with due discrimination. Mr Eve, without slavishly copying, appears originally to have modelled his work upon the admirable designs and ideas of the 'little masters' of German art in the sixteenth and seventeenth centuries. He afterwards progressed therefrom to a distinctive and very excellent style of his own. Mr Graham Johnson models his work upon Plantagenet and Tudor examples. The work of Père Anselm, and of Pugin, the first start towards the present ideas of heraldic art, embodying as it did so much of the beauty of the older work whilst possessing a character of its own, and developing ancient ideals by increased beauty of execution, has placed their reputation far above that of others, who, following in their footsteps, have not possessed their abilities. But with regard to most of the heraldic design of the present day as a whole it is very evident that we are simply picking and choosing tit-bits from the work of bygone craftsmen, and copying, more or less slavishly, examples of other periods. This makes for no advance in design either in its character or execution, nor will it result in any peculiarity of style which it will be possible in the future to identify with the present period. Our heraldry, like our architecture, though it may be dated in the twentieth century, will be a heterogeneous collection of isolated specimens of Gothic, Tudor, or Queen Anne style and type, which surely is as anachronistic as we consider to be those Dutch paintings which represent Christ and the Apostles in modern clothes.[193]

Roughly the periods into which the types of mantlings can be divided, when considered from the standpoint of their fashioning, are somewhat as follows. There is the earliest period of all, when the mantling depicted approximated closely if it was not an actual representation of the capelote really worn in battle. Examples of this will be found in the *Armorial de Gelre* and the Zurich *Wappenrolle*. As the mantling worn lengthened and evolved itself into the lambrequin, the mantling depicted in heraldic art was similarly increased in size, terminating in the long mantle drawn in profile but tasselled and with the scalloped edges, a type which is found surviving in some of the early Garter plates. This is the transition stage. The next definite period is when we find the mantling depicted on both sides of the helmet and the scalloped edges developed, in accordance with the romantic ideas of the period, into the slashes and cuts of the bold and artistic mantlings of Plantagenet armorial art.

Slowly decreasing in strength, but at the same time increasing in elaboration, this mantling and type continued until it had reached its highest pitch of exuberant elaboration in Stuart and early Georgian times. Side by side with this over-elaboration came the revulsion to a Puritan simplicity of taste which is to be found in other manifestations of art at the same time, and which made itself evident in heraldic decoration by the use as mantling of the plain uncut cloth suspended behind the shield. Originating in Elizabethan days, this plain cloth was much made use of, but towards the end of the Stuart period came that curious evolution of British heraldry which is peculiar to these countries alone. That is the entire omission of both helmet and mantling. How it originated it is difficult to under-

193. That heraldic art has blossomed since the World War was evidenced in an exhibition of work by contemporary artists held under the auspices of The Heraldry Society in London in 1968. This is probably due to a number of distinct factors: a conscious return to ancient principles; a greatly increased demand for impersonal arms, where, for advertising purposes, the arms are required to be bold and dramatic; a relaxation of many conventions, such as those that ordained the colours of wreath and mantling, which made design less elastic than it now is; an increased knowledge and awareness of heraldry, which has helped to put both designers and artists on their mettle, and sufficient work to employ a number of excellent artists who, in other circumstances, might have defected for more regular and lucrative employment.

stand, unless it be due to the fact that a large number, in fact a large proportion, of English families possessed a shield only and neither claimed nor used a crest, and that consequently a large number of heraldic representations give the shield only. It is rare indeed to find a shield surmounted by helmet and mantling when the former is not required to support a crest. At the same time we find, among the official records of the period, that the documents of chief importance were the Visitation Books. In these, probably from motives of economy or to save needless draughtsmanship, the trouble of depicting the helmet and mantling was dispensed with, and the crest is almost universally found depicted on the wreath, which is made to rest upon the shield, the helmet being omitted. That being an accepted official way of representing an achievement, small wonder that the public followed, and we find as a consequence that a large proportion of the bookplates during the seventeenth and eighteenth centuries had no helmet or mantling at all, the elaboration of the edges of the shield, together with the addition of decorative and needless accessories bearing no relation to the arms, fulfilling all purposes of decorative design. It should also be remembered that from towards the close of the Stuart period onward, England was taking her art and decoration almost entirely from Continental sources, chiefly French and Italian. In both the countries the use of crests was very limited indeed in extent, and the elimination of the helmet and mantling, and the elaboration in their stead of the edges of the shield, we probably owe to the effort to assimilate French and Italian forms of decoration to English arms. So obsolete had become the use of helmet and mantling that it is difficult to come across examples that one can put forward as mantlings typical of the period.

Helmets and mantlings were of course painted upon grants and upon the Stall plates of the knights of the various orders, but whilst the helmets became weak, of a pattern impossible to wear, and small in size, the mantling became of a stereotyped pattern, and of a design poor and wooden according to our present ideas.

Unofficial heraldry had sunk to an even lower style of art, and the regulation heraldic stationer's types of shield, mantling, and helmet are awe-inspiring in their ugliness.

The term 'mantle' is sometimes employed, but it would seem hardly quite correctly, to the parliamentary robe of estate upon which the arms of a peer of the realm were so frequently depicted at the end of the eighteenth and in the early part of the nineteenth centuries. Its popularity is an indication of the ever-constant predilection for something which is denied to others and the possession of which is a matter of privilege. Woodward, in his *Treatise on Heraldry*, treats of and dismisses the matter in one short sentence: 'In England the suggestion that the arms of peers should be mantled with their Parliament robes was never generally adopted.' In this statement he is quite incorrect, for as the accepted type in one particular opportunity of armorial display its use was absolutely universal. The opportunity in question was the emblazonment of arms upon carriage panels. In the early part of the nineteenth and at the end of the eighteenth centuries armorial bearings were painted of some size upon carriages, and there were few such paintings executed for the carriages, chariots, and state coaches of peers that did not appear upon a background of the robe of estate. With the modern craze for ostentatious unostentation (the result, there can be little doubt, in this respect of the wholesale appropriation of arms by those without a right to bear these ornaments), the decoration of a peer's carriage nowadays seldom shows more than a simple coronet, or a coroneted crest, initial, or monogram; but the State chariots of those who still possess them almost all, without exception, show the arms emblazoned upon the robe of estate. The Royal and many other State chariots made or refurbished for the coronation ceremonies in 1901 show that, when an opportunity of the fullest display properly arises, the robe of estate is not yet a thing of the past. 665 is from a photograph of a carriage panel, and shows the arms of a

665 Carriage Panel of Georgiana, Marchioness of Cholmondeley.

former Marchioness of Cholmondeley displayed in this manner. Incidentally it also shows a practice frequently resorted to, but quite unauthorised, of taking one supporter from the husband's shield and the other (when the wife was an heiress) from the arms of her family. The arms are those of Georgiana Charlotte, widow of George James, first Marquess of Cholmondeley, and younger daughter and coheir of Peregrine, third Duke of Ancaster. She became a widow in 1827 and died in 1838, so the panel must have been painted between those dates. The arms shown are: 'Quarterly, 1 and 4, gules, in chief two esquires' helmets proper, and in base a garb or (for Cholmondeley); 2. gules, a chevron between three eagles' heads erased argent; 3. or, on a fesse between two chevrons sable, three cross crosslets or (for Walpole), and on an escutcheon of pretence the arms of Bertie, namely: argent, three battering-rams fesswise in pale proper, headed and garnished azure.' The supporters shown are: 'Dexter, a griffin sable, armed, winged, and membered or (from the Cholmondeley achievement); sinister, a friar vested in russet with staff and rosary or' (one of the supporters belonging to the Barony of Willoughby D'Eresby, to which the Marchioness of Cholmondeley in her own right was a coheir until the abeyance in the Barony was determined in favour of her elder sister).

'In later times the arms of sovereigns—the German Electors, &c.—were mantled, usually with crimson velvet fringed with gold, lined with ermine, and crowned; but the mantling armoyé was one of the marks of dignity used by the Pairs de France, and by Cardinals resident in France; it was also employed by some great nobles in other countries. The mantling of the Princes and Dukes of Mirandola was chequy argent and azure, lined with ermine. In France the mantling of the Chancelier was of cloth of gold; that of Présidents, of scarlet, lined with alternate strips of ermine and *petit gris*. In France, Napoleon I, who used a mantling of purple semé of golden bees, decreed that the princes and grand dignitaries should use an azure mantling thus semé; those of Dukes were to be plain, and lined with vair instead of ermine. In 1817 a mantling of azure, fringed with gold and lined with ermine, was appropriated to the dignity of Pair de France.'

The *Pavilion* is a feature of heraldic art which is quite unknown to British heraldry, and one can call to mind no single instance of its use in this country; but as its use is very prominent in Germany and other countries, it cannot be overlooked. It is confined to the arms of sovereigns, and the pavilion is the tent-like erection within which the heraldic achievement is displayed. The pavilion seems to have originated in France, where it can be traced back upon the Great Seals of the kings to its earliest form and appearance upon the seal of Louis XI. In the case of the Kings of France, it was of azure semé-de-lis or. The pavilion used with the arms of the German Emperor was of gold semé alternately of Imperial crowns and eagles displayed sable, and is lined with ermine. The motto is carried on a crimson band, and it is surmounted by the Imperial crown, and a banner of the German colours gules, argent, and sable. The pavilion used by the German Emperor as King of Prussia was of crimson, semé of black eagles and gold crowns, and the band which carries the motto was blue. The pavilions of the King of Bavaria and the Grand Duke of Baden, the King of Saxony, the Grand Dukes of Hesse, of Mecklenburg-Schwerin, of Saxe-Weimar-Eisenach, of Saxe-Meiningen-Hildburghausen, of Saxe-Altenburg, and Anhalt, were all of crimson.

In Germany heraldry a rather more noticeable distinction is drawn than with ourselves between the lambrequin (*Helmdecke*) and the mantle (*Helmmantel*). This more closely approximates to the robe of estate, though the *helmmantel* has not in Germany the rigid significance of peerage degree that the robe of estate has in this country. The German *helmmantel* with few exceptions is always of purple lined with ermine, and whilst the mantel always falls directly from the coronet or cap, the pavilion is arranged in a dome-like form which bears the crown upon its summit. The pavilion is supposed to be the invention of the Frenchman Philip Moreau (1680), and found its way from France to Germany, where both in the Greater and Lesser Courts it was enthusiastically adopted. Great Britain, Austria-Hungary, Spain, Portugal, and Württemberg are the only Royal Arms in which the pavilion does not figure.

25 · The torse, or wreath

The actual helmet, from the very *earliest* heraldic representations which have come down to us, would sometimes appear not to have had any mantling, the crest being affixed direct to the (then) flat top of the helmet in use. But occasional crests appear very early in the existence of 'ordered' armory, and at much about the same time we find the 'textile' covering of the helmet coming into heraldic use. In the earliest times we find that frequently the crest itself was continued into the mantling. But where this was not possible, the attaching of the crest to the helmet when the mantling intervened left an unsightly joining. The unsightliness very soon called forth a remedy. At first this remedy took the form of a coronet or a plain fillet or ribbon round the point of juncture, sometimes with and sometimes without the ends being visible. If the ends were shown they were represented as floating behind, sometimes with and sometimes without a representation of the bow or knot in which they were tied. The plain fillet still continued to be used long after the torse had come into recognised use. The consideration of crest coronets has been already included, but with regard to the wreath an analysis of the Plantagenet Garter plates will afford some definite basis from which to start deduction.

Of the eighty-six achievements reproduced in Mr St John Hope's book, five have no crest. Consequently we have eighty-one examples to analyse. Of these there are ten in which the crest is not attached to the lambrequin and helmet by anything perceptible, eight are attached with fillets of varying widths, twenty-one crests are upon chapeaux, and twenty-nine issue from coronets. But at no period governed by the series is it possible that either fillet, torse, chapeau, or coronet was in use to the exclusion of another form. This remark applies more particularly to the fillet and torse (the latter of which undoubtedly at a later date superseded the former), for both at the beginning and at the end of the series referred to we find the fillet and the wreath or torse, and at both periods we find crests without either coronet, torse, chapeau, or fillet. The fillet must soon afterwards (in the fifteenth century) have completely fallen into desuetude. The torse was so small and unimportant a matter that upon seals it would probably equally escape the attention of the engraver and the observer, and probably there would be little to be gained by a systematic hunt through early seals to discover the date of its introduction, but it will be noticed that no wreaths appear in some of the early Rolls. General Leigh[194] says, 'In the time of Henry the Fifth, and long after, no man had his badge set on a wreath under the degree of a knight. But that order is worn away.' It probably belongs to the end of the fourteenth century. There can be little doubt that its twisted shape was an evolution from the plain fillet suggested by the turban

194. This is clearly meant to be Gerard Leigh or Legh, who wrote the well-known, though not particularly accurate or scholarly, *The Accedence of Armorie* (1564).

of the East. We read in the old romances, in Mallory's *Morte d'Arthur* and elsewhere, of valiant knights who in battle or tournament wore the favour of some lady, or even the lady's sleeve, upon their helmets. It always used to be a puzzle to me how the sleeve could have been worn upon the helmet, and I wonder how many of the present-day novelists, who so glibly make their knightly heroes of olden time wear the 'favours' of their lady-lovers, know how it was done? The favour did not take the place of the crest. A knight did not lightly discard an honoured, inherited, and known crest for the sake of wearing a favour only too frequently the mere result of a temporary flirtation; nor to wear her colours could he at short notice discard or renew his lambrequin, surcoat, or the housings and trappings of his horse. He simply took the favour—the colours, a ribbon, or a handkerchief of the lady, as the case might be—and twisted it in and out or over and over the fillet which surrounded the joining-place of crest and helmet. To put her favour on his helmet was the work of a moment. The wearing of a lady's sleeve, which must have been an honour greatly prized, is of course the origin of the well-known 'maunch', the solitary charge in the arms of Conyers, Hastings, and Wharton. Doubtless the sleeve twined with the fillet would be made to encircle the base of the crest, and it is not unlikely that the wide hanging mouth of the sleeve might have been used for the lambrequin. The dresses of ladies at that period were decorated with the arms of their families, so in each case would be of the 'colours' of the lady, so that the sleeve and its colours would be quickly identified, as it was no doubt usually intended they should be. The accidental result of twining a favour in the fillet, in conjunction with the pattern obviously suggested by the turban of the East, produced the conventional torse or wreath. As the conventional slashings of the lambrequin hinted at past hard fighting in battle, so did the conventional torse hint at past service to and favour of ladies, love and war being the occupations of the perfect knight of romance. How far short of the ideal knight of romance the knight of fact fell, perhaps the frequent bordures and batons of heraldry are the best indication. At first, as is evident from the Garter plates, the colours of the torse seem to have had little or no compulsory relation to the 'livery colours' of the arms. The instances to be gleaned from the Plantagenet Garter plates which have been reproduced are as follows:

Sir John Bourchier, Lord Bourchier. Torse: sable and vert. Arms: argent and gules.

Sir John Grey, Earl of Tankerville. Torse: vert, gules, and argent. Arms: gules and argent.

Sir Lewis Robsart, Lord Bourchier. Torse: azure, or, and sable. Arms: vert and or. [The crest, derived from his wife (who was a daughter of Lord Bourchier) is practically the same as the one first quoted. It will be noticed that the torse differs.]

Sir Edward Cherleton, Lord Cherleton of Powis. Torse: gules and sable. Arms: or and gules.

Sir Gaston de Foix, Count de Longueville. Torse: or and gules. Arms: or and gules.

Sir William Nevill, Lord Fauconberg. Torse: argent and gules. Arms: gules and argent.

Sir Richard Wydville, Lord Rivers. Torse: vert. Arms: argent and gules.

Sir Henry Bourchier, Earl of Essex. Torse: sable and vert. Arms: argent and gules. [This is the same crest above alluded to.]

Sir Thomas Stanley, Lord Stanley. Torse: or and azure. Arms: or and azure.

Sir John Bourchier, Lord Berners. Torse: gules and argent. Arms: argent and gules. [This is the same crest above alluded to.]

Sir Walter Devereux, Lord Ferrers. Torse: argent and sable. Arms: argent and gules. [The crest really issues from a coronet upon a torse in a previous case; this crest issues from a torse only.]

Sir Francis Lovel, Viscount Lovel. Torse: azure and or. Arms: or and gules.

Sir Thomas Burgh, Lord Burgh. Torse: azure and sable. Arms: azure and ermine.

Sir Richard Tunstall, K.G. Torse: argent and sable. Arms: sable and argent.

I can suggest no explanation of these differences unless it be, which is not unlikely, that they perpetuate 'favours' worn; or perhaps a more likely supposition is that the wreath or torse was of the 'family colours', as these were actually worn by the servants or retainers of each person. If this be not the case, why are the colours of the wreath termed the livery colours? At the present time in an English or Irish grant of arms the colours are not specified, but the crest is stated to be 'on a wreath of the colours'. In Scotland, however, the crest is granted in the following words: 'and upon a wreath of his liveries is set for crest'. Consequently, I have very little doubt, the true state of the case is that originally the wreath was depicted of the colours of the livery which was worn. Then new families came into prominence and eminence, and had no liveries to inherit. They were granted arms and chose the tinctures of their arms as their 'colours', and used these colours for their personal liveries. The natural consequence would be in such a case that the torse, being in unison with the livery, was also in unison with the arms. The consequence is that it has become a fixed, unalterable rule in British heraldry that the torse shall be of the principal metal and of the principal colour of the arms.[195] I know of no recent exception to this rule, the latest, as far as I am aware, being a grant in the early years of the eighteenth century. This, it is stated in the patent, was the regranting of a coat of foreign origin. Doubtless the formality of a grant was substituted for the usual registration in this case, owing to a lack of formal proof of a right to the arms, but there is no doubt that the peculiarities of the foreign arms, as they had been previously borne, were preserved in the grant. The peculiarity in this case consisted of a torse of three tinctures. The late Lyon Clerk once pointed out to me, in Lyon Register, an instance of a coat there matriculated with a torse of three colours, but I unfortunately made no note of it at the time. Woodward alludes to the curious chequy wreath on the seals of Robert Stewart, Duke of Albany, in 1389. This appears to have been repeated in the seals of his son Murdoch.

The wreath of Patrick Hepburn appears to be of roses in the Gelre 'Armorial', and a careful examination of the plates in this volume will show many curious Continental instances of substitutes for the conventional torse. Though by no

195. The 'unalterable rule' has now been altered. Wreaths may be of any colour and metal, or colours and metals. For example, the wreath in the arms of The Heraldry Society is or, azure and gules. This is really a return to early practice, and gives the designer of arms much more scope than when limited to the principal metal and colour in the arms.

means peculiar to British heraldry, there can be no manner of doubt that the wreath in the United Kingdom has obtained a position of legalised necessity and constant usage and importance which exists in no other country.

As has been already explained, the torse should fit closely to the crest, its object and purpose being merely to hide the joining of crest and helmet. Unfortunately in British heraldry this purpose has been ignored. Doubtless resulting first from the common practice of depicting a crest upon a wreath and without a helmet, and secondly from the fact that many English crests are quite unsuitable to place on a helmet, in fact impossible to affix by the aid of a wreath to a helmet, and thirdly from our ridiculous rules of position for a helmet, which result in the crest being depicted (in conjunction with the representation of the helmet) in a position many such crests never could have occupied on any helmet, the effect has been to cause the wreath to lose its real form, which encircled the *helmet*, and to become considered as no more than a straight support for and relating only to the crest. When, therefore, the crest and its supporting basis is transferred from indefinite space to the helmet, the support, which is the torse, is still represented as a flat resting-place for the crest, and it is consequently depicted as a straight and rigid bar, balanced upon the apex of the helmet. This is now and for long has been the only accepted official way of depicting a wreath in England. Certainly this is an ungraceful and inartistic rendering, and a rendering far removed from any actual helmet wreath that can ever have been actually borne. Whilst one has no wish to defend the 'rigid bar', which has nothing to recommend it, it is at the same time worth while to point out that the heraldic day of actual helmets and actual usage is long since over, never to be revived, and that our heraldry of today is merely decorative and pictorial. The rigid bar is none other than a conventional-ised form of the actual torse, and is perhaps little more at variance with the reality than is our conventionalised method of depicting a lambrequin.[196] Whilst this conventional torse remains the official pattern, it is hopeless to attempt to banish such a method of representation: but Lyon King of Arms, happily, will have none of it in his official register or on his patents, and few heraldic artists of any repute now care to so design or represent it. As always officially painted it must consist of six links alternately of metal and colour (the 'livery colours' of the arms), of which the metal must be the first to be shown to the dexter side. The torse is now supposed to be and represented as a skein of coloured silk intertwined with a gold or silver cord.

196. The 'rigid bar' has, happily, long been forsworn by artists, but the problem of a helm facing dexter and a crest frontwards remains, although artists more and more twist helm and crest to-wards each other to such degree as the kings of arms will tolerate. There has always been a clamour to abolish the helmet rule, but there is one great objection to this, namely that it has existed now for some three and a half hundred years. If it were abolished, then overnight the man whose crest was a lion's head and he whose crest was a lion's head affronty would at once have identical crests. If only the position of the crest had not been regarded as a material difference, then all would be well; but such has not been the case. Crests are still officially blazoned as being 'on a wreath', whereas if they were regarded as modelled in the round it would be logical to alter the blazon to 'within a wreath'.

26 · Supporters

In this country a somewhat fictitious importance has become attached to supporters, owing to their almost exclusive reservation to the highest rank. The rules which hold at the moment will be recited presently, but there can be no doubt that originally they were in this country little more than mere decorative and artistic appendages, being devised and altered from time to time by different artists according as the artistic necessities of the moment demanded. The subject of the origin of supporters has been very ably dealt with in *A Treatise on Heraldry* by Woodward and Burnett, and with all due acknowledgement I take from that work the subjoined extract:

'Supporters are figures of living creatures placed at the side or sides of an armorial shield, and appearing to support it. French writers make a distinction, giving the name of *Supports* to animals, real or imaginary, thus employed; while human figures or angels similarly used are called *Tenants*. Trees, and other inanimate objects which are sometimes used, are called *Soutiens*.

'Menêtrier and other old writers trace the origin of supporters to the usages of the tournaments, where the shields of the combatants were exposed for inspection, and guarded by their servants or pages disguised in fanciful attire: "C'est des Tournois qu'est venu cet usage parce que les chevaliers y faisoient porter leurs lances, et leurs écus, par des pages, et des valets de pied, deguisez en ours, en lions, en mores, et en sauvages' (*Usage des Armoiries*, p. 119).

'The old romances give us evidence that this custom prevailed; but I think only after the use of supporters had already arisen from another source.

'There is really little doubt now that Anstis was quite correct when, in his *Aspilogia*, he attributed the origin of supporters to the invention of the engraver, who filled up the spaces at the top and sides of the triangular shield upon a circular seal with foliage, or with fanciful animals. Any good collection of medieval seals will strengthen this conviction. For instance, the two volumes of Laing's *Scottish Seals* afford numerous examples in which the shields used in the thirteenth and fourteenth centuries were placed between two creatures resembling lizards or dragons. (See the seal of ALEXANDER DE BALLIOL, 1295; Laing, ii, 74.)

★　★　★　★　★

'The seal of John, Duke of Normandy, eldest son of the King of FRANCE, before 1316 bears his arms (FRANCE-ANCIENT, *a bordure gules*) between two lions rampant away from the shield, and an eagle with expanded wings standing above it. The *secretum* of Isabelle de FLANDRES (*c.* 1308) has her shield placed between three lions, each charged with a bend (Vrée, *Gen. Com. Flanr.*, Plates XLIII, XLIV, XCII). In 1332 AYMON OF SAVOY places his arms (SAVOY, *with a label*) between a winged lion in chief and a lion without wings at either side. Later, on the seal of AMADEUS VI, a lion's head between wings became the crest of SAVOY. In 1332 AMADEUS bears SAVOY on a lozenge between in chief two eagles, in base two lions. (Cibrario, Nos. 61, 64; and Guichenon, tome i, No. 130). In Scotland the shield of REGINALD CRAWFORD in 1292 is placed between two dogs, and surmounted by a fox; in the same year the paly shield of REGINALD, Earl of ATHOLE, appears between two lions in chief and as many griffins in flanks. (Laing, i, 210, 761.

'The seal of HUMBERT II, Dauphin de Viennois in 1349, is an excellent example of the fashion. The shield of DAUPHINY is in the centre of a quatrefoil. Two savages mounted on griffins support its flanks; on the upper edge an armed knight sits on a couchant lion, and the space in base is filled by a human face between two wingless dragons. The spaces are sometimes filled with the Evangelistic symbols, as on the seal of YOLANTE DE FLANDRES, Countess of BAR (c. 1340). The seal of JEANNE, Dame de PLASNES, in 1376 bears her arms *en bannière* a quatrefoil supported by two kneeling angels, a demi-angel in chief, and a lion couchant guardant in base.'

Corporate and other seals afford countless examples of the interstices in the design being filled with the figures similar to those from which in later days the supporters of a family have been deduced. But I am myself convinced that the argument can be carried further. Fanciful ornamentation or meaningless devices may have first been made use of by seal engravers, but it is very soon found that the badge is in regular use for this purpose, and we find both animate and inanimate badges employed. Then where this is possible the badge, if animate, is made to support the helmet and crest, and, later on, the shield, and there can be no doubt the badge was in fact acting as a supporter long before the science of armory recognised the existence of supporters.

Before passing to supporters proper, it may be well to briefly allude to various figures which are to be found in a position analogous to that of supporters. The single human figure entire, or in the form of a demi-figure appearing above the shield, is very frequently to be met with, but the addition of such figures *was and remains purely artistic*, and I knew of no single instance in British armory where one figure, animate or inanimate, had ever existed alone in the character of a single supporter, and as an integral part of the heritable armorial achievement, until in 1906 the arms of Falkirk were matriculated in Lyon Register with a single supporter, described as such, viz., 'a lion rampant affronté gules,' etc. Of course I except those figures upon which the arms of certain families are properly displayed. These will be presently alluded to, but though they are certainly exterior ornaments, I do not think they can be properly classed as supporters unless to this term is given some elasticity, or unless the term has some qualifying remarks of reservation added to it. There are, however, many instances of armorial ensigns depicted, and presumably correctly, in the form of banners supported by a single animal, but it will always be found that the single animal is but one of the pair of duly allocated supporters. Many instances of arms depicted in this manner will be found in *Prince Arthur's Book*. The same method of display was adopted in some number of cases, and with some measure of success, in Foster's *Peerage* Single figures are very frequently to be met with in German and Continental heraldry, but on these occasions, as with ourselves, the position they occupy is

PLATE VIII

CONCILIO ET LABORE

The Arms of Manchester

merely that of an artistic accessory, and bears no inseparable relation to the heraldic achievement. The single exception to the foregoing statement of which I am aware is to be found in the arms of the Swiss Cantons. These thirteen coats are sometimes quartered upon one shield, but when displayed separately each is accompanied by a single supporter. Zurich, Lucerne, Uri, Unterwalden, Glarus, and Basle all bear the supporter on the dexter side; Bern, Schwyz, Zug, Freiburg, and Solothurn on the sinister. Schaffhausen (a ram) and Appenzell (a bear) place their supporters in full aspect behind the shield.

On the corbels of Gothic architecture, shields of arms are frequently supported by *Angels*, which, however, cannot generally be regarded as heraldic appendages —being merely supposed to indicate that the owners have contributed to the erection of the fabric. Examples of this practice will be found on various ecclesiastical edifices in Scotland, and among others at Melrose Abbey, St Giles', Edinburgh, and the church of Seton in East Lothian. An interesting instance of an angel supporting a shield occurs on the beautiful seal of Mary of Gueldres, Queen of James II (1459); and the Privy Seal of David II, a hundred years earlier, exhibits a pretty design of an escutcheon charged with the ensigns of Scotland, and borne by two arms issuing from clouds above, indicative of divine support.★

Of instances of single objects from which shields are found depending or supported the *Treatise on Heraldry* states:

'Allusion has been made to the usage by which on vesica-shaped shields ladies of high rank are represented as supporting with either hand shields of arms. From this probably arose the use of a single supporter. MARGUERITE DE COURCELLES in 1284, and ALIX DE VERDUN in 1311, bear in one hand a shield of the husband's arms, in the other one of their own. The curious seal of MURIEL, Countess of STRATHERNE, in 1284, may be considered akin to these. In it the shield is supported partly by a falcon, and partly by a human arm issuing from the sinister side of the *vesica*, and holding the falcon by the jesses (LAING, i. 764). The early seal of BOLESLAS III, King of POLAND, in 1255, bears a knight holding a shield charged with the Polish eagle (VOSSBERG, *Die Siegel des Mittelalters*). In 1283 the seal of FLORENT of HAINAULT bears a warrior in chain mail supporting a shield charged with a lion impaling an eagle dimidiated.

★   ★   ★   ★   ★

'On the seal of HUMPHREY DE BOHUN in 1322 the *guige* is held by a swan, the badge of the Earls of HEREFORD; and in 1356 the shield of the first Earl of DOUGLAS is supported by a lion whose head is covered by the crested helm, a fashion of which there are many examples. A helmed lion holds the shield of MAGNUS I, Duke of BRUNSWICK, in 1326.

★   ★   ★   ★   ★

'On the seal of JEAN, Duc de BERRI, in 1393 the supporter is a helmed swan (compare the armorial slab of HENRY of LANCASTER, in BOUTELL, Plate LXXIX).[197]

197. This is Plate LXIII, facing page 210, in the 1863 Edition of *Heraldry, Historical and Popular*, by the Reverend Charles Boutell.

★ Plate XI, 10, Laing's *Catalogue*, No. 29. At each side of the King's seated figure on the counter-seal of Robert II (1386) the arms of Scotland are supported from behind by a skeleton within an embattled buttress (*Catalogue*, No. 34).

Jean IV, Comte d'Alençon (1408), has a helmed lion sejant as supporter. In 1359 a signet of Louis van Male, Count of Flanders, bears a lion sejant, helmed and crested, and mantled with the arms of Flanders between two small escutcheons of Nevers, or the county of Burgundy ['Azure, billetty, a lion rampant or'], and Rethel ('Gules, two heads of rakes fesswise in pale or').

★   ★   ★   ★   ★

'A single lion sejant, helmed and crested, bearing on its breast the quartered arms of Burgundy between two or three other escutcheons, was used by the Dukes up to the death of Charles the Bold in 1475. In Litta's splendid work, *Famiglie celebri Italiane*, the Buonarotti arms are supported by a brown dog sejant, helmed, and crested with a pair of dragon's wings issuing from a crest-coronet. On the seal of Thomas Holland, Earl of Kent, in 1380 the shield is buckled round the neck of the white hind lodged, the badge of his half-brother, Richard II. Single supporters were very much in favour in the thirteenth and fourteenth centuries, and the examples are numerous. Charles, Dauphin de Viennois (c. 1355), has his shield held by a single dolphin. In 1294 the seal of the Dauphin Jean, son of Humbert I, bears the arms of Dauphiné pendent from the neck of a griffon. The shields of arms of Bertrand de Bricquebec, in 1325; Pierre de Tournebu, in 1339; of Charles, Count of Alençon, in 1356; and of Oliver de Clisson in 1397, are all supported by a warrior who stands behind the shield. In England the seal of Henry Percy, first Earl, in 1346, and another in 1345, have similar representations.

'On several of our more ancient seals only one supporter is represented, and probably the earliest example of this arrangement occurs on the curious seal of William, first Earl of Douglas (c. 1356), where the shield is supported from behind by a lion "sejant", *with his head in the helmet*, which is surmounted by the crest.

'On the seal of Archibald, fourth Earl of Douglas (c. 1418), the shield is held, along with a club, in the right hand of a savage *erect*, who bears a helmet in his left; while on that of William, eighth Earl (1446), a *kneeling* savage holds a club in his right hand, and supports a couché shield on his left arm.'

An example reproduced from Jost Amman's *Wappen und Stammbuch*, published at Frankfurt, 1589, will be found in 666. In this the figure partakes more of the character of a shield guardian than a shield supporter. The arms are those of Sigmund Hagelshaimer, otherwise Helt, living at Nürnberg. The arms are 'Sable, on a bend argent, an arrow gules'. The crest is the head and neck of a hound sable, continued into a mantling sable, lined argent. The crest is charged with a pale argent, and thereupon an arrow as in the arms, the arrow-head piercing the ear of the hound.

Seated figures as supporters are rare, but one occurs in 667, which shows the arms of the Vöhlin family. They bear: 'Argent, on a fesse sable, three "P's" argent.' The wings which form the crest are charged with the same device. This curious charge of the three letters is explained in the following saying:

> Piper Peperit Pecuniam,
> Pecunia Peperit Pompam,
> Pompa Peperit Pauperiem,
> Pauperies Peperit Pietatem.

666 *Arms of Sigmund Hagelshaimer.*

667 *Arms of Vöhlin of Augsburg.*

There are, however, certain exceptions to the British rule that there can be no single supporters, if the objects upon which shields of arms are displayed are accepted as supporters. It was always customary to display the arms of the Lord High Admiral on the sail of the ship. In the person of King William IV, before he he succeeded to the throne, the office of Lord High Admiral was vested for a short time, but it had really fallen into desuetude at an earlier date and has not been revived again, so that to all intents and purposes it is now extinct, and this recognised method of depicting arms is consequently also extinct. But there is one other case which forms a unique instance which can be classified with no others. The arms of Campbell of Craignish are always represented in a curious manner, the gyronny coat of Campbell appearing on a shield displayed in front of a lymphad (Plate II). What the origin of this practice is it would be difficult to say; probably it merely originated in the imaginative ideas of an artist when making a seal for that family, artistic reasons suggesting the display of the gyronny arms of Campbell in front of the lymphad of Lorne. The family, however, seem to have universally adopted this method of using their arms, and in the year 1875, when Campbell of Inverneil matriculated in Lyon Register, the arms were matriculated in that form. I know of no other instance of any such coat of arms, and this branch of the Ducal House of Campbell possesses armorial bearings which, from the official standpoint, are absolutely unique from one end of Europe to the other.

In Germany the use of arms depicted in front of the eagle displayed, either single-headed or double-headed, is very far from being unusual. Whatever may have been its meaning originally in that country, there is no doubt that now and for some centuries past it has been accepted as meaning, or as indicative of, princely rank or other honours of the Holy Roman Empire. But I do not think it can always have had that meaning. About the same date the Earl of Menteith placed his shield on the breast of an eagle, as did Alexander, Earl of Ross, in 1338; and in 1394 we find the same ornamentation in the seal of Euphemia, Countess of Ross. The shield of Ross is borne in her case on the breast of an eagle, while the arms of Leslie and Comyn appear on its displayed wings. On several other Scottish seals of the same era, the shield is placed on the breast of a displayed eagle, as on those of Alexander Abernethy and Alexander Cumin of Buchan (1292), and Sir David Lindsay, Lord of Crawford. English heraldry supplies several similar examples, of which we may mention the armorial insignia of Richard, Earl of Cornwall, brother of Henry III, and of the ancient family of Latham, in the fourteenth century. A curious instance of a shield placed on the breast of a *hawk* is noticed by Hone in his *Table Book*, viz. the arms of the Lord of the Manor of Stoke-Lyne, in the county of Oxford. It appears therefrom that when Charles I held his Parliament at Oxford, the offer of knighthood was gratefully declined by the then Lord of Stoke-Lyne, who merely requested, and obtained, the Royal permission to place the arms of his family upon the breast of a hawk, which has ever since been employed in the capacity of single supporter. What authority exists for this statement it is impossible to ascertain, and one must doubt its accuracy, because in England at any rate no arms, allocated to any particular *territorial estate*, have ever received official recognition.

In later years, as indicative of rank in the Holy Roman Empire, the eagle has been rightly borne by the first Duke of Marlborough and by Henrietta his daughter, Duchess of Marlborough, but the use of the eagle by the later Dukes of Marlborough would appear to be entirely without authority, inasmuch as the princedom, created in the person of the first duke, became extinct on his death. His daughters, though entitled of right to the courtesy rank of princess and its accompanying privilege of the right to use the eagle displayed behind their arms, could not transmit it to their descendants upon whom the title of Duke of Marlborough was specially entailed by English Act of Parliament.

The Earl of Denbigh and several members of the Fielding family have often made use of it with their arms, in token of their supposed descent from the Counts of Hapsburg, which, if correct, would apparently confer the right upon them. This descent, however, has been much questioned, and in late years the claim thereto would seem to have been practically dropped. The late Earl Cowper, the last remaining Prince of the Holy Roman Empire in the British Peerage, was entitled to use the double eagle behind his shield, being the descendant and representative of George Nassau Clavering Cowper, third Earl Cowper, created a Prince of the Holy Roman Empire by the Emperor Joseph II, the patent being dated at Vienna, 31 January 1778, and this being followed by a Royal Licence from King George III to accept and bear the title in this country.

There are some others who have the right by reason of honours of lesser rank of the Holy Roman Empire, and amongst these may be mentioned Lord Methuen, who bears the eagle by Royal Warrant dated 4 April 1775. Sir Thomas Arundel, who served in the Imperial army of Hungary, having in an engagement with the Turks near Strignum taken their standard with his own hands, was by Rodolph II created Count of the Empire to hold for him and the heirs of his body for ever, dated at Prague 14 December 1595. This patent, of course, means that every one of his descendants in the male line has the rank of a Count of the Empire, and that every daughter of any such male descendant is a Countess, but this does not confer the rank of count or countess upon descendants of the daughters. It was this particular patent of creation that called forth the remark from Queen Elizabeth I that she would not have her sheep branded by any foreign shepherd, and we believe that this patent was the origin of the rule translated in later times (*temp.* George IV) into a definite Royal Warrant, requiring that no English subject shall, without the express Royal Licence of the Sovereign conveyed in writing, accept or wear any foreign title or decoration. No Royal Licence was subsequently obtained by the Arundel family, who therefore, according to British law, are denied the use of the privileged Imperial eagle. Outside those cases in which the double eagle is used in this country to denote rank of the Holy Roman Empire, the usage of the eagle displayed behind the arms or any analogous figure is in British heraldry most limited.

One solitary authoritative instance of the use of the displayed eagle is found in the coat of arms of the city of Perth. These arms are recorded in Lyon Register, having been matriculated for that Royal Burgh about the year 1672. The official blazon of the arms is as follows: 'Gules ane holy lambe passant regardant staff and cross argent, with the banner of St Andrew proper, all within a double tressure counter-flowered of the second, the escutcheon being surmounted on the breast of ane eagle with two necks displayed or. The motto in ane Escroll, "Pro Rege Lege et Grege."'

Another instance of usage, though purely devoid of authority, occurs in the case of a coat of arms set up on one of the panels in the Hall of Lincoln's Inn. In this case the achievement is displayed on the breast of a single-headed eagle. What reason led to its usage in this manner I am quite unaware, and I have not the slightest reason for supposing it to be authentic. The family of Stuart-Menteith also place their arms upon a single-headed eagle displayed gules, as was formerly to be seen in Debrett's *Peerage*, but though arms are matriculated to them in Lyon Register, this particular adornment forms no part thereof, and it has now disappeared from the printed *Peerage* books. The family of Britton have, however, recently recorded as a badge a double-headed eagle displayed ermine, holding in its claws an escutcheon of their arms (Plate XI).

Occasionally batons or wands or other insignia of office are to be found in conjunction with armorial bearings, but these will be more fully dealt with under the heading of Insignia of Office. Before dealing with the usual supporters, one perhaps may briefly allude to 'inanimate' supporters.

Probably the most curious instance of all will be found in the achievement of the Earls of Errol as it appears in the MS. of Sir David Lindsay. In this two ox-yokes take the place of the supporters. The curious tradition which has been attached to the Hay arms is quoted as follows by Sir James Balfour Paul, Lyon King of Arms, in his *Heraldry in relation to Scottish History and Art*, who writes:

313

'Take the case of the well-known coat of the Hays, and hear the description of its origin as given by Nisbet: "In the reign of Kenneth III, about the year 980, when the Danes invaded Scotland, and prevailing in the battle of Luncarty, a country Scotsman with his two sons, of great strength and courage, having rural weapons, as the yokes of their plough, and such plough furniture, stopped the Scots in their flight in a certain defile, and upbraiding them with cowardice, obliged them to rally, who with them renewed the battle, and gave a total overthrow to the victorious Danes; and it is said by some, after the victory was obtained, the old man lying on the ground, wounded and fatigued, cried, 'Hay, Hay,' which word became a surname to his posterity. He and his sons being nobilitate, the King gave him the aforesaid arms (argent, three escutcheons gules) to intimate that the father and the two sons had been luckily the three shields of Scotland, and gave them as much land in the Carse of Gowrie as a falcon did fly over without lighting, which having flown a great way, she lighted on a stone there called the Falcon Stone to this day. The circumstances of which story is not only perpetuated by the three escutcheons, but by the exterior ornaments of the achievement of the family of Errol; having for crest, on a wreath, a falcon proper; for supporters two men in country habits, holding the oxen-yokes of a plough over their shoulders; and for motto, 'Serva jugum.'"'

'Unfortunately for the truth of this picturesque tale there are several reasons which render it utterly incredible, not the least being that at the period of the supposed battle armorial bearings were quite unknown, and could not have formed the subject of a royal gift. Hill Burton, indeed, strongly doubts the occurrence of the battle itself, and says that Hector Boece, who relates the occurrence, must be under strong suspicion of having entirely invented it. As for the origin of the name itself, it is, as Mr Cosmo Innes points out in his work on *Scottish Surnames*, derived from a place in Normandy, and neither it nor any other surname occurred in Scotland till long after the battle of Luncarty.[197a] I have mentioned this story in some detail, as it is a very typical specimen of its class; but there are others like unto it, often traceable to the same incorrigible old liar, Hector Boece.'

It is not unlikely that the ox-yoke was a badge of the Hays, Earls of Errol, and a reference to the variations of the original arms, crest, and supporters of Hay will show how the changes have been rung on the shields, falcon, ox-yokes, and countrymen of the legend.

Another instance is to be found in the arms of the Mowbray family as they were at one time depicted with an ostrich feather on either side of the shield (675, p. 357), and at first one might be inclined to class these amongst the in-animate supporters. The Garter plate, however, of John Beaufort, Duke of Somerset, probably supplies the key to the whole matter, for this shows not only the ostrich feathers but also supporters of the ordinary character in their usual position. From the last-mentioned instance, it is evident the ostrich feathers can

197a. G. F. Black (*The surnames of Scotland* (1946), p. 350) derives the name from Old High German *haga* through French *haie* of the time of Charles the Bald. The word appears as a French place-name element in the middle of the 11th century. The first Scots appearance he records is that of William de Haya, who obtained the lands of (H)errol in Gowrie towards the end of the following century.

be only representations of the badge, their character doubtless being peculiarly adaptable to the curious position they occupy. They are of course the same in the case of the Mowbray arms, and doubtless the ox-yoke of the Earl of Errol is similarly no more than a badge.

A most curious instance of supporters is to be found in the case of the arms of Viscount Montgomery.[198] This occurs in a record of them in Ulster's Office, where the arms appear without the usual kind of supporters, but represented with an arm in armour, on either side issuing from clouds in base, the hands supporting the shield.

When supporters are inanimate objects, the escutcheon is said to be cottised —a term derived from the French word *coté* (a side)—in contradistinction to supported. An old Scottish term for supporters was 'bearers'.

Amongst other cases where the shield is cottised by inanimate objects may be mentioned the following. The Breton family of 'Bastard' depict their shield cottised by two swords, with the points in base. The Marquises Alberti similarly use two lighted flambeaux, and the Dalzells (of Binns) the extraordinary device of a pair of tent-poles. Whether this last has been officially sanctioned I am unaware. The 'Pillars of Hercules' used by Charles V are, perhaps, the best known of this group of supporters. In many cases (notably foreign) the supporters appear to have gradually receded to the back of the shield, as in the case of the Comte d'Erps, Chancellor of Brabant, where two maces (or) are represented saltirewise *behind* the shield. Generally, however, this variation is found in conjunction with purely official or corporate achievements.

A curious example of inanimate supporters occurs on the English seal of William, Lord Botreaux (1426), where, on each side of a couché shield exhibiting a griffin 'segreant' and surmounted by a helmet and crest, a buttress is quaintly introduced, in evident allusion to the owner's name. A somewhat similar arrangement appears on the Scottish seal of William Ruthven (1396), where a tree growing from a mount is placed on each side of the escutcheon. Another instance is to be found in the seal of John de Segrave, where a garb is placed on either side of the shield. Perhaps mention should here be made of the arms (granted in 1826) of the National Bank of Scotland, the shield of which is 'surrounded with two thistles proper disposed in orle'.[199]

Heraldic supporters as such, or badges occupying the position and answering the purpose of supporters, and not merely as artistic accessories, in England date from the early part of the fourteenth century. Very restricted in use at first, they later rapidly became popular, and there were few peers who did not display them upon their seals. For some reason, however, very few indeed appear on the early Garter plates. It is a striking fact that by far the larger number of the ancient standards display as the chief device not the arms but one of the supporters, and I am

198. The reference is to Viscount Montgomery of the Great Ardes (created 1622). The Viscount was created Earl of Mount Alexander in 1661, and the peerages became extinct in 1757. There is a record of the arms of Lord Mount Alexander with human supporters, which suggests that the curious supporters referred to by Fox-Davies may have been no more than artistic embellishments.
199. Inanimate supporters are rarely found. Those of Lord Boyd-Orr (a Scottish grant) are two wheatsheaves on a compartment of stubble proper. The supporters of Pine Rivers Shire Council, granted on 1 February 1965, afford an English example; they are: on either side a Norfolk Pine Tree, in front of that to the sinister, and beside the stock of a tree, a felling axe proper.

inclined to think that in this fact we have further confirmation of my belief that the origin of supporters is found in the badge.

Even after the use of two supporters had become general, a third figure is often found placed behind the shield, and forms a connecting link with the old practice of filling the void spaces on seals, to which we have already referred. On the seal of WILLIAM STERLING, in 1292, two lions rampant support the shield in front of a tree. The shield on the seal of OLIVER ROUILLON, in 1376, is supported by an angel, and by two demi-lions couchant-guardant in base. That of PIERRE AVOIR, in 1378, is held by a demi-eagle above the shield, and by two mermaids. On many ancient seals the supporters are disposed so that they hold the crested helm above a couché shield.

The counter-seals of RUDOLF IV, Archduke of AUSTRIA, in 1359 and 1362, afford instances in which a second set of supporters is used to hold up the crested helm. The shield of AUSTRIA is supported by two lions, on whose volets are the arms of HAPSBURG and PFIRT; the crested helm (coroneted, and having a panache of ostrich feathers) is also held by two lions, whose volets are charged with the arms of STIRIA, and of CARINTHIA (HUEBER, *Austria Illustrata*, tab. xviii).

In 1372 the seal of EDMUND MORTIMER represents his shield hanging from a rose-tree, and supported by two lions couchant (of MARCH), whose heads are covered by coroneted helmets with a panache (azure) as crest.

Boutell directs attention to the fact that the shield of EDMUND DE ARUNDEL (1301–26) is placed between similar helms and panaches, without the supporting beasts (*Heraldry, Historical and Popular*, pp. 271–418).

Crested supporters have sometimes been misunderstood, and quoted as instances of double supporters—for instance, by LOWER, *Curiosities of Heraldry*, who gives (p. 144) a cut from the achievement of the French D'ALBRETS as 'the most singular supporters, perhaps, in the whole circle of heraldry'. These supporters are two lions couchant (or), each helmed, and crested with an eagle au vol levé. These eagles certainly assist in holding the shield, but the lions are its true supporters; nor is this arrangement by any means unique. The swans which were used as supporters by JEAN, DUC DE BERRI, in 1386, are each mounted upon a bear. Two wild men, each *à cheval* on a lion, support the escutcheons of GERARD D'HARCHIES (1476) and of NICOLE DE GIRESME (1464). Two lions sejant, helmed and crested (the crest is a human head with the ears of an ass), were the supporters of ARNAUD D'ALBREY in 1368.

In 1919 new arms were designed for Iceland which, I think, form the most amazing heraldic composition I have ever seen, for the shield has apparently FOUR supporters.

Scotland, which is the home of curiosities of heraldry, gives us at least two instances of the use of supporters which must be absolutely unique—that is, the surcharging of an escutcheon with an inescutcheon, to the latter of which supporters are attached. The first instance occurs in the cases of Baronets of Nova Scotia, a clause appearing in all the earlier patents which ordained 'that the Baronets, and their heirs-male, should, as an *additament of honour* to their armorial ensigns, bear, either on a canton or inescutcheon, in their option, the ensign of Nova Scotia, being *argent*, a cross of St Andrew *azure* (the badge of Scotland counterchanged), charged with an inescutcheon of the Royal Arms of Scotland, supported on the dexter by the Royal unicorn, and on the sinister by a savage, or wild man, proper; and for crest, a branch of laurel and a thistle issuing from two hands conjoined, the one being armed, the other naked; with the motto, 'Munit hæc et altera vincit.' The incongruity of these exterior ornaments within a shield of arms is noticed by Nisbet, who informs us, however, that they are very soon removed. In the year 1629, after Nova Scotia was sold to the French, the Baronets of Scotland and their heirs-male, were authorised by Charles I 'to wear and carry about their necks, in all time coming, an orange-tawny silk ribbon, whereon shall be pendent, in a scutcheon *argent*, a saltire *azure*, thereon an inescutcheon, of the arms of Scotland, with an Imperial crown above the scutcheon and encircled with this motto: "Fax mentis honestæ gloria."' According to the same authority, this badge was never much used 'about their necks', but was carried, by way of canton or inescutcheon, on their armorial bearings, without the motto, and, of course, since then the superimposed supporters have been dropped.

The same peculiarity of supporters being surcharged upon a shield will be found, however, in the matriculation (1795) to Gordon Cumming of Altyre. These arms are depicted on Plate IV. In this the entire achievement (arms, crest, motto, and supporters) of Gordon of Gordon is placed upon an inescutcheon superimposed over the arms of Cumming.

In Scotland the arms, and the arms only, constitute the mark of a given family, and whilst due difference is made in the respective shields, no attempt is made as regards crest or supporters to impose any distinction between the figures granted to different families even where no blood relationship exists. The result is that whilst the same crests and supporters are duplicated over and over again, they at any rate remain in Scotland simple, graceful, and truly heraldic, even when judged by the most rigid medieval standard. They are, of course, necessarily of no value whatever for identification. In England the simplicity is relinquished for the sake of distinction, and it is held that equivalent differentiation must be made, both in regard to the crests and the supporters, as is made between the shields of different families. The result as to modern crests is truly appalling, and with supporters it is almost equally so, for by their very nature it is impossible to design adequate differences for crests and supporters, as can readily be done in the charges upon a shield, without creating monstrosities. With regret one has to admit that the dangling shields, the diapered chintz-like bodies, and the fasces and other footstools so frequently provided for modern supporters in England would seem to be pedantic, unnecessary, and inartistic strivings after a useless ideal.

In England the right to bear supporters is confined to those to whom they have been granted or recorded, but such grant or record is very rigidly confined to peers, to Knights of the Garter, Thistle, and St Patrick, and to Knights Grand Cross, or Knights Grand Commanders (as the case may be) of other Orders. Before the Order of the Bath was divided into classes, Knights of the Bath had supporters. As by an unwritten but nowadays invariably accepted law, the Orders of the Garter, Thistle, and St Patrick[200] are confined to members of the peerage, those entitled to claim (upon their petitioning) a grant of supporters in England

200. The Orders of the Garter and the Thistle are not now confined to members of the peerage. Classic examples are to be found in the persons of the late Sir Winston Churchill, K.G., and of Sir Robert Menzies, K.T. The Order of St Patrick must now be regarded as obsolescent.

are in practice limited to peers and Knights Grand Cross or Knights Grand Commanders. In the cases of peers, the grant is always attached to a particular peerage, the 'remainder' in the limitations of the grant being to 'those of his descendants upon whom the peerage may devolve', or some other words to this effect. In the cases of life peers and Knights Grand Cross the grant has no hereditary limitation, and the right to the supporters is personal to the grantee. There is nothing to distinguish the supporters of a peer from those of a Knight Grand Cross. Baronets of England, Ireland, Great Britain, and the United Kingdom as such are not entitled to claim grants of supporters, but there are some number of cases in which, by special favour of the sovereign, specific Royal Warrants have been issued—either as marks of favour or as augmentations of honour— conveying the pleasure of the sovereign to the kings of arms, and directing the latter to grant supporters — to descend with the baronetcy. Of the cases of this nature the following may be quoted: Guise (Royal Warrant, dated July 12, 1863), Prevost (Royal Warrant, October 1816), Guinness, afterwards Lord Ardilaun (Royal Warrant, dated 15 April 1867), Halford (Royal Warrant, 19 May 1827), Otway (Royal Warrant, 10 June 1845), and Laking. These, of course, are exceptional marks of favour from the sovereign, and this favour in at least two instances has been extended to untitled families. In 1815 Mr George Watson-Taylor, an especial intimate of the then Prince Regent, by Royal Warrant dated 28 September 1815, was granted the following supporters: 'On either side a leopard proper, armed and langued gules, collared and chained or.' A more recent instance, and, with the exception of an Irish case presently to be referred to, the only other one within the knowledge of the writer, is the case of the Speke★ arms. It is recited in the Royal Warrant, dated 26 July 1867, that Captain John Hanning Speke 'was by a deplorable accident suddenly deprived of his life before he had received any mark of our Royal favour' in connection with the discovery of the sources of the Nile. The Warrant goes on to recite the grant to his father, William Speke, of Jordans, co. Somerset, of the following augmentations to his original arms (argent, two bars azure) namely: on a chief representation of flowing water superinscribed with the word 'Nile', and for a crest of honourable augmentation a 'crocodile', also the supporters following—that is to say, on the dexter side a crocodile, and on the sinister side a hippopotamus. Some number of English baronets have gone to the trouble and expense of obtaining grants of supporters in Lyon Office; for example Sir Christopher Baynes, by grant dated 10 June 1805, obtained two savages, wreathed about the temples and loins, each holding a club over the exterior shoulder. It is very doubtful to what extent such grants in Scotland to domiciled Englishmen can be upheld. Many other baronets have at one time or another assumed supporters without any official warrant or authority in consequence of certain action taken by an earlier committee of the baronetage, but

★ Armorial bearings of William Speke, Esq.: Argent, two bars azure, over all an eagle displayed with two heads gules, and as an honourable augmentation (granted by Royal Licence, dated 26 July 1867, to commemorate the discoveries of the said John Hanning Speke), a chief azure, thereon a representation of flowing water proper, superinscribed with the word 'Nile' in letters gold. Upon the escutcheon is placed a helmet befitting his degree, with a mantling azure and argent; and for his crests: 1. (of honourable augmentation) upon a wreath of the colours, a crocodile proper; 2. upon a wreath of the colours, a porcupine proper; and as a further augmentation for supporters (granted by Royal Licence as above to the said William Speke, Esq., for and during his life)—on the dexter side, a crocodile; and on the sinister side, a hippopotamus, both proper; with the motto, 'Super æthera virtus.'

cases of this kind are slowly dropping out of the Peerage books and this, combined with the less ostentatious taste of the present day in the depicting of armorial bearings upon carriages and elsewhere, is slowly but steadily reducing the use of supporters to those who possess official authority for their display.

Another fruitful origin of the use of unauthorised supporters at the present day lies in the fact that grants of supporters personal to the grantee for his life only have been made to Knights Grand Cross or to life peers in cases where a hereditary title has been subsequently conferred. The limitations of the grant of supporters having never been extended, the grant has naturally expired with the death of the life honour to which the supporters were attached.

In addition to these cases there is a very limited number of families which have always claimed supporters by prescriptive right, amongst whom may be mentioned Tichborne of Tichborne (two lions guardant gules), De Hoghton of Hoghton (two bulls argent), Scrope of Danby (two choughs), and Stapylton. Concerning such cases it can only be said that in England no official sanction has ever been given to such use, and no case exists of any official recognition of the right of an untitled family to bear supporters to their arms save those few exceptional cases governed by specific Royal Warrants. In many cases, notably Scrope, Luttrel, Hilton, and Stapylton, the supporters have probably originated in their legitimate adoption at an early period in connection with peerage or other titular distinction, and have continued inadvertently in use when the titular distinctions to which they belonged have ceased to exist or have devolved upon other families. Possibly their use in some cases has been the result of a *claim* to *de jure* honours. The cases where supporters are claimed 'by prescriptive right' are few indeed in England, and need not be further considered.

Whilst the official laws in Ireland are, and have apparently always been, the same as in England, there is no doubt that the heads of the different septs assert a claim to the right to use supporters. On this point Sir Bernard Burke, Ulster King of Arms, wrote: 'No registry of supporters to an Irish chieftain appears in Ulster's Office, in right of his chieftaincy only, and without the honour of peerage, nor does any authority to bear them exist.' But nevertheless 'The O'Donovan' uses, dexter, a lion guardant, and sinister, a griffin; 'The O'Gorman' uses, dexter, a lion, and sinister, a horse; 'The O'Reilly' uses two lions or. 'The O'Connor Don,' however, is in the unique position of bearing supporters by unquestionable right, inasmuch as the late Queen Victoria, on the occasion of her last visit to Dublin, issued her Royal Warrant conferring the right upon him. The supporters granted to him were 'two lions rampant gules, each gorged with an antique crown, and charged on the shoulder with an Irish harp or'.

The right to bear supporters in Scotland is on a widely different basis from that in any other country. As in England and Ireland, peers and Knights Grand Cross are permitted to obtain grants of these distinctions. But outside and beyond these there are many other families who bear them by right. At the official inquiry concerning the Lyon Office, the Lyon-Depute, Mr George Tait, put in a Note of Persons whom he considered might lawfully bear supporters under Scottish Heraldic Law. The following is the text of the note in question:

'NOTE OF PERSONS who are considered by GEORGE TAIT, Esq., Lyon-Depute, to be entitled to supporters, furnished to the Commissioners of Inquiry by their desire, intimated to him at his examination this day, 27 June 1821.

'1. *Peers*. By immemorial usage, Peers have right to supporters, and supporters are commonly inserted in modern patents of Peerage. This includes Peeresses in their own right.

'2. *Ancient Usage*. Those private gentlemen, and the lawful heirs-male of their bodies, who can prove immemorial usage of carrying supporters, or a usage very ancient, and long prior to the Act 1672, are entitled to have their supporters recognised, it being presumed that they received them from lawful authority, on account of feats of valour in battle or in tournament, or as marks of the Royal favour (see *Murray of Touchadam's Case*, 24 June 1778).

'3. *Barons*. Lawful heirs-male of the bodies of the smaller Barons, who had the full right of free barony (not mere freeholders) prior to 1587, when representation of the minor Barons was fully established, upon the ground that those persons were Barons, and sat in Parliament as such, and were of the same as the titled Barons. Their right is recognised by the writers on heraldry and antiquities. Persons having right on this ground, will almost always have established it by ancient usage, and the want of usage is a strong presumption against the right.

'4. *Chiefs*. Lawful heirs-male of Chiefs of tribes or clans which had attained power, and extensive territories and numerous members at a distant period, or at least of tribes consisting of numerous families of some degree of rank and consideration. Such persons will in general have right to supporters, either as Barons (great or small) or by ancient usage. When any new claim is set up on such a ground, it may be viewed with suspicion, and it will be extremely difficult to establish it, chiefly from the present state of society, by which the traces of clanship, or the patriarchal state, are in most parts of the country almost obliterated; and indeed it is very difficult to conceive a case in which a new claim of that kind could be admitted. Mr Tait has had some such claims, and has rejected them.

'5. *Royal Commissions*. Knights of the Garter and Bath, and any others to whom the King may think proper to concede the honour of supporters.

'These are the only descriptions of persons who appear to Mr Tait to be entitled to supporters.

'An idea has gone abroad, that Scots Baronets are entitled to supporters; but there is no authority for this in their patents, or any good authority for it elsewhere. And for many years subsequent to 1672, a very small portion indeed of their arms which are matriculated in the Lyon Register, are matriculated with supporters; so small as necessarily to lead to this inference, that those whose arms are entered with supporters had right to them on other grounds, *e.g.* ancient usage, chieftainship, or being heirs of Barons. The arms of few Scots Baronets are matriculated during the last fifty or sixty years; but the practice of assigning supporters gradually gained ground during that time, or rather the practice of assigning supporters to them, merely as such, seems to have arisen during that period; and it appears to Mr Tait to be an erroneous practice, which he would not be warranted in following.

'British Baronets have also, by recent practice, had supporters assigned to them, but Mr Tait considers the practice to be unwarranted; and accordingly, in a recent case, a gentleman, upon being created a Baronet, applied for supporters to the King—having applied to Mr Tait, and been informed by him that he did not conceive the Lord Lyon entitled to give supporters to British Baronets.

'No females (except Peeresses in their own right) are entitled to supporters, as the representation of families is only in the male line. But the widows of Peers, by courtesy, carry their arms and supporters; and the sons of Peers, using the lower titles of the peerage by courtesy, also carry the supporters by courtesy.

'Mr Tait does not know of any authority for the Lord Lyon having a discretionary power of granting supporters, and understands that only the King has such a power.

'Humbly submitted by   (signed)   'G. TAIT.'

Though this statement would give a good general idea of the Scottish practice, its publication entails the addition of certain qualifying remarks. Supporters are most certainly not 'commonly inserted in modern patents of peerage'. Supporters appertaining to peerages are granted by special and separate patents. These to English subjects are now under the hand and seal of Garter alone. In the event of a grant following upon the creation of an Irish peerage, the patent of supporters would be issued by Ulster King of Arms. But it is competent to Lyon King of Arms to matriculate the arms of Scottish peers with supporters, or to grant these to such as may still be without them. Both Lyon and Ulster would appear to have the right to grant supporters to Peers of the United Kingdom who are heraldically their domiciled subjects. With regard to the second paragraph of Mr Tait's memorandum, there will be few families within its range who will not be included within the range of the paragraph which follows, and the presumption would rather be that the use of supporters by an untitled family originated in the right of barony than in any mythical grant following upon mythical feats of valour.

Mr Tait, however, is clearly wrong in his statement that 'no females (except peeresses in their own right) are entitled to supporters'. They have constantly been allowed to the heir of line, and their devolution through female heirs must of necessity presuppose the right thereto of the female heir through whom the inheritance is claimed. A recent case in point occurs with regard to the arms of Hunter-Weston, matriculated in 1880, Mrs Hunter-Weston being the heir of line of Hunter of Hunterston. Widows of peers, providing they have arms of their own to impale with those of their husbands, cannot be said to only bear the supporters of their deceased husbands by courtesy. With them it is a matter of right. The eldest sons of peers bearing courtesy titles most certainly do not bear the supporters of the peerage to which they are heirs. Even the far more generally accepted 'courtesy' practice of bearing coronets is expressly forbidden by an Earl-Marshal's Warrant.

Consequently it may be asserted that the laws concerning the use of supporters in Scotland are as follows: In the first place, no supporters can be borne of right unless they have been the subject of formal grant or matriculation. The following classes are entitled to obtain, upon payment of the necessary fees, the grant or matriculation of supporters to themselves, or to themselves and their descendants according as the case may be: (1) Peers of Scotland, and other peers who are domiciled Scotsmen. (2) Knights of the Garter, Knights of the Thistle, and Knights of St Patrick, being Scotsmen, are entitled as such to obtain grants of supporters to themselves for use during life, but as these three orders are now confined to members of the peerage★, the supporters used would be probably those appertaining to their peerages, and it is unlikely that any further grants for life will be made under these circumstances. (3) Knights of the Bath until the revision of the order were entitled to obtain grants of supporters to themselves for use during their lifetimes, and there are many instances in the Lyon Register where such grants have been made. (4) Knights Grand Cross of the Bath, of St Michael and St George, and of the Royal Victorian Order, and the Order of the British Empire, and Knights Grand Commanders of the Orders of the Star of India, and of the Indian Empire, are entitled to obtain grants of supporters for use during their lifetimes. (5) The lawful heirs of the minor barons who had the full right of free barony prior to 1587 may matriculate supporters if they can show their ancestors used them, or may now obtain grants. Though practically the whole of these have been at some time or other matriculated in Lyon Register, there still remain a few whose claims have never been officially adjudicated upon. For example, it is only quite recently that the ancient Swinton supporters have been formally enrolled on the official records (Plate V). (6) There are certain others, being chiefs of clans and the heirs of those to whom grants have been made in times past, who also have the right, but as no *new* claim is likely to be so recognised in the future, it may be taken that these are confined to those cases which have been already entered in the Lyon Register.

During the latter part of the eighteenth century, the executive of Lyon Office had fallen into great disrepute. The office of Lyon King of Arms had been granted to the Earls of Kinnoul, who had contented themselves with appointing deputies and drawing fees. The whole subject of armorial jurisdiction in Scotland had become lax to the last degree, and very many irregularities had crept in. One, and probably the worst result, had been the granting of supporters in many cases where no valid reason other than the payment of fees could be put forward to warrant the obtaining of such a privilege. And the result was the growth and acceptance of the fixed idea that it was within the power of Lyon King of Arms to grant supporters to any one whom he might choose to so favour. Consequently many grants of supporters were placed upon the records, and many untitled families of Scotland apparently have the right under these patents of grant to add supporters to their arms. Though it is an arguable matter whether the Lord Lyon was justified in making these grants, there can be no doubt that, so long as they remain upon the official register, and no official steps are taken to cancel the patents, they must be accepted as existing by legal right. Probably the most egregious instance of such a grant is to be found in the case of the grant to the first baronet of the family of Antrobus, who on purchasing the estate of Rutherford, the seat of the extinct Lords Rutherford, obtained from the then Lyon King of Arms a grant of the peerage supporters carried by the previous owners of the property.

With regard to the devolution of Scottish supporters, the large proportion of those registered in Lyon Office are recorded in the terms of some patent which specifies the limitations of their descent, so that there are a comparatively small number only concerning which there can be any uncertainty as to whom the

★ See above, n. 200.

supporters will descend to. The difficulty can only arise in those cases in which the arms are matriculated with supporters as borne by ancient usage in the early years of the Lyon Register, or in the cases of supporters still to be matriculated on the same grounds by those families who have so far failed to comply with the Act of 1672. Whilst Mr Tait, in his memorandum which has been previously quoted, would deny the right of inheritance to female heirs, there is no doubt whatever that in many cases such heirs have been allowed to succeed to the supporters of their families. Taking supporters as an appanage of right of barony (either greater or lesser), there can be no doubt that the greater baronies, and consequently the supporters attached to them, devolved upon heirs female, and upon the heir of line inheriting through a female ancestor; and, presumably, the same considerations must of necessity hold good with regard to those supporters which are borne by right of lesser barony, for the greater and the lesser were the same thing, differing only in degree, until in the year 1587 the lesser barons were relieved of compulsory attendance in Parliament. At the same time there can be no doubt that the headship of a family must rest with the heir male, and consequently it would seem that in those cases in which the supporters are borne by right of being head of a clan or chief of a name, the right of inheritance would devolve upon the heir male. There must of necessity be some cases in which it is impossible to determine whether the supporters were originally called into being by right of barony or because of chieftainship, and the consequence has been that concerning the descent of the supporters of the older untitled families there has been no uniformity in the practice of Lyon Office, and it is impossible from the precedents which exist to deduce any certain and unalterable rule upon the point. Precedents exist in each case, and the well-known case of Smith-Cunningham and Dick-Cunningham, which is often referred to as settling the point, did nothing of the kind, inasmuch as that judgment depended upon the interpretation of a specific Act of Parliament, and was not the determination of a point of heraldic law. The case, however, afforded the opportunity to Lord Jeffrey to make the following remarks upon the point (see Seton, p. 355):

'If I may be permitted to take a common-sense view, I should say that there is neither an inflexible rule nor a uniform practice in the matter. There may be cases where the heir of line will exclude the heir male, and there may be cases where the converse will be held. In my opinion the common-sense rule is that the chief armorial dignities should follow the more substantial rights and dignities of the family. *If the heir male succeed to the title and estates, I think it reasonable that he should also succeed to the armorial bearings of the head of the house.* I would think it a very difficult proposition to establish that the heir of line, when denuded of everything else, was still entitled to retain the barren honours of heraldry. But I give no opinion upon that point.'

Mr Seton, in his *Law and Practice of Heraldry in Scotland*, sums up the matter of inheritance in these words (see p. 357): 'As already indicated, however, by one of the learned Lords in his opinion on the case of Cuninghame, the practice in the matter in question has been far from uniform: and accordingly we are very much disposed to go along with his relative suggestion, that "the chief armorial dignities should follow the more substantial rights and dignities of the family"; and that when the latter are enjoyed by the female heir of line, such heir should also be regarded as fairly entitled to claim the principal heraldic honours.'

The result has been in practice that the supporters of a family have usually been matriculated to whoever has carried on the name and line of the house, unless the supporters in question have been governed by a specific grant, the limitations of which exist to be referred to, but in cases where both the heir of line and the heir male have been left in a prominent position, the difficulty of decision has in many cases been got over by allowing supporters to both of them. The most curious instance of this within our knowledge occurs with regard to the family of Chisholm.

Chisholm of Erchless Castle appears undoubtedly to have succeeded as head and chief of his name—'The Chisholm'—about the end of the seventeenth century. As such supporters were carried, namely: 'On either side a savage wreathed about the head and middle with laurel, and holding a club over his exterior shoulder.'

At the death of Alexander Chisholm—'The Chisholm'—7 February 1793, the chieftainship and the estates passed to his half-brother William, but his heir of line was his only child Mary, who married James Gooden of London. Mrs Mary Chisholm or Gooden in 1827 matriculated the *undifferenced* arms of Chisholm ['Gules, a boar's head couped or'], without supporters, but in 1831 the heir male *also* matriculated the same *undifferenced* arms, in this case with supporters.

The chieftainship of the Chisholm family then continued with the male line until the death of Duncan Macdonell Chisholm—'The Chisholm'—in 1859, when his only sister and heir became heir of line of the later chiefs. She was then Jemima Batten, and by Royal Licence in that year she and her husband assumed the additional surname of Chisholm, becoming Chisholm-Batten, and, contrary to the English practice in such cases, the arms of Chisholm *alone* were matriculated in 1860 to Mrs Chisholm-Batten and her descendants. These once again were the *undifferenced* coat of Chisholm, viz.: 'Gules, a boar's head couped or.' Arms for Batten have since been granted in England, the domicile of the family being English, and the arms of Chisholm-Batten, though including the quartering for Chisholm, is usually marshalled as allowed in the College of Arms by English rules.

Though there does not appear to have been any subsequent rematriculation in favour of the heir male who succeeded as 'The Chisholm', the undifferenced arms were also considered to have devolved upon him together with the supporters. On the death of the last known male heir of the family, Roderick Donald Matheson Chisholm, The Chisholm, in 1887, Mr James Chisholm Gooden-Chisholm claimed the chieftainship as heir of line, and in that year the Gooden-Chisholm arms were again rematriculated. In this case supporters were added to the again undifferenced arms of Chisholm, but a slight alteration in the supporters was made, the clubs being reversed and placed to rest on the ground.

Amongst the many other untitled Scottish families who rightly bear supporters, may be mentioned Gibsone of Pentland, Barclay of Urie, Barclay of Towie, Drummond of Megginch, Maclachlan of that Ilk, 'Cluny' Macpherson, Cunninghame, and Brisbane of the Ilk.

Armorial matters in the Channel Islands present a very unsatisfactory state of affairs. There never appears to have been any Visitation, and the arms of Channel Island families which officially pass muster must be confined to those of the very few families (for example, De Carteret, Dobrée, and Tupper) who have found it necessary or advisable on their own initiative to register their arms in the official English sources. In none of these instances have supporters been allowed, nor I believe did any of these families claim to use them, but some (Lemprière, De Saumerez, and other families) assert the possession of such a distinction by pre-scriptive right. If the right to supporters be a privilege of peerage, or if, as in Scotland, it anciently depended upon the right of free barony, the position of these Channel Island families in former days as seignorial lords was much akin. But it is highly improbable that the right to bear supporters in such cases will ever be officially recognised, and the case of De Saumerez, in which the supporters were bedevilled and regranted to descend with the peerage, will probably operate as a decisive precedent upon the point and against such a right. There are some number of families of foreign origin who bear supporters or claim them by the assertion of foreign right. Where this right can be established their use has been confirmed by Royal Licence in this country in some number of cases; for example, the cases of Rothschild and De Salis. In other cases (for example, the case of Chamier) no official record of the supporters exists with the record of the arms, and presumably the foreign right to the supporters could not have been established at the time of registration.

With regard to impersonal arms, the right to supporters in England is not easy to define. In the case of counties, crests and supporters are granted if the county likes to pay for them.

In the case of towns, the rule in England was that an ordinary town might not have supporters but that a city could, and instances are numerous where sup-porters have been granted upon the elevation of a town to the dignity of a city. Birmingham, Sheffield, and Nottingham are all modern instances in point. This rule, however, was not absolutely rigid, and an exception may be pointed to in the case of Liverpool, the supporters being granted in 1797, and the town not being created a city until a subsequent date. At the present time the rule is regarded as quite exploded, supporters having been granted in 1915 even to Southend. In Scotland, where, of course, until quite recently supporters were granted practi-cally to anybody who chose to pay for them, a grant will be found for the county of Perth dated in 1800, in which supporters were included. But as to towns and cities it is no more than a matter of fees, any town in Scotland eligible for arms being at liberty to obtain supporters also if they are desired. In grants of arms to corporate bodies it is difficult to draw the line or to deduce any actual rule. In 23rd of Henry VIII the Grocers' Livery Company were granted 'two griffins per fess gules and or', and many other of the Livery Companies have supporters to their arms. Others, for no apparent reason, are without them. The 'Merchant Adventurers' Company or Hamburg Merchants' have supporters, as had both the old and the new East India Companies. The arms of Jamaica and Cape Colony and of the British North Borneo Company have supporters, but on the other hand no supporters were assigned to Canada or to any of its provinces in the original warrant. In Ireland the matter appears to be much upon the same footing as in England, and as far as impersonal arms are concerned it is very difficult to say what the exact rule is, if this is to be deduced from known cases and past precedents.[201]

Probably the freedom— amounting in many cases to great laxity— with which in English heraldic art the positions and attitudes of supporters are changed, is the one point in which English heraldic art has entirely ignored the trammels of conventionalised officialism. There must be in this country scores of entrance gates where each pillar of the gateway is surmounted by a shield held in the paws of a single supporter, and the Governmental use of the Royal supporters in an amazing variety of attitudes, some of which are grossly unheraldic, has not helped towards a true understanding. The reposeful attitude of watchful slumber in which the Royal lion and unicorn are so often depicted, may perhaps be in the nature of submission to the Biblical teaching of Isaiah that the lion shall lie down with the lamb (and possibly therefore also with the unicorn), in these times of peace which have succeeded those earlier days when 'the lion beat the unicorn round and round the town.'

668 *The Arms used by Kilmarnock, Ayrshire:*
Azure, a fess chequy gules and argent.
Crest: a dexter hand raised in benediction.
Supporters: on either side a squirrel sejant proper.

In official minds, however, the sole attitude for the supporters is the rampant, or as near an approach to it as the nature of the animal will allow. A human being, a bird, or a fish naturally can hardly adopt the attitude. In Scotland, the land of heraldic freedom, various exceptions to this can be found. Of these one can call to mind the arms used by the town of Kilmarnock (668), in which the supporters, 'squirrels proper', are depicted always as sejant.[202] These particular creatures, however, would look strange to us in any other form. These arms unfortunately have never been matriculated as the arms of the town (being really the arms of the

201. It is current practice to grant supporters to counties, county boroughs, cities and boroughs, but not to urban and rural district councils. Corporations incorporated by Royal Charter are normally allowed supporters, as are well constituted professional bodies. It is wisest, however, to regard grants of supporters as being made purely on an *ad hoc* basis. It is up to Garter Kings of Arms to advise the Earl Marshal on each particular case.
202. The arms were matriculated on 18 September 1929 but certain small alterations were made. The field became purpure and the fess chequy or and vert. Above the arms was placed a mural crown proper masoned sable but the crest, supporters and mottoes were not altered.

Boyd family, the attainted Earls of Kilmarnock), and consequently can hardly as yet be referred to as a definite precedent, because official matriculation might result in a similar 'happening' to the change which was made in the case of the arms of Inverness. In all representations of the arms of earlier date than the matriculation, the supporters, (dexter) a camel and (sinister) an elephant, are depicted *statant* on either side of the shield, no actual contact being made between the escutcheon and the supporters. But in 1900, when in a belated compliance with the Act of 1672 the armorial bearings of the Royal Burgh of Inverness were matriculated, the position was altered to that more usually employed for supporters.

The supporters always used by Sir John Maxwell Stirling-Maxwell of Pollok were two lions sejant guardant. These, as appears from an old seal, were in use as far back as the commencement of the fifteenth century, but the supporters officially recorded for the family are two apes. In English armory one or two exceptional cases may be noticed; for example, the supporters of the city of Bristol, which are: 'On either side, on a mount vert, a unicorn sejant or, armed, maned, and unguled sable.' Another instance will be found in the supporters of Lord Rosmead, which are: 'On the dexter side an ostrich and on the sinister side a kangaroo, both regardant proper.' From the nature of the animal, the kangaroo is depicted sejant.

Supporters in Germany date from the same period as with ourselves, being met with on seals as far back as 1276. At first they were similarly purely artistic adjuncts, but they have retained much of this character and much of the purely permissive nature in Germany to the present day. It was not until about the middle of the seventeenth century that supporters were granted or became hereditary in that country. Grants of supporters can be found in England at an earlier date, but such grants were isolated in number. Nevertheless supporters had become hereditary very soon after they obtained a regularly heraldic (as opposed to a decorative) footing. Their use, however, was governed at that period by a greater freedom as to alteration and change than was customary with armory in general. Supporters were an adjunct of the peerage, and peers were not subject to the Visitations. With his freedom from arrest, his high social position, and his many other privileges of peerage, a peer was 'too big' a person formerly to accept the dictatorial armorial control which the Crown enforced upon lesser people. Short of treason, a peer in any part of Great Britain for most practical purposes of social life was above the ordinary law. In actual fact it was only the rights of one peer as opposed to the rights of another peer that kept a Lord of Parliament under any semblance of control. When the great lords of past centuries could and did raise armies to fight the King a peer was hardly likely to, nor did he, brook much interference.

Of the development of supporters in Germany Ströhl writes:

'Only very late, about the middle of the seventeenth century, were supporters granted as hereditary, but they appear in the arms of burghers in the first half of the fifteenth century, and the arms of many towns also possess them as decorative adjuncts.

'The first supporters were human figures, generally portraits of the arms-bearers themselves; then women, young men, and boys, so-called *Schildbuben*. In the second half of the fourteenth century animals appear: lions, bears, stags, dogs,

327

griffins, &c. In the fifteenth century one frequently encounters angels with richly curling hair, saints (patrons of the bearer or of the town), then later, nude wild men and women (*Waldmenschen*) thickly covered with hair, with garlands round their loins and on their heads. The thick, hairy covering of the body in the case of women is only to be met with in the very beginning. Later the endeavour was to approach the feminine ideal as nearly as possible, and only the garlands were retained to point out the origin and the home of these figures.

'At the end of the fifteenth and in the sixteenth century, there came into fashion lansquenets, huntsmen, pretty women and girls, both clothed and unclothed.' Speaking of the present day, and from the executive standpoint, he adds:

'Supporters, with the exception of flying angels, should have a footing on which they can stand in a natural manner, whether it be grass, a pedestal, a tree, or line of ornament, and to place them upon a ribbon of a motto is less suitable because a thin ribbon can hardly give the impression of a sufficiently strong support for the invariably heavy-looking figures of the men or animals. The supporters of the shield may at the same time be employed as bearers of the helmets. They bear the helmets either over the head or hold them in their hands. Figures standing near the shield, but not holding or supporting it in any way, cannot in the strict sense of the word be designated supporters; such figures are called *Schildwächter* (shield-watchers or guardians).

Human figures as supporters

Of all figures employed as supporters probably human beings are of most frequent occurrence, even when those single and double figures referred to on an earlier page, which are not a real part of the heraldic achievement, are excluded from consideration. The endless variety of different figures perhaps gives some clue to the reason of their frequent occurrence.

Though the nude human figure appears (male) upon the shield of Dalziel and (female) in the crest of Ellis (Agar-Ellis, formerly Viscount Clifden), one cannot call to mind any instance of such an occurrence in the form of supporters, though possibly the supporters of the Glaziers' Livery Company ['Two naked boys proper, each holding a long torch inflamed of the last'] and of the Joiners' Livery Company ['Two naked boys proper, the dexter holding in his hand an emblematical female figure, crowned with a mural coronet sable, the sinister holding in his hand a square'] might be classed in such a character.[203] Nude figures in armory are practically always termed 'savages', or occasionally 'woodmen' or 'wildmen', and garlanded about the loins with foliage.

With various adjuncts— clubs, banners, trees, branches, &c.— *Savages* will be found as the supporters of the arms of the German Emperor, and in the sovereign

203. The arms and supporters of the Glaziers' Company were entered in the 1634 Visitation of London, and a certificate was issued on 1 February 1965 as the original patent had been destroyed. The Joiners' Company's arms were granted on 10 August 1571, but the supporters are of no authority. The arms of Earl Poulett are supported by a wild man and a woman, wreathed about the loins with oak. I am not certain when the floral cache-sex was introduced, but in a seventeenth century manuscript at the College of Arms (Vincent 183) the supporters are clearly shown as naked woodhouses or wild people of the woods, covered with fur except for their faces, hands, feet, elbows and knees.

arms of Brunswick, Denmark, Schwarzburg-Sondershausen, and Rudolstadt, as well as in the arms of the kingdom of Prussia. They also appear in the arms of the kingdom of Greece, though in this case they should perhaps be more properly described as figures of Hercules.

In British armory—amongst many other families—two savages are the supporters of the Marquess of Ailesbury, Lord Calthorpe, Viscount de Vesci, Lord Elphinstone, the Earl of Elgin and Kincardine, the Duke of Fife, Earl Fitzwilliam (each holding in the exterior hand a tree eradicated), Lord Kinnaird, the Earl of Morton; and amongst the baronets who possess supporters, Menzies, Douglas of Carr, and Williams-Drummond have on either side of their escutcheons a 'savage'. Earl Poulett alone has both man and woman, his supporters being: 'Dexter, a savage man; sinister, a savage woman, both wreathed with oak, all proper.' As some one remarked on seeing a realistic representation of this coat of arms by Catton, R.A., the blazon might more appropriately have concluded 'all improper'.

Next after savages, the most favourite variety of the human being adopted as a supporter is the *Man in Armour*.

Even as heraldic and heritable supporters angels are not uncommon, and are to be met with amongst other cases in the arms of the Marquess of Waterford, the Earl of Dudley, and Viscount Dillon.

It is rare to find supporters definitely stated to represent any specific person, but in the case of the arms of Arbroath (669) the supporters are 'Dexter: "St

669 Arms of Arbroath: Gules, a portcullis with chains pendent or. Motto: 'Propter Libertatem.' Supporters: dexter, St. Thomas à Becket in his archiepiscopal robes all proper; sinister, a Baron of Scotland armed cap-à-pie, holding in his exterior hand the letter from the Convention of the Scottish Estates, held at Arbroath in the year of 1320, addressed to Pope John XXII, all proper.

329

Thomas à Becket," and sinister, a Baron of Scotland.' Another instance, again from Scotland, appears in a most extraordinary grant by the Lyon in 1816 to Sir Jonathan Wathen Waller, Bart, of Braywick Lodge, co. Berks, and of Twickenham, co. Middlesex. In this case the supporters were two elaborately 'harnessed' ancient warriors, 'to commemorate the surrender of Charles, Duke of Orleans, at the memorable battle of Agincourt (that word being the motto over the crest) in the year 1415, to Richard Waller of Groombridge in Kent, Esq., from which Richard the said Sir Jonathan Wathen Waller is, according to the tradition of his family, descended.' This pedigree is set out in Burke's Peerage, which assigns as arms to this family the old coat of Waller of Groombridge, with the augmented crest, viz.: 'On a mount vert, a walnut-tree proper, and pendent therefrom an escutcheon of the arms of France with a label of three points argent.' Considerable doubt, however, is thrown upon the descent by the fact that in 1814, when Sir Jonathan (then Mr Phipps) obtained a Royal Licence to assume the name and arms of Waller, a very different and much bedevilled edition of the arms and not the real coat of Waller of Groombridge was exemplified to him. These supporters (the grant was quite *ultra vires*, Sir Jonathan being a domiciled Englishman) do not appear in any of the Peerage books, and it is not clear to what extent they were ever made use of, but in a painting which came under my notice the Duke of Orleans, in his surcoat of France, could be observed handing his sword across the front of the escutcheon to Mr (or Sir) Richard Waller. The supporters of the Needlemakers' Company are commonly known as Adam and Eve, and the motto of the Company ['They sewed fig-leaves together and made themselves aprons'] bears this supposition out. The blazon, however, is: 'Dexter, a man; sinister, a woman, both proper, each wreathed round the waist with leaves of the last, in the woman's dexter hand a needle or.'[204] The supporters of the Earl of Aberdeen are, 'dexter an Earl and sinister a Doctor of Laws, both in their robes all proper.'

Highlanders in modern costume figure as supporters to the arms of Maconochie-Wellwood, and in more ancient garb in the case of Cluny Macpherson, and soldiers in the uniforms of every regiment, and savages from every clime, have at some time or other been pressed into heraldic service as supporters; but a work on Armory is not a handbook on costume, military and civil, nor is it an ethnographical directory, which it would certainly become if any attempt were to be made to enumerate the different varieties of men and women, clothed and unclothed, which have been used for the purposes of supporters.

Animals as supporters

When we turn to animals as supporters, we at once get to a much wider range, and but little can be said concerning them beyond stating that though usually rampant, they are sometimes sejant, and may be guardant or regardant. The *Lion* naturally first claims one's attention. 670 shows an interesting and curious instance of the use of a single lion as a supporter. This is taken from a drawing in the possession of the town library at Breslau (*Herold*, 1888, No. 1), and represents the arms of Dr Heinrich Rubisch, Physician to the King of Hungary and Bohemia.

204. Unfortunately this rather romantic coat is of no authority. There have been many versions of it since it first appeared in the late seventeenth century.

670 *Arms of Dr Heinrich Rubisch.*

The arms are, 'per fesse', the chief argent, a 'point' throughout sable, charged with a lion's face, holding in the jaws an annulet, and the base also argent charged with two bars sable. The mantling is sable and argent. Upon the helmet as crest are two buffalo's horns of the colours of the shield, and between them appears (apparently as a part of the heritable crest) a lion's face holding an annulet as in the arms. This, however, is the face of the lion, which, standing behind the escutcheon, is employed as the supporter, though possibly it is intended that it should do double duty. This employment of one animal to serve a double armorial purpose is practically unknown in British armory, except possibly in a few early examples of seals, but in German heraldry it is very far from being uncommon.

Winged lions are not very usual, but they occur as the supporters of Lord Braye: 'On either side a lion guardant or, winged vair.' A winged lion is also one of the supporters (the dexter) of Lord Leconfield, but this, owing to the position of the wings, is quite unique. The blazon is: 'A lion with wings inverted azure, collared or.' Two lions rampant double-queued, the dexter or, the sinister sable, are the supporters of the Duke of Portland, and the supporters of both the Earl of Feversham and the Earl of Dartmouth afford instances of lions crowned with a coronet, and issuing therefrom a plume of ostrich feathers.

Sea-lions will be found as supporters to the arms of Viscount Falmouth ['Two sea-lions erect on their tails argent, gutté-de-l'armes'], and the Earls of Howth bore: 'Dexter, a sea-lion as in the crest; sinister, a mermaid proper, holding in her exterior hand a mirror.'

The *heraldic tyger* is occasionally found as a supporter, and an instance occurs in the arms of the Marquess of Dufferin and Ava. It also occurs as the sinister supporter of the Duke of Leeds, and of the Baroness Darcy de Knayth, and was the dexter supporter of the Earls of Holderness. Two heraldic tygers are the supporters both of Sir Andrew Noel Agnew, Bart, and of the Marquess of Anglesey. Of recent years the *natural tiger* has taken its place in the heraldic menagerie, and instances of its appearance will be found in the arms of Sir Mortimer Durand, and as one of the supporters of the arms of the city of Bombay. When occurring in heraldic surroundings it is always termed for distinction a 'Bengal tiger', and two Royal Bengal tigers are the supporters of Sir Francis Outram, Bart: 'On either side a Royal Bengal tiger guardant proper, gorged with a wreath of laurel vert, and on the head an Eastern crown or.'

The *griffin* is perhaps the next most favourite supporter. Male griffins are the supporters of Sir George John Egerton Dashwood: 'On either side a male gryphon argent, gorged with a collar flory counterflory gules.'

A very curious supporter was borne by Mr Styleman Le Strange. Of course, as a domiciled English commoner, having no Royal Licence to bear supporters, his claim to these additions would not be recognised, but their use no doubt originated in the fact that he represented the lines of several coheirships to different baronies by writ, to some one of which, no doubt, the supporters may have at some time belonged. The dexter supporter in question is 'a stag argent with a lion's forepaws and tail, collared.'

The supporters granted to Lord Milner are two 'springbok', and the same animal (an 'oryx' or 'springbok') is the sinister supporter of the arms of Cape Colony.

Goats are the supporters of the Earl of Portsmouth (who styles his 'chamois or wild goats'), of Lord Bagot and Lord Cranworth, and they occur in the achievements of the Barony of Ruthven and the Marquess of Normanby. The supporters of Viscount Southwell are two 'Indian' goats.

Rams are the supporters of Lord de Ramsey and Lord Sherard. A ram is also one of the supporters attached to the Barony of Ruthven, and one of the supporters used by the town of New Galloway.[205] These arms, however, have never been matriculated, which on account of the curious charge upon the shield is very much to be regretted.

The supporters of Lord Mowbray and Stourton afford an example of a most curious and interesting animal. Originally the Lords Stourton used two antelopes azure, but before the seventeenth century these had been changed to two 'sea-dogs'. When the abeyance of the Barony of Mowbray was determined in favour of Lord Stourton the dexter supporter was changed to the lion of Mowbray, but the sinister supporter still remained a 'sea-dog'.

The *horse* and the *pegasus* are constantly met with supporting the arms of peers and others in this country. A bay horse regardant figures as the dexter supporter of the Earl of Yarborough, and the horses which support the shield of Earl Cowper are very specifically detailed in the official blazon: 'Two dun horses close cropped (except a tuft upon the withers) and docked, a large blaze down the

---

205. The Royal Burgh of New Galloway matriculated arms on 26 April 1938. The arms are blazoned: gules, a cross couped and reversed argent, ensigned with a boar's head erased and encircled in chief with a viscount's coronet of sixteen pearls proper. The arms are ensigned with a mural crown proper, masoned sable and the motto beneath the arms is 'Cruce crescimus'. There are no supporters.

face, a black list down the back, and three white feet, viz. the hind-feet and near fore-foot.' Lord Joicey has two Shetland ponies and Lord Winterstoke has 'two horses sable, maned, tailed, and girthed or'.

The arms of the City of London are always used with *dragons* for supporters, but these supporters are not officially recorded. The arms of the City of London are referred to at greater length elsewhere in these pages. The town of Appleby uses dragons with wings expanded (most fearsome creatures), but these are not official, nor are the 'dragons sejant addorsed gules, each holding an ostrich feather argent affixed to a scroll' which some enterprising artist designed for Cheshire.[206] Dragons will be found as supporters to the arms of the Earl of Enniskillen, Lord St Oswald, the Earl of Castlestuart, and Viscount Arbuthnot.[207] The heraldic dragon is not the only form of the creature now known to armory. The Chinese dragon was granted to Lord Gough as one of his supporters, and it has since also been granted as a supporter to Sir Robert Hart, Bart.

Wyverns are the supporters of the Earl of Meath and Lord Burghclere, and the sinister supporter of both Lord Raglan and Lord Lyveden.

The arms of the Royal Burgh of Dundee are quite unique. The official blazon runs: 'Azure, a pott of growing lillies argent, the escutcheon being supported by two dragons, their tails nowed together underneath vert, with this word in an escroll above a lilie growing out of the top of the shield as the former, "Dei Donum".' Though blazoned as dragons, the creatures are undoubtedly wyverns.

Wyverns when figuring as supporters are usually represented standing on the one claw and supporting the shield with the other, but in the case of the Duke of Marlborough, whose supporters are two wyverns, these are generally represented sejant erect, supporting the shield with both claws. This position is also adopted for the wyvern supporters of Sir Robert Arbuthnot, Bart, and the Earl of Eglinton.

Two *cockatrices* are the supporters of Lord Donoughmore, the Earl of Westmeath, and Sir Edmund Nugent, Bart, and the dexter supporter of Lord Lanesborough is also a cockatrice.

The *basilisk* is the same creature as the cockatrice, and in the arms of the town of Basle (German Basel), is an example of a supporter blazoned as a basilisk. The arms are: 'Argent, a crosier sable.' The supporter is a basilisk vert, armed and jelloped gules.

The supporters of the Plasterers' Company, which were granted with the arms (15 January 1556), are: 'Two opinaci (figures very similar to griffins) vert pursted (? purfled) or, beaked sable, the wings gules.' The dexter supporter of the arms of Cape Colony is a 'gnu'.

The *zebra*, the *giraffe*, and the *okapi* are as yet unclaimed as supporters, though the giraffe, under the name of the camelopard, figures in some number of cases as a crest, and there is at least one instance (Kemsley) of a zebra as a crest. The ass,

206. Both the town of Appleby and Cheshire County Council now have arms. The grant to Appleby was made on 1 June 1959, and the supporters are blazoned: two dragons proper, resting the interior hind claw on an apple slipped and leaved vert. That to Cheshire was made on 3 May 1938, and the supporters consist of two lions or, supporting between the forepaws an ostrich feather argent.

207. The Viscount Arbuthnot is properly styled The Viscount of Arbuthnott; the baronet's family spells the name with only one 't' at the end.

though there are some number of cases in which it appears as a crest or a charge, does not yet figure anywhere as a supporter, nor does the mule. The *hyena*, the *sacred cow* of India, the *bison*, the *giant sloth*, and the *armadillo* are all distinctive animals which still remain to be withdrawn from the heraldic 'lucky bag' of Garter. The mythical human-faced *winged bull* of Egyptian mythology, the *harpy*, and the *female centaur* would lend themselves well to the character of supporters.

Robertson of Struan has no supporters matriculated with his arms, and it is difficult to say for what length of time the supporters now in use have been adopted. But he is chief of his name, and the representative of one of the minor barons, so that there is no doubt that supporters would be matriculated to him if he cared to apply. Those supporters in use, viz. 'Dexter, a serpent; sinister, a dove, the heads of each encircled with rays,' must surely be no less unique than is the strange compartment, 'a wild man lying in chains', which is borne below the arms of Struan Robertson, and which was granted to his ancestor in 1451 for arresting the murderers of King James I.

The supporters belonging to the city of Glasgow★ are also unique, being two salmon, each holding a signet-ring in the mouth.

The supporters of the city of Waterford, though not recorded in Ulster's Office, have been long enough in use to ensure their official 'confirmation' if a request to this effect were to be properly put forward. They are, on the dexter side a lion, and on the sinister side a dolphin. Two dolphins azure, finned or, are the supporters of the Watermen and Lightermen's Livery Company, and were granted 1655.

Birds as supporters

Whilst *eagles* are plentiful as supporters, nevertheless if eagles are eliminated the proportion of supporters which are birds is not great.

A certain variety and differentiation is obtained by altering the position of the wings, noticeably in regard to eagles, but these differences do not appear to be by any means closely adhered to by artists in pictorial representations of armorial bearings.

671 ought perhaps more properly to have been placed amongst those eagles which, appearing as single figures, carry shields charged upon the breast, but in the present case, in addition to the shield charged upon it in the usual manner, it so palpably supports the two other escutcheons, that we are tempted to include it amongst definite supporters. The figure represents the arms of the free city of Nürnberg, and the design is reproduced from the title-page of the German edition of Andreas Vesalius' *Anatomia*, printed at Nürnberg in 1551. The eagle is that of the German Empire, carrying on its breast the impaled arms of Castile and

★ Arms of Glasgow: Argent, on a mount in base vert an oak-tree proper, the stem at the base thereof surmounted by a salmon on its back also proper, with a signet-ring in its mouth or, on the top of the tree a redbreast, and in the sinister fess point an ancient hand-bell, both also proper. Above this shield is placed a suitable helmet, with a mantling gules, doubled argent; and issuing from a wreath of the proper liveries is set for crest, the half-length figure of St Kentigern affronté, vested and mitred, his right hand raised in the act of benediction, and having in his left hand a crosier, all proper. On a compartment below the shield are placed for supporters, two salmon proper, each holding in its mouth, a signet-ring or, and in an escroll entwined with the compartment this motto, 'Let Glasgow flourish.'

Austria. The shields it supports may now be said both to belong to Nürnberg. The dexter shield, which is the coloured seal device of the old Imperial city, is: 'Azure, a harpy (in German *Frauenadler* or maiden eagle) displayed and crowned or.' The sinister shield (which may more properly be considered the real arms of Nürnberg) is: 'Per pale or, a double-headed Imperial eagle displayed, dimidiated with bendy of six gules and argent.'

The supporters of Lord Amherst of Hackney are two *Herons*: 'On either side a heron proper, collared or.'

The city of Calcutta, to which arms and supporters were granted in 1896, has for its supporters *Adjutant Birds*, which closely approximate to storks. Two woodpeckers have recently been granted as the supporters of Lord Peckover.[208]

208. The great increase during the past fifteen years in the proportion of arms granted to corporations, both in this country and throughout the Commonwealth, has meant many more grants of supporters. This in its turn has produced a host of animals, birds, monsters and humans which previously had not done duty as supporters. It would be pointless to list these; sufficient to state that almost anything, even if its ability to support is minimal, can probably be granted as a supporter.

671 *The Arms of Nürnberg.*

27 · The compartment

A compartment is anything depicted below the shield as a foothold or resting-place for the supporters, or indeed for the shield itself. Sometimes it is a fixed part of the blazon and a constituent part of the heritable heraldic bearings. At other times it is a matter of mere artistic fancy, and no fixed rules exist to regulate or control nor even to check the imagination of the heraldic artist. The fact remains that supporters must have something to stand upon, and if the blazon supplies nothing, the discretion of the artist is allowed considerable laxity.

On the subject of compartments a great deal of diversity of opinion exists. There is no doubt that in early days and early examples supporters were placed to stand upon some secure footing, but with the decadence of heraldic art in the seventeenth century came the introduction of the gilded 'freehand copy' scroll with which we are so painfully familiar, which one writer has aptly termed the heraldic gas-bracket. Arising doubtless from and following upon the earlier habit of balancing the supporters upon the unstable footing afforded by the edge of the motto scroll, the 'gas-bracket' was probably accepted as less open to objection. It certainly was not out of keeping with the heraldic art of the period to which it owed its evolution, or with the style of armorial design of which it formed a part. It still remains the accepted and 'official' style and type in England, but Scotland and Ireland have discarded it, and 'compartments' in those countries are now depicted of a nature requiring less gymnastic ability on the part of the animals to which they afford a foothold. The style of compartment is practically always a matter of artistic taste and design. With a few exceptions it is always entirely disregarded in the blazon of the patent, and the necessity of something for the supporters to stand upon is as much an understood thing as is the existence of a shield whereon the arms are to be displayed. But as the shape of the shield is left to the fancy of the artist, so is the character of the compartment, and the Lyon Register nowadays affords examples of achievements where the supporters stand on rocks and flowery mounds or issue from a watery abiding-place. The example set by the Lyon Register has been eagerly followed by most heraldic artists.

672.

It is a curious commentary upon the heraldic art of the close of the eighteenth and the early part of the nineteenth centuries that whilst the gymnastic capabilities of animals were admitted to be equal to 'tight-rope' exhibitions of balancing upon the ordinary scroll, these feats were not considered practicable in the case of human beings, for whom little square platforms were always provided. 672, which represents the sinister supporter of Lord Scarsdale (viz. the figure of Liberality represented by a woman habited argent, mantled purpure, holding a cornucopia proper) shows the method by which platform accommodation was provided for human figures when acting as supporters.

At the same time this greater freedom of design may occasionally lead to

673 *Arms of Cape Town:*
Or, an anchor erect sable, stock proper, from the ring a riband flowing azure,
and suspended therefrom an escocheon gules charged with three annulets of the field;
and for the crest, on a wreath of the colours, upon the battlements of a tower proper,
a trident in bend dexter or, surmounted by an anchor and cable in bend sinister sable.

mistakes in relation to English supporters and their compartments. Following
upon the English practice already referred to of differentiating the supporters of
different families, it has apparently been found necessary in some cases to place
the supporters to stand upon a definite object, which object is recited in the blazon
and becomes an integral and unchangeable portion of the supporter. Thus Lord
Torrington's supporters are each placed upon dismounted ships' guns ['Dexter,
an heraldic antelope ermine, horned, tusked, maned and hoofed or, standing on a
ship gun proper; sinister, a sea-horse proper, on a like gun'], Lord Hawke's★
dexter supporter rests his sinister foot upon a dolphin, and Lord Herschell's
supporters each stand upon a fasces ['Supporters: on either side a stag proper,
collared azure, standing on a fasces or']. The supporters of Lord Iveagh each rest
a hind-foot upon an escutcheon ['Supporters: on either side a stag gules, attired
and collared gemel or, resting the inner hoof on an escutcheon vert charged with
a lion rampant of the second'], whilst the inner hind-foot of each of Lord Burton's
supporters rests upon a stag's head caboshed proper. Probably absurdity could
go no further. But in the case of the supporters granted to Cape Town (673), the
official blazon runs as follows: 'On the dexter side, standing on a rock, a female

★ Supporters of Lord Hawke: Dexter, Neptune, his mantle of sea-green colour, edged argent, crowned with
an Eastern coronet or, his dexter arm erect, darting downwards his trident sable, headed silver, resting his
sinister foot on a dolphin, also sable; sinister a sea-horse or, sustaining in his forefins a banner argent the staff
broken proper.

337

figure proper, vested argent, mantle and sandals azure, on her head an estoile radiated or, and supporting with her exterior hand an anchor also proper; and on the sinister side, standing on a like rock, a lion rampant guardant gules.' In this case it will be seen that the rocks form an integral part of the supporters, and are not merely an artistic rendering of the compartment. The illustration, which was made from an official drawing supplied from the Heralds' College, shows the curious way in which the motto scroll is made to answer the purpose of the compartment.

Occasionally the compartment itself—as a thing apart from the supporters—receives attention in the blazon, *e.g.* in the case of the arms of Baron de Worms, which are of foreign origin, recorded in this country by Royal Warrant. His supporters are: 'On a bronze compartment, on either side a lion gold, collared and chained or, and pendent from the compartment a golden scroll, thereon in letters gules the motto, "Vinctus non victus."'

In the Royal Arms of the United Kingdom the motto 'Dieu et mon Droit' is required to be on the compartment below the shield, and thereon the Union Badge of the Rose, Thistle, and Shamrock engrafted on the same stem.

The city of Norwich is not officially recognised as having the right to supporters, and doubtless those in use have originated in the old artistic custom, previously referred to, of putting escutcheons of arms under the guardianship of angels. They may be so deciphered upon an old stone carving upon one of the municipal buildings in that city. The result has been that two angels have been regularly adopted as the heraldic supporters of the city arms. The point that renders them worthy of notice is that they are invariably represented each standing upon its own little pile of clouds.

The arms of the Royal Burgh of Montrose (Forfarshire) afford an official instance of another variety in the way of a compartment, which is a fixed matter of blazon and not depending upon artistic fancy. The entry in Lyon Register is as follows:

'The Royal Burgh of Montrose gives for Ensignes Armoriall, Argent, a rose gules. The shield adorned with helmet, mantling, and wreath suteable thereto. And for a crest, a hand issuing from a cloud and reaching down a garland of roses proper, supported by two mermaids aryseing from the sea proper. The motto, "Mare ditat Rosa decorat." And for a revers, Gules, St Peter on the cross proper, with the keyes hanging at his girdle or. Which Arms, &c. Ext. 16 December 1694.'

An English example may be found in the case of the arms of Boston,* which are depicted with the supporters, again two mermaids, rising from the sea, though to what extent the sea is a fixed and unchangeable part of the achievement in this case is less a matter of certainty.

Probably of all the curious 'supporters' to be found in British armory, those of the city of Southampton (Plate X) must be admitted to be the most unusual. As far as the actual usage of the arms by the corporation is concerned, one seldom if ever sees more than the simple shield employed. This bears the arms: 'Per fess gules and argent, three roses counterchanged.' But in the official record of the

---

* Arms of Boston: Sable, three coronets composed of crosses patté and fleurs-de-lis in pale or. Crest: A woolpack charged with a ram couchant all proper, ducally crowned azure.

arms in one of the Visitation books a crest is added, namely: 'Upon a mount vert, a double tower or, and issuing from the upper battlements thereof a demi-female affronté proper, vested purpure, crined and crowned with an Eastern coronet also or, holding in her dexter hand a sword erect point upwards argent, pommel and hilt of the second, and in her sinister hand a balance sable, the pans gold. The shield in the Visitation book rests upon a mount vert, issuing from waves of the sea, and thereupon placed on either side of the escutcheon a ship of two masts at anchor, the sails furled all proper, the round top or, and from each masthead flying a banner of St George, and upon the stern of each vessel a lion rampant or, supporting the escutcheon.'

From the fact that in England the compartment is so much a matter of course, it is scarcely ever alluded to, and the *term* 'Compartment' is practically one peculiar to Scottish heraldry. It does not appear to be a very ancient heraldic appendage, and was probably found to be a convenient arrangement when shields were depicted erect instead of couché, so as to supply a resting-place (or standpoint) for the supporters. In a few instances the compartment appears on seals with couché shields, on which, however, the supporters are usually represented as resting *on the sides of the escutcheon*, and bearing up the helmet and crest, as already mentioned. Sir George Mackenzie conjectures that the compartment 'represents the bearer's land and territories, though sometimes (he adds) it is bestowed in recompense of some honourable action.' Thus the Earls of Douglas are said to have obtained the privilege of placing their supporters with a pale of wood wreathed, because the doughty lord, in the reign of King Robert the Bruce, defeated the English in Jedburgh Forest, and 'caused wreathe and impale', during the night, that part of the wood by which he conjectured they might make their escape. Such a fenced compartment appears on the seal of James Douglas, second Earl of Angus, 'Dominus de Abernethie et Jedworth Forest' (1434), on that of George Douglas, fourth Earl (1459), and also on those of several of his successors in the earldom (1511–1617). A still earlier example, however, of a compartment 'representing a park with trees, &c., enclosed by a wattled fence', occurs on the seal of Walter Stewart, Earl of Atholl (*c.* 1430), where the escutcheon is placed in the entrance to the park between two trees. Nisbet refers to a seal of William, first Earl of Douglas (1377), exhibiting a single supporter (a lion) 'sitting on a compartment like to a rising ground, with a tree growing out of it, and semé of hearts, mullets, and cross crosslets', these being the charges of Douglas and Mar in the escutcheon.

According to Sir George Mackenzie, these compartments were usually allowed only to sovereign princes; and he further informs us that, besides the Douglases, he knows of no other subject in Britain, except the Earl of Perth, whose arms stand upon a compartment. In the case of the Perth family, the compartment consists of a green hill or mount, semé of caltraps★ (or cheval-traps), with the relative motto, 'Gang warily', above the achievement. 'Albeit of late,' says Mackenzie, 'compartments are become more common, and some families in Scotland have some creatures upon which their achievement stands, as the Laird of Dundas, whose achievement has for many hundreds of years stood upon a

---

★ The caltrap was an instrument thrown on the ground to injure the feet of horses, and consisted of four iron spikes, of which one always pointed upwards.

salamander in flames proper (a device of the kings of France), and Robertson of Struan has a monstrous man lying under the escutcheon chained, which was given him for his taking the murderer of James I . . .' Such figures, however, as Nisbet remarks, cannot properly be called compartments, having rather the character of devices; while, in the case of the Struan achievement, the chained man would be more accurately described as 'an honourable supporter'. Sir George Mackenzie engraves 'the coat of Denham of ould', viz. a stag's head 'caboshed', below a shield couché charged with three lozenges, or fusils, conjoined in bend. In like manner, Nisbet represents the crest and motto of the Scotts of Thirlstane, 'by way of compartment', below the escutcheon of Lord Napier, and a blazing star, with the legend 'Luceo boreale', under that of Captain Robert Seton, of the family of Meldrum; while in the case of the illumination which accompanies the latest entry in the first volume of the Lyon Register (1804), relative to the arms of John Hepburn Belshes of Invermay, the trunk of an oak-tree sprouting forth anew is placed on a compartment under the shield, with the motto, 'Revirescit.'

Two other instances of regular compartments are mentioned by Nisbet, viz. those carried by the Macfarlanes of that Ilk and the Ogilvies of Innerquharity. The former consists of a wavy representation of Loch Sloy, the gathering-place of the clan, which word is also inscribed on the compartment as their *cri-de-guerre* or slogan; while the latter is a 'green hill or rising terrace', on which are placed two serpents, 'nowed', spouting fire, and the motto, 'Terrena pericula sperno,' For some of the foregoing instances I am indebted to Seton's well-known *Law and Practice of Heraldry in Scotland*.[209]

209. The present Garter King of Arms will not normally show a compartment on a grant of arms unless it is specially requested. In recent grants which have compartments of grass, earth or water, or a combination of these elements, the compartment is not blazoned; but if a charge is included in a compartment, then it is blazoned in the body of the patent. The supporters granted to Sir Henry Drummond Hancock are blazoned as being upon a compartment of grass bounded with palings proper. The supporters of the city of Wagga Wagga in New South Wales stand on a compartment of grass divided by water barry wavy argent and azure. The blazon of the supporters granted on 8 August 1946 to Queen Elizabeth Training College for the Disabled is interesting as the compartment is an integral part of the blazon of the supporters, thus: on either side a swan in front of a cedar tree proper, the whole resting on a bridge of fourteen arches over water also proper.

28 · Mottoes

To the uninitiated, the subject of the motto of a family has a far greater importance than is conceded to it by those who have spent any time in the study of armory. Perhaps it may clear the ground if the rules presently in force are first recited. It should be carefully observed that the status of the motto is vastly different in England and in other countries. Except in the cases of impersonal arms (and not always then), the motto is never mentioned or alluded to in the terms of the patent in a grant of arms in England; consequently they are not a part of the 'estate' created by the Letters Patent, though if it be desired a motto will always be painted below the emblazonment in the margin of the patent. Briefly speaking, the position in England with regard to personal armorial bearings is that mottoes are *not hereditary*. No one is compelled to bear one, nor is any authority needed for the adoption of a motto, the matter is left purely to the personal pleasure of every individual; but if that person elects to use a motto, the officers of arms are perfectly willing to paint any motto he may choose upon his grant, and to add it to the record of his arms in their books. There is no necessity expressed or implied to use a motto at all, nor is the slightest control exercised over the selection or change of mottoes, though, as would naturally be expected, the officers of arms would decline to record to any private person any motto which might have been appropriated to the sovereign or to any of the orders of knighthood. In the same way no control is exercised over the position in which the motto is to be carried or the manner in which it is to be displayed.

In Scotland, however, the matter is on an entirely different footing. The motto is included within the terms of the patent, and is consequently made the subject of grant. It therefore becomes inalienable and unchangeable without a rematriculation, and a Scottish patent moreover always specifies the position in which the motto is to be carried. This is usually 'in an escroll over the same' (*i.e.* over the crest), though occasionally it is stated to be borne on 'a compartment below the arms'. The matter in Ireland is not quite the same as in either Scotland or England. Sometimes the motto is expressed in the patent—in fact this is now the more usual alternative—but the rule is not universal, and to a certain extent the English permissiveness is recognised. Possibly the subject can be summed up in the remark that if any motto has been granted or is recorded with a particular coat of arms in Ireland, it is expected that that shall be the motto to be made use of therewith.

As a general practice the use of mottoes in England did not become general until the eighteenth century—in fact there are very few, if any, grants of an earlier date on which a motto appears. The majority, well on towards the latter part of the eighteenth century, had no motto added, and many patents are still issued without such an addition.[210] With rare exceptions, no mottoes are to be met with in the Visitation books, and it does not appear that at the time of the Visitations the motto was considered to be essentially a part of the armorial bearings. The one or two exceptions which I have met with where mottoes are to be found on Visitation pedigrees are in every case the arms of a peer. There are at least two such in the Yorkshire Visitation of 1587, and probably it may be taken for granted that the majority of peers at that period had begun to make use of these additions to their arms. Unfortunately we have no exact means of deciding the point, because peers were not compelled to attend a Visitation, and there are but few cases in which the arms or pedigree of a peer figure in the Visitation books. In isolated cases the use of a motto can, however, be traced back to an even earlier period. There are several instances to be met with upon the early Garter plates.

Many writers have traced the origin of mottoes to the 'slogan' or war-cry of battle, and there is no doubt whatever that instances can be found in which an ancient war-cry has become a family motto. For example, one can refer to the Fitzgerald 'Crom-a-boo': other instances can be found amongst some of the Highland families, but the fact that many well-known war-cries of ancient days never became perpetuated as mottoes, and also the fact that by far the greater number of mottoes, even at a much earlier period than the present day, cannot by any possibility have ever been used for or have originated with the purposes of battle-cries, inclines me to believe that such a suggested origin for the motto in general is without adequate foundation. There can be little if any connection between the war-cry as such and the motto as such. The real origin would appear to be more correctly traced back to the badge. As will be found explained elsewhere, the badge was some simple device used for personal and household purposes and seldom for war, except by persons who used the badge of the leader they followed. No man wore his own badge in battle. It generally partook of the nature of what ancient writers would term 'a quaint conceit', and much ingenuity seems to have been expended in devising badges and mottoes which should at the same time be distinctive and should equally be or convey an index or suggestion of the name and family of the owner. Many of these badges are found in conjunction with words, mottoes, and phrases, and as the distinction between the badge in general and the crest in general slowly became less apparent, they eventually in practice became interchangeable devices, if the same device did not happen to be used for both purposes. Consequently the motto from the badge became attached to the crest, and was thence transferred to its present connection with the coat of arms. Just as at the present time a man may and often does adopt a maxim upon which he will model his life, some pithy proverb, or some trite observation, without any question or reference to armorial bearings—so, in the old days, when learning was less diffuse and when proverbs and sayings had a

---

210. In fact more mottoes were included in late sixteenth- and early seventeenth-century grants, often being blazoned in the body of the grant, than Fox-Davies suggests. Here are a few examples. A grant by William Dethick to Edward Chysnall on 20 January 1595 contains the motto *Aixus Adversa Sperno*. John Wolstenholme, granted arms by William Camden on 10 August 1604, had the motto *In Ardua Virtus* inscribed beneath his shield. In the grant to the Scriveners' Company of London, made by Sir Richard St George on 11 November 1634, the motto *Scribite Scientes* appears above the crest, probably forming part of it, and also beneath the shield.

wider acceptance and vogue than at present, did many families and many men adopt for their use some form of words. We find these words carved on furniture, set up on a cornice, cut in stone, and embroidered upon standards and banners, and it is to this custom that we should look for the beginning of the use of mottoes. But because such words were afterwards in later generations given an armorial status, it is not justifiable to presume such status for them from their beginnings. The fact that a man put his badges on the standard that he carried into battle, and with his badges placed the mottoes that thereto belonged, has led many people mistakenly to believe that these mottoes were *designed for* war-cries and for use in battle. That was not the case. In fact it seems more likely that the bulk of the standards recorded in the books of the heralds which show a motto were never carried in battle.

With regard to the mottoes in use at the moment, some of course can be traced to a remote period, and many of the later ones have interesting legends connected therewith. Of mottoes of this character may be instanced the 'Jour de ma vie' of West, which was formerly the motto of the La Warr family, adopted to commemorate the capture of the King of France at the battle of Poictiers. There are many other mottoes of this character, amongst which may be mentioned the 'Grip fast' of the Leslies, the origin of which is well known. But though many mottoes relate to incidents in the remote past, true or mythical, the motto and the incident are seldom contemporary. Nothing would be gained by a recital of a long list of mottoes, but I cannot forbear from quoting certain curious examples which by their very weirdness must excite curiosity as to their origin. A family of Martin used the singular words, 'He who looks at Martin's ape, Martin's ape shall look at him,' whilst the Curzons use, 'Let Curzon hold what Curzon helde.' The Cranston motto is still more grasping, being, 'Thou shalt want ere I want'; but probably the motto of the Dakyns is the most mysterious of all, 'Strike Dakyns, the devil's in the hempe.' The motto of Corbet, 'Deus pascit corvos,' evidently alludes to the raven or ravens (corby crows) upon the shield. The mottoes of Trafford, 'Now thus,' and 'Gripe griffin, hold fast'; the curious Pilkington motto, 'Pilkington Pailedown, the master mows the meadows'; and the 'Serva jugum' of Hay have been the foundation of many legends. The 'Fuimus' of the Bruce family is a pathetic allusion to the fact that they were once kings, but the majority of ancient mottoes partake rather of the nature of a pun upon the name, which fact is but an additional argument towards the supposition that the motto has more relation to the badge than to any other part of the armorial bearings. Of mottoes which have a punning character may be mentioned 'Mon Dieu est ma roche,' which is the motto of Roche, Lord Fermoy; 'Cavendo tutus,' which is the motto of Cavendish; 'Forte scutum salus ducum,' which is the motto of Fortescue; 'Set on,' which is the motto of Seton; 'Da fydd' of Davies, and 'Ver non semper viret,' the well-known pun of the Vernons. Another is the apocryphal 'Quid rides' which Theodore Hook suggested for the wealthy and retired tobacconist. This punning character has of late obtained much favour, and wherever a name lends itself to a pun the effort seems nowadays to be made that the motto shall be of this nature. Perhaps the best pun which exists is to be found in the motto of the Barnard family, who, with arms 'Argent, a bear rampant sable, muzzled or,' and crest 'A demi-bear as in the arms,' use for the motto, 'Bear and Forbear,'

343

or in Latin, as it is sometimes used, 'Fer et perfer.' Others that may be alluded to are the 'What I win I keep' of Winlaw; the 'Libertas' of Liberty; the 'Ubi crux ibi lux' of Sir William Crookes; the 'Bear thee well' of Bardwell; the 'Gare le pied fort' of Bedford; the 'Gare la bête' of Garbett; and the 'Cave Deus videt' of Cave. Other mottoes—and they are a large proportion—are of some saintly and religious tendency. However desirable and acceptable they may be, and however accurately they may apply to the first possessor, they sometimes are sadly inappropriate to later and more degenerate successors.

In Germany, a distinction appears to be drawn between their 'Wahlsprüche' (*i.e.* those which are merely dictated by personal choice) and the 'armorial mottoes' which remained constantly and heritably attached to the armorial bearings, such as the 'Gott mit uns' ('God with us') of Prussia and the 'Nihil sine Deo' of Hohenzollern.

The Initial or Riddle Mottoes appear to be peculiar to Germany. Well-known examples of these curiosities are the 'W. G. W.' (*i.e.* 'Wie Gott will'—'As God wills'), or 'W. D. W.' (*i.e.* 'Wie du willst'—'As thou wilt'), which are both frequently to be met with. The strange but well-known alphabet or vowel-motto 'A. E. I. O. V' of the Emperor Frederick III has been variously translated, 'Aquila Electa Juste Omnia Vincit' ('The chosen eagle vanquishes all by right'), 'Aller Ehren Ist Oesterrich Voll' ('Austria is full of every honour'), or perhaps with more likelihood, 'Austriae Est Imperare Orbe Universo' ('All the earth is subject to Austria').

The *cri-de-guerre*, both as a heraldic fact and as an armorial term, is peculiar, and exclusively so, to British and French heraldry. The national *cri-de-guerre* of France, 'Montjoye Saint Denis,' appeared above the pavilion in the old Royal Arms of France, and probably the English Royal motto, 'Dieu et mon Droit,' is correctly traced to a similar origin. A distinction is still made in modern heraldry between the *cri-de-guerre* and the motto, inasmuch as it is considered that the former should always of necessity surmount the crest. This is very generally adhered to in Scotland in the cases where both a motto and a *cri-de-guerre* (or, as it is frequently termed in that country, a 'slogan') exist, the motto, contrary to the usual Scottish practice, being then placed below the shield. It is to be hoped that a general knowledge of this fact will not, however, result in the description of every motto found above a crest as a *cri-de-guerre*, and certainly the concentrated piety now so much in favour in England for the purposes of a motto can be quite fitly left below the shield.

Artists do not look kindly on the motto for decorative purposes. It has been usually depicted in heraldic emblazonment in black letters upon a white scroll, tinted and shaded with pink, but with the present revival of heraldic art, it has become more general to paint the motto ribbon in conformity with the colour of the field, the letters being often shown thereon in gold. The colour and shape of the motto ribbon, however, are governed by no heraldic laws, and except in Scottish examples should be left, as they are purely unimportant accessories of the achievement, wholly at the discretion of the artist.[211]

211. It is interesting to note how conservative grantees are with regard to the language they choose for their mottoes. Of 125 mottoes adopted between 1965 and 1966, 88 were in Latin, 25 in English and 12 in other languages, notably, French, Welsh and Greek. Of an equal number of mottoes

adopted between 1822 and 1824, 105 were in Latin, 14 in English and 6 in other languages, illustrating a slight switch from Latin to English, but nothing very significant.

It appears to have been customary to deny women mottoes. The only example that I have found of a woman having a motto was that assigned to Baroness Holland (Catherine, wife of the Rt Hon. Henry Fox) when she was granted supporters on 14 May 1762; but in a way this is a bad example, as the motto *Re E Marito* was to be borne and used by holders of the peerage. Recently, however, there has been a change of heart and, although emancipated woman is still denied shield and crest, some gentle aphorism may be placed on a scroll beneath her lozenge.

29 · Badges

The exact status of the badge in this country, to which it is peculiar, has been very much misunderstood. This is probably due to the fact that the evolution of the badge was gradual, and that its importance increased unconsciously. Badges do not formerly appear to have ever been made the subjects of grants, and the instances which can be referred to showing their control, or attempted control, by the Crown in past times are *very rare indeed*. As a matter of fact, the Crown seems to have perhaps purposely ignored them. They are not, as we know them, found in the earliest times of heraldry, unless we are to presume their existence from early seals, many of which show isolated charges taken from the arms; for if in the cases where such charges appear upon the seals we are to accept those seals as proofs of the contemporary existence of those devices as heraldic badges, we should often be led into strange conclusions.

There is no doubt that these isolated devices which are met with were not only a part of the arms, but in many cases the *origin* of the arms. Devices possessing a more or less personal and possessive character occur in many cases before record of the arms they later developed into can be traced. This will be noticed in relation to the arms of Swinton, to which reference is made elsewhere. If these are badges, then badges go back to an earlier date than arms. Such devices occur many centuries before such a thing as a shield of arms existed.

The *Heraldic Badge, as we know it*, came into general use about the reign of Edward III, that is, the heraldic badge as a separate matter having a distinct existence in addition to concurrent arms, and having at the same time a distinctly heraldic character. But long before that date, badges are found with an allied reference to a particular person, which very possibly are rightly included in any enumeration of badges. Of such a character is the badge of the broom plant, which is found upon the tomb of Geoffrey, Count of Anjou, from which badge the name of the Plantagenet dynasty originated (Plantagenet, by the way, was never a personal surname, but was the name of the dynasty).

It is doubtful, however, if at that early period there existed much if indeed any opportunity for the use of heraldic badges. At the same time, as far back as the reign of Richard I—and some writers would take examples of a still more remote period—these badges must have been occasionally depicted upon banners, for Richard I appears to have had a dragon upon one of his banners.

These banner decorations, which at a later date have been often accepted as badges, can hardly be quite properly so described, for there are many cases where no other proof of usage can be found, and there is no doubt that many such are instances of no more than banners prepared for specific purposes; and the record of such and such a banner cannot necessarily carry proof that the owner of the banner claimed or used the objects depicted thereupon as personal badges. If they are to be so included some individuals must have revelled in a multitude of badges.

But the difficulty in deciding the point very greatly depends upon the definition of the badge; and if we are to take the definition according to the manner of acceptance and usage at the period when the use of badges was greatest, then many of the earliest cannot be taken as coming within the limits.

In later Plantagenet days, badges were of considerable importance, and certain characteristics are plainly marked. They were never worn by the owner—in the sense in which he carried his shield, or bore his crest; they were his sign-mark indicative of ownership; they were stamped upon his belongings in the same way in which Government property is marked with the broad arrow, and they were worn by his servants. They were worn not only by his retainers, but very probably were also worn more or less temporarily by adherents of his party if he were big enough to lead a party in the State. At all times badges had very extensive decorative use.

There was never any fixed form for the badge; there was never any fixed manner of usage. I can find no fixed laws of inheritance, no common method of assumption. In fact the use of a badge, in the days when everybody who was anybody possessed arms, was quite subsidiary to the arms, and very much akin to the manner in which nowadays monograms are made use of. At the same time care must be taken to distinguish the 'badge' from the 'rebus', and also from the temporary devices which we read about as having been so often adopted for the purpose of the tournament when the combatant desired his identity to be concealed. Modern novelists and poets give us plenty of illustrations of the latter kind, but proof of the fact even that they were ever adopted in that form is by no means easy to find, though their professedly temporary nature of course militates against the likelihood of contemporary *record*. The rebus had never an heraldic status, and it had seldom more than a temporary existence. A fanciful device adopted (we hear of many instances) for the temporary purpose of a tournament could generally be so classed, but the rebus proper has some device, usually a pictorial rendering of the name of the person for whom it stood. In such a category would be included printers' and masons' marks, but probably the definition of Dr Johnson of the word rebus, as a word represented by a picture, is as good a definition and description as can be given. The rebus in its nature is a different thing from a badge, and may best be described as a pictorial signature, the most frequent occasion for its use being in architectural surroundings, where it was constantly introduced as a pun upon some name which it was desired to perpetuate. The best-known and perhaps the most typical and characteristic rebus is that of Islip, the builder of part of Westminster Abbey. Here the pictured punning representation of his name had nothing to do with his armorial bearings or personal badge; but the great difficulty, in dealing with both badges and rebuses, is the difficulty of knowing which is which, for very frequently the same or a similar device was used for both purposes. Parker, in his glossary of heraldic terms, gives several typical examples of rebuses which very aptly illustrate their status and meaning. At Lincoln College at Oxford, and on other buildings connected with Thomas Beckynton, Bishop of Bath and Wells, will be found carved the rebus of a beacon issuing from a tun. This is found in conjunction with the letter T for his Christian name, Thomas. Now this design was not his coat of arms, and was not his crest, nor was it his badge. Another rebus which is found at Canterbury shows an ox and the letters N, E, as the rebus of John Oxney. A rebus which indicates Thomas Conyston, Abbot of Cirencester, which can be found in Gloucester Cathedral, is a comb and a tun, and the printer's mark of Richard Grifton, which is a good example of a rebus and its use, was a tree, or graft, growing on a tun. In none of these cases are the designs mentioned on any part of the arms, crest, or badge of the persons mentioned. Rebuses of this character abound on all our ancient buildings, and their use has lately come very prominently into favour in connection with the many allusive bookplates, the design of which originates in some play upon the name. The words 'device', 'ensign', and 'cognisance' have no definite heraldic meaning, and are used impartially to apply to the crest, the badge, and sometimes to the arms upon the shield, so that they may be eliminated from consideration. There remains therefore the crest and the badge between which to draw a definite line of distinction. The real difference lay in the method of use, though there is usually a difference of form, recognisable by an expert, but difficult to put into words. The crest was the ornament upon the helmet, seldom if ever actually worn, and never used except by the person to whom it belonged. The badge, on the other hand, was never placed upon the helmet, but was worn by the servants and retainers, and was used right and left on the belongings of the owner as a sign of his ownership. So great and extensive at one period was the use of these badges, that they were far more generally employed than either arms or crest, and whilst the knowledge of a man's badge or badges would be everyday knowledge and common repute throughout the kingdom, few people would know that man's crest, fewer still would ever have seen it worn.

It is merely an exaggeration of the difficulty that we are always in uncertainty whether any given device was merely a piece of decoration borrowed from the arms or crest, or whether it had continued usage as a badge. In the same way many families who had never used crests, but who had used badges, took the opportunity of the Visitations to record their badges as crests. A notable example of the subsequent record of a badge as a crest is met with in the Stourton family. Their crest, originally a buck's head, but after the marriage with the heiress of Le Moigne a demi-monk, can be readily substantiated, as can their badge of the drag or sledge. At one of the Visitations, however, a cadet of the Stourton family recorded the sledge as a crest. Uncertainty also arises from the lack of precision in the diction employed at all periods, the words badge, device, and crest having so often been used interchangeably.

Another difficulty which is met with in regard to badges is that, with the exception of the extensive records of the Royal badges and some other more or less informal lists of badges of the principal personages at different periods, badges were never a subject of official record, and whilst it is difficult to determine the initial point as to whether any particular device is a badge or not, the difficulty of deducing rules concerning badges becomes practically impossible, and after most careful consideration I have come to the conclusion that there were never any hard and fast rules relating to badges, that they were originally and were allowed to remain matters of personal fancy, and that although well-known cases can be found where the same badge has been used generation after generation, those cases may perhaps be the exception rather than the rule. Badges should be considered and accepted in the general run as not being matters of permanence, and as of little importance except during the time from about the reign of Edward III to about the reign of Henry VIII. Their principal use upon the clothes of the retainers came to an end by the creation of the standing army, the beginning of which can be traced to the reign of Henry VIII, and as badges never had any ceremonial use to perpetuate their status, their importance almost ceased altogether at that period except as regards the Royal family.

Speaking broadly, regularised and *recorded* heraldic control as a matter of operative fact dates little if any further back than the end of the reign of Henry VIII; consequently badges originally do not appear to have been taken much cognisance of by the Heralds. Their actual use from that period onwards rapidly declined, and hence the absence of record.

Though the use of badges has become very restricted, there are still one or two occasions on which badges are used as badges, in the style formerly in vogue. Perhaps the case which is most familiar is the broad arrow which is used to mark Government stores. It is a curious commentary upon heraldic officialdom and its ways that though this is the only badge which has really any extensive use, it is not a Crown badge in any degree. Although this origin has been disputed it is said to have originated in the fact that one of the Sydney family, when Master of the Ordnance, to prevent disputes as to the stores for which he was responsible, marked everything with his private badge of the broad arrow, and this private badge has since remained in constant use. One wonders at what date the officers of Her Majesty will observe that this has become one of Her Majesty's recognised badges, and will include it with the other Royal badges in the warrants in which they are recited. Already more than two centuries have passed since it first came into use, and either they should represent to the Government that the pheon is not a Crown mark, and that some recognised Royal badge should be used in its place, or else they should place its status upon a definite footing.[212]

Another instance of a badge used at the present day in the ancient manner is the conjoined rose, thistle, and shamrock which is embroidered front and back

212. See note 103 for a description of the augmented badge for Wales.

On 17 July 1917, by Royal Proclamation, King George V declared that his house and family should thenceforth be known by the name of Windsor, and in 1938 King George VI adopted a badge for the House of Windsor. It is a representation of the Round Tower of Windsor Castle with a banner of the royal arms flying from the turret, the Tower being enclosed by two branches of oak and ensigned by the royal crown.

upon the tunics of the Beefeaters and the Yeomen of the Guard. The crowned harps which were worn by the Royal Irish Constabulary are another instance of the kind, but though a certain number of badges are recited in the warrant each time any alteration or declaration of the Royal Arms occurs, their use has now become very limited. Present badges are the crowned rose for England, the crowned thistle for Scotland, and the crowned trefoil and the crowned harp for Ireland; whilst for the Union there is the conjoined rose, thistle, and shamrock under the crown, and the crowned shield which carries the device of the Union Jack. The badge of Wales, which has existed for long enough, is the uncrowned dragon upon a mount vert, and the crowned cyphers, one within and one without the Garter, are also depicted upon the warrant. These badges, which appear on the Sovereign's warrant, are never assigned to any other member of the Royal Family, of whom the Prince of Wales is the only one who rejoices in the possession of officially assigned badges. The badge of the eldest son of the Sovereign, as such, and not as Prince of Wales, is the plume of three ostrich feathers, enfiled with the circlet from his coronet.[213] An additional badge (on a mount vert, a dragon passant gules, charged on the shoulder with a label of three points argent) has been assigned to His Royal Highness. This action was taken with the desire to in some way gratify the forcibly expressed wishes of Wales, and it is probable that, the precedent having been set, it will be assigned to all those who may bear the title of Prince of Wales in future.[214]

213. Fox-Davies has omitted to mention that beneath the coronet and entwined about the ends of the feathers is a blue scroll containing the motto *Ich Dien* in gold letters.

214. This precedent has been followed and the present Prince of Wales uses the dragon badge with a label. His full achievement of arms as approved by the Queen, shows in the compartment the feathers and dragon badges, and also the arms of the duchy of Cornwall: Sable, fifteen bezants, five, four, three, two and one or. The illustration is of the achievement as approved for use on souvenirs at the Investiture of the Prince in 1969 (FF).

FF *Arms of H.R.H. Charles, Prince of Wales.*

The only instances I am personally aware of in which a real badge of ancient origin is still worn by the servants are the cases of the state liveries of the Earl of Yarborough, whose servants wear an embroidered buckle, and of Lord Mowbray and Stourton, whose servants wear an embroidered sledge. The family of Daubeney of Cote still bear the old Daubeney badge of the pair of bat's wings; Lord Stafford still uses his 'Stafford knot'. I believe the servants of Lord Braye still wear the badge of the hemp-brake, and those of the Earl of Loudoun wear the Hastings maunch; and doubtless there are a few other instances. When the old families were becoming greatly reduced in number, and the nobility and the upper classes were being recruited from families of later origin, the wearing of badges, like so much else connected with heraldry, became lax in its practice.

The servants of all the great nobles in ancient days appear to have worn the badges of their masters in a manner similar to the use of the royal badge by the Yeomen of the Guard, although sometimes the badge was embroidered upon the sleeve; and the wearing of the badge by the retainers is the chief and principal use to which badges were anciently put. Nisbet alludes on this point to a paragraph from the Act for the Order of the Riding of Parliament in 1681, which says that 'the noblemen's lacqueys may have over their liveries velvet coats with their badges, *i.e.* their crests and mottoes done on plate, or embroidered on the back and breast conform to ancient custom.' A curious survival of these plates is to be found in the large silver plaques worn by so many bank messengers. Badges appear, however, to have been frequently depicted semé upon the lambrequins of armorial achievements, as will be seen from many of the old Garter plates; but here, again, it is not always easy to distinguish between definite badges and artistic decoration, nor between actual badges in use and mere appropriately selected charges from the shield.

The water-bougets of Lord Berners, the knot of Lord Stafford, popularly known as 'the Stafford knot'; the Harington fret; the ragged staff or the bear and the ragged staff of Lord Warwick (this being really a conjunction of two separate devices); the Rose of England, the Thistle of Scotland, and the sledge of Stourton, the hemp-brake of Lord Braye wherever met with are readily recognised as badges, but there are many badges which it is difficult to distinguish from crests, and even some which in all respects would appear to be more correctly regarded as coats of arms.

It is a point worthy of consideration whether or not a badge needs a background; here, again, it is a matter most difficult to determine, but it is singular that in any matter of *record* the badge is almost invariably depicted upon a background, either of a standard or a mantling, or upon the 'field' of a roundel, and it may well be that their use in such circumstances as the two cases first mentioned may have only been considered correct when the colour of the mantling or the standard happened to be the right colour for the background of the badge.

Badges are most usually met with in stained glass upon roundels of some colour or colours, and though one would hesitate to assert it as an actual fact, there are many instances which would lead one to suppose that the background of a badge was usually the livery colour or colours of its then owner, or of the family from which it was originally inherited. Certain is it that there are very few contemporary instances of badges which, when emblazoned, are not upon the known livery colours; and if this fact be accepted, then one is perhaps justified in assuming all to be livery colours, and we get at once a ready explanation on several points which have long puzzled antiquaries. The name of Edward 'the Black Prince' has often been a matter of discussion, and the children's history books tell us that the nickname originated from the colour of his armour. This may be true enough, but as most armour would be black when it was unpolished, and as most armour was either polished or dull, the probabilities are not very greatly in its favour. Though there can be found instances, it was not a usual custom for any one to paint his armour red or green. Even if the armour of the prince were enamelled black it would be so usually hidden by his surcoat that he is hardly likely to have been nicknamed from it. It seems to me far more probable that black was the livery colour of the Black Prince, and that his own retainers and followers wore the livery of black. If that were the case, one understands at once how he would obtain the nickname. The nickname is doubtless contemporary. A curious confirmation of my supposition is met with in the fact that his shield for peace was: 'Sable, three ostrich feathers two and one, the quill of each passing through a scroll argent.' There we get the undoubted badge of the ostrich feather, which was originally borne single, depicted upon his livery colour—black.

The badges represented in Prince Arthur's Book in the College of Arms (an important source of our knowledge upon the subject) are all upon backgrounds; and the curious divisions of the colours on the backgrounds would seem to show that each badge had its own background, several badges being only met with upon the same ground when that happens to be the true background belonging to them. But in attempting to deduce rules, it should be remembered that in all and every armorial matter there was greater laxity of rule at the period of the actual use of arms as a reality of life than it was possible to permit when the multiplication of arms as paper insignia made regulation necessary and more restrictive; so that an occasional variation from any deduction need not necessarily vitiate the conclusion, even in a matter exclusively relating to the shield. How much more, then, must we remain in doubt when dealing with badges which appear to have been so largely a matter of personal caprice.

It is a striking comment that of all the badges presently to be referred to of the Stafford family, each single one is depicted upon a background. It is a noticeable fact that of the eighteen 'badges' exemplified as belonging to the family of Stafford, nine are upon parti-coloured fields. This is not an unreasonable proportion if the fields are considered to be the livery colours of the families from whom the badges were originally derived, but it is altogether out of proportion to the number of shields in any roll of arms which would have the field party per pale, or party in any other form of division. With the exception of the second badge, which is on a striped background of green and white, all the party backgrounds are party per pale, which was the most usual way of depicting a livery in the few records which have come down to us of the heraldic use of livery colours, and of the eighteen badges, no less than eight are upon a parti-coloured field of which the dexter is sable and the sinister gules. Scarlet and black are known to have been the livery colours of Edward Stafford, Duke of Buckingham, who was beheaded in 1521. The arms of the town of Buckingham are on a field per pale sable and gules.

With regard to the descent of badges and the laws which govern their descent still less is known. The answer to the question, 'How did badges descend?' is simple: 'Nobody knows.' One can only hazard opinions more or less pious, of more or less value. It is distinctly a point upon which it is risky to be dogmatic, and we must wait for the development which will follow the recent revival of the granting of standards. As cases occur for decision precedents will be found and disclosed. Whilst the secrecy of the records of the College of Arms is so jealously preserved it is impossible to speak definitely at present, for an exact and comprehensive knowledge of exact and authoritative instances of fact is necessary before a decision can be definitely put forward. Unless some officer of arms will carefully collate the information which can be gleaned from the records in the College of Arms which are relevant to the subject, it does not seem likely that our knowledge will advance greatly.[215]

The grant of supporters to the Earl of Stafford, as under, is worthy of attention.

'To all and singular to whom these Presents shall come, John Anstis Esq[r] Garter principal King of Arms, sends greeting, Whereas his late Majesty King James the Second by Letters Patents under the Great Seal, did create Henry Stafford Howard to be Earl of Stafford, to have and hold the same to him and the heirs males of his body; and for default thereof to John and Francis his Brothers and the heirs males of their bodies respectively, whereby the said Earldom is now legally vested in the right Hon[ble] William Stafford Howard Son and Heir of the said John; And in regard that y[e] said Henry late Earl of Stafford omitted to take any Grant of Supporters, which the Peers of this Realm have an indisputable Right to use and bear, the right Hon[ble] Henry Bowes Howard Earl of Berkshire Deputy (with the Royal Approbation) of his Grace Thomas Howard Duke of Norfolk Earl Marshall and Hereditary Marshall of England hath been pleased to direct me to grant to the said right Hon[ble] William Stafford Howard Earl of Stafford the Supporters formerly granted to y[e] late Viscount Stafford, Grandfather to the said Earl; as also to order me to cause to be depicted in the Margin of my said Grant y[e] Arms of Thomas of Woodstock Duke of Gloucester quartered with the Arms of the said Earl of Stafford, together with the Badges of the said Noble Family of Stafford: Now these presents Witness that according to the consent of the said Earl of Berkshire signified under his Lordship's hand and seal I do by the Authority and power annexed to my Office hereby grant and assign to y[e] said Right Honourable William Stafford Howard Earl of Stafford, the following Supporters which

---

215. Unfortunately there is little to add to Fox-Davies' comments. It is true that by a Warrant dated 18 June 1906 the Earl Marshal empowered the kings of arms to grant badges to armigerous people, provided always an Earl Marshal's Warrant for the grant was first obtained in the same way as for a grant of arms. A badge is granted 'for use on Standards or otherwise according to the law of arms,' but no one has laid down what the law of arms is. If required, a standard will be painted on letters patent granting a badge, but the standard itself is not blazoned in the grant.

It is certain that a person could have more than one badge, and that badges were used in connection with specific lands or activities. That this fact is recognised today is demonstrated by the grant of no less than three badges to the British Transport Commission in 1956.

It would seem, and I hesitate to put it more strongly, that, whilst an armiger cannot licence another to use his arms, he can issue such a licence or permission with regard to his badge or badges. Certainly a number of corporations grant such licences.

The devolution of a personal badge is still a matter for speculation. Whilst Fox-Davies' theory that it descends in the same way as a quartering is interesting, it remains only theory.

were heretofore borne by the late Lord Viscount Stafford, that is to say, on the Dexter side a Lion Argent, and on the Sinister Side a Swan surgiant Argent Gorged with a Ducal Coronet per Pale Gules and sable beaked and membered of the Second; to be used and borne at all times and upon all occasions by the said Earl of Stafford and the heirs males of his body, and such persons to whom the said Earldom shall descend according to the Law and Practice of Arms without the let or interruption of any Person or Persons whatsoever. And in pursuance of the Warrant of the said Earl of Berkshire, The Arms of Thomas of Woodstock Duke of Gloucester, as the same are on a Plate remaining in the Chapel of St George within ye Castle of Windsor, set up there for his Descendant the Duke of Buckingham are depicted in the margin, and quartered in such place and manner as the same were formerly borne the Staffords Dukes of Buckingham, together with Eighteen badges belonging to the said most ancient and illustrious Family of Stafford, as the same are represented in a Manuscript remaining in the College of Arms (674). In Witness whereof I the said Garter have hereto subscribed my Name and affixed the Seal of my Office this First Day of August Anno Domini 1720.

'JOHN ANSTIS Garter
'Principal King of Arms.'

It may be of interest to call attention to the fact that in this exemplification the Royal Arms are displayed before those of Stafford. On the face of it, the document—as far as it relates to the badges—is no more than a certificate or exemplification, in which case it is undoubted evidence that badges descend to the heir-general as do quarterings; but there is the possibility that the document is a re-grant in the nature of an exemplification following a Royal Licence, or a re-grant to remove uncertainty as to the attainder. And if the document—as far as its relation to the badges goes—has any of the character of a grant, it can have but little value as evidence of the descent of badges. It is remarkable that it is absolutely silent as to the future destination of the badges. The real fact is that the whole subject of the descent and devolution of badges is shrouded in mystery. Each of the badges (674) is depicted within a circle adorned with a succession of Stafford knots, as is shown in the one instance at the head. Five of these badges appear upon a well-known portrait of Edward, Duke of Buckingham. The fact that some of these badges are really crests depicted upon wreaths goes far as an authority for the use of a crest upon livery buttons for the purposes of a badge.

In ancient days all records seemed to point to the fact that badges were personal, and that though they were worn by the retainers, they were the property of *the head* of the family, rather than (as the arms) of the whole family, and though the information available is meagre to the last degree, it would appear probable that in all cases where their use by other members of the family than the head of the house can be proved, the likelihood is that the cadets would render feudal service and would wear the badge as retainers of the man whose standard they followed into battle, so that we should expect to find the badge following the same descent as the peerage, together with the lands and liabilities which accompanied it. This undoubtedly makes for the inheritance of a badge upon the same line of descent as a barony by writ, and such a method of inheritance accounts for the known

674 *The Stafford Badges as exemplified in 1720 to William Stafford Howard, Earl of Stafford.*

descent of most of the badges heraldically familiar to us. Probably we shall be right in so accepting it as the ancient rule of inheritance. But, on the other hand, a careful examination of the *Book of Standards*, now preserved in the College of Arms, provides several examples charged with marks of cadency. But here again one is in ignorance whether this is an admission of inheritance by cadets, or whether the case should be considered as grants of differenced versions to cadets. This then gives us the badge, the property in and of which would descend to the heir-general (and perhaps also to cadets), whilst it would be used (if there were no inherited right) in token of allegiance or service, actual, quasi-actual, or sentimental, by the cadets of the house and their servants; for whilst the use of the cockade is a survival of the right to be waited on and served by a soldier servant, the use of a badge by a cadet may be a survival and reminder of the day when (until they married heiresses and continued or founded other families) the cadets of a house owed and gave military service to the head of their own family, and in return were supported by him.

354

From the wording of the recent grants of badges I believe the intention, however, is that the badge is to descend of right to all of those people on whom a right to it would devolve if it were a quartering.

The use of badges having been so limited, the absence of rule and regulation leaves it very much a matter of personal taste how badges, where they exist, shall be heraldically depicted, and perhaps it is better to leave their manner of display to artistic requirements. The most usual place, when depicted in conjunction with an achievement, is on either side of the crest, and they may well be placed in that position. Where they exist, however, they ought undoubtedly to be continued in use upon the liveries of the servants, and the present practice is for them to be placed on the livery buttons, and embroidered upon the epaulettes or on the sleeves of state liveries. Undoubtedly the former practice of placing the badge upon the servants' livery is the precursor of the present vogue of placing crests upon livery buttons, and many heraldic writers complain of the impropriety of placing the crest in such a position. I am not sure that I myself may not have been guilty in this way; but when one bears in mind the number of cases in which the badge and the crest are identical, and when, as in the above instance, devices which are undoubtedly crests are exemplified as and termed badges, even as such being represented upon wreaths, and even in that form granted upon standards, whilst in other cases the action has been the reverse, it leaves one under the necessity of being careful in making definite assertions.

Having dealt with the laws (if there ever were any) and the practice concerning the use and display of badges in former days, it will be of interest to notice some of those which were anciently in use.

I have already referred to the badge of the ostrich feathers, now borne exclusively by the heir-apparent to the throne. The old legend that the Black Prince won the badge at the battle of Crecy by the capture of John, King of Bohemia, together with the motto 'Ich dien', has been long since exploded. Sir Harris Nicolas brought to notice the fact that among certain pieces of plate belonging to Queen Philippa of Hainault was a large silver-gilt dish enamelled with a black escutcheon with ostrich feathers, 'vno scuch nigro cum pennis de ostrich', and upon the strength of that, suggested that the ostrich feather was probably originally a badge of the Counts of Hainault derived from the County of Ostrevaus, a title which was held by their eldest sons. The suggestion in itself seems probable enough and may be correct, but it would not account for the use of the ostrich feathers by the Mowbray family, who did not descend from the marriage of Edward III and Philippa of Hainault. Contemporary proof of the use of badges is often difficult to find. The Mowbrays had many badges, and certainly do not appear to have made any very extensive use of the ostrich feathers. But there seems to be very definite authority for the existence of the badge. There is in one of the records of the College of Arms (R. 22, 67), which is itself a copy of another record, the following statement:

'The discent of Mowbray written at length in lattin from the Abby booke of newborough wherein Rich 2 gaue to Thomas Duke of norff. & Erle Marshall the armes of Saint Edward Confessor in theis words:

'Et dedit eidem Thome ad pertandum in sigillo et vexillo suo arma S^{ti} Edwardi. Idcirco arma bipartata portavit scilt Sci Edwardi et domini marcialis

355

Angliæ cum duabus pennis strutionis erectis et super crestam leonem et duo parva scuta cum leonibus ex utraq' parte predictorum armorum.'

Accompanying this is a rough-tricked sketch of the arms upon which the illustration (675) has been based. Below this extract in the College Records is written in another hand: 'I find this then in ye chancell window of Effingham by Bungay in the top of the cot window with Mowbraye & Segrave on the side in glass there.'

Who the writer was I am unaware. He appends a further sketch to his note, which slightly differs. No helmet or crest is shown, and the central shield has only the arms of Brotherton. The feathers which flank it are both enfiled below the shield by one coronet. Of the smaller shields at the side, the dexter bears the arms of Mowbray and the sinister those of Segrave. Possibly the Mowbrays, as recognised members of the Royal Family, bore the badge by subsequent grant and authorisation and not on the simple basis of inheritance.

An ostrich feather piercing a scroll was certainly the favourite badge of the Black Prince and so appears on several of his seals, and triplicated it occurs on his 'shield of peace' (478), which, set up under the instructions in his will, still remains on his monument in Canterbury Cathedral. The arms of Sir Roger de Clarendon, the illegitimate son of the Black Prince, were derived from this 'shield for peace', which I take it was not really a coat of arms at all, but merely the badge of the Prince depicted upon his livery colour, and which might equally have been displayed upon a roundle. In the form of a shield bearing three feathers the badge occurs on the obverse of the second seal of Henry IV in 1411. A single ostrich feather with the motto 'Ich dien' upon the scroll is to be seen on the seal of Edward, Duke of York, who was killed at the battle of Agincourt in 1415. Henry IV as Duke of Lancaster placed on either side of his escutcheon an ostrich feather with a garter or belt carrying the motto 'Sovereygne' *twined around* the feather, John of Gaunt used the badge with a chain laid along the quill, and Thomas, Duke of Gloucester, used it with a garter and buckle instead of the chain; whilst John Beaufort, Duke of Somerset, placed an ostrich feather on each side of his shield, the quills in his case being compony argent and azure, like the bordure round his arms.

There is a note in Harl. MS. 304, folio 12, which, if it be strictly accurate, is of some importance. It is to the effect that the 'feather silver with the pen gold is the King's, the ostrich feather pen and all silver is the Prince's (*i.e.* the Prince of Wales), and the ostrich feather gold the pen ermine is the Duke of Lancaster's.' That statement evidently relates to a time when the three were in existence contemporaneously, *i.e.* before the accession of Henry IV. In the reign of Richard II there was no Prince of Wales. During the reign of Edward III from 1376 onwards, Richard, afterwards Richard II, was Prince of Wales, and John of Gaunt was Duke of Lancaster (so cr. 1362). But John of Gaunt used the feather in the form above stated, and to find a Duke of Lancaster *before* John of Gaunt we must go back to before 1360, when we have Edward III as King, the Black Prince as Prince, and Henry of Lancaster (father-in-law of John of Gaunt) as Duke of Lancaster. He derived from Henry III, and like the Mowbrays had no blood descent from Philippa of Hainault. A curious confirmation of my suggestion that black was the livery colour of the Black Prince is found in the fact that there was in a window in St Dunstan's Church, London, within a wreath of roses a roundle per pale sanguine and azure (these being unquestionably livery colours), a plume of ostrich feathers argent, quilled or, enfiled by a scroll bearing the words 'Ich dien'. Above was the Prince's coronet and the letters E. & P., one on each side of the plume. This was intended for Edward VI, doubtless being erected in the reign of Henry VIII. The badge in the form in which we know it, *i.e.* enfiled by the princely coronet, dates from about the beginning of the Stuart dynasty, since when it appears to have been exclusively reserved for the eldest son and heir-apparent to the throne. At the same time the right to the display of the badge would appear to have been reserved by the Sovereign, and Woodward remarks:

'On the Privy Seals of our Sovereigns the ostrich feather is still employed as a badge. The shield of arms is usually placed between two lions sejant guardant addorsed, each holding the feather. On the Privy Seal of Henry VIII the feathers are used without the lions, and this was the case on the majority of the seals of the Duchy of Lancaster. On the reverse of the present seal of the Duchy the feathers appear to be ermine.'

676 shows the seal of James II for the Duchy of Lancaster.[216] The first seal of

216. The arms at present used by the Queen as Duke of Lancaster were exemplified and approved in June 1962. The arms are those of England differenced by a label azure, each file charged with three fleurs-de-lis or. The shield is surmounted by a gold peer's helm with a red mantling doubled ermine. The crest is a lion statant guardant gorged with a label as in the arms, and crowned with a coronet composed of four crosses formy and four fleurs-de-lis or. Beneath the shield is the motto *Sovereyne*. There are no supporters.

675 *The arms granted by King Richard II to Thomas de Mowbray, Duke of Norfolk, and showing the ostrich feather badges.*

676 *Seal of King James II for the Duchy of Lancaster.*

357

677 *Badge of King Henry II.*

678 *Badge of Edward IV.*

679 *Compound Badge of
Henry VIII
and Catharine of Aragon.
(From the Westminster
Tournament Roll.)*

680 *Badge of Richard I.*

681 *Two badges of Henry
VII, viz. the 'sun-burst'
and the crowned portcullis.*

the Lancashire County Council shows a shield supported by two talbots sejant addorsed, each supporting in the exterior paw an ostrich feather semé-de-lis. It is possible that the talbots may be intended for lions and the fleurs-de-lis for ermine spots. The silver swan, one of the badges of King Henry V, was used also by Henry IV. It was derived from the De Bohuns, Mary de Bohun being the wife of Henry IV. From the De Bohuns it has been traced to the Mandevilles, Earls of Essex, who may have adopted it to typify their descent from Adam Fitz Swanne, *temp.* Conquest. 33 on the same plate is the white hart of Richard II. Although some have traced this badge from the white hind used as a badge by Joan, the Fair Maid of Kent, the mother of Richard II, it is probably a device punning upon his name, 'Rich-hart'. Richard II was not the heir of his mother. The heir was his half-brother, Thomas Holand, Earl of Kent, who *did* use the badge of the hind, and perhaps the real truth is that the Earl of Kent having the better claim to the hind, Richard was under the necessity of making an alteration which the obvious pun upon his name suggested. There is no doubt that the crest of Ireland originated therefrom. The stag in this case was undoubtedly 'lodged' in the earliest versions, and I have been much interested in tracing the steps by which the springing attitude has developed owing to the copying of badly drawn examples.

Amongst the many Royal and other badges in this country there are some of considerable interest. 677 represents the famous badge of the 'broom-cod' or 'planta genista', from which the name of the dynasty was derived. It appears to have been first used by King Henry II, though it figures in the decoration of the tomb of Geoffrey, Count of Anjou. 'Peascod' Street in Windsor of course derives its name therefrom. The well-known badges of the white and red roses of York and Lancaster have been already referred to, and 678, the well-known device of the 'rose-en-soliel' used by King Edward IV, was really a combination of two distinct badges, viz. 'the blazing sun of York' and the 'white rose of York'. The rose again appears in 679, here dimidiated with the pomegranate of Catharine of Aragon. This is taken from the famous Tournament Roll (now in the College of Arms), which relates to the Tournament, 13th and 14th of February 1510, to celebrate the birth of Prince Henry.

Richard I, John, and Henry III are all said to have used the device of the crescent and star (680). Henry VII is best known by his two badges of the crowned portcullis and the 'sun-burst' (681). The suggested origin of the former, that it was a pun on the name Tudor (*i.e.* two-door) is confirmed by the motto 'Altera securitas' which was used with it, but at the same time is rather vitiated by the fact that it was also used by the Beauforts, who had no Tudor descent. Save a very tentative remark hazarded by Woodward, no explanation has as yet been suggested for the sun-burst. My own strong conviction, based on the fact that this particular badge was principally used by Henry VII, who was always known as Henry of Windsor, is that it is nothing more than an attempt to represent pictorially the name 'Windsor' by depicting 'winds' of 'or'. The badge is also attributed to Edward III, and he, like Henry VII, made his principal residence at Windsor. Edward IV also used the white lion of March (whence is derived the shield of Ludlow: 'Azure, a lion couchant guardant, between three roses argent,' Ludlow being one of the fortified towns in the Welsh Marches), and the black bull which, though often termed 'of Clarence', is generally associated with the Duchy of Cornwall. Richard III, as Duke of Gloucester, used a white boar.

The Earl of Northumberland used a silver crescent; the Earl of Douglas, a red hart; the Earl of Pembroke, a golden pack-horse with collar and traces; Lord Hastings bore as badge a black bull's head erased, gorged with a coronet; Lord Stanley, a golden griffin's leg, erased; Lord Howard, a white lion charged on the shoulder with a blue crescent; Sir Richard Dunstable adopted a white cock as a badge; Sir John Savage, a silver unicorn's head erased; Sir Simon Montford, a golden lily; Sir William Gresham, a green grasshopper.

Two curious badges are to be seen in 682 and 683. The former is an ape's clog argent, chained or, and was used by William de la Pole, Duke of Suffolk (*d.* 1450). 683, 'a salet silver' (MS. Coll. of Arms, 2nd M. 16), is the badge of Thomas Howard, Duke of Norfolk (*d.* 1524). Various families used knots of different design, of which the best known is the Stafford knot (684). The wholesale and improper appropriation of this badge with a territorial application has unfortunately caused it to be very generally referred to as a 'Staffordshire' knot, and that it was the personal badge of the Lords Stafford is too often overlooked. Other badge knots are the Wake or Ormonde knot (685), the Bourchier knot (686), and the Heneage knot (687).

683 Badge of Thomas Howard, Duke of Norfolk.

The personal badges of the members of the Royal Family continued in use until the reign of Queen Anne, but from that time forward the Royal badges obtained a territorial character; the rose of England, the thistle of Scotland, and the shamrock of Ireland. To these popular consent has added the lotus-flower for India, the maple for Canada, and in a lesser degree the wattle or mimosa for Australia; but at present these lack any official confirmation as badges, although they appear in the respective Armorial Bearings. The two first named, nevertheless, figured on Coronation Invitation Cards.

684 *Stafford Knot.*

685 *Wake or Ormonde Knot.*

686 *Bourchier Knot.*

687 *Heneage Knot.*

30 · Heraldic flags, banners, and standards

When it comes to the display of flags, the British-born individual usually makes a hash of the whole business, and flies either the Sovereign's personal coat of arms, which really should only be made use of over a residence of the Sovereign when the Sovereign is actually there, or flown at sea when the Sovereign is on board; or else he uses the national flag, colloquially termed the 'Union Jack', which, strictly speaking, and as a matter of law, ought never to be made use of on land except over the residence of the Sovereign in his absence, or on a fortress or other Government building. But an official answer has been given in Parliament, declaring what is presumably the pleasure of the Sovereign, to the effect that the Union Jack is the National Flag, and may be flown as such on land by any British subject. If this is the intention of the Crown, it is a pity that this permission has not been embodied in a Royal warrant.[217]

The banner of St George, which is a white flag with a plain red cross of St George throughout, is now appropriated to the Order of the Garter, of which St George is the patron saint, though I am by no means inclined to assert that it would be incorrect to make use of it upon a church which happened to be specifically placed under the patronage of St George.

The white ensign, which is a white flag bearing the cross of St George and in the upper quarter next to the staff a reproduction of the Union device, belongs to the Royal Navy, and certain privileged individuals to whom the right has been given by a specific warrant. The blue ensign, which is a plain blue flag with the Union device on a canton in the upper corner next the staff, belongs to the Royal Naval Reserve; and the red ensign, which is the same as the former, except that a red flag is substituted for the blue one, belongs to the ships of the merchant service. These three flags have been specifically called into being by specific warrants for certain purposes which are stated in these warrants, and these purposes being wholly connected with the sea, neither the blue, the red, nor the white ensign ought to be hoisted on land by anybody. Of course there is no penalty for doing so on land, though very drastic penalties can be enforced for misuse of these ensigns on the water, a step which is taken frequently enough. For a

217 This general permission to fly the Union Flag is based on an oral reply given by Sir John Gilmor, the then Home Secretary, to a question asked in the House of Commons on 27 June 1933. He said: "The Union Flag is the national flag and may properly be flown by any British subject on land." It is indeed a pity that the matter has not been made the subject of a Royal Warrent, as the Union Flag is currently not only widely used but frequently also abused.

private person to use any one of these three flags on land for a private purpose, the only analogy which I can suggest to bring home to people the absurdity of such action would be to instance a private person for his own private pleasure adopting the exact uniform of some regiment whenever he might feel inclined to go bathing in the sea. If he were to do so, he would find under the Act of 1967 that he had incurred the penalty, which would be promptly enforced, for bringing Her Majesty's uniform into disrepute. It is much to be wished that the penalties exacted for the wrongful display of these flags at sea should be extended to their abuse on shore.

The development of the Union Jack and the warrants relating to it are dealt with herein by the Rev. J. R. Crawford, M.A., in a subsequent chapter, and I do not propose to further deal with the point, except to draw attention to a proposal, which has been often mooted, that some change or addition to the Union Jack should be made to typify the inclusion of the Commonwealth.

But to begin with, what is the Union Jack? Probably most would answer, 'The flag of the Commonwealth.' It is nothing of the kind. It is in a way stretching the definition to describe it as the Queen's flag. Certainly the design of interlaced crosses is a badge of the Queen's, but that badge is of a later origin than the flag.

The flag itself is the fighting emblem of the Sovereign, which the Sovereign has declared shall be used by his soldiers or sailors for fighting purposes under certain specified circumstances. That it is used, even officially, in all sorts of circumstances with which the Queen's warrants are not concerned is beside the matter, for it is to the Royal Warrants that one must refer for the theory of the thing.

Now let us go further back, and trace the 'argent, a cross gules', the part which is England's contribution to the Union Jack, which itself is a combination of the 'crosses' of St George, St Andrew, and St Patrick. The theory of one is the theory of the three, separately or conjoined.

'Argent, a cross gules' was never the coat of arms of England (except under the Commonwealth, when its use for armorial purposes may certainly be disregarded), and the reason it came to be regarded as the flag of England is simply and solely because fighting was always done under the supposed patronage of some saint, and England fought, *not* under the arms of England, but under the flag of St George, the patron saint of England and of the Order of the Garter. The battle-cry 'St George for Merrie England!' is too well known to need more than the passing mention. Scotland fought under St Andrew; Ireland, by a similar analogy, had for its patron saint St Patrick (if indeed there was a Cross of St Patrick before one was needed for the Union flag, which is a very doubtful point), and the Union Jack was not the combination of three territorial flags, but the combination of the recognised emblems of the three recognised saints, and though England claimed the sovereignty of France, and for that reason quartered the arms of France, no Englishman bothered about the patronage of St Denis, and the emblem of St Denis was never flown in this country. The fact that no change was ever made in the flag to typify Hanover, whilst Hanover duly had its place upon the arms, proves that the flag was recognised to be, and allowed to remain, the emblem of the three patron saints under whose patronage the British fought, and not the badge of any sovereignty or territorial area. If the colonies had already any saint of their own under whose patronage they had fought in bygone days, or in whose name they wished to fight in the future, there might be reason *for including the emblem of that saint* upon the fighting flag of the Empire; but they have no recognised saintly patrons, and they may just as well fight for our saints as choose others for themselves at so late a day; but having a flag which is a *combination* of the emblems of three saints, and which contains nothing that is not a part of those emblems, to make any addition heraldic or otherwise to it now would, in my opinion, be best expressed by the following illustration. Imagine three soldiers in full and complete uniform, one English, one Scottish, and one Irish, it being desired to evolve a uniform that should be taken from all three for use by a Union regiment. A tunic from one, trousers from another, and a helmet from a third, might be blended into a very effective and harmonious composite uniform. Following the analogy of putting a bordure, which is not the emblem of a saint, round the recognised emblems of the three recognised saints, and considering it to be in keeping because the bordure was heraldic and the emblems heraldic, one might argue, that because a uniform was clothing as was also a ballet-dancer's skirt, therefore a ballet-dancer's skirt outside the whole would be in keeping with the rest of the uniform. For myself I should dislike any addition to the Union device, as much as we should deride the donning of tulle skirts outside their tunics and trousers by the brigade of Guards.

The flag which should float from a church tower should have no more on it than the recognised ecclesiastical emblems of the saint to whom it is dedicated: the keys of St Peter, the wheel of St Catherine, the sword of St Paul, the cross and martlets of St Edmund, the lily of St Mary, the emblem of the Holy Trinity, or whatever the emblem may be of the saint in question. (The alternative for a church is the banner of St George, the patron saint of the realm).[218] The flags upon public buildings should bear the arms of the corporate bodies to whom those buildings belong. The flag to be flown by a private person, as the law now stands, should bear that person's private arms, if he has any, and if he has not he should be content to forego the pleasures arising from the use of bunting. A private flag should be double its height in length. The entire surface should be occupied by the coat of arms.

These flags of arms are *banners*, and it is quite a misnomer to term the banner of the Royal Arms the Royal Standard. The flags of arms hung over the stalls of the Knights of the Garter, St Patrick, and the former Knights of the Bath are properly, and are always termed *banners*. The term *standard* properly refers to the long tapering flag used in battle, and under which an overlord mustered his retainers in battle.[219] This did *not* display his armorial bearings. Next to the staff

218. In an Earl Marshal's Warrant dated 9 February 1938 it was laid down that 'the Banner or Flag proper to be flown in the Provinces of Canterbury and York to be the Cross of St George and in the first quarter an escutcheon of the Arms of the See in which such Church is ecclesiastically situate'. The resulting flag has been adversely criticised, and with some justification, because the representation of the arms of the see must necessarily be exiguous, and consequently difficult to identify from any distance. This visual problem, together with the cost of having such a flag made, is probably the main reason why most churches continue to fly the undifferenced Cross of St George.
219. The proper shape for an heraldic banner is square or even slightly deeper than it is wide, as are the banners illustrated in the Caerlaverock Poem (1302) and other early manuscripts. However, although such shapes generally make for good heraldic dimensions, being akin to the shape of the shield, they are not practical for flying from a high mast. Reasonable proportions for a fair weather flag are 5 to 3 and for a storm flag 4 to 3.

usually came the cross of St George, which was depicted, of course, on a white field. This occupied rather less than one-third of the standard. The remainder of the standard was of the colour or colours of the livery, and thereupon was represented all sorts of devices, usually the badges and sometimes the crest. The motto was usually on transverse bands, which frequently divided the standard into compartments for the different badges. These mottoes from their nature are *not* war-cries, but undoubtedly relate and belong to the badges with which they appear in conjunction. The whole banner was usually fringed with the livery colours, giving the effect of a bordure compony. The use of standards does not seem, except for the ceremonial purposes of funerals, to have survived the Tudor period, this doubtless being the result of the creation of the standing army in the reign of Henry VIII. The few exotic standards, *e.g.*, remaining from the Jacobite rebellion, seldom conform to the old patterns, but although the shape is altered, the artistic character largely remains in the regimental colours of the present day with their assorted regimental badges and scrolls with the names of battle honours.

With the recent revival of the granting of badges the standard has again been brought into use as the vehicle to carry the badge (Plate XI). The arms are now placed next the staff, and upon the rest of the field the badge is repeated or alternated with the crest. Badges and standards are now granted to any person already possessing a right to arms and willing to pay the necessary fees.

The armorial use of the banner in connection with the display of heraldic achievements is very limited in this country. In the case of the Marquess of Dufferin and Ava the banner or flag is an integral and unchangeable part of the heraldic supporters, and in Ross-of-Bladensburg, *e.g.*, it is similarly an integral part of the crest. In the warrant of augmentation granted to H.M. Queen Victoria Eugenie of Spain on her marriage, banners of the Royal Arms of England were placed in the paws of her supporters. Other cases where arms have been depicted on banners are generally no more than matters of artistic design; but in the arms of Scotland as matriculated in Lyon Register for King Charles II the supporters are accompanied by banners, the dexter being of the arms of Scotland, and the sinister the banner of St Andrew. These banners possess rather a different character, and approach very closely to the German use. The same practice has been followed in the seals of the Duchy of Lancaster, inasmuch as on the obverse of the seal of George IV and the seal of Queen Victoria the Royal supporters hold banners of the arms of England and of the Duchy (*i.e.* England, a label for difference). James I on his Great Seal had the banners of Cadwallader (azure, a cross patté fitché or) and King Edgar (azure, a cross patonce between four martlets or), and on the Great Seal of Charles I the dexter supporter holds a banner of St George, and the sinister a banner of St Andrew.

Of the heraldic use of the banner in Germany Ströhl writes:

'The banner appears in a coat of arms, either in the hands or paws of the supporters (688), also set up behind the shield, or the pavilion, as, for instance, in the larger achievement of his Majesty the German Emperor, in the large achievement of the kingdom of Prussia, of the dukedom of Saxe-Altenburg, and further in the Arms of State of Italy, Russia, Roumania, &c.

'Banners on the shield as charges, or on the helmet as a crest, are here, of

688 *'Middle' arms of the Duchy of Saxe-Altenburg.*
(*From Ströhl's* Deutsche Wappenrolle.)

course, not in question, but only those banners which serve as *Prachtstücke* (appendages of magnificence).

'The banners of the twelfth and thirteenth centuries are long and narrow, and frequently run in stripes, like battlements. However, in the second half of the thirteenth century flags were also to be met with, with the longer side attached to the stick. Later on the banners became more square, and show on the top a long strip, generally of another colour, the *Schwenkel* (*i.e.* something that flourishes), waves to and fro. To bear a red *Schwenkel* was a special privilege, similar to the right of sealing with red wax.

'The ecclesiastical banner has three points, and is provided with rings on the top in order that it may be fastened to the stick by them, in an oblique position.

'The banner always represents the field of the shield, and assumes accordingly its tincture. The charges of the shield should be placed upon the banner without the outline of a shield, and the edge against the flag-staff is considered the dexter; it follows from this that the figure must be turned towards it.

'For instance, if the shield bear the following arms, argent an eagle gules, the same figure, suited to the size of the flag, appears on the banner, with its head turned towards the staff. If it be wished to represent only the *colours* of the arms upon the flag, that of the charge is placed above, and that of the field below. Thus, for example, the Prussian flag is black and white, corresponding to the black eagle on the silver field; the flag of Hohenzollern is white and black, corresponding to their coat of arms, quartered silver and black, because in the latter case, so soon as a heraldic representation is available, from the position of the coloured fields, the correct order of the tinctures is determined.'[220]

220. Fox-Davies does not touch on historic flags, such as the guidon, presumably because they were essentially medieval battle flags which only survived the Middle Ages as part of the panoply of the

heraldic funeral, which, in its turn, did not really survive the seventeenth century. The principal flags used were the guidon mentioned above, the pennon, the banner, the standard, the cornet and the collonel. The guidon was almost certainly a rallying flag, at one time bearing the national emblem as well as the badge of the commander and later the commander's arms. It was a long flag like a small standard, usually with rounded end. The pennon was like a small guidon, but was a personal flag used by commanders below the rank of knight banneret. The banneret cut off the fly of his pennant, and was left with the banner from which he was named. Small pennons are sometimes called pencels; these were armorial lance pennons of various shapes. The cornet and collonel were simply livery flags.

Since the Second World War a new flag has been born: the royal personal flag. The first such flag was a square blue flag, fringed with gold and charged with the Queen's initial E ensigned with the royal crown, all within a chaplet of gold roses. This was adopted by the Queen in 1960 just before she visited India and Pakistan, on which visit the flag was used in place of the royal banner. Thereafter, whenever the Queen has visited a Commonwealth country she has adopted for use in that country, a personal flag consisting of a banner of the arms of the country, with the central motif from her original personal flag in the centre.

The most recent royal personal flag is that of the Prince of Wales for use in Wales, which was approved by the Queen in 1968. It consists of a banner of the arms of the Principality of Wales (the ancient arms of Llywelln, Prince of North Wales) charged with an inescutcheon vert, thereon a representation of the coronet of the heir apparent proper (GG).

GG *Personal flag of the Prince of Wales, for use in Wales.*

31 · Marks of cadency

The manner in which cadency is indicated in heraldic emblazonment forms one of the most important parts of British armory, but our own intricate and minutely detailed systems are a purely British development of armory. I do not intend by the foregoing remark to assert that the occasional use, or even, as in some cases, the constant use of altered arms for purposes of indicating cadency is unknown on the Continent, because different branches of one family are constantly found using, for the purposes of distinction, variations of the arms appertaining to the head of their house; in France especially the bordure has been extensively used, but the fact nevertheless remains that in no other countries is there found an organised system or set of rules for the purpose. Nor is this idea of the indication of cadency wholly a modern development, though some, in fact most, of the rules presently in force are no doubt a result of modern requirements, and do not date back to the earliest periods of heraldry in this country.

The obligation of cadet lines to difference their arms was recognised practically universally in the fourteenth century; and when, later, the systematic use of differencing seemed in danger of being ignored, it was made the subject of specific legislation. In the treatise of ZYPŒUS, *de Notitia juris Belgici*, lib. xii, quoted also in MENÊSTRIER, *Recherches du Blazon*, p. 218, we find the following:

'Ut secundo et ulterius geniti, quinimo primogeniti vivo patre, integra insignia non gerant, sed aliqua nota distincta, ut perpetuo linæ dignosci possint, et ex qua quique descendant, donec anteriores defecerint. Exceptis Luxenburgis et Gueldris, quibus non sunt ii mores.' (The exception is curious.)

The choice of these *brisures*, as marks of difference are often termed, was, however, left to the persons concerned; and there is, consequently, a great variety of differences or differentiation marks which seem to have been used for the purpose. The term 'brisure' is really French, whilst the German term for these marks is 'Beinzeichen'.

British heraldry, on the contrary, is remarkable for its use of two distinct sets of rules— the English and the Scottish— the Irish system being identical with the former.

To understand the question of cadency it is necessary to revert to the status of a coat of arms in early periods. In the first chapter we dealt with the origin of armory; and in a subsequent chapter with the status of a coat of arms in Great Britain, and it will therefrom have been apparent that arms, and a right to them, developed in this country as an adjunct of, or contemporaneously with, the extension of the feudal system. Every landowner was at one time required to have his seal— presumably, of arms— and as a result arms were naturally then considered to possess something of a territorial character. I do not by this mean to say that the arms belonged to the land and were transferable with the sale and purchase thereof. There never was in this country a period at which such an idea held; nor were arms originally entirely personal or individual. They belonged rather to a position half-way between the two. They were the arms of a given family, originating because that family held land and accepted the consequent responsibilities thereto belonging, but the arms appertained for the time being to the member of that family who owned the land, and that this is the true idea of the former status of a coat of arms is perhaps best evidenced by the Grey and Hastings controversy, which engaged the attention of the Court of Chivalry for several years prior to 1410. The decision and judgment in the case gave the undifferenced arms of Hastings to the heir-general (Grey de Ruthyn), the heir-male (Sir Edward Hastings) being found only capable of bearing the arms of Hastings subject to some mark of difference.

This case, and the case of Scrope and Grosvenor, in which the king's award was that the bordure was not sufficient difference for a stranger in blood, being only the mark of a cadet, show clearly that the status of a coat of arms in early times was that in its undifferenced state it belonged to one person only for the time being, and that person the head of the family, though it should be noted that the term 'Head of the Family' seems to have been interpreted into the one who held the lands of the family—whether he were heir-male or heir-general being apparently immaterial.

This much being recognised, it follows that some means were needed to be devised to differentiate the armorial bearings of the younger members of the family. Of course the earliest definite instances of any attempt at a systematic 'differencing' for cadency which can be referred to are undoubtedly those cases presented by the arms of the younger members of the Royal Family in England. These cases, however, it is impossible to take as precedents. Royal Arms have always, from the very earliest times, been a law unto themselves, subject only to the will of the Sovereign, and it is neither safe nor correct to deduce precedents to be applied to the arms of subjects from proved instances concerning the Royal Arms.

Probably, apart from these, the earliest mark of cadency which is to be met with in heraldry is the label (689) used to indicate the eldest son, and this mark of difference dates back far beyond any other regularised methods applicable to 'younger' sons. The German name for the label is 'Turnierkragen', i.e. Tournament Collar, which may indicate the origin of this curious figure. Probably the use of the label can be taken back to the middle or early part of the thirteenth century, but the opportunity and necessity of marking the arms of the heir-apparent temporarily, he having the expectation of eventually succeeding to the undifferenced arms, is a very different matter to the other opportunities for the use of marks of cadency. The lord and his heir were the two most important members of the family, and all others sunk their identity in their position in the household of their chief unless they were established by marriage, or otherwise, in lordships of their own, in which cases they are usually found to have preferred the arms of the family from whom they inherited the lordships they enjoyed; and their identities being to such a large extent overlooked, the necessity for any system of marking the arms of a younger son was not so early apparent as the necessity for marking the arms of the heir.

The label does not appear to have been originally confined exclusively to the

689 *The label.*

690 *Arms of John de Lacy, Earl of Lincoln (d. 1240): Quarterly, or and gules, a bend sable, and a label argent. (MS. Cott. Nero, D. 1.)*

691 *Arms of John de la Pole, Earl of Lincoln (son of John, Duke of Suffolk), d. 1487: Quarterly, 1 and 4, azure, a fess between three leopards' faces or; 2 and 3, per fess gules and argent, a lion rampant queue fourché or, armed and langued azure, over all a label argent. (From his seal.)*

692 *Arms of William Le Scrope, Earl of Wiltes (d. 1399): Quarterly, 1 and 4, the arms of the Isle of Man, a label argent; 2 and 3, azure, a bend or, a label gules. (From Willement's Roll, sixteenth century.)*

heir. It was at first the only method of differencing known, and it is not therefore to be wondered at that we find that it was frequently used by other cadets, who used it with no other meaning than to indicate that they were not the Head of the House. It has, consequently, in some few cases (for example, in the arms of Courtenay (246), Babington, and Barrington) become stereotyped as a charge, and is continuously and unchangeably used as such, whereas doubtless it may have been no more originally than a mere mark of cadency. The label was originally drawn with its upper edge identical with the top of the shield (520), but later its position on the shield was lowered. The number of points on the label was at first without meaning, a five-pointed label occurring in 690 and a seven-pointed one in 235.

In the Roll of Caerlaverock the label is repeatedly referred to. Of Sir MAURICE DE BERKELEY it is expressly declared that

'. . . un label de asur avoit,
Porce qe ces peres vivoit.'

Sir PATRICK DUNBAR, son of the Earl of LOTHIAN (*i.e.* of MARCH), then bore arms similar to his father, with the addition of a label 'azure'. On the other hand, Sir JOHN DE SEGRAVE is said to bear his deceased father's arms undifferenced, while his younger brother NICHOLAS carries them with a label 'gules'; and in the case of EDMUND DE HASTINGS the label is also assigned to a younger brother. Further proof of its being thus borne by cadets is furnished by the evidence in the Grey and Hastings controversy in the reign of HENRY IV, from which it appeared that the younger line of the HASTINGS family had for generations differenced the paternal coat by a label of three points; and, as various knights and esquires had deposed to this label being the cognisance of the nearest heir, it was argued that the defendant's ancestors would not have borne their arms in this way had they not been the reputed next heirs of the family of the Earl of PEMBROKE. The label will be seen in 690, 691, and 692, though its occurrence in the last case in each of the quarters is most unusual. The argent label on the arms for the Sovereignty of Man is a curious confirmation of the reservation of an argent label for Royalty.

WILLIAM RUTHVEN, Provost of PERTH, eldest son of the Master of RUTHVEN, bore a label of four points in 1503. Two other instances may be noticed of a label borne by a powerful younger brother. One is WALTER STEWART, Earl of MENTEITH, the fourth High Steward, in 1292; and we find the label again on the seal of his son ALEXANDER STEWART, Earl of MENTEITH.

At Caerlaverock, HENRY of Lancaster, brother and successor of THOMAS, Earl of LANCASTER—

'Portait les armes son frère
Au beau bastoun sans label,'

i.e. he bore the Royal Arms, differenced by a bendlet 'azure'.

JANE FENTOUN, daughter and heir-apparent of WALTER FENTOUN of Baikie, bore a label in 1448, and dropped it after her father's death. This is apparently an instance quite unique. I know of no other case where the label has been used by a woman as a mark of difference.

In FRANCE the label was the chief recognised mode of difference, though the bend and the bordure are frequently to be met with.

368

In GERMANY, Spener tells us that the use of the label, though occasional, was not infrequent: 'Sicuti in Gallia vix alius discerniculorum modus frequentior est, ita rariora exempla reperimus in Germania,' and he gives a few examples, though he is unable to assign the reason for its assumption as a hereditary bearing. The most usual method of differencing in Germany was by the alteration of the tinctures or by the alteration of the charges. As an example of the former method, the arms of the Bavarian family of Parteneck may be instanced (693 to 697), all representing the arms of different branches of the same family.

Next to the use of the label in British heraldry came the use of the bordure, and the latter as a mark of cadency can at any rate be traced back *as a well-established matter of rule* and precedent as far as the Scrope and Grosvenor controversy in the closing years of the fourteenth century.

At the period when the bordure as a difference is to be most frequently met with in English heraldry, it never had any more definite status or meaning than a sign that the bearer was *not* the head of the house, though one cannot but think that in many cases in which it occurs its significance is a doubt as to legitimate descent, or a doubt of the probability of an asserted descent. In modern *English* practice the bordure as a difference for cadets only continues to be used by those whose ancestors bore it in ancient times. Its other use as a modern mark of illegitimacy is dealt with in the chapter upon marks of illegitimacy, but the curious and unique *Scottish* system of cadency bordures will be presently referred to.

In Germany of old the use of the bordure as a difference does not appear to have been very frequent, though it was used to distinguish the arms of the Crown Prince. In Italian heraldry, although differences are known, there is no system whatever. In Spain and Portugal marks of cadency, in our sense of the word, are almost unknown, but nevertheless the bordure, especially as indicating descent from a maternal ancestor, is very largely employed. The most familiar instance is afforded by the Royal Arms of Portugal, in which the arms of PORTUGAL are surrounded by a 'bordure' of CASTILE.

Differencing, however, had become a necessity at an earlier period than the period at which we find an approach to the systematic usage of the label, bordure, and bend, but it should be noticed that those who wished, and needed, to difference were those younger members of the family who by settlement, or marriage, had themselves become lords of other estates, and heads of distinct houses. For a man must be taken as a 'Head of a House' for all intents and purposes as soon as by his possession of lands 'held in chief' he became *himself* liable to the Crown to provide stated military service, and as a consequence found the necessity for a banner of arms, under which his men could be mustered. Now having these positions as overlords, the inducement was rather to set up arms for themselves than to pose merely as cadets of other families, and there can be no doubt whatever that at the earliest period, differencing, for the above reason, took the form of and was meant as a *change in the arms*. It was something quite beyond and apart from the mere condition of a right to recognised arms, with an indication thereupon that the bearer was not the person chiefly entitled to the display of that particular coat. We therefore find cadets bearing the arms of their house with the tincture changed, with subsidiary charges introduced, or with some similar radical alteration made. Such coats should properly be considered essentially *different* coats,

693 *Parteneck.*

694 *Cammer.*

695 *Cammerberg.*

696 *Hilgertshauser.*

697 *Massenhauser.*

369

merely *indicating* in their design a given relationship rather than as the *same* coat regularly differenced by rule to indicate cadency. For instance, the three original branches of the Conyers family bear: 'Azure, a maunch ermine; azure, a maunch or; azure, a maunch ermine debruised by a bendlet gules.' The coat differenced by the bend, of course, stands self-confessed as a differenced coat, but it is by no means certain, nor is it known whether 'azure, a maunch ermine', or 'azure, a maunch or' indicates the original Conyers arms, for the very simple reason that it is now impossible to definitely prove which branch supplies the true head of the family. It is known that a wicked uncle intervened, and usurped the estates to the detriment of the nephew and heir, but whether the uncle usurped the arms with the estates, or whether the heir changed his arms when settled on the other lands to which he migrated, there is now no means of ascertaining.

Similarly we find the D'Arcy arms ['Argent, three cinquefoils gules,' which is probably the oldest form, 'Argent, crusuly and three cinquefoils gules,' and 'Azure, crusuly and three cinquefoils argent,'] and countless instances can be referred to where, for the purpose of indicating cadency, the arms of a family were changed in this manner. This reason, of which there can be no doubt, supplies the origin and the excuse for the custom of assigning *similar* arms when the descent is but doubtful. Similarity originally, though it *may* indicate consanguinity, was never intended to be proof thereof.

The principal ancient methods of alteration in arms, which nowadays are apparently accepted as former modes of differencing merely to indicate cadency, may perhaps be classified into: (*a*) Change of tincture; (*b*) the addition of small charges to the field, or to an ordinary; (*c*) the addition of a label or (*d*) of a canton or quarter; (*e*) the addition of an inescutcheon; (*f*) the addition (or change) of an ordinary; (*g*) the changing of the lines of partition enclosing an ordinary, and perhaps also (*h*) diminishing the number of charges; (*i*) a change of some or all of the minor charges. At a later date came (*j*) the systematic use of the label, the bordure, and the bend; and subsequently (*k*) the use of the modern systems of 'marks of cadency'. Perhaps, also, one should include (*l*) the addition of quarterings, the use of (*m*) augmentations and official arms, and (*n*) the escutcheon *en surtout*, indicating a territorial and titular lordship, but the three last-mentioned, though useful for distinction and frequently obviating the necessity of other marks of cadency, did not originate with the theory or necessities of differencing, and are not properly marks of cadency. At the same time, the warning should be given that it is not safe always to presume cadency when a change of tincture or other slight deviation from an earlier form of the arms is met with. Many families when they exhibited their arms at the Visitations could not substantiate them, and the heralds, in confirming arms, frequently deliberately changed the tinctures of many coats they met with, to introduce distinction from other authorised arms.

Practically contemporarily with the use of the bordure came the use of the bend, then employed for the same purpose. In the *Armorial de Gelre*, one of the earliest armorials now in existence which can be referred to, the well-known coat of Abernethy is there differenced by the bendlet engrailed, and the arms of the King of Navarre bear his quartering of France differenced by a bendlet compony. Amongst other instances in which the bend or bendlet appears originally as a mark of cadency, but now as a charge, may be mentioned the arms of Fitzherbert,

Fulton, Stewart (Earl of Galloway), and others. It is a safe presumption with regard to ancient coats of arms that any coat in which the field is semé is in nine cases out of ten a differenced coat for a junior cadet, as is also any coat in which a charge or ordinary is debruised by another. Of course in more modern times no such presumption is permissible. An instance of a semé field for cadency will be found in the case of the D'Arcy arms already mentioned. Little would be gained by a long list of instances of such differences, because the most careful and systematic investigations clearly show that in early times no definite rules whatever existed as to the assumption of differences, which largely depended upon the pleasure of the bearer, and no system can be deduced which can be used to decide that the appearance of any given difference or kind of difference meant a given set of circumstances. Nor can any system be deduced which has any value for the purposes of precedent.

Certain instances are appended which will indicate the style of differencing which was in vogue, but it should be distinctly remembered that the object was not to allocate the bearer of any particular coat of arms to any specific place in the family pedigree, but merely to show that he was not the head of the house, entitled to bear the undifferenced arms, if indeed it would not be more accurate to describe these instances as simply examples of different coats of arms used by members of the same family. For it should be remembered that anciently, before the days of 'black and white' illustration, prominent change of tincture was admittedly a sufficient distinction between strangers in blood. Beyond the use of the label and the bordure there does not seem to have been any recognised system of differencing until at the earliest the fifteenth century—probably any regulated system does not date much beyond the commencement of the series of Visitations.

Of the four sons of GILLES DE MAILLY, who bore, 'Or, three mallets vert', the second, third, and fourth sons respectively made the charges 'gules', 'azure', and 'sable'. The 'argent' field of the DOUGLAS coat was in some branches converted into 'ermine' as early as 1373; and the descendants of the DOUGLASES of Dalkeith made the chief 'gules' instead of 'azure'. A similar mode of differencing occurs in the Lyon Register in many other families. The MURRAYS of Culbin in the North bore a 'sable' field for their arms in lieu of the more usual 'azure', and there seems reason to believe that the Southern Frasers originally bore their field 'sable', the change to 'azure' being an alteration made by those branches who migrated northwards. An interesting series of arms is met with in the case of the differences employed by the Earls of Warwick. Waleran, Earl of Warwick (d. 1204), appears to have added to the arms of Warenne (his mother's family) 'a chevron ermine'. His son Henry, Earl of Warwick (d. 1229), changed the chevron to a bend, but Thomas, Earl of Warwick (d. 1242), reverted to the chevron, a form which was perpetuated after the earldom had passed to the house of Beauchamp. An instance of the addition of mullets to the bend in the arms of Bohun is met with in the cadet line created Earls of Northampton.

The shield of WILLIAM DE ROUMARE, Earl of LINCOLN, who died in 1198, is adduced by Mr Planché as an early example of differencing by crosses crosslet; the principal charges being seven mascles conjoined, three, three, and one. We find in the Rolls of Arms of the thirteenth and early part of the fourteenth century many instances of coats crusily, billetty, bezanty, and 'pleyn d'escallops', fleurette, and 'a les trefoiles d'or'. With these last Sir EDMOND DACRE of Westmoreland powdered the shield borne by the head of his family: 'Gules, three escallops or' (Roll of Edward II). The coat borne by the ACTONS of Aldenham, 'Gules, crusily or, two lions passant argent,' is sometimes quoted as a gerated coat of LESTRANGE; for EDWARD DE ACTON married the coheiress of LESTRANGE (living 1387), who bore simply: 'Gules, two lions passant argent.' That the arms of Acton are derived from Lestrange cannot be questioned, but the probability is that they were *a new invention* as a distinct coat, the charges suggested by Lestrange. The original coat of the House of Berkeley in England (Barclay in Scotland) appears to have been: 'Gules, a chevron or' (or 'argent'). The seals of ROBERT DE BERKELEY, who died 4 Henry III, and MAURICE DE BERKELEY, who died 1281, all show the shield charged with a chevron only. MORIS DE BARKELE, in the Roll *temp*. Henry III, bears: 'Goules, a chevron argent.'

But THOMAS, son of MAURICE, who died 15 EDWARD II, has the present coat: 'Gules, a chevron between ten crosses patée argent'; while in the roll of Edward II, 'De goules od les rosettes de argent et un chevron de argent' is attributed to Sir THOMAS DE BERKEELEY. In Leicestershire the BERKEELEYS gerated with cinquefoils, an ancient and favourite bearing in that county, derived of course from the arms or badge of the Earl of Leicester. In Scotland the BARCLAYS differenced by change of tincture, and bore: 'Azure, a chevron argent between (or in chief) three crosses patée of the same.' An interesting series of differences is met with upon the arms or NEVILLE of Raby, which are: 'Gules, a saltire argent,' and which were differenced by a crescent 'sable'; a martlet 'gules'; a mullet 'sable' and a mullet azure; a 'fleur-de-lis'; a rose 'gules'; a pellet, or annulet, 'sable', this being the difference of Lord Latimer; and two interlaced annulets 'azure', all borne on the centre point of the saltire. The interlaced annulets were borne by Lord Montagu, as a *second* difference on the arms of his father, Richard Nevill, Earl of Salisbury, he and his brother the King-maker *both* using the curious compony label of azure and argent borne by their father, which indicated their descent from John of Gaunt. One of the best known English examples of differencing by a change of charges is that of the coat of the COBHAMS, 'Gules, a chevron or,' in which the ordinary was charged by various cadets with three pierced estoiles, three lions, three crossed crosslets, three 'fleurs-de-lis', three crescents, and three martlets, all of 'sable'.

The original GREY coat ['Barry of six argent and azure'] is differenced in the Roll of Edward I by a bend gules for JOHN DE GREY; at Caerlaverock this is engrailed.

The SEGRAVE coat ['Sable, a lion rampant argent'] is differenced by the addition of 'a bendlet or'; or 'a bendlet gules'; and the last is again differenced by engrailing it.

In the Calais Roll the arms of WILLIAM DE WARREN ['Chequy or and azure'] are differenced by the addition of a canton said to be that of FITZALAN (but really that of NERFORD).

Whilst no regular system of differencing has survived in France, and whilst outside the Royal Family arms in that country show comparatively few examples of difference marks, the system as regards the French Royal Arms was well observed and approximated closely to our own. The Dauphin of France bore the Royal Arms undifferenced but never alone, they being always quartered with the

PLATE IX

The Arms of Fox-Davies

The Arms of Drake

The Arms of Dodge

The Arms of Swindon

698 *Seal of Elizabeth, widow of Philip, Duke of Orleans.*

sovereign arms of his personal sovereignty of Dauphiné: 'Or, a dolphin embowed azure, finned gules.' This has been more fully referred to on page 190. It is much to be regretted that the arms of H.R.H. the Prince of Wales do not include the arms of his sovereignty of the Duchy of Cornwall, nor any allusion to his dignities of Prince of Wales or Earl of Chester.[221]

The arms of the Dukes of Orleans were the arms of France differenced by a label argent. This is to be observed, for example, upon the seal (698) of the Duchess Charlotte Elizabeth of Orleans, widow of Philip of Orleans, brother of King Louis XIV of France. She was a daughter of the Elector Charles Louis. The arms of the old Dukes of Anjou were the ancient coat of France (azure, semé-de-lis or) differenced by a label of five points gules, but the younger house of Ançou bore the modern arms of France differenced by a bordure gules. The Dukes d'Alençon also used the bordure gules, but charged this with eight plates, whilst the Dukes de Berri used a bordure *engrailed* gules.

The Counts d'Angoulême used the arms of the Dukes of Orleans, adding a crescent gules on each point of the label, whilst the Counts d'Artois used France (ancient) differenced by a label gules, each point charged with three castles (towers) or.

The rules which govern the marks of cadency at present in England are as follows, and it should be carefully borne in mind that the Scottish system bears no relation whatever to the English system. The eldest son during the lifetime of his father differences his arms by a label of three points couped at the ends. This is placed in the centre chief point of the escutcheon. There is no rule as to its colour, which is left to the pleasure of the bearer; but it is usually decided as follows: (1) That it shall not be metal on metal, or colour on colour; (2) that it shall not be argent or white; and, if possible, that it shall differ from any colour or metal in which any component part of the shield is depicted. Though anciently the label was drawn throughout the shield, this does not now seem to be a method officially adopted. [222] At any rate drawn throughout it apparently obtains no official

221. The arms of the Prince of Wales now contain those of the ancient Princes of North Wales on an inescutcheon, as arms for the Principality of Wales (see page 365). The approved design of the arms of the present Prince of Wales also includes a representation of the arms of the Duchy of Cornwall.

222. Fortunately, there has been a welcome return to the medieval practice, and the ugly, truncated, dovetailed label is now seldom used; the Royal family is setting the new, or more truly old, fashion. I must confess that, although I have long sought evidence that the label argent is reserved for royalty, I have so far found nothing of an official nature to support this widely publicised theory.

countenance for the arms of subjects, though many of the best heraldic artists always so depict it. The eldest son bears this label during his father's lifetime, succeeding to the undifferenced shield on the death of his father. His children—being the grandchildren of the then head of the house—difference upon the label, but such difference marks are, like their father's, only contemporary with the life of the grandfather, and, immediately upon the succession of their father, the children remove the label, and difference upon the original arms. The use of arms by a junior grandson is so restricted in ordinary life that to all intents and purposes this may be ignored, except in the case of the heir-apparent of the heir-apparent, *i.e.* of the grandson in the lifetimes of his father and grandfather. In his case one label of *five* points is used, and to place a label upon a label is not correct when both are marks of cadency, not charges. But the grandson on the death of his father, during the lifetime of the grandfather, and when the grandson succeeds as heir-apparent of the grandfather, succeeds also to the label of three points, which may therefore more properly be described as the difference mark of the heir-apparent than the difference mark of the eldest son. It is necessary, perhaps, having said this, to add the remark that heraldry knows no such thing as disinheritance, and heirship is an inalienable matter of blood descent, and not of worldly inheritance. No woman can ever be an heir-apparent. Though now the number of points on a label is a matter of rule, this is far from having been always the case, and prior to the Stuart period no deductions can be drawn with certainty from the number of the points in use. It seems a very great pity that no warrants were issued for the children of the then Duke of York during the lifetime of Queen Victoria, as labels for *great*-grandchildren would have been quite unique.

If the eldest son succeeds through the death of his mother to her arms and quarterings during his father's lifetime, he must be careful that the label which he bears as heir-apparent to his father's arms does not cross the quartering of his mother's arms.

If his father bears a quarterly shield, the label is so placed that it shall apparently debruise all his father's quarterings, *i.e.* in a shield quarterly of four the label would be placed in the centre chief point, the centre file of the label being upon the palar line, and the other files in the first and second quarters respectively, whilst the colour would usually depend, as has been above indicated, upon the tinctures of the pronominal arms. Due regard, however, must be had that a label of gules, for example, is not placed on a field of gules. A parti-coloured label is not nowadays permissible, though instances of its use can occasionally be met with in early examples. Supposing the field of the first quarter is argent, and that of the second azure, in all probability the best colour for the label would be gules, and indeed gules is the colour most frequently met with for use in this purpose.

If the father possess the quarterly coat of, say, four quarterings, which are debruised by a label by the heir-apparent, and the mother die, and the heir-apparent succeed to her arms, he would of course, after his father's death, arrange his mother's quarterings with these, placing his father's pronominal arms 1 and 4, the father's quartering in the second quarter, and the mother's arms in the third quarter. This arrangement, however, is not permissible during his father's lifetime, because otherwise his label in chief would be held to debruise *all* the four coats, and the only method in which such a combination could be properly displayed in the lifetime of the father but after the death of his mother is to place the father's arms in the grand quartering in the first and fourth quarters, each being debruised by the label, and the mother's in the grand quartering in the second and third quarters without any interference by the label.

The other marks of difference are: For the second son a crescent; for the third son a mullet; for the fourth son a martlet; for the fifth son an annulet; for the sixth son a fleur-de-lis; for the seventh son a rose; for the eighth son a cross moline; for the ninth son a double quatrefoil (699).

699 The English marks of cadency.

Of these the first six are given in BOSSEWELL's *Workes of Armorie* (1572), and the author adds: 'If there be any more than six brethren the devise or assignment of further difference only appertaineth to the kingis of armes especially when they visite their severall provinces; and not to the father of the children to give them what difference he list, as some without authoritie doe allege.'[223]

The position for a mark of difference is in the centre chief point, though it is not incorrect (and many such instances will be found) for it to be charged on a chevron or fess, in the centre point. This, however, is not a very desirable position for it in a simple coat of arms. The second son of the second son places a crescent upon a crescent, the third son a mullet on a crescent, the fourth son a martlet on a crescent, and so on; and there is an instance in the Visitation of London in which the arms of Cokayne appear with *three* crescents one upon another: this instance has been already referred to on page 258. Of course, when the English system is carried to these lengths it becomes absurd, because the crescents charged one upon each other become so small as to be practically indistinguishable. There are, however, very few cases in which such a display would be correct—as will be presently explained. This difficulty, which looms large in theory, amounts to very little in the practical use of armory, but it nevertheless is the one outstanding objection to the English system of difference marks. It is constantly held up to derision by those people who are unaware of the next rule upon the subject, which is, that as soon as a quartering comes into the possession of a cadet branch— which quartering is not enjoyed by the head of the house—all necessity for any marks of difference at all is considered to be ended, provided that that quartering is always displayed—and that cadet branch then begins afresh from that generation to redifference.

Now there are few English families in whose pedigree during three or four generations one marriage is not with an heiress in blood, so that this theoretical difficulty very quickly disappears.

No doubt there is always an inducement to retain the quarterings of an historical or illustrious house which may have been brought in in the past, but if the honours and lands brought in with that quartering are wholly enjoyed by the head of the house, it becomes, from a practical point of view, mere affectation to prefer that quartering to another (brought in subsequently) of a family, the entire

223. The buckle, escallop and links of a chain are given as marks for the tenth, eleventh and twelfth sons in a book of Lincolnshire church notes at the College of Arms for the family of Tournay.

representation of which belongs to the junior branch and not to the senior. If the old idea of confining a shield to four quarters be borne in mind, concurrently with the necessity—for purposes of distinction—of introducing new quarterings, the new quarterings take the place of the old, the use of which is left to the senior branch. Under such circumstances, and the regular practice of them, the English system is seldom wanting, and it at once wipes out the difficulty which is made much of—that under the English system there is no way of indicating the difference between the arms of uncle and nephew. If the use of impalements is also adhered to, the difficulty practically vanishes.

To difference a *single* coat the mark of difference is placed in the centre chief point; to difference a *quarterly* coat of four quarters the same position on the shield is most generally used, the mark being placed over the palar line, though occasionally the difference mark is placed, and not incorrectly, in the centre of the quarterings. A coat of six quarters, however, is always differenced on the fess line of partition, the mark being placed in the fess point, because if placed in the centre chief point it would only appear as a difference upon the second quartering, so that on all shields of six or more quarterings the difference mark must be placed on some line of partition at the nearest possible point to the true centre fess point of the escutcheon. It is then understood to difference the whole of the quarterings over which it is displayed, but directly a quartering is introduced which has been inherited subsequently to the cadency which produced the difference mark, that difference mark must be either discarded or transferred to the first quartering only.

The use of these difference marks is optional. Neither officially nor unofficially is any attempt made to enforce their use in England—they are left to the pleasure and discretion of the bearers, though it is a well-understood and well-accepted position that, unless differenced by quarterings or impalement, it is neither courteous nor proper for a cadet to display the arms of the head of his house: beyond this, the matter is usually left to good taste.

There is, however, one position in which the use of difference marks is compulsory. If under a Royal Licence, or other exemplification—for instance, the creation of a peerage—a difference mark is painted upon the arms, or even if an exemplification of the arms differenced is placed at the head of an official record of pedigree, those arms would not subsequently be exemplified, or their use officially admitted, without the difference mark that has been recorded with them.

The differencing of crests for cadency is very rare. Theoretically, these should be marked equally with the shield, and when arms are exemplified officially under the circumstances above referred to, crest, supporters, and shield are all equally differenced, but the difficulty of adding difference mark on difference mark when no marriage or heiress can ever bring in any alteration to the crest is very generally recognised and admitted, even officially, and it is rare indeed to come across a crest carrying more than a single difference mark.

The grant of an augmentation to any cadet obviates the slightest necessity for any further use of difference marks inherited before the grant.

There are no difference marks whatever for daughters, there being in English common law no seniority between the different daughters of one man. They succeed equally, whether heiresses or not, to the arms of their father for use during their lifetimes, and they must bear them on their own lozenges or impaled on the

376

shields of their husbands, with the difference marks which their father needed to use. It would be permissible, however, to discard these difference marks of their fathers if subsequently to his death his issue succeeded to the position of head of the family. For instance, suppose the daughters of the younger son of an earl are under consideration. They would bear upon lozenges the arms of their father, which would be those of the earl, charged with the mullet or crescent which their father had used as a younger son. If by the extinction of issue the brother of these daughters succeed to the earldom, they would no longer be required to bear their father's difference mark.

There are no marks of difference between illegitimate children. In the eye of the law an illegitimate person has no relatives, and stands alone. Supposing it be subsequently found that a marriage ceremony had been illegal, the whole issue of that marriage becomes of course illegitimate. As such, no one of them is entitled to bear arms. A Royal Licence, and exemplification following thereupon, is necessary for each single one. Of these exemplifications there is one case on record in which I think nine follow each other on successive pages of one of the Grant Books: all differ in some way—usually in the colour of the bordure; but the fact that there are illegitimate brothers of the same parentage does not prevent the descendants of any daughter quartering the differenced coat exemplified to her. As far as heraldic law is concerned, she is the heiress of herself, representing only herself, and consequently her heir quarters her arms.[224]

Marks of difference are never added to an exemplification following upon a Royal Licence *after illegitimacy*. Marks of difference are to indicate cadency, and there is no cadency vested in a person of illegitimate birth—their right to the arms proceeding only from the regrant of them in the exemplification. What is added in lieu is the *mark of distinction* to indicate the bastardy.

The method of differencing the English Royal Arms is quite unique, and has no relation to the method ordinarily in use in this country for the arms of subjects. The Royal Arms are not personal. They are the sovereign arms of dominion, indicating the sovereignty enjoyed by the person upon the throne. Consequently they are in no degree hereditary, and from the earliest times, certainly since the reign of Edward I, the right to bear the undifferenced arms has been confined exclusively to the sovereign upon the throne. In early times there were two methods employed, namely, the use of the bordure and of varieties of the label, the label of the heir-apparent to the English throne being originally of azure. The arms of Thomas of Woodstock, the youngest son of Edward I, were differenced by a bordure argent; his elder brother, Thomas de Brotherton, having had a label of three points argent; whilst the eldest son, Edward II, as Prince of Wales used a label of three points azure. From that period to the end of the Tudor period the use of labels and bordures seems to have continued concurrently, some members of the Royal Family using one, some the other, though there does not appear to have been any precise rules governing a choice between the two. When Edward

224. This opinion is legally unimpeachable, but there is an interesting precedent to the contrary. When King William IV assigned arms to his bastard children on 30 May 1831, those of the five girls were shown impaled by their husband's arms and not, as one would expect in the cases of heraldic heiresses, placed on escutcheons of pretence. This could be more easily written off as a whim of royal heraldry were it not for the fact that each girl was treated as an heiress herself, inasmuch as each had an individual mark of distinction.

700 *King John, before his accession to the throne. (From MS. Cott., Julius, C. vii.)*

701 *Edmund 'Crouch-back', Earl of Lancaster, second son of Henry III. (From his tomb.) His arms are elsewhere given: De goules ove trois leopardes passantz dor, et lambel dazure florete d'or.*

702 *Thomas, Earl of Lancaster, d. 1322 (son of preceding): England with a label azure, each point charged with three fleurs-de-lis. (From his seal, 1301.)*

703 Henry of Lancaster, 1295–1324 (brother of preceding, before he succeeded his brother as Earl of Lancaster): England with a bend azure. (From his seal, 1301.) After 1324 he bore England with a label as his brother.

704 Henry, Duke of Lancaster, son of preceding. (From his seal, 1358.)

705 Edward of Carnarvon, Prince of Wales (afterwards Edward II), bore before 1307: England with a label azure. (From his seal, 1305.)

706 John of Eltham (second son of Edward II): England with a bordure of the arms of France. (From his tomb.)

707 Arms of Edmund of Woodstock, Earl of Kent, 3rd son of Edward I: England within a bordure argent. The same arms were borne by his descendant, Thomas de Holland, Earl of Kent.

708 Arms of John de Holand, Duke of Exeter (d. 1400): England, a bordure of France. (From his seal, 1381.)

709 John de Holand, Duke of Exeter, son of preceding, Arms as preceding. (From his seal.)

710 Henry de Holand, Duke of Exeter, son of preceding. Arms as preceding. (From his seal, 1455.)

711 Thomas of Brotherton, Earl of Norfolk, second son of Edward I: Arms of England, a label of three points argent.

712 Thomas de Mowbray, Duke of Norfolk (d. 1400.) (From a drawing of his seal, MS. Cott., Julius, C. vii., f. 166.) Arms, see page 357.

713 John de Mowbray, Duke of Norfolk (d. 1432): Arms as 711. (From his Garter plate.)

714 John de Mowbray, Duke of Norfolk (d. 1461): Arms as 711. (From his seal.)

715 Edward the Black Prince: Quarterly, 1 and 4 France (ancient); 2 and 3 England, and a label of three points argent. (From his tomb.)

716 Richard, Prince of Wales (afterwards Richard II), son of preceding: Arms as preceding. (From his seal, 1377.)

717 Edmund of Langley, Duke of York, fifth son of King Edward III: France (ancient) and England quarterly, a label of three points argent, each point charged with three torteaux. (From his seal, 1391.) His son, Edward, Earl of Cambridge, until he succeeded his father, i.e. before 1462, bore the same with an additional difference of a bordure of Spain (316). Vincent attributes to him, however, a label as 719, which possibly he bore after his father's death.

718 Richard, Duke of York (son of Edward, Earl of Cambridge and Duke of York): Arms as preceding. (From his seal, 1436.)

722 Richard, Duke of Gloucester (afterwards Richard III): A label of three points ermine, on each point a canton gules.

725 Thomas, Duke of Clarence, second son of Henry IV. France and England quarterly, a label of three points ermine. (From his seal, 1413.)

728 Jasper Tudor, Duke of Bedford: France and England quarterly, a bordure azure, charged with martlets or. (From his seal.) Although uncle of Henry VII, Jasper Tudor had no blood descent whatever which would entitle him to bear these arms. His use of them is very remarkable.

719 Referred to under 717.

723 Humphrey of Lancaster, Duke of Gloucester, fourth son of Henry IV: France (modern) and England quarterly, a bordure argent. (From his seal.)

726 George Plantagenet, Duke of Clarence, brother of Edward IV: France and England quarterly, a label of three points argent, each charged with a canton gules, (From MS. Harl. 521.)

729 Thomas de Beaufort, Earl of Dorset, brother of John, Earl of Somerset (724): France and England quarterly, a bordure compony ermine and azure. (From his Garter plate.)

720 Thomas of Woodstock, Earl of Buckingham, seventh son of Edward III: France (ancient) and England quarterly, a bordure argent. (From a drawing of his seal, 1391, MS. Cott., Julius, C vii.)

724 John de Beaufort, Earl and Marquis of Somerset, son of John of Gaunt. Arms subsequent to his legitimation: France and England quarterly, within a bordure gobony azuer and argent. Prior to his legitimation he bore: Per pale argent and azure (the livery colours of Lancaster), a bend of England (i.e. a bend gules charged with three lions passant guardant or) with a label of France.

727 John, Duke of Bedford, third son of Henry IV: France and England quarterly, a label of five points, the two dexter ermine, the three sinister azure, charged with three fleurs-de-lis or. (From MS. Add. 18,850.)

730 John of Gaunt Duke of Lancaster, bore: France (ancient) and England quarterly, a label of three points ermine (i.e. each point charged with three ermine spots).

721 Henry of Monmouth, afterwards Henry V: France (modern) and England quarterly, a label of three points argent. (From his seal.)

III claimed the throne of France and quartered the arms of that country with those of England, of course a portion of the field then became azure, and a blue label upon a blue field was no longer possible. The heir-apparent therefore differenced his shield by the plain label of three points argent, and this has ever since, down to the present day, continued to be the 'difference' used by the heir-apparent to the English throne. A label of gules upon the gules quartering of England was equally impossible, and consequently from that period all labels used by any member of the Royal Family have been argent, charged with different objects, these being frequently taken from the arms of some female ancestor. 700 to 730 are a somewhat extensive collection of variations of the Royal Arms.

Lionel of Antwerp, Duke of Clarence, third son of Edward III, bore: France (ancient) and England quarterly, a label of three points argent, and on each point a canton gules.

The use of the bordure as a legitimate difference upon the Royal Arms ceased about the Tudor period, and differencing between members of the Royal Family is now exclusively done by means of these labels. A few cases of bordures to denote illegitimacy can, however, be found. The method of deciding these labels is for separate warrants under the hand and seal of the sovereign to be issued to the different members of the Royal Family, assigning to each a certain coronet, and the label to be borne over the Royal Arms, crest, and supporters. These warrants are personal to those for whom they are issued, and are *not* hereditary. Of late their use, or perhaps maybe their issue, has not been quite so particularly conformed proof of its being thus borne by cadets is furnished by the evidence in the Grey and Hastings controversy in the reign of HENRY IV, from which it appeared that to as is desirable, and the official records show the arms of their Royal Highnesses the Duchess of Fife, the Princess Victoria, and the Queen of Norway, still bearing the label of five points indicative of their position as grandchildren of the sovereign, which of course they were when the warrants were issued in the lifetime of Queen Victoria. In spite of the fact that the warrants have no hereditary limitation, I am only aware of three modern instances in which a warrant has been issued to the son of a cadet of the Royal House who had previously received a warrant. One of these was the Duke of Cambridge. The warrant was issued to him in his father's lifetime, and to the label previously assigned to his father a second label of three points gules, to be borne directly below the other, was added. The other case was that of his cousin, afterwards Duke of Cumberland and King of Hanover. In his case the second label, also gules, was charged with the white horse of Hanover. Prince Arthur of Connaught has, I believe, received a warrant.[225]

The label of the eldest son of the heir-apparent to the English throne is not, as may be imagined, a plain label of five points, but the plain label of three points, the centre point only being charged. The Duke of Clarence charged the centre point of his label of three points with a cross couped gules. After his death the Duke of York relinquished the label of five points which he had previously borne, receiving one of three, the centre point charged with an anchor. In every other case all of the points are charged. The following examples of the labels in use will show how the system has obtained:

225. Prince Arthur's label was assigned on 11 November 1904. It was of five points charged with crosses gules and fleurs-de-lis azure alternately.

Prince of Wales. A label of three points argent.

Princess Royal (Louise, Duchess of Fife). A label of five points argent, charged on the centre and outer points with a cross of St George gules, and on the two others with a thistle proper.

Princess Victoria. A label of five points argent, charged with three roses and two crosses gules.

Princess Maud (H.M. The Queen of Norway). A label of five points argent, charged with three hearts and two crosses gules.

The Duke of Edinburgh (Duke of Saxe-Coburg and Gotha). A label of three points argent, the centre point charged with a cross gules, and on each of the others an anchor azure. His son, the hereditary Prince of Saxe-Coburg and Gotha, who predeceased his father, bore a label of five points, the first, third, and fifth each charged with a cross gules, and the second and fourth each with an anchor azure (731). This, I think, was not an English exemplification.

731 *Label of the late hereditary Prince of Saxe-Coburg and Gotha.*

The Duke of Connaught. A label of three points argent, the centre point charged with St George's cross, and each of the other points with a fleur-de-lis azure.

The former Princess Royal (German Empress). A label of three points argent, the centre point charged with a rose gules, and each of the others with a cross gules.

The Grand Duchess of Hesse. A label of three points argent, the centre point charged with a rose gules, and each of the others with an ermine spot sable.

Princess Christian of Schleswig-Holstein. A label of three points, the centre point charged with St George's cross, and each of the other points with a rose gules.

Princess Louise (Duchess of Argyll). A label of three points, the centre point charged with a rose, and each of the other two with a canton gules.

Princess Henry of Battenburg. A label of three points, the centre point charged with a heart, and each of the other two with a rose gules.

The Duke of Albany. A label of three points, the centre point charged with a St George's cross, and each of the other two with a heart gules.

The Dukes of Cambridge. The first Duke had a label of three points argent, the centre point charged with a St George's cross, and each of the other two with *two* hearts in pale gules. The warrant to the last Duke assigned him the same label with the addition of a second label, plain, of three points gules, to be borne below the former label.

The first Duke of Cumberland. A label of three points argent, the centre point charged with a fleur-de-lis azure, and each of the other two points with a cross of St George gules.

Of the foregoing formerly employed labels all were borne over the plain English arms (1 and 4 England, 2 Scotland, 3 Ireland), charged with the escutcheon of Saxony, except those of the Dukes of Saxe-Coburg and Gotha, Cambridge, and Cumberland[226]. The use of the escutcheon of Saxe-Coburg has recently been dis-

226. By Royal Proclamation dated 17 July, 1919, all crowns, coronets and titles of German degree cr provenance and the use of the inescutcheon of the arms of Saxony were forbidden to British subjects.

continued. In the two latter cases the labels were borne over the *latest* version of the arms of King George III, *i.e.* with the inescutcheon of Hanover, but, of course, neither the electoral bonnet nor the later crown which surmounted the inescutcheon of Hanover was made use of, and the smaller inescutcheon bearing the crown of Charlemagne was also omitted for the children of George III, except in the case of the Prince of Wales, who bore the plain inescutcheon of gules, but without the crown of Charlemagne thereupon.

The labels for the other sons and daughters of King George III were as follows:

The Duke of York. A label of three points argent, the centre point charged with a cross gules. The Duke of York bore upon the inescutcheon of Hanover an inescutcheon argent (in the place occupied in the Royal Arms by the inescutcheon charged with the crown of Charlemagne) charged with a wheel of six spokes gules, for the Bishopric of Osnaburgh, which he possessed.

The Duke of Clarence (afterwards William IV). A label of three points argent, the centre point charged with a cross gules, and each of the others with an anchor erect azure.

The Duke of Kent had his label charged with a cross gules between two fleurs-de-lis azure.

The Duke of Sussex. The label argent charged with two hearts in pale gules in the centre point between two crosses gules.

The Princess Royal (Queen of Württemberg). A rose between two crosses gules.

The Princess Augusta. A like label, charged with a rose gules between two ermine spots.

The Princess Elizabeth (Princess of Hesse-Homburg). A like label charged with a cross between two roses gules.

The Princess Mary (Duchess of Gloucester). A like label, charged with a rose between two cantons gules.

The Princess Sophia. A like label, charged with a heart between two roses gules.

The Princess Amelia. A like label, charged with a rose between two hearts gules.

The Duke of Gloucester (brother of George III). A label of *five* points argent, charged with a fleur-de-lis azure between four crosses gules. His son (afterwards Duke of Gloucester) bore an additional plain label of three points during the lifetime of his father.[227]

The Royal labels are placed across the shield, on the crest, and on each of the supporters. The crest stands upon and is crowned with a coronet identical with the circlet of any coronet of rank assigned in the same patent; the lion supporter is crowned and the unicorn supporter is gorged with a similar coronet. It may perhaps be of interest to note that no badges and no motto are ever now assigned in these Royal Warrants except in the case of the Prince of Wales.

227. The following are the labels which have been assigned to living members of the Royal family. On labels of three points: Prince Andrew, an anchor azure on the centre file; Princess Anne, a heart between two crosses gules; Princess Margaret, a thistle proper between two roses gules; the Duke of Windsor, the royal crown on the centre file; the Duke of Gloucester, a lion passant guardant between two crosses gules. On labels of five points: The Duke of Kent, anchors azure and crosses gules alternately; Prince Michael of Kent, crosses gules and anchors azure alternately; Princess Alexandra of Kent, hearts gules and anchors azure alternately; Prince William of Gloucester, lions passant guardant and crosses gules alternately and Prince Richard of Gloucester, crosses and lions passant guardant gules alternately.

F.-M. H.S.H. Prince Leopold of Saxe-Coburg, the Consort of H.R.H. the Princess Charlotte (only child of George IV), received by warrant dated 7 April 1818, the right 'to use and bear the Royal Arms (without the inescocheon of Charlemagne's crown, and without the Hanoverian Royal crown) differenced with a label of five points argent, the centre point charged with a rose gules, quarterly with the arms of his illustrious House ["Barry of ten sable and or, a crown of rue in bend vert"], the Royal Arms in the first and fourth quarters.'

By Queen Victoria's desire this precedent was followed in the case of the Prince Consort, the label in his case being of three points argent, the centre point charged with a cross gules, and, by a curious coincidence, the arms of his illustrious House, with which the Royal Arms were quartered, were again the arms of Saxony, these appearing in the second and third quarters.

The Royal Warrant issued for H.M. Queen Alexandra assigned, upon a single shield within the Garter, the undifferenced arms of Edward VII impaled with the undifferenced arms of Denmark. The shield is surmounted by the Royal Crown. The supporters are: (dexter) the lion of England, and (sinister) a savage wreathed about the temples and loins with oak and supporting in his exterior hand a club all proper. This sinister supporter was taken from the Royal Arms of Denmark. This precedent was followed for Queen Mary. She impaled quarterly 1 and 4 the arms of Cambridge, 2 and 3 the arms of Teck, and for her master supporter had a stage proper.[228]

Abroad there is now no equivalent whatever to our methods of differencing the Royal Arms. An official certificate has been issued to me from Denmark of the undifferenced Royal Arms of Denmark certified as correct for the 'Princes and Princesses' of that country. But the German Crown Prince bears his shield within a bordure gules, and anciently in France (from which country the English system was very probably originally derived) the differencing of the Royal French Arms for the younger branches seems to have been carefully attended to, as has been already specified.

Differencing in Scotland is carried out on an entirely different basis from differencing in England. In Scotland the idea is still rigidly preserved and adhered to that the coat of arms of a family belongs only to the head of the family for the time being, and the terms of a Scottish grant are as follows: 'Know ye therefore that we have devised and do by these presents assign ratify and conform to the said ———— and his descendants *with such congruent differences as may hereafter be matriculated for them the following ensigns armorial.*' Under the accepted interpretation of Scottish armorial law, whilst the inherent gentility conferred by a patent of arms is not denied to cadets, no right to make use of arms is conceded to them until such time as they shall elect to matriculate the arms of their ancestor in their own names. This point has led to a much purer system of heraldry in Scotland than in England, and there is far less heraldic abuse in that country as a result, because the differences are decided not haphazardly by the user himself, as is the case in England, but by a competent officer of arms. Moreover the constant occasions of matriculation bring the arms frequently under official review.

228. This precedent of using the sinister paternal supporter with the dexter royal supporter has been followed in the case of the arms of Queen Elizabeth the Queen Mother, as indeed it was for Queen Mary.

There is no fixed rule which decides *ipse facto* what difference shall be borne, and consequently this decision has retained in the hands of the heraldic executive an amount of control which they still possess far exceeding that of the executive in England, and perhaps the best way in which to state the rules which hold good will be to reprint a portion of one of the Rhind Lectures, delivered by Sir James Balfour Paul, which is devoted to the point:

'I have said that in Scotland the principle which limited the number of paternal coats led to a careful differencing of these coats as borne by the junior branches of the family. Though the English system was sometimes used, it has never obtained to any great extent in Scotland, the practice here being generally to difference by means of a bordure, in which way many more generations are capable of being distinguished than is possible by the English method. The weak point of the Scottish system is that, whilst the general idea is good, there is no definite rule whereby it can be carried out on unchanging lines; much is left to the discretion of the authorities.

'As a general rule, it may be stated that the second son bears a plain bordure of the tincture of the principal charge in the shield, and his younger brothers also bear plain bordures of varying tinctures. In the next generation the eldest son of the second son would bear his father's coat and bordure without change; the second son would have the bordure engrailed; the third, invected; the fourth, indented, and so on, the other sons of the younger sons in this generation differencing their father's bordures in the same way. The junior members of the next generation might have their bordures parted per pale, the following generations having their bordures parted per fess and per saltire, per cross or quarterly, gyronny or compony, that is, divided into alternate spaces of metal or colour in a single trace— this, however, being often in Scotland a mark of illegitimacy— counter-compone or a similar pattern in two tracts, or chequy with three or more tracts.

'You will see that these modifications of the simple bordure afford a great variety of differences, and when they are exhausted the expedient can then be resorted to of placing on the bordures charges taken from other coats, often from those of a maternal ancestor; or they may be arbitrarily assigned to denote some personal characteristic of the bearer, as in the case of James Maitland, Major in the Scots regiment of Foot Guards, who carries the dismembered lion of his family within a bordure wavy azure charged with eight hand grenades or, significant, I presume, of his military profession.

'You will observe that, with all these varieties of differencing we have mentioned, the younger branches descending from the original eldest son of the parent house are still left unprovided with marks of cadency. These, however, can be arranged for by taking the ordinary which appears in their father's arms and modifying its boundary lines. Say the original coat was "argent, a chevron gules", the second son of the eldest son would have the chevron engrailed, but without any bordure; the third, invected, and so on; and the next generations the systems of bordures accompanying the modified chevron would go on as before. And when all these methods are exhausted, differences can still be made in a variety of ways, *e.g.* by charging the ordinary with similar charges in a similar manner to the bordure as Erskine of Shielfield, a cadet of Balgownie, who bore: "Argent, on a pale sable, a cross crosslet fitchée or within a bordure azure"; or by the introduction of an ordinary into a coat which had not one previously, a bend or the ribbon (which is a small bend) being a favourite ordinary to use for this purpose. Again, we occasionally find a change of tincture of the field of the shield used to denote cadency.

'There are other modes of differencing which need not be alluded to in detail, but I may say that on analysing the earlier arms in the Lyon Register, I find that the bordure is by far the most common method of indicating cadency, being used in no less than 1080 cases. The next most popular way is by changing the boundary lines of an ordinary, which is done in 563 shields; 233 cadets difference their arms by the insertion of a smaller charge on the ordinary and 195 on the shield. A change of tincture, including counterchanging, is carried out in 155 coats, and a canton is added in 70 cases, while there are 350 coats in which two or more of the above methods are used. From these figures, which are approximately correct, you will see the relative frequency of the various modes of differencing. You will also note that the original coat of a family can be differenced in a great many ways so as to show the connection of cadets with the parent house. The drawback to the system is that heralds have never arrived at a uniform treatment so as to render it possible to calculate the exact relationship of the cadets. Much is left, as I said, to the discretion of the officer granting the arms; but still it gives considerable assistance in determining the descent of a family.'

The late Mr Stodart, Lyon Clerk Depute, who was an able herald, particularly in matters relating to Scotland, had elaborated a definite system of these bordures for differencing which would have done much to simplify Scottish cadency. Its weak point was obviously this, that it could only be applied to new matriculations of arms by cadets; and so, if adopted as a definite and unchangeable matter of rule,

732 *The scheme of Cadency Bordures devised by Mr Stodart.*

it might have occasioned doubt and misunderstanding in future times with regard to many important Scottish coats now existing, without reference to Mr Stodart's system. But the scheme elaborated by Mr Stodart is now accepted as the broad basis of the Scottish system for matriculations (732).

In early Scottish seals the bordures are to so large an extent engrailed as to make it appear that the later and present rule, which gives the plain bordure to immediate cadets, was not fully recognised or adopted. Bordures charged appear at a comparatively early date in Scotland. The bordure compony in Scotland and the bordure wavy in England, which are now used to signify illegitimacy, will be further considered in a subsequent chapter, but neither one nor the other originally carried any such meaning. The doubtful legitimacy of the Avondale and Ochiltree Stewarts, who bore the bordure compony in Scotland, along with its use by the Beauforts in England, has tended latterly to bring that difference into disrepute in the cadency of lawful sons—yet some of the bearers of that bordure during the first twenty years of the Lyon Register were unquestionably legitimate, whilst others, as SCOTT of Gorrenberry and Patrick SINCLAIR of Ulbester, were illegitimate, or at best only legitimated. The light in which the bordure compony had come to be regarded is shown by a Royal Warrant granted in 1679 to John LUNDIN of that Ilk, allowing him to drop the coat whichh is family had hitherto carried, and, as descended of a natural son of WILLIAM THE LION, to bear the arms of Scotland within a bordure compony argent and azure.

The bordure counter-compony is assigned to fifteen persons, none of them, it is believed, of illegitimate descent, and some expressly said to be 'lineallie and lawfulie descended' from the ancestor whose arms they bore thus differenced. The idea of this bordure having been at any time a mark of bastardy is a very modern error, arising from a confusion with the bordure compony.

In conclusion, attention needs to be pointedly drawn to the fact that all changes in arms are not due to cadency, nor is it safe always to presume cadency from proved instances of change. Instead of merely detailing isolated instances of variation in a number of different families, the matter may be better illustrated by closely following the successive variations in the same family, and an instructive instance is met with in the case of the arms of the family of SWINTON of that Ilk. This is peculiarly instructive, because at no point in the descent covered by the arms referred to is there any doubt or question as to the fact of legitimate descent.

Claiming as they do a male descent and inheritance from Liulf the son of Edulf, Vicecomes of Northumbria, whose possession before 1100 of the lands of Swinton is the earliest contemporary evidence which has come down to us of landowning by a Scottish subject, it is unfortunate that we cannot with authority date their armorial ensigns before the later half of the thirteenth century. Charters there are in plenty. Out of the twenty-three earliest Scottish writings given in the National MSS. of Scotland, nine, taken from the Coldingham documents preserved at Durham, refer to the village and lands of Swinton. Among these are two confirmations by David I, *i.e.* before 1153, of Swinton 'in hereditate sibi et heredibus' to 'meo militi Hernulfo' or 'Arnolto isti meo Militi', the first of the family to follow the Norman fashion, and adopt the territorial designation of de Swinton; while at Durham and elsewhere, Cospatric de Swinton and his son Alan and grandson Alan appear more than eighty times in charters before 1250.

733 *Seal of Alan de Swinton, c. 1271.*

734 *Seal of Henry de Swinton, 1378.*

But it is not till we come to *c.* 1271 that we find a Swinton seal still attached to a charter. This is a grant by a third Alan of the Kirk croft of Lower Swinton to God and the blessed Cuthbert and the blessed Ebba and the Prior and Monks of Coldingham. The seal is of a very early form (733), and may perhaps have belonged to the father and grandfather of the particular Alan who uses it.

Of the Henry de Swinton who came next, and who swore fealty to Edward the First of England at Berwick in 1296, and of yet a fourth Alan, no seals are known. These were turbulent days throughout Scotland: but then we find a distinct advance; a shield upon a diapered ground, and upon it the single boar has given place to the three boars' heads which afterwards became so common in Scotland. Nisbet lends his authority to the tradition that all the families of Border birth who carried them—Gordon, Nisbet, Swinton, Redpath, Dunse, he mentions, and he might have added others—were originally of one stock, and if so, the probability must be that the breed sprung from Swinton.

This seal (734) was put by a second Henry de Swynton to one of the family charters, probably of the date of 1378, which have now been placed for safe keeping in the Register House in Edinburgh.

His successor, Sir John, the hero of Noyon in Picardy, of Otterburn, and Homildon, was apparently the first of the race to use supporters. His seal (735) belongs to the second earliest of the Douglas charters preserved at Drumlanrig. Its date is 1389, and Sir John de Swintoun is described as Dominus de Mar, a title he bore by right of his marriage with Margaret, Countess of Douglas and Mar. This probably also accounts for his coronet, and it is interesting to note that the helmet, coronet, and crest are the exact counterpart of those on the Garter plate of Ralph, Lord Basset, in St George's Chapel at Windsor. It is possibly more than a coincidence, for Froissart mentions them both as fighting in France ten to twenty years earlier.

Of his son, the second Sir John, 'Lord of that Ilk', we have no seal. His lance it was that overthrew Thomas, Duke of Clarence, the brother of Henry V, at Beaugé in 1421, and he fell, a young man, three years later with the flower of the Scottish army at Verneuil; but in 1475 his son, a third Sir John, uses the identical crest and shield which his descendants carry to this day (736). John had become a common name in the family, and the same or a similar seal did duty for the next three generations; but in 1598 we find the great-great-grandson, Robert Swinton of that Ilk, who represented Berwickshire in the first regularly constituted Parliament of Scotland, altering the character of the boars' heads (737). He would also appear to have placed upon the chevron something which is difficult to decipher, but is probably the rose so borne by the Hepburns, his second wife having been a daughter of Sir Patrick Hepburn of Whitecastle.

Whatever the charge was, it disappeared from the shield (738) erected on the outer wall of Swinton Church by his second son and eventual heir, Sir Alexander, also member for his native county; but the boars' heads are turned the other way, perhaps in imitation of those above the very ancient effigy of the first Sir Alan inside the church.

Sir Alexander's son, John Swinton, 'Laird Swinton' Carlyle calls him, wrecked the family fortunes. According to Bishop Burnet he was 'the man of all Scotland most trusted and employed by Cromwell', and he died a Quaker, excommunicated

735 *Seal of Sir John de Swinton, 1389.*

736 *Seal of Sir John de Swinton, 1475.*

737 *Seal of Robert Swinton, of that Ilk, 1598.*

738 *Arms of Swinton. (From Swinton Church, 163–.)*

739 Bookplate of Sir John Swinton of that Ilk, 1707.

740 Bookplate of Archibald Swinton of Kimmerghame.

and forfeited. To the circumstance that when, in 1672, the order went out that all arms were to be officially recorded, he was a broken man under sentence that his arms should be 'laceret and delete out of the Heralds' Books', we probably owe it that until of late years no Swinton arms appeared on the Lyon Register.

Then to come to less stirring times, and turn to book-plates. His son, yet another Sir John of that Ilk, in whose favour the forfeiture was rescinded, sat for Berwickshire in the last Parliament of Scotland and the first of Great Britain. His bookplate (739) is one of the earliest Scottish dated plates.

His grandson, Captain Archibald Swinton of Kimmerghame, county Berwick (740), was an ardent book collector up to his death in 1804, and Archibald's great-grandson, Captain George C. Swinton (741), walked as March Pursuivant in the procession in Westminster Abbey at the coronation of King

741 Bookplate of Captain George S. Swinton, March Pursuivant of Arms.

Edward the Seventh of England in 1902, and smote on the gate when that same Edward as First of Scotland claimed admission to his castle of Edinburgh in 1903.

The arms as borne today by the head of the family, John Edulf Blagrave Swinton of Swinton Bank, a lieutenant in the Lothians and Berwickshire Imperial Yeomanry, are as given (Plate V).

388

32 · Marks of bastardy

It has been remarked that the knowledge of 'the man in the street' is least incorrect when he knows nothing. Probably the only heraldic knowledge that a large number possess is summed up in the assertion that the heraldic sign of illegitimacy is the 'bar sinister'.

No doubt it is to the novelists—who, seeking to touch lightly upon an unpleasant subject, have ignorantly adopted a French colloquialism—that we must attribute a great deal of the misconception which exists concerning illegitimacy and its heraldic marks of indication. I assert most unhesitatingly that there are not now and never have been any unalterable laws as to what these marks should be, and the colloquialism which insists upon the 'bar sinister' is a curiously amusing example of an utter misnomer. To any one with the most rudimentary knowledge of heraldry it must plainly be seen to be radically impossible to depict a bar sinister, for the simple reason that the bar is neither dexter nor sinister. It is utterly impossible to draw a bar sinister—such a thing does not exist. But the assertion of many writers with a knowledge of armory that 'bar sinister' is a mistake for 'bend sinister' is also somewhat misleading, because the real mistake lies in the spelling of the term. The 'barre sinistre' is merely the French translation of bend sinister, the French word 'barre' meaning a *bend*. The French 'barre' is not the English 'bar'.

In order to properly understand the true significance of the marks of illegitimacy, it is necessary that the attempt should be made to transplant oneself into the environment when the laws and rules of heraldry were in the making. At that period illegitimacy was of little if any account. It has not debarred the succession of some of our own sovereigns, although, from the earliest times, the English have always been more prudish upon the point than other nations. In Ireland, even so late as the reign of Queen Elizabeth I, it is a striking genealogical difficulty to decide in many noble pedigrees which if any of the given sons of any person were legitimate, and which of the ladies of his household, if any, might be legally termed his wife. In Scotland we find the same thing, though perhaps it is not quite so blatant to so late a date, but considering what are and have been the Scottish laws of marriage, it is the *fact* or otherwise of marriage which has to be ascertained; and though in England the legal status was recognised from an earlier period, the social status of the illegitimate offspring of a given man depended little upon the legal legitimacy of birth, but rather upon the amount of recognition the bastard received from his father. If a man had an unquestionably legitimate son, that son undoubtedly succeeded; but if he had not, any technical stain upon the birth of the others had little effect in preventing their succession. A study of the succession to the Barony of Meinill clearly shows that the illegitimate son of the second Lord Meinill succeeded to the estates and peerage of his father in preference to his legitimate uncle.[229] There are many other analogous cases. And when the Church juggled at its pleasure with the sacrament of marriage—dispensing and annulling or recognising marriages for reasons which we nowadays can only term whimsical—small wonder is it that the legal fact, though then admitted, had little of the importance which we now give to it. When the actual fact was so little more than a matter at the personal pleasure of the person most concerned, it would be ridiculous to suppose that any perpetuation of a mere advertisement of the fact would be considered necessary, whilst the fact itself was so often ignored; so that until comparatively recent times the Crown certainly never attempted to enforce any heraldic marks of illegitimacy. Rather were these enforced by the legitimate descendants if and when such descendants existed.

The point must have first arisen when there were both legitimate and illegitimate descendants of a given person, and it was desired to make record of the true line in which land or honours should descend. To effect this purpose, the arms of the illegitimate son were made to carry some charge or alteration to show that there was some reason which debarred inheritance by their users, whilst there remained those entitled to bear the arms without the mark of distinction. But be it noted that this obligation existed equally on the legitimate cadets of a family, and in the earliest periods of heraldry there is little or no distinction either in the marks employed or in the character of the marks, which can be drawn between mere marks of cadency and marks of illegitimacy. Until a comparatively recent period it is absolutely unsafe to use these marks as signifying or proving either legitimate cadency or illegitimacy. The same mark stood for both, the only object which any distinctive change accomplished, being the distinction which it was necessary to draw between those who owned the right to the undifferenced arms, and owned the land, and those who did not. The object was to safeguard the right of the real possessors and their true heirs, and not to penalise the others. There was no particular mark either for cadency or for illegitimacy, the distinctions made being dictated by what seemed the most suitable and distinctive mark applicable to the arms under consideration.

When that much has been thoroughly grasped, one gets a more accurate understanding of the subject. One other point has to be borne in mind (and to the present generation, which knows so well how extensively arms have been improperly assumed, the statement may seem startling), and that is, that the use of arms was formerly evidence of pedigree. As late as the beginning of the nineteenth century evidence of this character was submitted to the Committee of Privileges at the hearing of a Peerage case. The evidence was *admitted* for that purpose, though doubt (in that case very properly) was thrown upon its value.

Therefore, in view of the two foregoing facts, there can be very little doubt

---

229. This is a specious argument; Nicholas, bastard son of Nicholas, Lord Meinill, was summoned to Parliament by writs dated from 22 January 1335–6 to 3 March 1340–1. He did not *succeed* his father; modern peerage doctrine would hold that these writs created a new peerage with limitation to the heirs general of the recipient of the writ. The Crown may have preferred to address writs to the bastard son rather than to the brother and heir male, which could suggest a broadminded view of illegitimacy; but it is not evidence of succession to an hereditary dignity by a bastard in preference to the legitimate heir. Had this peerage been created by patent rather than have been inferred at a later date to have been created by writ, the situation would be quite different.

that the use of armorial marks of bastardy *was not invented or instituted, nor were these marks enforced, as punishment or as a disgrace.*

It is a curious instance how a careful study of words and terms employed will often afford either a clue or confirmation, when the true meaning of the term has long been overlooked.

The official term for a mark of cadency is a 'difference' mark, *i.e.* it was a mark to show the difference between one member of a family and another. The mark used to signify a lack of blood relationship, and a mark used to signify illegitimacy are each termed a 'mark of distinction', *i.e.* a mark that shall make something plainly 'distinct'. What is that something? The fact that the use of the arms is not evidence of descent through which heirship can be claimed or proved. This, by the way, is a patent example of the advantage of adherence to precedent.

The inevitable conclusion is that a bastard was originally only required to mark his shield sufficiently that it should be distinctly apparent that heirship would never accrue. The arms had to be distinct from those borne by those members of the family upon whom heirship might devolve. The social position of a bastard as 'belonging' to a family was pretty generally conceded, therefore he carried their arms, sufficiently marked to show he was not in the line of succession.

This being accepted, one at once understands the great variety of the marks which have been employed. These answered the purpose of distinction, and nothing more was demanded or necessary. Consequently a recapitulation of marks, of which examples can be quoted, would be largely a list of isolated instances, and as such they are useless for the purposes of deduction in any attempt to arrive at a correct conclusion as to what the ancient rules were. In brief, there were no rules until the eighteenth, or perhaps even until the nineteenth century. The only rule was that the arms must be sufficiently marked in *some* way. This is borne out by the dictum of Menêstrier.

Except the label, which has been elsewhere referred to, the earliest marks of either cadency or illegitimacy for which accepted use can be found are the bend and the bordure; but the bend for the purpose of illegitimacy seems to be the earlier, and a bend superimposed over a shield remained a mark of illegitimate cadency until a comparatively late period. This bend as a difference naturally was originally depicted as a bend dexter, and as a mark of legitimate cadency is found in the arms of the *younger* son of Edmund Crouchback, Earl of Lancaster, before he succeeded his elder brother.

There are scores of other similar instances which a little research will show. Whether the term 'left-handed marriage' is the older, and the sinister bend is derived therefrom, or whether the slang term is derived from the sinister bend, it is perhaps not necessary to inquire. But there is no doubt that from an early period the bend of cadency, when such cadency was illegitimate, is frequently met with in the sinister form. But concurrently with such usage instances are found in which the dexter bend was used for the same purpose, and it is very plainly evident that it was never at that date looked upon as a penalty, but was used merely as a *distinction*, or for the purpose of showing that the wearer was not the head of his house or in possession of the lordship. The territorial idea of the nature of arms, which has been alluded to in the chapter upon marks of cadency, should be borne in mind in coming to a conclusion.

Soon after the recognition of the bend as a mark of illegitimacy we come across the bordure; but there is some confusion with this, bordures of all kinds being used indiscriminately to denote both legitimate and illegitimate cadency. There are countless other forms of marking illegitimacy, and it is impossible to attempt to summarise them, and absolutely impossible to draw conclusions as to any family from marks upon its arms when this point is under discussion. To give a list of these instances would rather seem an attempt to deduce a rule or rules upon the point, so I say at once that there was no recognised mark, and any plain distinction seems to have been accepted as sufficient; and no distinction whatever was made when the illegitimate son, either from failure of legitimate issue or other reason, succeeded to the lands and honours of his father. Out of the multitude of marks, the bend, and subsequently the bend sinister, emerge as most frequently in use, and finally the bend sinister exclusively;[230] so that it has come to be considered, and perhaps correctly as regards one period, that its use was equivalent to a mark of illegitimacy in England.

But there has always remained to the person of bastard descent the right of discarding the bastardised coat, and adopting a new coat of arms, the only requirement as to the new coat being that it shall be so distinct from the old one as not to be liable to confusion therewith. And it is a moot point whether or not a large proportion of the instances which are tabulated in most heraldic works as examples of marks of bastardy are anything whatever of the kind. My own opinion is that many are not, and that it is a mistake to so consider them; the true explanation undoubtedly in some—and outside the Royal Family probably in most—being that they are new coats of arms adopted *as* new coats of arms, doubtless bearing relation to the old family coat, but sufficiently distinguished therefrom to rank as new arms, and were never intended to be taken as, and never were bastardised examples of formerly existing coats. It is for this reason that I have refrained from giving any extensive list such as is to be found in most other treatises on heraldry, for all that can be said for such lists is that they are lists of the specific arms of specific bastards, which is a very different matter from a list of heraldic marks of illegitimacy.

Another objection to the long lists which most heraldic works give of early instances of marks of bastardy as data for deduction lies in the fact that most are instances of the illegitimate children of Royal personages. It is singularly unsafe to draw deductions, to be applied to the arms of others, from the Royal Arms, for these generally have laws unto themselves.

The bend sinister in its bare simplicity, as a mark of illegitimacy, was seldom used, the more frequent form being the sinister bendlet, or even the diminutive of that, the cottise. There is no doubt, of course, that when a sinister bend or bendlet debruises another coat that that is a bastardised version of an older coat, but examples can be found of the sinister bend as a charge which has no reference whatever to illegitimacy. Two instances that come to mind, which can be found by reference to any current peerage, are the arms of Shiffner and Burne-Jones. Certainly in these cases I know of no illegitimacy, and neither coat is a bastardised version of an older existing coat. Anciently the bendlet was drawn across arms

230. As Fox-Davies later states, it was the bendlet rather than the bend sinister which was commonly used to denote bastardy. Frequently it debruised all the quarterings of the reputed father.

and quarterings, and an example of a coat of arms of some number of quarterings debruised for an illegitimate family is found in the registration of a Talbot pedigree in one of the Visitation Books. As a mark of distinction upon arms the bend sinister for long past has fallen out of use, though for the purpose of differencing crests a bendlet wavy sinister is still made use of, and will be again presently referred to.

Next to the bend comes the bordure.[231] Bordures of all kinds were used for the purposes of cadency from practically the earliest periods of heraldic differencing. But they were used indiscriminately, as has been already stated, both for legitimate and illegitimate cadency. John of Gaunt, as is well known, was the father of Henry IV and the ancestor of Henry VII, the former being the issue of his legitimate wife, the latter coming from a son who, as one of the old chroniclers puts it, 'was of double advowtrie begotten'. But, as everyone knows, John of Gaunt's children by Catherine Roet or Swynford were legitimated by Act of Parliament, the Act of Parliament not excepting the succession to the Throne, a disability later introduced in Letters Patent of the Crown when giving a subsequent confirmation of the Act, but which, nevertheless, they could not overrule. But taking the sons of the latter family as legitimate, which (whatever may have been the moral aspect of the case) they were undoubtedly in the eyes of the common law after the passing of the Act referred to, they existed concurrently with the undoubtedly senior descendants of the first marriage of John of Gaunt with Blanche of Lancaster, and it was necessary—whether they were legitimate or not —to distinguish the arms of the junior from the senior branch. The result was that as legitimate cadets, and not as bastards, the arms of John of Gaunt were differenced for the line of the Dukes of Somerset by the addition of the bordure compony argent and azure—the livery colours of Lancaster. It is a weird position, for these colours were derived from the family of the legitimate wife.

The fight as to whether these children were legitimate or illegitimate was, of course, notorious, and a matter of history; but from the fact that they bore a bordure compony, an idea grew up both in this country and in Scotland also from the similarity of the cases of the doubtful legitimacy of the Avondale and Ochiltree Stewarts, who both used the bordure compony, that the bordure compony was a sign of illegitimacy, whereas in both countries at an earlier period it undoubtedly was accepted as a mark of legitimate cadency.

As a mark of bastardy it had subsequently some extensive use in both countries, and it still remains the only mark now used for the purpose in Scottish heraldry. Whether it was that it was not considered as of a fixed nature, or whether it was

---

231. Of all the bordures used as marks of bastardy, the bordure engrailed was the most popular. On 17 July 1623 Sir Thomas Sackville, knight, received an exemplification of nine quarterings within a bordure engrailed, the then Earl of Dorset having attested that Sir Thomas was his grandfather's bastard. Another interesting example of the use of the bordure occurs in the case of Sir Ralph Bourchier. He was the son of James Bourchier, bastard son of Sir John Bourchier, Lord Berners. In the 1584 Visitation of Yorkshire the arms and quarterings of his reputed grandfather are shown within a bordure sable as an indivisible coat quartering other quarterings acquired after the illegitimacy. The bordure was later dropped as in the case of Norris, Egerton, Herbert and others. There is, however, no apparent justification for dropping marks of bastardy after a few generations of clean living. They are, after all, not stigmas or punishments, but marks illustrating a certain type of descent carrying with it the blood but not the right of inheritance.

that it had become notorious and unacceptable, it is difficult to say, though the officers of arms have been blamed for making a change on the assumption that it was the latter.

Some writers who clamour strongly for the *penalising* of bastard arms, and for the plain and recognisable marking of them as such (a position adopted rather vehemently by Woodward, a singularly erudite heraldic writer), are rather uncharitable, and at the same time rather lacking in due observation and careful consideration of ancient ideas and ancient precedents. That the recognised mark has been changed at different periods, and as a consequence that to a certain extent the advertisement it conveys has been less patent is, of course, put down to the 'venality' of medieval heralds (happily their backs are broad) by those who are too short-sighted to observe that the one thing an official herald moves heaven and earth to escape from is the making of a new precedent; and that, on the score of signs of illegitimacy, the official heralds, when the control of arms passed into their hands, found no established rule. So far from having been guilty of venality, as Woodward suggests, they have erred on the other side, and by having worked only on the limited number of precedents they found they have stereotyped the advertisement, and thereby made the situation more stringent than they found it.

We have it from biblical sources that the sins of the fathers shall be visited upon the children unto the third and fourth generations, and this spirit has undoubtedly crept into the views of many writers, but to get into the true perspective of the matter one needs to consider the subject from the point of view of less prudish days than our own.

I have no wish to be misunderstood. In these days much heraldic reviewing of the blatant and baser sort depends not upon the value of the work performed, a point of view which is never given a thought, but entirely upon the identity of the writer whose work is under review, and is largely composed of misquotation and misrepresentation. It may perhaps be as well, therefore, to state that I am not seeking to condone illegitimacy or to combat opinions upon the point. I merely state that our present opinions are a modern growth, and that in the thirteenth, fourteenth, fifteenth, and sixteenth centuries, when the fundamental principles of heraldry were in the making, it was not considered a disgrace to have an illegitimate son, nor was it considered then that to be of illegitimate birth carried the personal stigma that came later.

At any rate, the fact remains that a new mark was called into being in England about the year 1780 when in a grant to Zachary to quarter the arms of Sacheverell, from which family he was in the female line illegitimately descended, the bordure wavy was first met with as a sufficient and proper mark of illegitimacy. The curious point is that before that date in Scotland and in England the bordure wavy possessed nothing of this character, and to the present day the bordure wavy in Scotland is undoubtedly nothing more than a legitimate mark of legitimate cadency, for which mark Mr Stodart provides a place in the scheme of differencing which he tabulated as the basis of cadency marks in Scotland (732). Since that date the bordure wavy has remained the mark which has been used for the purpose in England, as the bordure compony has remained the mark in Scotland.

Bearing in mind that the only necessity was some mark which should carry sufficient *distinction* from the arms of the family, it follows, as a natural consequence

394

of human nature, that as soon as any particular mark became identified with illegitimacy (after that was considered to be a stigma), that mark was quietly dropped and some other substituted, and no one should be surprised to find the bordures wavy and compony quietly displaced by something else. If any change is to be made in the future it is to be hoped that no existing mark will be adopted, and that the marks in England and Scotland shall not conflict even if they do not coincide.

The bendlet sinister, however, survives in the form of the baton sinister, which is a bendlet couped placed across the centre of the shield. The baton sinister, however, is a privilege which, as a charge on a shield, is reserved, such as it is, for Royal bastards. The latest instance of this was in the exemplification of arms to the Earl of Munster and his brothers and sisters early in the nineteenth century. Other surviving instances are met with in the arms of the Duke of St Albans and the Duke of Grafton. Another privilege of Royal bastards is that they may have the baton of *metal*, a privilege which is, according to Berry, denied to those of humbler origin.[232]

According to present law the position of an illegitimate person heraldically is based upon the common law of the country, which practically declares that an illegitimate child has no name, no parentage, and no relations. The illegitimacy of birth is an insuperable bar to inheritance, and a person of illegitimate birth inherits no arms at all, the popular idea that he inherits a right to the arms subject to a mark of distinction being quite incorrect. He has none at all. There has never been any mark which, as a matter of course and of mere motion, could attach itself automatically to a shield, as is the case with the English marks of difference, *e.g.* the crescent of the second son or the mullet of the third. This is a point upon which I have found mistaken ideas very frequently held, even by those who have made some study of heraldry.

But a very little thought should make it plain that by the very nature of the fact there cannot be either a recognised mark, compulsory use, or an *ipse facto* sign. Illegitimacy is negative, not positive— a fact which many writers hardly give sufficient weight to.

If any one of illegitimate birth desires to obtain a right to arms he has two courses open to him. He can either (not disclosing the fact of his illegitimacy, and not attempting to prove that he is a descendant of any kind from any one else) apply for and obtain a new grant of arms on his own basis, and worry through the College the grant of a coat as closely following in design that of the old family as he can get, which means that he would be treated and penalised with such

---

232. I can find no justification for Berry's opinion here quoted. Indeed, most royal bastards, whose arms have been differenced with the baton sinister, sport either a coloured baton (that of the Duke of St Albans in gules, whilst the Earl of Munster's is azure) or like the Duke of Grafton, a baton compony of colour and metal. Curiously, I have not found an example of the use of the baton sinister outside the Royal family, although Elizabeth Colleton, in a petition addressed to the Deputy Earl Marshal in 1714, states that by the law and practice of arms her bastard daughter by Richard, Earl Rivers, could not bear the paternal arms of Savage but with a baton sinister. In consequence she begs for the Deputy Earl Marshal's special consent and allowance that her daughter may be assigned some other mark. The end of this story was that on 31 July 1714 her daughter was granted the arms of Savage within a bordure sable, bezanty. It is, of course, possible that Miss Colleton may have been misinformed as to the law and practice of arms!

alterations (not 'marks of distinction') as would be imposed upon a stranger in blood endeavouring to obtain arms founded upon a coat to which he had no right. The cost of such a proceeding in England is £76 10s., the usual fees upon an ordinary grant.

The alternative course is simple. He must avow himself a bastard, and must prove his paternity or maternity, as the case may be (for in the eye of the law—common and heraldic—he bears the same relation, which is nil, and the same right to the name and arms, which is nil, of both his father and his mother).[233]

Illegitimacy under English law affords one of the many instances in which anomalies exist, for, strange as the statement is, a bastard comes into the world without any name at all.

Legally, at birth a bastard child has then no name at all, and no arms. It must subsequently acquire such right to a name (whatever right that may amount to) as user of and reputation therein may give him. He inherits no arms at all, no name, and no property, save by specific devise or bequest. The lack of parents operates as a *chasm* which it is impossible to bridge. It is not a case of a peculiar bridge or a faulty bridge; there is no bridge at all.

Names, in so far as they are matters of law, are subject to canon law; at any rate, the law upon the subject, such as it is, originated in canon law, and not in statute or common law. Canon law was first made at a time when surnames as we now understand them were not in existence. A bastard no more inherits the surname of the mother than it does the surname of its father; and the spirit of petty officialism, so rampant amongst the clergy, which seeks to impose upon a bastard *nolens volens* the surname of its mother, has no justification in law or fact. A bastard has precisely as little right to the surname of its mother as it has to the surname of its father. Obviously, however, under the customs of our present social life, every person must have a surname of one kind or another; and it is here that the anomaly in the British law exists, inasmuch as neither statute nor canon law provide any means of conferring a surname. That the Crown has the prerogative, and exercises it, of conferring or confirming surnames is, of course, unquestioned, but it is hardly to be supposed that the Queen will trouble herself to provide a surname for every illegitimate child which may be born; and outside this prerogative, which probably is exercised about once a year, there is no method provided or definitely recognised by the law to meet this necessity. To obviate the difficulty, the surname has to be that which is conferred upon the child by general custom; and as an illegitimate child is in ninety-nine cases out of a hundred brought up by its mother, it is usually by the same custom which confers the surname of its owner upon a dog in so many parts of the country that a bastard child gets known by its mother's surname, and consequently has that surname conferred upon it by general custom. The only names that an illegitimate child has an inalienable right to are the names by which it is baptized; and if two names are given, and the child

---

233. If a bastard follows the first procedure advocated, the fee will be £157 10s., not £76 10s. Not surprisingly the fees on grants of arms have risen since Fox-Davies wrote, though not nearly as dramatically as the cost of other and more transient commodities. If a bastard acknowledges his origin and proves paternity, then, to be granted the differenced arms of his reputed father, he must now first obtain a Royal licence. In the case of Australian and Canadian citizens he need only obtain the consent of the kings of arms.

or its guardians elect that it should be known only by those baptismal names, and if common repute and general custom, as would be probable, uses the last of those names as a surname, there is no legal power on earth which can force upon the child any other name; and if the last of the baptismal names happens to be its father's surname, the child will have an absolute right to be known only by its Christian names, which to all intents and purposes will mean that it will be known by its father's surname.

In the same way that an illegitimate child inherits no surname at all, it equally inherits no arms. Consequently it has no shield upon which to carry a mark of bastardy, if such a mark happened to be in existence. But if under a will or deed of settlement an illegitimate child is required to assume the name and arms of its father or of its mother, a Royal Licence to assume such name and arms is considered to be necessary. It may be here noted that voluntary applications to assume a name and arms in the case of an illegitimate child are not entertained unless it can be clearly shown (which is not always an easy matter) what the parentage really was.

It will be noticed that I have said he will be required to prove his paternity. This is rigorously insisted upon, inasmuch as it is not fair to penalise the reputation of a dead man by inflicting upon him a record of bastard descendants whilst his own life might have been stainless. An illegitimate birth is generally recorded under the name of the mother only, and even when it is given, the truth of any statement as to paternity is always open to grave suspicion. There is nothing, therefore, to prevent a person asserting that he is the son of a duke, whereas his real father may have been in a very plebeian walk in life; and to put the arms of the duke's family at the mercy of any fatherless person who chose to fancy a differenced version of them would be manifestly unjust, so that without proof in a legal action of the actual paternity, or some recognition under a will or settlement, it is impossible to adopt the alternative in question. But if such recognition or proof is forthcoming, the procedure is to petition the Sovereign for a Royal Licence to use (or continue to use) the name desired and to bear the arms of the family. Such a petition is always granted, on proper proof of the facts, if made in due form through the proper channels. The Royal Licence to that effect is then issued. But the document contains two conditions, the first being that the arms shall be exemplified according to the laws of arms 'with due and proper marks of distinction', and that the Royal Licence shall be recorded in the College of Arms, otherwise 'to be void and of none effect'. The invariable insertion of this clause puts into the hands of the College one of the strongest weapons the officers of arms possess.

Under the present practice the due and proper marks of distinction are, for the arms, a bordure wavy round the shield of the most suitable colour, according to what the arms may be, but if possible of some colour or metal different from any of the tinctures in the arms. The crest is usually differenced by a bendlet sinister wavy, but a pallet wavy is sometimes used, and sometimes a saltire wavy, couped or otherwise. The choice between these marks generally depends upon the nature of the crest. But even with this choice, the anomaly is frequently found of blank space being carefully debruised. Seeing that the mark of the debruising is not a tangible object or thing, but a mark painted upon another object, such a result seems singularly ridiculous, and ought to be avoided. Whilst the ancient practice certainly appears to have been to make some slight change in the crest it does not seem to have been debruised in the present manner. There are some number of more recent cases where, whilst the existing arms have been charged with the necessary marks of distinction, entirely new, or very much altered crests have been granted without any recognisable 'marks of distinction'. There can be no doubt that the bendlet wavy sinister upon the crest is a palpable penalising of the bearer, and I think the whole subject of the marks of bastardy in the three kingdoms might with advantage be brought under official consideration, with a view to new regulations being adopted. A bendlet wavy sinister is such an absolute defacement of a crest that few can care to make use of a crest so marked. It carries an effect far beyond what was originally the intention of marks of distinction.

A few recent bastardised exemplifications which have issued from Ulster's Office have had the crest charged with a baton couped sinister. The baton couped sinister had always hitherto been confined to the arms of Royal bastards, but I am not aware of any Royal crest so bastardised. Of course no circumstances can be conceived in which it is necessary to debruise supporters, as under no circumstances can these be the subject of a Royal Licence of this character, except in a possible case where they might have been granted as a simple augmentation to a man and his descendants, without further limitation. I know of no bastardised version consequent upon such a grant. Supporters signify some definite honour which cannot ordinarily survive illegitimacy.

The bordure wavy is placed round the pronominal arms only, and no right to any quarterings the family may have enjoyed previously is conferred, except such right to a quarterly coat as might ensue through the assumption of a double name. Quartering is held to signify representations which cannot be given by a Royal Licence,[234] but a quartering of augmentation or a duplicate coat for the pronominal name which had been so regularly used with the alternative coat as to constitute the two something in the nature of a compound coat, would be exemplified 'all within a bordure wavy'. Each illegitimate coat stands on its own basis, and there is a well-known instance in which a marriage was subsequently found to be illegal, or to have never taken place, after which, I believe, some number of brothers and sisters obtained Royal Licences and exemplifications. The descendants of one of the brothers will be found in the current Peerage Books, and those who know their peerage history well will recognise the case I allude to. All the brothers and sisters had the same arms exemplified, each with a bordure wavy *of a different colour*. If there were descendants of any of the sisters, those descendants would have been entitled to quarter the arms, because the illegitimacy made each sister an heiress for heraldic purposes.[235] This is a curious anomaly, for had they been legitimate the descendants would have enjoyed no such right.

In Scotland the mark of illegitimacy for the arms is the bordure compony,

234. I take issue with Fox-Davies with regard to his statement that a quartering cannot be given by Royal Licence. Quite apart from the fact that the Crown, as fount of honour, cannot be restricted, save by constitutional means, from doing what it pleases, it was, as we have seen, common practice for quarterings to be assigned to bastards without the intervention of any higher authorities than the reputed father, the kings of arms and the Earl Marshal.
235. See note 224.

which is usually but not always indicative of the same. The bordure counter-company has been occasionally stated to have the same character. This is hardly correct, though it may be so in a few isolated cases, but the bordure chequy has nothing whatever of an illegitimate character. It will be noticed that whilst the bordure company and the bordure counter-company have their chequers or 'panes', to use the heraldic term, following the outline of the shield, by lines parallel to those which mark its contour, the bordure chequy is drawn by lines parallel to and at right angles to the palar line of the shield, irrespective of its outline. A bordure chequy must, of course, at one point or another show three distinct rows of checks.

The bastardising of crests even in England is a comparatively modern practice. I know of no single instance ancient or modern of the kind in Scottish heraldry, though I could mention scores of achievements in which the shields carry marks of distinction. This is valuable evidence, for no matter how lax the official practice of Scottish armory may have been at one period, the theory of Scottish armory far more nearly approaches the ancient practices and rules of heraldry than does the armory of any other country. That theory is much nearer the ideal theory than the English one, but unfortunately for the practical purposes of modern heraldic needs, it does not answer so well. At the present day, therefore, a Scottish crest is not marked in any way.

Most handbooks refer to a certain rule which is supposed to exist for the differencing of a coat to denote illegitimacy when the coat is that of the mother and not the father, the supposed method being to depict the arms under a surcoat, the result being much the same as if the whole of the arms appeared in exaggerated flaunches, the remainder of the shield being left vacant except for the tincture of the surcoat. As a matter of fact only one instance is known, and consequently we must consider it as a new coat devised to bear reference to the old one, and not as a regularised method of differencing for a particular set of circumstances.

In Ireland the rules are to all intents and purposes the same as in England, with the exception of the occasional use of a sinister baton instead of a bendlet wavy sinister upon the crest. In Scotland, where Royal Licences are unknown, it is merely necessary to prove paternity, and rematriculate the arms with due and proper marks of distinction.

It was a very general idea during a former period, but subsequently to the time when the bend and bendlet sinister and the bordure were recognised as in the nature of the accepted marks of bastardy, and when their penal nature was admitted, that whatever mark was adopted for the purpose of indicating illegitimacy need only be borne for three generations. Some of the older authorities tell us that after that length of time had elapsed it might be discarded, and some other and less objectionable mark be taken in its place. The older writers were striving, consciously or unconsciously, to reconcile the disgrace of illegitimacy, which they knew, with heraldic facts which they also knew, and to reconcile in certain prominent families undoubted illegitimacy with unmarked arms, the probability being that their sense of justice and regard for heraldry prompted them to the remark that some other mark of distinction *ought* to be added, whilst all the time they knew it never was. The arms of Byron, Somerset, Meinill, and Herbert are all cases where the marks of illegitimacy have been quietly dropped, entire reversion being had to the undifferenced original coat. At a time when marks of illegitimacy, both in fact and in theory, were nothing more than marks of cadency and difference from the arms of the head of the house, it was no venality of the heralds, but merely the acceptance of current ideas, that permitted them to recognise the undifferenced arms for the illegitimate descendants when there were no legitimate owners from whose claim the arms of the others needed to be differentiated, and when lordships and lands had lapsed to a bastard branch. To this fact must be added another. The armorial control of the heralds after the days of tournaments was exercised through the Visitations and the Earl Marshal's Court. Peers were never subject to the Visitations, and so were not under control unless their arms were challenged in the Earl Marshal's Court by the rightful owner. The cases that were notorious are cases of the arms of peers.

The Visitations gave the officers of arms greater control over the arms of commoners than they had had theretofore, and the growing social opinions upon legitimacy and marriage brought social observances more into conformity with the technical law, and made that technical law of no inheritance and no paternity an operative fact. The result is that the hard legal fact is now rigidly and rightly insisted upon, and the claim and right to arms of one of illegitimate descent depends and is made to depend solely upon the instruments creating that right, and the conditions of 'due and proper marks of distinction' always subject to which the right is called into being. Nowadays there is no release from the penalty of the bordures wavy and compony save through the avenue of a new and totally different grant and the full fees payable therefor. But, as the bearer of a bordure wavy once remarked to me, 'I had rather descend illegitimately from a good family and bear their arms marked than descend from a lot of nobodies and use a new grant.' But until the common law is altered, if it ever is, the game must be played fairly and the conditions of a Royal Licence observed, for the sins of the fathers are visited upon the children.

Although I have refrained from giving any extended list of bastardised coats as examples of the rules for indicating illegitimacy, reference may nevertheless be made to various curious examples.

The canton has occasionally been used. Sir John de Warren, a natural son of John, Earl of Surrey, Sussex, and Warenne (d. 1347), bore a canton of the arms of his mother, Alice de Nerford ['Gules, a lion rampant ermine'], over the chequy shield of Warren. A similar instance can be found in modern times, the arms of Charlton of Apley Castle, co. Salop, being bastardised by a sinister canton which bears two coats quarterly, these coats having formerly been quarterings borne in the usual manner.

The custom of placing the paternal arms upon a bend has been occasionally adopted, but this of course is the creation of a *new* coat. It was followed by the Beauforts before their legitimation, and by Sir Roger de Clarendon, the illegitimate son of the Black Prince. The Somerset family, who derived illegitimately from the Beauforts, Dukes of Somerset, first debruised the Beaufort arms by a bendlet sinister, but in the next generation the arms were placed upon a wide fess, this on a plain field of or. Although the Somersets, Dukes of Beaufort, have discarded all signs of bastardy from their shield, the version upon the fess was continued as one of the quarterings upon the arms of the old Shropshire family of Somerset

Fox. One of the most curious bastardised coats is that of Henry Fitz-Roy, Duke of Richmond and Somerset, illegitimate son of Henry VIII. This shows the Royal Arms within a bordure quarterly ermine and counter-compony or and azure, debruised by a baton sinister argent, an inescutcheon quarterly gules and vairé, or and vert (possibly hinting at the Blount arms of his mother, barry nebuly or and sable), over all a lion rampant argent, on a chief azure a tower between two stags' heads caboshed argent, attired or.[236]

236. A new chapter in the arms of illegitimate children has been opened by recent legislation. Under the Legitimacy Act 1959, an adulterine bastard can be legitimised by the subsequent marriage of its parents, but such legitimisation does not affect succession to honours or dignities. As arms are in the nature of an honour rather than property, it has been construed that a person legitimised under the terms of this act has no right to the paternal arms. He can, of course, seek a Royal Licence for a grant of arms, but such arms will have to bear some mark of distinction. At the time of writing, the nature of this mark has not been settled. It is also essential to distinguish on a pedigree legitimised children from those born in wedlock, and this has been effected by using a straight descent line with three waves in it, a cross between the ordinary descent line and the wavy line used to indicate bastardy.

The attitude of society towards adopted children has also had its effect upon armory. It is now quite usual for an adopted child to be granted a Royal Licence to bear the arms of its adoptive father differenced by two links of a chain. In Scotland a voided canton on the arms of the adoptive father is used.

33 · The marshalling
of arms

The science of marshalling is the conjoining of two or more coats of arms upon one shield for the purpose of indicating sovereignty, dominion, alliance, descent, or pretension, according to recognised rules and regulations, by the employment of which the story of any given achievement shall be readily translatable.

The methods of marshalling are (1) dimidiation, (2) impalement, (3) quartering, (4) superimposition.

Instances of quartered shields are to be met with possibly before impalements or dimidiation. The earliest attempt at anything like a regularised method of procedure to signify marriage was that usually males *quartered* the arms of their wives or ancestresses from whom they acquired their lands; whilst impaled coats were to all intents and purposes the armorial bearings of married women, or more frequently of widows who took an immediate interest in their husbands' property. This ancient usage brings home very forcibly the former territorial connection of arms and land. The practice of the husband impaling the wife's arms, whether heiress or not, probably arose near the close of the fifteenth century. Even now it is laid down that the arms of a wife should not in general be borne upon the husband's banner, surcoat, or official seal.

But impalement as we now know it was preceded by dimidiation. Dimidiation, which was but a short-lived method, was effected by the division of the shield down the centre. On the dexter side was placed the dexter half of the husband's arms, and on the sinister side was placed the sinister half of the wife's arms. With some coats of arms no objection could be urged against the employment of this method. But it was liable to result (*e.g.* with two coats of arms having the same ordinary) in the creation of a design which looked far more like one simple coat than a conjunction of two. The dimidiation of 'argent, a bend gules' and 'argent, a chevron sable' would simply result in a single coat 'argent, a bend per pale gules and sable'. This fault of the system must have made itself manifest at an early period, for we soon find it became customary to introduce about two-thirds of the design of each coat for the sake of demonstrating their separate character. It must soon thereafter have become apparent that if two-thirds of the design of a coat of arms could be squeezed into half of the shield there was no valid reason why the whole of the design could not be employed. This therefore became customary under the name of impalement, and the practice has ever since remained with us. Few examples indeed of dimidiation are to be met with, and as a practical method of conjunction, the practice was chiefly in vogue during the earlier part of the fourteenth century.

402

Occasionally quartered coats were dimidiated, in which case the first and third quarters of the husband's coat were conjoined with the second and fourth of the wife's. As far as outward appearance went, this practice resulted in the fact that no distinction existed from a plain quartered coat. Thus the seal of Margaret of Bavaria, Countess of Holland, and wife of John, Count de Nevers, in 1385 (afterwards Duke of Burgundy), bears a shield on which is apparently a simple instance of quartering, but really a dimidiated coat. The two coats to the dexter side of the palar line are: In chief Burgundy-Modern ('France-Ancient, a bordure compony argent and gules'), and in base Burgundy-Ancient. On the sinister side the coat in chief is Bavaria ('Bendy-lozengy argent and azure'); and the one in base contains the quartered arms of Flanders (' Or, a lion rampant sable'); and Holland ('Or, a lion rampant gules'); the lines dividing these latter quarters being omitted, as is usually found to be the case with this particular shield.

Certain examples can be found amongst the Royal Arms in England which show earlier instances of dimidiation. The arms of Margaret of France, who died in 1319, the second queen of Edward I, as they remain on her tomb in Westminster Abbey, afford an example of this method of conjunction. The arms of England appear on the dexter side of the escocheon; and this coat undergoes a certain amount of curtailment, though the dimidiation is not complete, portions only of the hindmost parts of the lions being cut off by the palar line. The coat of France, on the sinister side, of course does not readily indicate the dimidiation.

Boutell, in his chapter on marshalling in *Heraldry, Historical and Popular*, gives several early examples of dimidiation. The seal of Edmond Plantagenet, Earl of Cornwall (*d.* 1300), bears his arms (those of Richard, Earl of Cornwall, and King of the Romans) dimidiating those of his wife, Margaret de Clare. Here only the sinister half of his bordure is removed, while the Clare coat ('Or, three chevrons gules') is entirely dimidiated, and the chevrons are little distinguishable from bends. Both coats are dimidiated in other examples mentioned by Boutell, viz. William de Valence and his wife, and Alianore Montendre and her husband Guy Ferre. On the seal of Margaret Campbell, wife of Alexander Napier, in 1531, the shield shows upon the dexter side the arms of Lennox, and on the sinister the dimidiated coat (the sinister half of the quartered arms) of Campbell and Lorn. This results in the galley of Lorn being in chief, and the Campbell gyrons in base.

An early and interesting Irish example of this kind of marshalling is afforded by a dimidiated coat of Clare and Fitzgerald, which now figures on the official seal of the Provosts of Youghal (Clare: 'Or, three chevrons gules.' Fitzgerald: 'Argent, a saltire gules, with a label of five points in chief'). Both these coats are halved. They result from the marriage of Richard Clare, Earl of Hertford, with Juliana, daughter and heir of Maurice Fitzgerald, feudal lord of Inchiquin and Youghal.

An even more curious case of dimidiation comes to light in the arms formerly used by the Abbey of St Etienne at Caen, in which the arms of England and those attributed to the Duchy of Normandy ['Gules, two lions passant guardant or'] were dimidiated, so that in the former half three of the fore-quarters of the lions appear, while in the sinister half only two of the hind-quarters are represented.

Dimidiation was not always effected by conjunction down the palar line, other partition lines of the shield being occasionally, though very rarely, employed in this manner.

Certain curious (now indivisible) coats of arms remain which undoubtedly originated in the dimidiation of two separate coats, *e.g.* the arms of Yarmouth, Sandwich, Hastings, Rye and Chester. In all cases some Royal connection can be traced which has caused the Royal Arms of England to be conjoined with the earlier devices of fish, ships, or garbs which had been employed by the towns in question. It is worth the passing thought, however, whether the conjoined lions and hulks used by the Cinque Ports may not originally have been a device of the Sovereign for naval purposes, or possibly the naval version of the Royal Arms (see page 140).

One other remainder from the practice of dimidiation still survives amongst the presently existing rules of heraldry. It is a rule to which no modern authoritative exception can be mentioned. When a coat within a bordure is impaled with another coat, the bordure is not continued down the centre of the shield, but stops short at top and bottom when the palar line is reached. This rule is undoubtedly a result of the ancient method of conjunction by dimidiation, but the curious point is that, at the period when dimidiation was employed and during the period which followed, some number of examples can be found where the bordure is continued round the whole coat which is within it.

The arms of man and wife are now conjoined according to the following rules: If the wife is not an heraldic heiress the two coats are impaled. If the wife be an heraldic heir on coheir, in lieu of impalement the arms of her family are placed on an inescutcheon superimposed on the centre of her husband's arms, the inescutcheon being termed an escutcheon of pretence, because *jure uxoris* she being an heiress of her house, the husband 'pretends' to the representation of her family.

For heraldic purposes it therefore becomes necessary to define the terms heir and heiress. It is very essential that the point should be thoroughly understood, because quarterings other than those of augmentation can only be inherited from or through female ancestors who are in themselves heirs or coheirs (this is the true term, or, rather, the ancient term, though they are now usually referred to colloquially as heiresses or coheiresses) in blood, or whose issue subsequently become in a later generation the representatives of any ancestor in the male line of that female ancestor. A woman is an 'heir' or 'heiress' (1) if she is an only child; (2) if all her brothers die without leaving any issue to survive, either male or female; (3) she becomes an heiress 'in her issue', as it is termed, if she die leaving issue herself if and when all the descendants male and female of her brothers become absolutely extinct. The term 'coheir' or 'coheiress' is employed in cases similar to the foregoing when, instead of one daughter, there are two or more.

No person can be 'heir' or 'coheir' of another person until the latter is dead, though he or she may be heir-apparent or heir-presumptive. Though the word 'heir' is frequently used with regard to material matters, such usage is really there incorrect, except in cases of intestacy. A person benefiting under a will is a legatee of money, or a devisee of land, and not an heir to either. The table on page 407 may make things a little clearer, but in the following remarks intestacy is ignored, and the explanations apply solely to heirship of blood.

Charles in the accompanying pedigree is, after 1800, *heir* of David. Thomas is

PLATE X

The Arms of Dublin

The Arms of Southampton

heir-apparent of Charles, being a son and the eldest born. He dies *v.p.* (*vita patris, i.e.* in the lifetime of his father) and never becomes heir. A daughter can never become an heir-apparent, as there is always, during the lifetime of her father, the possibility of a son being born. Mary, Ellen, and Blanche are coheirs of Thomas their father, whom they survive, and they are also coheirs of their grandfather Charles, to whom they succeed, and they would properly in a pedigree be described as both. They are heirs-general of Thomas, Charles, and David, and, being the heirs of the senior line, they are heirs-general or coheirs-general of their house. David being possessed of the barony 'by writ' of Cilfowyr, it would 'fall into abeyance' at the death of Charles between the three daughters equally.

In Scotland Mary, Ellen, and Blanche would be termed 'heirs portioners', and Mary, being an heiress and the eldest born in the direct and senior line, would be termed the 'heir of line'. David being possessed of an ancient Scottish peerage not limited to males (the Earldom of Edinburgh), Mary, the heir of line, would at once succeed in her own right as Countess of Edinburgh on the death of her grandfather Charles. If the family were an untitled Scottish family entitled to supporters, these would descend to Mary unless they had been specifically granted with some other limitation.

At the death of Thomas in 1830 Edmond becomes heir male apparent, and at the death of his father in 1840 Edmond becomes heir male of his house until his death. David having been created a peer (Duke of London) with remainder to the heirs male of his body, Edmond succeeded as Duke of London at the death of Charles in 1840. Grace and Muriel are coheirs of Edmond after his death. They are *not* either coheirs or heirs-general of Charles, in spite of the fact that their father was his heir male. At the death of Charles in 1840, when Edmond succeeded as heir male, John succeeded as heir male presumptive to Edmond. He was not heir-apparent, because a son might at any moment have been born to Edmond. An heir-apparent and an heir-presumptive cannot exist at the same time, for whilst there is an heir-apparent there cannot be an heir-presumptive. John succeeded as heir male of his house, and therefore as Duke of London, in 1850, at the death of his elder brother Edmond; but, though John was the 'heir male' of his said elder brother, he was *not* his 'heir' (Grace and Muriel being the coheirs of Edmond), nor was he the 'heir male of the body' of Edmond, not being descended from him. John, however, was 'heir male of the body' of Charles. George is heir-apparent of John until his death in 1870, when George succeeds as 'heir' of his father and heir male of his house, and consequently Duke of London. At his death in 1880 Dorothy becomes the 'sole heir', or, more properly, the 'sole heir-general', of her father George; but his kinsman Robert becomes his 'heir male', and therefore Duke of London, in spite of the fact that there was a much nearer male relative, viz. a nephew, Arthur, son of George's sister. Robert also becomes the heir male of the body of Owen and heir male of his house, and as such Duke of London. He would also be generally described as the heir male of the body of David.

At the death of Dorothy in 1885 her coheirs were her aunt Alice and her cousin Arthur equally, and though these really were the coheirs of *Dorothy* (the claims of Alice and Annie being equal, and the rights of Annie having devolved upon Arthur), they would more usually be found described as the coheirs of George or of John. Annie was never *herself* really a coheir, because she died before her brother, but 'in her issue' she became the coheir of Dorothy, though she would, after 1885, be usually described as 'in her issue' a coheir of George, or possibly even of John, though this would be an inexact description. Arthur was heir of his mother after 1870, heir of his father after 1872, and heir-apparent of his father before that date; after 1885 he is a coheir of Dorothy, and after 1887 sole heir of Dorothy and sole heir of Alice. He would also be usually described as heir-general of George, and heir-general of John. Let us suppose that John had married Edith Torkington, an English baroness (*suo jure*) by writ (Baroness Neville), who had died in 1862. At that date the barony would have descended to her eldest son George until his death in 1880, when Dorothy, *suo jure*, would have succeeded. At her death in 1885 the barony would have fallen into abeyance between Alice and Arthur. At the death of Alice in 1887 the abeyance would be at an end, and the barony in its entirety would have devolved upon Arthur, who would have enjoyed it until at his death in 1888 the barony would have again fallen into abeyance between Maria, Jane, and Hannah equally. It is not unlikely that Her Majesty might have 'determined the abeyance', or 'called the barony out of abeyance' (the meanings of the terms are identical) in favour of Maria, who would consequently have enjoyed the barony in its entirety. At her death in 1889 it would again fall into abeyance between Jane and Hannah. At Jane's death in 1890 Hannah became sole heir, and the abeyance came to an end when Hannah succeeded to the barony. At her death it would pass to her aunt Lilian. Hannah would usually be described as 'coheir and subsequently sole heir of' Arthur. If the Baroness Neville had been possessed of an ancient Scottish Peerage (the Earldom of Torkington) it would have passed undividedly and in full enjoyment to the heir of line, *i.e.* in 1862 to George, 1880 to Dorothy, 1885 to Alice, 1887 to Arthur, 1888 to Maria, 1889 to Jane, 1890 to Hannah, and 1896 to Lilian, the last (shown on the pedigree) in remainder. Lilian does not become an heiress until 1896, when the whole issue of her brother becomes extinct. Irene and Isabel never become heirs at all.

Robert, as we have seen, became heir male of his house and Duke of London in 1880. At his death (1896) Harriet becomes sole heir of Robert, but at her death in 1897 his niece Ada, the only child of his younger brother Philip, who had predeceased him, would be usually referred to as heir of Robert, whilst Cecil is heir male of his house.

When the term 'of the body' is employed, *actual descent* from that person is signified, *e.g.* Arthur after 1885 is 'collateral' heir-general of Dorothy, but 'heir-general of the body' of Edith Torkington.

An 'heir of entail', or, to use the Scottish term, the 'heir of tailzie', is merely the person succeeding to property under a specific remainder contained in a deed of entail. This has no relation to heirship in blood, and the term, from an armorial point of view, might be entirely disregarded, were it not that some number of Scottish coats of arms, and a greater number of Scottish supporters, and some Scottish peerages and baronetcies, are specifically granted and limited to the heirs of entail. There are a few similar English grants following upon Royal Licences for change of name and arms.

The term 'heir in expectancy' is sometimes heard, but it is not really a proper term, and has no exact or legal meaning. When George was alive his daughter

DAVID CILFOWYR, created Duke of London in the Peerage of the United Kingdom, remainder to him and the heirs male of his body, was Earl of Edinburgh in the Peerage of Scotland (with remainder to his heirs male), and Lord Cilfowyr by writ in the Peerage of England (with remainder to his heirs-general). Died 1800.

CHARLES CILFOWYR, elder son and heir; head of his house, Duke of London, Earl of Edinburgh, and Lord Cilfowyr. Died 1840.

OWEN CILFOWYR, Esq., commonly called Lord Owen Cilfowyr by courtesy. Died 1870.

ROBERT CILFOWYR, Esq., eldest son, becomes heir male of his house in 1880 at the death of George, and as such succeeds as Duke of London. Died 1896.

PHILIP CILFOWYR, Esq., second son. Died 1879.

CECIL CILFOWYR, Esq., third son. When his brother succeeds in 1880 as Duke of London he petitions the Queen for that style and precedence which he would have enjoyed had his father lived to inherit the Dukedom. His petition being granted, he becomes by courtesy Lord Cecil Cilfowyr, until he succeeds in 1896, at the death of his brother, to the Dukedom of London.

ISABEL CILFOWYR, styled by courtesy as Lady Isabel Cilfowyr. Living 1900.

HARRIET CILFOWYR, only child, by courtesy after 1880 Lady Harriet Cilfowyr. Died 1897.

ADA, only child, has no courtesy title. Living 1900.

THOMAS CILFOWYR, Esq., eldest son and heir-apparent, styled Earl of Edinburgh by courtesy. Died v.p. 1830, so never succeeds.

EDMOND CILFOWYR, Esq., second son, styled by courtesy Lord Edmond Cilfowyr until 1840, when he succeeds as Duke of London. Died 1850.

JOHN CILFOWYR, Esq., third son, styled by courtesy Lord John Cilfowyr until 1850, when he succeeds as Duke of London. Died 1870.

EDITH TORKINGTON, succeeds in 1861 as suo jure Baroness Neville by writ in England and Countess of Torkington (to herself and her heirs) in Scotland. Died 1862.

IRENE CILFOWYR, styled by courtesy as Lady Irene Cilfowyr. Living 1900.

MARY CILFOWYR, Countess of Edinburgh. Living 1900. Heir of Line.

ELLEN CILFOWYR, styled by courtesy Lady Ellen Cilfowyr. Living 1900.

BLANCHE CILFOWYR, styled by courtesy Lady Blanche Cilfowyr. Living 1900.

GRACE CILFOWYR, styled by courtesy Lady Grace Cilfowyr, elder dau. Living 1900.

MURIEL CILFOWYR, styled by courtesy Lady Muriel Cilfowyr. Living 1900.

GEORGE CILFOWYR, Esq., only son, and so styled until 1850, when his father succeeds as Duke of London. As son of a Duke he then becomes by courtesy Lord George Cilfowyr, and this is his proper description, because his father has no minor title which he could assume. But by a quite modern custom which has sprung up of late years he would very probably call himself 'Lord Cilfowyr'. In 1861 his mother succeeds in her own right to two titles, and by courtesy he would thenceforward be styled by her minor title as Lord Neville until her death in 1862, when he becomes Earl of Torkington in his own right and also Lord Neville. At his father's death in 1870 he becomes Duke of London. Died 1880.

ALICE CILFOWYR, styled by courtesy Lady Alice Cilfowyr until 1885, when she succeeds as Countess of Torkington. Died 1887, s.

ANNIE CILFOWYR, styled by courtesy Lady Annie Cilfowyr and Lady Annie Sherwin. Died 1870.

REGINALD SHERWIN. Died 1872.

DOROTHY CILFOWYR, styled Lady Dorothy Cilfowyr until 1880, when she becomes suo jure Countess of Torkington and Baroness Neville. Died s.p. 1885.

ARTHUR SHERWIN, only son and heir, succeeds as Earl of Torkington and Lord Neville in 1887, at the death of his aunt. Died 1888.

LILIAN SHERWIN, only daughter, known as Lady Lilian Sherwin until 1896, when she succeeds as Countess of Torkington and Baroness Neville. Living 1900.

The Barony of Cilfowyr falls into abeyance between these three equally. In Scottish phraseology they are termed heirs portioners.

MARIA SHERWIN, called by courtesy Lady Maria Sherwin, succeeds in 1888 as Countess of Torkington and senior coheir to the Barony of Neville, which falls into abeyance between herself and her sisters. The Queen determines the abeyance in her favour, and she consequently becomes also Baroness Neville. Died s.p. 1889.

JANE SHERWIN, by courtesy Lady Jane Sherwin, succeeds as Countess of Torkington in 1889, but the Barony of Neville again falls into abeyance between herself and her younger sister. Died s.p. 1890.

HANNAH SHERWIN, called by courtesy Lady Hannah Sherwin. She succeeds in 1890 as sole heir of her father, and consequently the abeyance determines of itself, and she becomes both Countess of Torkington and Baroness Neville. Died s.p. 1896.

742.

743.

744.

Dorothy was his heir-presumptive, but supposing that Dorothy were a Catholic nun and Alice a lunatic, in each of which cases there would be very little likelihood of any marriage ever taking place, Arthur would very generally be described as 'heir in expectancy', for though he was neither heir-apparent nor heir-presumptive, all probability pointed to the eventual succession of himself or his issue.

Anybody is said to be 'in remainder' to entailed property or a peerage if he is included within the recited limits of the entail or peerage. The 'heir in remainder' is the person next entitled to succeed after the death of the existing holder.

Thus (excluding heirs in expectancy and women who are heirs-presumptive) a marriage with any woman who is an heir or coheir results in her arms being placed upon an escutcheon of pretence over the arms of the husband. In the cases of all other women the arms are 'impaled' only. To 'impale two coats' the shield is divided by a straight line down the centre, the whole design of the arms of the husband being placed on the dexter side of the escutcheon, and the whole design of the wife's arms being placed on the sinister side (742).

It may perhaps be as well to here exemplify the different methods of the conjunction of the arms of men and wife, arranging the same two coats in the different methods in which they might be marshalled before reverting to ancient practices.

An ordinary commoner impales his wife's arms as in 742. If she be an heiress, he places them on an escutcheon of pretence as in 743. If the husband, not being a Knight, is, however, a Companion of an Order of Knighthood, this does not (except in the case of the Commanders of the Victorian Order) give him the right to use the circle of his Order round his arms, and his badge is simply hung below the escutcheon, the arms of the wife being impaled or placed on an escutcheon of pretence thereupon as the case may necessitate.[237] The wife of a Knight Bachelor shares the state and rank with her husband, and the only difference is in the helmet (744). But if the husband be a knight of any order, the ensigns of that order are personal to himself, and cannot be shared with his wife, and consequently two shields are employed. On the dexter shield are the arms of the husband with the circle of his order of knighthood, and on the sinister shield are the arms of the husband impaling the arms of the wife. Some meaningless decoration, usually a wreath of oak-leaves, is placed round the sinister shield to 'balance', from the artistic point, the ribbon, or the ribbon and collar, as the case may be, of the order of knighthood of the husband (745). A seeming exception to this rule in the case of the warrant to Queen Alexandra, whose arms, impaled by those of Edward VII, are depicted impaled within the Garter, is perhaps explained by the fact that Her Majesty was herself a member of that Order. The same remarks apply to the warrant for Queen Mary. A Knight Grand Cross (or Commander in Indian orders), of course, adds his collar to the dexter shield, and if he has supporters, these are placed outside the *two* shields.

A peer impales the arms of his wife as in the case of a commoner, the arms of the wife being, of course, under the protection of the supporters, coronet, and helmet of the peer (746). If, in addition to being a peer, he is also a knight of an

237. The statutes of all the Orders of Knighthood are constantly being revised, and the reader should consult Chapter 36 with regard to what insignia can be used by whom in a full achievement of arms.

order, he follows the rules which prescribe the use of two shields as already described.

Supposing the wife to be a peeress in her own right, she cannot nowadays confer any rank whatever upon her husband; consequently, if she marry a commoner, the husband places her arms upon an escutcheon of pretence surmounted by a coronet of her rank, but the supporters belonging to her peerage cannot be added to his shield. The arms of the wife are consequently repeated alone, but in this case upon a lozenge on the sinister side of the husband's shield. Above this lozenge is placed the coronet of her rank, and the supporters belonging to her peerage are placed on either side of the lozenge (747). But the arms of a peeress in her own right are frequently represented on a lozenge without any reference to the arms of her husband. In the case of a peeress in her own right marrying a peer, the arms of the peeress are placed upon an escutcheon of pretence in the centre of her husband's shield, the only difference being that this escutcheon of pretence is surmounted by the coronet belonging to the peerage of the wife; and on the sinister side the arms of the wife are repeated upon a lozenge with the supporters and coronet belonging to her own peerage. It is purely an artistic detail, but it is a happy conceit in such an instance to join together the compartments upon which the two pairs of supporters stand to emphasise the fact that the whole is in reality but one achievement (748).

Now, it is not uncommon to see an achievement displayed in this manner, for there have been several instances in recent years of peeresses in their own right who have married peers. Every woman who *inherits* a peerage must of necessity be an heir or coheir, and, as will have been seen, the laws of armory provide for this circumstance; but supposing that the peeress were a peeress by creation and were not an heiress, how would her arms be displayed? Apparently it would not be permissible to place them on an escutcheon of pretence, and consequently there is no way upon the husband's shield of showing that his wife is a peeress in her own right. Such an instance did arise in the case of the late Baroness Stratheden, who was created a peeress whilst not being an heiress. Her husband was subsequently created Baron Campbell. Now, how were the arms of Lord Campbell and Lady Stratheden and Campbell displayed? I think I am correct in saying that not a single textbook on armory recites the method which should be employed, and I candidly confess that I myself am quite ignorant upon the point.

All the foregoing are simply instances of how to display the arms of man and wife, or, to speak more correctly, they are instances of the methods *in which a*

745.

746.

747.

748.

409

749.

750.

751.

752.

man should bear arms for himself and his wife when he is married; for the helmet and mantling clearly indicate that it is the man's coat of arms, and not the woman's. In olden days, when the husband possessed everything, this might have been enough for all the circumstances which were likely to occur.

A lady whilst unmarried bears arms on a lozenge (749), and, upon becoming a widow, bears again upon a lozenge the arms of her husband impaled with the arms borne by her father (750), or with the latter upon an escutcheon of pretence if the widow be herself an heiress (751). The widow of a knight has no way whatever of indicating that her husband was of higher rank than an ordinary untitled gentleman. The widow of a baronet, however, places the inescutcheon with the hand of Ulster upon her husband's arms (752). I have often heard this disputed, but a reference to the Grant Books at the College of Arms (*vide* a grant of arms many years ago to Lady Pearce) will provide the necessary precedent. If, however, the baronetcy is of Nova Scotia, this means of indicating the rank cannot be employed. The widow of a peer (not being a peeress in her own right) uses a lozenge of her husband's and her own arms, with his supporters and his coronet (753).

If a peeress, after marriage with a commoner, becomes a widow, she bears on the dexter side a lozenge of her late husband's arms and superimposed thereupon her own on an escutcheon of pretence surmounted by a coronet. (The coronet, it should be noted, is over the escutcheon of pretence and not above the lozenge.) On the sinister side she bears a lozenge of her own arms alone with her supporters and with her coronet above the lozenge. The arms of the former Baroness Kinloss would show an example of such an arrangement of two lozenges, but as Lady Kinloss did not possess supporters these additions could not be introduced.

The laws of arms provide no way in which a married woman (other than a peeress in her own right) can display arms in her own right during the lifetime of her husband, unless this is to be presumed from the method of depicting the arms of a wife upon a hatchment. In such a case, a *shield* is used, usually suspended from a ribbon, identical with the shield of the husband, but omitting the helmet, crest, mantling, and motto.[238]

Impalement is used occasionally in other circumstances than marriage, *i.e.* to effect conjunction of official and personal arms.

With rare exceptions, the official arms which exist are those of Archiepiscopal and Episcopal Sees, of the Kings of Arms, and of the Regius Professors at Cambridge. Here, certainly in the ecclesiastical cases, the theory of marriage remains, the official arms being placed on the dexter side and the personal arms on the sinister, inasmuch as the laws of armory for ecclesiastics were made at a time when the clergy were celibate. The personal helmet and crest are placed above the

238. Recent grants to peeresses in their own right have shown different marshallings on the Letters Patent. Lady Northchurch (wife of Viscount Davidson) and Lady Swanborough (widow of the Marquess of Reading) have their paternal arms only on a lozenge with supporters and coronets. This may be because both are entitled to encircle their arms with the insignia of the second and first class respectively of the Order of the British Empire. Lady Elliot of Harwood, a Scot, has her arms impaled by those of her late husband on a lozenge with supporters, coronet and motto all displayed on the robe of a Baron. On the other hand, in the grant of supporters to Lady Emmet of Amberley only her late husband's arms are depicted, there being no reference to her paternal arms of Rodd.

impaled coat, except in the cases of bishops and archbishops, who, of course, use a mitre in place thereof. It is not correct to impale the arms of a wife upon the same shield which carries the impalement of an official coat of arms, because the wife does not share the office. In such a case it is necessary to make use of two shields placed side by side, as is done in conjoining the arms of a Knight of any Order with those of his wife.

753.

In impaling the arms of a wife, it is not correct to impale more than her pronominal coat. This is a definite rule in England, somewhat modified in Scotland, as will be presently explained. Though it has never been considered good form to impale a quartered shield, it is only recently that the real fact that such a proceeding is definitely incorrect has come to light. It appears from the State Papers, Domestic Series, Eliz. xxvi. 31, 1561:

'At a Chapitre holden by the office of Armes at the Embroyderers' Hall in London, anno 4° Reginæ Elizabethæ it was agreed that no inhiritrix eyther mayde wife or widow should bear or cause to be borne any Crest or cognizance of her Ancestors otherwise than as followeth. If she be unmarried to bear in her ringe, cognizaunce or otherwise, the first coate of her ancestors in a Lozenge. And during her widowhood to set the first coate of her husbande in pale with the first coate of her Auncestors. And if she mary on who is noe gentleman, then she to be clearly exempted from the former conclusion.'

Whilst this rule holds in England, it must, to a certain extent, be modified in relation to the arms of a Scottish wife. Whilst the inalienable right to quarter arms derived from an heiress cannot be said to be non-existent in Scotland, it should be noted that the custom of indiscriminately quartering is much less frequent than in England, and comparatively seldom adopted, unless estates, or chief representation in an important or appreciable degree, follow the technical heraldic representation. In England the claim is always preferred to quarter the arms of an ancestress who had no brothers whether she transmitted estates or not. Of course, technically and theoretically the claim is perfectly correct, and cannot, and should not, be denied. But in practice in England it has in some cases reached a rather absurd extent, when a man on marrying an only daughter of the youngest son of the youngest branch of a family consequently acquires the right to display with his own ensigns the full arms and quarterings of the head of a house from which he has inherited no lands, and which is still thriving in the senior male line. In Scottish practice such an event would be ignored, and in that country it is not usual to add quarterings to a shield, nor are these officially recognised without a rematriculation of the arms. In England it is merely a question of recording the pedigree and proving heirship, and many quarterings are proved and recorded that there is not the slightest intention to use regularly. Rematriculation has a more permanent character than mere registration, inasmuch as the coat with its quarterings upon matriculation as far as usage is concerned becomes indivisible, and, consequently, for a Scottish wife the impalement should be of the indivisible arms and quarterings matriculated to her father in Lyon Register, with his bordure and other 'difference' marks.

All the old armorists provide ways of impaling the arms of several wives, and consequently the idea has grown up that it is permissible and correct to bear and use the arms of two wives at the same time. This is a mistake, because, strictly and technically speaking, the right to impale the arms of a wife ceases at her death. Impalement means marriage, and when the marriage is dissolved the impalement becomes meaningless, and should be discontinued. A man cannot be married to two people at one time, nor can he as a consequence impale two coats of arms at the same time.

The matter is more clearly apparent if the question of an escutcheon of pretence be considered in place of an impalement. The escutcheon of pretence means that the husband pretends to represent the family of his wife. This *jure uxoris* he undoubtedly does whilst she is alive, but the moment she dies the actual representation of her family passes to her son and heir, and it is ridiculous for her husband to pretend to represent when there is an undoubted representative in existence, and when the representation, such as it was when vested in himself, has come to an end, and passed elsewhere. If his heiress-wife had been a peeress, he would have borne her escutcheon of pretence surmounted by her coronet; but it is ridiculous for him to continue to do so when the right to the coronet and to the peerage has passed to his wife's heir. The same argument holds good with regard to impalement. That, of course, raises the point that in every authority (particularly in those of an earlier period) will be found details of the methods to be adopted for impaling the arms of several wives. People have quite failed to appreciate the object of these rules. Armory from its earliest introduction has had great memorial use, and when a monument or hatchment is put up to a man it has been usual, prior to these utilitarian days of funeral reform, to memorialise all the wives he has been possessed of. In the same way, in a pedigree it is necessary to enumerate the names and arms of all the wives of a man. Consequently for tombs and pedigrees — when all being dead, there is no reason to indicate any particular woman as the present wife — plans have been devised for the combination of several coats into one memorial achievement, plans necessitated by the circumstances of the cases, and plans to which no objection can be taken. Tombs, pedigrees, and other memorials are the usual form in which the records of arms have chiefly come down to us, and from the frequency in which cases of achievements with double impalements have been preserved, a mistaken idea has arisen that it is correct to bear, and actually use and carry, two impalements at one and the same time. Outside memorial instances, I have utterly failed to find any instance in former days of a man himself using in his own lifetime two impalements, and I believe and state it to be absolutely incorrect for a man to use, say on a carriage, a bookplate, or a seal, the arms of a deceased wife. You may *have been* married to a presently deceased woman, therefore impale her arms in a record or memorial; but no one *is* married to a deceased woman, therefore it is wrong to advertise that you are married to her by impaling her arms; and as you cannot be married to two people at the same time, it is illogical and wrong to use or carry two impalements. I know of no instance of a grant to a man of arms to bear in right of a deceased wife. It is for these occasions of memorial and record that methods have been devised to show a man's marriage with several wives. They certainly were not devised for the purpose of enabling him to bear and use for contemporary purposes the arms of a series of dead women, the representation of whom is no longer vested in himself.

Whilst admitting that for the purposes of record or memorial rules *do* exist, it should at the same time be pointed out that even for such occasions it is much more usual to see two shields displayed, each carrying its separate impalement, than to find two impalements on one shield. The use of a separate shield for each marriage is the method that I would strongly advocate, but as a knowledge of past observances must be had fully, if one is to read aright the records of the tombs, I recite what the rules are:

(1) *To impale the arms of two wives.* Either the husband's arms are placed in the centre, with the first wife on the dexter and the second wife on the sinister, or else the husband's arms are placed on the dexter side, and the sinister side is divided in fess, the arms of the first wife being placed in chief and those of the second in base. The former method is the one more generally employed of the two.

(2) *Three wives.* Husband's arms in centre, first wife's on dexter side, second wife's on sinister side in chief, and third wife in base.

(3) *Four wives.* Husband's in centre, first and second wives' in chief and base respectively on the dexter side, and third and fourth similarly on the sinister.

If one of two wives be an heiress her arms might be found in pretence and the other coat or coats impaled, but it is impossible in such a case to place a number to the wife, and it is impossible to display an escutcheon of pretence for more than one wife; if the escutcheon of pretence is removed from the exact centre, it at once ceases to be an escutcheon of pretence. Consequently, if more than one wife be an heiress, separate escutcheons should be used for each marriage. Plans have been drawn up and apparently accepted providing for wives up to nearly twenty in number, but no useful purpose will be served by repeating them. A man with more than four wives is unusual in this country.

Divorce nullifies marriage, and both husband and wife must at once revert to bachelor and maiden achievements respectively.[239]

It is difficult to deduce any certain conclusions as to the ancient rules connected with impalement, for a simple reason which becomes very noticeable on an examination of ancient seals and other armorial records. In early times there can be no doubt whatever that men did not impale, or bother about the arms of wives who were not great heiresses. A man bore his own arms, and he left his father-in-law, or his brother-in-law, to bear those of the family with which he had matched. Of course, we find many cases in which the arms of a wife figure upon the husband's shield, but a careful examination of them shows that in practically every case the reason is to be found in the fact that the wife was an heiress. Husbands were called to Parliament in virtue of the peerages vested in their wives, and we cannot but come to the conclusion that whenever one finds use in early times of the arms of a wife, it is due to the fact that the husband was bearing them not because of his mere marriage, but because he was enjoying the estates, or peerage, of his wife.

For that reason we find in many cases the arms of the wife borne in preference

239. The statement that divorce nullifies marriage is a little misleading, inasmuch as a decree of nullity means that the marriage is declared invalid for reasons of insanity, wilful refusal to consummate the marriage and so forth. It would be truer to say that divorce terminates a marriage which validly took place and the issue of which marriage are unquestionably legitimate. For this reason it seems a little absurd that a divorced woman should resume her paternal arms, with the addition of a mascle, without reference to her former husband's arms, since she frequently bears his name and is the mother of his children.

to the paternal arms of descent, or meet with them quartered with the arms of the husband, and frequently being given precedence over his own; and on the analogy of the coats of arms of wives at present borne with the wife's surname by the husband under Royal Licence, there can be little doubt that at a period when Royal Licences had not come into regular vogue the same idea was dominant, and the appearance of a wife's coat of arms meant the assumption of those arms by the husband as his own, with or without the surname of the wife.

The connection between name and arms was not then so stereotyped as it is at present; rather was it a connection between arms and land, and perhaps more pointedly of arms and a peerage title where this existed, for there are many points and many facts which conclusively show that at an early period a coat of arms was often considered to have a territorial limitation; or perhaps it should be said that, whilst admittedly personal, arms have territorial attributes or connection.

This is borne out by the pleadings and details remaining to us concerning the Grey and Hastings controversy, and if this territorial character of a coat of arms is admitted, together with another characteristic no less important—and certainly equally accepted—that a coat of arms could belong to but one person at the same time, it must be recognised that the appearance of a wife's arms on a husband's shield is not an instance of a sign of mere marriage or anything analogous thereto. But when we turn to the arms of women, the condition of affairs is wholly reversed. A woman, who of course retained her identity, drew her position from her marriage and from her husband's position, and from the very earliest period we find that whilst a man simply bore his own arms, the wife upon her seal displayed both the arms of her own family and the arms of her husband's. Until a much later period it cannot be said to have been ordinarily customary for the husband to bear the arms of his wife unless she were an heiress, but from almost the beginning of armory the wife conjoined the arms of her husband and herself. But the instances which have come down to us from an early period of dimidiated or impaled coats are chiefly instances of the display of arms by a widow.

The methods of conjunction which can be classed as above, however, at first seem to have been rather varied.

Originally separate shields were employed for the different coats of arms, then dimidiated examples occur; at a later period we find the arms impaled upon one shield, and at a subsequent date the escutcheon of pretence comes into use as a means of indicating that the wife was an heiress.

The origin of this escutcheon is easy to understand. Taking arms to have a territorial limitation—a point which still finds a certain amount of acceptance in Scottish heraldry—there was no doubt that a man, in succeeding to a lordship in right of his wife, would wish to bear the arms associated therewith. He placed them, therefore, upon his own, and arms exclusively of a territorial character have certainly very frequently been placed 'in pretence'. His own arms he would look upon as arms of descent; they consequently occupied the field of his shield. The lordship of his wife he did not enjoy through descent, and consequently he would naturally incline to place it 'in pretence', and from the constant occasions in which such a proceeding would seem to be the natural course of events (all of which occasions would be associated with an heiress-wife), one would be led to the conclusion that such a form of display indicated an heiress-wife; and consequently the rule deduced, as are all heraldic rules, from past precedents became established.

In the next generation, the son and heir would have descent from his mother equally with his father, and the arms of her family would be equally arms of descent to him, and no longer the mere territorial emblem of a lordship. Consequently they became on the same footing as the arms of his father. The son would naturally, therefore, quarter the arms. The escutcheon of pretence being removed, and therefore having enjoyed but a temporary existence, the association thereof with the heiress-wife becomes emphasised in a much greater degree.

This is now accepted as a definite rule of armory, but in reciting it as a rule it should be pointed out, first, that no man may place the arms of his wife upon an escutcheon of pretence during the lifetime of her father, because whilst her father is alive there is always the opportunity of a re-marriage, and of the consequent birth of a son and heir. No man is compelled to bear arms on an escutcheon of pretence, it being quite correct to impale them merely to indicate the marriage—if he so desires. There are many cases of arms which would appear meaningless and undecipherable when surmounted by an escutcheon of pretence.

'Sometimes, also,' says Guillim, 'he who marries an heretrix may carry her arms in an inescutcheon upon his own, because the husband pretends that his heirs shall one day inherit an estate by her; it is therefore called an escutcheon of pretence; but this way of bearing is not known abroad upon that occasion.'

A man on marrying an heiress-wife has no great space at his disposal for the display of her arms, and though it is now considered perfectly correct to place any number of quarterings upon an escutcheon of pretence, the opportunity does not in fact exist for more than the display of a limited number. In practice, three or four are as many as will usually be found, but theoretically it is correct to place the whole of the quarterings to which the wife is entitled upon the escutcheon of pretence.

Two early English instances may be pointed out in the fifteenth century, in which a husband placed his wife's arms *en surtout*. These are taken from the Garter Plates of Sir John Neville, Lord Montagu, afterwards Marquess of Montagu (elected K.G. *circa* 1463), and of Richard Beauchamp, fifth Earl of Warwick and Albemarle (elected K.G. *circa* 1400); but it was not until about the beginning of the seventeenth century that the regular practice arose by which the husband of an heiress places his wife's arms in an escutcheon *en surtout* upon his personal arms, whether his coat be a quartered one or not. Another early instance is to be found in 754, which is interesting as showing the arms of both wives of the first Earl of Shrewsbury. His first was *suo jure* Baroness Furnivall. Her arms are, however, impaled. His second wife was the daughter (but not the heir) of Richard Beauchamp, Earl of Warwick, but she was coheir of her mother, the Baroness Lisle.

It should be borne in mind that even in Great Britain an inescutcheon *en surtout* does not always mean an heiress-wife. The Earl of Mar and Kellie bears an inescutcheon surmounted by an earl's coronet for his Earldom of Kellie, and another instance is to be found in the arms of Gordon Cumming (see Plate IV), whilst Sir Hector Maclean Hay, Bart, thus bears his pronominal arms over his quarterings in continental fashion. Inescutcheons of augmentation occur in the arms of

754 *Arms of John Talbot, Earl of Shrewsbury, K.G.: Quarterly, 1 and 4, gules, a lion rampant within a bordure engrailed or (Talbot); 2 and 3, argent, two lions passant in pale gules (Strange); impaling the arms of his first wife whose Peerage he enjoyed, viz.: quarterly, 1 and 4, argent, a bend between six martlets gules (Furnival); 2 and 3, or, a fret gules (Verdon); and upon an escutcheon of pretence the arms of the mother of his second wife (to whom she was coheir, conveying her mother's Peerage to her son), viz.: 1 and 4, gules, a lion passant guardant argent, crowned or (Lisle); 2 and 3, argent, a chevron gules (Tyes). (From MS. Reg. 15, E. vi.)*

415

the Dukes of Marlborough and Wellington, Lord Newton, and on the shields of Newman, Wolfe, and others.

Under the Commonwealth the Great Seals of Oliver Cromwell and his son Richard, as Protectors, bore a shield of arms: 'Quarterly, 1 and 4, argent, a cross gules (for England); 2. azure, a saltire argent (for Scotland); 3. azure, a harp or, stringed argent (for Ireland);' and upon these quarterings *en surtout* an escutcheon of the personal arms of Cromwell: 'Sable, a lion rampant argent.'

In the heraldry of the Continent of Europe it has long been the custom for an elected sovereign to place his hereditary arms in an escutcheon *en surtout* above those of his dominions. As having obtained the crown by popular election, the Kings of the Hellenes also place *en surtout* upon the arms of the Greek kingdom ('Azure, a Greek cross couped argent') an escutcheon of their personal arms. Another instance is to be found in the arms of the Dukes of Saxe-Coburg and Gotha. Whilst all the descendants of the Prince Consort (other than His Majesty King Edward VII) formerly bore in England the Royal Arms of this country, differenced by their respective labels with an escutcheon of Saxony *en surtout* as Dukes and Duchesses of Saxony, the Duke of Saxe-Coburg and Gotha bore the arms of Saxony, placing the differenced Royal shield of this country *en surtout*.

We now come to the subject of quartering. Considering the fact that every single text-book on armory gives the ordinary rules for the marshalling of quarterings, it is strange how many mistakes are made, and how extremely funny are the ideas of some people upon the subject of quartering. As has already been stated, the rules of quartering are governed by the simple, but essential and important fact, that every quartering exhibited means the representation in blood of some particular person. Quarterings, other than those of augmentation, can only be inherited from or through those female ancestors who are in themselves heirs or coheirs in blood, or whose issue subsequently become in a later generation the representatives of any ancestor in the male line of that said female ancestor. Briefly speaking, a woman is an heiress, first, if she is only child; second, if all her brothers die without issue in her own lifetime; and third, if the entire issue, male and female, of her brothers, becomes extinct in her own lifetime. A woman becomes an 'heiress in her issue', as it is termed, if she die before her brothers, if and when all the descendants of her brothers become absolutely extinct.

If the wife be either an heir or coheir, she transmits after her death to *all* her children the arms and quarterings—as quarterings to add to their paternal arms, and as such only—which she was entitled to place upon her own lozenge.

The origin and theory of quartering is as follows: If the daughter be an heiress or coheiress she represents either wholly or in part her father and his branch of the family, even if 'his branch' only commenced with himself. Now in the days when the science of armory was slowly evolving itself there was no Married Women's Property Act, and the husband *ipso facto* became to all intents and purposes possessed of and enjoyed the rights of his wife. But it was at the same time only a possession and enjoyment by courtesy, and not an actual possession in fee, for the reversion remained with the wife's heirs, and did not pass to the heirs of the husband; for in cases where the husband or wife had been previously married, or where there was no issue of their marriage, their heirs would not be identical. Of course during the lifetime of his wife he could not actually *represent* his wife's family, and consequently could not quarter the arms, but in right of his wife he 'pretended' to the representation of her house, and consequently the inescutcheon of her arms is termed an 'escutcheon of pretence'.

After the death of a wife her children immediately and actually become the representatives of their mother, and are as such *entitled* of right to quarter the arms of their mother's family.

The earliest example which has been discovered at the present time of the use of a quartered coat of arms is afforded by the seal of Joanna of Ponthieu, second wife of Ferdinand III, King of Castile and Leon, in 1272. This seal bears on its reverse in a vesica the triple-towered castles of Castile, and the rampant lion of Leon, repeated as in the modern quarterings of Spain. There is, however, no separation of the quarters by a line of partition. This peculiarity will be also noticed as existing in the quartered coats of Hainault a quarter of a century later. The quartered coat of Castile and Leon remains upon the monument in Westminster Abbey erected in memory of Eleanor of Castile, who died in 1290, the first wife of Edward I.

Providing the wife be an heiress—and for the remainder of this chapter, which deals only with quarterings, this will be assumed—the son of a marriage *after the death of his mother* quarters her arms with those of his father; that is, he divides his shield into four quarters, and places the arms of his father in the first and fourth quarters, and the arms of his mother in the second and third. That is the root, basis, and original rule of all the rules of quartering, but it may be here remarked, that no man is entitled to quarter the arms of his mother whilst she is alive, inasmuch as she is alive to represent herself and her family, and her issue cannot assume the representation whilst she is alive.

But it should not be imagined that the definite rules which exist at the moment had any such unalterable character in early times. Husbands are found to have quartered the arms of their wives if they were heiresses, and if important lordships devolved through the marriage. Territorial arms of dominion were quartered with personal arms (755), quarterings of augmentation were granted, and the present system is the endeavour to reconcile all the varying circumstances and precedents which exist. One point, however, stands out clearly from all ancient examples, viz. that quartering meant quartering, and a shield was supposed to have but four quarters upon it. Consequently we find that instead of the elaborate schemes now in vogue showing 10, 20, 50, or 100 quarterings, the shield had but four; and this being admitted and recognised, it became essential that the four most important should be shown, and consequently we find that quarterings were selected in a manner which would seem to us haphazard. Paternal quarterings were dropped and the result has been that many coats of arms are now known as the arms of a family with quite a different surname from that of the family with which they originated. The matter was of little consequence in the days when the 'upper-class' and arms-bearing families were few in number. Every one knew how Stafford derived his Royal descent, and that it was not male upon male, so no confusion resulted from the Earls of Buckingham giving the Royal coat precedence before their paternal quartering of Stafford (see 756), or from their using only the Woodstock version of the Royal Arms; but as time went on the upper classes became more numerous, arms-bearing ancestors by the succession of

755 *Arms of Thomas Stanley, Earl of Derby (d. 1572); Quarterly, 1. quarterly, i. and iiii., argent, on a bend azure, three bucks' heads caboshed or (Stanley); ii. and iii., or, on a chief indented azure, three bezants (Lathom); 2 and 3, gules, three legs in armour conjoined at the thigh and flexed at the knee proper, garnished and spurred or (for the Lordship of Man); 4. quarterly, i. and iii., gules, two lions passant in pale argent (for Strange); ii. and iii., argent, a fess and a canton gules (for Wydeville). The arms on the escutcheon of pretence are not those of his wife (Anne Hastings), who was not an heiress, and they seem difficult to account for unless they are a coat for Rivers or some other territorial lordship inherited from the Wydeville family. The full identification of the quarterings borne by Anthony, Lord Rivers, would probably help in determining the point.*

417

756 *Arms of Edward Stafford, Duke of Buckingham (d. 1521): Quarterly, 1 and 4, quarterly, i. and iiii., France; ii. and iii., England, within the bordure argent of Thomas of Woodstock; 2 and 3, or, a chevron gules (for Stafford). (From MS. Add. 22, 306.)*

757 *Arms of George Nevill, Baron Abergavenny (d. 1535): Quarterly, 1. gules, on a saltire argent, a rose of the field (Nevill); 2. chequy or and azure (Warenne); 3. or, three chevrons gules (Clare); 4. quarterly argent and gules, in the second and third quarters a fret or, over all a bend sable (Le Despencer); 4. gules, on a fess between six cross crosslets or, a crescent sable (for Beauchamp). (Add. MS. 22,306.)*

generations increased in number, and while in the thirteenth and fourteenth centuries it would be a physical impossibility for any man to have represented one hundred different heiresses of arms-bearing families, in later days such became the case. The result has been the necessity to formulate those strict and rigid rules which for modern purposes must be conformed to, and it is futile and childish to deduce a set of rules from ancient and possibly isolated examples originating in and suitable for the simpler genealogical circumstances of an earlier day, and assert that it is equally permissible to adopt them at the moment, or to marshal a modern shield accordingly.

The first attempt to break away from the four quarters of a shield was the initiation of the system of grand quarters (see 755 and 756). By this means the relative importance could roughly be shown. Supposing a man had inherited a shield of four quarters and then married a wife in whom was vested a peerage, he naturally wished to display the arms connected with that peerage, for these were of greater importance than his own four quarterings. The problem was how to introduce the fifth. In some cases we find it borne in pretence, but in other cases, particularly in a later generation, we find that important quarter given the whole of a quarter of the shield to itself, the other four being conjoined together and displayed so as to occupy a similar space. These, therefore, became sub-quarters. The system also had advantages, because it permitted coats which by constant quartering had become indivisible to be perpetuated in this form. So definite was this rule, that in only one of the series of Garter plates anterior to the Tudor period is any shield found containing more than four quarters, though many of these are grand quarters containing other coats borne sub-quarterly. The one instance which I refer to as an exception is the shield of the Duke D'Urbino, and it is quite possible that this should not be quoted as an instance in point. He appears to have borne in the ordinary way four quarters, but he subsequently added thereto two quarterings which may or may not have been one and the same coat of arms by way of augmentation. These he placed in pale in the centre of the others, thus making the shield apparently one of six quarters.

But one is safe in the assertion that during the Plantagenet period no more than four quarters were ordinarily placed upon a shield. Then we come to the brief period of 'squeezed in' quarterings (757 and 758). In the early Visitations we get instances of six, eight, and even a larger number, and the start once being made, and the number of four relinquished, there was of course no reason why it should not be extended indefinitely. This appears to have rapidly become the case, and we find that schemes of quarterings are now proved and recorded officially in England and Ireland some of which exceed 200 in number. The record number of officially proved and recorded quarterings is at present held by the family of Lloyd, of Stockton in Chirbury, co. Salop, but many of the quarterings of this family are mere repetition owing to constant intermarriages, and to the fact that a single Welsh line of male descent often results in a number of different shields. Welsh arms did not originally have the hereditary unchangeability we are accustomed to in English heraldry, and moreover a large proportion are later inventions borne to denote descent and are not arms actually used by those they stand for, so that the recorded scheme of the quarterings of Mr Money-Kyrle, or of the sister Countesses of Yarborough and Powis, respectively Baroness Fauconberg and

Conyers and Baroness Darcy de Knayth, are decidedly more enviable. Nobody of course attempts to bear such a number. In Scotland, however, even to the present day, the system of four quarterings is still adhered to. The result is that in Scotland the system of grand quarterings is still pursued, whilst in England it is almost unknown, except in cases where coats of arms have for some reason or another become indivisible. This is a very patent difficulty when it becomes necessary to marshal indivisible Scottish coats with English ones, and the system of cadency adopted in Scotland, which has its chief characteristic in the employment of bordures, makes the matter sometimes very far from simple. The system adopted at the present time in the case of a Royal Licence, for example, to bear a Scottish name and arms where the latter is a coat of many quarterings within a bordure, is to treat such coat as made indivisible by and according to the most recent matriculation. That coat is then treated as a grand quartering of an equivalent value to the pronominal coat in England.

But reverting to the earlier chart, by the aid of which heirship was demonstrated, the following were entitled to transmit the Cilfowyr arms as quarterings: Mary, Ellen, Blanche, Grace, Muriel, and Dorothy all had the right to transmit. By the death of Dorothy v.p., Alice and Annie both became entitled. Maria, Jane and Hannah would have been entitled to transmit Sherwin and Cilfowyr, but not Cilfowyr alone, if there had been no arms for Sherwin, though they could have transmitted Sherwin alone if there had been arms for Sherwin and none for Cilfowyr. Harriet would have transmitted the arms of Cilfowyr if she had survived, and Ada would, each subject to differences as has been previously explained.

As has been already explained, every woman is entitled to bear upon a lozenge in her own lifetime the arms, quarterings, and difference marks which belonged to her father. If her mother were an heiress she adds her mother's arms to her father's, and her mother's quarterings also, marshalling the whole into a correct sequence, and placing the said sequence of quarterings upon a lozenge. Such are the armorial bearings of a daughter. If the said daughter be not an heraldic heiress in blood she cannot transmit either arms or quarterings to her descendants. Needless to say, no woman, heiress or non-heiress, can now transmit a crest, and no woman can bear either crest, helmet, mantling, or motto.[240] A daughter not being an heiress simply confers the right upon her husband to impale upon his shield such arms and difference marks as her father bore in his own right. If an heiress possessing arms marry a man with illegal arms, or a man making no pretensions to arms, her children have no arms at all, and really inherit nothing; and the rights, such as they are, to the arms of the mother as a quartering remain, and must remain, dormant unless and until arms are established for their father's line, inasmuch as they can only inherit armorially from their mother through their father. In England it is always optional for a man to have arms assigned to him to fill in any blanks which would otherwise mar his scheme of quarterings.

Let us now see how various coats of arms are marshalled as quarterings into one achievement.

The original theory of quartering upon which all rules are based is that after a marriage with an heiress, necessitating for the children the combination of the

240. As has been mentioned elsewhere, the rules have been relaxed, and there are recent examples of a woman having a motto shown on her grant of arms.

758 Arms of Henry Algernon Percy, Earl of Northumberland (d. 1527): Quarterly, 1. quarterly, i. and iiii., or, a lion rampant azure (Percy); ii. and iii., gules, three lucies haurient argent (Lucy); 2. azure, five fusils conjoined in fess or (for Percy); 3. barry of six or and vert, a bendlet gules (Poynings); 4. gules, three lions passant in pale argent, a bendlet azure (FitzPayne), or three piles azure (Brian).

759.

760.

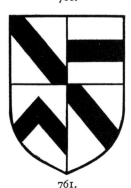

761.

two coats, the shield is divided into four quarters. These four are numbered from the top left-hand (the dexter) corner (No. 1) across towards the sinister (No. 2) side of the shield; then the next row is numbered in the same way (Nos. 3 and 4). This rule as to the method of numbering holds good for any number of quarterings.

In allocating the position of the different coats to their places in the scheme of quarterings, the pronominal coat must always be in the first quartering.

In a simple case (the exceptions will presently be referred to) that places the arms of the father in the first and fourth quarters, and the arms of the mother in the second and third; such, of course, being on the assumption that the father possessed only a simple coat without quarterings, and that the mother was in the same position. The children therefore possess a coat of four quarters (759). Suppose a son of theirs in his turn marries another heiress, also possessing only a simple coat without quarterings, he bears arms as 760, and the grandchildren descending from the aforesaid marriage put that last-mentioned coat in the third quarter, and the coat, though still of only four quarters, is: 1 and 4, the pronominal coat; 2, the first heiress; 3, the second (761).

If another single quartering is brought in, in a later generation, that takes the place of No. 4. So far it is all plain sailing, but very few text-books carry one beyond this point. Another single quartering inherited gives five quarterings to be displayed on one shield. The usual plan is to repeat the first quartering, and gives you six, which are then arranged in two rows of three. If the shield be an impaled shield one sometimes sees them arranged in three rows of two, but this is unusual though not incorrect. But five quarterings are sometimes arranged in two rows, three in the upper and two in the lower, and with a shield of the long pointed variety this plan may be adopted with advantage. Subsequent quarterings, as they are introduced by subsequent marriages, take their places, Nos. 6, 7, 8, 9, 10, and so on *ad infinitum*.

In arranging them on one shield, the order in which they devolve (according to the pedigree and not necessarily according to the date order in which they are inherited) must be rigidly adhered to; but a person is perfectly at liberty (1) to repeat the *first* quartering at the end to make an even number or not at his pleasure, but no more than the first quartering must be repeated in such cases; (2) to arrange the quarters in any number of rows he may find most convenient according to the shape of the space the quarterings will occupy.

Upon the Continent it is usual to specify the number and position of the lines by which the shield is divided. Thus, while an English herald would say simply, *Quarterly of six*, and leave it to the painter's or engraver's taste to arrange the quarterings in three rows of two, or in two rows of three, a French or German herald would ordinarily specify the arrangement to be used in distinct terms.

If a man possessing only a simple coat of arms without quarterings marry an heiress with a number of quarterings (*e.g.* say twenty), he himself places the arms and quarterings of his wife in pretence. Their children eventually, as a consequence, inherit twenty-one quarterings. The first is the coat of their father, the second is the first coat of the mother, and the remaining nineteen follow in a regular sequence, according to their position upon their mother's achievement.

To sum the rule up, it is necessary first to take *all* the quarterings inherited from the father and arrange them in a proper sequence, and then follow on *in the same sequence* with the arms and quarterings inherited from the mother.

The foregoing explanations should show how generation by generation quarterings are added to a paternal shield, but I have found that many of those who possess a knowledge of the laws to this extent are yet at a loss, given a pedigree, to marshal the resulting quarterings in their right order.

Given your pedigree, the first quartering must be the pronominal coat (I am here presuming no change of name or arms has occurred), which is the coat of the strict male line of descent. Then follow this male line back as far as it is known. The second quartering is the coat of the first heiress who married your earliest ancestor in the male line who is known to have married an heiress. Then after her coat will follow all the quarterings which she was entitled to and which she has 'brought in' to your family. Having exhausted these, you then follow your male line *down* to the next heiress, adding her arms as a quartering to those already arranged, and following it by her quarterings. The same plan must be pursued until you arrive at your own name upon the pedigree. Unless some exceptional circumstance has arisen (and such exceptions will presently be found detailed at length), all the quarterings are of equal heraldic value, and must be the same size when displayed.

If after having worked out your quarterings you find that you have more than you care to use, you are quite at liberty to make a selection, omitting any number, but it is entirely wrong to display quarterings without those quarterings which brought them into the paternal line. Supposing your name to be Brown, you *must* put the Brown arms in the first quarter, but at your pleasure you can quarter the arms of each single heiress who married an ancestor of yours in the male line (*i.e.* who herself became Mrs Brown), or you can omit the whole or a part. But supposing one of these, Mrs Brown (*née* Smith), was entitled to quarter the arms of Jones, which arms of Jones had brought in the arms of Robinson, you are not at liberty to quarter the arms of Jones without quartering Smith, and if you wish to display the arms of Robinson you *must* also quarter the arms of Jones to bring in Robinson and the arms of Smith to bring in Robinson and Jones to your own Brown achievement. You can use Brown only: or quarterly, 1 and 4, Brown; 2 and 3, Smith: or 1 and 4, Brown; 2. Smith; 3. Jones: or quarterly, 1. Brown; 2. Smith; 3. Jones; 4. Robinson; but you are *not* entitled to quarter: 1 and 4, Brown; 2. Jones; 3. Robinson, because Smith, which brought in Jones and Robinson, has been omitted, and there was never a match between Brown and Jones.

Quarterings signifying nothing beyond mere representation are not compulsory, and their use or disuse is quite optional.

So much for the general rules of quartering. Let us now consider certain cases which require rules to themselves.

It is possible for a daughter to be the sole heir or coheir of her mother whilst not being the heir of her father, as in the following imaginary pedigree:

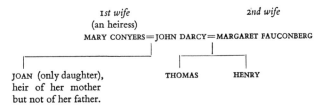

421

In this case Joan is not the heir of her father, inasmuch as he has sons Thomas and Henry, but she is the heir of her mother and the only issue capable of inheriting and transmitting the Conyers arms and quarterings. Joan is heir of her mother but not of her father.

The husband of Joan can either impale the arms of Darcy as having married a daughter of John Darcy, or he can place upon an escutcheon of pretence arms to indicate that he has married the heiress of Conyers. But it would be quite incorrect for him to simply place Conyers in pretence, because he has not married a Miss Conyers. What he must do is to charge the arms of Conyers with a dexter canton of the arms of Darcy and place this upon his escutcheon of pretence.★ The children will quarter the arms of Conyers with the canton of Darcy and inherit likewise all the quarterings to which Mary Conyers succeeded, but the Conyers arms must always thereafter charged with the arms of Darcy on a canton, and no right accrues to the Darcy quarterings.

The following curious, but quite genuine case, which was pointed out to me by a former Ulster King of Arms, presents a set of circumstances absolutely unique, and it still remains to be decided what is the correct method to adopt:

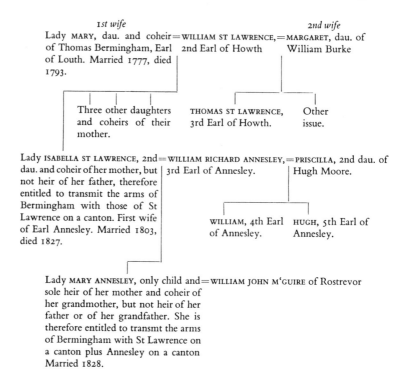

How the arms of Bermingham are to be charged with both St Lawrence and Annesley remains to be seen. I believe Ulster favoured two separate cantons, dexter and sinister respectively, but the point did not come before him officially, and I know of no official decision which affords a precedent.

The reverse of the foregoing affords another curious point when a woman is the heir of her father but not the heir of her mother:

★ Arms borne on a sinister canton suggest illegitimacy.

It is officially admitted (see the introduction to Burke's *General Armory*) that the claim is accurately made. The process of reasoning is probably thus. John Williams places upon an escutcheon of pretence the arms of Smith, and Alice Williams succeeds in her own right to the arms of her mother because the latter was an heiress, and for herself is entitled to bear, as would a son, the arms of the two parents quarterly; and having so inherited, Alice Williams being herself an heiress, is entitled to transmit. At any rate Arthur Ellis is entitled to impale or place upon his escutcheon of pretence Williams and Smith quarterly. To admit the right for the descendants to quarter the arms Arthur Ellis so bore is no more than a logical progression, but the eventual result appears faulty, because we find Theodore Ellis quartering the arms of Smith, whilst the representation of Smith is in the line of Edward Roberts. This curious set of circumstances, however, is rare in the extreme.

It frequently happens, in devising a scheme of quarterings, that a person may represent heiresses of several families entitled to bear arms, but to whom the pedigree must be traced through an heiress of another family which did not possess arms. Consequently any claim to quarterings inherited through the non-armorial heiress is dormant, and the quarterings must not be used or inserted in any scheme drawn up. It is always permissible, however, to petition for arms to be granted to be borne for that non-armorial family for the purpose of introducing the quarterings in question, and such a grant having been made, the dormant claim then becomes operative and the new coat is introduced, followed by the dormant quartering in precisely the same manner as would have been the case if the arms granted had always existed. Grants of this character are constantly being obtained.

When a Royal Licence to assume or change name and arms is granted it very considerably affects the question of quartering, and many varying circumstances attending these Royal Licences make the matter somewhat intricate. If the Royal Licence is to assume a name and arms in lieu of those previously used, this means that for everyday use the arms are *changed*, the right to the old arms lapsing except for the purpose of a scheme of quarterings. The new coat of arms under the terms of the Royal Licence, which requires it first 'to be exemplified in our Royal College of Arms,[241] otherwise this our Royal Licence to be void and of none effect', is always so exemplified, this exemplification being from the legal point of view equivalent to a new grant of the arms to the person assuming them.

241. The College of Arms is not the Royal College of Arms, nor was it, nor is it so styled in Royal Warrants and Licences.

The terms of the Royal Licence have always carefully to be borne in mind, particularly in the matter of remainder, because sometimes these exemplifications are for a limited period or intended to devolve with specified property, and a Royal Licence only nullifies a prior right to arms to the extent of the terms recited in the Letters Patent of exemplification. In the ordinary way, however, such an exemplification is equivalent to a new grant affecting all the descendants. When it is assumed in lieu, for the ordinary purpose of use the new coat of arms takes the place of the old one, but the right to the old one remains in theory to a certain extent, inasmuch as its existence is necessary in any scheme of quartering to bring in any quarterings previously inherited, and these cannot be displayed with the new coat unless they are preceded by the old one. Quarterings, however, which are brought into the family through a marriage in the generation in which the Royal Licence is obtained, or in a subsequent generation, can be displayed with the new coat without the interposition of the old one.

If the Royal Licence be to bear the name of a certain family in lieu of a present name, and to bear the arms of that family quarterly with the arms previously borne, the quarterly coat is then exemplified. In an English or Irish Royal Licence the coat of arms for the name assumed is placed in the first and the fourth quarters, and the old paternal arms figure in the second and third. This is an invariable rule. The quarterly coat thus exemplified becomes an indivisible coat for the new name, and it is not permissible to subsequently divide these quarterings. They become as much one coat of arms as 'azure, a bend or' is the coat of arms of Scrope. If this quarterly coat is to be introduced in any scheme of quarterings it will only occupy the same space as any other single quartering and counts only as one, though it of course is in reality a grand quartering. In devising a scheme of quarterings for which a sub-quarterly coat of this character exemplified under a Royal Licence is the pronominal coat, that sub-quarterly coat is placed in the first quarter. Next to it is placed the original coat of arms borne as the pronominal coat before the Royal Licence and exemplified in the second and third sub-quarters of the first quarter. When here repeated it occupies an entire quarter. Next to it are placed the whole of the quarterings belonging to the family in the order in which they occur. If the family whose name has been assumed is represented through an heiress that coat of arms is also repeated in its proper position and in that place in which it would have appeared if unaffected by the Royal Licence. But if it be the coat of arms of a family from whom there is no descent, or of whom there is no representation, the fact of the Royal Licence does not give any further right to quarter it beyond its appearance in the pronominal grand quartering. The exact state of the case is perhaps best illustrated by the arms of Reid-Cuddon. The name of the family was originally Reid, and representing an heiress of the Cuddons of Shaddingfield Hall they obtained a Royal Licence to take the name and arms of Cuddon in addition to the name and arms of Reid, becoming thereafter Reid-Cuddon. The arms were exemplified in due course, and the achievement then became: Quarterly, 1 and 4, Reid-Cuddon sub-quarterly, 2. the arms of Reid, 3. the arms of Cuddon. In Scotland no such thing as a Royal Licence exists, the matter being determined merely by a rematriculation following upon a voluntary change of name. There is no specified order or position for the arms of the different names, and the arrangement of the various quarterings is left to be determined by the circumstances of the case. Thus in the arms of Anstruther-Duncan the arms of Anstruther are in the first quarter, and the matter is always largely governed by the importance of the respective estates and the respective families. In England this is not the case, because it is an unalterable rule that the arms of the last or principal surname if there be two, or the arms of the one surname if that be the case when the arms of two families are quartered, must always go in the 1st and 4th quarters. If three names are assumed by Royal Licence, the arms of the last name go in the 1st and 4th quarters, and the last name but one in the second quarter, and of the first name in the third. These cases are, however, rare. But no matter how many names are assumed, and no matter how many original coats of arms the shield as exemplified consists of, it thereafter becomes an indivisible coat.

When a Royal Licence is issued to an illegitimate person to bear the name and arms of another family, no right is conferred to bear the quarterings of that family even subject to difference marks. The Royal Licence is only applicable to whatever arms were the pronominal coat used with the name assumed. Though instances certainly can be found in some of the Visitation Books and other ancient records of a coat with quarterings, the whole debruised by a bendlet sinister, notably in the case of a family of Talbot, where eight quarters are so marked, the fact remains that this practice has long been definitely considered incorrect, and is now never permitted. If a Royal Licence is issued to an illegitimate woman the exemplification is to herself personally, for in the eyes of the law she has no relatives; and though she may be one of a large family, her descendants are entitled to quarter the arms with the marks of distinction exemplified to her because such quartering merely indicates the representation of that one woman, who in the eyes of the law stands alone and without relatives.[242] In the case of a Royal Licence to take a name and arms subject to these marks of distinction for illegitimacy, and in cases where the arms to be assumed are a sub-quarterly coat, the mark of distinction, which in England is now invariably a bordure wavy, will surround both quarterings, which remain an indivisible coat.

If an augmentation is granted to a person whose pronominal coat is sub-quarterly, that augmentation, whatever form it may assume, is superimposed upon all quarterings. Thus a chief of augmentation would go across the top of the shield, the four quarters being displayed below, and the whole of this shield would be only one quartering in any scheme of quartering. An inescutcheon is superimposed over all. If the augmentation take the form of a quartering, then the pronominal coat is a grand quartering, equivalent in size to the augmentation. If a person entitled to a sub-quarterly coat and a double name obtains a Royal Licence

242. A less obvious case is that of a woman who is a grantee of arms and therefore sole heir to such arms, but who is not heir in blood to her father; that is, there are sons (or their male descendants) of her father living. Now she is in one sense an heiress, yet in another sense she is not. Does she or does she not transmit her arms as a quartering? This problem has only been recently resolved, and the answer is that she transmits her arms impaled by those of her husband, all within a bordure of suitable tincture, as a quartering to her issue. Should she become an heiress in her issue by the extinction of the male descendants in the male line of her father, then her issue will quarter her arms in the normal way. Thus, if Mr Smith married Miss Jones, a non-heiress grantee, on her death their issue will bear, quarterly, 1 and 4, Smith; 2 and 3, Smith impaling Jones within a bordure. If Miss Jones, albeit a grantee, were an heiress in blood, then her arms would be inherited as a quartering in the normal way.

to bear another name and arms, and to bear the arms he has previously borne quarterly with those he has assumed, the result would be: Quarterly, 1 and 4, the new coat assumed, quarterly 2 and 3, the arms he has previously borne sub-quarterly. But it should be noticed that the arrangements of coats of arms under a Royal Licence largely depends upon the wording of the document by which authority is given by the Sovereign. The wording of the document in its terms is based upon the wording of the petition, and within reasonable limits any arrangement which is desired is usually permitted, so that care should be taken as to the wording of the petition.

A quartering of augmentation is always placed in the first quarter of a shield, but it becomes indivisible from and is depicted sub-quarterly with the paternal arms; for instance, the Dukes of Westminster for the time being, but not other members of the family, bear as an augmentation the arms of the city of Westminster in the 1st and 4th quarters of his shield, and the arms of Grosvenor in the 2nd and 3rd, but this coat of Westminster and Grosvenor is an indivisible sub-quarterly coat which together would only occupy the first quarter in a shield of quarterings. Then the second one would be the arms of Grosvenor alone, which would be followed by the quarterings previously inherited.

If under a Royal Licence a name is assumed and the Royal Licence makes no reference to the arms of the family, the arms for all purposes remain unchanged and as if no Royal Licence had ever been issued. If the Royal Licence issued to a family simply exemplifies a single coat of arms, it is quite wrong to introduce any other coat of arms to convert this single coat into a sub-quarterly one.

To all intents and purposes it may be stated that in Scotland there are still only four quarters in a shield, and if more than four coats are introduced grand quarterings are employed. Grand quarterings are very frequent in Scottish armory. The Scottish rules of quartering follow no fixed principle, and the constant rematriculations make it impossible to deduce exact rules; and though roughly approximating to the English ones, no greater generalisation can be laid down than the assertion that the most recent matriculation of an ancestor governs the arms and quarterings to be displayed.

A royal quartering is never subdivided.

In combining Scottish and English coats of arms into one scheme of quartering, it is usual if possible to treat the coat of arms as matriculated in Scotland as a grand quartering equivalent in value to any other of the English quarterings. This, however, is not always possible in cases where the matriculation itself creates grand quarterings and sub-quarterings; and for a scheme of quarterings in such a case it is more usual for the Scottish matriculation to be divided up into its component parts, and for these to be used as simple quarterings in succession to the English ones, regardless of any bordure which may exist in the Scottish matriculation. It cannot, of course, be said that such a practice is beyond criticism, though it frequently remains the only practical way of solving the difficulty.

Until comparatively recent times, if amongst quarterings inherited the Royal Arms were included, it was considered a fixed, unalterable rule that these should be placed in the first quarter, taking precedence of the pronominal coat, irrespective of their real position according to the date or pedigree place of introduction. This rule, however, has long since been superseded, and Royal quarterings now take their position on the same footing as the others. It very probably arose from the misconception of the facts concerning an important case which doubtless was considered a precedent. The family of Mowbray, after their marriage with the heiress of Thomas de Brotherton, used either the arms of Brotherton alone, these being England differenced by a label, or else placed them in the first quarter of their shield. Consequently from this precedent a rule was deduced that it was permissible and correct to give a Royal quartering precedence over all others. The position of the Mowbrays, Dukes of Norfolk, as Earls Marshal no doubt led to their own achievement being considered an exemplary model. But it appears to have been overlooked that the Mowbrays bore these Royal Arms of Brotherton not as an inherited quartering but as a grant to themselves. Richard II apparently granted them permission to bear the arms of Edward the Confessor impaled with the arms of Brotherton, the whole between the two Royal ostrich feathers (675), and consequently, the grant having been made, the Mowbrays were under no necessity to display the Mowbray or the Segrave arms to bring in the arms of Brotherton. A little later a similar case occurred with the Stafford family, who became sole heirs-general of Thomas of Woodstock, and consequently entitled to bear his arms as a quartering. The matter appears to have been settled at a chapter of the College of Arms, and the decision arrived it was as follows:

B.M. Cott. MS., Titus, C. i. fol. 404, in handwriting of end of sixteenth century.

[An order made for Henry Duke of Buckingham to beare the Armes of Thomas of Woodstock alone without any other Armes to bee quartered therewith. Anno 13 E 4.]

Memorandum that in the yeare of the Reigne of our Soveraign Lord King Edward the iij^th, the Thurtein in the xviij^tin day of ffeverir, it was concluded in a Chapitre of the office of Armes that where a nobleman is descended lenyalle Ineritable to iij. or iiij. Cotes and afterward is ascended to a Cotte neir to the King and of his royall bloud, may for his most onneur bere the same Cootte alone, and none lower Coottes of Dignite to be quartered therewith. As my Lord Henry Duke of Buckingham, Eirll of Harford, Northamton, and Stafford, Lord of Breknoke and of Holdernes, is assended to the Coottes and ayer to Thomas of Woodstoke, Duke of Glocestre and Sonne to King Edward the third, hee may beire his Cootte alone. And it was so Concluded by [Claurancieulx King of Armes, Marche King of Armes, Gyen King of Armes, Windesor Herauld, Fawcon Herauld, Harfford Herald].

But I imagine that this decision was in all probability founded upon the case of the Mowbrays, which was not in itself an exact precedent, because with the Staffords there appears to have been no such Royal grant as existed with the Mowbrays. Other instances at about this period can be alluded to, but though it must be admitted that the rule existed at one time, it has long since been officially overridden. It has, however, governed the warrants to Queen Mary and the Duchess of Fife.

A territorial coat or a coat of arms borne to indicate the possession of a specific title is either placed in the first quarter or borne in pretence; see the arms of the Earl of Mar and Kellie. A singular instance of a very exceptional method of marshalling occurs in the case of the arms of the Earl of Caithness. He bears four coats of arms, some being stated to be territorial coats, quarterly, dividing them by the cross engrailed sable from his paternal arms of Sinclair. The arms of the Earls of Caithness are thus marshalled: 'Quarterly, 1. azure, within a Royal tressure a ship with furled sails all or.' For Orkney: '2 and 3, or, a lion rampant tules.' For Spar (a family in possession of the Earldom of Caithness before the Sinclairs): '4. Azure, a ship in sail or, for Caithness'; and over all, dividing the quarters, a cross engrailed 'sable', for Sinclair. The Barons Sinclair of Sweden (so created 1766, but extinct ten years later) bore the above quartered coats as cadets of Caithness, but separated the quarters, not by the engrailed cross sable of Sinclair, but by a cross patée throughout ermine. In an escutcheon *en surtout* they placed the Sinclair arms: 'Argent, a cross engrailed sable'; and, as a mark of cadency, they surrounded the main escutcheon with 'a bordure chequy or and gules'. This arrangement was doubtless suggested by the Royal Arms of Denmark, the quarterings of which have been for so many centuries separated by the cross of the Order of the Dannebrog: 'Argent, a cross patée throughout fimbriated gules.' In imitation of this a considerable number of the principal Scandinavian families use a cross patée throughout to separate the quarters of their frequently complicated coats. The quarterings in these cases are often not indicative of descent from different families, but were all included in the original grant of armorial bearings. On the centre of the cross thus used, an escutcheon, either of augmentation or of the family arms, is very frequently placed *en surtout*.

The main difference between British and foreign usage with regard to quartering is this, that in England quarterings are usually employed to denote simply descent from an heiress, or representation in blood; in Scotland they also implied the possession of lordships. In foreign coats the quarterings are often employed to denote the possession of fiefs acquired in other ways than by marriage (*e.g.* by bequest or purchase), or the *jus expectationis*, the right of succession to such fiefs in accordance with certain agreements.

In foreign heraldry the base of the quartered shield is not infrequently cut off by a horizontal line, forming what is known as a *Champagne*, and the space thus made is occupied by one or more coats. At other times a pile with curved sides runs from the base some distance into the quartered shield, which is then said to be *enté en point*, and this space is devoted to the display of one or more quarterings. The definite and precise British regulations which have grown up on the subject of the marshalling of arms have no equivalent in the armorial laws of other countries.

Very rarely quartering is affected *per saltire*, as in the arms of Sicily and in a few coats of Spanish origin, but even as regards foreign armory the practice is so rare that it may be disregarded.

The laws of marshalling upon the Continent, and particularly in Germany, are very far from being identical with British heraldic practices.

The British method of impaling two coats of arms upon one shield to signify marriage is abroad now wholly discarded, and two shields are invariably made use of. These shields are placed side by side, the dexter shield being used to display the man's arms and the sinister those of the woman's family. The shields are tilted towards each other (the position is not quite identical with that which we term accollé). But—and this is a peculiarity practically unknown in England—the German practice invariably reverses the charges upon the dexter shield, so that the charges upon the two shields 'respect' each other. This perhaps can be readily understood by reference to 762 and 763. The former shows the simple arms of

762 *Arms of Hans Wolf von Bibelspurg.*

763 *Arms of Hans Wolf von Bibelspurg and his wife Catherina Waraus married in 1507 at Augsburg.*

764.

765.

766 *Arms of Loschau or Lexaw, of Augsburg.*

767.

768 *Arms of the Elector and Archbishop of Treves.*

Von Bibelspurg, the latter the same coat allied with another. But it should be noted that letters or words, if they appear as charges upon the shield, are not reversed. This reversing of the charges is by no means an uncommon practice in Germany for other purposes. For instance, if the arms of a State are depicted surrounded by the arms of provinces, or if the arms of a reigning Sovereign are grouped within a bordure of the shields of other people, the charges on the shields to the dexter are almost invariably shown in reflection regarding the shield in the centre. This practice, resting only on what may be termed 'heraldic courtesy', dates back to very early times, and is met with even in Rolls of Arms where the shields are all turned to face the centre. Such a system was adopted in Siebmacher's *Book of Arms*. But what the true position of the charges should be when represented upon a simple shield should be determined by the position of the helmet. It may be of interest to state that in St George's Chapel of Windsor the early Stall plates as originally set up were all disposed so that helmets and charges alike faced the High Altar.

The conjunction of three coats of arms in Germany is effected as shown in 764. Although matrimonial alliance does not in Germany entail the conjunction of different coats of arms on one shield, such conjunction does occur in German heraldry, but it is comparable (in its meaning) with our rules of quartering and not with our rules of impalement. No such exact and definite rules exist in that country as are to be met with in our own to determine the choice of a method of conjunction, nor to indicate the significance to be presumed from whatever method may be found in use. Personal selection and the adaptability to any particular method of the tinctures and the charges themselves of the coats to be conjoined seem to be the determining factors, and the existing territorial attributes of German armory have a greater weight in marshalling than the principle of heirship which is now practically the sole governing factor in British heraldry. One must therefore content oneself with a brief recital of some of the various modes of conjunction which have been or are still practised. These include impalement per pale or per fess (765) and dimidiation (766), which is more usual on the Continent than it ever was in these kingdoms. The subdivision of the field, as with ourselves, is most frequently adopted; though we are usually confined to quartering, German armory knows no such restrictions. The most usual subdivisions are as given in 767. The ordinary quartered shield is met with in 768, which represents the arms of James III, von Eltz, Elector and Archbishop of Treves (1567–81), in which his personal arms of Eltz ('Per fess gules and argent, in chief a demi-lion issuing or') are quartered with the impersonal arms of his

429

769.

770.

771.

archbishopric, 'Argent, a cross gules.' Another method of conjunction is super-imposition, by which the design of the one shield takes the form of an ordinary imposed upon the other (769). A curious method of conjoining three coats is by engrafting the third in base (770). The constant use of the inescutcheon has been already referred to, and even early English armory (706 and 710) has examples of the widespread Continental practice (which obtains largely in Spanish and Portuguese heraldry) of surrounding one coat with a bordure of another.

The German method of conjunction by incorporation has been frequently pleaded in British heraldry, in efforts to account for ancient arms, but with us (save for occasional use for cadency differencing at an early and for a limited period) such incorporation only results in and signifies an originally *new* coat, and not an authorised marshalling of existing arms of prior origin and authority. The German method can best be explained by two examples. Let us suppose a coat 'per fess argent and gules', with which another coat 'gules, a fleur-de-lis argent', is to be marshalled. The result would be 'per fess argent and gules, a fleur-de-lis counter-changed'. With smaller objects a more usual method would duplicate the charges, thus 'per bend argent and azure', and 'argent, a star of six points azure' would result in 'per bend argent and azure, two stars of six points counterchanged' (771).

34 · The armorial insignia of knighthood

It hardly falls within the scope of the present work to detail or discuss the various points concerning the history or statutes of the different British Orders of Knighthood, and still less so of the Foreign Orders. The history of the English Orders alone would make a bulky volume. But it is necessary to treat of the matter to some limited extent, inasmuch as in modern heraldry in every country in Europe additions are made to the armorial achievement whenever it is desired to signify rank in any of the Orders of Knighthood.

Though a large numbers of the early Plantagenet Garter Stall plates date as far back as the year 1420, it is evident that nothing in the armorial bearings with which they are emblazoned bears any relation to the order of knighthood to which they belonged until the year 1469 or thereabouts, when Charles the Bold, Duke of Burgundy, was elected a Knight of the Garter. His Stall plate, which is of a very exceptional style and character, is the first to bear the garter encircling the shield. It is curious to notice, by the way, that upon the privy seal of the Duke of Burgundy, which shows the same arms depicted upon his Garter plate, the shield is surrounded by the collar, from which depends the badge of the Order of the Golden Fleece, so that it is highly probable that the custom of adding marks of knighthood to a shield came to us from the Continent. The next Garter plate, which shows the garter around the shield, is that of Viscount Lovel, who was elected in 1483; and the shield of the Earl of Derby, who was elected in the same year, also is encircled by the Garter. The Garter itself encircling the shields of knights of that order remained the only mark of knighthood used armorially in this country for a considerable period, though we find that the example was copied in Scotland soon afterwards with regard to the Order of the Thistle. At the commencement of the present Lyon Register, which dates from the year 1672, the arms of the King of Scotland, which are given as such and not as the King of England and Scotland, are described as encircled by the collar of the Order of the Thistle. This probably was used as the equivalent of the garter in England, for we do not find the collar of the Garter, together with the garter itself, or the ribbon circle of the Thistle, together with the collar of that order, until a much later period. The use of collars of knighthood upon the Continent to encircle coats of arms has been from the fifteenth century very general and extensive; examples are to be found at an earlier date; but the encircling of arms with the garter carrying the motto of the order, or with the ribbon (which is termed the circle) and motto of any other order is an entirely English practice, which does not appear to have been copied in any other country. It, of course, arose from the fact that the actual garter as worn by the knight of the order carried the motto of the order, and that by representing the garter round the shield, the motto of the order was of necessity also added. The Lyon Register, however, in the entry of record (dated 1672), states that the shield is 'encircled with the Order of Scotland, the same being composed of rue and thistles having the image of St Andrew with his crosse on his brest y'unto pendent', and it is by no means improbable that occasional instances of the heraldic use of the collar of the garter might be discovered at the same period. But it is not until the later part of the eighteenth century that it obtained anything like a regular use.

During the Hanoverian period it became customary to encircle the shield first with the garter, and that in its turn with the collar of the order whenever it was desired to display the achievement in its most complete style; and though even then, as at the present day, for less elaborate representations the garter only was used without the collar, it still remains correct to display both in a full emblazonment of the arms. An impetus to the practice was doubtless given by the sub-division of the Order of the Bath, which will be presently referred to. In speaking of the garter, the opportunity should be taken to protest strongly against the objectionable practice which has arisen of using a garter to encircle a crest or shield and to carry the family motto. No matter what motto is placed upon the garter, it is both bad form and absolutely incorrect for any one who is not a Knight of the Garter to use a garter in any heraldic display.[243]

But to tabulate the existing practice, the present rules as to the display of the arms of knights of the different orders are as follows:

A Knight of the Most Noble Order of the Garter encircles his escutcheon by a representation of the garter he wears. This is a belt of dark blue velvet edged with gold and ornamented with a heavy gold buckle and ornament at the end. It carries the motto of the Order, 'Honi soit qui mal y pense', in gold letters of plain Roman character. Anciently the motto was spelled 'Hony soit qy mal y pense', as may be noticed from some of the early Garter plates, and the style of the letter was what is now known as 'Old English'. The garter is worn buckled, with the end tucked under and looped in a specified manner, which is the method also adopted in heraldic representations. It is quite permissible to use the garter alone, but a Knight of the Order is allowed to add outside the garter the representation of the collar of the order. This is of gold, consisting of twenty-six buckled garters enamelled in the correct colour, each surrounding a rose, the garter alternated with gold knots all joined up by chain links of gold. From the collar depends the 'George', or figure of St George on horseback encountering the dragon, enamelled in colours. In heraldic representations it is usual to ignore the specified number of links in the collar. A Knight of the Garter as such is entitled to claim the privilege of a grant of supporters, but as nowadays the order is reserved for those of the

---

243. It may be bad form to encircle the crest with a 'garter' carrying the motto, but I doubt if it is 'absolutely incorrect', particularly in view of an accepted Scottish custom; for in Scotland Lord Lyon King of Arms allows clansmen to use the chief's crest within a 'belt and buckle' inscribed with the motto. The widespread use of these 'garters' throughout the United Kingdom suggests that there is nothing too heinously wrong with it.

rank of earl and upwards, supporters will always have a prior existence in connection with the peerage.[244]

Knights of the Most Ancient and Most Noble Order of the Thistle are entitled to surround their arms with a plain circle of green edged with gold and bearing the motto in gold letters, 'Nemo me impune lacessit.' They are also entitled to surround their arms with the collar of the order, which is of gold, and composed of sprigs of thistle and rue (Andrew) enamelled in their proper colours. From the collar the badge (the figure of St Andrew) depends.

Knights of the Most Illustrious Order of St Patrick are entitled to surround their arms by a plain circle of sky-blue edged with gold, bearing the motto, 'Quis Separabit. MDCCLXXXIII', as enamelled on the star of the order. This is encircled by the collar of the order, which is of 'gold, composed of roses and harps alternately, tied together with knots of gold, the said roses enamelled alternately, white leaves within red and red leaves within white; and in the centre of the said collar shall be an Imperial crown surmounting a harp of gold, from which shall hang the badge'.[245]

Knights of the Thistle and St Patrick are entitled as such to claim a grant of supporters on payment of the fees, but these orders are nowadays confined to peers.

The Most Honourable Order of the Bath. Knights of the Bath, who have existed from a remote period, do not appear as such to have made any additions to their arms prior to the revival of the order in 1725. At that time, similarly to the Orders of the Garter and the Thistle, the order was of one class only and composed of a limited number of knights. Knights of that order were then distinguished by the letters K.B., which, it should be noted, mean Knight of the Bath, and not Knight Bachelor, as so many people now imagine. There is nobody at the present time who is entitled to use these letters. Upon those of the Bath plates which now remain in the chapel of Henry VII in Westminster Abbey, no instance will be found in which the collar is represented outside the circle, which is pretty good evidence that although isolated examples may possibly be found at an earlier date, it was not the usual custom up to the end of the eighteenth century to encircle a shield with a collar of knighthood. These Knights of the Bath (K.B.), as they were termed, surrounded their escutcheons with circlets of crimson edged with gold, and bearing thereupon the motto of the order, 'Tria juncta in uno', in gold letters.

Although at that time it does not appear that the collar of the order was ever employed for armorial purposes, instances are to be found in which the laurel wreath surrounded the circlet with the motto of the order.

In the year 1815, owing to the large number of officers who had merited reward in the Peninsular Campaign, it was considered necessary to largely increase the extent and scope of the order. For this purpose it was divided into two Divi-

244. This is not now true. Sir Austen Chamberlain, who became a Knight of the Garter in 1925, was never a peer; but he had a grant of supporters on 30 January 1926, at the same time as arms were granted to him and his descendants and to the other descendants of his late grandfather Joseph Chamberlain. The arms granted were: gules, a key in bend between two lions rampant or. Crest: issuant from the battlements of a tower a demi-lion proper, holding between its paws a key erect or. Supporters: on either side a dove proper, charged on the breast with a key erect, ward inwards or.
245. The Order of St Patrick is obsolescent. Apart from the Sovereign, the only knights left are the Dukes of Windsor and Gloucester.

sions—the Military Division and the Civil Division—and each of these were divided into three classes, namely, Knights Grand Cross (G.C.B.), Knights Commanders (K.C.B.), and Companions (C.B.). The then existing Knights of the Bath became Knights Grand Cross. The existing collar served for all Knights Grand Cross, but the old badge and star were assigned for the civil division of the order, a new pattern being designed for the military division. The number of stalls in Henry VII's Chapel being limited, the erection of Stall plates and the display of banners ceased; those then in position were allowed to remain, and remained there until the present century, when it was decided to erect the plates, banners, and crests of the Knights Grand Cross by seniority. A Knight Grand Cross of the Order of the Bath surrounds his arms with the circlet as was theretofore the case, and in addition he surrounds the circlet by his collar, from which depends the badge (either military or civil) of the division to which he belongs. The collar is really for practical purposes the distinguishing mark of a Knight Grand Cross, because although as such he is entitled upon payment of the fees to claim a grant of supporters, he is under no compulsion to do so, and comparatively few avail themselves of the privilege. All Knights of the Bath, before the enlargement of the order, had supporters. A Knight Grand Cross of the military division encircles his arms with the laurel wreath in addition, this being placed outside the circlet and within the collar of the order. The collar is composed of gold having nine Imperial crowns and eight devices of the rose, the thistle, and shamrock issuing from a sceptre placed alternately and enamelled in their proper colours, the links being connected with seventeen knots enamelled white. The badges of the military and civil divisions differ considerably.

Knights Commanders of the Bath have no collar and cannot claim a grant of supporters, but they encircle their shields with the circlet of the order, suspending their badge below the shield by the ribbon from which it is worn. Knights Commanders of the military division use the laurel wreath as do Knights Grand Cross, but no members of any class of the civil division are entitled to display it.

Companions of the order (C.B.) do not use the helmet of a knight as does a G.C.B. or a K.C.B.; in fact, the only difference which is permissible in their arms from those of an undistinguished commoner is that they are allowed to suspend the badge of a C.B. from a ribbon below their shields. They do not use the circlet of the order. Certain cases have come under my notice in which a military C.B. has added a laurel wreath to his armorial bearings, but whether such a practice is correct I am unaware, but I think it is not officially recognised.[246]

The Most Exalted Order of the Star of India (like the Order of the Bath as at present constituted) is divided into three classes, Knights Grand Commanders, Knights Commanders, and Companions. Knights Grand Commanders place the circlet of the order around their shields. This is of light blue inscribed with the motto, 'Heaven's light our guide'. This in its turn is surrounded by the collar of the order, which is composed of alternate links of the Indian lotus flower, crossed palm-branches, and the united red and white rose of England. In the centre of the

246. Companions of the Order of the Bath may place the circlet of the order round the shield of their arms and suspend the badge beneath it. In the military division the circlet is enclosed by two branches of laurel enamelled in colour issuing from a blue scroll bearing the words *Ich Dien* in gold.

434

collar is an Imperial crown from which depends the badge of the order, this being an onyx cameo of the effigy of Queen Victoria within the motto of the order, and surmounted by a star, the whole being richly jewelled. The surrounding of the shield by the circlet of the order doubtless is a consequence and follows upon the original custom of the armorial use of the garter, but this being admitted, it is yet permissible to state that that practice came from the Continent, and there is little reason to doubt that the real meaning and origin of the custom of using the circlet is derived from the Continental practice which has for long been usual of displaying the shield of arms upon the star of an order of knighthood. The star of every British order—the Garter included—contains the circlet and motto of the order, and it is easy to see how, after depicting the shield of arms upon the star of the order, the result will be that the circlet of the order surrounds the shield. No armorial warrant upon the point is ever issued at the creation of an order; the thing follows as a matter of course, the circlet being taken from the star to surround the shield without further authorisation. Upon this point there can be no doubt, inasmuch as the garter which surrounds the shield of a K.G. is in *all* authoritative heraldic paintings buckled in the peculiar manner in which it is worn and in which it is depicted upon the star. The Star of the Thistle shows the plain circlet, the Star of St Patrick the same, and the arms of a Knight of St Patrick afford a curious confirmation of my contention, because whilst the motto of the order is specified to be, 'Quis separabit', the circlet used for armorial purposes includes the date (MDCCLXXXIII) as shown upon the star. The Order of the Bath, again, has a plain circlet upon the star, and the badges and stars of the military knights have the laurel wreath represented in heraldic drawings, the laurel wreath being absent from the stars and the shields of those who are members of the civil division. Now with regard to the Order of the Star of India the motto on the star is carried upon a representation of a ribbon which is tied in a curious manner, and my own opinion is that the circlet used to surround the shield of a G.C.S.I. or K.C.S.I. should (as in the case of the Garter) be represented not as a simple circlet like the Bath or Thistle, but as a ribbon tied in the curious manner represented upon the star. This tying is not, however, duplicated upon the badge, and possibly I may be told that the circlet and its use are taken from the badge and not from the star. The reply to such a statement is, first, that there is no garter upon the badge of that order, there is no circlet on the badge of the Thistle, and the circlet on the badge of St Patrick is surrounded by a wreath of trefoils which in that case ought to appear round the shield of a K.P. This wreath of trefoils is absent from the K.P. star. Further, no Companion of an Order is permitted to use the Circlet of the Order, whilst every Companion has his badge. No Companion has a star. Though I hold strongly that the circlet of the Star of India should be a ribbon tied as represented on the star of the order, I must admit I have never yet come across an official instance of it being so represented. This, however, is a point upon which there is no definite warrant of instruction, and is not the conclusion justifiable that on this matter the officers of arms have been led into a mistake in their general practice by an oversight and possible unfamiliarity with the actual star?[247] A Knight Grand Commander is entitled to claim a grant of

247. As this order is obsolescent, no appointments to it having been made since 1947, this problem need not be explored here.

supporters on payment of the fees. A Knight Commander encircles his shield with the circlet of the order and hangs his badge from a ribbon below, a Companion or the Order simply hangs the badge he wears below his shield.

The Most Distinguished Order of St Michael and St George. This order again is divided into three classes—Knights Grand Cross, Knights Commanders, and Companions. Knights Grand Cross place the circlet of the order and the collar with the badge around their shields, and, like other Knights Grand Cross, they are entitled to claim a grant of supporters. The circlet of the order is of blue edged with gold, and bearing in gold letters the motto of the order, 'Auspicium melioris ævi'. The collar is composed alternately of lions of England, of Maltese crosses, and of the ciphers S.M. and S.G., and having in the centre an Imperial crown over two lions passant guardant, each holding a bunch of seven arrows. At the opposite point of the collar are two similar lions. The whole is of gold except the crosses, which are of white enamel, and the various devices are linked together by small gold chains. Knights Commanders of the Order encircle their shields with a similar circlet of the order, and hang their badges below. A Companion simply suspends his badge from a ribbon below his shield.[248]

The Most Eminent Order of the Indian Empire. This order is divided into three classes—Knights Grand Commanders, Knights Commanders, and Companions. Knights Grand Commanders and Knights Commanders encircle their shields with the circlet of the order, which is of purple inscribed in letters of gold, with the motto of the order, 'Imperatricis auspiciis'. The collar of the order, which is used by the Knights Grand Commanders, in addition to the circle, is composed of elephants, lotus flowers, peacocks in their pride, and Indian roses, and in the centre is an Imperial crown, the whole being linked together by chains of gold. Knights Commanders suspend their badges from their shields. Companions are only permitted to suspend their badges from a ribbon, and, as in the cases of the other orders, are not allowed to make use of the circlet of the order.[249]

The Royal Victorian Order is divided into five classes. Knights Grand Cross surround their shields with the collar and the circlet of the order, which is of dark blue carrying in letters of gold the motto, 'Victoria'. Knights Commanders and Commanders also use the circlet, with the badge suspended from the ribbon. Members of the fourth and fifth classes of the Order suspend the badge which they are entitled to wear below their shields. The 'Victorian Chain' is quite apart from the Victorian Order, and up to the present time has only been conferred upon a very limited number. It apparently exists by the pleasure of the Sovereign, no statutes having been ordained.

The Order of the British Empire follows the same rules. It was instituted in 1917. There are already 26,257 members of the Order. The population of the United Kingdom is somewhere about forty-six millions.[250]

248. According to the latest statues of this order, Companions may place the circlet with motto round the shield of their arms and suspend the badge from a riband beneath it.
249. Like the Order of the Star of India, no appointments have been made to this order since 1947.
250. Although the rules regarding the display of insignia by those belonging to the Order of the British Empire are the same as those which apply to the Royal Victorian Order, the last two classes are differently designated. The fourth class is called Officer, rather than Member of the fourth class, and the fifth class is simply styled Member. There are both Civil and Military divisions,

PLATE XI

Standard of Vickers

Standard of Noble

Standard of Britton

Standard of Scott-Gatty

The Distinguished Service Order, the Imperial Service Order, and the Order of Merit are each of but one class only, none of them conferring the dignity of knighthood. They rank heraldically with the Companions of the other Orders, and for heraldic purposes merely confer upon those people entitled to the decorations the right to suspend the badges they wear below their shields or lozenges, as the case may be, following the rules observed by other Companions. The Victoria Cross, the Albert Medal, the Edward Medal, the Conspicuous Service Cross, the Order of Merit, the Companions of Honour, the Imperial Service Order, the Distinguished Service Cross, the Order of Victoria and Albert, the Flying Cross, the Police Medal, the Special Constabulary Medal, the Kaisar-i-Hind Medal, the Royal Red Cross, the Volunteer Officers' Decoration, the Territorial Decoration, and the Decoration of the League of Mercy all rank as decorations. Though none confer any style or precedence of knighthood, those entitled to them are permitted to suspend representations of such decorations as are enjoyed below their shields.

The members of the Orders of Victoria and Albert and of the Crown of India are permitted to display the badges they wear below their lozenges.[251]

Some people, notably in the early part of the nineteenth century, adopted the practice of placing war medals below the escutcheons amongst other decorations. It is doubtful, however, how far this practice is correct, inasmuch as a medal does not technically rank as a decoration or as a matter of honour. That medals are 'decorations' is not officially recognised, with the exception, perhaps, of the Jubilee Medal, the Diamond Jubilee Medal, and the Coronation medals, which have been given a status more of the character of a decoration than of simple medals.

The Order of the Hospital of St John of Jerusalem in England does not rank with other orders or decorations, inasmuch as it was initiated without Royal intervention, and carries no precedence or titular rank. In 1888, however, a Royal charter of incorporation was obtained, and the distribution of the highest offices of the order in the persons of the Sovereign, the Prince of Wales, and other members of the Royal Family has of late years very much increased its social status. The Order is, however, now recognised to a certain extent, and its insignia is worn at Court by duly appointed authority. The Crown is gradually acquiring a right of veto, which will probably eventually result in the order becoming a recognised honour, of which the gift lies with the Crown. In the charter of incorporation, Knights of Justice and Ladies of Justice were permitted to place as a chief over their arms the augmentation anciently used by knights of the English language of the original Roman Catholic Celibate Order. The chief used is: 'Gules, charged with a cross throughout argent, the cross embellished in its

the only difference in their insignia being in the ribbon: that of the Civil division is of rose pink edged with a pearl grey stripe; a like vertical stripe down the centre of the ribbon distinguishes the Military division. There is also a Military and Civil medal connected with the Order, called the British Empire Medal.

251. To this list should be added the George Cross (instituted 23 September 1940), the Military Cross (28 December 1914), the Distinguished Flying Cross (3 June 1918), and the Air Force Cross (3 June 1918). The Kaisar-i-Hind Medal has not been awarded since 1947, and the last appointment to the Imperial Order of the Crown of India was made in 1948.

angles with lions passant guardant and unicorns passant alternately both or', as in the cross of the order. The omission, which is all the more inexplicable owing to the fact that Garter King of Arms is the officer for the order, that the heraldic provisions of this charter have never been conveyed, as should have been the case, in a Royal Warrant to the Earl Marshal, has caused some confusion, for the officers of the College of Arms, when speaking officially, decline to admit the insignia of the order in any official emblazonment of arms. Lyon King of Arms has been less punctilious.

Knights of Justice, Knights of Grace, and Esquires of the Order all suspend the badges they wear from a black watered-silk ribbon below their shields and Ladies of Justice and Ladies of Grace do the same below their lozenges. The arms of members of the Order are frequently depicted superimposed upon the Cross. By the Statutes of the Order Knights of Justice were required to show that all their four grandparents were legally entitled to bear arms, but so many provisions for the exercise of discretion in dispensing with this requirement were at the same time created that to all intents and purposes such a regulation might never have been included. Some of the Knights of Justice even yet have no arms at all, others are themselves grantees, and still others would be unable to show what is required of them if the claims of their grandparents were properly investigated.[252]

It should perhaps be stated that supporters, when granted to Knights Grand Cross of any order as such, are personal to themselves, and in the patents by which they are granted the grant is made for life only, no hereditary limitation being added.[253]

Any person in this country holding a Royal Licence to wear the insignia of any foreign order is permitted to adopt any heraldic form, decoration, or display

252. The style or title of this order is now 'The Grand Priory in the British Realm of the Most Venerable Order of the Hospital of St John of Jerusalem'. Regulations have been laid down for the use of the insignia of the order in connection with arms, and these are listed in the schedule attached to the Royal charters of 15 March 1955 and 14 November 1958. The regulations are as follows: 1. Bailiffs and Dames Grand Cross may be granted supporters, use a chief of the arms of the order (see below), and place their shield or lozenge on the badge of the order (the eight-pointed star with the lions and unicorns in the four principal angles). 2. Knights and Ladies of Justice who held their grade before the Royal Charter of 12 June 1926 may continue to use a chief of the arms of the order. 3. Knights and Dames, either of Justice or of Grace, and Chaplains may display their arms on the Badge of the Order. 4. All members of the order of any grade may suspend from their arms the riband and badge of their grade. By Royal Warrant dated 1 February 1926 the following arms were assigned to the order: gules, a cross argent, in the first quarter a representation of the Sovereign's crest. To become a Knight or Dame of Justice rather than of Grace, a person must satisfy the genealogist of the Grand Priory or of the Priory of Scotland that he or she is entitled to bear arms.

253. This also applies to life peers and peeresses who are granted supporters. By the provisions of the Peerage Act 1963 a peer may, in certain circumstances, disclaim his peerage for life. Such a disclaimer, which is irrevocable, has the effect of divesting the peer, and if he be married, his wife, of 'all right or interest to or in the peerage, and all titles, rights, offices, privileges and precedence attaching thereto'. Also it relieves him of all obligations and disabilities arising therefrom. Armorial bearings are not specifically referred to in the Act, but the insignia of peerage, including supporters, may be construed as being privileges of peerage and are therefore forfeited. The status of the children of a peer who has disclaimed is nowhere mentioned in the Act, but the Earl Marshal and his officers and Lord Lyon King of Arms will accord such children their courtesy titles and presumably also their precedence.

438

which that order confers in the country of origin. Official recognition exists for this, and many precedents can be quoted.

The rules which exist in foreign countries concerning heraldic privileges of the knights of different orders are very varied, and it is impossible to briefly summarise them. It may, however, be stated that the most usual practice is to display the shield alone in the centre of the star (772). As with us, the collars of the orders are placed around the shields, and the badges depend below, but the use of the circlet carrying the motto of the order is exclusively a British practice. In the case of some of the Orders, however, the official coat of arms of the order is quartered, impaled, or borne in pretence with the personal arms, and the cross patée of the Order of the Dannebrog is to be met with placed in front of a shield of quarterings, the charges thereupon appearing in the angles of the cross. I am not sure, however, that the cases which have come under my notice should not be rather considered definite and hereditary grants of augmentation, this being perhaps a more probable explanation than that such a method of display followed as a matter of course on promotion to the order. The Grand Masters of the Teutonic Order quarter the arms of that order with those of their families. The Knights of the Order of St Stephen of Tuscany bear the arms of that order in chief over their personal arms. 772 represents the manner in which a 'Bailli-profès' (Grand Cross) of the real Catholic and Celibate Order of St John of Malta places the chief of the order on his shield, the latter being imposed upon a Maltese star (this being white) and the badge of the order depending below. The 'Knight-profès' does not use the chief of the order.[254] In the German Protestant Order of Malta (formerly Bailiwick of Brandenburg) the Commendatores place the shield of their arms upon the Cross of Malta. The Knights of Justice ('Richtsritter') on the contrary assume the cross upon the shield itself, whilst the Knights of Grace suspend it from the bottom of the shield. The members of the ancient Order of La Cordelière formerly encircled their lozenges with a representation of the Cordelière, which formed a part of their habit; and the officers of the Ecclesiastical Orders frequently surround their escutcheons with rosaries from which depend crucifixes. Whether this latter practice, however, should be considered merely a piece of artistic decoration, or whether it should be regarded as an ecclesiastical matter or should be included within the purview of armory, I leave others to decide.

By a curious fiction, for the origin of which it is not easy to definitely account, unless it is a survival of the celibacy required in certain orders, a knight is not supposed to share the insignia of any order of knighthood with his wife. There is not the slightest doubt that his own knighthood does confer upon her both precedence and titular rank, and why there should be any necessity for the statement to be made as to the theoretical position has long been a puzzle to me. Such a theory, however, is considered to be correct, and as a consequence in modern

772 'Bailli-profès' of the Catholic Order of the Knights Hospitallers or the Order of Malta.

254. There have been considerable changes in the Sovereign Military Order of St John of Jerusalem of Rhodes and of Malta since this was written but, as the Order is not officially recognised in this country, it would be pointless to detail the present grades and the armorial insignia they may use. However, it was and is misleading to refer to the Order as the 'Catholic and Celibate Order'. Catholic it certainly is, but not celibate; only a few of the knights are professed, taking the vows of poverty, chastity and obedience.

times it has become a rigid rule that the arms of the wife of a knight must not be impaled upon a shield when it is displayed within the circlet of an order. No such rule existed in ancient times, and many instances can be found in which impaled shields, or the shield of the wife only, are met with inside a representation of the Garter. In the warrant issued for Queen Alexandra the arms of England and Denmark were impaled within a Garter. This may have been quite exceptional and consequent upon the fact that Her Majesty was herself a member of the Order. The same precedent was followed for Queen Mary. Nevertheless, the modern idea is that when a Knight of any Order impales the arms of his wife, he must use two shields placed accollé, the dexter surmounting the sinister (745). Upon the dexter shield is represented the arms of the knight within the circlet, or the circlet and collar, as the case may be, of his Order; on the sinister shield the arms of the knight are impaled with those of his wife, and this shield, for the purpose of artistic balance, is usually surrounded with a meaningless and inartistic floral or laurel wreath to make its size similar to the dimensions of the dexter shield.

The widow of a knight of any Order is required at present to immediately discontinue the use of the ensigns of that Order, and to revert to the plain impaled lozenge which she would be entitled to as the widow of an undecorated gentleman. As she retains her titular rank, such a regulation seems absurd, but it undoubtedly exists, and until it is altered must be conformed to.

Knights Grand Cross and Knights Commanders, as also Knights Bachelors, use the open affronté helmet of a knight. Companions of any order, and members of those orders which do not confer any precedence or title of knighthood, use only the close profile helmet of a gentleman. A Knight Bachelor, of course, is at liberty to impale the arms of his wife upon his escutcheon without employing the double form. It only makes the use of the double escutcheon for Knights of Orders the more incomprehensible.

Reference should also be made to the subject of impalement, which will be found in the chapter upon Marshalling.

35 · The armorial bearings of a lady

Bearing in mind that armory was so deeply interwoven with all that was best in chivalry, it is curious that the armorial status of a woman should have been left so undefined. A query as to how a lady may bear arms will be glibly answered for her as maid (749) and as widow (750, 751, and 752) by the most elementary heraldic text-book. But a little consideration will show how far short our knowledge falls of a complete or uniform set of rules.

Let what is definitely known be first stated. In the first place, no woman (save a Sovereign) can inherit, use, or transmit crest or motto, nor may she use a helmet or mantling. All daughters, if unmarried, bear *upon a lozenge* the paternal arms and quarterings of their father, with his difference marks. If their mother were an heiress, they quarter her arms with those of her father. In England (save in the Royal Family, and in this case even it is a matter of presumption only) there is no seniority amongst daughters, and the difference marks of all daughters are those borne by the father, and none other. There are no marks of distinction as between the daughters themselves. In Scotland, however, seniority does exist, according to priority of birth; and, though Scottish heraldic law provides no marks of cadency as between sister and sister, the laws of arms north of the Tweed recognise seniority of birth in the event of a certain set of circumstances arising.

In Scotland, as doubtless many are aware, certain untitled Scottish families, for reasons which may or may not be known, have been permitted to use supporters to their arms. When the line vests in coheirs, the eldest born daughter, as heir of line, assumes the supporters, unless some other limitation has been attached to them. Scottish supporters are peculiar things to deal with, unless the exact terms of the patent of grant or matriculation are known.

The lozenge of an unmarried lady is frequently surmounted by a true lover's knot of ribbon, usually painted blue (749). It has no particular meaning and no official recognition, though plenty of official use, and practically its status is no more than a piece of supposedly artistic ornament.

Concerning the law for unmarried ladies, therefore, there is neither doubt nor dispute. A widow bears arms upon a lozenge, this showing the arms of her late husband impaled with those of her own family (750), or with these latter displayed on an escutcheon of pretence if she be an heir or coheir (751).

The other state in the progress of life in which a lady may hope or expect to find herself is that of married life. Now, how should a married lady display arms? Echo and the text-books alike answer, 'How?' Does *anybody* know? This 'fault', for such it undoubtedly is, is due to the fact that the laws of arms evolved themselves in that period when a married woman was little accounted of. As an unmarried heiress she undoubtedly was a somebody; as a widowed and richly-jointured dowager she was likewise of account, but as a wedded wife her identity was lost, for the Married Women's Property Act was not in existence, nor was it thought of. So completely was it recognised that all rights and inheritance of the wife devolved of right upon the husband, that formerly the husband enjoyed any peerage honours which had descended to the wife, and was summoned to Parliament as a peer in his wife's peerage. Small wonder, then, that the same ideas dominated the rules of armory. These only provide ways and methods for the husband to bear the wife's arms. This is curious, because there can be no doubt that at a still earlier period the practice of impalement was entirely confined to women, and that, unless the wife happened to be an heiress, the husband did not trouble to impale her arms. But a little thought will show that the two are not at variance, for if monuments and other matters of record are ignored, the earliest examples of impalement which have come down to us are all, almost without exception, examples of arms borne by widows. One cannot get over the fact that a wife during coverture had practically no legal status at all. The rules governing impalement, and the conjunction of the arms of man and wife, as they are to be borne by the husband, are recited in the chapter upon Marshalling, which also details the ways in which a widow bears arms in the different ranks of life. Nothing would be gained by repeating them here.

It may be noted, however, that it is not considered correct for a widow to make use of the true lover's knot of blue ribbon, which is sometimes used in the case of an unmarried lady. A divorce puts matters *in statu quo ante*.

There still remains, however, the question of the bearing of arms in her own right by a married woman under coverture at the present day.

The earliest grant of arms that I can put my hands upon to a woman is one dated 1558.[255] It is, moreover, the only grant of which I know to one single person, that person being a wife. The grant is decidedly interesting, so I print it in full:

'To ALL AND SINGULAR as well kinges heraldes and officers of armes as nobles gentlemen and others which these presents shall see or here Wyllyam Hervye Esquire otherwise called Clarencieux principall heralde and kinge of armes of the south-east and west parties of England fendith due comendacõns and greting. fforasmuch as aunctientlye ffrom the beginnynge the valyant and vertuous actes off excellent parsons have ben comended to the worlde with sondry monumentes and remembrances off theyr good desertes among the which one of the chefist and most usuall hath ben the beringe of figures and tokens in shildes called armes beinge none other thinges then Evidences and demonstracõns of prowes and valoure diverselye distributed accordinge to the quallyties and desertes of the parsons. And for that Dame Marye Mathew daughter and heyre of Thomas Mathew of Colchester in the counte of Essex esquire hath longe contynued in nobylyte she and her auncestors bearinge armes, yet she notwithstandinge being ignorant of the same and ffor the advoydinge of all inconvenyences and troubles that dayleye happeneth in suche cases and not wyllinge to preiudyce anye person hath instantlye requyred me The sayde Clarencieux kinge of armes accordinge to

255. At least one earlier grant to a woman is known to me, namely that made to Annys Samson, 37 Henry VIII. In this grant, as in that to Marye Mathew, the arms are shown on a lozenge.

my registers and recordes To assigne and sett forthe ffor her and her posterite The armes belonging and descendinge To her ffrom her saide auncesters. In consideraçon whereof I have at her ientle request assigned geven and granted unto her and her posterite The owlde and auncient armes of her said auncesters as followeth. That is to saye—partye per cheveron sables and argent a Lyon passant in chefe off the second the poynt goutey* of the firste as more plainly aperith depicted in this margent. Which armes I The Saide Clarencieux kinge of Armes by powre and authorite to myne office annexed and graunted By the Queenes Majesties Letters patentes under The great Seale of England have ratefyed and confirmed and By These presentes do ratefye and confyrme unto and for the saide dame marye Mathew otherwise called dame Mary Jude wiffe to Sir Andrew Jude Knight late Mayor and Alderman off London and to her posterite To use bear and show for evermore in all places of honour to her and theyr wourshipes at theyr Lybertie and pleasur without impediment lett or interupçon of any person or persons.

'IN WITNESS WHEREOF the saide Clarencieux Kinge of Armes have signed these presentes with my hand and sett thereunto The Seale off myne office and The Seale of myne armes geven at London The xth daye off October in the Yeare of owre Lord Godd 1558 and in the ffourth and ffifth yeares off the reignes off owre Souereignes Lorde and Layde Phellip and Marye by the grace of God Kinge and Queene of England france both cycles Jerusalem Irland deffendors of the faythe Archedukes of Austrya Dukes of Burgoyne myllain & braband erles of haspurgie, Flanders and Tyrrell.

'W. HERVEY alṡ CLARENCIEUX
'King of Armes.

'Confirmation of Arms to Dame Mary Mathew, "otherwise called Dame Marye Jude, wyffe to Sir Andrew Jude, Knight, Late Lord Mayor and Alderman off London", 1558.'

In this grant the arms are painted upon a *shield*. The grant was made in her husband's lifetime, but his arms are not impaled therewith. Evidently, therefore, the lady bears arms *in her own right*, and the presumption would seem to be that a married lady bears her arms without reference to her husband, and bears them upon a shield. On the other hand, the grant to Lady Pearce, referred to on an earlier page, whilst not blazoning the Pearce arms, shows the painting upon the patent to have been a lozenge of the arms of Pearce, charged with a baronet's hand impaled with the arms then granted for the maiden name of Lady Pearce. On the other hand, a grant is printed in vol. i of the Notes to the 'Visitation of England and Wales'. The grant is to Dame Judith Diggs, widow of Sir Maurice Diggs, Bart, now wife of Daniel Sheldon, and to Dame Margaret Sheldon, her sister, relict of Sir Joseph Sheldon, Knight, late Alderman, and sometime Lord Mayor of the City of London, daughters and coheirs of Mr George Rose, of Eastergate. The operative clause of the grant is: 'do by these Presents grant and assign to yᵉ said Dame Judith and Dame Margaret the Armes hereafter mentioned Vizᵗ: Ermine, an Eagle displayed Sable, membered and beaked Gules, debruised

* Gutté-de-poix.

with a Bendlet Componè Or and Azure, as in the margin hereof more plainly appears depicted. To be borne and used for ever hereafter by them yᵉ said Dame Judith Diggs and Dame Margaret Sheldon, and the descendants of their bodies respectively, lawfully begotten, according to the Laws, Rules and practice of Armes.'

In each case it will be noted that the sisters were respectively wife and widow of some one of the name of Sheldon; and it might possibly be supposed that these were arms granted for the name of Sheldon. There seems, however, to be very little doubt that these are the arms for Rose. The painting is, however, of the single coat of Rose, and one is puzzled to know why the arms are not painted in conjunction with those of Sheldon. The same practice was followed in the patent which was granted to Nelson's Lady Hamilton. This patent, which both heraldically and historically is excessively interesting, was printed in full on p. 168, vol. i. of the *Genealogical Magazine*. The arms which in the grant are specifically said to be the arms of Lyons (not of Hamilton) are painted upon a lozenge, with no reference to the arms of Hamilton. In each of these cases, however, the grantee of arms has been an heiress, so that the clause by which the arms are limited to the descendants does not help. An instance of a grant to a man and his wife, where the wife was not an heiress, is printed in *The Right to Bear Arms*; and in this case the painting shows the arms impaled with those of the husband. The grant to the wife has no hereditary limitations, and presumably her descendants would never be able to quarter the arms of the wife, no matter even if by the extinction of the other issue she eventually became a coheir. The fact that the arms of man and wife are herein granted together prevents any one making any deduction as to what is the position of the wife alone.

There was a patent issued in the year 1784 to a Mrs Sarah Lax, widow of John Lax, to take the name and arms of Maynard, such name and arms to be borne by herself and her issue. The painting in this case is of the arms of Maynard alone upon a lozenge, and the crest which was to be borne by her male descendants is quite a separate painting in the body of the grant, and not in conjunction with the lozenge. Now, Mrs Maynard was a widow, and it is manifestly wrong that she should bear the arms as if she were unmarried; yet how was she to bear them? She was bearing the name of Lax because that had been her husband's name, and she took the name of Maynard, which presumably her husband would have taken had he been alive; she herself was a Miss Jefferson, so would she have been entitled to have placed the arms of Jefferson upon an escutcheon of pretence, in the centre of the arms of Maynard? Presumably she would, because suppose the husband had assumed the name and arms of Maynard in his lifetime, he certainly would have been entitled to place his wife's arms of Jefferson on an escutcheon of pretence.

On 9 March 1878, Francis Culling Carr, and his second wife, Emily Blanche, daughter of Andrew Morton Carr, and niece of the late Field-Marshal Sir William Maynard Gomm, G.C.B., both assumed by Royal Licence the additional surname and arms of Gomm. Neither Mr nor Mrs Carr-Gomm appear to have had any blood descent from the Gomm family; consequently the Gomm arms were granted to both husband and wife, and the curious part is that they were not identical, the marks (showing that there was no blood relationship) being a canton for the husband and a cross crosslet for the wife. In this case the arms were impaled. One is puzzled to know why the grant to the wife was necessary as well as the grant to the husband.

In 1865 Mrs Massy, widow of Hugh Massy, assumed the name and arms of Richardson in lieu of Massy. Mrs Massy was the only child of Major Richardson Brady, who had previously assumed by Royal Licence the arms of Brady only. The painting upon the patent is a lozenge, bearing the arms of Massy, and upon an escutcheon of pretence the arms of Richardson. Of course, the arms of Mrs Massy, as a widow, previously to the issue of the Royal Licence were a lozenge of the arms of Massy, and on an escutcheon of pretence the arms of Brady.

An interesting Grant of Arms was issued to a Mrs Sharpe, widow of Major Sharpe. The arms were to be borne by herself and the descendants of her late husband, and by the other descendants of her husband's father, so that there is no doubt whatever that these were the arms of Sharpe. I have no idea who Mrs Sharpe was, and I do not know that she possessed any arms of her own. Let us presume she did not. Now, unless a widow may bear the arms of her late husband on a lozenge, whether she has arms to impale with them or not, how on earth is she to bear arms at all? And yet the grant most distinctly was primarily to Mrs Sharpe.

After the death of General Ross, the victor of Bladensburg, a grant of an augmentation was made to be placed upon the monument to the memory of the General (Plate II). The grant also was for the augmentation to be borne by his widow during her widowhood. But no mention appears of the arms of Mrs Ross, nor, as far as I can ascertain, was proof officially made that Mrs Ross was in her own right entitled to arms; consequently, whether she really was or was not, we may assumed that as far as the official authorities officially knew she was not, and the same query formulated with regard to the Sharpe patent holds good in this case. The painting on the patent shows the arms upon a shield, and placed above is a helmet surmounted by the crest of augmentation and the family crest of Ross.

So that from the cases we have mentioned instances can be found of the arms of a wife upon a shield alone, and of a widow having arms depicted upon a lozenge, such arms being on different occasions the impaled arms of her husband and herself, or the arms of herself alone or of her husband alone; and we have arms granted to a wife, and depicted as an impalement or upon a lozenge. So that from grants it seems almost impossible to deduce any decided and unquestionable rule as to how wife or widow should bear a coat of arms. There is, however, one other source from which profitable instruction may be drawn. I refer to the methods of depicting arms upon hatchments, and more particularly to the hatchment of a married woman. Now a hatchment is strictly and purely personal, and in the days when the use of such an article was an everyday matter, the greatest attention was paid to the proper marshalling of the arms thereupon.[256] There are so many varying circumstances that we have here only space to refer to the three simple

256. It is true that great care should have been taken when marshalling arms on hatchments, but, as the marshalling was often in the hands of amateurs, many hatchments are not only wrongly marshalled but, even more frequently, also depict bogus arms. The student of heraldry would be well advised to study hatchments, but not to accept the story they tell as gospel truth until he has substantiated it with evidence culled from a more disinterested source than the relatives of those commemorated.

rules, and these uncomplicated by any exceptional circumstances, which governed the hatchments of maid, wife, and widow. In the first case, the hatchment of an unmarried lady showed the whole of the background black, the paternal arms on a lozenge, and this suspended by a knot of blue ribbon. In the hatchment of a widow the background again was all black, the arms were upon a lozenge (but without the knot of ribbon), and the lozenge showed the arms of husband and wife impaled, or with the wife's in pretence, as circumstances might dictate. The hatchment of a wife was entirely different. Like the foregoing, it was devoid, of course, of helmet, mantling, crest, or motto; but the background was white on the dexter side (to show that the husband was still alive), and black on the sinister (to show the wife was dead). But the impaled arms were not depicted upon a lozenge, but upon a shield, and the shield was surmounted by the true lover's knot of blue ribbon.

I have already stated that when the rules of arms were in the making the possibility of a married woman bearing arms in her own right was quite ignored, and theoretically even now the husband bears his wife's arms for her upon his shield. But the arms of a man are never depicted suspended from a true lover's knot. Such a display is distinctly feminine, and I verily believe that the correct way for a married woman to use arms, if she desires the display thereof to be personal to herself rather than to her husband, is to place her husband's arms impaled with her own upon a shield suspended from a true lover's knot, and without helmet, mantling, crest, or motto. At any rate such a method of display is a correct one; it is in no way open to criticism on the score of inaccuracy, it has precedent in its favour, and it affords a very desirable means of distinction. My only hesitation is that one cannot say it is the only way, or that it would be 'incorrect' for the husband. At any rate it is the only way of drawing a distinction between the 'married' achievements of the husband and the wife.

The limitations attached to a lady's heraldic display being what they are, it has long been felt, and keenly felt, by every one attempting heraldic design, that artistic treatment of a lady's arms savoured almost of the impossible. What delicacy of treatment can possibly be added to the hard outline of the lozenge? The substitution of curvilinear for straight lines in the outline, and even the foliation of the outline, goes but a little way as an equivalent to the extensive artistic opportunities which the mantling affords to a designer when depicting the arms of a man.

To a certain extent, two attempts have been made towards providing a remedy. Neither can properly claim *official* recognition, though both have been employed in a quasi-official manner. The one consists of the knot of ribbon; the other consists of the use of the cordelière. In their present usage the former is meaningless and practically senseless, whilst the use of the latter is radically wrong, and in my opinion, little short of imposture. The knot of ribbon, when employed, is usually in the form of a thin streamer of blue ribbon tied in the conventional true lover's knot (749). But the imbecility and inconsistency of its use lies in the fact that except upon a hatchment it has been denied by custom to married women and widows, who have gained their lovers; whilst its use is sanctioned for the unmarried lady, who, unless she be affianced, neither has nor ought to have anything whatever to do with lovers or with their knot. The women who are fancy-free display the tied-up knot; women whom love has fast tied up, unless the foregoing opinion as to the correct way to display the arms of a married lady which I have expressed be correct, must leave the knot alone. But as matters stand heraldically at the moment the ribbon may be used advantageously with the lozenge of an unmarried lady.

With reference to the cordelière some writers assert that its use is optional, others that its use is confined to widow ladies. Now as a matter of fact it is nothing whatever of the kind. It is really the insignia of the old French Order of the Cordelière, which was founded by Anne of Bretagne, widow of Charles VIII, in 1498, its membership being confined to widow ladies of noble family. The cordelière was the waist girdle which formed a part of the insignia of the Order, and it took its place around the lozenges of the arms of the members in a manner similar to the armorial use of the garter for Knights of that Order. Though the Order of the Cordelière is long since extinct, it is neither right nor proper that any part of its insignia should be adopted unaltered by those who can show no connection with it or membership of it.

36 · Official heraldic insignia

The armory of all other nations than our own is rich in heraldic emblems of office. In France this was particularly the case, and France undoubtedly for many centuries gave the example, to be followed by other civilised countries, in all matters of honour and etiquette.

If English heraldry were entirely destitute of official heraldic ensigns, perhaps the development elsewhere of this branch of armory might be dismissed as an entirely foreign growth. But this is far from being the case, as there are some number of cases in which these official emblems do exist. In England, however, the instances are governed by no scale of comparative importance, and the appearance of such tokens can only be described as capricious. That a more extended usage might with advantage be made no one can deny, for usage of this character would teach the general public that armory had a meaning and a value, it would increase the interest in heraldry, and also assist greatly in the rapidly increasing revival of heraldic knowledge. The existence of these heraldic emblems would manifestly tend towards a revival of the old and interestingly excellent custom of regularly setting up in appropriate public places the arms of those who have successively held various offices. The Inns of Court, St George's Chapel, the Public Office at the College of Arms, and the halls of some of the Livery Companies are amongst the few places of importance where the custom still obtains. And yet what an interesting memorial such a series always becomes! The following list may not be entirely complete, but it is fairly so as far as France is concerned, and I think also complete as to England.

The following are from the Royal French Court:

The High Constable of France: Two swords held on each side of the shield by two hands in armour issuing from the clouds.

The Chancellor: In saltire behind his arms two great maces, and over his helmet a mortier or cap sable crossed by two bands of gold lace and turned up ermine; thereon the figure of a demi-queen as an emblem of France, holding a sceptre in her right hand and the great seal of the kingdom in her left.

The Marshal: Two batons in saltire behind the arms azure, semé-de-lis or.

The Admiral: Two anchors in saltire behind the arms, the stocks of the anchors in chief azure, semé-de-lis or.

The General of the Galleys: Two anchors in saltire behind the arms.

Vice-Admiral: One anchor in pale behind the arms.

Colonel-General of the Infantry: Under his arms in saltire six flags, three on each side, white crimson, and blue.

Colonel of the Cavalry: Over the arms four banners of the arms of France, fringed, &c., two to the dexter and two to the sinister.

Grand Master of the Artillery: Two field-pieces of ordnance under the arms, one pointing to the dexter and one to the sinister.

448

The Superintendent of the Finance: Two keys imperially crowned and endorsed in pale, one on each side of the arms, the dexter or, the sinister-argent.

Grand Master of the Household to the King: Two grand batons of silver gilt in saltire behind the arms.

Grand Almoner: Under his arms a blue book, on the cover the arms of France and Navarre within the Orders of St Michael and the Holy Ghost, over the Orders the Crown.

Grand Chamberlain: Two keys, both imperially crowned or, in saltire behind the arms endorsed, the wards-in-chief.

Grand Esquire: On each side of the shield a royal sword erect, the scabbard azure, semé-de-lis, hilt and pommel or, the belts folded round the scabbard azure, semé-de-lis. or.

Grand Pannetier, who by virtue of his office had all the bakers of Paris under his jurisdiction, and had to lay the king's cover at his table, bore under his arms a rich cover and a knife and fork in saltire.

Grand Butler or Cupbearer: On each side of the base of the shield, a grand silver flagon gilt, with the arms of the King thereon.

Gamekeeper to the King: Two bugle-horns appending from the ends of the mantling.

Grand Falconer: Two lures appending from the ends of the mantling.

Grand Wolf-hunter: On each side of the shield a wolf's head caboshed.

Captain of the King's Guards: Two small batons sable, headed gold, like a walking-cane.

Captain of the Hundred Swiss Guards: Two batons in saltire sable, headed argent, and under the arms two black velvet caps with feathers.

First Master of the Household: Under his arms two batons in saltire.

Grand Carver to His Majesty: Under his arms a knife and fork in saltire proper, the handles azure, semé-de-lis or.

Grand Provost of the Household: Under his arms two Roman fasces or, corded azure.

Grand Quartermaster: A mace and battle-axe in saltire.

Captain of the Guards of the Gate: Two keys in pale, crowned argent, one on each side the arms.

The President of the Parliament: On his helmet a black cap with two bands of gold lace.

Under the Empire (of France) the Vice-Connétable used arms holding swords, as had been the case with the Constable of the Kingdom, but the swords were sheathed and semé of golden bees. The Grand Chamberlain had two golden keys in saltire, the bows thereof enclosing the imperial eagle, and the batons of the Maréchaux de French were semé of bees instead of fleurs-de-lis.

The Pope bears a cross with three arms,[257] an archbishop one with two arms, a bishop one with a single arm. Besides this, two crossed keys appertain to the Pope, the golden key to bind, in bend dexter, the silver key to loose, in sinister bend. British archbishops and bishops will be presently referred to. Ecclesiastical

257. The triple-traversed cross does not form part of the papal insignia. The Pope bears, as stated, the keys in saltire behind his arms. Above is placed the tiara, and anciently also the pavillion or ombrellino.

princes, who were at the same time sovereign territorial princes, bore behind their shield a pendum or pastorale (crosier), crossed with the sword of penal judicature. A bishop bears the crosier with an outward bend, an abbot with an inward bend, thus symbolising the range of their activity or dominion.[258] The arch and hereditary offices of the old German Empire had also their own attributes; thus the 'Erztruchsess', Lord High Steward (Palatinate-Bavaria), bore a golden Imperial globe, which arose from a misinterpretation of the double dish, the original attribute of this dignity. The Lord High Marshal of the Empire (Saxony) expressed his office by a shield divided 'per fess argent and sable', bearing two crossed swords gules. The Hereditary Standard-bearer (Württemberg) bore: 'Azure, a banner or, charged with an eagle sable'; the Lord High Chamberlain (Brandenburg): 'Azure, a sceptre or', while the Hereditary Chamberlain (Hohenzollern) used: 'Gules, two crossed sceptres or'.

In Italy the Duca de Savelli, as Marshal of the Conclave, hangs on either side of his shield a key, the cords of which are knotted beneath his coronet.

In Holland Admirals used the naval Crown, and added two anchors in saltire behind the shield.

In Spain the Admirals of Castile and of the Indies placed an anchor in bend behind the shield.

The instances I am aware of which have official sanction already in this country are as stated in the list which follows:

I have purposely (to make the list absolutely complete) included insignia which may possibly be more properly considered ensigns of rank, because it is not particularly easy always to distinguish offices from honours and from rank.

The Kings of England (George I to William IV), as Arch Treasurers of the Holy Roman Empire, bore: Upon an inescutcheon gules, in the centre of the arms of Hanover, a representation of the Crown of Charlemagne.

An Archbishop has: (1) His official coat of arms, which he impales (placing it on the dexter side) with his personal arms; (2) his mitre, which, it should be noted, is the same as the mitre of a Bishop, and not having a coronet encircling its band; (3) his archiepiscopal staff (of gold, and with two transverse arms), which is placed in pale behind his escutcheon; (4) two crosiers in saltire behind the escutcheon. It is curious to note that the pallium which occurs in all archiepiscopal coats of arms (save that of York) is now very generally conceded to have been more in the nature of an emblem of the rank of Archbishop (it being a part of his ecclesiastical costume) than a charge in a concrete impersonal coat of arms for a defined area of archiepiscopal jurisdiction. In this connection it is interesting to observe that the Archbishops of York anciently used the pallium in lieu of the official arms now regularly employed.

A Bishop has: (1) His official coat of arms, (2) his mitre, (3) two crosiers in saltire behind his escutcheon.[259]

The Bishop of Durham has: (1) His official coat of arms, (2) his coronetted

258. Whilst I am prepared to believe that there may have been a temporary fashion for bending the end of the crozier inwards for an abbot and outwards for a bishop, this custom never appears to have received any form of official sanction, nor was it in any sense an universal practice.

259. For details of the insignia used by Roman Catholic Prelates and clergy see note 271 in chapter 38.

mitre, which is peculiar to himself, and (which is another privilege also peculiar to himself alone) he places a *sword* and a crosier in saltire behind his arms. Reference should also be made to the chapter upon Ecclesiastical Heraldry.

A Peer has: (1) His coronet, (2) his helmet of rank, (3) his supporters, (4) his robe of estate.[260]

A Scottish Peer has, in addition, the ermine lining to his mantling.

A Baronet of England, of Ireland, or Great Britain, or of the United Kingdom has: (1) His helmet of rank, (2) his badge of Ulster upon an inescutcheon or canton (argent, a sinister hand erect, couped at the wrist gules).

A Baronet of Nova Scotia has: (1) His helmet of rank, (2) his badge (an orange tawny ribbon, whereon shall hang pendent in an escutcheon argent, a saltire azure, thereon an inescutcheon of the arms of Scotland, with an imperial crown over the escutcheon, and encircled with this motto, 'Fax Mentis Honestæ Gloria', pendent below the escutcheon).

A Knight of the Garter has: (1) His Garter to encircle the shield, (2) his collar and badge, (3) supporters. The Prelate of the Order of the Garter (an office held by the Bishops of Winchester) is entitled to encircle his arms with the Garter. The Chancellor of the Order of the Garter encircles his arms with the Garter. Formerly the Bishops of Salisbury always held this office, but in 1836 when the county of Berks (which of course includes Windsor, and therefore the chapel of the order) was removed from the Diocese of Salisbury to the Diocese of Oxford, the office of Chancellor passed to the Bishops of Oxford.[261] The Dean of Windsor, as Registrar of the Order, displays below his shield the ribbon and badge of his office.

A Knight of the Thistle has: (1) The ribbon or circlet of the order, (2) his collar and badge, (3) supporters. The Dean of the Chapels Royal in Scotland, as Dean of the Order, used the badge and ribbon of his office.

A Knight of St Patrick has: (1) The ribbon or circlet of the order, (2) his collar and badge, (3) supporters. The Prelate of the Order of St Patrick was as such entitled to encircle his escutcheon with the ribbon or circlet of that order, from which his official badge depends. The office, of course, came to an end with the disestablishment of the Irish Church. It was held by the Archbishops of Armagh. The Chancellor of the Order of St Patrick is as such entitled to encircle his escutcheon with the ribbon or circlet of that order, from which his official badge depends. This office, formerly held by the Archbishops of Dublin, has since the disestablishment been enjoyed by the Chief Secretaries for Ireland. The Deans of St Patrick's were similarly Registrars of the Order, and as such used the badge and ribbon of their office.

Knights Grand Cross or *Knights Grand Commanders* of the Orders of the Bath, the Star of India, St Michael and St George, the Indian Empire, or the Victorian Order, have: (1) The circlets or ribbons of their respective Orders, (2) their

---

260. As has been noted elsewhere, the peer's robe of estate does not normally form part of his full achievement, although it is sometimes used in Scotland and there are isolated examples in English grants of arms.

261. The Chancellor of the Order of the Garter is no longer an ecclesiastic, but one of the Knights. The present Chancellor is the Marquess of Salisbury, K.G.

collars and badges, (3) their helmets of degree, (4) supporters, if they incline to pay the fees for these to be granted.[262]

Knights Commanders of the aforesaid Orders have: (1) The circlets or ribbons of their respective Orders, (2) their badges pendent below the shield, (3) their helmets of degree.

Commanders of the Victorian Order have: (1) The circlet of the Order, (2) the badge pendent below the shield.

Companions of the aforesaid Order, and Members of the Victorian Order, as also Members of the Distinguished Service Order, the Imperial Service Order, the Order of Merit, the Order of Victoria and Albert, the Order of the Crown of India, and those entitled to the Victoria Cross, the Albert Medal, the Edward Medal, the Conspicuous Service Cross, the Kaiser-i-Hind Medal, the Royal Red Cross, the Volunteer Officers' Decoration, the Territorial Decoration, and the Decoration of the League of Mercy, are entitled to suspend their respective decorations below their escutcheons. The officers of these orders of knighthood are of course entitled to display their badges of office. The Dean of Westminster is always Dean of the Order of the Bath.

Knights Grand Cross and *Knights Commanders of the Bath*, if of the Military Division, are also entitled to place a wreath of laurel round their escutcheons.

Knights of Justice of the Order of the Hospital of St John of Jerusalem in England are entitled to place upon their escutcheons a chief of the arms of the Order (gules, a cross throughout argent, embellished in the angles with a lion guardant and a unicorn, both passant or).

Knights of Grace and other Members of the Order suspend whatever badge they are entitled to wear below their shield from a black watered-silk ribbon.

(Some members of the Order display their arms upon the Cross of the Order, as was done by Knights of the original Order, from which the present Order is copied, but how far the practice is sanctioned by the Royal Charter, or in what manner it is controlled by the rules of the Order, I am not aware.)

The Lord High Constable of England is entitled to place behind his escutcheon two batons in saltire similar to the one which is delivered to him for use at the Coronation, which is now the only occasion when the office is enjoyed. As the office is only held temporarily, the existing privilege does not amount to much.

The Lord High Constable of Scotland is entitled to place behind his escutcheon, in saltire, two silver batons tipped with gold at either end. The arms of the Earl of Errol (Hereditary Lord High Constable of Scotland) have only once, at an early period, been matriculated in Lyon Register, and then without any official insignia, but there can be no doubt of the right to the crossed batons.[263]

The Lord High Chamberlain of Scotland (I am not sure this office still exists): Two golden keys in saltire behind the escutcheon.

The Earl Marshal and Hereditary Marshal of England places two batons of gold tipped with sable in saltire behind his arms.

262. For details of alterations in the use of insignia connected with the various orders of chivalry, see notes 244–52 in chapter 34.

263. The Lord High Constable of Scotland (at present the Countess of Erroll) also bears on either side of her lozenge an arm gauntleted proper, issuing out of a cloud and grasping a sword in pale argent, hilt and pommel or.

(*A Deputy Earl Marshal* places one similar baton in bend behind his shield.)

The Earl Marischal of Scotland (until the office was extinguished by attainder) placed saltirewise behind his shield two batons gules, semé of thistles, each ensigned on the top with an Imperial Crown or.

The Hereditary Marshal of Ireland (an office for long past in abeyance) used two batons in saltire behind his arms. According to MS. Harl. 6589, f. 39: 'Les armes des office du Mareschall d'Ireland sont de Goulz et cinque fucelles bendes d'Argent.' These certainly do not appear to be the personal arms of those who held the office, but there is other record that some such coat was used.

The Hereditary Lord Great Seneschal of Ireland (the Earl of Shrewsbury) places a white wand in pale behind his escutcheon.

The Duke of Argyll places in saltire behind his arms: (1) In bend dexter, a baton gules, semé of thistles or, ensigned with an Imperial Crown proper, thereon the crest of Scotland (as Hereditary Great Master of the Household in Scotland); (2) in bend sinister, a sword proper, hilt and pommel or (as Hereditary Justice-General of Scotland) (*vide* Plate III).

The Earl of Mar and Kellie, as Hereditary Keeper of Stirling Castle, bears a key and a baton in saltire behind his arms.

The Master-General of the Ordnance (by warrant of King Charles II) bears on each side of his arms a field-piece.

The Lord Justice Clerk of Scotland places two swords in saltire behind his shield.

The Lord Chief Justice of England encircles his arms with his Collar of SS.

The Walker Trustees place behind their shield two batons in saltire, each ensigned with a unicorn salient supporting a shield argent, the unicorn horned or, and gorged with an antique crown, to which is affixed a chain passing between the fore-legs and reflexed over the back of the last, for the office of Heritable Usher of the White Rod of Scotland, now vested in the said Trustees. Before the Court of Claims the claim was made to exercise the office by deputy, and such claim was allowed.

The Master of the Revels in Scotland has an official coat of arms: Argent, a lady rising out of a cloud in the nombril point, richly apparelled, on her head a garland of ivy, holding in her right hand a poignard crowned, in her left a vizard all proper, standing under a veil or canopy azure garnished or, in base a thistle vert.

Serjeants-at-Arms encircle their arms with their Collars of SS.

Garter King of Arms has: (1) His official coat of arms (argent, a cross gules, on a chief azure, a ducal coronet encircled with a Garter, between a lion passant guardant on the dexter, and a fleur-de-lis on the sinister, all or); (2) his crown; (3) his Collar of SS (the collar of a King of Arms differs from that of a Herald, inasmuch as it is of *silver-gilt*, and on each shoulder a portcullis is inserted); (4) his badge as Garter pendent below his shield. His sceptre of silver-gilt has been sometimes placed in bend behind his escutcheon, but this has not been regularly done. The practice, however, has now been reverted to by Garter.[264]

Lyon King of Arms has: (1) His official coat of arms (argent, a lion sejant, erect and affronté gules, holding in his dexter paw a thistle slipped vert, and in the sinister a shield of the second, on a chief azure a St Andrew's cross—*i.e.* a saltire—of the

264. The present Garter King of Arms, Sir Anthony Wagner, favours two sceptres in saltire behind his shield of arms.

field); (2) his crown; (3) two batons, representing that of his office in saltire behind his shield, these being azure semé of thistles and fleurs-de-lis or, tipped at either end with gold; (4) his Collar of SS; (5) his triple chain of gold, from which depends his badge as Lyon King of Arms.

Ulster King of Arms has: (1) His official coat of arms (or, a cross gules, on a chief of the last a lion of England between a harp and a portcullis, all of the first); (2) his crown; (3) his Collar of SS; (4) his two staves in saltire behind the shield; (5) his chain and badge as Ulster King of Arms; (6) his badge as Registrar of the Order of St Patrick.

Clarenceux King of Arms has: (1) His official coat of arms (argent, a cross gules, on a chief of the second a lion passant guardant or, crowned of the last); (2) his crown; (3) his Collar of SS.

Norroy King of Arms has: (1) His official coat of arms (argent, a cross gules, on a chief of the second[265] a lion of England passant guardant or, crowned with an open crown, between a fleur-de-lis on the dexter and a key on the sinister of the last); (2) his crown; (3) his Collar of SS.

Bath King of Arms has: (1) His crown; his Collar of SS.

I am not aware that any official arms have been assigned to Bath up to the present time; but if none exist, there would not be the slightest difficulty in obtaining these.

An English Herald encircles his shield with his Collar of SS.

A Scottish Herald is entitled to do the same, and has also his badge, which he places below the escutcheon pendent from a ribbon of blue and white.

An *Irish Herald* has his Collar of SS, and his badge suspended from a sky-blue ribbon. An *Irish Pursuivant* has a similar badge.

The Regius Professors (or 'Readers') in the University of Cambridge, for 'Phisicke', 'Lawe', 'Devinity', 'Hebrew', and 'Greke', have official arms as follows (see grant by Robert Cooke, Clarenceux, 1590: *Genealogical Magazine*, vol. ii. p. 125):

Of Phisicke: Azure, a fesse ermines (? ermine) between three lozenges or, on a chief gules a lion passant guardant of the third, charged on the side with the letter M sable. Crest: on a wreath or and azure, a quinquangle silver, called 'simbolum sanitatis'. Mantling gules and argent.

Of Lawe: Purpure, a cross moline or, on a chief gules, a lion passant guardant of the second, charged on the side with the letter L sable. Crest: on a wreath 'purple and gold', a bee volant or. Mantling gules and argent.

Of Devinity: Gules, on a cross ermine, between four doves argent, a book of the first, the leaves or, charged in the midst with the Greek letter θ (Theta) sable. Crest: on a wreath 'silver and gules', a dove volant argent, with an olive-branch vert in his beak. Mantling gules, double argent.

Of Hebrew: Argent, the Hebrew letter ת (Tawe) sable, on a chief gules, a lion passant guardant or, charged on the side with the letter H sable. Crest: on a wreath 'silver and sables', a turtle-dove azure. Mantling gules, double argent.

Of Greke: Per chevron argent and sable, in chief the two Greek letters A

265. The chief in the arms of office of Norroy King of Arms is not gules, but per pale azure and gules. The office of Norroy is now amalgamated with that of Ulster, and when Mr A. J. Toppin was Norroy and Ulster King of Arms he used a seal showing the arms of office of Norroy impaling those of Ulster.

(Alpha) and Ω (Omega) of the second, and in base a 'cicado' or grasshopper of the first, on a chief gules, a lion passant guardant or, charged on the side with the letter G sable. Crest: on a wreath 'silver and sables', an owl argent, legs beak, and ears or. Mantling gules and argent.

The following insignia of office I quote subject to the reservation that I am doubtful how far they enjoy official sanction:

The Lord Chancellor of England: Two maces in saltire (or one in pale) behind the shield and the purse containing the Great Seal below it.

The Lord Great Chamberlain of England: Two golden keys in saltire; and

The Lord Chamberlain of the Household: A golden key in pale behind the shield.

At Exeter the Dean, Precentor, Chancellor, and Treasurer have used official arms impaled with their own insignia. These were:

The Dean: Azure, a stag's head caboshed and between the horns a cross patée fitchée argent.

The Precentor: Argent, on a saltire azure a fleur-de-lis or.

The Chancellor: Gules, a saltire argent between four crosslets or.

The Treasurer: Gules, a saltire between four leopards' heads or.

The Dean of the Savoy Chapel may perhaps employ the complicated coat of the chapel to impale his personal arms, placing the escutcheon on the breast of an eagle sable, crowned or.

Many English Deaneries claim to possess arms which presumably the occupant may use to impale his own coat with, after the example of the Dean of Exeter. Such are London, Winchester, Lincoln, Salisbury, Lichfield, Durham, which all difference the arms of the see with a letter D of gold or sable.

St David's reverses the tinctures of the arms of the see.

Norwich and Carlisle carry: Argent, a cross sable.

Canterbury: Azure, on a cross argent the monogram ✗ sable.

York differences the arms of the see by changing the crown into a mitre, and adding three plates in flanks and base.[266]

266. Few of the decanal coats used are authoritative, although there are official records of two or three of them.

★　★　★　★　★

A new use of insignia is that of the baton by Field Marshals. When Sir Gerald Templer, K.G., was granted supporters, two Field Marshal's batons were shown in saltire behind his arms.

★　★　★　★　★

Mayors of towns may impale their arms with those of the Town Council during their tenure of office. This custom has been extended, although it would seem unofficially, to Chairmen of Urban and Rural District Councils and of other armigerous bodies, and to Principals of Colleges and the like. The custom seems a harmless one, although the legal suggestion is that the principal officer in the Corporation is in fact himself a corporation sole in law, whereas he is usually no more than *primus inter pares*.

37 · Augmentations of honour

Of all heraldic distinctions the possession of an augmentation of honour is the one most prized. The Sovereign is of course the fountain of honour, and though ordinary grants of arms are made by Letters Patent under the hands and seals of the Kings of Arms, by virtue of the powers expressly and specifically conferred upon them in the Letters Patent respectively appointing them to their offices, a grant of arms is theoretically a grant from the Crown. The privilege of the possession of arms in the ordinary event is left in the discretion of the Earl Marshal, whose warrant is a condition precedent to the issue of a Grant. Providing a person is palpably living in that style and condition of life in which the use of arms is usual, subject always to the Earl Marshal's pleasure and discretion, a Grant of Arms can ordinarily be obtained upon payment of the usual fees. The social status of present-day grantees of arms is considerably in advance of the status of grantees in the Tudor period. An augmentation of arms, however, is on a totally and entirely different footing. It is an especial mark of favour from the Sovereign, and the effective grant is a Royal Warrant under the hand and Privy Seal of the Sovereign. The warrant recites and requires that the augmentation granted shall be exemplified and recorded in the College of Arms. Augmentations have been less frequently conferred in recent years than was formerly the case. Technically speaking, a gift of arms by the Sovereign direct where none previously existed is not an augmentation, though one is naturally inclined to include such grants in the category. Such an example is met with in the shield granted to Colonel Carlos by King Charles to commemorate their mutual adventures in the oak tree ('Or, issuing from a mount in base vert, an oak tree proper, over all on a fess gules, three Imperial crowns also proper') (Plate II).

There are many gorgeous legends relating to augmentations and arms which are said to have been granted by William the Conqueror as rewards after the Battle of Hastings. Personally I do not believe in a single one. There was a certain augmentation borne by the Dodge family, which, if it be correct, dates from the thirty-fourth year of Edward I, but whether this be authentic it is impossible to say. Most people consider the alleged deed of grant a forgery, and if this be so, the arms only exist by right of subsequent record and the question of augmentation rests upon tradition. The curious charge of the woman's breast distilling drops of milk to typify the nourishment afforded to the king's army is at any rate most interesting (Plate IX). The earliest undoubted one in this country that I am aware of dates from the reign of Edward III. Sir John de Pelham shared in the glory of the Battle of Poictiers, and in the capture of the French King John. To commemorate this he was granted two round buckles with thongs. The Pelham family arms were 'Azure, three pelicans argent', and as will be seen, these family arms were quartered with the buckles and thongs on a field gules as an augmentation. The quarterly coat forms a part of the arms both of Lord Chichester and of Lord Yarborough at the present day, and 'the Pelham buckle' has been the badge of the Pelham family for centuries[267].

Piers Legh fought with the Black Prince and took the Count de Tanquervil prisoner at the Battle of Crecy, 'and did valiantly rere and advance the said princes Banner att the bataile of Cressy to the noe little encouragement of the English army', but it was not until the reign of Queen Elizabeth I that the augmentation to commemorate this was granted.

The Battle of Flodden was won by the Earl of Surrey, afterwards the Duke of Norfolk, and amongst the many rewards which the King showered upon his successful Marshal was the augmentation to his arms of 'a demi-lion pierced in the mouth with an arrow, depicted on the colours for the arms of the Kingdom of Scotland, which the said James, late King of Scots, bore'. According to the Act of Parliament under which it was granted, this augmentation would seem now to belong exclusively to Lord Mowbray and Stourton and the Hon. Mary Petre, but it is borne apparently with official sanction, or more likely perhaps by official inadvertence, by the Duke of Norfolk and the rest of the Howard family.

The victory over the Scots at Solway Moss in 1542 was recorded in the bordure of augmentation 'on a bordure or eight pairs of lion's gambs erased in saltire gules' granted by Edward VI to Lord Wharton, and in his sinister supporter 'a lion gules, fretty or'. In other words, he had 'cut the claws' of the Scottish King and put his lion in a net.

The Battle of Agincourt is referred to by Shakespeare, who puts these words into King Henry's mouth on the eve of that great battle (Act iv, sc. 3):

> We few, we happy few, we band of brothers;
> For he to-day that sheds his blood with me
> Shall be my brother; be he ne'er so vile,
> This day shall gentle his condition.

There is actual foundation in fact for these lines. For in a writ couched in very stringent and severe terms issued by the same king in after years decreeing penalties for the improper assumption and use of false arms, specific exception is made in favour of those 'who bore arms with us at the Battle of Agincourt'. Evidently this formed a very extensive kind of augmentation.

The reign of Queen Elizabeth I furnishes an interesting example of the gift of a complete coat in the case of Sir Francis Drake, who had been using the arms of another family of the same name. The representative of that family complained to the Queen that Sir Francis, whom he styled an upstart, should take such liberties

267. I can find no justification for either the Dodge or Pelham legends. There was certainly no grant to Dodge in 34 Edward I. To my mind the charge of a woman's breast, the dug distilling drops of milk, is no more than a cant on the name Dodge. In the case of the Pelham family, it is true that the buckle has long been used as a badge by this family, but the so called 'coat of augmentation' is certainly foreign to Pelham heraldry (as exhibited in rolls and on seals) until at least the middle of the fifteenth century, and I suspect that further research would reveal that this coat is, in fact, of Tudor provenance.

with his arms; whereupon the Queen said she would give Sir Francis arms which should outrival those of his namesake. At least, such is the legend, and though the arms themselves were granted by Clarenceux King of Arms, and I have not yet found any Royal Warrant indicating that the grant was made by specific Royal command, it is possible the story is correct. The arms are: 'Sable, a fess wavy between two stars argent. Crest: a ship under reef, drawn round a terrestrial globe with a cable by a hand issuing from clouds all proper' (Plate IX). The stars upon the shield are the two pole stars, and the wavy band between them typifies Drake's voyage round the world, as does also the peculiar crest in which the Divine hand is shown guiding his ship around the globe.

At the Battle of Naseby Dr Edward Lake fought bravely for the King, and in the service of his Majesty received no less than sixteen wounds. At the end of the battle, when his left arm was useless, he put the bridle of his horse between his teeth and still fought on. The quartering of augmentation given to him was: 'Gules, a dexter arm embowed in armour holding in the hand a sword erect all proper, thereto affixed a banner argent charged with a cross between sixteen escutcheons of the field, on the cross a lion of England'. The sixteen shields upon the banner typify his sixteen wounds.

After the Commonwealth was established in England, Charles II made a desperate effort to regain his crown, an effort which culminated in his disastrous defeat at the Battle of Worcester. The King escaped through the gate of the city solely through the heroic efforts of Colonel Newman, and this is kept in remembrance by the inescutcheon of augmentation, viz.: 'Gules, a portcullis imperially crowned or'. Every one has heard how the King was accompanied in his wanderings by Colonel Carlos, who hid with him in the oak tree at Boscobel. Afterwards the king accompanied Mistress Jane Lane on horseback as her servant to the coast, whence he fled to the Continent. The reward of Colonel Carlos was the gift of the entire coat of arms already referred to. The Lanes, though not until after some years had passed and the King had come back to his own again, were granted two remarkable additions to their family arms. First of all 'the canton of England' (that is, the arms of England upon a canton) was added to their shield. They are the only family to whom such an honour has been given, and a most curious result has happened. When the use of armorial bearings was taxed by Act of Parliament the Royal Arms were specially exempted, and on account of this canton the Lane family claimed and obtained exemption from the tax. A few years later a crest was granted to them, namely, a strawberry-roan horse, 'couped at the flanks', holding in its feet the Royal crown (Plate II). It was upon a horse of this colour that the King and Mistress Lane had escaped and thereby saved the crown. Mr Francis Wolfe, of Madeley, who also was a party to the escape, received the grant of an inescutcheon gules charged with a lion of England. Another family which bears an augmentation to commemorate King Charles' escape is Whitgreave.[268]

268. These augmentations were granted by Sir Edward Walker, who was Garter in exile during the Commonwealth. After King Charles II was restored to the throne, he issued a warrant under the Royal sign manual directing Garter Walker to grant 'unto any person of Eminent quality, fidelity and extraordinary meritt, that shall desire it, such augmentation of any of our Royall Badges to be added unto his Armes, as you shall judge most proper to testify the same'. The warrant also stated that if such a person had no arms, then arms should be granted to him.

The reign of Queen Anne produced in the Duke of Marlborough one of the finest generals the world has ever seen; and in the Battle of Blenheim one of its greatest victories. The augmentation which commemorates this is a shield bearing the cross of St George and in the centre a smaller shield with the golden lilies of France.

In the year 1797 the Battle of Camperdown was fought, when Admiral Duncan defeated the Dutch Fleet and was created Lord Camperdown. To his family arms were added a naval crown and a representation of the gold medal given by George III to Lord Camperdown to commemorate his victory.

The arms of Nelson are most interesting, inasmuch as one version of the arms carries two separate and distinct augmentations. It is not, however, the coat as it was granted to and borne by the great Admiral himself. After the Battle of the Nile he received the augmentation on the chief, a landscape showing the palm-tree, the disabled ship, and the battery in ruins. The one crest was the plume of triumph given to the Admiral by the Sultan Selim III, and his second crest, which, however, is not a crest of augmentation, was the stern of the Spanish ship *San Josef*. After his death at the Battle of Trafalgar his brother was created Earl Nelson, and a second augmentation, namely, a fess wavy sable with the word 'Trafalgar' upon it in gold letters, was added to the arms. This, however, has since been discontinued, except by Lord Bridport, who quarters it, whilst the Nelson family has reverted to the arms as they were borne by the great Admiral.[269]

After the death of Nelson at the Battle of Trafalgar, Lord Collingwood took command, and though naval experts think that the action of Collingwood greatly minimised the number of prizes which would have resulted from the victory, Lord Collingwood received for an augmentation a chief wavy gules, thereon the lion of England, navally crowned, with the word 'Trafalgar' above the lion. He also received an additional crest, namely, the stern of his ship, the *Royal Sovereign*, between a wreath of oak on the one side and a wreath of laurel on the other.

The heroic story of the famous fight between the *Shannon* and the *Chesapeake* has been often told. Captain Broke sent in a challenge to the *Chesapeake* to come out and fight him, and, though a banquet was prepared by the Mayor of Boston for that evening 'to meet the English officers', Captain Broke defeated the *Chesapeake* in an engagement which only lasted a very short time. He was granted an additional crest, namely, an arm holding a trident and issuing from a naval crown, together with the motto, 'Sævumque tridentem servamus'.

General Ross fought and won the Battle of Bladensburg, and took the city of Washington, dying a few days afterwards. The story is that the family were offered their choice of a baronetcy or an augmentation, and they chose the latter. The augmentation (Plate II), which was specially granted with permission for it to be placed upon the monument to the memory of General Ross, consists of the arm holding the flag of the United States with a broken flag-staff which will be

269. This sounds as if the Nelson family cavalierly discontinued the use of a mark of royal favour. When Earl Nelson died in 1835 he was succeeded in the peerage, by virtue of a special remainder, by his sister's son, Thomas Bolton. Under the terms of an act for securing the Nelson annuity (46 George III, chapter 146), he assumed the name and arms of Admiral, Viscount Nelson, not those of his brother the Earl. The Earl's arms, complete with the 'Trafalgar' augmentation, were inherited by the issue of his only surviving child and heiress, Charlotte Mary, Baroness Bridport

seen both on the shield itself, and as an additional crest. The shield also shows the gold cross for previous services at Corunna and in the Peninsula. The family were also given the surname of 'Ross-of-Bladensburg'.

The capture of Curaçoa by Admiral Sir Charles Brisbane, K.C.B., is commemorated by the representation of his ship passing between the two Dutch forts; and by the additional crest of an arm in a naval officer's uniform grasping a cutlass. Admiral Sir Robert Otway, for his distinguished services, was granted: 'On a chief azure an anchor between two branches of oak or, and on the dexter side a demi-Neptune and on the sinister a mermaid proper', to add to his shield. Admiral Sir George Pocock, who captured Havannah, was given for an augmentation: 'On a chief wavy azure a sea-horse' (to typify his naval career), between two Eastern crowns (to typify his services in the East Indies), with the word 'Havanna', the scene of his greatest victory.

Sir Edward Pellew, who was created Viscount Exmouth for bombarding and destroying the fort and arsenal of Algiers, was given upon a chief a representation of that fort, with an English man-of-war in front of it, to add to his arms. It is interesting to note that one of his supporters, though not a part of his augmentation, represents a Christian slave, in memory of those in captivity at Algiers when he captured the city.

There were several augmentations won at the Battle of Waterloo, and the Waterloo medal figures upon many coats of arms of Waterloo officers. Colonel Alexander Clark-Kennedy, with his own hand, captured the French Eagle of the 105th French Regiment. For this he bears a representation of it and a sword crossed upon a chief over his arms, and his crest of augmentation is a demi-dragoon holding the same flag. Of the multitude of honours which were showered upon the Duke of Wellington, not the least was his augmentation. This was a smaller shield to be superimposed upon his own, and charged with those crosses of St George, St Andrew, and St Patrick, which we term 'the Union Jack'. Sir Edward Kerrison, who distinguished himself so greatly in the Peninsula and at Waterloo, was granted a sword with a wreath of laurel and representations of his medals for Orthes and Waterloo, and, for an additional crest, an arm in armour holding a banner inscribed 'Peninsula'.

Sir Thomas Munro, who will be long remembered as the Governor of Madras, was rewarded for his capture of Badamy by a representation of that hill-fort in India. The augmentation of Lord Keane is very similar, being a representation of the Fortress of Ghuznee in Afghanistan, which he captured. Other instances of a similar character are to be found in the arms of Cockburn-Campbell and Hamilton-Grace.

The arms of Lord Gough are most remarkable, inasmuch as they show no less than two distinct and different augmentations both earned by the same man. In 1816, for his services in the Peninsula, he received a representation of the Spanish Order of Charles III, and on a chief the representation of the Fortress of Tarifa, with the crest of the arm holding the colours of his own regiment, the 87th, and a French eagle reversed and depressed. After his victories in the East, particularly at Goojerat, and for the subjugation and annexation of the Punjab, he was granted, in 1843, an additional quartering to add to his shield. This has the Lion of England holding up the Union Jack below the words 'China' and 'India'. The third crest, which was then granted to him, shows a similar lion holding the Union Jack and a Chinese flag.

Sir George Pollock, 'of the Khyber Pass', Bart, earned everlasting fame for himself in the first Afghan War, by forcing the Khyber Pass and by the capture of Cabul. For this he was given an Eastern crown and the word 'Khyber' on a chief as well as three cannon upon a canton, and at the same time he was granted an additional crest—a lion holding an Afghan banner with the staff thereof broken. With him it seemed as if the practice of granting augmentations for military services had ceased. Lord Roberts had none, neither had Lord Wolseley. But recently the old practice was reverted to in favour of Lord Kitchener. His family arms were: 'Azure, a chevron cottised between three bustards', and in the centre chief point a bezant; with a stag's head for a crest; but for 'smashing the Khalifa' he has been given the Union Jack and the Egyptian flag with the staves encircled by a coronet bearing the word 'Khartoum', all on a pile superimposed over his family arms. He also received a second crest of an elephant's head holding a sword in its trunk issuing from a mural crown. At the conclusion of the South African War a second augmentation was granted to him, this taking the form of a chief.

Two other very interesting instances of augmentation of arms are worthy of mention.

Sir Ralph Abercromby, after a distinguished career, fought and won the Battle of Aboukir Bay, only to die a few days later on board H.M.S. *Foudroyant* of his wounds received in the battle. But long before he had fought and conquered the French at Valenciennes, and in 1795 had been made a Knight of the Bath. The arms which are upon his Stall plate in Westminster Abbey include his augmentation, which is an arm in armour encircled by a wreath of laurel supporting the French Standard.

Sir William Hoste gained the celebrated victory over the French fleet off the Island of Lissa in 1811, and the augmentation which was granted was a representation of his gold medal hanging from a naval crown, and an additional crest, an arm holding a flag inscribed with the word 'Cattaro', the scene of another of his victories.

Peace has its victories no less than war, but there is generally very much less fuss made about them. Consequently, the augmentations to commemorate entirely pacific actions are considerably fewer in number. The Speke augmentation has been elsewhere referred to, and reference may be made to the Ross augmentation to commemorate the Arctic exploits of Sir John Ross.

It is a very common idea that arms were formerly to be obtained by conquest in battle. Like many other heraldic ideas, there is a certain amount of truth in the idea, from which very erroneous generalisations have been made. The old legend as to the acquisition of the plume of ostrich feathers by the Black Prince no doubt largely accounts for the idea. That legend, as has been already shown, lacks foundation. Territorial or sovereign arms doubtless would be subject to conquest, but I do not believe that because in battle or in a tournament *à outrance* one person defeated another, he therefore became entitled to assume, of his own motion, the arms of the man he had vanquished. The proposition is too absurd. But there is no doubt that in some number of historic cases his Sovereign has subsequently conferred upon the victor an augmentation which has closely approximated to the

773 *Arms of Robert de Vere,*
Duke of Ireland
and Earl of Oxford:
Quarterly, 1 and 4
(of augmentation),
azure, three crowns or,
within a bordure argent;
2 and 3, quarterly gules
and or, in the first
quarter a mullet argent.

arms of his victim. Such cases occur in the arms of the Clerkes, Barts, of Hitcham, Bucks, who bear: 'On a sinister canton azure, a demi-ram salient of the first, and in chief two fleurs-de-lis or, debruised by a baton', to commemorate the action of Sir John Clerke of Weston, who captured Louis D'Orleans, Duke of Longueville, at Borny, near Terouenne, 5 Henry VII. The augmentation conferred upon the Duke of Norfolk at the battle of Flodden has been already referred to, but the family of Lloyd of Stockton, co. Salop, carry a remarkable augmentation, inasmuch as they are permitted to bear the arms of Sir John Oldcastle, Lord Cobham, to commemorate his recapture by their ancestor after Lord Cobham's escape from the Tower.

Augmentations which have no other basis than mere favour of kings, or consanguinity to the Royal Family, are not uncommon. Richard II, who himself adopted the arms of St Edward the Confessor, bestowed the right to bear them also upon Thomas Mowbray, Duke of Norfolk (675). No difference was added to them in his case, which is the more remarkable as they were borne by the Duke impaled with the arms of England. In 1397 the King conferred the same arms upon John de Holland, Duke of Exeter, differenced by a label argent, and upon Thomas de Holland, Duke of Surrey, within a bordure ermine. Richard II seems to have been inclined to the granting of augmentations, for in 1386, when he created the Earl of Oxford (Robert de Vere) Duke of Ireland, he granted him as an augmentation the arms of Ireland ('Azure, three crowns or') within a bordure argent (773). The Manners family, who were of Royal descent, but who, not being descended from an heiress, had no right to quarter the Royal Arms, received the grant of a chief 'quarterly azure and gules, in the first and fourth quarters two fleurs-de-lis, and in the second and third a lion passant guardant or'. This precedent, no doubt, suggested the augmentation assigned in the case of Queen Victoria Eugenie of Spain. The Waller family, of Groombridge, co. Kent, one of whom, Richard Waller, captured Charles, Duke of Orleans, at the Battle of Agincourt, received as an augmentation the right to suspend from the crest ('On a mount a walnut-tree proper') an escutcheon of the arms of that Prince, viz.: 'Azure, three fleurs-de-lis or, a label of three points argent'. Lord Polwarth bears one of the few augmentations granted by William III, viz.: 'An inescutcheon azure charged with an orange ensigned with an Imperial crown all proper', whilst the titular King James III and VIII granted to John Græme, Earl of Alford, a coat of augmentation, viz.: 'The Royal Arms of Scotland on the field and cross of St Andrew counterchanged', the date of the grant being 20 January 1734. Sir John Keith, Earl of Kintore, Knight Marischal of Scotland, saved the regalia of Scotland from falling into the hands of Cromwell, and in return the Keith arms (now quartered by Lord Kintore) were augmented with 'an inescutcheon gules, a sword in bend sinister surmounted by a sceptre in bend dexter, in chief an imperial crown, the whole within an orle of eight thistles'.

The well-known augmentation of the Seymour family: 'Or, on a pile gules, between six fleurs-de-lis azure, three lions of England', is borne to commemorate the marriage of Jane Seymour to Henry VIII, who granted augmentations to all his wives except Catharine of Aragon and Anne of Cleves. The Seymour family is, however, the only one in which the use of the augmentation has been continued. The same practice was followed by granting the arms of England to the

Consort of the Princess Caroline and to the Prince Consort. See page 383.

The frequent grant of the Royal tressure in Scotland, probably usually as an augmentation, has been already referred to. King Charles I granted to the Earl of Kinnoull as a quartering of augmentation: 'Azure, a unicorn salient argent, armed, maned, and unguled or, within a bordure of the last charged with thistles of Scotland and roses gules of England dimidiated'. The well-known augmentation of the Medicis family, viz.: 'A roundle azure, charged with three fleurs-de-lis or', was granted by Louis XII to Pietro de Medicis. The Prussian Officers, ennobled on the 18 of January 1896, the twenty-fifth anniversary of the foundation of the new German Empire, bore as a device a chief purpure, and thereupon the Prussian sceptre and a sword in saltire interlaced by two oak-branches vert (774). The Right Hon. Sir Thomas Thornton, G.C.B., received a Royal Licence to accept the Portuguese title of Conde de Cassilhas and an augmentation. This was an inescutcheon (ensigned by his coronet as a Conde) 'or, thereon an arm embowed vested azure, the cuff gold, the hand supporting a flagstaff therefrom flowing the Royal Standard of Portugal'. The same device issuing from his coronet was also granted to him as a crest of augmentation. Sir Woodbine Parish, K.C.H., by legislative act of the Argentine Republic received in 1839 a grant of the arms of that country, which was subsequently incorporated in the arms granted to him and registered in the Heralds' College in this country. He had been Consul-General and Chargé d'Affaires at Buenos Aires, 1823–32; he was appointed in 1824 Plenipotentiary, and concluded the first treaty by which the Argentine Republic was formally recognised. Reference has been already made (p. 318) to the frequent grant of supporters as augmentations, and perhaps mention should also be made of the inescutcheons for the Dukedom of Aubigny, borne by the Duke of Richmond and Gordon, and for the Duchy of Chatelherault, borne by the Duke of Abercorn. Possibly these should more properly be ranked as territorial arms and not as augmentations. A similar coat is the inescutcheon borne by the Earl of Mar and Kellie for his Earldom of Kellie. This, however, is stated by Woodward to be an augmentation granted by James VI to Sir Thomas Erskine, one of several granted by that King to commemorate the frustration of the Gowrie Plot in 1600.

The Marquess of Westminster, for some utterly inexplicable reason, was granted as an augmentation the right to bear the arms of the city of Westminster in the first quarter of his arms. Those who have rendered very great personal service to the Crown have been sometimes so favoured. The Halford and Gull (see p. 188) augmentations commemorate medical services to the Royal Family, and augmentations have been conferred upon Sir Frederick Treves and Sir Francis Laking in connection with the illness of King Edward VII at the time of his Coronation.

The badges of Ulster and Nova Scotia borne as such upon their shields by Baronets are, of course, augmentations.

Two cases are known of augmentations to the arms of towns. The arms of Derry were augmented by the arms of the city of London in chief, when, after its fearful siege, the name of Derry was changed to Londonderry to commemorate the help given by the city of London. The arms of the city of Hereford had an azure bordure semé of saltires couped argent added to its arms after it had successfully withstood its Scottish siege, and this, by the way, is a striking example of

463

colour upon colour, the field of the coat being gules. Perhaps the grant of arms to the County of Norfolk by the King's Royal Warrant in 1904 is really a case of an augmentation.[270]

There are many grants in the later part of the eighteenth and the beginning of the nineteenth centuries recorded in Lyon Register which at first sight appear to be augmentations. Perhaps they are rightly so termed, but as the additions usually appear to be granted by the Lyon without specific Royal Warrants, they are hardly equivalent to the English ones issued during the same period. Many ordinary grants made in England which have borne direct reference to particular achievements of the grantee have been (by the grantees and their descendants) wrongly termed augmentations. A rough and ready (though not a certain) test is to imagine the coat if the augmentation be removed, and see whether it remains a properly balanced design. Few of such coats will survive the test. The additions made to a coat to make it a different design, when a new grant is founded upon arms improperly used theretofore, are not augmentations, although spoken departures from the truth on this detail are by no means rare.

270. A recent augmentation to a civic coat was made on 19 October 1956, when the Augmented Royal Badge for Wales was added to the supporters of the arms of the city of Cardiff. The badge is suspended from the neck of each supporter by a gold chain. This grant was made to commemorate the declaration of Cardiff as the capital city of the Principality of Wales. The grant of arms to the Norfolk County Council can hardly be regarded as a grant of augmentation, but rather as a mark of special royal favour.

774 *Device from the chief of the*
"Prussian Sword Nobility".

38 · Ecclesiastical heraldry

Ecclesiastical heraldry has nothing like the importance in British armory that it possesses elsewhere. It may be said to consist in this country exclusively of the official arms assigned to and recorded for the archiepiscopal and episcopal sees, and the mitres and crosiers which are added to the shields, and a certain number of ecclesiastical symbols which occur as charges. In Pre-Reformation days there were, of course, the many religious houses which used armorial emblems, but with the suppression of the monasteries these vanished. The cardinal's hat was recognised in former days, and would still be officially certified in England as admittedly correctly displayed above the arms of a Roman cardinal. But the curious and intricate development of other varieties of the ecclesiastical hat which will be found in use in all other European countries is not known to British armory. Nor has the English College of Arms recognised the impersonal arms of the Catholic communities. Those arms, with and without the ecclesiastical hats, play a conspicuous part in Continental heraldry.[271]

It is difficult to assign a proper value or a definite status to the arms of the abbeys and other religious houses in this country in Pre-Reformation times. The principal, in fact the only important sources of information concerning them are the impressions of seals which have come down to us. Many of these seals show the effigies of saints or patrons, some show the impersonal arms of the religious order to whose rule the community conformed, some the personal arms of the official of the moment, others the personal arms of the founder. In other cases arms

271. As the law stands, it seems that arms cannot be granted to Roman Catholic Sees, as the bishops are not recognised as corporations sole and their use of territorial titles is contrary to certain provisions contained in the 'Catholic Emancipation' Act 1829. Arms can, however, be granted to most Roman Catholic institutions, and to prelates and clergy as individuals.

By an Earl Marshal's warrant dated 17 July 1967, certain insignia was approved for use in connection with the personal arms of Roman Catholic prelates and clergy. The approved insignai is as follows: 1. Cardinals place over their arms a red hat having thirty red tassels interlaced with gold thread. 2. Archbishops place over their arms a precious mitre (*mitra pretiosa*) and/or a green hat having twenty tassels, and a doubled traversed cross in pale behind the shield. 3. Bishops and Abbots Nullius Dioceseos place over their arms a precious mitre and/or a green hat having twelve tassels, and a single traversed cross or crosier either in pale or in bend behind the shield. 4. Abbots place over their arms a simple mitre (the white *mitra simplex*) or a black hat having six tassels, and a crozier either in pale or in bend behind the shield. 5. Protonotaries Apostolic, Vicars, and Prefects Apostolic place over their arms a crimson hat having twelve tassels. 6. Religious Superiors General or Provincial and Honorary or Titular Protonotaries Apostolic place over their arms a black hat having twelve tassels. 8. Privy Chamberlains and Chaplains to the Pope place over their arms a black hat having twelve violet tassels. 9. Canons of Cathedral Chapters place over their arms a black hat having six tassels. 10. Priests place over their arms a black hat having two tassels. If any prelate or clergyman is also a Cardinal, he will substitute the Cardinal's hat for the hat belonging to his degree and use it in conjunction with such other insignia as may be appropriate.

465

presumably those of the particular foundation or community occur, but in such cases the variations in design are so marked, and so often we find that two, three, or more devices are used indifferently and indiscriminately, that one is forced to arrive at the conclusion that a large proportion of the devices in use, though armorial in character, had no greater status than a temporary existence as seal designs. They distinctly lack the unchanging continuity one associates with armorial bearings. But whatever their status may once have been, they have now completely passed out of being and may well be allowed to rest in the uncertainty which exists concerning them. The interest attaching to them can never be more than academic in character and limited in extent. The larger abbeys, the abbots of which were anciently summoned to Parliament as Lords of Parliament, appear to have adhered rather more consistently to a fixed device in each case, though the variations of design are very noticeable even in these instances. A list of them will be found in the *Genealogical Magazine* (vol. ii, p. 3).

The suppression of the monasteries in this country was so thorough and so ruthless, that the contemporary instances of abbatical arms remaining to us from which deduction as to armorial rules and precedents can be made are singularly few in number, but it would appear that the abbot impaled the arms of his abbey on the dexter side of his personal arms, and placed his mitre above the shield.

The mitre of an abbot differed from that of a bishop, inasmuch as it had no labels— or *infulæ*— depending from within it. The Abbot used a crosier, which doubtless was correctly added to his armorial bearings, but it is found in pale behind the shield, in bend, and also two in saltire, and it is difficult to assert which was the most correct form.

The crosier of an abbot was also represented with the crook at its head curved inwards, the terminal point of the crook being entirely contained within the hook. The point of a bishop's, on the other hand, was turned outwards at the bottom of the crook. The difference is said to typify the distinction between the confined jurisdiction of the abbot— which was limited to the abbey and the community under his charge— and the more open and wider jurisdiction of the bishop. Although this distinction has been much disputed as regards its recognition for the actual crosiers employed, there can be no doubt that it is very generally adhered to in heraldic representations, though one hesitates to assert it as an absolute rule.[272] The official arms for the archiepiscopal and episcopal sees are of some interest. With the single exception of York, the archiepiscopal coats of arms all have, in some form or another, the pallium which forms part of an archbishop's vestments or insignia of rank, but it is now very generally recognised and conceded that the pallium is not merely a charge in the official coat for any specified jurisdiction, but is itself the sign of the rank of an archbishop of the same character and status as is the mitre, the pallium being displayed upon a shield as a matter of convenience for artistic representation. This view of the case has been much strengthened by the discovery that in ancient instances of the archiepiscopal

272. There is no truth in the statement that the mitres of abbots are shown without the infulæ— certainly not in English heraldry, as an early Tudor manuscript at the College of Arms (L. 10) clearly indicates. Likewise there is no significance in the form of crozier. In some continental countries the crosier of an abbot is distinguished from that of a bishop, not by the direction of the crook, but by the addition of a short veil beneath it.

466

arms of York the pallium is found, and not the more modern coat of the crown and keys; but whether the pallium is to be still so considered, or whether under English armorial law it must now be merely ranked as a charge in an ordinary coat of arms, in general practice it is accepted as the latter; but it nevertheless remains a point of very considerable interest (which has not yet been elucidated) why the pallium should have been discarded for York, and another coat of arms substituted.

The various coats used by the archbishops of England and Ireland are as follows:

Canterbury. Azure, an episcopal staff in pale or, and ensigned with a cross pateé argent surmounted of a pall of the last, charged with four crosses formée fitchée sable, edged and fringed or.

York. Gules, two keys in saltire argent, in chief a Royal crown or.

Armagh. Azure, an episcopal staff argent, ensigned with a cross patée or, surmounted by a pallium of the second, edged and fringed or, charged with four crosses formée fitchée sable.

Dublin. The arms of this archbishopric are the same as those of Armagh, only with five crosses charged on the pallium instead of four.

The arms of the episcopal sees have no attribute at all similar to the charge of the pallium in the coat of an archbishop, and are merely so many different coats of arms. The shield of every bishop and archbishop is surmounted by his mitre, and it is now customary to admit the use of the mitre by all persons holding the title of bishop who are recognised as bishops by the English law.

This, of course, includes Colonial and Suffragan bishops, retired bishops, and bishops of the Episcopal Churches in Scotland and in Ireland. It is a moot point whether the bishops of the Episcopal Churches in Ireland, in Scotland, and in Wales are entitled to make use of the official arms formerly assigned to their Sees at a period when those Churches were State-established; but, looking at the matter from a strictly official point of view, it would not appear that they are any longer entitled to make use of them.

The mitres of an archbishop and of a bishop—in spite of many statements to the contrary—are exactly identical, and the mistaken idea which has of late years (the practice is really quite a modern one) encircled the rim of an archbishop's mitre with the circlet of a coronet is absolutely incorrect.

There are several forms of mitre which, when looked upon as an ecclesiastical ornament, can be said to exist; but from the heraldic point of view only one mitre is recognised, and that is of gold, the labels being of the same colour. The jewelled variety is incorrect in armorial representations, though the science of armory does not appear to have enforced any particular shape of mitre.[273]

The 'several forms' of the mitre—to which allusion has just been made—refer to the use in actual practice which prevailed in Pre-Reformation England, and still holds amongst Roman Catholic bishops at the present day. These are three in

273. The heraldic mitre (except in the arms of Roman Catholic Prelates where the precise variety of mitre is specified) is of indeterminate form. It is chased to look like the *mitra pretiosa* but is usually painted a rather washy blue and white. It is certainly not the unadorned *mitra simplex*, nor is it the *mitra aurifereta* or plain gold mitre. I think Fox-Davies is right when he says it should be of gold, but I also think it should be jewelled, or at least chased as jewelled, as in Tudor armorials.

number, *i.e.* the 'precious' (*pretiosa*), the gold (*auriferata*), and the simple (*simplex*). The two former are both employed at a Pontifical Mass (being alternately assumed at different parts of the service); the second only is worn at such rites as Confirmation, &c.; while the third (which is purely of white linen) is confined to Services for the Dead, and on Good Friday. As its name implies, the first of these is of cloth of gold, ornamented to a greater or less degree with jewels, while the second —though likewise of cloth of gold—is without any design or ornament. The short Gothic mitre of Norman days has now given place to the modern Roman one, an alteration which, with its great height and arched sides, can hardly perhaps be considered an artistic improvement. Some individual Roman Catholic bishops at the present day, however (in England at any rate), wear mitres more allied to the Norman and Gothic shape.

The past fifteen or so years have seen a revival—though in a purely eclectic and unofficial manner—of the wearing of the mitre by Church of England bishops. Where this has been (and is being) done, the older form of mitre has been adhered to, though from the informal and unofficial nature of the revival no rules as to its use have been followed, but only individual choice.

At the recent Coronations, mitres were not worn; which they undoubtedly would have been had this revival now alluded to been made authoritatively.[274]

All bishops and archbishops are entitled to place two crosiers in saltire behind their shields. Archbishops of the Roman Catholic Church have continuously placed in pale behind their shields what is known as the archbishop's cross. In actual practice, the cross carried before an archbishop is an ordinary one with one transverse piece, but the heraldic archiepiscopal cross is always represented as a double cross, *i.e.* having two transverse pieces one above the other. In the Established Church of England the archiepiscopal cross—as in the Roman Catholic Church—is the plain two-armed variety, and though the cross is never officially recognised as an armorial attribute and is not very frequently met with in heraldic representations, there can be no doubt that if this cross is used to typify archiepiscopal rank, it should be heraldically represented with the double arms. The actual cross borne before archbishops is termed the provincial cross, and it may be of interest to here state that the Bishops of Rochester are the official cross-bearers to the Archbishops of Canterbury.

To the foregoing rules there is one notable exception, *i.e.* the Bishop of Durham. The Bishopric of Durham, until the earlier part of the nineteenth century, was a Palatinate, and in earlier times the Bishops of Durham, who had their own parliament and Barons of the Palatinate, exercised a jurisdiction and regality, limited in extent certainly, but little short in fact or effect of the power of the Crown. If ever any ecclesiastic can be correctly said to have enjoyed temporal power, the Bishops of Durham can be so described. The Prince-Bishops of the Continent had no such attributes of regality vested in themselves as were enjoyed by the Bishops of Durham. These were in truth kings within their bishoprics, and even to the present day—though modern geographies and modern social

274. The revival of the use of the mitre by bishops and archbishops of the Established Church now seems to be at least semi-official, and the precious mitre is frequently worn on high festal and sacramental occasions. The simple mitre is also occasionally used in services for the dead as in the Roman Church.

PLATE XII

St. George's Cross

St. Andrew's Cross

The Union Jack

St. Patrick's Cross

*Union Flag of
England and Scotland*

legislation have divided the bishopric into other divisions—one still hears the term employed of 'within' or 'without' the bishopric.

The result of this temporal power enjoyed by the Bishops of Durham is seen in their heraldic achievement. In place of the two crosiers in saltire behind the shield, as used by the other bishops, the Bishops of Durham place a sword and a crosier in saltire behind their shield to signify both their temporal and spiritual jurisdiction.

The mitre of the Bishop of Durham is heraldically represented with the rim encircled by a ducal coronet, and it has thereby become usual to speak of the coronetted mitre of the Bishop of Durham; but it should be clearly borne in mind that the coronet formed no part of the actual mitre, and probably no mitre has ever existed in which the rim has been encircled by a coronet. But the Bishops of Durham, by virtue of their temporal status, used a coronet, and by virtue of their ecclesiastical status used a mitre, and the representation of both of these at one and the same time has resulted in the coronet being placed to encircle the rim of the mitre. The result has been that, heraldically, they are now always represented as one and the same article.

It is, of course, from this coronetted mitre of Durham that the wholly inaccurate idea of the existence of coronet on the mitre of an archbishop has originated. Apparently the humility of these Princes of the Church has not been sufficient to prevent their appropriating the peculiar privileges of their ecclesiastical brother of lesser rank.

A crest is never used with a mitre or ecclesiastical hat. Many writers deny the right of any ecclesiastic to a crest. Some deny the right also to use a motto, but this restriction has no general acceptance.

Therefore ecclesiastical heraldry in Britain is summed up in (1) its recognition of the cardinal's hat, (2) the official coat of arms for ecclesiastical purposes, (3) the ensigns of ecclesiastical rank above alluded to, viz. mitre, cross, and crosier.

Ecclesiastical heraldry—notably in connection with the Roman Church—in other countries has, on the contrary, a very important place in armorial matters. In addition to the emblems officially recognised for English heraldry, the ecclesiastical hat is in constant use.

The use of the ecclesiastical hat is very general outside Great Britain, and affords one of the few instances where the rules governing heraldic usages are identical throughout the Continent.

This curious unanimity is the more remarkable because it was not until the seventeenth century that the rather intricate rules concerning the colours of the hats used for different ranks and the number of tassels came into vogue.

Other than the occasional recognition of the cardinal's hat in former days, the only British official instance of the use of the ecclesiastical hat is met with in the case of the matriculation of arms in Lyon Register to the Right Rev. Æneas Chisholm, Roman Catholic Bishop of Aberdeen.[275] I frankly admit I

275. The assignment of an Archbishop's hat to Bishop Chisholm was an error. Today Lord Lyon's practice with regard to the insignia used in connection with the arms of Roman Catholic prelates and clergy is similar to that employed in England (see note 271, page 465), as both English and Scottish jurisdictions have based their systems on the accepted practice of the Holy See. Lyon has also granted ecclesiastical hats to clergy outside the Roman obedience. The Minister of the Canon-

am unaware why the ecclesiastical hat assigned to the bishop in the official matriculation of his arms has ten tassels on either side. The Continental usage would assign him but six, and English armory has no rules of its own which can be quoted in opposition thereto. Save as an acceptance of Roman regulations (Roman Holy Orders, it should not be forgotten, are recognised by the English Common Law to the extent that a Roman Catholic priest is not reordained if he becomes an Anglican clergyman), the heraldic ecclesiastical hat of a bishop has no existence with us, and the Roman regulations would give him but six tassels.

The mitre is to be met with as a charge and as a crest, for instance, in the case of Barclay and Berkeley ['A mitre gules, labelled and garnished or, charged with a chevron between ten crosses patée, six and four argent. Motto: "Dieu avec nous"']; and also in the case of Sir Edmund Hardinge, Bart, whose crests are curious ['1. of honourable augmentation, a hand fesswise couped above the wrist habited in naval uniform, holding a sword erect surmounting a Dutch and a French flat in saltire, on the former inscribed 'Atalanta', on the latter 'Piedmontaise', the blade of the sword passing through a wreath of laurel near the point and a little below through another of cypress, with the motto, "Postera laude recens"; 2. a mitre gules charged with a chevron argent, fimbriated or, thereon three escallops sable.']

The cross can hardly be termed exclusively ecclesiastical, but a curious figure of this nature is to be met with in the arms recently granted to the Borough of Southwark. It was undoubtedly taken from the device used in Southwark before its incorporation, though as there were many bodies who adopted it in that neighbourhood, it is difficult to assign it to a specific origin.[276]

Pastoral staves and passion-nails are elsewhere referred to, and the figures of saints and ecclesiastics are mentioned in the chapter on 'The Human Figure'.

The emblems of the saints, which appear to have received a certain amount of official recognition—both ecclesiastical and heraldic—supply the origin of many other charges not in themselves heraldic. An instance of this kind will be found in the sword of St Paul, which figures on the shield of London. The cross of St Cuthbert, which has been adopted in the unauthorised coat for the See of Newcastle-on-Tyne, and the keys of St Peter, which figure in many ecclesiastical coats, are other examples. The lilies of the Virgin are, of course, constantly to be met with in the form of fleurs-de-lis and natural flowers; the wheel of St Catherine is familiar, and the list might be extended indefinitely.

gate, which includes Holyrood House, has a black hat, with red strings and two purple tassels. The Dean of the Thistle has a similar hat, but with black strings and red tassels. On 4 February 1960 the Moderator of the General Assembly of the Church of Scotland was granted arms surmounted by a black hat with twenty blue tassels, whilst in pale behind the shield was a Moderator's staff, a cuirgrich or, its staff sable, the crook stoned purpure and saltire-banded azure. The effect was very Roman, and in consequence alternative insignia was granted on 5 April 1963. Encircling the shield was an annulet or, stoned sable (the ring of investiture) and over it a Geneva Bonnet sable with, on either side a string ending in a single blue tassel.

276. This is a type of merchant mark associated with Bridge House, headquarters for the London Bridge Authority, which was situated in the old Metropolitan Borough of Southwark.

39 · Arms of dominion and sovereignty

Royal arms in many respects differ from ordinary armorial bearings, and it should be carefully borne in mind that they stand, not for any particular area of land, but for the intangible sovereignty vested in the rulers thereof. They are not necessarily, nor are they in fact, hereditary. They pass by conquest. A dynastic change which introduces new sovereignties introduces new quarterings, as when the Hanoverian dynasty came to the throne of this country the quartering of Hanover was introduced, but purely personal arms in British heraldry are never introduced. The personal arms of Tudor and Stewart were never added to the Royal Arms of this country.

The origin of the English Royal Arms was dealt with on page 133. 'Gules, three lions passant guardant in pale or', as the arms of England, were used by Kings John, Henry III, Edward I, and Edward II. The quartering for France was introduced by Edward III, as explained on page 206, and the Royal shield: Quarterly 1 and 4, France, ancient [azure, semé-de-lis or]; 2 and 3, England [gules, three lions passant guardant in pale or], was in use in the reigns of Edward III, Richard II [who, however, impaled his arms with those of St Edward the Confessor], and Henry IV. The last-mentioned king about 1411[277] reduced the number of fleurs-de-lis to three, and the shield remained without further change till the end of the reign of Edward VI. Queen Mary did not alter the arms of this country, but during the time of her marriage with Philip of Spain they were always borne impaled with the arms of Spain. Queen Elizabeth I bore the same shield as her predecessors. But when James I came to the throne the arms were: 'Quarterly 1 and 4, quarterly i. and iiii. France, ii. and iii. England; 2. Scotland (or, a lion rampant within a double tressure flory and counterflory gules); 3. Ireland (azure, a harp or, stringed argent).' The shield was so borne by James I, Charles I, Charles II, and James II.

When William III and Mary came to the throne an inescutcheon of the arms of Nassau ('Azure, billetty and a lion rampant or') was superimposed upon the Royal Arms as previously borne, for William III, and he impaled the same coat without the inescutcheon for his wife. At her death the impalement was dropped. After the Union with Scotland in 1707 the arms of England ('Gules, three lions', &c.) were impaled with those of Scotland (the tressure not being continued down

277. There are many examples of the use of France Modern (three fleurs-de-lis) superseding France Ancient earlier than 1411, when a new Great Seal was struck embodying the revised coat. It is reasonable to suppose that the change was gradually effected, as no official pronouncement on the subject has ever been discovered.

471

the palar line), and the impaled coat of England and Scotland was placed in the first and fourth quarters, France in the second, Ireland in the third.

At the accession of George I the arms of Hanover were introduced in the fourth quarter. These were: 'Tierced in pairle reversed, 1. Brunswick, gules, two lions passant guardant in pale or; 2. Lüneburg, [or semé of hearts gules, a lion rampant azure]; 3. (in point), Westphalia [gules, a horse courant argent, and on an inescutcheon (over the fourth quarter) gules, the crown of Charlemagne (as Arch Treasurer of the Holy Roman Empire)].

At the union with Ireland in 1801 the opportunity was taken to revise the Royal Arms, and those of France were then discontinued. The escutcheon decided upon at that date was: 'Quarterly, 1 and 4, England; 2. Scotland; 3. Ireland and the arms of Hanover were placed upon an inescutcheon'. This inescutcheon was surmounted by the Electoral cap, for which a crown was substituted later when Hanover became a kingdom.

At the death of William IV, by the operation of the Salic Law, the crowns of England and Hanover were separated, and the inescutcheon of Hanover disappeared from the Royal Arms of this country, and by Royal Warrant issued at the beginning of the reign of Queen Victoria the Royal Arms and badges were declared to be: 1 and 4, England; 2. Scotland; 3. Ireland. The necessary alteration of the cyphers are the only alterations since made.

The supporters date from the accession of James I. Before that date there had been much variety. Some of the Royal badges have been already alluded to in the chapter on that subject.

The differences used by various junior members of the Royal Family will be found in the Chapter on Marks of Cadency.

40 · Hatchments

A custom formerly prevailed in England, which at one time was of very considerable importance. This was the setting up of a hatchment after a death. No instances of hatchments of a very early date, as far as I am aware, are to be met with, and it is probably a correct conclusion that the custom, originating rather earlier, came into vogue in England during the seventeenth century and reached its height in the eighteenth. It doubtless originated in the carrying of ceremonial shields and helmets (afterwards left in the church) at funerals in the sixteenth century, and in the earlier practice of setting up in the church the actual shield of a deceased person. The cessation of the ceremonial funeral, no doubt, led to the cult of the hatchment. Hatchments cannot be said even yet to have come entirely to an end, but instances of their use are nowadays extremely rare, and since the early part of the nineteenth century the practice has been steadily declining, and at the present time it is seldom indeed that one sees a hatchment in use. The word 'hatchment' is, of course, a corruption of the term 'achievement', this being the heraldic term implying an emblazonment of the full armorial bearings of any person.

The manner of use was as follows. Immediately upon the death of a person of any social position a hatchment of his or her arms was set up over the entrance to his house, which remained there for twelve months, during the period of mourning. It was then taken down from the house and removed to the church, where it was set up in perpetuity. There are few churches of any age in this country which do not boast one or more of these hatchments, and some are rich in their possession. Those now remaining—for example, in St Chad's Church in Shrewsbury—must number, I imagine, over a hundred. There does not appear to have been any obligation upon a clergyman either to permit their erection, or to allow them to remain for any specified period. In some churches they have been discarded and relegated to the vestry, to the coal-house, or to the rubbish-heap, whilst in others they have been carefully preserved.

The hatchment was a diamond-shaped frame, painted black, and enclosing a painting in oils upon wood, or more frequently canvas, of the full armorial bearings of the deceased person. The frame was usually about five feet six in height and the rules for the display of arms upon hatchments afford an interesting set of regulations which may be applied to other heraldic emblazonments. The chief point, however, concerning a hatchment, and also the one in which it differs from an ordinary armorial emblazonment, lay in the colour of the groundwork upon which the armorial bearings were painted. For an unmarried person the whole of the groundwork was black, but for a husband or wife half was black and half white, the groundwork behind the arms of the deceased person being black, and of the surviving partner in matrimony white. The background for a widow or widower was entirely black.

473

41 · The Union Jack

By Rev. J. R. CRAWFORD

Orders in Council and other official documents refer to this flag as the Union Flag, The Union Jack, Our Jack, The King's Colours, and the Union Banner, which last title precise Heraldry usually adopts. In patriotic songs it is toasted as 'The Red, White, and Blue', whilst in the Services men affectionately allude to it as 'the dear old duster'. But Britons at large cling to the title which heads this chapter; to them it is '*The Union Jack*'.

Why *Union*? Obviously because it unites three emblems of tutelar saints on one flag, and thereby denotes the union of three peoples under one Sovereign. It is the motto '*Tria juncta in Uno*' rendered in bunting.

Why *Jack*? Two theories are propounded, one fanciful, the other probable. Some say 'Jack' is the anglicised form of 'Jacques', which is the French signature of James I, in whose reign and by whose command the first Union Flag was called into being. Against this at least three reasons may justly be urged: (1) The term '*Jack*' does not appear—so far as we can discover—in any warrant referring to the Jacobean Flag of 1606. It is rather in later documents that this term occurs. (2) If the earliest Union Flag be a '*Jack*' just because it is the creation of James, then surely it follows that, to be consistent, later Union Flags, the creations of later sovereigns, should have borne those Sovereigns' names; for example *The Union Anne, The Union George*! (3) The English way of pronouncing 'Jacques' is not, and probably never was, *Jack*, but *Jaikes*. The other, and more feasible theory, is as follows: The term 'Jaque' (e.g. *jaque de mailles*) was borrowed from the French and referred to any jacket or coat on which, especially, heraldic emblems were blazoned. In days long prior to those of the first Stuart king, mention is made of '𝖜𝖍𝖞𝖙𝖙𝖊 𝖈𝖔𝖙𝖊𝖘 𝖜𝖎𝖙𝖍 𝖗𝖊𝖉 𝖈𝖗𝖔𝖘𝖘𝖊𝖘 𝖜𝖔𝖗𝖓 𝖇𝖞 𝖘𝖍𝖞𝖕𝖕𝖊𝖘𝖒𝖊𝖓 𝖆𝖓𝖉 𝖒𝖊𝖓 𝖔𝖋 𝖙𝖍𝖊 𝖈𝖊𝖙𝖙𝖊 𝖔𝖋 𝕷𝖔𝖓𝖉𝖔𝖓,' from which sentence we learn that the emblem of the nation's tutelar saint was (as in yet earlier Crusaders' days) a *fighter's* emblem. When such emblem or emblems were transferred to a flag, the term *Jaque* may well, in course of time, have been also applied to that flag, as previously to the jacket.

Glance now at the story of those Orders in Council which created the various Union flags. The very union of the two kingdoms of England and Scotland seems to have accentuated the pettier national jealousies, so that Southrons annoyed Northerners by hoisting the St George above the St Andrew, and the Scotsmen retaliated by a species of *tu quoque*. The King sought to allay these quarrels by creating a British, as other than a purely English or Scottish, flag. But let the Proclamation speak for itself.

474

'By the King.

'*Whereas, some differences hath arisen between Our subjects of South and North Britaine travelling by Seas, about the bearing of their Flagges; For the avoiding of all contentions hereafter, Wee have, with the advice of our Council, ordered; That from henceforth all our Subjects of this Isle and Kingdome of Great Britaine, and all our members thereof, shall beare in their main-toppe the Red Crosse, commonly called St George's Crosse, and the White Crosse, commonly called St Andrew's Crosse, joyned together according to the forme made by our heralds, and sent by Us to our Admerall to be published to our Subjects; and in their fore-toppe our Subjects of South Britaine shall weare the Red Crosse onely as they were wont, and our Subjects of North Britaine in their fore-toppe the White Crosse onely as they were accustomed.*'— 1606.

This attempt at conciliating differences deserved but did not win success. *The King's Owne Shipps*' deemed themselves slighted, since all vessels were treated alike in this matter, and so persistent was the agitation that at last, in Charles I's reign (1634), another Proclamation was issued '*for the honour of Oure Shipps in Oure Navie Royall*, whereby those ships alone had the right of hoisting '*the Union Flagge*'. The days of the Commonwealth brought another change, for with the King the King's Flag disappeared. The Protector caused two new flags to be made, viz. *The Great Union* (a flag little used, however, although it figured at his funeral obsequies), and which may be thus blazoned: *Quarterly* 1 *and* 4, *The St George*; 2. *The St Andrew*; 3. *azure, a harp or, for Ireland; over all on an inescutcheon of pretence, sable, a lion rampant or*, for the Protector's personal arms, and *The Commonwealth Ensign*, which latter Parliament treated as the paramount flag. The most interesting features of this flag are that it was of three kinds, one red, one white, one blue, and that Ireland but not Scotland had a place on its folds. When the King came to his own again yet another change was witnessed. By this Proclamation ships in the Navy were to carry *The Union*, and all merchantmen *The St George*, whilst these latter vessels were also to wear 'The Red Ensign with the St George, on a Canton'. Passing on, we reach the days of Queen Anne, who as soon as the union of the two Parliaments was accomplished, issued a famous Proclamation often quoted. Suffice it here to outline its effect.

The two crosses of *St George* and *St Andrew* were—as the Treaty of Union had agreed should be—'*conjoyned in such a manner as we should think fit*'; and what that manner was is '*described on the margent*' in the shape of a sketch. But further, in place of the *St George* being placed on the canton of the *Red Ensign* of Charles II (itself the *Commonwealth Ensign*, minus the harp) the Proclamation ordered the '*Union*' as a canton, and finally this new Red Ensign was confined to the merchant ships, whilst '*Our Jack*' was reserved for the use of the Navy, unless by particular warrant. Thus things continued until the union of Ireland with England and Scotland. The Proclamation referring to this Act of Union closes with the Herald's verbal blazon of the full Union Flag: 'The Union Flag shall be Azure, the Crosses Saltire of St Andrew and St Patrick, Quarterly per saltire, countercharged Argent and Gules, the latter fimbriated of the second, surmounted by the Cross of St George of the third, fimbriated as the Saltire.' Thus the Union, as displayed in bunting, was perfected.

475

Fig. 1

Danish

Fig. 2

Swedish

Fig. 3

Norwegian

Fig. 4

Union Flag Sweden & Norway

775.

Our *Union Flag* is very remarkable, even amongst the flags of Christendom, both as a blending of crosses, and crosses only, and also as an emblem of the union of two or more countries. Yet it is not unique, for the flags of Denmark, Sweden, and Norway have a somewhat similar story to tell. The last two countries separated at different dates from Denmark, and then together formed a United Scandinavian Kingdom. In separating, they each took to themselves a separate flag, and again, in uniting, they called into being a Union Banner. How they treated these changes 775 will illustrate. Notwithstanding these acts of union both Scandinavians and Britons have had, and we still have, differences over these Union Flags. Whilst, however, they based their protests on the sentiment of independence, we ground our grumblings on questions of heraldic precedence, and of the interpretation of verbal blazons. Leaving our neighbours to settle their differences, let us examine our own. Take the subject of precedence. Very early in the flag's history, Scotsmen were indignant because the St Andrew was not placed over the St George. All kinds of variations have been suggested to lessen this crux of precedence, but such attempts must plainly be in vain. Do what you will, some kind of precedence is unavoidable. The St George, then, as representing the paramount partner, occupies the centre of the flag, whilst the St Andrew, as senior in partnership to the St Patrick, is placed *above the St Patrick, in the first quarter*, although throughout it is counterchanged. The words in italic are important, for when the order is reversed, then that particular flag is flying upside down.

The mode of procedure in creating flags has been much the same from one reign to another. Briefly it is this: The Sovereign seeks the advice of, and receives a report from, the Lords of the Privy Council. These councillors are '*attended by the King of Arms and Heralds, with diverse drafts prepared by them*'. A decision being arrived at, an Order in Council, followed by a Royal Proclamation, makes known the character of the flag. In both Order and Proclamation it is usual to make reference to the verbal blazon, and to '*the form made by our heralds*'. Thus there are three agents recognised—(1) the Sovereign, the fountain of all honours; (2) the heralds, who authoritatively blazon, outline, and register all achievements; and (3) the naval authority, as that in which are vested the duty and the power of seeing the actual bunting properly made up and properly flown. In keeping with this, the general mode of procedure, the Proclamations demand our attention. *The Proclamation of James I (1606).* A high official of the College of Arms informs us that neither verbal blazon nor drawing of the first Union Flag is extant. On the other hand, in the *Proclamations of 1707 and 1801* we have both blazon and drawing. The blazon has already been given of the 1801 flag (which is the one most needing a verbal blazon), and the drawings of both flags we here produce (776 and 777). These drawings—though slightly reduced in these pages—are most careful copies of the signed copies supplied to us by the official already alluded to. In forwarding them he writes: 'They are not drawn to scale'; and he adds, further on, 'they are exactly the same size as recorded in our books'. So then we have, in these two drawings, the heralds' interpretation, *at the time*, of their own verbal blazon. Now comes the Admiralty part of the work. In the Admiralty Regulations we have a '*Memorandum relative to the origin of the Union Flag in its present form*'. In this there is a brief history of the changes made in the flag from time to time, with quotations from the warrants, together with the verbal blazon and two

776 *The Union Flag of 1707.* 777 *The Union Flag of 1801.*

coloured drawings (778 and 779). The Admiralty has also appended to the Memorandum the following interesting and ingeniously worked out *Table of proportions, adapted for a flag 15 feet by 7½ feet.* Presumably this table forms the basis upon which all Union Flags are made up under Admiralty supervision:

$$
\text{The } + \text{ of}
\begin{cases}
\text{St George} & \cdots \cdots \frac{1}{5} \\
\text{Two borders } \frac{1}{15} \text{ each} \cdots \frac{2}{15}
\end{cases}
\Big\}\text{together } \frac{1}{3}
\begin{cases}
\text{I} & 6 \\
\text{I} & 0
\end{cases}\Big\}\frac{1}{3}
$$

$$
\text{The } \times \text{ of}
\begin{cases}
\text{St Patrick} & \cdots \cdots \frac{1}{15} \\
\text{Its border} & \cdots \cdots \frac{1}{30} \\
\text{St Andrew} & \cdots \cdots \frac{1}{10}
\end{cases}
\begin{cases}
\text{together } \frac{1}{10}
\begin{cases}
0 & 6 \\
0 & 3 \\
0 & 9
\end{cases}\Big\}\frac{1}{5}
\end{cases}
$$

The student of heraldry will observe that this table is based on the proportions of the Ordinaries and Sub-Ordinaries figuring on the flag, as those proportions are regulated by English Rules of Armory. These rules give a cross as $\frac{1}{3}$, a saltire as $\frac{1}{5}$, a fimbriation about $\frac{1}{20}$, of the flag's width. By the way, we notice here, yet only to dismiss it as hypercritical, the objection taken to the employment (in the verbal blazon of 1801) of the term 'fimbriated'. To our mind this objection seems a storm in a teacup. Further, it is always admissible in armory to lessen the size of charges when these crowd a field, and although we are fully aware that the laws of armory are not always nor all of them applied to flags, yet there is sufficient evidence to show that the heralds and the Admiralty did recognise the cases of shields and flags to be somewhat analogous. But there are two features in the Admiralty pattern which cannot but arrest the attention of all those who have made a study of armory. The one is that the sub-ordinaries, *i.e.* the fimbriations, have

778 *Admiralty Pattern of 1707 Flag.*

779 *Admiralty Pattern of 1801 Flag.*

different proportions given to them, although they are repetitions of the same sub-ordinary, and also seem guarded against such treatment by the very wording of the blazon, and by the practice usual in such cases. And the other is that, after counterchanging the saltires, the St Patrick is attenuated by having its fimbriation taken off its own field, instead (as the common custom is) off the field of the flag.

All Warrants dealing with flags provide for their being flown *at sea* (Queen Anne's Proclamation is apparently the first that adds '*and land*'), and gradually reserve for the Royal Navy—or fighting ships—the honour of alone bearing the Union Jack. The accompanying diagram shows at a glance the changes made by the several Proclamations. The latest word on this subject is *The Merchant Shipping (Colours) Act of Queen Victoria, 1894.* This Act sets forth among other things that—(1) '*The red ensign usually worn by merchant ships, without any defacement or modification whatsoever, is hereby declared to be the proper national colours for all ships and boats belonging to any British subject, except in the case of Her Majesty's ships or boats, or in the case of any other ship or boat for the time being allowed to wear any other national colours in pursuance of a warrant from Her Majesty or from the Admiralty. (2) If any distinctive national colours except such red ensign, or except the Union Jack with a white border, or if any colours usually worn by Her Majesty's ships, &c. . . . are or is hoisted on board any ship . . . without warrant . . . for each offence . . . a fine not exceeding five hundred pounds.*

42 · 'Seize-Quartiers'

PROOF OF ANCESTRY

If any heraldic term, other than 'bar sinister', has been misunderstood in this country, 'Seize-Quartiers' is that term. One hears 'Seize-Quartiers' claimed right and left, whereas in British armory it is only on the very rarest occasions that proof of it can be made. In England there is not, and never has been, for any purpose a real 'test' of blood. By the statutes of various Orders of Knighthood, esquires of knights of those orders are required to show that their grandparents were of gentle birth and entitled to bear arms, and a popular belief exists that Knights of Justice of the Order of the Hospital of St John of Jerusalem in England need to establish some test of birth. The wording of the statute, however, is very loose and vague, and in fact, judging from the names and arms of some of the knights, must be pretty generally ignored. But Peer, K.G., or C.B., alike need pass no test of birth. The present state of affairs in this country is the natural outcome of the custom of society, which always recognises the wife as of the husband's status, whatever may have been her antecedents, unless the discrepancy is too glaring to be overlooked. In England few indeed care or question whether this person or that person has even a coat of arms; and in the decision of Society upon a given question as to whether this person or the other has 'married beneath himself', the judgment results solely from the circle in which the wife and her people move. By many this curious result is claimed as an example of, and as a telling instance to demonstrate, the broad-minded superiority of the English race, as evidenced by the equality which this country concedes between titled and untitled classes, between official and unofficial personages, between the land-owning and the mercantile communities. But such a conclusion is most superficial. We draw no distinction, and rightly so, between titled and untitled amongst the few remaining families who have held and owned their lands for many genera-tions; but outside this class the confusion is great, and to a close observer it is plainly enough apparent that great distinctions are drawn. But they are often mistaken ones. That the rigid and definite dividing line between patrician and plebeian, which still exists so much more markedly upon the Continent, can only be traced most sketchily in this country is due to two causes—(1) the fact that in early days, when Society was slowly evolving itself, many younger sons of gentle families embarked upon commercial careers, natural family affection, because of such action, preventing a rigid exclusion from the ranks of Society of every one tainted by commerce; (2) the absence in this country of any equivalent of the patent distinguishing marks 'de', 'van', or 'von', which exist among our neigh-bours in Europe.

The result has been that in England there is no possible way (short of specific

479

genealogical investigation) in which it can be ascertained whether any given person is of gentle birth, and the corollary of this last-mentioned fact is that any real test is ignored. There are few families in this country, outside the Roman Catholic aristocracy (whose marriages are not quite so haphazard as are those of other people), who can show that all their sixteen great-great-grandparents were in their own right entitled to bear arms. That is the true definition of the 'Proof of Seize-Quartiers'.

In other words, to prove Seize-Quartiers you must show this right to have existed for

Self	Parents	Grand-parents	Gt.-grand-parents	Gt.-gt.-grand-parents
1. Your	Father's	Father's	Father's	Father
2. Your	Father's	Father's	Father's	Mother
3. Your	Father's	Father's	Mother's	Father
4. Your	Father's	Father's	Mother's	Mother
5. Your	Father's	Mother's	Father's	Father
6. Your	Father's	Mother's	Father's	Mother
7. Your	Father's	Mother's	Mother's	Father
8. Your	Father's	Mother's	Mother's	Mother
9. Your	Mother's	Father's	Father's	Father
10. Your	Mother's	Father's	Father's	Mother
11. Your	Mother's	Father's	Mother's	Father
12. Your	Mother's	Father's	Mother's	Mother
13. Your	Mother's	Mother's	Father's	Father
14. Your	Mother's	Mother's	Father's	Mother
15. Your	Mother's	Mother's	Mother's	Father
16. Your	Mother's	Mother's	Mother's	Mother

It should be distinctly understood that there is no connection whatever between the list of quarterings which may have been inherited, which it is permissible to display, and 'Seize-Quartiers', which should never be marshalled together or displayed as quarterings.

Few people indeed in this country can prove the more coveted distinction of 'Trente Deux Quartiers', the only case that has ever come under my notice being that of the late Alfred Joseph, Baron Mowbray, Segrave, and Stourton, for whom an emblazonment of his thirty-two quarters was prepared under the direction of Stephen Tucker, Esq., Somerset Herald.

After many futile trials (in order to add an existing English example), which have only too surely confirmed my opinion as to the rarity of 'Seize-Quartiers' in this country, it has been found possible in the case of the late Duke of Leinster, and details of the 'proof' follow:

The following are the heraldic particulars of the shields which would occur were this proof of 'Seize-Quartiers' emblazoned in the ordinary form adopted for such a display. The arms are numbered across from left to right in rows of 16, 8, 4, 2, and 1.

1. *Duke's Coronet* (Ribbon of St Patrick): Argent, a saltire gules (Fitz Gerald).
2. *Lozenge:* Argent, a chief azure, over all a lion rampant gules, ducally crowned or (St George).
3. *Earl's Coronet* (Ribbon of Hanoverian Guelphic Order): Quarterly ermine and gules, in the centre a crescent on a crescent for cadency (Stanhope).

(1) WILLIAM ROBERT (FITZ GERALD), 2nd Duke of Leinster, K.P., born 13 March 1749, married 7 November 1775, died 20 October 1804 =

(2) Hon. EMILIA OLIVIA ST GEORGE, dau. of Usher (St George), Baron St George of Hatley St George.

(3) CHARLES (STANHOPE), 3rd Earl of Harrington, G.C.H., born 17 March 1753 married 23 May 1779, died 5 September 1829. =

(4) JANE, dau. and co-heir of Sir John Fleming, Bart., of Brompton Park.

(5) GEORGE GRANVILLE (LEVESON-GOWER), 1st Duke of Sutherland, K.G., born 9 January 1758, married 4 September 1785, died 5 July 1833. =

(6) ELIZABETH, *suo jure* Countess of Sutherland, born 24 May 1765, died 29 January 1839.

(7) GEORGE (HOWARD), 6th Earl of Carlisle, K.G., born 17 September 1773 married 11 March 1801, died 7 October 1848. =

(8) Lady GEORGIANA CAVENDISH, eldest dau. and co-heir of William, 5th Duke of Devonshire, K.G.

(9) CHARLES (DUNCOMBE), 1st Baron Feversham, born 5 December 1764, married 24 September 1795, died 16 July 1841. =

(10) Lady CHARLOTTE LEGGE, only dau. of William, 2nd Earl of Dartmouth, died 5 November 1848.

(11) GEORGE (STEWART), 8th Earl of Galloway, K.T., born 24 March 1768, married 18 April 1797, died 27 March 1834. =

(12) Lady JANE PAGET, dau. of Henry, 1st Earl of Uxbridge, died 30 June 1842.

(13) Sir JAMES GRAHAM, 1st Bart, of Netherby, born April 1761, married 28 September 1782, died 13 April 1824. =

(14) Lady CATHERINE STEWART, dau. of John, 7th Earl of Galloway, died 20 October 1836.

(15) Colonel JAMES CALLANDER of Craigforth, born 1774, died ——, married (as his 3rd wife) 1776. =

(16) Lady ELIZABETH MACDONNEL, dau. of Alexander, 5th Earl of Antrim, died 1796

AUGUSTUS FREDERICK (FITZ GERALD) 3rd Duke of Leinster, born 21 August 1791, married 16 June 1818, died 10 October 1874=

Lady CHARLOTTE AUGUSTA (STANHOPE), born 15 February 1793, died 15 February 1859.

GEORGE GRANVILLE (SUTHERLAND-LEVESON-GOWER, formerly Leveson-Gower), 2nd Duke of Sutherland, K.G., born 8 August 1786, married 28 May 1823, died 28 February 1861=

Lady HARRIET ELIZABETH GEORGINA HOWARD, born 21 May 1806, died 27 October 1868.

WILLIAM (DUNCOMBE), 2nd Baron Feversham, born 14 January 1798, married 18 December 1823, died 11 February 1867==

Lady LOUISA STEWART, died 5 March 1889.

Right Hon. Sir JAMES ROBERT GEORGE GRAHAM, 2nd Bart, P.C., G.C.B., born 1 June 1792, married 8 July 1819, died 25 October 1861 =

FANNY CALLANDER, died 25 October 1857.

CHARLES WILLIAM (FITZ GERALD), 4th Duke of Leinster, born 30 March 1819, married 30 October 1847, died 10 February 1887=

Lady CAROLINE SUTHERLAND-LEVESON-GOWER, born 15 April 1827, died 13 May 1887.

WILLIAM ERNEST (DUNCOMBE), 1st Earl of Feversham (created 1868), born 28 January 1829, married 7 August 1851, died 13 January, 1915=

MABEL VIOLET GRAHAM.

GERALD (FITZ GERALD), 5th Duke of Leinster, born 16 August 1851, married 17 January 1884, died 1 December 1893=

Lady HERMOINE WILHELMINA DUNCOMBE, born 30 March 1864, died 19 March 1895.

The Most Noble MAURICE (FITZ GERALD), Duke of Leinster, Marquess and Earl of Kildare, co. Kildare, Earl and Baron of Offaly, all in the Peerage of Ireland; Viscount Leinster of Taplow, co. Bucks, in the Peerage of Great Britain; and Baron Kildare of Kildare in the Peerage of the United Kingdom; Premier Duke, Marquess, and Earl of Ireland; born 1 March 1887, died 4 February, 1922.

481

4. *Lozenge:* Argent, a chevron gules, a double tressure flory and counterflory of the last (Fleming).

5. *Duke's Coronet* (Garter): Quarterly, 1 and 4, barry of eight or and gules, over all a cross flory sable; 2 and 3, azure, three laurel leaves or (Leveson-Gower).

6. *Lozenge* (surmounted by Earl's coronet): Gules, three mullets or, on a bordure of the second a tressure flory counterflory of the first (Sutherland).

7. *Earl's Coronet* (Garter): Quarterly of six, 1. gules, on a bend between six cross crosslets fitchée argent, an inescutcheon or, charged with a demi-lion rampant, pierced through the mouth with an arrow, within a double tressure flory counterflory of the first; 2. gules, three lions passant guardant in pale or, in chief a label of three points argent; 3. chequy or and azure; 4. Gules, a lion rampant argent; 5. gules, three escallops argent; 6. barry of six argent and azure, three chaplets gules, in the centre of the quarters a mullet for difference (Howard).

8. *Lozenge:* Sable, three bucks' heads caboshed argent (Cavendish).

9. *Baron's Coronet:* Per chevron engrailed gules and argent, three talbots' heads erased counterchanged (Duncombe).

10. *Lozenge:* Azure, a buck's head caboshed argent (Legge).

11. *Earl's Coronet* (Ribbon of Thistle): Or, a fess chequy argent and azure, surmounted of a bend engrailed gules, within a tressure flory counterflory of the last (Stewart).

12. *Lozenge:* Sable, on a cross engrailed between four eagles displayed argent, five lions passant guardant of the field (Paget).

13. *Baronet's Badge:* Or, on a chief sable, three escallops of the field (Graham).

14. *Lozenge:* Arms as on No. 11 (Stewart).

15. *Shield:* Quarterly, 1 and 4, sable, a bend chequy or and gules between six billets of the second; 2. azure, a stag's head caboshed or; 3. gules, three legs armed proper, conjoined in the fess point and flexed in triangle, garnished and spurred or (Callander).

16. *Lozenge:* Quarterly, 1. or, a lion rampant gules; 2. or, a dexter arm issuant from the sinister fess point out of a cloud proper, the hand holding a cross crosslet fitchée erect azure; 3. argent, a ship with sailes furled sable; 4. per fess azure and vert, a dolphin naiant in fess proper (Macdonell).

17. As 1. but no ribbon of K.P.

18. *Lozenge:* Arms as 3.

19. *Duke's Coronet* (Garter): Quarterly, 1 and 4. as in 5; 2, as in 5; 3. as in No. 6.

20. *Lozenge:* As No. 7.

21. *Baron's Coronet:* As No. 9.

22. *Lozenge:* As No. 14.

23. As No. 13, but with ribbon of a G.C.B.

24. *Lozenge:* As No. 15.

25. As 17.

26. *Lozenge:* As No. 19.

27. As 21, but Earl's coronet.

28. *Lozenge:* As No. 13, but no Baronet's Badge.

29. As 17.

30. *Lozenge:* As No. 9.

31. *Arms:* Argent, a saltire gules. Crest: a monkey statant proper, environed about the middle with a plain collar, and chained or. Supporters: two monkeys (as the crest). Mantling gules and argent. Coronet of a duke. Motto: 'Crom a boo.'

Epilogue

By J. P. Brooke-Little

The enjoyment and value of any game depends on the players learning and conscientiously observing the rules. Heraldry is like this. To enjoy heraldry fully—and heraldry ought to be enjoyed—it is essential that one be well grounded in the grammar, learning the conventions and something of the history of the subject. Just as the rules of boxing have changed considerably during the past century, so some of the conventions of armory have altered, and it is necessary to know how they have altered if today's heraldry is to be understood and appreciated as a living science and not simply as an antiquarian study.

The enduring value of Fox-Davies' book is that it provides a readable, accurate and complete guide to the grammar and practice of modern heraldry seen against a backcloth of its history.

Fox-Davies wrote at the time of a pronounced revival of interest in armory, but he was regarded as a pedantic, legalistic reactionary by the apostles of the revival, men like Oswald Barron, W. H. St John Hope, and J. Horace Round, the great debunker of long cherished genealogical myths. The reason was simply that the revivalists were scholarly, heraldic pre-Raphaelites; they wanted a return to medieval practice. They sought to clear the pure field of armory of the tortuous undergrowth of jargon and banality, representationism and stylised artistry. They saw in Fox-Davies the champion of the dull, pedestrian heraldry that came from the College of Arms, with its lugubrious blazon, everlasting copper-plate, meretricious, though faultlessly executed, painting and general air of portentous self-satisfaction. But though Fox-Davies provided a whipping-boy, he was not really a very satisfactory one, for he, too, deprecated representational arms and yearned for a more lively approach to heraldry, although always within the confines of what he understood to be the law of arms. His real fight with the revivalists was not with their mediaevalism nor their aesthetic sensibilities, but with their efforts to sweep away centuries of heraldic evolution in order to impose the method of heraldry, which grew up with the feudal system, on a democratic, sophisticated, industrial society. He knew it was the pipe dream it later proved to be. Yet the twentieth century has shown that both Fox-Davies and his scholarly critics were right. They were right inasmuch as it has been possible to re-introduce into heraldry many medieval practices without upsetting the natural evolution of the science. This is particularly true in the field of artistry. Letters Patent granting arms more and more often contain beautiful illuminated capitals and decorated borders; arms are depicted in a wide variety of styles and the standard of painting is as high as, and infinitely more versatile than, it ever was. The revival of the heraldic badge has given both the armorist and the armiger more scope both to use arms

483

correctly and to display them in a wide variety of ways. Now that badges are becoming more and more popular, that magnificent medieval flag, the standard, is reappearing, and it is to be hoped that this trend will continue. Multi-coloured wreaths, parti-coloured mantlings and mantlings strewn with the badge frequently appear. The dreary practice of the mantling and wreath being of the principal colour and metal in the arms, and the earlier, but almost equally dreary (because inelastic), convention of the mantling always being gules doubled argent are now only followed when artistically desirable. Happily the rule of eye has triumphed over the rule of thumb.

The revivalists' combination of scholarship and aesthetics has been emulated by at least two people in high places in the twentieth century, and their mark on the continuous story of heraldry must not be underrated. I refer to Sir George Bellew, Garter King of Arms from 1950–1961, and his successor, Sir Anthony Wagner, who currently fills with distinction this honourable office. Sir George had (indeed 'has', for he is very much alive) a natural sense of design and a great feeling for living heraldry. It was he who freed heraldic practice from the shackles of many of the 'obsolete rules' which Fox-Davies quotes so frequently. It is perhaps too early properly to assess his influence on armory, but my own opinion is that it will be found to have been considerable, both in its own right and as a vital link in a chain of considered liberalisation.

Sir Anthony Wagner, his successor, has done much scholarly research, and has revealed a vast amount of information concerning early heralds and heraldry which has helped, and will increasingly help, to put heraldry into its proper historical context. It is often forgotten that the true meaning of heraldry is 'the business of the heralds'. Not just coats of arms but ceremonial, precedence, genealogy and kindred disciplines. Living heraldry is entirely dependent on the heralds; their enthusiasms, whims, excellencies and defects are all reflected in the armory of the day. Heraldry is the heralds and the heralds are heraldry; their history is therefore to a large extent the history of heraldry and it is in this particular field that Sir Anthony has concentrated much of his very considerable ability. His two books, *Heralds and Heraldry in the Middle Ages* and *The Heralds of England*, probably contain more original material about the heralds than has ever been published before. Some of it is scarcely complimentary, but if all the heralds had always been perfect, heraldry would never have been less than excellent, and the officers of arms would truly have been 'herald angels'. In fact, the chequered history of the heralds helps in great measure to explain the ups and downs which have characterised the art and science of heraldry through the centuries.

Many of the ideas and aspirations of the reformers thus have come to pass; but Fox-Davies also has been vindicated. He firmly believed that the use and display of arms must be governed by rules and conventions. His extreme critics argued that most of the rules had been made after true heraldry—that is, feudal heraldry—had become a dead letter, and that they should, therefore, be abolished. Up to a point the critics were right; as heraldry evolved, it left the battle-field and tournament field for the drawing board, and so concerned an ever widening circle of society. Naturally it became more complex, and the ingenuity of the heralds was constantly challenged trying to introduce new charges and methods of displaying them. Early heraldic grammarians, like Gerard Legh (died 1563), John Guillim (born

1565; died 1621) and Randle Holme (born 1571; died 1655) had a profound effect on heraldry, as they to some extent codified and rationalised the capricious growth of early sixteenth-century heraldic design and terminology, and provided basic text-books for professional as well as dilettante armorists. Later writers tended to draw heavily from their works, and the inevitable result was the stagnation against which Barron and his followers so understandably rebelled.

Whilst Fox-Davies believed in orderly conventions and could not see how the clock could be put back, this was not a fetish with him. His real hobby-horse was the law, not the lore, of arms. He saw heraldry as a legal system governed by law, and had no time for those who claimed that there was such a thing as prescriptive right to arms. He constantly referred to 'bogus' arms, and this was a red rag to the bulls of Barron. Fox-Davies and W. P. W. Phillimore ranged their forces against Horace Round and W. Paley Baildon, who both wrote scathing attacks on Fox-Davies in *The Ancestor*, an excellent quarterly journal founded and edited by Barron from 1902 until 1905.

In the end, I think victory must be conceded to Fox-Davies, for today few doubt that there is a law of arms and that it is enforceable in the Court of Chivalry. The case of the Lord Mayor, Aldermen and Citizens of the City of Manchester versus The Manchester Palace of Varieties Ltd held before the Court on 21 December 1954 established that the Court, which had not sat since 1737, was still a court of law, and had jurisdiction in matters related to armorial bearings. Fox-Davies has, in great measure, to thank G. D. Squibb, Q.C., Norfolk Herald Extraordinary for taking over the torch. By diligent and scholarly research he has managed, and with arguments far more valid than Fox-Davies ever propounded, to place the law of arms and the Court of Chivalry in their proper perspective. Those interested in this important aspect of heraldry are referred to an excellent pamphlet by Squibb and published by the Heraldry Society, entitled *The Law of Arms in England* (revised edition 1967).

The result of these battles at the beginning of this century has been to stir up a wide and informed interest in armory which is reflected in the number of books, both scholarly and otherwise, which have been published, especially since the last war; the several excellent exhibitions, wholly devoted to heraldry which have been mounted; and the foundation of a flourishing Society in 1947, and later the formation of similar societies throughout the Commonwealth. Also, nine International Congresses of Genealogical and Heraldic Sciences have been held in different parts of Europe. Under the auspices of the Heraldry Society the first purely English congress was successfully held at Oxford in 1967, and in 1968, under the same patronage, the first exhibition of heraldic art—*Heraldic Design Today*—was staged at the premises of the Reed Paper Group Ltd and with their generous co-operation, in Piccadilly, London.

Barron, whose very great merits were recognised in 1937 when he became Maltravers Pursuivant Extraordinary, would have rejoiced to have seen the revival of interest in the art and origins of heraldry, the paring down of jargon and the less aloof approach of the officers of arms. For his part, Fox-Davies would have been happy to see the law of arms firmly established and, like Barron, I am sure he would have approved of the way in which much of the manual-writer's trash has been discarded.

Bibliography

By W. K. FORD

AUBREY, John. Brief Lives. Edited by O. L. Dick. Third Edition. London, Secker and Warburg, 1958.

BARRON, Arthur Oswald. 'Heraldry'. *In:* Shakespeare's England. Oxford, Clarendon Press, 1916.

BERRY, William. Encyclopedia heraldica; or, complete dictionary of heraldry. London, Sherwood, Gilbert and Piper, [1828]. 4 v., including volume of plates and supplement.

BOSSEWELL, John. Workes of armorie. London, Tottel, 1572. 3 v.

BOUTELL, Charles. Boutell's heraldry. 5th edition by C. W. Scott-Giles and J. P. Brooke-Little. London, Warne, 1966.

BOUTON, Victor, *ed.* Wapenboeck, ou Armorial de 1334 à 1372. ... Par Gelre, Heraut d'Armes. Paris et Bruxelles, 1881–6. 4 v.

BURKE, (John) Bernard. The general armory of England, Scotland, Ireland and Wales. Comprising a registry of armorial bearings. London, Harrison, 1878; new ed. with supplement, 1883.

CAMDEN, William. Brittania, sive florentissimorun regnorum . . . chorographica descriptio. London, Newbery, 1586. Various editions; English translation, 1610.

DALLAWAY, James. Inquiries into the origin and progress of the science of heraldry in England. Gloucester, Cadell, 1793.

DAVENPORT, Cyril. 'History of personal jewelry from prehistoric times'. *In:* Journal of the Royal Society for the Encouragement of Art . . ., vol. 50 (1902), pp. 769–90, 793–804.

DAVENPORT, Cyril. The English regalia. London, Kegan Paul, 1897.

DAVIS, Cecil T. Monumental brasses of Gloucestershire. London, Phillimore, 1899.
> Volume covering Herefordshire and Worcestershire publications 1885.

DENHOLM-YOUNG, Noel. History and heraldry, 1254–1310: a study of the historical value of the rolls of arms. Oxford, Clarendon Press, 1965.

DICKSON, Thomas. Accounts of the Lord High Treasurer of Scotland. Edinburgh, H.M. General Register House.
> Vol. 1 (1877), pp. ccxcii–cccv, gives an account of pursuivants.

EDMONDSON, Joseph. A complete body of heraldry. London, the author, 1780. 2 v.

ELVIN, Charles Norton. Dictionary of heraldry. London, Kent; East Dereham, W. H. Brown, [1889].

EVANS, Sloane. Grammar of heraldry. London, R. Smith, 1847; 1854.

EVE, George W. Heraldry as art: an account of its development and practice, chiefly in England. London, Batsford, 1907.

EVE, George W. Decorative heraldry: a handbook of its description and treatment. London, Bell, 1908.

FAIRBAIRN, James. Crests of the families of Great Britain. Fourth edition. London, Jack, 1905. 2 v.

FOSTER, Joseph. Two Tudor books of arms: being Harleian MSS 2179 and 6163. Privately printed, 1904. (Howard de Walden Library).

FOSTER, Joseph. Peerage, baronetage and knightage ... for 1882. Westminster, Nicholls, Chapman and Hall, 1882.

FOX-DAVIES, A. C. The right to bear arms, by 'X'. 2nd ed. London, Stock, 1900.

FOX-DAVIES, A. C. The book of public arms. New edition. London, Jack, 1915.
> First edition with M. E. B. Crookes, 1894.

GAYRE, Robert, *of Gayre and Nigg.* Heraldic standards and other ensigns. Edinburgh, Oliver and Boyd, 1959.

GELRYE: *See* BOUTON.

GUILLIM, John. A display of heraldrie. London, W. Hall, 1610. Third edition, enlarged: T. Cotes, 1638; sixth edition: London, Bonwick, 1724.

HARDYNG, John. The chronicle of John Hardyng from the firste begynning of England. London, Grafton, 1543.
>   Two editions of this work were issued with the same date; see: BENNETT, H. S. *English books and readers, 1475–1557* (Cambridge, 1952), p. 129. Grafton's continuation to the original chronicle was edited by Henry Ellis, 1812.

HOPE, W. H. St. John. Heraldry for craftsmen and designers. London, Pitman, 1913; J. Hogg, 1913. (The Artistic Crafts Series.)

HOPE, W. H. St. John. A grammar of English heraldry. Second edition by A. R. Wagner. Cambridge University Press, 1953.

INNES, Thomas, *of Learney*. Scots heraldry: a . . . handbook on the historical principles and modern applications of the art and science. Second edition. Edinburgh, Oliver and Boyd, 1956.

KNIGHT, F., and RUMLEY, J. Heraldic illustrations. Edinburgh, [1870].

LAING, Henry. Descriptive catalogue of impressions from ancient Scottish seals. Edinburgh, 1850; supplement, 1866.

LAWRANCE, Henry. Heraldry from military monuments before 1350 in England and Wales. London, Harleian Society, 1946. (Volume 96.)
>   A catalogue of surviving examples, arranged by family.

LEGH, Gerard. Accedens of armory. Tottel, 1562.

LELAND, J. De rebus Britannicis collectanea, ed. T. Hearn. Oxford, 1715. 6 v.

LONDON, H. S. 'A catalogue of the English officers of arms'. *In:* PINE, L. G., *ed.* Burke's genealogical and heraldic history of the landed gentry. 17th edition. London, Burke's Peerage, 1952. Pp. cvii–cxxi.

LOWER, Mark A. Curiosities of heraldry. London, R. Smith, 1845.

MENESTRIER, Claude F. Origine des armoiries. Paris, 1680.

MENESTRIER, Claude F. L'art du blason justifié . . . . Lyon, B. Coral, 1661.

MENESTRIER, Claude F. Le véritable art du blason. Lyon, 1671.
>   *Les recherches du blason* refers to 3rd ed., 1673.

PAPWORTH, John W. and MORANT, Alfred W. An alphabetical dictionary of coats of arms . . . Ordinary of British armorials. London, T. Richards, 1874; reprinted with introductions by G. D. Squibb and A. R. Wagner. London, Tabard Publications, 1961.

PARKER, James, *publ.* Glossary of the terms used in heraldry. New edition. Oxford, 1894.

PAUL, James B. Ordinary of Scottish arms. Edinburgh, Green, 1903.

PAUL, James B. Heraldry in relation to Scottish history and art. Edinburgh, Douglas, 1900.

PERCEVAL, Charles S., *with* WALFORD, W. S. Three rolls of arms of the 13th century. London, 1864.

PLANCHÉ, J. R. The Pursuivant of Arms. London, 1851; 1873.

POOLE, Austin L. *ed.* Medieval England. Revised edition, Oxford, Clarendon Press, 1958.
>   Vol. 1 has chapters on Arms and armour by Sir James Mann, The art of war by R. C. Smail, and Heraldry by A. R. Wagner.

RIETSTAB, J. B. Armorial général. Second edition, 1884, reprinted, London, Heraldry Today, 1965. 2 v.
>   Plates of armorial bearings were published separately by Institut Heraldique Universal, Paris, between 1903 and 1926. 6 vols in 7.

ROBERTSON, William. An index drawn up about the year 1629 of many records of charters granted . . . 1306 to 1413, most of which records have long been missing. Edinburgh, Murray and Cochrane, 1798.

ROBSON, Thomas. British herald; or cabinet of armorial bearings. Sunderland, 1830. 2 v.

ROUND, J. Horace. Studies in peerage and family history. London, Constable, 1901.

ROUND, J. Horace. Peerage and pedigree: studies in peerage law and family history, London, Nisbet, 1910. 2 v.

ROUND, J. Horace. Family origins and other studies. London, Constable, 1930.

SANDFORD, Francis. A genealogical list of the kings and queens of England. Ed. Samuel Stebbing. 1775.

SCOTT-GILES, C. Wilfred. Civic heraldry of England and Wales. London, Dent, 1953.

SIEBMACHER, Johann. Das erneurte Teutschen Wappen-buch. Nürnberg, 1655.

ANTHONY VON SIEGENFELD, A. The territorial arms of Styria. Graz. 1898.

SQUIBB, G. D. The law of arms in England. Revised edition. London, Heraldry Society, 1967.

SQUIBB, G. D. Reports of heraldic cases in the Court of Chivalry 1623–1732. London, Harleian Society 1956. (Volume 107).

SQUIBB, G. D. Visitation pedigrees and the genealogist. London, Phillimore, 1964.

SQUIBB, G. D. The High Court of Chivalry; a study of the Civil Law in England . . . Oxford, Clarendon Press, 1959.

STENTON, Frank M., *ed.* The Bayeux tapestry: a comprehensive survey. London, Phaidon Press, 1957.

STRÖHL, H. G. Heraldische Atlas: eine Sammlung von heraldische Musterblättern. Stuttgart, Hoffmann, 1909.

STRÖHL, H. G. Deutsche Wappenrolle. Stuttgart, Hoffmann, 1897.

TAUNTON, William, G. The Tauntons of Oxford, by one of them. London, Stock, 1902.

TRIVICK, Henry H. The craft and design of monumental brasses. London, Baker, 1969.

WAGNER, Anthony R. Heralds of England: a history of the Office and College of Arms. London, H.M.S.O., 1967.

WAGNER, Anthony R. Heralds and heraldry in the Middle Ages. London, Oxford University Press, 1939; 1956.

WAGNER, Anthony R. Historic heraldry of Britain. London, Oxford University Press, 1939.

WAGNER, Anthony R. A catalogue of English medieval rolls of arms. Oxford, University Press, 1950. (Harleian Society, Vol. 100; Aspilogia, Vol. 1).

WOODWARD, John. A treatise on ecclesiastical heraldry. Edinburgh, W. and A. K. Johnston, 1894.

WOODWARD, John and BURNETT, George. A treatise on heraldry, British and foreign, with English and French glossaries. Edinburgh, Johnston, 1892. 2 v. Revised edition by Woodward alone, 1896, 2 v.

Index